W9-AVT-040

Public Relations

FOR THE PROFESSOR:

An Instructor's Manual with Test Bank is available for this text. Please contact your local HarperCollins sales representative or write: Communications Editor, College Division, HarperCollins Publishers Inc., 4th floor, 10 East 53rd Street, New York, NY 10022.

Public Relations

STRATEGIES AND TACTICS

THIRD EDITION

With a Foreword by Edward L. Bernays
and an Afterword by Robert L. Dilenschneider

DENNIS L. WILCOX
San Jose State University

PHILLIP H. AULT
South Bend *Tribune*

WARREN K. AGEE
University of Georgia

HarperCollins*Publishers*

Credits for part-opening photos

Page 1: Reuters, Bettmann / *page 147:* UPI, Bettmann / *page 231:* Reuters, Bettmann / *page 325:* Hamilton, Monkmeyer Press Photo / *page 541:* Gottlieb, Monkmeyer Press Photo.

Sponsoring Editor: Melissa A. Rosati
Project Editor: Susan Goldfarb
Design Supervisor: Lucy Krikorian
Text Design: Circa 86, Inc.
Cover Design: Jan Kessner
Photo Researcher: Mira Schachne
Production Administrator: Jeffrey Taub
Compositor: York Graphic Services, Inc.
Printer and Binder: R. R. Donnelley & Sons Company
Cover Printer: The Lehigh Press, Inc.

PUBLIC RELATIONS: Strategies and Tactics, Third Edition

Library of Congress Cataloging-in-Publication Data

Wilcox, Dennis L.
Public relations : strategies and tactics / Dennis L. Wilcox, Phillip H. Ault, Warren K. Agee. — 3rd ed. / with a foreword by Edward L. Bernays and an afterword by Robert L. Dilenschneider.
p. cm.
Includes bibliographical references and index.
ISBN 0-06-500100-1
1. Public relations. 2. Public relations—United States. I. Ault, Phillip H., 1914- . II. Agee, Warren Kendall. III. Title.
HM263.W49 1992
659.2—dc20 91-21307
CIP

93 94 9 8 7 6 5 4

CONTENTS

CHAPTER 23 SPOKEN TACTICS 595

CHAPTER 24 VISUAL TACTICS 633

FOREWORD

BY EDWARD L. BERNAYS*

One of the basic requirements of a vocation is that it have a literature of its own. In 1923 I wrote *Crystalizing Public Opinion,* published by Boni and Liveright, the first book on public relations. It defined the principles and practices of the new vocation of public relations and laid down the principles of ethics by which it should be governed.

Today there are more than 16,000 items in the bibliography of public relations. Every new volume, like this one, that discusses the old and new problems the vocation faces should be welcomed.

With the increasing complexity of our society, the public relations practitioner, an applied social scientist, must gain new and old knowledge from books before he or she can practice effectively. That is the pattern pursued consistently by lawyers, medical doctors, and those in other vocations.

With people power the most dominant force in society, it is essential that the public relations practitioner have the broadest understanding possible of the vocation. This book meets that need.

The past is prelude to the future. That is why the historical treatment of public relations in this volume is so important. Historical perspective provides proof why people must be given such serious consideration. Every activity depends on people for its survival, whether profit or nonprofit. By taking up various steps to pursue, this book provides basic approaches for teacher, student, and practitioner.

In my practice of 77 years books have been my greatest, most valuable resource.

Many people in public relations, as in other fields, think of themselves as Columbuses and Magellans in tackling their problems, as if they were the first ever to burst upon a particular issue. But the real Columbuses and Magellans read a book like this and then proceed to use books like this one as their greatest resource in the practice of their vocation.

There are serious problems concerning public relations that readers of this book must face if the vocation is to survive. The words *public relations* are in the public domain. Unlike true professions, public relations has not been defined by law. In the American language, words have the stability of soap bubbles. Anyone can misuse the term *public relations*. And many people unfitted by education, experience, or ethics use the term to mean whatever they want it to mean.

I noted in one directory of a public relations association 14 different appellations. None of them gave the least indication of an individual's education, experience, or ethics. Today any car salesperson or paperhanger can call himself or herself a ''public

---

*New York University commemorated the sixty-second anniversary of the teaching of public relations at a ceremony in 1985, during which NYU President John Brademas presented Dr. Bernays with a presidential citation.

relations practitioner.'' I have seen help-wanted advertisements for tourist-guide public relations practitioners who are required to ''love people.'' It is in the interest of all the readers of this book to strengthen the status of public relations by making it a profession.

Public relations is an art applied to a science—social science—in which the public interest rather than financial motivation is the primary consideration. A professional practitioner in public relations would turn down Somoza, Franco, and Hitler as clients, as I did.

Public relations today has all the characteristics of a profession except one. Public relations lacks licensing and registration by the state with legal sanctions.

The public relations vocation has its literature, an earmark of a profession. With more than 16,000 items published as of this writing, the literature grows every year.

Public relations has its educational courses, another earmark of a profession. In this and most other countries, instruction is offered in public relations. But what is actually taught as public relations often differs from school to school. Obviously, education would be standardized if licensing and registration were adopted in public relations, as is currently the case with instruction in the professions.

Public relations has its associations. They exist both in this country and internationally. There is an International Public Relations Association, with members in more than sixty-six countries.

Ethics is still another earmark of a profession. The public relations societies have their codes of ethics. In the case of licensed and registered professions, these codes of ethics are enforced by law. In public relations, no legal sanctions exist.

A group of practitioners is trying to bring about needed change. A committee calling for registration and licensing with legal sanctions has been established, not only to preserve and codify the standards of the field but also to prevent unqualified individuals from calling themselves public relations practitioners. It would also standardize the teaching of public relations in the United States.

In my judgment, degrees in public relations should be given on completion of a liberal arts program. In the two years following, M.S. degree graduates in public relations would study the social science disciplines, including economics and history. Additionally, universities could set up a double-degree program for students who plan a career in a specific area of public relations—for example, degrees in medicine and public relations for a career in medical public relations.

In sum, this book promises to be a good preparation for life in a public relations career.

Edward L. Bernays has received honorary doctorates from Boston University, Babson College, Ball State University, and Northeastern University for his contributions to the fields of public relations and social science.

PREFACE

The world of public relations expands and changes so rapidly that a textbook covering the entire field, as *Public Relations: Strategies and Tactics* does, requires frequent revision to stay abreast of developments. This third edition does precisely that. It examines public relations of the 1990s in both theory and practice, with emphasis on emerging trends.

Basic organization of the textbook remains the same as in the second edition. In a survey, users of the text told us overwhelmingly to keep it that way. Within that format, much up-to-the-minute new material drawn from real-world public relations practice has been added.

Four expanding aspects of public relations in particular receive strong emphasis:

- The environment
- International practice
- Ethics and professionalism
- The public relations–marketing relationship

As public concern for preserving the global environment multiplies, so do challenges to public relations practitioners. Corporations must show the public that they do not cause pollution or, if they do, that they are working to clean it up. Environmental organizations depend on public relations techniques as a principal way to promote their causes. We examine these organizations and how they work. Examples of what can be done in this field are spread throughout the book.

Development of worldwide conglomerate corporations and global communications companies, as well as growing international involvement of smaller organizations, has opened an intriguing new area of public relations work. Not only does this edition contain a detailed chapter on international practice, but it also has been "internationalized" throughout.

Our chapter on ethics and professionalism in previous editions has been commended for its depth, perception of the problems, and frankness. In this edition the chapter has been expanded to cover recent developments. Ethical questions also are addressed in the context of other chapters.

Public relations practice and the work of marketing departments have become increasingly interlocked. The student needs to understand how the two areas can cooperate to achieve corporate and institutional goals. We discuss this issue at some length in Chapter 14, "Corporations," and include examples elsewhere.

As every instructor knows, examples, anecdotes, and case histories are extremely valuable in helping students grasp principles and theories. *Public Relations: Strategies and Tactics* has won a reputation for its abundance of this material, mostly drawn from professional practice. This edition is filled with new material.

A detailed examination of the *Exxon Valdez* oil spill as the wrong way to handle a public relations crisis is contrasted with success stories about the British Petroleum oil spill and the classic example of Johnson & Johnson's management of the Tylenol poisoning deaths.

A sampling of other new examples and cases in the third edition: AT&T's handling of a nationwide telephone service failure, R. J. Reynolds' blunder in introducing a cigarette for black smokers, the tuna packers' decision against netting dolphins, the broccoli growers' publicity bonanza at the White House, a Spokane bank's loss of a $1 million account, and the Globe Theater's $10 million capital fund campaign in San Diego.

This book is divided into five parts:

- Part One: ''Role''
- Part Two: ''Process''
- Part Three: ''Strategy''
- Part Four: ''Application''
- Part Five: ''Tactics''

The organization is based on the fact that diversity exists in the teaching of introductory courses in public relations. At some colleges and universities, the course is offered as an overview of the entire field, covering theories, strategies, and on-the-job tactics. Other universities concentrate on theory and strategy, teaching the technical applications in public relations writing courses. Therefore, we concentrate the tactical material in Part Five. Instructors may include it or not, as they desire. Thus the book may be used under both teaching approaches.

The first four parts examine the principles, theories, and strategies in a natural teaching sequence. The fifth part explains the techniques of day-by-day public relations practice—such assignments as preparing a news release, writing a speech, coaching a client for a television appearance, and staging a news conference. For the reader's convenience, we have grouped the techniques into three categories, with a chapter on each: ''Written Tactics,'' ''Spoken Tactics,'' and ''Visual Tactics.''

We also draw readers' attention to Chapter 21, ''Public Relations and New Technologies.'' Discussion centers on the spectacular advances worldwide in message-delivery methods and electronic research sources. It explains how such tools as facsimile, video news releases, desktop publishing, and satellite transmission are used in public relations practice.

Supplementing the body of the text are a glossary of public relations terms and a comprehensive bibliography at the back of the book, as well as lists of suggested readings and review questions at the end of each chapter.

Supplements to the text include the following:

- Instructor's Manual w/Test Bank
- TestMaster
- HarperCollins Mass Communications Video Library

ACKNOWLEDGMENTS

A textbook of such scope as this one could not have been written without the assistance of many academic and professional advisers and consultants. We particularly wish to thank the following academics who read drafts of the first edition manuscript and provided many helpful suggestions: Robert L. Bishop, University of Georgia; Michael B. Hesse, University of Alabama; Robert L. Kendall, University of Florida; Norman R. Nager, California State University at Fullerton; Walt Seifert, Ohio State University; Judy VanSlyke Turk, University of Oklahoma; and Albert Walker, Northern Illinois University.

We express our gratitude also to those who reviewed the manuscript of the second edition: Glenn Butler, University of Florida; Fred Casmir, Pepperdine University; Lois Conn, Grand Valley State College; Bill Day, University of Toledo; Jerry Hudson, Texas Tech University; Bruce Renfro, Southwest Texas State University; and Maria Russell, Syracuse University.

Others in the academic world who assisted us include James E. Grunig, College of Journalism, University of Maryland, College Park; Randall Murray, California Polytechnic State University, San Luis Obispo; and Glen T. Cameron, Ruth Ann W. Lariscy, Roland Page, and R. Barry Wood, University of Georgia, Athens.

We also thank those who reviewed the third edition manuscript: Fred L. Casmir, Pepperdine University; Marilyn Kern-Foxworth, Texas A & M University; Norman R. Nager, California State University at Fullerton.

The following people provided specialized information for the third edition: Joe Andrews, publicity coordinator, Pillsbury Brands, Minneapolis, MN; John F. Budd, Jr., vice-chairman, Carl Byoir & Associates, New York; Laura Elmore and Gabriele Schindler, Regis McKenna, Inc., Palo Alto, CA; Richard Harmon, product press relations, Hewlett-Packard Company, Palo Alto, CA; Grant H. Horne, vice president of corporate communications, Pacific Gas & Electric Co., San Francisco; Walter K. Lindenmann, director of research, Ketchum Public Relations, New York; Michael A. McLeod, creative services, American Cancer Society, Atlanta; Alfredo Pedroso, account executive, Bruce Rubin Associates, Miami; Julie Ross, vice president, Ketchum Public Relations, San Francisco; Keith Sheldon, features editor, Southern California Edison, Rosemead, CA; and Michael Sullivan, Neale-May & Partners, Los Altos, CA.

The Public Relations Society of America and the International Association of Business Communicators generously supplied information and illustrations, as did dozens of professional practitioners.

Our special gratitude is extended to Edward L. Bernays for writing the Foreword to this textbook and to Robert L. Dilenschneider, former president and chief executive officer of Hill & Knowlton, Inc., for contributing the Afterword. Also, we thank Melissa Rosati, sponsoring editor, and the staff of HarperCollins for their numerous valuable suggestions.

Dennis L. Wilcox
Phillip H. Ault
Warren K. Agee

PART ONE
Role

WELCOME TO PUBLIC RELATIONS!

A company makes a "green audit" to determine the ways in which it may be damaging the environment . . . a march by AIDS activists demands more intensive research against the disease . . . TV shows and magazines interview Madonna about her new movie *Dick Tracy* . . . Exxon encounters a crisis of public confidence after its Alaskan oil spill . . . 800,000 people walk across the Golden Gate Bridge in San Francisco to celebrate its fiftieth birthday . . .

This is merely a sampling of the projects and events included under the broad, loosely defined term *public relations*.

Inform . . . create ideas . . . persuade . . . make things happen . . .

These are some of the things public relations people do.

This book explains the principles and theories of public relations, examines the ethical standards governing it, and describes the techniques used in putting the principles to work. Examples, anecdotes, and illustrations give the text the zest of real-world professional practice. We hope that in its pages you will discover what the combination of imagination and tactical skill can achieve in a field whose scope and possibilities expand constantly.

CHAPTER

What Is Public Relations?

People frequently define public relations by some of its most visible techniques and activities—whether it is publicity in a newspaper, a television interview with an organization's spokesperson, or even the appearance of a celebrity at a special event.

What people fail to understand is that public relations has many aspects that are more subtle and far-reaching. Public relations is essential in today's complex world to facilitate communication and understanding. It involves research and analysis, policy formation, programming, communication, and feedback from a variety of publics. Its practitioners operate on two distinct levels: as advisers to their clients or to an organization's top management, and as technicians who produce and disseminate a variety of messages in multiple media channels.

This chapter defines the term *public relations* as the management of an organization's relationships with its various publics (themselves discrete segments of the audience). We will discuss the versatile role of the public relations professional and the importance of public relations as a systematic process. We also will discuss how public relations differs from advertising and marketing—and in what ways the three areas overlap and reinforce each other.

THE CHALLENGE OF PUBLIC RELATIONS

Humanity has at its disposal tools of communication so swift, so abundant, and so pervasive that their potential is not yet fully comprehended. Messages are flashed around the world by satellite within seconds. Computers produce almost instantaneous calculations and pour out information at the rate of thousands of words a minute. Immense warehouses of information stored in electronic databases are available at the touch of a keyboard.

Yet in the midst of this information revolution, and in general agreement that we live in a "global information society," misunderstanding, lack of comprehension, and antagonism abound. Time after time, a crisis or conflict is caused by failure to communicate effectively.

Research and analysis also have provided knowledge of the motivation behind individual behavior, the dynamics of group conduct, and the sociological factors that create conflict among different groups. Our tools and accumulated knowledge, however, far surpass our ability to harness the concepts for effective conflict resolution, negotiation, and compromise between groups that take different sides on such varying issues as economic development and preservation of the environment, abortion, and cigarette smoking.

More than ever, today the world needs—not more information—but sensitive communicators and facilitators who can explain the goals and methods of organizations, individuals, and governments to others in a socially responsible manner. Equally, these experts in communication and public opinion must provide their employers with knowledge of what others are thinking, to guide them in setting their policies wisely for the common good.

Patrick Jackson, a former president of the Public Relations Society of America (PRSA) and publisher of *PR Reporter,* makes the case for this public relations role. He once wrote:

> As soon as there was Eve with Adam, there were relationships, and in every society, no matter how small or primitive, public communication needs and problems inevitably emerge and must be resolved. Public relations is devoted to the essential function of building and improving human relationships.

Indeed, those who fill this need are in the challenging field of public relations. The U.S. Bureau of Labor Statistics estimates that 159,000 men and women are employed in public relations in the United States. It is difficult to estimate worldwide figures, but *Reed's Worldwide Directory of Public Relations Organizations* (1990) lists 155 public relations organizations with an aggregate membership of 137,000 people. There are probably considerably more public relations specialists than the numbers indicate, however. Professor Robert L. Kendall of the University of Florida, after analyzing U.S. Census Bureau figures, estimates the number of public relations people in the United States alone to be almost 400,000.

Whatever the figure, there is every indication that the numbers will increase throughout the 1990s. A recent issue of the *U.S. Employment Opportunities Handbook* predicts a growth rate for public relations "much faster than average for all occupations through the year 2000."

The publication notes an increasing demand for workers in corporations, associations, and health agencies coupled with a rise in public relations operations in smaller businesses. The report predicts an expanding role for public affairs specialists to influence the general business environment through efforts directed toward local and national legislators. Other growth areas and trends in employment are discussed in Chapter 5.

The public relations industry is most developed in the United States, where companies spend an estimated $9.5 billion annually in such an effort. Considerable growth is also taking place in Europe and Asia. Claudio Belli, head of international operations for America's largest public relations firm, Hill and Knowlton, estimates that European companies spend $3 billion annually on public relations, a figure that will increase with the full implementation of the European Community (EC) and the opening of Eastern Europe to private enterprise. In addition, Shandwick, the world's largest public relations firm, sees growth of 20 to 30 percent annually in Asian nations on the Pacific Rim.

In sum, public relations is a global activity with excellent prospects for growth. The challenge is to define and practice public relations in such a way that it fosters greater understanding and harmonious relationships between organizations and the public interest.

A PLETHORA OF DEFINITIONS

Formulating a definition of public relations is a game any number may play. Pioneer public relations educator Rex Harlow once compiled about 500 definitions from almost as many sources.

Harlow found definitions ranging from the simple to the complex. Some of the more succinct:

- Good performance, publicly appreciated.
- PR stands for *P*erformance and then *R*ecognition.
- Doing good and getting credit for it.
- Actions taken to promote a favorable relationship with the public.
- An organization's efforts to win the cooperation of groups of people.

Textbook authors have also formulated various definitions. Scott M. Cutlip, Allen H. Center, and Glen M. Broom state in *Effective Public Relations* (Sixth Edition) that "public relations is the management function that identifies, establishes, and maintains mutually beneficial relationships between an organization and the various publics on whom its success or failure depends." The management function is also emphasized in *Managing Public Relations* by James E. Grunig and Todd Hunt. They state that public relations is "the management of communication between an organization and its publics."

The Public Relations Society of America (PRSA), the world's largest organization of public relations professionals, sought to define public relations operationally in an official statement, reprinted later in this chapter. The statement begins:

> Public relations helps our complex, pluralistic society to reach decisions and function more effectively by contributing to mutual understanding among groups and institutions. It serves to bring private and public policies into harmony.

Other national and international public relations organizations also have formulated definitions, broad enough to apply anywhere in the world, including the following:

- "Public relations is the deliberate, planned, and sustained effort to establish and maintain mutual understanding between an organization and its publics." (British Institute of Public Opinion, whose definition has also been adopted in a number of Commonwealth nations)
- "Public relations is the conscious and legitimate effort to achieve understanding and the establishment and maintenance of trust among the public on the basis of systematic research." (Deutsche Public Relations Gesellschaft of the Federal Republic of Germany—note that there is no term equivalent to *public relations* in the German language)
- "Public relations is the sustained and systematic managerial effort through which private and public organizations seek to establish understanding, sympathy, and support in those public circles with which they have or expect to obtain contact." (Dansk Public Relations Klub of Denmark, which also uses the English term)
- "Public relations practice is the art and social science of analyzing trends, predicting their consequences, counseling organization leaders, and implementing planned programs of action which serve both the organization's and the public's interest." (A definition approved at the World Assembly of Public Relations in Mexico City in 1978 and endorsed by 34 national public relations organizations)

Careful study of these explanations should enable anyone to formulate his or her own definition of public relations; committing any single one to memory is unnecessary. The key words to remember in defining public relations follow:

Deliberate. Public relations activity is intentional. It is designed to influence, gain understanding, provide information, and obtain *feedback* (reaction from those affected by the activity).

Planned. Public relations activity is organized. Solutions to problems are discovered and logistics are thought out, with the activity taking place over a period of time. It is systematic, requiring research and analysis.

Performance. Effective public relations is based on actual policies and performance. No amount of public relations will generate goodwill and support if the organization is unresponsive to community concerns. A Pacific Northwest timber company, despite an advertising campaign with the theme "For Us, Every Day Is Earth Day," became known as the villain of Washington State because of its insistence on logging old-growth forests and bulldozing a logging road into a prime elk habitat.

Public Interest. The rationale for any public relations activity is to serve the public interest, and not simply to achieve benefits for the organization. Ideally, public relations activity is mutually beneficial to the organization and the public; it is the alignment of the organization's self-interests with the public's concerns and interests. For example, the Mobil Corporation sponsors quality programming on public television because it enhances the company's image; by the same token, the public benefits from the availability of such programming.

Two-way Communication. Dictionary definitions often give the impression that public relations consists only of the dissemination of informational materials. It is equally important, however, that the definition include feedback from audiences. The ability to listen is an essential part of communication expertise.

Management Function. Public relations is most effective when it is part of the decision-making of top management. Public relations involves counseling and problem-solving at high levels, not just the releasing of information after a decision has been made. Public relations is defined by Denny Griswold, founder and owner of *PR News*, as "the management function which evaluates public attitudes, identifies the policies and procedures of an organization with the public interest, and executes a program of action (and communication) to earn public understanding and acceptance."

To summarize, a person can grasp the essential elements of public relations by remembering the following words: *deliberate . . . planned . . . performance . . . public interest . . . two-way communication . . . management function.*

In his own definition, based on the interpretations of public relations that he assembled, Rex Harlow strongly emphasized the role of management:

> Public relations is a distinctive management function which helps establish and maintain mutual lines of communication, understanding, acceptance, and cooperation between an organization and its publics; involves the management of problems or issues; helps management to keep informed on and responsive to public opinion; defines and emphasizes the responsibility of management to serve the public interest; helps management keep abreast of and effectively utilize change, serving as an early warning system to help anticipate trends; and uses research and ethical communication techniques as its principal tools.

Other definitions stress the importance of counseling management. As public relations pioneer Edward L. Bernays once explained to the World Assembly of Public Relations, professional counsel advises management on attitudes and actions to gain social objectives. He added:

> The public relations counsel first ascertains adjustments and maladjustments between the principals and the publics . . . then gives the principal advice to modify indicated attitudes and actions . . . then advises on how to inform and persuade relevant publics on services, products or ideas. Counseling covers adjustment, information and persuasion.

THE VERSATILE ROLE OF THE PRACTITIONER

Public relations practitioners play a dual role. On one level, they serve as advisers and counselors to management. On another level, they often function as technicians using a

Defense Secretary Richard B. Cheney and General Colin L. Powell, chairman of the Joint Chiefs of Staff, hold a televised news conference in Washington to summarize the progress of the Persian Gulf war. Such briefings were a major source of official news about the conflict.
(Reuters/Bettmann)

tool bag of communication techniques (news releases, slide presentations, special events, and so forth) to tell the public about management actions and decisions. People working in the field often define public relations by the activities they perform on a regular basis. Public relations people, for example, do the following:

Advise management on policy
Participate in policy decisions
Plan public relations programs
Sell programs to top management
Get cooperation of middle management
Get cooperation from other employees
Listen to speeches
Make speeches
Write speeches for others
Obtain speakers for organizational meetings
Place speakers on radio and television programs
Attend meetings

Plan and conduct meetings
Prepare publicity items
Talk to editors and reporters
Hold press conferences
Write feature articles
Research public opinion
Plan and manage events
Conduct tours
Write letters
Plan and write booklets, leaflets, reports, and bulletins
Edit employee newsletters
Supervise bulletin boards
Design posters

Plan films and videotapes
Plan and prepare slide presentations
Plan and produce exhibits
Take pictures or supervise photographers
Make awards
Greet visitors
Screen charity requests
Evaluate public relations programs
Design company symbols
Conduct fund-raising drives

These activities are elaborated on throughout this book, especially in Chapters 2 and 5.

PUBLIC RELATIONS AS A PROCESS

Public relations can also be defined as a *process*—that is, as a series of actions, changes, or functions that bring about a result. One popular way to describe the process, and to remember its components, is to use the RACE acronym, first articulated by John Marston in his book *The Nature of Public Relations*. Essentially, RACE means that public relations activity consists of four key elements:

1. *R*esearch—What is the problem?
2. *A*ction and Planning—What is going to be done about it?

FIGURE 1.1
Companies frequently use cartoon or photographic symbols to identify themselves and their products in the public's mind. The Pillsbury Doughboy, personifying the company's bakery goods, is among the most famous. Pillsbury celebrated the Doughboy's twenty-fifth birthday in 1990 with a public party in Minneapolis hosted by Steve Allen. (Courtesy of Pillsbury Brands)

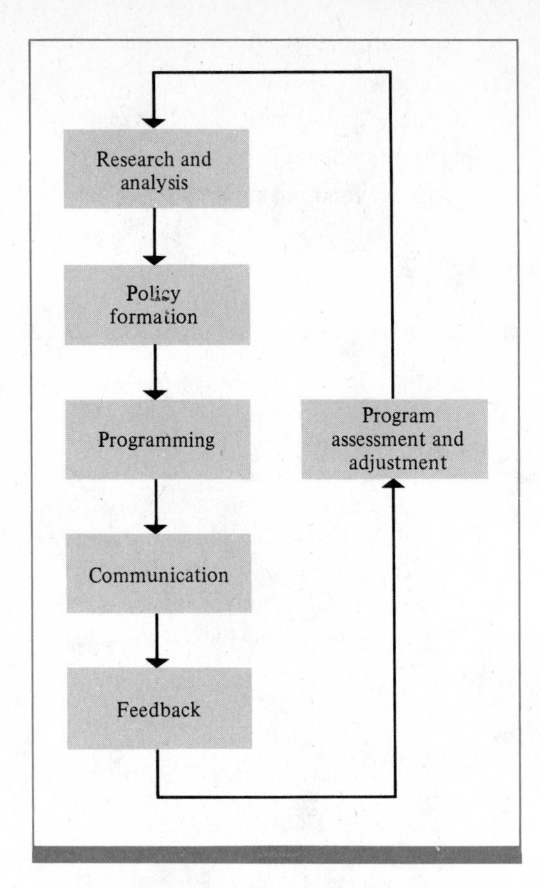

FIGURE 1.2
In the conceptualization of public relations as a cyclical process, feedback—or audience response—leads to assessment of the program, which then becomes an essential element in the development of another public relations project.

3. *C*ommunication—How will the public be told?

4. *E*valuation—Was the audience reached and what was the effect?

Part Two of the text discusses this key four-step process.

Another approach is to think of the process as a never-ending cycle in which six components are links in a chain. Figure 1.2 shows the process.

The public relations process also may be conceptualized as follows:

Level 1

A. Public relations personnel obtain insights into the problem from numerous sources.

B. Public relations personnel analyze these inputs and make recommendations to management.

C. Management makes policy and action decisions.

Level 2

D. Public relations personnel execute a program of action.

E. Public relations personnel evaluate the effectiveness of the action.

OFFICIAL STATEMENT ON PUBLIC RELATIONS

(Formally adopted by PRSA Assembly, November 6, 1982.)

Public relations helps our complex, pluralistic society to reach decisions and function more effectively by contributing to mutual understanding among groups and institutions. It serves to bring private and public policies into harmony.

Public relations serves a wide variety of institutions in society such as businesses, trade unions, government agencies, voluntary associations, foundations, hospitals, and educational and religious institutions. To achieve their goals, these institutions must develop effective relationships with many different audiences or publics such as employees, members, customers, local communities, shareholders and other institutions, and with society at large.

The managements of institutions need to understand the attitudes and values of their publics in order to achieve institutional goals. The goals themselves are shaped by the external environment. The public relations practitioner acts as a counselor to management, and as a mediator, helping to translate private aims into reasonable, publicly acceptable policy and action.

As a management function, public relations encompasses the following:

- Anticipating, analyzing, and interpreting public opinion, attitudes, and issues which might impact, for good or ill, the operations and plans of the organization.
- Counseling management at all levels in the organization with regard to policy decisions, courses of action and communication, taking into account their public ramifications and the organization's social or citizenship responsibilities.
- Researching, conducting and evaluating, on a continuing basis, programs of action and communication to achieve informed public understanding necessary to the success of an organization's aims. These may include marketing, financial, fund-raising, employee, community or government relations and other programs.
- Planning and implementing the organization's efforts to influence or change public policy.
- Setting objectives, planning, budgeting, recruiting and training staff, developing facilities—in short, *managing* the resources needed to perform all of the above.
- Examples of the knowledge that may be required in the professional practice of public relations include communication arts, psychology, social psychology, sociology, political science, economics and the principles of management and ethics. Technical knowledge and skills are required for opinion research, public issues analysis, media relations, direct mail, institutional advertising, publications, film/video productions, special events, speeches and presentations.

In helping to define and implement policy, the public relations practitioner utilizes a variety of professional communication skills and plays an integrative role both within the organization and between the organization and the external environment.

Step A consists of inputs that determine the nature and extent of the public relations problem. These may include feedback from the public, media reporting and editorial comment, analysis of trend data, other forms of research, personal experience, and government pressures and regulations.

In Step B, public relations personnel assess these inputs, establish objectives and an agenda of activity, and convey their recommendations to management. As previously noted, this is the adviser role of public relations.

After management makes its decisions, in Step C, public relations personnel execute the action program in Step D through such means as news releases, publications, speeches, and community relations programs. In Step E, the effect of these efforts is measured by feedback from the same components that made up Step A. The cycle is then repeated to solve related aspects of the problem that may require additional decision-making and action.

Note that public relations plays two distinct roles in this process, thus serving as a ''middle ground'' or ''linking agent.'' On Level 1, public relations interacts directly with external sources of information, including the public, media, and government, and relays these inputs to management along with recommendations. On Level 2, public relations becomes the vehicle through which management reaches the public with assorted messages. Veteran public relations counselor Philip Lesly explains:

> Public relations people have the role of being always in the middle—pivoted between their clients/employers and the public. They must be attuned to the thinking and needs of the organizations they serve or they cannot serve well. They must be attuned to the dynamics and needs of the publics so they can interpret the publics to the clients, as well as interpret the clients to the publics.

Diffusion-of-knowledge theorists call public relations people ''linking agents.'' Sociologists refer to them as ''boundary spanners'' that act to transfer information between two systems. As the last lines of the official statement on public relations by the Public Relations Society of America note: ''The public relations practitioner utilizes a variety of professional communication skills and plays an integrative role both within the organization and between the organization and the external environment.''

OTHER NAMES FOR PUBLIC RELATIONS

Public relations is used as an umbrella term on a worldwide basis. Sixty-four of the 69 national associations and societies of practitioners outside the United States identify themselves with that term.

O'Dwyer's Directory of Corporate Communications identifies 98 Fortune 500 firms that have either public relations or corporate public relations departments. Another 13 corporations use *public relations* as a partial title in conjunction with other terms such as *advertising, marketing, investor relations,* and *employee relations.*

A total of 154 companies have what they call a *corporate communications* or *communications* department. Other popular designations include *corporate relations, corporate affairs, public affairs,* and *investor relations*. Still other firms perform the public relations function in such departments as corporate marketing, marketing communications, and even advertising and sales promotion. (Public relations in a marketing context will be discussed later in this chapter.)

Surprisingly, 71 of the Fortune 500 firms do not have a formal public relations unit and no doubt rely on the contracted services of public relations firms. *Public informa-*

tion is the term most widely used by social service agencies, universities, and government agencies. The implication is that only information is being disseminated, in contrast to persuasive communication, generally viewed as the purpose of public relations. Most state and federal legislation permits government entities only to provide information and not to advocate any particular idea or program. In reality, much hairsplitting is done because information in itself can be persuasive. Social service agencies also use the term *community relations,* and the military is fond of *public affairs*.

In many cases it is clear that companies and organizations use *public information, public affairs,* or *corporate communications* as euphemisms for *public relations*. This is, in part, a reaction to the misuse of the original term by the public and the media. On more than one occasion, a reporter or a government official will use the term *public relations gimmick* or *ploy* to imply that the activities or statements of an organization are without substance or sincerity.

Other companies, however, use a term that better describes the primary activity of a department. It is clear, for example, that a department of investor relations deals primarily with stockholders, institutional investors, and the financial press. Likewise, a department of media relations is self-explanatory. Public affairs, on the other hand, can mean more emphasis on legislative bodies and government agencies. A department of marketing communications primarily emphasizes product publicity.

Like departments, individuals also specialize in subcategories of public relations. A person who deals exclusively with placement of stories in the media is, to be precise, a *publicist*. A *press agent* also is a specialist, operating within the subcategory of public relations that concentrates on planning staged events to attract media attention—a stunt by an aspiring Hollywood performer, for example, or an attempt to be listed in the *Guinness Book of Records* by baking the world's largest apple pie.

Unfortunately, the public and the press often use the general term *public relations expert* to describe publicists, press agents, and former government officials such as Michael Deaver who illegally traded on his Washington contacts under the guise of "public affairs." (Chapter 15 provides details of the Deaver case.) A number of newspapers also continue the practice of using *flack*, a derisive slang term for a press agent, or for anyone working in the public relations field. Irate letters of protest usually follow from professional public relations practitioners.

Within the public relations community, some feeling also exists that *PR* is a slang term and carries a somewhat denigrating connotation. The authors of this text have eliminated as much as possible its use as an abbreviation. In more formal writing, use of slang words generally is avoided. In informal conversation, however, the term *PR* probably never will be eliminated from the common language.

HOW PUBLIC RELATIONS DIFFERS FROM ADVERTISING

Just as many people mistakenly equate publicity with public relations, there is also some confusion about the distinction between publicity (one area of public relations) and advertising.

Publicity—or information about an event, an individual or group, or a product—is disseminated through the news media and other channels to attract favorable public

FOUR IMPORTANT FUNCTIONS OF PUBLIC RELATIONS

The chairman of one of the world's largest public relations firms, Harold Burson of Burson-Marsteller, believes public relations has four important functions in today's society:

Sensor of Social Change The public relations professional perceives those rumblings at the heart of society that augur good or ill for the organization and helps management prepare for the onslaught and impact of those issues.

Corporate Conscience Henry David Thoreau wrote: "It is truly enough said that a corporation has no conscience; but a corporation of conscientious men is a corporation with a conscience." Those are powerful words and ones that the public relations professional should always bear in mind. These qualities are basic to the job description of public relations officers.

Communicator Many people think communications is the main public relations role. Most likely, they think that way because they spent a lot of time mastering communication skills and very little time honing their social judgments. Communications is not the main role; it is one of four important roles.

Corporate Monitor This function seeks to make corporate policies and programs match public expectations. The spirit of the ombudsman should pervade the public relations person's job. And this is perhaps the best reason for the senior public relations officer to report to the highest level of management.

Source: PR Reporter (Tips and Tactics), March 23, 1987.

notice. The practitioner who prepares and distributes the information is often called a *publicist*.

Advertising is paid space and time in print, including billboards, and in electronic media. Organizations and individuals contract to purchase space and time, and an advertisement is almost always broadcast or printed exactly as the purchaser has prepared it.

Publicity, as distinguished from advertising, appears in broadcast news programs and in newspaper and magazine stories. The prepared copy is sent to the news department (not the advertising department) and *gatekeepers* (reporters and editors) modify the material according to news requirements. In other words, there is no guarantee that an organization's news release will be used or will appear in the form in which it was prepared.

There are other differences between public relations activities and advertising. Here are some of them:

- Advertising deals with the selling of goods and services; public relations generates public understanding and fosters goodwill for an organization.

- Advertising works almost exclusively through mass media outlets; public relations relies on a number of communication tools—brochures, slide presentations, special events, speeches, news releases, feature stories, and so forth.
- Advertising is addressed to external audiences—primarily consumers of goods and services; public relations presents its message to specialized external audiences (stockholders, vendors, community leaders, environmental groups, and so on) and internal publics (employees).
- Advertising is readily identified as a specialized communication function; public relations is broader in scope, dealing with the policies and performance of the entire organization, from the morale of employees to the way telephone operators respond to calls.
- Advertising often is used as a communication tool in public relations, and public relations activity often supports advertising campaigns. Advertising's function is to sell goods and services; the public relations function is to create an environment in which the organization can thrive. The latter calls for dealing with economic, social, and political factors that can affect the organization.

The major disadvantage of advertising, of course, is the cost. Typically, a full-page ad in *Parade* magazine, distributed weekly in almost 350 dailies, costs $421,000. Advertising campaigns on network television can run into the millions of dollars. Because of this, companies increasingly are using a tool of public relations—product publicity—that is more cost-effective and often more credible because the message appears in a news context.

The strong relationship between the techniques of public relations and marketing is discussed next.

HOW PUBLIC RELATIONS SUPPORTS AND DIFFERS FROM MARKETING

Philip Kotler, professor of marketing at Northwestern University and author of a leading marketing textbook, says public relations is the fifth "P" of marketing strategy, which includes four other Ps—Product, Price, Place, and Promotion. As he wrote in the *Harvard Business Review,* "Public relations takes longer to cultivate, but when energized, it can help pull the company into the market."

Indeed, the new buzzword of the 1990s seems to be *integrated marketing,* in which management orchestrates advertising, product promotions, corporate sponsorships of events, and public relations to achieve the success of a product or service in the marketplace.

Public relations firms and departments often do "marketing communications" and "marketing public relations," which support the overall advertising and marketing objectives of a company or client. This means that the tools of public relations—product publicity, news conferences, exclusive interviews, trade show seminars, customer receptions, open houses, and even speeches to local professional and industry groups—essentially are cost-effective sales messages to potential customers.

Dennis L. Wilcox and Lawrence W. Nolte, in their text *Public Relations Writing and Media Techniques*, list eight ways in which product publicity contributes to fulfilling marketing objectives by

- Developing new prospects for new markets, such as people who inquire after seeing or hearing a product release in the news media
- Providing third-party endorsements—via newspapers, magazines, radio, and television—through news releases about a company's products or services, community involvement, inventions, and new plans
- Generating sales leads, usually through articles in the trade press about new products and services
- Paving the way for sales calls
- Stretching the organization's advertising and promotional dollars through timely and supportive releases about it and its products
- Providing inexpensive sales literature, because articles about the company and its products can be reprinted as informative pieces for prospective customers
- Establishing the corporation as an authoritative source of information on a given product
- Helping to sell minor products that don't have large advertising budgets

One example of how public relations tools can make a difference is the introduction of Keebler Cookie Company's Soft-Batch brand. The company didn't have the massive advertising resources of competitors such as Procter & Gamble and Nabisco, so it used a marketing public relations program that included an unusual press kit designed in the form of Keebler's "Magic Oven." The resulting media publicity, valued at $3 million in national television exposure alone, helped Keebler take a 30 percent market share with only modest advertising expenditures.

The effective use of public relations tools in an integrated marketing program should not be underestimated, but the specialty function of "marketing communications" or "marketing public relations" is not public relations. To say otherwise is the same as saying "publicity is public relations."

Public relations is distinct from marketing in several ways, although the boundaries between them often overlap. A recent colloquium at San Diego State University brought together distinguished educators and practitioners from public relations and marketing and, after a day of discussion and debate, they agreed that both fields deal with an organization's relationships and employ similar processes. They also agreed that the major difference is the outcome that each function seeks to achieve. Marketing almost exclusively is concerned with sales.

Joe Epley, president of the Public Relations Society of America, describes the goal of public relations differently:

> The mission of public relations is to build trust; to ensure that the public good is considered in setting corporate strategies and to develop effective communications programs that build mutual understanding and acceptance. Without favorable public opinion, it is difficult to do business.

The panelists at the San Diego colloquium also sought to distinguish between the two fields. Their definition of public relations:

Public relations is the management process whose goal is to attain and maintain accord and positive behaviors among social groupings on which an organization depends in order to achieve its mission. Its fundamental responsibility is to build and maintain a hospitable environment for an organization.

FIGURE 1.3
News headlines illustrate some of the widely varied aspects and challenges of public relations work.

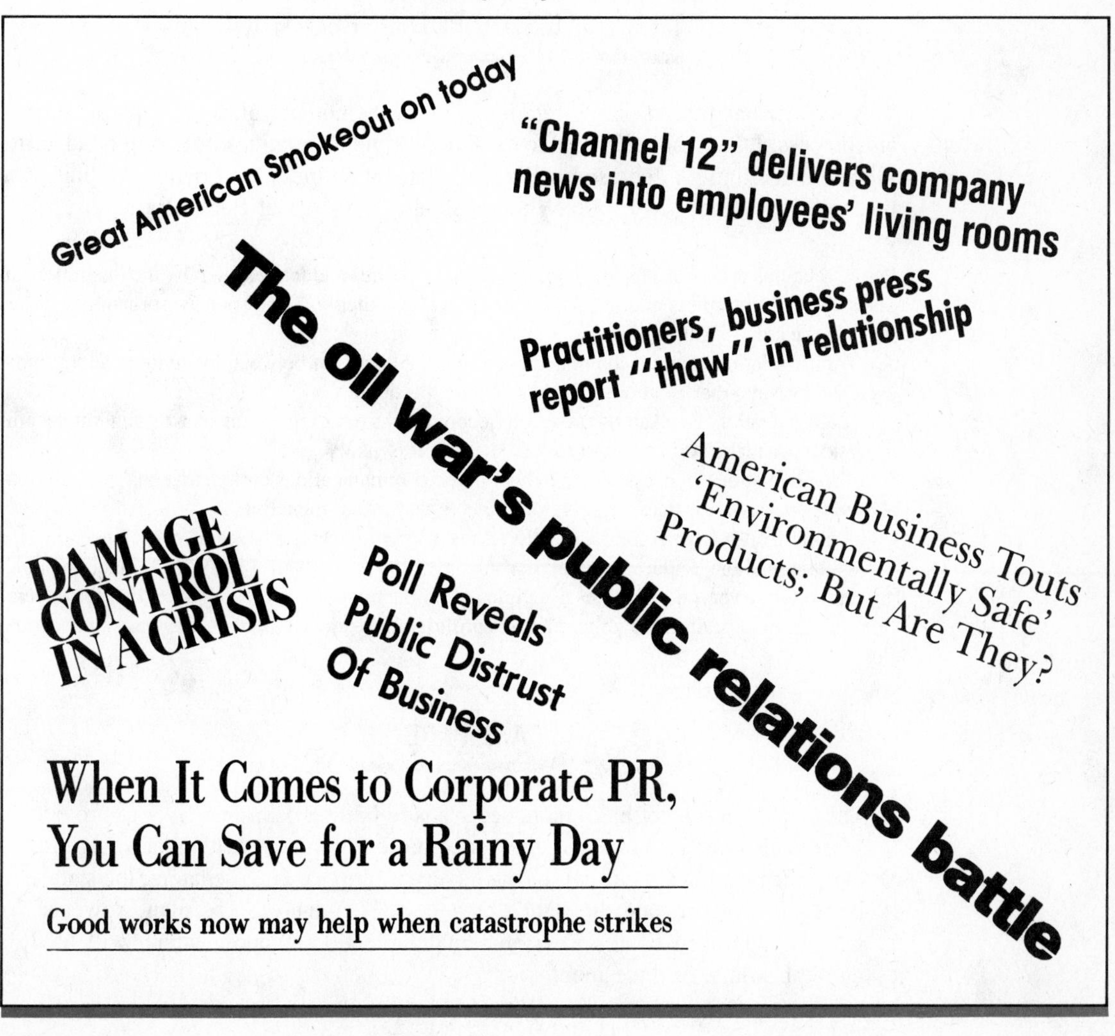

The group defined marketing's goal in different terms:

Marketing is the management process whose goal is to attract and satisfy customers (or clients) on a long-term basis in order to achieve an organization's economic objectives. Its fundamental responsibility is to build and maintain a market for an organization's products or services.

Patrick Jackson, mentioned earlier as publisher of *PR Reporter*, says that chief executive officers (CEOs) can and do differentiate between public relations and marketing. Public relations is not simply a "cash register problem-solving solution" for marketing, but a way of dealing with such matters as environmental concerns that often are impediments to sales success. "The marketing department," according to Professor Glen Broom of San Diego State University, "points to the 'bottom line' despite threats by environmental and wildlife groups."

Marketing communications are discussed further in Chapter 14.

THE VALUES OF PUBLIC RELATIONS

This chapter has placed public relations within the context of definitions, activities, and process. It has also attempted to explain how public relations differs from advertising and marketing. A good summarizing statement on the role of public relations was prepared by PRSA's Task Force on the Stature and Role of Public Relations:

Public relations is a means for the public to have its desires and interests felt by the institutions in our society. It interprets and speaks for the public to otherwise unresponsive organizations, as well as speaking for those organizations to the public.

Public relations is a means to achieve mutual adjustment between institutions and groups, establishing smoother relationships that benefit the public.

Public relations is a safety valve for freedom. By providing means of working out accommodations, it makes arbitrary action or coercion less likely.

Public relations is an essential element in the communications system that enables individuals to be informed on many aspects of subjects that affect their lives.

Public relations personnel can help activate the organization's social conscience.

Public relations (either systematic or unconscious) is a universal activity. It functions in all aspects of life. Everyone practices principles of public relations in seeking acceptance, cooperation, or affection of others. Public relations professionals practice public relations as an occupation.

CASE PROBLEM

The state government has announced plans to build a dam on a river to provide additional water resources for the economic development of the state's largest city. The plan has the support of the governor, the two U.S. senators, the state's largest newspaper, and the state's chamber of commerce. The plan, however, must be approved by the Environmental Protection Agency, which will hold public hearings in three months.

A coalition of environmental groups opposes the dam because it would flood 30 miles of prime wild trout habitat on a river that the U.S. Fish and Wildlife Service calls "unique, irreplaceable and of national significance."

Using Figure 1.2 as a guide, outline what the coalition should do in each step of the process to design and execute an effective public relations program to rally public opinion against the building of the dam.

QUESTIONS FOR REVIEW AND DISCUSSION

1. How many people work in public relations in the United States? Is public relations a growing career field?

2. There are many definitions of public relations. Of those listed in Chapter 1, select the one that you find most satisfying and discuss the reasons for your preference.

3. What ten words characterize the essential elements of public relations?

4. Name ten activities in which public relations practitioners frequently are engaged.

5. The RACE acronym is a popular way of describing the public relations process. For what procedure does each initial stand?

6. How would you summarize the official statement on public relations issued by the Public Relations Society of America?

7. Public relations is often described as a *loop process*. What does that mean?

8. Harold Burson says that public relations serves four important functions. What are they?

9. What other terms are used by companies and organizations to describe the public relations function?

10. Why do public relations practitioners resent calling publicists and press agents "public relations experts"?

11. Do you consider *PR* a slang term that should be avoided? Why or why not?

SUGGESTED READINGS

Bolland, Eric J. "Advertising vs. Public Relations." *Public Relations Quarterly*, Fall 1989, pp. 10–12.

Broom, Glen M., and Tucker, Kerry. "An Essential Double Helix: Marketing Public Relations." *Public Relations Journal,* November 1989, pp. 39–40.

Culbertson, Hugh M. ''Breadth of Perspective: An Important Concept for Public Relations.'' Chapter 1 of *Public Relations Research Annual,* edited by James and Larissa Grunig, Volume 1, Hillsdale, NJ: Lawrence Erlbaum Associates, 1989, pp. 3–26.

Cushman, Aaron. ''Why Marketing Directors Are Listening Now.'' *Public Relations Journal*, May 1990, pp. 17–19.

Dilenschneider, Robert L. *Power and Influence*. New York: Prentice Hall, 1990.

Grunig, James E. ''Theory and Practice of Interactive Media Relations.'' *Public Relations Quarterly,* Fall 1990, pp. 18–23.

Harlow, Rex F. ''Building a Public Relations Definition.'' *Precision Public Relations,* edited by Ray E. Hiebert. New York: Longman, 1988, pp. 7–16.

Lesly, Philip. ''Public Relations Numbers Are Up but Stature Down.'' *Public Relations Review*, Winter 1988, pp. 3–7.

Levy, Dorothy. ''What Public Relations Can Do Better Than Advertising.'' *Public Relations Quarterly*, Fall 1989, pp. 7–9.

Paluszek, John. ''Public Relations in the Coming Global Economy.'' *Vital Speeches of the Day,* October 15, 1989.

Ryan, Joan Aho, and Lemmond, George H. ''Thinking Like a Brand Manager.'' *Public Relations Journal,* August 1989, pp. 24–28.

Webster, Philip J. ''Strategic Corporate Public Relations: What's the Bottom Line?'' *Public Relations Journal,* February 1990, pp. 18–21.

White, Jon. ''The Vantage Point of Public Relations.'' *Public Relations Review,* Summer 1988, pp. 3–11.

CHAPTER

2

Types of Public Relations Work

Chapter 1 examined definitions of public relations and its basic principles and purposes. Now it is time to discuss the specifics of contemporary practice, to learn where and how these concepts are applied. Just what do public relations practitioners do? To what aspects of business, education, government, and nonprofit organizations do these specialists devote their skills?

Although the same principles apply in all areas of public relations, practitioners work in diverse fields and seek to reach hundreds of different publics. The tasks they perform are almost infinite in variety. One practitioner might seek to increase public awareness of a major health danger such as heart disease, while another's job may be to inform consumers about a new product on the market. Others may work in corporate employee communications, recruit volunteers for a community fund drive, or even publicize the winning streak of a major league football team.

Virtually all commercial and noncommercial organizations that deal with the public, from computer manufacturers to hospitals to art museums, need public relations guidance and service. Public relations practitioners apply their skills across a richly varied spectrum. This chapter will reveal the field's scope and variety.

This ''door-opening'' chapter gives a concise summary of the principal types of public relations work. With this broad picture in mind, we will examine each type of work in detail in later chapters.

CORPORATIONS

A substantial majority of public relations professionals work to further the goals and objectives of profit-earning organizations. They do so either as members of a public relations department or as part of a counseling firm employed by the corporation. Especially in large companies, public relations programs have many facets, each of which requires development of specialized knowledge and techniques.

The primary areas of corporate public relations work are the following:

1. *Reputation—protection and enhancement.* The role of tending to company reputation involves preserving and building goodwill for a company by demonstrating to the public that the firm is an efficient producer of well-made products, an honest seller of goods and services, a fair and equitable employer, and a responsible corporate citizen. This function includes: (*a*) protecting the company against attacks; (*b*) telling its story well when controversy arises; (*c*) initiating programs to explain company goals and policies; (*d*) making early identification of developing problems so the company can act quickly to solve them; (*e*) displaying concern for environmental problems; (*f*) protecting and promoting corporate trademarks and logos; (*g*) showing that the company cares for the welfare of its employees and the communities in which its facilities are located; and (*h*) explaining the company position on political, social, and economic issues.

This role, performed in many ways, uses a variety of communication tools to build a positive image of the company. "Image" in this sense means the personality or character of the company projected to the public.

Some public relations experts dislike the term *image* because it has the connotation of being illusionary, suggesting deceptive manipulation. Since effective public relations is presenting "images" that actually reflect a company's policies and actions, many companies describe this broad-based role as building *corporate identity*.

2. *Information service.* Part of building a company's reputation is the role of supplying information to a variety of publics. One important area is *media relations*. Companies send news releases to the media in order to inform the public about earnings, acquisitions, new products, and so forth. They hold news conferences, and the public relations staff sometimes arranges interviews for reporters with company executives. Companies must respond to inquiries from customers, distributors, government officials, and community residents. Prompt, comprehensive, and gracious responses build friends; perceived "brush-offs" make enemies.

3. *Marketing communications.* Two important corporate functions are the introduction of new products and the creation of campaigns to put fresh life into the sale of established products. Much of this work is in the form of product publicity; this includes placement of articles about product developments, application stories about how the product is used, and interviews with people who developed the product. Public relations practitioners work closely with the marketing department to develop this material.

Closely but unhappily linked with product publicity is the problem of *product recall*. Companies face this when a belatedly discovered defect requires recall of a product from the market for repair or replacement. Proctor-Silex, for example, recalled 800,000 coffeemakers in late 1990 after receiving 181 reports of fires involving the appliance. It offered safe new coffeemakers in return. The company advertised a toll-free number for owners of the unsafe appliances to call.

When the quality and safety of a company's product are under severe criticism, public relations representatives must use a wide range of techniques either to recall the product or convince the public that the product is safe and a recall unnecessary.

4. *Investor relations*. The corporate function of investor relations is also called *stockholder communications*. Essentially, it means providing information to individuals who own stock or have a special interest in the corporation. Elaborate annual reports, quarterly reports mailed with dividend checks, and other printed materials are sent to stockholders on a regular basis. At an annual meeting stockholders may ask questions of management, voice complaints, and have their resolutions for policy changes put to a vote. If a proxy fight erupts (conflict involving rival solicitations of support from absent stockholders), or one company attempts the forced takeover of another, public relations personnel often mount a campaign to convince stockholders not to sell their stock. Conversely, staff members may be called upon to convince stockholders that an acquisition or merger is in their best interest.

For example, in 1990 Lockheed Corporation successfully fought off an attempt by billionaire Harold Simmons to capture control of its board of directors in a bitter proxy battle. Solicitation of proxies by both sides was so intense that 83.4 percent of Lockheed's 63.2 million outstanding shares were voted at the annual meeting. Lockheed employees, who owned 19 percent of the stock, voted 90 percent of it in favor of their bosses—a major factor in management's victory. Total cost of the proxy fight for the two sides: $14 million. Both sides made extensive use of public relations counsel and employed such techniques as letters to stockholders, full-page advertisements in the *Wall Street Journal,* and video news releases to institutional investors.

5. *Financial relations*. A parallel function of investor relations is to provide extensive information to the financial community. Security analysts at brokerage houses, large banks, and similar institutions weigh the information and make judgments on a company's financial strength and prospects. On the basis of their recommendations, institutional investors and brokerage firms buy or sell a company's stock.

Public relations staff members prepare printed materials and arrange for high company officials to address meetings of financial analysts. Failure to communicate the company's message well can cause major losses, as in the case of the Amdahl Corporation. Its stock immediately declined three points after a key analyst covering the computer industry removed the company from a recommended list. This meant a paper loss to the company of millions of dollars.

A thorough knowledge of finance, as well as Securities and Exchange Commission (SEC) rules, is essential for a public relations person specializing in financial relations. (For a further discussion, see Chapter 14.)

6. *Community relations*. A company is a citizen in a local community, and such citizenship implies certain obligations. Corporations often take an active role in supporting community organizations. Encouraging employees to do volunteer work, giving a grant to the local symphony orchestra, lending executives to the United Way effort, having executives serve on civic advisory boards—these are a few of the steps a company can take. Good relations include an effort to assure company compliance with environmental regulations and to work with other civic groups to improve the quality of life.

7. *Employee relations.* An open flow of information from management to employees, and from employees to management, is recognized as essential by most corporations. To achieve this, the public relations department works closely with the personnel or human resources department.

Among the functions it performs are (*a*) publication of an employee magazine, newspaper, or video news magazine; (*b*) the writing of brochures for employees explaining company policies and benefits; (*c*) preparation of audiovisual materials for training and policy-transmission purposes; (*d*) the scheduling of staff meetings and seminars; (*e*) the training of speakers among managers and supervisors who serve as communicators to employees; and (*f*) coordination of employee productivity or energy conservation campaigns. The public relations staff of FMC Corporation, for example, coordinated an employee campaign to generate awareness about the company's code of ethics.

8. *Special events management.* A relatively new role for public relations personnel is special events management, as companies increasingly sponsor everything from rock concerts to the fiftieth anniversary celebration of San Francisco's Golden Gate Bridge (see Chapter 20). Corporate sponsorship of such events requires public relations staff members who have an eye for detail, organization, logistics, and publicity opportunities.

9. *Public affairs.* The actions of government on the local, state, and national level have major effects on corporations and how they conduct their affairs. Thus, a number of public relations people work in the area often referred to as *governmental relations*. In this role public affairs executives seek to influence legislation through contact with legislators and governmental regulatory agencies.

Public affairs work is done on several levels. On one level is the public affairs manager. He or she, according to the public affairs section of PRSA, must be "concerned with the management function covering the relationship between the organization and its external environment and involving key tasks of intelligence gathering and analysis, external action program directed at government, communities and the general public as well as strategic issue management and internal communications." A *lobbyist,* in contrast, has a narrower function: the lobbyist is "concerned with direct or indirect means of exercising influence on passage or defeat of legislative bills or regulatory actions, and [seeks] to influence their outcomes."

10. *Issues management.* The role of issues management, often carried out by public relations professionals, is the management process of determining how various public issues will affect the company. R. Howard Chase, a counselor specializing in issues management, says there are five steps in the process: (1) identifying the issue, (2) analyzing it, (3) ascertaining options open to the company, (4) initiating a plan of action, and (5) evaluating the results. (A detailed discussion of issues management appears in Chapter 14.)

The way in which an American company would assess its operations and investments in the Republic of South Africa illustrates the process. Using Chase's model, the firm first identifies the issue as South Africa's apartheid policies and questions whether the company should stay in the country under them. Second, it determines the policy of the U.S. government about American investment in South Africa, the attitudes of key publics important to the company, and the actions of other corporations. Third, it sets priorities on the options available to it and the financial impact of each. Fourth, it decides on an action program (disinvest or justify remaining). The fifth step, of course, would be to evaluate the company's decision and the reaction to it.

Since the release of black leader Nelson Mandela from prison and the softening of apartheid policies under President F.W. de Klerk, companies with stringent anti–South African policies face a new task of deciding if and when they should relax those policies.

A corporation's relationship with the environment, both in the products it makes and the properties it owns, is a major issue of the 1990s. Astute managements are beginning to take the initiative to clean up operations vulnerable to criticism from environmental groups. Others try to ignore the issue and hope they won't get caught—a dangerously short-sighted policy.

A REFERENCE LIST

The ten principal areas in which public relations professionals work are the following:

- Reputation—protection and enhancement
  - Corporate identity programming
- Information service
  - Media relations
- Marketing communications
  - Product publicity
- Investor relations
  - Stockholder communications
- Financial relations
- Community relations
- Employee relations
- Special events management
- Public affairs
  - Governmental relations
- Issues management

The ten types of public relations activity just described also take place, in varying degrees, within other types of organizations. This work is described in greater detail in Part 4.

MEMBERSHIP ORGANIZATIONS

Significant among the communication channels that tie contemporary society together are organizations made up of individuals or separate businesses sharing strong common interests—financial, professional, social, cultural, or intellectual. Usually, these organizations advance the collective interests of their members. Public relations is essential to their success, for without public understanding and support, goals and objectives will not be realized. Four major types of associations are trade groups, labor unions, professional and cultural societies, and "cause" organizations.

TRADE ASSOCIATIONS

A *trade association* consists of member companies that produce the same type of product or provide similar services. Although they may compete for the consumer's dollar as individual businesses, they band together in an association to further common interests. Their association promotes or opposes legislation, informs the public about the industry, and undertakes statistical and other types of research for the benefit of its members. Examples of powerful trade associations are the National Association of Manufacturers, the Tobacco Institute, American Bankers Association, and the Pharmaceutical Manufacturers Association.

The food industry provides examples of how trade groups work together to promote a generic product. The California Milk Advisory Board carried out an extensive public relations campaign to convince customers that real butter is "100 percent natural" and lower in fat content than most health-conscious Americans believe. The objective, of course, was to woo consumers away from margarine, which has seriously eroded the butter market.

Another trade group, the Washington State Apple Commission, along with apple growers in other states, faced a crisis in 1989. The National Resources Defense Council (NRDC), a private group, asserted that Alar, a chemical used in some orchards to improve apple growth, was carcinogenic. It said that children were more likely than adults to be harmed by such pesticides.

In a Senate hearing, actress Meryl Streep emotionally condemned Alar and other pesticides. Frightened mothers stopped giving their children apples. New York, San Francisco, Los Angeles, and other school districts quit serving the fruit; the Los Angeles cutoff alone involved 5 million apples a year. A serious slump in national sales followed. Apple growers called the surge of bad publicity "unfair."

They soon received support from the federal government. Three agencies—the Food and Drug Administration, the Environmental Protection Agency, and the Department of Agriculture—jointly disputed the NRDC claim and declared apples safe to eat. The Washington State Association, representing a primary growing area, quickly followed with a $1.7 million public relations campaign that switched the focus away from an emphasis on taste by promoting the health value of apples. Other grower groups fought back similarly. These campaigns helped to diminish the public's fear, and sales increased. The use of Alar, already in decline when the fuss began, dwindled still further. The episode showed how volatile public opinion can be. (See Chapter 15 for a description of rival public relations efforts in this controversy.)

LABOR UNIONS

To serve members and build favorable public recognition, labor organizations must rely on public relations extensively. Union leadership administers pension plans, insurance programs, and the like; the members must be kept informed about how these

Actress Meryl Streep delivers an emotional appeal before a U.S. Senate committee condemning the use of the chemical Alar on apples. After her appearance, some school districts and many mothers stopped serving the fruit to children. (UPI/Bettmann)

programs may benefit them. Grievance procedures must be explained. New members must be sought and new locals formed. Before contract negotiations, union leadership must learn what the members desire and in turn keep them informed about negotiating strategy. Just as in corporate structures, two-way communication is essential.

If a breakdown in negotiations leads to a strike, or threatens to do so, unions must outline their positions and enlist public support. Since the public often is inconvenienced by strikes, unions must find ways to explain the justness of their cause. When agreement is reached, union leadership must present the contract provisions to the members in order to obtain ratification.

Labor organizations participate heavily in political affairs, from the federal to the local level, by endorsing and financing candidates and taking strong positions on issues. Union leadership urges members to vote according to its recommendations. Less evident, but continuous, is the task of developing and publicizing activities for members and their families, and of participating in community affairs as part of the union's efforts to be a constructive organizational citizen. Political participation and community affairs both require a wide variety of public relations activities. A major problem for unions in the 1990s is to recruit and retain membership, which has been falling. (See Chapter 17 for a detailed discussion.)

PROFESSIONAL AND CULTURAL SOCIETIES

Members of a profession band together in associations for their mutual benefit, including the exchange of information, just as trade associations do. The public relations work of professional societies includes (1) legislative campaigns, (2) advocacy of professional standards, (3) publication of information at both the skilled professional and general readership levels, (4) membership recruitment, and (5) general work to strengthen the profession's stature in the public mind. Associations of health professionals such as the American Medical Association and the American Dental Association, for instance, conduct vigorous campaigns to promote good health practices. Other representative professional societies are the American Bar Association and the American Chemical Society.

Cultural societies resemble professional groups, except that the common bond of members is interest in a cultural activity rather than career development and stature in the profession. The Metropolitan Museum of Art, Chicago Historical Society, and San Francisco Symphony Orchestra are examples. All use public relations personnel to (1) publicize their programs, (2) produce publications, (3) arrange speaking engagements and event openings, (4) recruit new members, (5) foster community participation and support, and (6) raise funds.

"CAUSE" ORGANIZATIONS

Still another group of organizations consists of those seeking to influence the public and generate support for their points of view on a variety of issues. Representative of this category are the National Safety Council, National Wildlife Federation, Sierra Club, American Association of Retired Persons, American Civil Liberties Union, Mothers Against Drunk Driving (MADD), the National Organization for Women (NOW), and Greenpeace.

Because raising public awareness is the first task, cause groups often stage events to generate media coverage. The protest march at the recent international AIDS conference in San Francisco is one example of this method. Arrests often follow, but so do media publicity and public awareness, some of it antagonistic.

FIGURE 2.1
Both the Greenpeace stamp promoting its dolphin campaign and the logo of the World Wildlife Fund symbolize the significant role environmental organizations play in public relations work.

SOCIAL AND RELIGIOUS AGENCIES

Nonprofit organizations that serve social welfare, health, and religious needs call extensively upon their staffs of public relations specialists. They must alert the public to the services offered and raise funds to finance those services. As a group, these agencies have inherent public approval because of the obviously valuable work they do. However, this abstract approval must be translated into tangible support.

Social service and religious agencies have four areas in which public relations techniques are essential:

1. Role promotion—stimulating public awareness of their work and demonstrating what can be accomplished through their services
2. Client services—making these services known to the public and convincing individuals to use them
3. Fund-raising
4. Enlistment of volunteers

The Salvation Army and Goodwill Industries are examples of social service agencies. So are the American Red Cross and the Visiting Nurse Association. On a different level are such health organizations as the American Heart Association and the American Cancer Society, which warn the public about the dangers of the diseases they combat. Hospital public relations is a rapidly expanding field as these institutions enlarge their work in preventive medicine and add ancillary services.

Religious organizations on state and national levels use public relations practices in much the same way that social services do. Their concerns are to increase the role of religion in contemporary life and to provide related social services. Some church groups also take active roles in such social issues as abortion and alcoholism.

ENTERTAINMENT AND SPORTS

Publicizing individuals and promoting entertainment constitute the aspect of contemporary public relations practice that comes closest to the traditional mantle of *press agentry*. This work requires intense contact with the media, by telephone and mail and in person. Name recognition is its primary goal.

The impact of television on the field of personality promotion is immense. An unknown person who appears on a nationally distributed television show may become an almost instant celebrity. Public relations firms specializing in personality buildup have staffs that book clients—show-business people, politicians, sports figures, and authors of promotional-type books in particular—in a highly organized manner for TV and radio talk shows. Distribution of news items about personalities to print media columnists and electronic media commentators, and the scheduling of interviews with newspapers and magazines, also are major functions. So are public relations tours by film and television stars.

FIGURE 2.2
This advertisement by the American Cancer Society urging proper nutrition was published free as a public service by 15 magazines with combined circulation of 10.5 million. (Paramount Pictures allowed the society to use the Spock photograph without charge.) (Courtesy of American Cancer Society, Inc.)

Promotion of entertainment events is a many-faceted activity, intensely competitive because many events compete for the consumer's time and money. Exposure in the print and electronic media is fundamental. The success of theatrical engagements, fairs and exhibitions, and entertainment centers such as Disney World depends on their public relations and publicity programs.

Professional and big-time college sports is another category in which energetic public relations efforts are necessary. Every professional team has its public relations specialist, and athletic departments of large universities have their sports information directors. (See Chapter 20.)

PUBLIC AFFAIRS, THE MILITARY, AND POLITICS

Many men and women pursue public relations careers by working for government agencies, the military services, and political figures.

The massive administrative and legislative structure of federal, state, and local governments needs to explain its work to the taxpayers who support it and to help them obtain the services it provides. This work is done by thousands of specialists, usually called *public information officers* or *public affairs officers*. Best known of these is the presidential press secretary at the White House, who has a sizable staff of assistants. Every government department and agency in Washington has its public information office. Similar but less elaborate establishments do the same work for state governments, large municipalities, and assorted other agencies such as regional water authorities.

The military services have an elaborate public information service network. Its principal functions are to (1) provide information about military policies and operations, (2) encourage recruiting, (3) maintain good relationships between military installations and their surrounding communities, and (4) distribute news about individuals in the service (see the example of the Navy's Blue Angels in this chapter). The way in which the U.S. military forces presented and distributed information about the Persian Gulf war between the allied coalition and Iraq is a graphic example of government public affairs in operation. The carefully designed content of the military briefings and the manner in which military commanders limited reporting by media correspondents strongly influenced the picture of war operations received by the public.

National political leaders frequently have personal public relations aides, although the functions of these assistants may be obscured by a title such as "administrative assistant." Governors and large-city mayors have them, too. Image-building is a constant preoccupation of politicians, who seek to give the impression that they are energetic practitioners of good government, working hard to help the people who elected them.

When a politician runs for major office, the press secretary is a key figure on the candidate's staff. Often a candidate hires a public relations firm that specializes in political campaigns to help plan strategy. Voter opinion polls help to form the strategy. Spot television commercials and ten-second "sound bites" on TV newscasts have become primary campaign tools.

EDUCATION

Public relations programs are essential to the well-being of universities and colleges. Practitioners on campus either conduct or assist in several important functions that further the school's cause among students, alumni, and the public. In large universities, the public relations staffs needed to perform these functions are substantial in size.

In Utah, for example, Brigham Young University mounted an extensive public relations campaign to publicize its "Ramses II: The Pharaoh and His Time" exhibit on loan from the Egyptian government. Public relations staff created visual and printed

HIGH-FLYING PUBLIC RELATIONS

The U.S. Navy and Marine Corps generate publicity and goodwill through performances by the Blue Angels precision flying team at numerous air shows throughout the nation. The mission and purpose of the Blue Angels was explained by the Navy as follows:

> By representing a faultless display of aerial artistry to what has now exceeded 201 million spectators, the Blue Angels seek to attract talented and qualified youth to join them in the U.S. Navy and Marine Corps. As "ambassadors of good will," the Blue Angels take naval aviation to the public as a means of demonstrating the quality of personnel and equipment comprising the U.S. Naval Service.

Blue Angels pilots create community goodwill by visiting hospitals and youth organizations and speaking to civic clubs. They also attend special functions arranged by local Navy recruiters and talk to prospective enlistees. Pilots are booked for media interviews. Extensive coverage is generated by offering rides to reporters so they can describe their experiences traveling at 600 miles per hour in a jet fighter.

The Blue Angels precision flying team roars past in tight formation.

materials for the event, organized the opening ceremonies and VIP ("very important person") activities, and reached 125,000 university alumni in a direct mail campaign. As a result, 520,000 people visited the exhibition.

Among the areas in which collegiate public relations practitioners may be involved are:

1. News releases—distribution to the news media of information about campus events, research, and faculty/student achievements
2. Publications—preparation of periodicals, brochures, and catalogues
3. Alumni contact work—various activities, including campus tours for returning alumni and other visitors
4. Relations with federal, state, and local governments
5. Fund-raising—solicitation of donations from foundations, alumni, federal and state governments, and special-interest groups. This work is vital to privately operated universities and colleges and also of great importance to tax-supported institutions.
6. Student recruitment
7. Internal public relations with faculty, staff, and student body

In urban areas, elementary and high school districts frequently have public relations officers to assist the news media and to work with parents and school groups. (More information on educational public relations may be found in Chapter 19.)

CASE PROBLEM

Teddy Bear, Inc., is a toy manufacturer located in Columbus, Ohio. Its specialty, "Fred Bear," can play back ten recorded messages at the touch of a button on its back. In its beginning years, the company emphasized product publicity. Now a large national company, it wishes to expand its public relations activities.

You are hired to be vice president of corporate communications and are asked to propose a project in each of the ten principal areas of public relations outlined in this chapter. What project would you recommend for each area?

QUESTIONS FOR REVIEW AND DISCUSSION

1. Protecting and enhancing a corporation's reputation is an important role for a public relations practitioner. Name three aspects of this function.

2. Some public relations people substitute the term *corporate identity* for *image-building*. Why?

3. Part of product publicity is knowing how to handle a product recall. What good and bad examples of how a company handled a recall can you remember?

4. What is the difference between *investor relations* and *financial relations*?

5. What kinds of activities are performed by public relations personnel in employee relations?

6. What kinds of publics are usually addressed in public affairs?

7. What are the five basic processes in *issues management*?

8. Describe the principal functions of a trade association.

9. How did the apple industry fight back against charges that the fruit might cause cancer in children?

10. Why do labor unions need public relations programs?

SUGGESTED READINGS

Bernstein, Jack. "PR Pivotal to Megamarketing, Expert Says." *Advertising Age*, April 28, 1986, p. 30.

Cantor, Bill. *Experts in Action*. New York: Longman, 1989. Chapters by various authors that highlight the variety of public relations activity.

Carlson, Peter. ''The Image Makers.'' Washington *Post* magazine, February 11, 1990, pp. 12–17, 30–35. Public relations in Washington, D.C.

Davids, Meryl. ''How Now, IR?'' *Public Relations Journal,* April, 1989, pp. 15–19. The field of investor relations.

Eilts, Catherine M. ''High-Tech Public Relations: An Upstart Matures.'' *Public Relations Journal,* February 1990, pp. 22–27.

''Financial Services PR: Booming New Area.'' *Communication World,* September 1987, pp. 31–33.

Foehrenbach, Julie, and Goldfarb, Steve. ''Employee Communication in the 1990s.'' *Communication World, May–June 1990, pp. 101–106.*

Lewton, Kathleen Larey. ''Health Care: Critical Conditions.'' *Public Relations Journal,* December 1989, pp. 18–22. Health-care public relations.

Lowengrad, Mary. ''Community Relations: New Approaches to Building Consensus.'' *Public Relations Journal,* October 1989, pp. 24–30.

CHAPTER

3

History of Public Relations

Practitioners who lack an understanding of how public relations evolved cannot consider themselves professionals. Knowledge of the history of the field is essential if today's practitioners are to benefit from the ideas generated by their predecessors. Every society, and every craft, owes a distinct debt to the past.

This chapter explores some of the opinion-influencing practices of past centuries, including the press agentry of the nineteenth century. It explains how modern counseling and other public relations functions evolved out of simple publicity at the beginning of the twentieth century.

We describe how a number of women advocates of feminist and other causes effectively used some of the techniques of public relations. We emphasize the little-recognized professional public relations role played by Doris E. Fleischman, wife and business partner of her fellow pioneer Edward L. Bernays.

Along the way we introduce some other interesting, imaginative people, including Phineas T. Barnum, Ivy Ledbetter Lee, Henry Ford, Paul W. Garrett, Carl O. Byoir, and Leone Baxter—individuals who have helped shape the course of public relations over the last 100 years.

We explore the steady growth and the current international development of public relations, and we close with a discussion by prominent leaders of the problems that seem to lie ahead for public relations nationally and internationally.

THE ROOTS OF PUBLIC RELATIONS

Public relations is a twentieth-century phenomenon whose roots extend deep into history; in a sense it is as old as human communication itself. In succeeding civilizations, such as those of Babylonia, Greece, and Rome, people were persuaded to accept the authority of government and religion through techniques that are still used: interpersonal communication, speeches, art, literature, staged events, publicity, and other such devices. None of these endeavors was called public relations, of course, but their purpose and their effect were the same as those of similar activities today.

The following remarks of Peter G. Osgood, president of Carl Byoir & Associates, provide a few examples of the early practice of the art of public relations:

> The art has many roots. For example, the practice of dispatching teams to prepare the way for a traveling dignitary or politician was not invented by Harry Truman or Richard Nixon. Their political ancestors in Babylonia, Greece, and Rome were quite adept at it.
>
> St. John the Baptist himself did superb advance work for Jesus of Nazareth.
>
> Publicity, community relations, speech writing, positioning, government relations, issues analysis, employee relations, even investor relations: when you think about these activities in terms of the skills needed to practice them, it's plain they have deep historical roots.
>
> Generating publicity for the Olympics in ancient Athens, for example, demanded the same skills as [it did in 1984] in Los Angeles.
>
> Speech writing in Plato's time meant the same thing as it does today at Byoir: you must know the composition of your audience, never talk down to them, and impart information that will enlighten their ignorance, change their opinion, or confirm their own good judgments.
>
> Businesses in the Republic of Venice in the latter half of the Fifteenth Century practiced as fine an art of investor relations as IBM does in the United States in the latter half of the Twentieth Century: perhaps even finer since it was practiced one-on-one, face-to-face, every day on the Rialto, just as it was under the spreading elm tree on Wall Street in the early days of the Stock Exchange.

Other examples abound. In the eleventh century, throughout the far-flung hierarchy of the Roman Catholic Church, Pope Urban II persuaded thousands of followers to serve God and gain forgiveness of their sins by engaging in the Holy Crusades against the Muslims. Six centuries later, the church was among the first to use the word *propaganda,* with the establishment by Pope Gregory XV of the College of Propaganda to supervise foreign missions and train priests to propagate the faith.

The stories that Spanish explorers publicized of the never-discovered Seven Cities of Gold, and even the fabled Fountain of Youth, induced others to travel to the New World. Some of the explorers probably believed those stories themselves. Two more blatant deceptions—examples of actions unacceptable to public relations people today—occurred when Eric the Red, in A.D. 1000, discovered a land of ice and rock and, to attract settlers, named it Greenland; and when Sir Walter Raleigh in 1584 sent back glowing accounts of what was actually a swamp-filled Roanoke Island, to persuade other settlers to travel to America.

It is clear, then, that the idea of using all forms of human communication—drama and storytelling among them—to influence the behavior of other people is nothing new.

THE EVOLVING FUNCTIONS

An excellent way to understand what public relations is all about today is to examine the evolution of its principal functions—press agentry, publicity, and counseling—along with the methods used to carry out those functions.

PRESS AGENTRY

''Hyping''—the promotion of movie and television stars, books, magazines, and so on through shrewd use of the media and other devices—is an increasingly lively phenomenon in today's public relations world. At the center of hyping is the press agent, whom the *American College Dictionary* defines as ''a person employed to attend to the advertising of a theater, performer, etc., through advertisements and notices to the press.''

Press agentry is simply an extension of the activities of those who, in ancient civilizations, promoted athletic events such as the Olympic games and built an aura of myth around emperors and heroes. Its modern expression may be found in the press agentry that, during the nineteenth century in America, promoted circuses and exhibitions; glorified Davy Crockett as a frontier hero in order to draw political support from Andrew Jackson; attracted thousands to the touring shows of Buffalo Bill and sharpshooter Annie Oakley; made a legend of frontiersman Daniel Boone; and promoted hundreds of other personalities, politicians, and theatrical performers with remarkable success.

The oldtime press agents and the show people they most often represented played upon the credulity of the public in its longing to be entertained, whether deceived or not. Advertisements and press releases were exaggerated to the point of being outright lies. Doing advance work for an attraction, the press agent dropped a sheaf of tickets on the desk of a newspaper city editor along with the announcements. Voluminous publicity generally resulted, and reporters, editors, and their families flocked to their free entertainment with scant regard for the ethical constraints that largely prohibit such practices today.

Small wonder then that today's public relations practitioner, exercising the highly sophisticated skills of evaluation, counseling, communication, and influencing management policies, shudders at the suggestion that public relations grew out of press agentry. And yet some aspects of modern public relations have their roots in the practice.

Phineas T. Barnum, the great American showman of the nineteenth century, for example, was the master of the *pseudoevent,* the planned happening that occurs primarily for the purpose of being reported—a part of today's public relations activities.

Barnum, who was born in Connecticut in 1810, was also a hardheaded businessman, devoted to his family, a generous contributor to charities, a nondrinker, an accumulator of property, imaginative and energetic, a man whose primary love in staging his circus performances was to make children smile. Beyond that, however, most of today's public relations people would like to part company—for Barnum used deception, hoax, and humbuggery in his operations and in his advertising and publicity. Even so, a public hungry for entertainment accepted his exaggerations, perhaps because they were audacious. Spectators thrilled to the wonders that he presented:

- Joice Heath was a slave who said she was 161 years old and claimed to have been George Washington's nurse. Barnum even produced a stained birth certificate, but an autopsy disclosed she was far younger.
- Tom Thumb became one of the sensations of the century. Barnum discovered Charles S. Stratton in Connecticut when Stratton was 5 years old, only an inch over 2 feet in stature and weighing 15 pounds. Barnum made a public relations event of "General" Tom Thumb's marriage to another midget. After triumphal tours of the United States, where Tom Thumb entertained audiences with singing, dancing, and comedy monologues, Barnum took his attraction to England. Europeans were already familiar with midgets, however—their use as entertainment dated back to the royal courts of the Middle Ages—so Barnum had to come up with something that made Tom Thumb special. A tiny carriage and ponies helped to attract attention, but Barnum decided that the best way to get public acceptance was first to involve the opinion leaders. Consequently, he invited London society leaders to his townhouse, where they met the quick-witted Tom Thumb. This meeting resulted in an invitation to the palace. Having entertained royalty, Tom Thumb drew full houses every night. Barnum, even in his day, knew the value of third-party endorsement.
- Jenny Lind, the "Swedish Nightingale," was one of Europe's most famous singers but was virtually unknown in the United States. Consequently, Barnum launched an unprecedented press campaign to acquaint the American public with her well-loved voice. He obtained full houses on opening nights in each community by donating part of the proceeds to charity. As a civic activity, the event attracted many of the town's opinion leaders, whereupon the general public flocked to attend succeeding performances—a device still employed today. Barnum also capitalized on the idea, current at the time, that anything from Europe must be culturally superior.
- Jumbo, the world's largest elephant, was brought by Barnum from England with enormous publicity. Posters and pamphlets featuring exaggerated woodcuts and inflated prose trumpeted the animal's size.
- The Barnum & Bailey Circus, with its 3 rings, 2 stands, and 800 employees, was proclaimed "The Greatest Show on Earth." Neil Harris, in his book *Humbug: The Art of P. T. Barnum,* describes the circus as the showman's "one enduring monument to fame; the legacy lies in his name left for the future."

Barnum owed much of his success to a corps of press agents headed by Richard F. "Tody" Hamilton. A famous circus clown, "Uncle" Bob Sherwood, described Hamilton as a verbal conjurer whose language was so polysyllabic that "an Oxford professor would have found it difficult to understand."

Upon Barnum's death in 1891, the London *Times* joined in almost universal acclaim of his life with the eulogy: "His death removes an almost classic figure, and his name is a proverb already, and a proverb it will continue until mankind has ceased to find pleasure in the comedy of the showman and his patrons—the comedy of the harmless deceiver and the willingly deceived.''

PUBLICITY

Early Development Publicity, which consists mainly of the issuing of news releases to the media about the activities of an organization or an individual, is one of the earliest forms of public relations. It has been used for virtually every purpose. Signs such as ''Vote for Cicero. He is a good man.'' have been found by archaeologists in ruins of ancient civilizations. In 59 B.C. Julius Caesar ordered the posting of a news sheet, *Acta Diurna,* outside the Forum to inform citizens of actions of Roman legislators; Caesar's *Commentaries* were published largely to aggrandize the achievements of the emperor.

The Colonial Era In 1620, broadsides were distributed in Europe by the Virginia Company offering 50 acres of free land to those bringing settlers to America by 1625. In 1641, Harvard College published a fund-raising brochure, and in 1758, Kings College (now Columbia University) issued its first press release, announcing commencement exercises.

Mainly through the use of newspapers and pamphlets, a staged event (the Boston Tea Party), and wide publicity accorded the so-called Boston Massacre, fiery Samuel Adams and the Boston Radicals achieved a propaganda triumph in helping persuade the American colonists to revolt against Great Britain. Also highly instrumental in bringing lukewarm citizens into the Revolutionary movement was Tom Paine's *Common Sense;* more than 120,000 copies of the pamphlet were sold in three months. Influencing public opinion both in the colonies and in England were the *Federalist Papers,* comprised of 85 letters written by Alexander Hamilton, James Madison, and John Jay, and a series of articles by John Dickinson titled ''Letters from a Farmer in Pennsylvania.'' The most frequently cited female propagandists of the era included Mercy Otis Warren, Abigail Adams, and Sarah Bache, daughter of Benjamin Franklin, who lent his journalistic skills to the American cause, too (see Figure 3.1).

Nineteenth Century Public affairs were controlled mainly by the aristocratic, propertied class until the revolt of the so-called common man placed rough-hewn Andrew Jackson in the White House in 1828. Amos Kendall, a former Kentucky newspaper editor, became an intimate member of Jackson's ''kitchen cabinet'' and probably the first presidential press secretary. The appointment demonstrated for the first time that public relations is integral to political policy-making and management.

Jackson's campaign and presidency represented the first attempt in American political life to gain broad-based support for a presidential candidate. Kendall sampled public opinion on issues, advised Jackson, and skillfully interpreted his rough ideas, putting them into presentable form as speeches and news releases. He served as Jackson's advance agent on trips, wrote glowing articles that he sent to supportive newspapers, and was probably the first to use newspaper reprints in public relations; almost every complimentary news story or editorial about Jackson was reprinted and circulated.

FIGURE 3.1
This famous cartoon was published in 1754 in Benjamin Franklin's *Pennsylvania Gazette* as part of the campaign to create unity among the American colonies.

After the Jacksonian era, American politicians increasingly used press releases, pamphlets, posters, and emblems to win favor. The effort reached a nineteenth-century crescendo during the presidential campaigns of William Jennings Bryan and William McKinley in 1896.

Throughout the century, publicity techniques helped populate western land. Newly sprung-up villages competed to attract printers, whose newspaper copies and pamphlets describing almost every community as "the garden spot of the West" were sent back East to induce increased settlement. Many settlers were lured to Illinois, for example, by gazettes that extolled the fertile land. Henry W. Ellsworth's *Valley of the Upper Wabash,* published in the 1830s, and another publication, *Illinois in 1837,* were subsidized by speculators seeking to lure land-buyers. One critic of the time called these gazettes downright puffery, "full of exaggerated statements, and high-wrought and false-colored descriptions."

In addition, the supporters of such causes as antislavery, antivivisectionism, women's rights, and prohibition employed publicity to maximum effect throughout the century. One of the most influential publicity ventures for the abolition of slavery was the publication of Harriet Beecher Stowe's *Uncle Tom's Cabin.* Stowe was among a number of women who, although they were not public relations people, extensively used the techniques of public relations to promote their causes. Sarah J. Hale, editor from 1836 to 1877 of *Godey's Ladies Book,* a best-selling magazine with 150,000 circulation, ardently promoted women's rights. After a women's rights convention in Seneca Falls, New York, in 1845, Amelia Bloomer became famous. Now associated with the loose-fitting trousers she wore in protest of the corset, she edited *The Lily,* a woman's rights publication. Noted temperance crusader Susan B. Anthony was business manager of *The Revolution,* which advocated a variety of radical causes. The American Woman Suffrage Association was formed in 1869 with Lucy Stone as editor of its weekly, *The Woman's Journal*. While adoption of the Nineteenth Amendment to the U.S. Constitution in 1920 gave women the right to vote, the movement ended without ensuring women greater property rights.

A wave of industrialization, mechanization, and urbanization swept the nation after the Civil War. Concentrations of wealth developed throughout manufacturing and trade. Amid the questioning of business practices, the Mutual Life Insurance Company in 1888 hired journalist Charles J. Smith to write press releases designed to improve its image. In 1889 Westinghouse Corporation established what is said to be the first in-house publicity department, with a former newspaper reporter, E. H. Heinrichs, as manager. In 1897 the term *public relations* was used by the Association of American Railroads in a company listing.

Twentieth Century As the use of publicity gained increased acceptance, the first publicity agency, known as the Publicity Bureau, was established in Boston in 1900. Harvard College was its most prestigious client. George F. Parker and Ivy Ledbetter Lee opened a publicity office in New York City in 1904. Parker remained in the publicity field, but Lee became an adviser to companies and individuals (as will be discussed in the section that follows). In Washington, D.C., William Wolf Smith established a firm to influence legislators through publicity.

A second Boston publicity business was opened in 1906 by James D. Ellsworth, who later joined the staff of the American Telephone & Telegraph Company. Theodore N. Vail greatly expanded the press and customer relations operations at AT&T after becoming its president in 1907. In 1909 another pioneer, Pendleton Dudley, established a public relations office in New York.

The Santa Fe Railway, at the beginning of the twentieth century, commissioned dozens of painters and photographers to depict scenes in the then little-known Southwest. The paintings unabashedly prettified the American Indian, and the photographs, colored by hand, showed the Indians weaving, grinding corn, and dancing. This corporate image-making attracted hundreds of tourists and contributed to the romanticizing of the Indian and the West.

The Chicago Edison Company broke new ground in public relations techniques under the skillful leadership of its president, Samuel Insull. Well aware of the special need of a public utility to maintain a sound relationship with its customers, Insull created a variety of techniques—he established an external magazine, *Chicago, The Electric City,* in 1903; used press releases extensively; was the first in business to use films for public relations purposes, in 1909; and started the "bill stuffer" idea in 1912 by inserting company information into customer bills.

Henry Ford probably was the first major industrialist to utilize thoroughly two basic public relations concepts. The first was the notion of *positioning*—the idea that credit and publicity always go to those who do something first—and the second idea was ready accessibility to the press. Joseph Epstein, author of *Ambition,* says, "He may have been an even greater publicist than mechanic."

In 1900 Ford obtained coverage of the prototype Model T by demonstrating it to a reporter from the Detroit *Tribune*. By 1903 Ford achieved widespread publicity by racing his cars—a practice that is still carried out today by automakers. Ford hired Barney Oldfield, a champion bicycle racer and a popular personality, to drive a Ford car at a record speed of 1 minute and 6 seconds per mile, or a bit less than 60 miles per hour. The publicity from these speed runs gave Ford financial backing and a ready market for the regular production of cars.

Ford also positioned himself as the champion of the common person and was the first automaker to envision that a car should be affordable for everyone. To this end, he produced his first Model T in 1908 for $850 and, by 1915–1916, was able to reduce its selling price to $360. Such price reductions made Ford dominant in the auto industry and on the front pages of the nation's newspapers. He garnered further publicity and became the hero of working men and women by being the first automaker to double his worker's wages to $5 per day.

Ford became a household word because he was willing to be interviewed by the press on almost any subject, including the gold standard, evolution, alcohol, foreign affairs, and even capital punishment. His comments, not always based on informed knowledge, were pithy and easily quotable. A populist by nature, he once said, "Business is a service, not a bonanza," an idea reiterated by many of today's top corporate executives who believe business has a social responsibility.

Although Ford was the first major industrialist to hire blacks in large numbers, he also wrote a number of anti-Semitic articles. In the 1930s, his earlier image as the champion of the working class was shattered by his resistance to organized labor, which led to several violent confrontations as the United Automobile Workers attempted to organize Ford workers.

In politics, President Theodore Roosevelt proved himself a master in generating publicity. Roosevelt was the first president to make extensive use of news conferences and interviews in drumming up support for his projects. He knew the value of the presidential tour for publicity purposes. For example, on a trip to what became Yosemite, designed to publicize the idea of national parks, Roosevelt was accompanied by a bevy of reporters and photographers who wrote glowing articles about the need to preserve the area for public recreational use.

Not-for-profit organizations joined the publicity bandwagon in the century's first decade. The American Red Cross and the National Tuberculosis Association began extensive publicity programs soon after their formation in 1908. Two other nonprofit organizations, the Knights of Columbus and the National Lutheran Council, opened press offices in 1918.

COUNSELING

Industrialists and Muckrakers In the latter part of the nineteenth century, the United States was transformed by mighty economic and social forces. Industrialization moved forward on a major scale; cities swelled with even more immigrants; production was rapidly being mechanized; and business firms grew through the use of vastly improved transportation and communication facilities, along with new interlocking corporate structures and financing methods.

It was the era of the so-called robber barons, exploiters of natural resources and labor, known in less accusatory terms as founders of great American industries. Heavy concentrations of power were held by John D. Rockefeller, Sr., in oil; Andrew Carnegie in steel; J. Pierpont Morgan, Cornelius Vanderbilt, and Jay Gould in finance; Leland Stanford, Collis P. Huntington, James J. Hill, and George Pullman in railroading; Gustavus F. Swift and Philip D. Armour in meat packing; and other industrial leaders. Labor strife intensified, and the government, upon the urging of populist and progressive forces, began to challenge big business with the enactment of such measures as the Interstate Commerce Act and the Sherman Antitrust Act.

Within the dozen years after 1900, several magazines developed a literature of exposure that Theodore Roosevelt called the work of "muckrakers." He was comparing the more sensational writers to the Man with the Muckrake in the seventeenth-century work *Pilgrim's Progress*—a character who did not look up to see the celestial crown but continued to rake the filth. Led by Ida M. Tarbell, these writers posed a serious threat to business. Tarbell wrote a series of articles published by *McClure's* in 1903 titled "History of the Standard Oil Company," an attack on the corruption and unfair practices of the Rockefeller oil monopoly. Other noted muckrakers included Upton Sinclair, who exposed unsanitary and fraudulent practices of the meat packers in his 1906 book *The Jungle*.

The First Public Relations Counsel The combination of stubborn management attitudes and improper actions, labor strife, and widespread public criticism produced the first public relations counselor, Ivy Ledbetter Lee. Although, as previously noted, this Princeton graduate and former business reporter for the New York *World* began his private practice as a publicist, he shortly expanded that role to become the first public relations counsel.

The emergence of modern public relations can be dated from 1906, when Lee was hired by the anthracite coal industry, then embroiled in a strike. Lee discovered that, although the miners' leader, John Mitchell, was supplying reporters with all the facts they requested, by contrast the leader of the coal proprietors, George F. Baer, had refused to talk to the press or even to President Theodore Roosevelt, who was seeking to arbitrate the dispute. Lee persuaded Baer and his associates to change their policy. He issued a press notice signed by Baer and the other leading proprietors that began: "The anthracite coal operators, realizing the general public interest in conditions in the mining regions, have arranged to supply the press with all possible information. . . ."

Lee issued a "Declaration of Principles," which signaled the end of the "public-be-damned" attitude of business and the beginning of the "public-be-informed" era. Eric Goldman said the declaration "marks the emergence of a second stage of public relations. The public was no longer to be ignored, in the traditional manner of business, nor fooled, in the continuing manner of the press agent." The declaration reads:

> This is not a secret press bureau. All our work is done in the open. We aim to supply news. This is not an advertising agency; if you think any of our matter ought properly to go to your business office, do not use it. Our matter is accurate. Further details on any subject treated will be supplied promptly, and any editor will be assisted most cheerfully in verifying directly any statement of fact. . . . In brief, our plan is, frankly and openly, in behalf of business concerns and public institutions, to supply to the press and the public of the United States prompt and accurate information concerning subjects which it is of value and interest of the public to know about.

Ivy Ledbetter Lee won recognition early in the twentieth century as the first public relations counsel. (UPI/Bettmann Archive.)

The continuance of Lee's policy of providing accurate information about corporate and institutional activities has saved American news media millions of dollars in reporter salaries during the intervening eight decades. Despite some misleading information given out by some public relations people, news releases quickly became extremely valuable—even a necessity—to the media.

Railroads at the time also were seeking to operate secretly in their dealings with the press. Retained by the Pennsylvania Railroad Company to handle press relations after a major rail disaster, Lee persuaded the president to alter his policy. Lee provided press facilities, released all available information, and enabled reporters to view the disaster scene. Although such action appeared to the conservative railway directors to constitute reckless indiscretion, they later acknowledged that the company had received fairer press comment than on any previous such occasion.

In 1914, John D. Rockefeller, Jr., hired Lee in the wake of the vicious strikebreaking activities known as the Ludlow Massacre at the Rockefeller family's Colorado Fuel and Iron Company plant. Lee went to Colorado and talked to both sides. He also persuaded Rockefeller to talk with the miners and their families. Lee made sure that the press was there to record Rockefeller's eating in the workers' dining hall, swinging a pick ax in the mine, and having a beer with the workers after hours. The press portrayed Rockefeller as seriously concerned about the plight of the workers, thus increasing his popularity with the striking miners. Meanwhile, Lee distributed a factsheet giving management's view of the strike and even convinced the governor of Colorado to write an article supporting the position taken by the company.

Rockefeller's visits with the miners led to policy changes and more worker benefits, but the company also prevented the United Mine Workers from gaining a foothold. George McGovern, former Democratic Party candidate for President, wrote his doctoral dissertation on the Ludlow Massacre. "It was the first time in any American labor struggle where you had an organized effort to use what has become modern public relations to sell one side of a strike to the American people."

Lee's success in transforming a labor dispute into a positive situation (and public image) for the Rockefeller family was based on the fact, according to Gordon M. Sears, president of T. J. Ross and Associates, that "Lee tried to solve the problem or at least establish the proper course toward solution before turning to communications." Lee's achievement led the Rockefeller family to hire him for a full-scale renovation of the Rockefeller name, badly damaged by the muckrakers who often pictured John D. Rockefeller, Sr., as an exploiter and the king of the greedy capitalists. Lee advised the Rockefellers to announce publicly the millions of dollars that they gave to charitable institutions. He also convinced John, Sr., to allow reporters and photographers to record his golf playing and socializing with family and friends. When John, Sr., died in 1937, he was mourned worldwide as a kindly old man and a great humanitarian and philanthropist.

In 1933 Lee assessed his contribution to the Rockefeller family: "It might interest you to know that in the 18 years I have been associated with Mr. Rockefeller, the only thing that has been done has been to assist Mr. Rockefeller in his interest in the development of sound policies and to let the public find out about those policies in a natural way."

Lee's public relations firm became Lee, Harris, and Lee in 1916. Three years later he was joined by Thomas J. Ross in the firm of Ivy Lee and T. J. Ross and Associates. Among other counseling activities, Lee advised the American Tobacco Company to initiate a profit-sharing plan, the Pennsylvania Railroad to beautify its stations, and the movie industry to stop inflated advertising and form a voluntary code of censorship.

Lee lost a measure of public trust by advocating diplomatic recognition and trade with the Bolsheviks in the 1920s. He defended his stand by arguing that such action was necessary to resolve differences between the United States and the Soviet Union.

John D. Rockefeller, Sr., often was photographed giving dimes to children during the 1920s. His public relations counselor, Ivy Ledbetter Lee, has been credited with suggesting that Rockefeller do so to improve his image, but Lee says he merely convinced Rockefeller to let news photographers show what he had been doing for years. Rockefeller gave millions to charity. Here he presents a dime to William Gebele, Jr., at Lakewood, New Jersey. (AP/Wide World Photos.)

His reputation was damaged more severely when a congressional hearing disclosed that he was working for the Hitler government while being paid by Germany's I. G. Farben chemical firm as a subterfuge in the early 1930s. Lee said he opposed Hitler and counseled the firm as a means of obtaining goodwill and product sales in the United States. The secret relationship caused Congress to pass the Foreign Agents Registration Act (see Chapter 15).

Lee died in 1934. He is remembered for four important contributions to public relations: (1) advancing the concept that business and industry should align themselves with the public interest, and not vice versa; (2) dealing with top executives and carrying out no program unless it had the active support and personal contribution of management; (3) maintaining open communication with the news media; and (4) emphasizing the necessity of humanizing business and bringing its public relations down to the community level of employees, customers, and neighbors.

PUBLIC RELATIONS ROOTS IN GERMANY, GREAT BRITAIN, AND AUSTRALIA

Germany As the Industrial Revolution swept through Europe, few owners, as in the United States, sensed a need to communicate with the public about their operations. In Germany, however, railroad companies and at least one share-holding corporation began publicity efforts as far back as the mid-nineteenth century. Alfred Krupp, founder of the Krupp Company, which became the premier industrial firm in Germany and the base of the Nazi war power, wrote to a financial adviser in 1866:

> We think . . . it is time that authoritative reports concerning factory matters in accordance with the facts should be propagated on a regular basis through newspaper reports which serve the enlightened public. We can supply the material for this purpose, and should qualified experts at times be unavailable, it is our wish to contact responsible newspaper editors ourselves.

Company documents reveal that Krupp was unable to find a qualified person to assist him in the effort. However, his son, Friedrich Alfred Krupp, hired Adolf Lauter in 1893 to establish a news bureau, and the department was integrated into the firm's operations in 1901.

As the Krupp public relations efforts expanded internationally, other major industries followed suit. Ivy Lee's involvement in 1933 with the I. G. Farben cartel, through its German Dye Trust, was mentioned previously.

Great Britain The industrial and communication systems of Great Britain were already developed in 1910, when the Marconi Company established a department to distribute news releases about its achievements in wireless telegraphy.

Professional public relations counseling was introduced in the country in 1924, when Sir Basil Clarke, a former government press officer, established Editorial Services Ltd. in London. For his first client, a dairy group, he promoted the idea of milk pasteurization, an innovation that had met with some resistance from the public.

The first public relations officer so styled in Britain was Sir John Elliott, appointed in 1925 by the Southern Railway Company.

Beginning in the mid-nineteenth century, the government enjoyed a close working relationship with the Reuters news agency for almost 100 years. Paul Julius Reuter,

Wartime Counsel to Government Both world wars saw a tremendous upsurge in the role of public relations on behalf of the government—especially the Creel Committee during World War I and the Office of War Information during World War II.

The Creel Committee. "Literally public relations counselors to the United States Government" during World War I is the description given to members of the Committee on Public Information by James O. Mock and Cedric Larson in their book *Words That Won the War*. President Wilson called upon George Creel, a former newspaper reporter, to organize a comprehensive public relations effort to advise him and his cabinet, to carry out programs, and to influence United States and world opinion. Wrote Mock and Larson:

agency owner, was granted use of cables linking the empire's outposts; in return, agency dispatches did much to further the nation's commercial and political interests, and there is little doubt that the news service was careful to say at crucial points what the British government wished it to say. With such an arrangement, historians have noted, government propaganda was particularly effective in bringing the United States to its side in World War I. Today, Reuters operates with scant if any government influence.

In 1911 the first government public relations campaign was carried out when, at the instigation of Prime Minister David Lloyd George, the Insurance Commission explained the benefits of the National Insurance Act, an unpopular measure that had attracted much adverse publicity. The Air Ministry appointed the first government press officer in 1919, and a year later the Ministry of Health selected Sir Basil Clarke, a former Reuters correspondent, as director of information.

Government public relations was substantially enlarged after World War II. The offices now are organized into three sections: press relations, publicity and inquiry, and intelligence. During recent extended freedom-of-information debates, however, the system was labeled the most secretive in the world (an obvious exaggeration), and demands were made that the service be disbanded and its work turned over to regular administrators.

Via shortwave, the British Broadcasting Company (BBC), chartered in 1922, carries a British point of view in its news dispatches and commentary to an estimated 75 million adults around the world each week.

Australia Public relations in Australia largely consisted of publicity efforts until after World War II. When U.S. General Douglas MacArthur arrived in Australia after his escape from Corregidor in 1942, he introduced the term *public relations* and, with a highly skilled staff, demonstrated numerous ways of promoting his image and war policy.

The industry grew steadily, and, in 1960, the Public Relations Institute of Australia (PRIA) was formed. It now includes more than 1500 practitioners throughout the country. Women, today comprising about one-third of the nation's public relations specialists, were among its founders.

Notable practitioners include George Fitzpatrick, credited with being the first Australian to conduct public relations, and Eric White, who, a Hill and Knowlton official said, "virtually created the public relations industry" in Australia. As early as the 1960s White oversaw extensions of his firm in six Pacific Rim countries.

> Mr. Creel assembled as brilliant and talented a group of journalists, scholars, press agents, editors, artists, and other manipulators of the symbols of public opinion as America had ever seen united for a single purpose. It was a gargantuan advertising agency, the like of which the country had never known, and the breathtaking scope of its activities was not to be equalled until the rise of the totalitarian dictatorship after the war. George Creel, Carl Byoir, Edgar Sisson, Harvey O'Higgins, Guy Stanton Ford, and their famous associates were literally public relations counselors to the United States Government, carrying first to the citizens of this country and then to those in distant lands, the ideas which gave motive power to the stupendous undertaking of 1917–1918.

Among numerous other activities, the committee persuaded newspapers and magazines to contribute volumes of news and advertising space to encourage Americans to save food and to invest heavily in Liberty Bonds, which more than 10 million people purchased. Thousands of businesses set up their own groups of publicity people to expand the effort. Wilson accepted Creel's advice that hatred of the Germans should be played down and loyalty and confidence in the government should be emphasized. The committee publicized the war aims and ideals of Woodrow Wilson—to make the world safe for democracy and to make World War I the war to end all wars. The American Red Cross, operating in cooperation with the committee, enrolled more than 19 million new members and received over $400 million in contributions during the period.

The massive effort had a profound effect upon the development of public relations by demonstrating the success of these full-blown techniques (see Figure 3.2). It also awakened an awareness in Americans of the power of persuasive approaches. This, coupled with postwar analysis of British propaganda devices alleged to have helped get the nation into the war, resulted in a number of scholarly books and college courses on the subject. Among the books was Walter Lippmann's classic *Public Opinion,* in which he pointed out how people are moved to action by "the pictures in our minds."

Another legacy was the training received by the noted public relations practitioners Carl Byoir, associate chairman of the committee, and Edward L. Bernays. Byoir in 1930 founded a company that for more than a half century was one of the largest public relations firms in the United States. Bernays's contributions to public relations will be discussed shortly.

Office of War Information (OWI). To head the vital war information operation during World War II, President Franklin Roosevelt turned to Elmer Davis, an Indiana-born journalist and a Rhodes Scholar. Davis had spent 15 years as a novelist and free-lance writer, 10 years as a New York *Times* reporter, and 3 years as a radio commentator for the Columbia Broadcasting System.

Profiting by knowledge of the techniques so successful in World War I, Davis orchestrated an even larger public relations effort during World War II. His job was exceptionally difficult because his office had to coordinate information from the military and numerous government agencies, wrestle for funds each year with a Congress suspicious that the OWI would become Roosevelt's personal propaganda vehicle, and overcome opposition from a large segment of the press that resented having to do business with an official spokesperson.

As in World War I, the OWI's campaigns were extremely successful in promoting the sale of war bonds and in obtaining press and broadcast support for other wartime

FIGURE 3.2
Howard Chandler Christy's poster stimulated recruiting during World War I long before women could join the U.S. Navy.

As director of the Office of War Information, Elmer Davis led the U.S. government's public relations program in World War II. (Courtesy ABC.)

necessities. These included food, clothing, and gasoline rationing; more "victory gardens"; higher productivity and less absenteeism; and secrecy regarding troop movements and weaponry development.

The OWI news bureau had 250 full-time employees, and 300 reporters and correspondents used its facilities. Davis established a Domestic Branch, which, according to the director, "did not withhold news because we did not like it, nor delay it to produce a greater effect." His Overseas Branch also provided news to foreign peoples but with selective timing and emphasis. The OWI worked harmoniously and effectively with the Office of Censorship.

Of the domestic operation, Davis declared: "It is the job of OWI not only to tell the American people how the war is going, but where it is going and where it came from—its nature and origins, how our government is conducting it, and what (besides national survival) our government hopes to get out of victory."

The Voice of America, established by the Department of State in 1942, carried news of the war to all parts of the world. The film industry provided support through such means as Frank Capra's documentary film for the U.S. Signal Corps, designed to build patriotism; bond-selling tours by film stars; and the production of commercial movies glorifying U.S. fighting forces.

The OWI was the forerunner of the U.S. Information Agency, established in 1953 under President Eisenhower to "tell America's story abroad." A number of the people who worked with Davis became public relations leaders during the ensuing decades.

Further Development of the Counseling Function The role of the public relations practitioner as an adviser to corporate and institutional managements grew in significance as the American economy expanded during the 1920s. The persons most responsible for defining this function and drawing public attention to it were Edward L.

Bernays and his wife and partner Doris E. Fleischman. Fleischman was a talented writer, ardent feminist, and former assistant women's page and assistant Sunday editor of the New York *Tribune*. Married in 1922, they became equal partners in the firm of Edward L. Bernays, Counsel on Public Relations. The partnership continued until Fleischman's death in 1980.

Fleischman indeed was an equal partner in the work of the firm, interviewing clients, writing news releases, editing the company's newsletter, and writing and editing books and magazine articles, among other duties. As a contributor to a 1989 book, *Women in Mass Communication: Challenging Gender Values,* edited by Pamela J. Creedon, historian Susan Henry, a professor of journalism at California State University, Northridge, says that Bernays called Fleischman "the brightest woman I'd ever met in my life" and "the balance wheel of our operation." At one point Bernays recalled that, "I used to say to her, 'It's great to have a George Gallup right in the house.'"

The male value system of the time, however, did not allow Fleischman to represent the firm to its clients or even to be included in the firm's title. Other historians have credited to Bernays both his own and their shared public relations achievements, included in the list of early examples of counseling that follows shortly.

The Concept Explained "In writing this book I have tried to set down the broad principles that govern the new profession of public relations counsel." With this opening sentence of *Crystallizing Public Opinion,* published in 1923, Bernays coined a

Edward L. Bernays is a legendary figure in public relations, with a career spanning almost three-quarters of a century. Bernays, who celebrated his ninety-ninth birthday in 1990, continues to lecture and write about public relations.

Doris Fleischman was the partner and wife of Edward L. Bernays in their pioneer public relations couseling firm. (Courtesy of Edward L. Bernays.)

term to describe a function that was to become the core of public relations. He illuminated the scope and function, methods and techniques, and social responsibilities of public relations. Following by a year Walter Lippmann's insightful treatise on public opinion, the book attracted much attention, and Bernays was invited by New York University to offer the first public relations course in the nation.

Even so, the name and definition that Bernays gave to the scope and function of public relations failed for years to gain acceptance by editors and scholars, most of whom equated the new business with press agentry. Stanley Walker, famed city editor of the New York *Herald Tribune,* wrote later:

> Bernays has taken the sideshow barker and given him a philosophy and a new and awesome language. . . . He is no primitive drum-beater. . . . He is devoid of swank and does not visit newspaper offices [as did the circus advance agents]; and yet, the more thoughtful newspaper editors, who have their own moments of worry about the mass mind and commercialism, regard Bernays as a possible menace, and warn their colleagues of his machinations.

This antipathy toward public relations still lingers among many journalists.

In 1955 Bernays refined his approach to public relations and, in a book titled *The Engineering of Consent,* he gave the field a new name. To many people, the word *engineering* implied manipulation through propaganda and other devices. Bernays, who himself later railed at use of the word *image* to mean reputation-building, defended his terminology and concept:

> The term engineering was used advisedly. In our society, with its myriads of group interests, interest groups, and media, only an engineering approach to the problems of adjustment, information, and persuasion could bring effective results. . . .

Public relations practiced as a profession is an art applied to a science, in which the public interest and not pecuniary motivation is the primary consideration. The engineering of consent in this sense assumes a constructive social role. Regrettably, public relations, like other professions, can be abused and used for anti-social purposes. I have tried to make the profession socially responsible as well as economically viable.

Early Examples of Counseling The following examples illustrate how effectively Bernays performed his public relations work:

- When, in the 1910s, the actor Richard Bennett wanted to produce *Damaged Goods,* a play about sex education, Bernays blunted the anticipated criticism of moralists, and possibly avoided a police raid, by organizing the Sociological Fund of the *Medical Review of Reviews* journal, with contributors paying $4 each to attend the play as an educational event.
- To help Procter & Gamble sell Ivory soap, Bernays attracted the attention of children and their parents to cleanliness by developing a nationwide interest in soap sculpture.
- In an effort to humanize President Calvin Coolidge, described by the writer Dorothy Parker as "weaned on a pickle," Bernays arranged a breakfast at the White House during which Al Jolson, the Dolly Sisters, and other celebrities performed. The unprecedented event brought nationwide publicity.
- To demonstrate the safety of radium when properly handled and to gain acceptance of radium in therapy for cancer and for use in luminous gauges, Bernays, in behalf of the U.S. Radium Corporation, carried a gram of the substance by rail to a state hospital in Buffalo.
- At a time when public opinion and some legislation kept women from smoking in public, Bernays was hired by George Washington Hill, president of the American Tobacco Company, to expand sales of Lucky Strike cigarettes. Bernays consulted a psychoanalyst, who told him that cigarettes might be perceived as "torches of freedom" by women seeking equality with men. Bernays helped break the barrier by inducing ten debutantes to "light up" while strolling in New York City's traditional Easter parade.
- Later, when research showed that sales of Lucky Strike cigarettes to women were down because many felt that the green package clashed with their clothes, Bernays tried to persuade Hill to change the color. Unsuccessful in the effort, Bernays made green fashionable by arranging a prestigious socialites' ball with that color scheme; getting makers of accessories to promote green shoes, hosiery, and gloves; and arranging for green fashion displays on the covers of *Harper's Bazaar* and *Vogue* on the date of the ball. (Only during World War II, when an ingredient in the color became an industrial scarcity, did Hill relent, nevertheless reaping continued sales with the slogan, "Lucky Strike Green Has Gone to War.")
- When the short-hair fashion introduced by dancer Irene Castle sharply reduced the sale of hairnets, Bernays, working for the Venida Company, emphasized the use of hairnets as a safety measure for women working with machinery, and laws were

passed requiring the protective devices. The sanitary aspect of hairnets worn by cooks and waitresses also was heralded.

Perhaps the most spectacular example of Bernays's skill took place in 1929. To celebrate the fiftieth anniversary of Thomas Edison's invention of the electric light bulb, Bernays arranged the worldwide-attention-getting Light's Golden Jubilee. On October 21, many of the world's utilities shut off their power all at one time, for one minute, in honor of Edison. President Herbert Hoover and many other dignitaries attended a banquet climaxing the celebration. The event achieved such fame that the U.S. Post Office, on its own, issued a commemorative two-cent postage stamp.

Sociologist Leonard W. Doob described the jubilee as "one of the most lavish pieces of propaganda ever engineered in this country during peace time." Bernays, wrote Doob, was working "not for Edison or for Henry Ford, but for very important interests [General Electric and Westinghouse had hired Bernays] which saw this historic anniversary as an opportunity to publicize the uses of the electric light." Of course, the worldwide publicity and media attention also were helped by the fact that Thomas Edison was already widely heralded as the godhead of American science and ingenuity.

Light's Golden Jubilee is considered one of Bernays's major accomplishments. It showed, in 1929, the potential of effective public relations. And when television commentator Bill Moyers interviewed Bernays in 1984 on a Public Broadcasting Service program about the early beginnings of public relations, Moyers said: "You know, you got Thomas Edison, Henry Ford, Herbert Hoover, and masses of Americans to do what you wanted them to do. You got the whole world to turn off its lights at the same time. You got American women to smoke in public. That's not influence. That's power."

Replied Bernays: "But you see, I never thought of it as power. I never treated it as power. People want to go where they want to be led."

Although he retired from full-time consulting in 1962, Bernays has continued to write, give interviews, and lecture about his favorite theme of public relations as a profession and an applied social science. He wrote regularly for the *Public Relations Quarterly,* often on the theme of licensing as a way to remove incompetent and unethical practitioners from the field. He is widely acknowledged as the founder of modern public relations; one historian has even described him as "the first and doubtless the leading ideologist of public relations." Sigmund Freud, founder of psychoanalysis, must have been proud of his nephew. In 1990 *Life* magazine cited Bernays as one of the 100 most important Americans of the twentieth century.

Other Public Relations Pioneers Benjamin Sonnenberg, Rex Harlow, and Leone Baxter loom large in the list of other early, influential public relations counselors.

BENJAMIN SONNENBERG. It was Sonnenberg who suggested that the Texaco Company sponsor performances of the Metropolitan Opera Company on national radio. Sponsorship of the Saturday afternoon series, which began in 1940, still continues. Sonnenberg, who believed that a brief mention of a client in the right context is better than a long-winded piece of flattery, proposed Texaco's sponsorship after some segments of the American public criticized the company for negotiating with Adolf Hitler on an oil deal in the mid-1930s. With time, Texaco emerged as a patron of the arts, and critics forgot about the dealings with Hitler before the outbreak of World War II.

REX HARLOW. Harlow was probably the first full-time public relations educator. As a professor in Stanford University's School of Education, Harlow began teaching a public relations course on a regular basis in 1939. In that same year he founded the American Council on Public Relations (which eventually became the Public Relations Society of America), serving as its president for eight years. He criss-crossed the country giving workshops and seminars for practitioners that continued for about twenty years. It is estimated that 10,000 people received their first formal instruction in public relations from this educator.

In 1952, Harlow founded the *Social Science Reporter,* one of the first newsletters in the field. In it he actively sought to show practitioners and top management how social science research findings benefit the practice of public relations. Harlow, a prolific writer, produced many articles and seven books on public relations.

LEONE BAXTER. A partner for more than 25 years with Clem Whitaker in the firms of Whitaker & Baxter, Campaigns Incorporated, W&B Advertising, and California Feature Service, Leone Baxter has headed Whitaker & Baxter International since her partner's death in 1961. As president, she counsels clients in the United States and abroad, formulates plans, and directs the staff that carries them out.

The firm is credited with being the first professional political campaign management organization in the United States, setting the pace for many thousands today.

Baxter has won the Gold Anvil, PRSA's highest personal award, for her distinguished career and for ethical contributions to the public relations profession. Her philosophy, often expressed—and not always popular—emphasizes that "the public

Leone Baxter, with Clem Whitaker, founded the first professional political campaign management firm in the United States during the early 1940s. The firm conducted campaigns for a number of California governors including Earl Warren, and gained national attention in General Dwight Eisenhower's presidential campaign of 1952. Whitaker died in 1961. Baxter, headquartering in San Francisco, heads Whitaker and Baxter International, counselors in national and international public affairs.

assessment of our profession in the final analysis must hinge very largely on the profession's candid assessment of itself, on its standards and its own efforts to create and maintain a highly capable, ethical, and responsible profession.''

Among the most widely known advocates of social causes in the twentieth century who effectively used some of the techniques of public relations were Margaret Sanger, founder of the Planned Parenthood Federation of America; singer Kate Smith, who sold thousands of dollars in U.S. bonds during World War II while making Irving Berlin's ''God Bless America'' almost the national anthem; Dorothy Day, founder of the widely respected *Catholic Worker* magazine in 1933 and its editor until 1980, an active pacifist and worker for the nonviolent achievement of social justice; Gloria Steinem, cofounder with Patricia Carbine of *Ms.* magazine, chronicler of the feminist movement for almost two decades; and Betty Friedan, originator of the National Organization of Women (NOW) in 1966, who promoted numerous women's causes and whose accomplishments included the adoption of a prochoice plank at the NOW convention in 1967.

Serving on the Management Team Public relations counseling is at its best when it functions at the very top level of management. American corporate executives have been slow to accept this viewpoint. Its recognition in recent years has resulted mostly from the experiences of companies whose leaders understood much of what public relations is all about.

Arthur Page, who became vice-president of the American Telephone & Telegraph Company in 1927, helped shape today's practice by advocating the philosophy that public relations is a management function and that it should have an active voice in management. He also expressed the belief that a company's performance, not press agentry, comprises its basis for public approval.

Alfred P. Sloan, then president of General Motors Corporation, also was among the first executives to place great trust in public relations. In 1931, during the early years of the Great Depression when business was attacked widely for its failures, Sloan hired Paul W. Garrett as his first public relations employee.

Garrett was charged with ascertaining public attitudes and executing a program to bring the company full public approval. For one thing, the board of directors felt that favor might be gained by making the billion-dollar corporation appear small. Garrett considered that approach neither reasonable nor possible. Instead, he informed management that it must interpret itself by words and deeds that had meaning to those outside the company; that it must put the broad interests of the public first; that it must develop sound internal relationships with its employees; and that it must be frank and honest and explain the company's policies clearly and simply through every possible medium.

Garrett's program proved highly effective, and his speechmaking and other activities during a 25-year career with General Motors broadened the understanding of leaders of many other major organizations about the full-fledged public relations function. *Fortune* magazine, in a series of articles in 1938 and 1939, praised the GM program, along with those of Chrysler, Ford, and AT&T, and also lauded public relations itself as a valuable economic, social, and political function. No important magazine had previously reported on a corporation's public relations and described the function as a vital management responsibility.

Another example of high-level management counseling that won wide attention was that provided by Earl Newsom for Henry Ford II. When Ford took over the reins of the company, he was relatively unknown, because Edsel Ford had been groomed as the heir apparent. There was widespread conjecture as to whether Henry Ford II could lead the company properly. The grandson of the pioneer automobile maker employed Newsom in 1945 to advise him during a strike by the United Automobile Workers. Planning was Newsom's forte: he issued no news releases and held no news conferences. By

FOUR MODELS OF PUBLIC RELATIONS

To aid in understanding the history of formal public relations as well as its practice today, Professors James E. Grunig of the University of Maryland, and Todd Hunt of Rutgers: The State University of New Jersey have constructed four models of public relations. All four models are practiced today, but the "ideal" one—that in increasing use—is the two-way symmetric model. They explain the models in their 1984 book *Managing Public Relations:*

Press Agentry/Publicity Propaganda is the purpose, sought through one-way communication that is often incomplete, distorted, or only partially true. The model is source → receiver. Communication is viewed as telling, not listening, and little if any research is undertaken. P. T. Barnum was the leading historical figure during this model's heyday from 1850 to 1900. Sports, theater, and product promotion are the main fields of practice today by about 15 percent of public relations operations.

Public Information Dissemination of information, not necessarily with a persuasive intent, is the purpose. The model is source → receiver. Research, if any, is likely to be confined to readability tests or readership studies. Ivy Lee is the leading historical figure during this model's early development period from about 1900 into the 1920s. Government, nonprofit associations, and business are primary fields of practice today by about 50 percent of public relations operations.

Two-way Asymmetric Scientific persuasion is the purpose, and communication is two-way, with imbalanced effects. The model is source → receiver, with feedback (←) to the source. Research is both formative, helping to plan an activity and to choose objectives, and evaluative, finding if the objective has been met. Ivy Lee is the leading historical figure during the model's period beginning in the 1920s. Competitive business and public relations firms are the primary places of practice today by about 20 percent of public relations operations.

Two-way Symmetric Gaining mutual understanding is the purpose, and communication is two-way with balanced effects. The model is group → group with feedback (←). Formative research is used mainly both to learn how the public perceives the organization and to determine what consequences the organization has for the public, resulting in the counseling of management about policies. Evaluative research is used to measure whether a public relations effort has improved both the understanding publics have of the organization and that which management has of its publics.

Edward L. Bernays, educators, and professional leaders have been the main historical figures of the two-way symmetric model, followed by some organizations since the 1960s and 1970s. Some practitioners are just beginning to adopt the model today.

preparing five major speeches for Ford II before major, influential audiences, Newsom achieved both public and press recognition for Ford's ability, along with much quotable copy.

PUBLIC RELATIONS COMES OF AGE

AFTER WORLD WAR II

The booming economy after World War II produced rapid growth in all areas of public relations. Companies opened public relations departments or expanded existing ones. Government staffs increased in size, as did those of nonprofit organizations such as educational institutions and health and welfare agencies. Television emerged in the late 1940s as a new challenge for public relations expertise. New firms sprang up in cities throughout the country, many discovering that they were required not only to sell their own services to potential clients but first to educate many managers on the value of public relations itself.

By 1950 an estimated 17,000 men and 2,000 women were employed as practitioners in public relations and publicity. Typical of the public relations programs of large corporations at midcentury was that of the Aluminum Company of America. Heading the operation was a vice president for public relations–advertising, aided by an assistant public relations director and an advertising manager. Departments included community relations, product publicity, motion pictures and exhibits, employee publications, news bureau, and industrial economics (speechwriting and educational relations). *Alcoa News* magazine was published for all employees, as well as separate publications for those in 20 plants. The main broadcast effort was sponsorship of Edward R. Murrow's "See It Now" television program.

A British scholar, J. A. R. Pimlott, wrote in 1951: "Public relations is not a peculiarly American phenomenon, but it has nowhere flourished as in the United States. Nowhere else is it so widely practiced, so lucrative, so pretentious, so respectable and disreputable, so widely suspected and so extravagantly extolled."

Census-takers in 1960 counted 23,870 men and 7,271 women engaged in public relations, although some observers put the total figure at approximately 35,000. Most were employed in fields of manufacturing, business services, finance, insurance, religion and other nonprofit groups, public administration, and communications.

Since 1960, the number of public relations practitioners has dramatically increased. The U.S. Bureau of Labor Statistics in 1986 estimated that 157,000 were employed in the field and that women, for the first time, comprised more than 50 percent of public relations personnel. The publication of public relations magazines and newsletters has stimulated and coordinated the activity of practitioners. Recent surveys show that four out of five large companies and trade organizations now have public relations departments. Additionally, there are more than 6000 public relations firms. In 1980 the top 50 public relations firms posted revenues of $200 million; in 1990 total revenues reached $1.01 billion.

Journalism and mass communications schools also have felt the impact of public relations majors. In 1989 an estimated 190 colleges and universities offered degrees or sequences in public relations—about 50 percent of the total number of institutions offering journalism and mass communications programs.

WHY PUBLIC RELATIONS IS GROWING

Ronald B. Millman, a partner of the Financial Relations Board Inc. of Chicago and president of that city's PRSA chapter, says public relations "came of age" during the 1980s. Citing the increasing number of practitioners and the rise in billings by the top ten U.S. public relations firms (to more than $910 million in 1990, more than seven times that of 1980), Millman offers seven reasons for the growth:

- *PR is cost-efficient.* An annual public relations campaign costs less than the production of most television commercials.
- *PR has won over management.* With issues such as ecology, civil rights, equal rights, and consumerism commanding increased attention, management has come to realize the value of its public relations operation.
- *The penalties of poor PR are viewed each night on the 10 o'clock news.* With the Exxon oil disaster as an example, good managers realize they must prepare for crises as though they were part of the year's business plan.
- *PR is no longer measured by the ink (or time) it produces.* Measurement tools are now far more sophisticated.
- *PR is becoming more specialized.* Many public relations firms now concentrate their efforts solely in one area, such as finance, consumer marketing, crisis communications, employee communications, and politics.
- *PR tools are becoming more complex.* For example, video news releases are a basic ingredient of almost every marketing public relations program, and faxing releases is an accepted means of distributing news not only to the media but also to the business community.
- *Markets are going international.* The stakes of competing in the global marketplace have increased along with the obstacles, such as different languages, cultures, and approaches. Public relations is the technique of choice as a global communication tool.

Public relations majors now constitute a healthy percentage of the declared majors in departments and schools of journalism and mass communications. By 1983, a survey by Professor Albert Walker of Northern Illinois University noted that in 60 percent of the institutions offering such studies, public relations sequences ranked first or second in total enrollment.

The popularity of public relations as a major field of study also is reflected in annual statistics gathered by the Association for Education in Journalism and Mass Communication (AEJMC). As early as 1987, Professor Paul Peterson of Ohio State University, who conducted the annual AEJMC survey for many years, declared, "Indications are clear that the areas of advertising and public relations are the leaders in attracting student interests." Data collected in 1989 by Professor Lee Becker, who now conducts the survey, projected that almost 22,000 majors were studying public relations in 190 American colleges and universities. This figure does not include many public relations sequences in departments and schools of communication. Reports from Australia, Singapore, England, and Germany also show major increases in public relations enrollments.

The Public Relations Student Society of America, founded in 1968, provides important professional training on campus. (See Chapter 5.) The International Association of Business Communicators (IABC) also has individual student members and some student chapters, but no national student organization.

Public Relations Literature A measurement of the growth of public relations in the twentieth century also may be found in its literature. From 1900 to 1928, only two books with "public relations" in their titles were listed in the catalogue *Books in Print*. Landmark publications include the following:

- 1902: "What Is Publicity?" by H. C. Adams, in the *American Review*. Perhaps the first magazine article dealing with public relations as a topic.
- 1915: *Publicity and Progress,* by H. H. Smith.
- 1920: *Winning the Public,* by S. M. Kennedy.
- 1922: *Getting Your Name in Print,* by Funk & Wagnalls, the dictionary publisher.
- 1923: *Crystallizing Public Opinion,* by Edward L. Bernays. By far the most lasting of the early books, and still available in print.
- 1924: *Public Relations: A Handbook of Publicity,* by John C. Long.
- 1944: Founding of *Public Relations Journal,* the monthly magazine of the Public Relations Society of America.
- 1947: *Practical Public Relations,* by Rex Harlow and Marvin Black. Perhaps the first regular public relations textbook.
- 1949: *Public Relations in Management,* by J. Handly Wright and Byron H. Christian. The first attempt to link public relations with management.
- 1952: *Effective Public Relations,* by Scott Cutlip and Allen Center. The best-known basic textbook for many years, now in its sixth edition.
- 1954: First doctoral dissertation on public relations. By Frederic J. O'Hare, Columbia University.
- 1955: Founding of *Public Relations Quarterly*.
- 1957: *A Public Relations Bibliography,* compiled by Scott M. Cutlip. The first in the field, and followed in 1974 by *Public Relations: A Comprehensive Bibliography,* compiled by Robert L. Bishop.
- 1970: Founding of *IABC Communication World,* monthly magazine of the International Association of Business Communicators.
- 1974: Founding of *Public Relations Review,* first quarterly refereed journal in public relations. By the Foundation for Public Relations Education and Research.
- 1976: Founding of *IPRA Review,* first magazine devoted to international public relations. By the International Public Relations Association.
- 1989: Founding of *Public Relations Research Annual,* edited by James E. Grunig and Larissa A. Grunig.

Each year hundreds of articles and numerous books are published about public relations and related fields; a wide selection of the most current titles is listed in the bibliography at the end of this book. The body of knowledge about the field has been abstracted and codified by PRSA and is available on computer diskette.

Public Relations Growth Public relations has become essential in modern life because of a multiplicity of reasons, including the following: heavy, continuing population growth, especially in cities where individual citizens have scant direct contact with Big Business, Big Labor, Big Government, Big Institutions, and other powerful organizations influencing their lives; scientific and technological advances, including automation and computerization; the communications revolution; mergers and consolidations, with bottom-line financial considerations often replacing the more personalized decision-making of previous, more genteel times; and the increased interdependence of a complex world society.

Many citizens feel alienated, bewildered by such rapid change, cut off from the sense of community that characterized the lives of previous generations. They seek power through innumerable pressure groups, focusing on causes such as environmentalism, human rights, and antinuclear campaigns. Public opinion, registered through continual polling, has become an increasingly powerful force in combatting or effecting change.

Both physically and psychologically separated from their publics, American business and industry have turned increasingly to public relations specialists for audience analysis, strategic planning, and issues management, among other functions. Corporate social responsibility has become the norm and the expectation. One of the most important tasks of these specialists is that of environmental surveillance—serving, in effect, much like the periscope of a submarine. The continued growth of companies, if not survival itself, depends in large part upon the skills of public relations people.

Research has assumed an importance never before known. Back in 1853, Theodore N. Vail, founder of the American Telephone & Telegraph Company, had sensed its importance, sending letters to his customers seeking their opinions. In 1912, public relations-wise Henry Ford had asked 1000 customers why they had purchased his Model T car. These were among the forerunners of the social science research techniques that were developed after World War I. In the 1930s, George Gallup, Elmo Roper, Claude Robinson, and others began to conduct modern public opinion and marketing surveys. They provided a tool by which public relations specialists and others could evaluate public attitudes quantitatively and obtain objective measurements to supplement personal estimates of public opinion. By the 1990s, aided by the computer, research had become invaluable as a means by which companies and institutions, through their public relations experts, could interact effectively with their many specialized publics.

PUBLIC RELATIONS IN THE 1990s

The field of public relations is constantly evolving, and the 1990s promise to be a decade of major growth, opportunities, and challenges.

Shandwick, the world's largest public relations firm, predicts after a study that public relations will experience a record growth at a compound rate of 20 percent until the mid-1990s. That means the public relations industry would double in four years.

On a worldwide basis Shandwick predicts that public relations expenditures will grow at a 26 percent rate each year in the United Kingdom, 28 percent in Germany, and 100 percent in some Asian nations.

The shape of public relations in the 1990s, according to public relations leaders, will be formed by a number of national and global issues confronting the profession. A digest of what is foreseen follows.

A Global Economy Every national economy and every business is part of an integrated global economy. The internationalization of business means that companies and public relations people must learn a great deal about foreign cultures, business practices, and languages. Accompanying this globalization thrust, the wealth of the world has largely shifted from the West to the Pacific Rim, especially to Japan, Taiwan, Singapore, and Korea. Of the largest 25 companies in the world, 19 are Japanese and one is European.

J. F. Coates, coauthor of a recent book titled *What Futurists Believe,* writes: "The primary challenge to American business is for better design, higher quality, more sure and speedy service, durable performance, and general reliability in schedules, claims, and effectiveness." And Daniel W. Bellack, chairman of TFB/BBDO Business Communications, Inc., says: "Global strategy really means localizing. . . . Be sure you understand each local market, culture, and, of course, language."

Quality of the Environment Concern for the environment is now a widespread issue, and people in many countries believe that protecting it is so important that no requirements and standards can be too high. Environmental issues also translate as a "quality of life" issue: people are concerned about their health and perceive a direct self-interest in such issues as the "greenhouse effect," acid rain, pollution, toxic wastes, and the spread of AIDS. Because such issues are transnational in scope, international dialogue and cooperation are prerequisites for effective solutions.

Corporations in the 1990s must be more sensitive to environmental concerns than in the past and show diverse publics that they are part of the solution, not the problem. At the same time, says C. J. Silas, chairman of Phillips Petroleum Company, "The challenge for industry and government will be to balance the two good, but seemingly paradoxical, objectives of environmental protection and economic growth and development." Companies deemed by the public to be insensitive to the environment, he states, will be the focus of consumer boycotts.

Increased Management Role for Public Relations Impediments to sales success such as environmental concerns require that public relations play a major role in the strategic planning and policy formulations of companies. John L. Clendenin, chairman of BellSouth Corporation, says, "I can't imagine any institution being able to operate successfully in today's environment without effective and proactive public relations management."

James A. Burke, former chairman of Johnson & Johnson, adds, "The CEO must have an understanding of how essential it is for public relations to be an intimate part of the decision-making process." Robert E. Allen, chairman of AT&T, puts it quite simply: "I need PR at my side, not in my wake." This means that in the 1990s "Public relations professionals had better be prepared to think and perform like senior-level

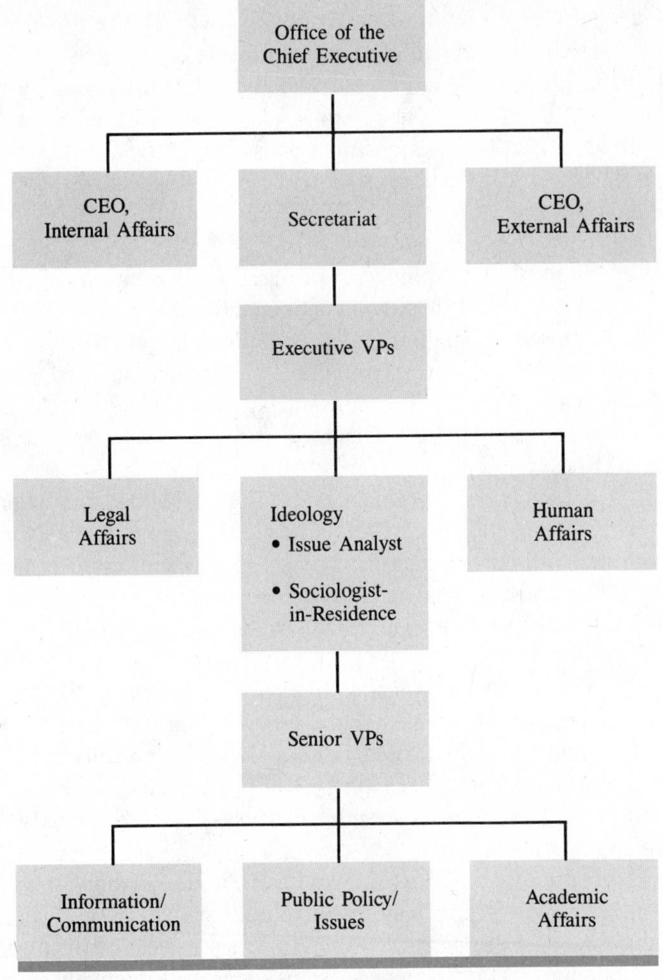

FIGURE 3.3
The organization chart of a future corporate structure in public relations, designed by veteran counselor John F. Budd, Jr. (Copyright 1989, John Budd, Jr.)

managers,'' says Lawrence G. Foster, vice president of public relations for Johnson & Johnson.

New Emphasis on Issues Management Many countries are seeking to cope with a flood of public policy issues. Governments as well as corporations are turning to experts skilled in problem analysis and conflict resolution to deal with the tough problems facing society and the planet Earth. Because of these pressures, John D. Francis, president of the Canadian Public Relations Society, says, ''Issues management—improving the potential for controlling situations by understanding the attitudes of the public, the media, and opinion leaders and planning accordingly—will also be increasingly important in the 1990s.'' (See Chapter 14.)

Increased Government Regulation and Intervention The resurgence of popular movements and activist groups will place more pressure on governments to make sure that corporations and other institutions are socially and environmentally responsible. The public also will demand ''right to know'' laws giving them access to full and complete information that corporations now consider proprietary. On another level, government will expect corporations to provide more financial resources (taxes) to clean up the environment.

Proliferation of Publics The splintering of mass markets into hundreds of smaller markets, begun mainly in the 1980s, will continue through the 1990s. Public relations personnel will use microdemographics (closely defining target audiences by age, sex, educational level, and the like) to reach multiple publics with tailored information. In addition to traditional publics such as consumers, stockholders, employees, and the community, audiences also will be fragmented into special-interest groups mobilized around specific issues.

Robert L. Dilenschneider, president and CEO of Hill & Knowlton, says the special-interest environmental groups with large membership that largely comprise the ''green movement'' will demonstrate their power in public affairs and public discussion. Other special-interest groups, he adds, will continue to crystallize around a number of social issues such as abortion, child care, and gun control.

Decline of Mass Media The fragmentation of publics also means the decline of mass media as vehicles with which to reach audiences. The big four media—newspapers, magazines, radio, and television (except cable)—will not be truly major players in public relations communication. Technology will provide an infinite number of avenues for transmitting messages to specific audiences; the key terms will be *niche programming* and *narrowcasting*.

Cynthia Pharr, president of Tracy-Locke Pharr Public Relations, puts it this way: ''With mass media rapidly giving way to specialized vehicles of communication, it is essential to tailor messages to narrow, well-defined audiences.'' This means identifying and understanding particular interest groups, working effectively with the media those groups trust, and developing a variety of messages to reach different audiences. The ''one-size-fits-all'' news release, she contends, is dead. ''Targeting demands multiple releases, each featuring an element or angle that appeals to the audience it hopes to capture,'' Pharr adds. (See Chapter 12.)

Advent of New Media Technologies ''The challenge of the nineties for the communicator is to catch up with, and master, the exploding field of high-tech communication tools,'' says John Armstrong, a veteran counselor and professor at the University of Portland, Oregon. (Technology is discussed in Chapter 21.) Futurist Joseph Coates adds: ''Information technology, by the end of the century, will put every worker in the global corporation in easy communication with any other worker in the global corporation, as well as with any customer, constituent, client, vendor, or regulator.'' For example, an international network permits General Electric Company employees to communicate worldwide, using voice, video, and computer data, by simply dialing seven digits on the telephone. In sum, such a large number of communication vehicles will undercut the influence of the mass media.

International Media Relations Worldwide announcements of new ventures will become the norm during the 1990s. Satellite transmission of press conferences and simultaneous briefings by teams of public relations professionals in various countries will increase. Corporations will maintain decentralized public relations offices in Asia and Africa, says Ann Wilkinson, manager of worldwide public relations for National Semiconductor. Corporations will publish customer and employee newsletters in a variety of languages. Her company, for example, now publishes a consumer newsletter in six.

Higher Priority on Employee Communications Employee relations and communications will be a priority for a number of reasons. First, because the wave of mergers and acquisitions, generally resulting in the discharge of some employees (downsizing), is likely to continue through the 1990s, employee loyalty and trust of their employers will remain at an all-time low. Says James H. Dowling, president of Burson-Marsteller Public Relations: ''The development of employee commitment to the venture—in the face of increased employee distrust of institutions and their leadership—may be the ultimate public relations challenge in the 1990s.''

Second, the composition of the American workforce is rapidly changing to include more women, minorities, and foreign-born persons. This will require management activity in job and literacy training, and in child care. Communicating to a multiethnic workforce will be a major public relations challenge, and the issues will be complex. For example, corporations increasingly will need to provide health education and information programs to reduce the staggering costs of health insurance.

Increased Research and Surveys Public relations people, according to Dilenschneider, will spend much more time analyzing information on a continuing basis. He adds, ''Public relations people will become masters of sampling and surveying, of focused research and intricate problem-solving.'' In employee communications, greater use will be made of attitude surveys and reader-viewer studies to measure the results of communications.

The Skilled Practitioner For the global corporation of the 1990s, public relations personnel will require training and professional experience in marketing, international business, finance, and government. They must be able to perform like senior-level managers, thinking, visualizing, and implementing strategies.

Richard G. Charlton, vice president of corporate communications for Parker Hannifin Corporation, believes the 1990s will mark the rise of the generalist in public relations. ''In the public relations department of the '90s,'' he explains, ''there will likely be more flexible staffing, so that a public relations generalist can cover a story for the corporate newsletter or video news program and at the same time prepare an external news release.'' In addition, the public relations professional will provide increased coaching for middle managers to make them effective speakers and small-group discussion leaders.

Dilenschneider believes that increasing numbers of lawyers, accountants, scientists, and senior government officials will select public relations as their second career fields. "Managers," he points out, "no longer want advice that isn't backed by seasoned operating experience." At the same time, he adds, opportunities for journalists to undertake second careers in public relations will decline.

CASE PROBLEM 1

The latter part of this chapter lists a number of national and global trends predicted to shape the practice of public relations during the 1990s. Select one of these issues and do some additional research. Write a short paper from the standpoint of what a public relations person should know about this issue and how it may affect his or her work in public relations.

CASE PROBLEM 2

The 100th anniversary of a U.S. global soft drinks company is approaching.

As head of the company's public relations department, you are directed to develop a program that will call the event—and the product—to the attention of people around the world.

It's a mammoth undertaking but you have an almost unlimited budget.

Outline some of the actions that you and your colleagues would take. How can the company's history be used?

QUESTIONS FOR REVIEW AND DISCUSSION

1. The roots of public relations extend deep into history. What are some of the early antecedents of today's public relations practice?

2. What is meant by "hyping"?

3. Which practices of press agent Phineas T. Barnum should modern practitioners use? Which should they reject?

4. Describe briefly the publicity practices used by Henry Ford and by Theodore Roosevelt.

5. Ivy Lee made four important contributions to public relations. Can you identify them?

6. What effect did the Creel Committee of World War I have upon the development of public relations?

7. Who was Doris E. Fleischman? Name at least three other women who used public relations techniques in pursuit of their causes.

8. Identify three of the successful public relations campaigns conducted by Edward L. Bernays.

9. What are some of the aspects of current American social and business life that make public relations essential?

10. What major national and global issues confront public relations practitioners today?

SUGGESTED READINGS

Badaracco, Claire. "Publicity and Modern Influence." *Public Relations Review,* Fall 1990, pp. 5–18. The history of publicity in American life.

Budd, John F. "PR Sages See Growth." *Communication World,* May–June 1990, pp. 95–98. Trends in public relations.

Coates, Joseph F. "Business Communication in Millennium III." *Communication World,* May–June 1990, pp. 129–134. Trends in public relations.

Creedon, Pamela J. "Public Relations History Misses 'Her' Story." *Journalism Educator,* Autumn 1989, pp. 26–36. Portrayal of women in histories of public relations.

Cutlip, Scott M. "Pioneering Public Relations for Foreign Governments." *Public Relations Review,* Spring 1987, pp. 13–34.

"Forecast 1991." *Public Relations Journal,* January 1991, pp. 22–27, 38. PRSA section leaders forecast what's ahead in the public relations field.

Fuhrman, Candice Jacobson. *Publicity Stunt: Great Staged Events that Made the News.* San Francisco: Chronicle Books, 1989.

Fullerton, Ronald A. "Art of Public Relations: U.S. Department Stores, 1876–1923." *Public Relations Review,* Fall 1990, pp. 68–79.

Gibson, Dirk. "The Making of the Hoover Myth: A Critical Analysis of FBI Public Relations." *Public Relations Quarterly,* Winter 1988–1989, pp. 7–15.

Nagy, Alex. "Word Wars at Home: U.S. Response to World War II Propaganda." *Journalism Quarterly,* Spring 1990, pp. 207–213.

Olasky, Marvin. "Engineering Social Change: Triumphs of Abortion Public Relations from the Thirties Through the Sixties." *Public Relations Quarterly,* Winter 1988–1989, pp. 17–21.

Pearson, Ron. "Perspectives on Public Relations History." *Public Relations Review,* Fall 1990, pp. 27–38.

"Public Relations in the Year 2000." *Public Relations Journal,* January, 1990. Entire issue devoted to articles exploring multiple trends in public relations.

Saxon, A. H. *P. T. Barnum: The Legend and the Man.* New York: Columbia University Press, 1990.

Wylie, Frank W. "The Challenge of Public Relations Education." *Syracuse Scholar,* vol. 10, no. 1, 1990, pp. 57–66. Historical development of public relations education.

CHAPTER

Public Relations Departments and Firms

The first three chapters have presented an introductory look at the many faces of public relations—the numerous types of activities that practitioners are involved in. This chapter will examine the operational structure of the industry. Two basic types of operations exist: the public relations department and the public relations counseling firm. We describe how both are organized and how they perform their functions.

A substantial majority of practitioners work for public relations or communications departments of companies and nonprofit organizations. A recent survey found that 85 percent of the 1500 largest corporations in the United States have such a department. According to another survey by the International Association of Business Communicators (IABC), nearly half of its members work in a corporate setting. Another 10 percent are employed in public relations departments of nonprofit organizations. The Public Relations Society of America (PRSA) reports that 45 percent of its members work in business and industry, while another 25 percent are in public relations firms. The remaining 30 percent are employed in nonprofit agencies, associations, educational institutions, and government.

Public relations firms offer a wide range of services and expert advice to clients on a fee basis. Their clients primarily are organizations that have limited public relations staffs or seek specialized services.

This chapter takes a look at the advantages and disadvantages of public relations work in each type of setting, and explores some of the problems that each area faces. Students can thus gain an understanding of the operational setup of the industry, as seen in an examination of its two major branches.

ROLE

ROLE

For a century, public relations departments have served companies and organizations. George Westinghouse is reported to have created the first corporate department in 1889 when he hired two men to publicize his pet project, alternating current (AC) electricity. Their work was relatively simple when compared to the melange of physical, sociological, and psychological elements that contemporary departments employ. Eventually Westinghouse won out over Thomas A. Edison's direct current system, and his method became the standard in the United States. Westinghouse's public relations department concept has also grown into a basic part of today's electronic world.

Today, public relations is expanding from its traditional functions, enlarged over the years as explained in Chapter 3, to exercise its influence in the highest levels of management.

Importance in the 1990s In a changing environment, and faced with the variety of pressures previously described, corporate executives increasingly see public relations not as publicity and one-way communication, but as a process of negotiation and compromise with a number of key publics. James Grunig, professor of public relations at the University of Maryland, calls the new approach "building good relationships with strategic publics," which will require public relations executives to be "strategic communication managers rather than communication technicians."

Grunig, head of a six-year, IABC Foundation research study on Excellence in Public Relations and Communications Management, continues:

> When public relations helps that organization build relationships, it saves the organization money by reducing the costs of litigation, regulation, legislation, pressure campaign boycotts, or lost revenue that result from bad relationships with publics—publics that become activist groups when relationships are bad. It also helps the organization make money by cultivating relationships with donors, customers, shareholders and legislators.

The preliminary results of the IABC study do seem to indicate that chief executive officers (CEOs) consider public relations a good investment. A survey of chief executives in 200 organizations, for example, showed that CEOs gave public relations operations a 235 percent return-on-investment, whereas public relations managers of the same organizations gave the function only a 205 percent rating.

Professional public relations people, ideally, assist management in developing policy and communicating with various groups. Research indicates, however, that the role of public relations in an organization often depends on its structure and even the capabilities of the public relations executive.

One study, by Professor Larissa Grunig of the University of Maryland, showed that large-scale, complex organizations have a greater tendency to include public relations in the policy-making process. A company such as IBM or Chevron, which operate in a highly competitive environment, is more sensitive than many others to policy issues, public attitudes, and establishing a solid corporate identity. Consequently, there is more emphasis on news conferences, formal contact with the media, writing executive speeches, and counseling management about issues that could potentially affect the corporation's bottom line.

In contrast, a small-scale organization manufacturing a standardized product feels few public pressures and little governmental regulatory interest. It has scant public relations activity, and staff members are relegated to such technician roles as producing the company newsletter and issuing routine news releases. Public relations has little or no input into management decisions and policy formulation.

Although corporate structure and the pressures of the external environment seem to shape the role of the corporate public relations department, the IABC Foundation research also seems to indicate that the power of the senior public relations person to affect organizational decisions may be limited by his or her background and capabilities. CEOs, for example, prefer strategic communication managers, but a large number of current senior managers—many of them former journalists by training—seem to be preoccupied by the mass media even though, as the IABC research points out, the mass media "generally are not the most effective way of communicating with strategic publics—especially at the stage of building relationships rather than responding to issues."

EXPECTATIONS OF MANAGEMENT

In today's environment every organization must be cognizant of many factors that can affect its success. Modern management recognizes that public relations is a tool for problem-solving as well as attention-getting, and has several expectations.

1. *Information analysis*. Public relations staff members should function as information analysts and information brokers, communicating both outward from management and inward to management with the views of the public and employees.

2. *Issues management*. The public relations staff should monitor trends in society and pinpoint public concerns before they erupt into full-fledged controversies. Indeed, as a PRSA Task Force on the Stature and Role of Public Relations pointed out:

> the greatest value of the public relations professional is in anticipating and shaping what is happening, not in reporting or coping with what has already been determined. By the time an organization is confronted with attitudes of its publics, it is usually too late for public relations thinking to have an effect on them. Dealing with existing attitudes is important, but helping to shape and direct future attitudes is far more valuable.

3. *Training*. Public relations personnel must counsel management on how to communicate the organization's position to the public effectively. Because of societal pressures, top management increasingly is spending more time on public affairs and in speaking to a variety of audiences. Peter Drucker, a management expert, estimates that top executives now spend up to 75 percent of their time on public affairs. Top executives also are less hesitant than previously to appear on television talk shows.

4. *Management expertise*. Public relations personnel—at least those who aspire to key positions in the organization—must master the techniques of management and strategic planning. They must understand such concepts as Management by Objective (MBO), allocation of resources, supervision of personnel, and use of cost-effective communication tools. James E. Burke, former chairman of Johnson & Johnson, says:

The public is more deeply involved in those events that affect the corporation than ever before imaginable. The CEO will increasingly be challenged to act swiftly, decisively and responsibly on all kinds of issues in a way that the public can comprehend. This means that the public relations executive should have easy and open access to the chairman's office. . . .

DEPARTMENT ORGANIZATION

The head executive of a public relations or similarly named department usually has one of three titles—manager, director, or vice president. A vice president of corporate communications may have direct responsibility for the additional activities of advertising and marketing communications.

A department usually is divided into specialized sections that have a coordinator or manager. Common sections found in a large corporation are media relations, investor relations, consumer affairs, governmental relations, community relations, marketing communications, and employee communications.

A typical organizational chart for a public relations department is shown in Figure 4.1.

One of the world's largest corporations, General Motors, has more than 300 public relations personnel and a wide range of job titles based on geography and operating

FIGURE 4.1
The organizational chart of the Hewlett-Packard Corporation's corporate public relations department. The corporate press relations unit is subdivided into "general press" and "product press" relations. The executive communication unit includes the function of investor relations, and the public relations services unit includes community relations. (Courtesy of Hewlett-Packard.)

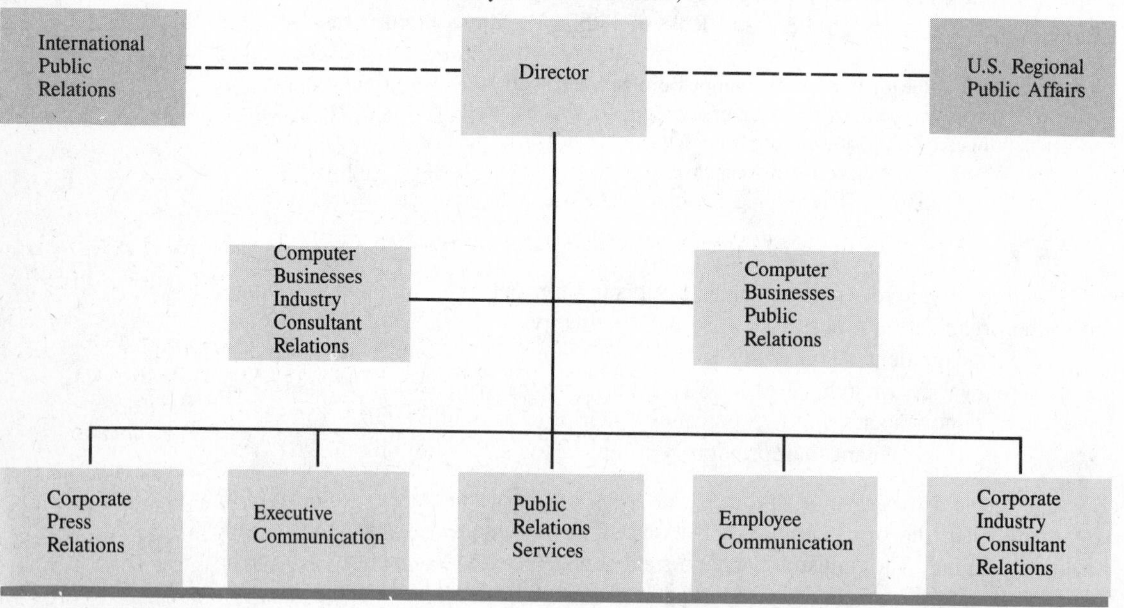

divisions. Each division, such as Buick or the Saginaw Steering Gear Division, has its own director of public relations. General Electric, another corporate giant, has several hundred persons in various public relations functions.

These examples should not mislead the reader about the size of public relations departments in American companies. Multimillion-dollar corporations often have small departments. Most public relations people work in departments that have fewer than ten on the staff.

Public relations personnel also may be dispersed throughout an organization in such a manner that an observer has difficulty in ascertaining the extent of public relations activity. Some may be housed under marketing communications in the marketing department. Others may be assigned to the personnel department as communication specialists producing newsletters and brochures. Still others may be in marketing, working exclusively on product publicity. Decentralization of the public relations function, and the frictions it causes, will be discussed later in this chapter.

LINE VERSUS STAFF FUNCTION

Traditional management theory divides an organization into *line* and *staff* functions. A line person—for example, a vice president of manufacturing—is concerned with achievement of an organization's objectives, such as the manufacture and sale of personal computers. A line manager accomplishes this goal through the delegation of authority, the assignment of projects, and the supervision of others, such as assembly-line workers. A staff person, in contrast, indirectly influences the work of others through the use of suggestions, recommendations, and advice.

According to accepted management theory, public relations is a staff function. Public relations personnel are experts in communication. Line managers, including the president of the organization, rely on public relations people to utilize their skills in preparing and processing data, making recommendations, and executing communication programs to implement the organization's policies.

Public relations staff members, for example, may find through a community survey that people have only a vague understanding of what the company manufactures. In order to improve community comprehension and create greater rapport, for instance, the public relations department may recommend to top management that a community open house be held at which product demonstrations, tours, and entertainment would be featured.

Notice that the department *recommends* this action. It would have no direct authority to decide arbitrarily on an open house and to order various departments within the company to cooperate. If top management approves the proposal, the department may take responsibility for organizing the event. Top management, as line managers, has the authority to direct all departments to cooperate in the activity.

Although public relations departments can function only with the approval of top management, there are varying levels of influence that departments may exert. These levels will be discussed shortly.

Access to Management The power and influence of a public relations department usually result from access to top management, which uses advice and recommendations to formulate policy. That is why public relations, as well as other staff functions, is located high in the organizational chart and is called upon by top management to make reports and recommendations on issues affecting the entire company. In today's environment, public acceptance or nonacceptance of a proposed policy is an important factor in decision-making—as important as costing and technological ability. This is why the former president of RJR Nabisco, F. Ross Johnson, told the *Wall Street Journal* in an interview that his senior public relations aide was "Numero Uno" and quipped, "He is the only one who has an unlimited budget and exceeds it every year."

The organizational chart of General Motors, for example, also shows public relations as a policy group reporting directly to the executive committee, consisting of the GM president and key board members. Other policy groups with the same status as public relations include engineering, marketing, personnel, and research—all of which have functions that affect every area of the corporation.

Levels of Influence Management experts state that staff functions in an organization operate at various levels of influence and authority. On the lowest level, the staff function may be only *advisory:* line management has no obligation to take recommendations or even request them.

When public relations is purely advisory, often it is not effective. A good example is the Alaska oil-spill crisis (see Chapter 14). Exxon generated a great deal of public, legislative, and media criticism because public relations was relegated to a low level and was, for all practical purposes, nonexistent.

Johnson & Johnson, on the other hand, gives its public relations staff function higher status. The Tylenol crisis, in which seven persons died after taking capsules containing cyanide, clearly showed that the company based much of its reaction and quick recall of the product on the advice of public relations staff. In this case, public relations was in a *compulsory-advisory* position (see the case study on Tylenol in Chapter 14).

Under the compulsory advisory concept, organization policy requires that line managers (top management) at least listen to the appropriate staff experts before deciding on a strategy. Don Hellriegel and John Slocum, authors of the textbook *Management,* state: "Although such a procedure does not limit the manager's decision-making discretion, it ensures that the manager has made use of the specialized talents of the appropriate staff agency."

Another level of advisory relationship within an organization is called *concurring authority*. For instance, an operating division wishing to publish a brochure cannot do so unless the public relations department approves the copy and layout. If differences arise, the parties must agree before work can proceed. Many firms use this mode to prevent departments and divisions from disseminating materials not in conformity with company standards. In addition, the company must ascertain that its trademarks are used correctly to ensure continued protection (see Chapter 13).

Concurring authority, however, also may limit the freedom of the public relations department. Many companies have a policy that all employee magazine articles and external news releases must be reviewed by the legal staff before publication. The material cannot be disseminated until legal and public relations personnel have agreed upon what will be said. The situation is even more limiting on public relations when the legal department has *command authority* to change a news release with or without the consent of public relations. This is one reason that newspaper editors find some news releases so filled with "legalese" as to be almost unreadable.

Editors are likely to find news releases in the high technology field particularly difficult to follow, because in some companies the engineering staff has command authority to insert technical terms and jargon without the consent of the public relations staff. In such a case, the unfortunate public relations person usually reaps the criticism of the news media for giving out material that is useless for publication or broadcast.

SOURCES OF FRICTION

Invariably, frictions arise between line and staff people. This problem results from such factors as personality conflicts, orientation, and place in the organizational chart.

Surveys show that line people are generally oriented to the advancement of the company and that their future is heavily dependent upon being loyal to the organization. Staff people, on the other hand, tend to be oriented toward the advancement of their profession, whether it be engineering, scientific research, advertising, marketing, or public relations. Staff people identify highly with an occupation rather than with an organization. Physicians, for example, have more loyalty to the standards of the medical profession than to the particular hospital in which they practice.

A major cause of friction is the fact that staff units are higher in the organizational structure than line units and enjoy a direct reporting relationship with top management. Staff people often acquire informal authority by having the ear of management. Staff recommendations accepted by top management are effective in shaping policies that line managers must carry out.

Friction also occurs between staff units. The public relations function often intrudes on the staff functions of legal, human resources, advertising, and marketing.

Legal The legal staff tends to be concerned about the possible effect of any public statement on present or impending lawsuits. Consequently, lawyers often frustrate public relations personnel by requiring revisions of news releases, sometimes excessively. The work of attorneys may take place in a court of law, while public relations people strive to represent the organization in what Professor Emeritus Walt Seifert of Ohio State University has called "the court of public opinion." Composing a clear, succinct news release while satisfying the legal department's needs often tests a writer's skill.

Human Resources The traditional personnel department has now evolved into the expanded role of "human resources," and in the 1990s experts predict a major turf battle over who will be responsible for employee communications. Public relations, on the one hand, is becoming the prime area of organizational relations through corporate strategy, risk, and crisis management. Human resources, according to *PR Reporter,* is striving to shed the confines of "personnel" and be a central overseer of employee relations in the broadest sense.

Human resources personnel believe they should control the flow of information. Public relations administrators say that satisfactory external communications cannot be achieved unless effective employee relations are conducted simultaneously. Public relations people also say personnel administrators often are poor communicators and

BANK OF AMERICA BOOSTS EMPLOYEE MORALE

The corporate communications department of the Bank of America, headquartered in San Francisco, played a key role in a novel program to let employees know that the bank appreciated their efforts.

Background From 1985 to 1987, Bank of America lost $1.8 billion. It suspended stock dividends, sold prime assets, reduced its staff, and fought a major takeover attempt. By 1989, recovery was in sight, but surveys found employee morale extremely low—a major stumbling block to achieving stability and increased productivity. Executive management asked corporate communications to formulate a plan that would give employees renewed confidence and enthusiasm.

The Plan Communications proposed that the bank present shares of stock to every employee who was, and continued to be, part of the company's turnaround effort. The managing committee endorsed the plan and decided to award ten shares of stock to each eligible employee. It also added a vacation day for each employee and cash awards to newcomers or part-time workers. The strategy was to make sure that every employee and manager—50,000 employees and 3,000 bank managers in seven states and 44 nations—would be rewarded.

Communications Strategy To make the award a ''major event,'' it was decided to hold surprise staff meetings at the same time worldwide and make the announcement through a personal letter from CEO Tom Clausen. More than 3000 information packets were prepared in strict secrecy, and a massive, specially handled mail delivery put the packages on managers' desks at the same time. On the appointed day, at meetings around the world, the managers surprised the employees with news of their stock awards. A special edition of the bank's employee newsletter was produced overnight and distributed. A month later managers reassembled staffs for a celebration and handed out the certificates and checks.

Results The surprise was total and the response overwhelming. Thousands of employees sent ''thank you'' notes and cards, and a phone survey showed virtually 100 percent of the managers and employees viewed this award as a major morale boost.

Costs Staff time and printing costs were approximately $50,000 for Corporate Communications and Human Resources. The awards cost nearly $20 million.

do not understand how a lack of effective communication generates rumors and morale problems.

One survey of 2,000 companies indicates that human resources dominates employee communications. On the other hand, surveys of companies with more than 10,000 employees show that in their organizations public relations departments handle employee communications.

Advertising Advertising and public relations departments often collide because they compete for funds to communicate with external audiences. Advertising's approach to communications is, ''Will it sell?'' Public relations asks, ''Will it make friends?'' These differing orientations frequently cause breakdowns in coordination of overall strategy. Marketing departments also compete with public relations departments for funds; marketing's emphasis is on product publicity.

To avoid conflicts between departments, the following suggestions are made:

1. Representatives of departments should serve together on key committees to enable an exchange of information.

2. Heads of departments should be equals in job title. In this way, the autonomy of one executive is not subverted by another.

3. All department heads should report to the same superior, so that all viewpoints can be considered before an appropriate decision is made.

4. Informal, regular contacts with representatives in other departments can help create mutual trust and respect.

5. Written policies should be established to spell out the responsibilities of each department. Such policies are helpful in settling disputes as to which department has authority to communicate with employees or alter a news release.

PLACE IN OVERALL STRUCTURE

In any modern organization, public relations is a management function as well as a staff function. Its power and influence are directly related to two factors.

First, as noted earlier, public relations efforts can be effective only if the head of the department has direct access to top management and is represented on key policy-making committees. The desirable model is for the public relations department to have a *compulsory-advisory* role.

Second, the head of public relations must be equal in status and rank to heads of other departments. It is important that all have the same title. If other department heads are at the vice presidential level, for instance, the head of public relations should be, too.

Not all companies realize the value of this organizational model. In some, a director of public relations reports directly to a vice president of marketing or advertising. This arrangement suggests that the organization narrowly defines the function of public relations. The department focuses on product publicity, to the detriment of other important activities.

Other large corporations have vice presidents of corporate communications who supervise public relations, advertising, and marketing communications. This setup tends to work much better, because the managers or directors of the three departments have equal status and report to a centralized person, who then coordinates a total communications strategy after weighing the recommendations of all three.

Some models for the public relations function in an organizational chart are shown in Figure 4.2.

ADVANTAGES AND DISADVANTAGES OF WORKING IN A DEPARTMENT

Work in a public relations department can be invigorating and can offer staff members a sense of accomplishment as they help the organization achieve its objectives. The

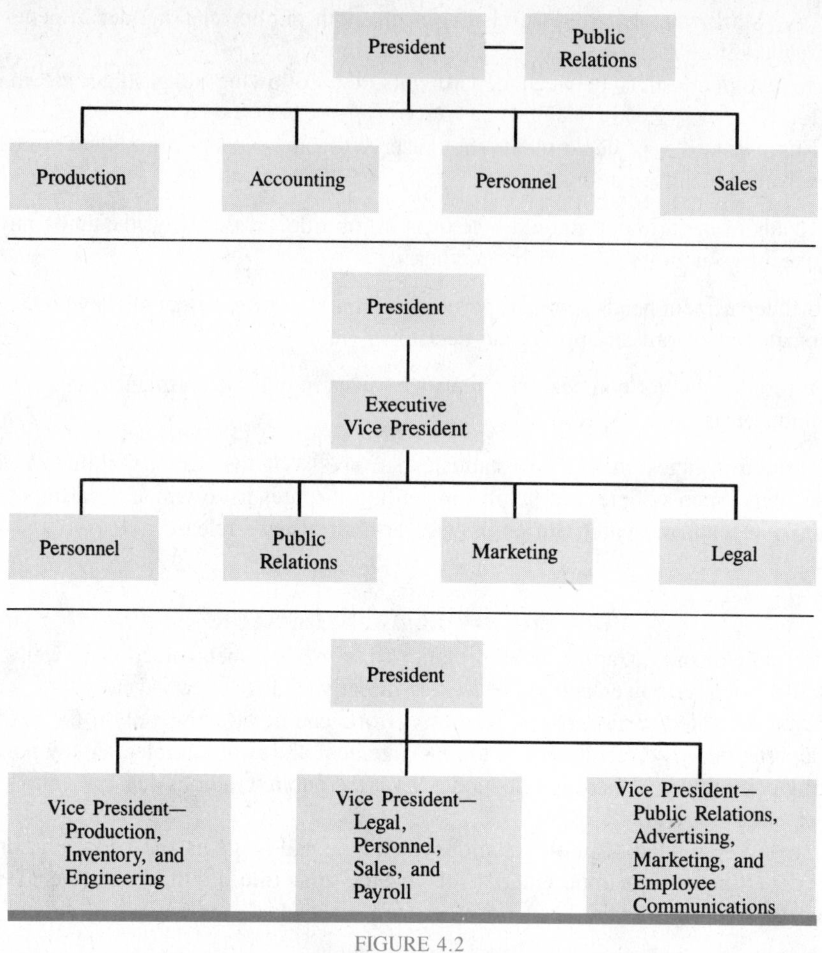

FIGURE 4.2
This chart depicts three examples of corporate management organization, showing the important position of public relations.

advantages of employment in a corporate setting are (1) generally good salaries, (2) extensive health and insurance benefits, (3) the opportunity to work with a group of professional peers, and (4) extensive resources. The disadvantages can be (1) a laborious approval process before production or dissemination of information, (2) lack of understanding by management of the public relations function, (3) lack of advancement opportunities in a small department, and (4) involvement in routine activities that change little over a period of time.

Although the general trend is for public relations to expand its role and influence in the corporation, it is also true that corporate downsizing and mergers are resulting in public relations staff cutbacks. Most RCA corporate public relations people, for example, lost their jobs when their company merged with the General Electric Company. And when Mobil Corporation moved its headquarters to Fairfax, Virginia, it closed its public relations office in New York. Only 28 of the 66 staff members followed the company to Virginia.

Public relations firms are the major beneficiaries of corporate retrenchment, and the major growth area in public relations employment is in this area.

PUBLIC RELATIONS FIRMS

In size, public relations firms range from one- or two-person staffs to giants such as Burson-Marsteller, which employs about 2000 people worldwide. The scope of services provided to clients varies accordingly. Big or small, each has an identical purpose: to give counsel and, to the extent a client wishes, perform the technical services required to carry out an agreed-upon program. The counseling firm may operate as an adjunct to an organization's public relations department or, if no department exists, conduct the entire public relations effort.

These firms have proliferated in proportion to the growth of American business and industry. As American companies expanded after World War II into booming domestic and worldwide markets, many corporations felt a need for public relations firms that could provide them with professional expertise in communications.

Stimulating the growth of public relations firms were increased urbanization, expansion of government bureaucracy and regulation, more sophisticated mass media systems, the rise of consumerism, and the demand for more information. Professionals

THE TEN LARGEST PUBLIC RELATIONS FIRMS

Name	Fee Income	Employees
Shandwick	$200 million +	2000 +
Hill & Knowlton (A)	$190 million +	1900 +
Burson-Marsteller (A)	$190 million +	2000 +
Ogilvy Public Relations Group (A)	$ 62.3 million	759
Omnicom PR Network (A)	$ 61.8 million	761
Edelman Public Relations Worldwide	$ 45.9 million	495
Fleishman-Hillard	$ 45.8 million	509
Ketchum Public Relations (A)	$ 42.3 million	401
Manning, Selvage & Lee (A)	$ 29.3 million	303
Ruder Finn	$ 25.2 million	296

"A" Denotes advertising agency subsidiary.
Source: Jack O'Dwyer's Newsletter, March 28, 1991. Copyright 1991 by the J. R. O'Dwyer Company, Inc.

were needed to maintain lines of communication in an increasingly complicated world and to provide much of the material to be distributed. Some experts, who point out that public relations services seem to grow best in an atmosphere of conflict, say that the number of firms multiplied as the American public placed less trust in large corporations and demanded more corporate responsibility in environmental and consumer matters. Whatever the reason, American Business Lists of Omaha has compiled a list of 6644 public relations firms operating in the United States.

THE SERVICES THEY PROVIDE

Counseling firms today offer services far more extensive than those provided by the nation's first firm, the Publicity Bureau, founded in 1900 in Boston. A full-fledged public relations firm provides a wide variety of services:

- *Executive speech training*. Top executives are coached on public affairs activities, including personal appearances.
- *Research and evaluation*. Scientific surveys to measure public attitudes and perceptions are conducted.
- *Diversified communication tools*. Slide presentations, videotapes, brochures, newsletters, and other materials are prepared and distributed.
- *Crisis communication*. Management is counseled on what to say and do in an emergency such as an oil spill or recall of an unsafe product.
- *Media analysis*. Appropriate media are examined for targeting specific messages to key audiences.
- *Community relations*. Management is counseled on ways to achieve official and public support for such projects as building or expanding a factory.
- *Product promotion*. Representatives are placed on radio and television talk shows; news releases, feature stories, and artwork are provided for print media.
- *Events management*. News conferences, anniversary celebrations, rallies, symposiums, and national conferences are planned and conducted.
- *Public affairs*. Materials and testimony are prepared for government hearings and regulatory bodies, and background briefings are prepared.
- *Employee communications*. Ways to motivate employees and raise productivity are discussed with management.
- *Positioning a company*. Advice is given on corporate identity programs that establish a place in the market for the company and its products.
- *Financial relations*. Management is counseled on ways to avoid takeover by another firm and effectively communicate with stockholders, security analysts, and institutional investors.

Increasingly, public relations firms emphasize the counseling aspect of their services, and a number of executives object to the idea that they operate public relations ''agencies.'' The say that public relations is a management consulting function and cannot be delegated to others, as the term ''agent'' implies. Advertising firms, in contrast, are properly called ''agencies'' because they serve as agents buying time or space on behalf of a client.

We approach public relations as a management and counseling function and, consequently, use the term ''public relations firm'' throughout the book. At the same time, we realize that a number of public relations ''agencies'' do exist because they simply act as agents preparing and distributing publicity materials on behalf of clients.

GLOBAL REACH

Public relations firms, large and small, tend to cluster in major metropolitan areas. On an international level, the firms and their affiliates are found in most major world cities. Burson-Marsteller, headquartered in New York, has 51 offices in 27 nations. Some of the major cities include Toronto, Montreal, San Juan, Brussels, The Hague, Frankfort, Geneva, London, Malmö, Milan, Paris, Hong Kong, Kuala Lumpur, Singapore, Tokyo, Melbourne, Sydney, Sao Paulo, and even Moscow.

Hill & Knowlton, also headquartered in New York, has a similar list of locations and even an office in Beijing. It has 62 offices in 22 nations and, with its affiliate-firm network, 125 offices in 60 nations. Shandwick, based in London, has 70 offices in 18 nations.

International outreach isn't only for the large firms, however. Small and medium-sized firms also are establishing bases abroad through networks of affiliated public relations firms. For example, about 60 firms around the world have established an affiliate network called Worldcom Group, Inc. Another network of affiliated firms, Pinnacle Group, Inc., has a combined size of 42 offices in various nations. Essentially, firms in an affiliation cooperate with each other to service clients with international needs. For example, a firm in India may call its affiliate firm in Los Angeles to handle the details of a news conference for a visiting Indian trade delegation. This approach gives small firms with limited resources an opportunity to offer the same kinds of services as the largest firms.

The major cities of Eastern Europe and the Soviet Union are next on the expansion lists of the large international firms, as well as various affiliated groups. (See Chapter 16.)

SHANDWICK: THE LARGEST FIRM

Perhaps one indication of globalism in the public relations business is the fact that a London-based firm, instead of one in New York, now holds the title of world's largest public relations firm.

Shandwick—which launched a three-year international buying spree of 38 public relations and related firms between 1986 and 1989—posted a fee income of $200 million during the calendar year 1990 to supersede Hill & Knowlton's fee income of $190 million.

Hill & Knowlton, recognized as the world's largest public relations firm until 1989, in turn had surpassed Burson-Marsteller, the 1986 title holder. Hill & Knowlton, like Shandwick, had gained its lead by acquiring other firms. One acquisition was

The future will not be the past.

FIGURE 4.3
With an eye to the future, Burson-Marsteller emphasizes the international aspect of public relations in this advertisement listing major events of the next decade in which the firm plans to be involved.

Gray & Co., one of Washington's most influential lobbying firms. Hill & Knowlton and Burson-Marsteller are by far the two largest public relations firms in the United States.

Although Hill & Knowlton is widely identified as an American firm, it actually is owned by the WPP Group, a London-based holding company.

The emergence of Shandwick as the largest firm, according to data collected by *Jack O'Dwyer's Newsletter* (March 28, 1990), did raise criticisms. Many contend that Shandwick is simply a holding company because all of the firms it acquired still operate under their original names. WPP Group, for example, claims that if it grouped all of its public relations operations together, including Hill & Knowlton and the

Ogilvy Public Relations Group, fees would total about $294 million (in 1990) and there would be 2950 employees. A New York *Times* article about the growth of public relations firms abroad noted, "Whether Shandwick emerges as a worldwide public relations powerhouse or just a directionless conglomerate probably rests on how well it coordinates its agency services."

ADVERTISING AND PUBLIC RELATIONS MERGERS

Until the 1970s, the largest American public relations firms were independently owned by their principal officers or, in some cases, by employee stockholders. A significant change began in 1973 when Carl Byoir & Associates, then the nation's third largest firm, was purchased by the advertising firm of Foote, Cone & Belding.

In rapid succession, Burson-Marsteller became part of the Young & Rubicam advertising conglomerate; Manning, Selvage & Lee was absorbed into Benton & Bowles; Doremus & Company joined BBDO advertising; and Hill & Knowlton became part of J. Walter Thompson, Inc.

Although ownerships have changed over the years, six of the ten largest public relations firms still are subsidiaries of advertising agencies or their holding companies (see the "top ten" table earlier in this chapter).

These firms, for the most part, have maintained their original names and continued to operate autonomously, with their own chief executives and staffs. This approach has somewhat diffused the concern that public relations would became a poor stepchild in the much larger advertising operation, and all facets of public relations counseling would be reduced to product publicity and promotion.

Initially, supporters of mergers between advertising agencies and public relations firms believed that it was only the natural evolution of integrating various communication disciplines into "total communications networks." They maintained that no single-function agency was really equipped with personnel and resources to handle complex, often global, marketing functions in an efficient way for a client. On a more practical level, joint public relations and advertising endeavors would both increase the pool of potential new clients and expand the number of geographical locations.

Although the premise was logical, the complexities of the marketplace have made "total communications networks" less than effective. In many cases, corporations bypassed the concept of "one-stop shopping" from a megafirm and preferred, instead, to use the services of independent, specialized firms. For example, of the 40 largest firms after the "big ten," less than one-fourth are owned by advertising companies. Other clients resisted because they perceived a possible conflict of interest if a subsidiary of a megafirm had the account of a business competitor. As a result, the advertising agency and the public relations firm owned by the same company often don't collaborate much and, more often than not, have their own client lists.

Acquisitions by advertising agencies have slowed considerably since the late 1970s, but public relations firms continue to expand by acquiring smaller ones. The most common method of expansion into a new geographic area is to buy an existing firm. This was Shandwick's approach. Another method is simply to buy equity in other firms, which MSL Worldwide does. Hill & Knowlton, in addition to opening its own offices, buys other firms. In 1990, for example, H&K acquired the Washington firm of Wexler, Reynolds, Fuller, Harrison, & Schule. Burson-Marsteller, responding to its rival, countered in early 1991 by purchasing the Washington lobbying firm of Black, Manafort, Stone & Kelly.

STRUCTURE OF A COUNSELING FIRM

A small public relations firm may consist only of the owner (president) and an assistant (vice president), supported by a secretary. Larger firms have a hierarchy something like this:

- President
- Executive vice president
- Vice president
- Account supervisor
- Account executive
- Assistant account executive
- Secretarial/clerical staff

The chart of Ketchum Public Relations/San Francisco is fairly typical. The president is based in the New York office of Ketchum Public Relations, so the executive vice president is the on-site director in San Francisco. A senior vice president is associate director of operations. Next in line are several vice presidents who primarily do account supervision or special projects.

An *account supervisor* is in charge of one major account or several smaller ones. An *account executive,* who reports to the supervisor, is in direct contact with the client and handles most of the day-to-day activity. At the bottom of the list is the *assistant account executive,* who does routine maintenance work compiling media lists, gathering information, and writing rough drafts of news releases.

A recent college graduate usually starts as an assistant account executive. Once he or she learns the firm's procedures and shows ability, promotion to account executive may occur within 6 to 18 months. After two or three years, it is not uncommon for an account executive to become an account supervisor.

Executives at or above the vice presidential level usually are heavily involved in selling their firm's services. In order to prosper, a firm must continually seek new business and sell additional services to current clients. Consequently, the upper management of the firm calls on prospective clients, prepares proposals, and makes new business presentations. In this very competitive field, a firm not adept at selling itself frequently fails.

Firms frequently organize account teams, especially to serve a client whose program is multifaceted. One member of the team, for example, may set up a nationwide media tour in which an organization representative is booked on television talk shows. Another may supervise all materials going to the print media, including news stories, feature articles, background kits, and artwork. A third may concentrate on the trade press or perhaps arrange special events.

Another approach is to assemble a team with expertise in a particular field. Large firms make it a point to hire staff members with individual backgrounds in such fields as law, business, science, journalism, engineering, and marketing, so that the appropriate people can be selected for a team depending upon the client's needs. In a modern public relations practice that emphasizes management counseling, problem-solving, and strategic positioning, the old idea that everyone should have a mass media background is increasingly passé.

WORKING IN A PUBLIC RELATIONS FIRM

To many, work in a public relations firm sounds glamorous. A person associates with a number of highly intelligent, creative people, and there is the stimulation of working on several exciting projects at any one time. One day may find the account executive at the opening of a plush restaurant, while the next finds the intrepid executive flying to New York or London to set up a press conference. Of course, there are the proverbial cocktail parties and the pleasure of learning that a well-written feature article has been picked up by 180 daily newspapers.

Although all these happenings do occur in public relations, they are less routine than one would suspect. On many days, an account person may sit in a small cubicle writing a standard news release about a new diesel engine and having a Big Mac for lunch. On other days, the person may spend fruitless hours on the phone trying to book a client's representative for radio and television interviews. It is not very exciting to write a brochure about the services of an engineering firm or to have a masterpiece of prose reduced to alphabet soup by a client's penchant for complex sentences.

The Frustrations and the Rewards Working for a public relations firm can be a source of both frustrations and rewards. Individuals often cite the following frustrations:

1. *Lack of privacy*. For their staff, most firms provide cubicles that are small, open at the top, and without doors. As one employee points out, "You have to think and work in a fishbowl."

2. *Constant documentation of work*. Great emphasis is placed on productivity, and account executives are expected to have 80 to 90 percent of their working hours billable to a client. Time sheets, accurate to the nearest 15 minutes and describing each activity in detail, must be recorded so that the firm may prepare the proper billings.

3. *Many demands on time*. An account executive usually works on several projects, and it is difficult to give each client the undivided attention that is often demanded.

4. *Client relationships*. Few clients have a good understanding of what public relations can or cannot accomplish. A firm's personnel must constantly educate clients about public relations.

5. *Extended workdays*. Many times an account person must attend night functions or work overtime to meet a deadline.

Despite these frustrations, many people thrive in a public relations firm. They enjoy the constant challenge of coming up with creative ideas—the psychic reward of observing their idea for a slogan become a household term or a planned special event achieve international publicity. Those who leave a public relations firm for jobs with corporations often miss the diversity of assignments.

What It Takes What, then, does it take to work in a public relations firm? Harold Burson, chairman of Burson-Marsteller, once told a national convention of the Public Relations Student Society of America (PRSSA) about the characteristics he seeks in a prospective employee.

First he asks a job applicant, ''What do you read?'' Burson wants individuals who are aware of the complex world around them. ''If you want to pursue a career in public relations, learn to read—everything,'' he exhorts. Burson has the feeling that those who don't read can't write. And, he points out, in order to succeed in public relations a person must perfect his or her writing skills.

Burson also searches for people who have strong self-discipline. He says:

> You are, to some considerable degree, able to do what you want to do and at your own pace. You can turn out a major feature article that sparkles or you can, in the same time frame, deliver up eight mundane news releases written to formula. You can go for a placement on the ''Today'' show or with the local town daily. You can take a day doing it—or two days. In most cases, you won't get much supervision. You're on your own for a lot of the work you do—almost regardless of who employs you.

Other public relations executives echo what Burson says about reading, writing, and self-discipline. They add such characteristics as the ability to (1) organize and plan; (2) juggle several projects at once without getting rattled; (3) give good, persuasive presentations; and (4) work well with others.

PROS AND CONS OF USING A PUBLIC RELATIONS FIRM

Because public relations is a service industry, a firm's major asset is the quality of its people. Potential clients thinking about hiring a public relations firm usually base their decisions on that fact, according to a survey of Fortune 500 corporate vice presidents.

Consultant Alfred Geduldig, who conducted the survey, also found that (1) quality of presentation, (2) possible conflicts, and (3) the writing ability of the firm's personnel also were important—more so than costs, size of client list, or even ''full service'' capability. He also found that projects accounted for 70 percent of the work assigned to public relations firms. Financial, product, and corporate positioning projects were popular assignments.

Advantages Public relations firms offer many services and capabilities:

- *Objectivity*. The firm can analyze a client's needs or problems from a new perspective and offer fresh insights.
- *Variety of skills and expertise*. The firm has specialists, whether in speechwriting, trade magazine placement, or helping with proxy battles.

- *Extensive resources*. The firm has abundant media contacts and works regularly with numerous suppliers of products and services. It has research materials, including data information banks, and experience in similar fields.
- *Offices throughout the country*. A national public relations program requires coordination in major cities. Large firms have on-site staffs or affiliate firms in many cities and even around the world.
- *Special problem-solving*. A firm may have extensive experience and a solid reputation in desired areas. For example, Burson-Marsteller is well known for expertise in crisis communications, health and medical issues, and international coordination of special projects. Hill & Knowlton is known for expertise in public affairs, and Ketchum Public Relations is the expert in consumer marketing.
- *Credibility*. A successful public relations firm has a solid reputation for professional, ethical work. If represented by such a firm, a client likely will get more attention among opinion leaders in mass media, government, and the financial community. Such is the reputation of Regis McKenna, Inc., for example, that an article in *Fortune* magazine stated, "Simply being a client of Regis McKenna, Inc., has become a kind of appointment for a high-tech business."

A SAMPLE OF PROGRAMS

Public relations firms handle a variety of assignments. Here are some examples:

- *PBN Company*. When Mikhail Gorbachev visited California after a summit meeting with President Bush, this firm handled the logistics of assisting 2800 media representatives covering the event. *Fenton Communications* handled press rela-

Mikhail Gorbachev emphasizes a point in a public appearance. The Soviet leader's tour of America after a summit meeting with President Bush in Washington, which attracted massive media coverage, was organized by an American public relations firm. (Reuters/Bettman)

tions for Nelson Mandela's 1990 tour of the United States after his release from prison in South Africa.

- *Edelman Public Relations*. Handled public relations for Star-Kist when the company announced that it no longer would use tuna caught by methods harmful to dolphins.
- *Paul Werth Associates*. Developed a public relations program for the Ohio Department of Health that informed youth about the social, medical, and economic consequences of teen pregnancy.
- *Anthony M. Franco, Inc*. Conducted a public information campaign on behalf of the Troy, Michigan, School District that convinced voters to approve a $33.5 million bond issue for a new high school.
- *Ketchum Public Relations*. Used the California Raisin characters in a program to generate enthusiasm for reading among children. The program, on behalf of the California Raisin Board and supported by the American Library Association, involved one million children through 5000 libraries nationwide.
- *L. C. Williams and Associates*. Created the official campaign kickoff for a new $25 million Hanes megabrand ad campaign for underwear, socks, and fleece.
- *Holt, Ross & Yulish*. Organized a program to regain community confidence in a New Jersey firm, Sybron Chemicals, after an accidental release of noxious chemical caused the evacuation of 60 residents. Through a series of public opinion surveys, a telephone hot-line, and a community open house, area residents felt more secure about the company as a responsible neighbor.
- *Russell, Karsh & Hagen Public Relations*. This Denver firm volunteered to assist an environmental coalition in opposing a project to dam the South Platte River. The groundswell of public opinion opposed to the dam caused the Denver Water Board to abandon the project.

Accounts accepted by public relations firms do not always meet with widespread public support. Chapter 6, for example, discusses the controversy that ensued after Hill & Knowlton signed a contract with the U.S. Catholic Conference to manage an anti-abortion campaign. And Burson-Marsteller was severely criticized by animal rights groups after agreeing to represent the fur industry in a campaign to counter the rhetoric of the anti-fur activists.

On the Minus Side Despite many successes, not everything goes smoothly between a firm and its client. There are several "complaints" about public relations firms:

- *Superficial grasp of a client's unique problems*. While objectivity is gained from an outsider's perspective, there is often a disadvantage in the public relations firm's not thoroughly understanding the client's business or needs.
- *Lack of full-time commitment*. A public relations firm has many clients to service. Therefore, no single client can monopolize its personnel and other resources.

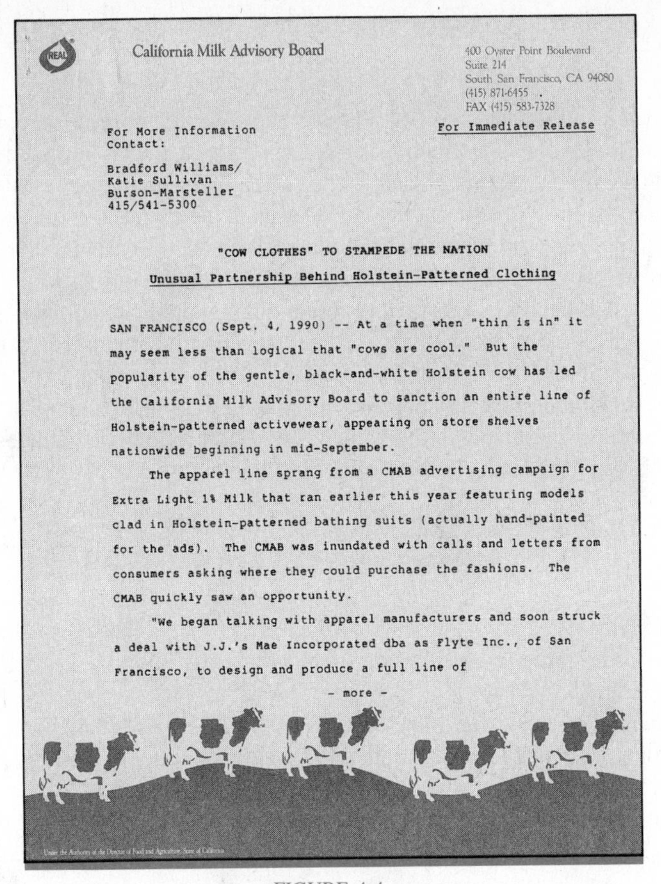

California Milk Advisory Board

400 Oyster Point Boulevard
Suite 214
South San Francisco, CA 94080
(415) 871-6455
FAX (415) 583-7328

For More Information
Contact:

Bradford Williams/
Katie Sullivan
Burson-Marsteller
415/541-5300

For Immediate Release

"COW CLOTHES" TO STAMPEDE THE NATION

Unusual Partnership Behind Holstein-Patterned Clothing

SAN FRANCISCO (Sept. 4, 1990) -- At a time when "thin is in" it may seem less than logical that "cows are cool." But the popularity of the gentle, black-and-white Holstein cow has led the California Milk Advisory Board to sanction an entire line of Holstein-patterned activewear, appearing on store shelves nationwide beginning in mid-September.

The apparel line sprang from a CMAB advertising campaign for Extra Light 1% Milk that ran earlier this year featuring models clad in Holstein-patterned bathing suits (actually hand-painted for the ads). The CMAB was inundated with calls and letters from consumers asking where they could purchase the fashions. The CMAB quickly saw an opportunity.

"We began talking with apparel manufacturers and soon struck a deal with J.J.'s Mae Incorporated dba as Flyte Inc., of San Francisco, to design and produce a full line of

- more -

FIGURE 4.4
Preparing and issuing news releases is an important function of public relations departments and firms. This first page of a release about a new product describes a clever promotional idea that increases awareness of milk among young people. It was prepared by Burson-Marsteller.

- *Need for prolonged briefing period.* Some companies become frustrated because time and money are needed for a public relations firm to research the organization and make recommendations. Consequently, the actual start of a public relations program may take weeks or months.
- *Resentment of internal staff.* The public relations staff members of a client organization may resent the use of outside counsel because they think it implies that they lack the ability to do the job.
- *Need for strong direction by top management.* High-level executives must take the time to brief outside counsel on specific objectives sought.
- *Need for full information and confidence.* A client must be willing to share all information, including the skeletons in the closet, with outside counsel.

- *Costs*. Outside counsel is expensive. In many situations, routine public relations work can be handled at lower cost by internal staff.

The problems often are two-way. Personnel in counseling firms complain at times that they cannot do a highly effective job for clients because (1) top corporate executives do not take time to define objectives and clarify what they want a public relations program to accomplish; (2) the clients fail to provide the information needed to tailor a program to the specific problem; and (3) clients often are penny-wise and pound-foolish in terms of not approving expenditures for key items.

Counselors also complain that clients often think of public relations as some sort of magical cure-all that can accomplish miracles. By the time counsel is called in, they say, the crisis has already occurred—and there really isn't much a public relations program can do. Public relations counsel must continually tell clients that they cannot (1) guarantee specified results, (2) change public perceptions or attitudes overnight, and (3) make any organization something that it is not.

FEES AND CHARGES

The Three Methods of Charging A public relations firm charges for its services in several ways. The three most common methods are as follows:

1. *Basic hourly fee, plus out-of-pocket expenses*. The number of hours spent on a client's account is tabulated each month and billed to the client. Work by personnel in the counseling firm is billed at various hourly rates—for example, a secretary typing envelopes at $20 an hour and an account executive working at $85 an hour. Out-of-pocket expenses, such as cab fares, car rentals, airline tickets, and meals, also are billed to the client.

2. *Retainer fee*. A basic monthly charge billed to the client covers ordinary administrative and overhead expenses for maintaining the account and being ''on call.'' Many retainer fees also specify the number of hours the counseling firm will spend on the account each month. Additional work is billed at normal hourly rates. Out-of-pocket expenses normally are billed separately.

3. *Fixed project fee*. The public relations firm agrees to do a specific project, such as an annual report, a newsletter, or a special event, for a fixed fee. For example, a counseling firm may write and produce a quarterly newsletter for $30,000 annually. The fixed fee is the least popular of the three methods because it is difficult to estimate accurately all work and expenses in advance.

The primary basis for all three methods is to estimate the number of hours that a particular project will take to plan, execute, and evaluate. The first method—the basic hourly fee—is the most flexible and most widely used among large firms. It is preferred by public relations people because they are paid for the exact number of hours spent on a project and because it is the only sound way that a fee can be determined intelligently. The retainer fee and the fixed project fee are based on an estimate of how many hours it will take to counsel a client.

Clients, however, like to have a fixed budget for their public relations expenses so that the proper allocation of funds can be made. Often a compromise agreement is reached as to the financial parameters of a program. The public relations firm estimates the number of staff members and hours a project will take, and this estimate then becomes the budget for the program. The counseling firm, for example, may estimate that a program will take 200 hours over 3 months at a cost of $10,500. The client signs an agreement to pay the firm $3,500 a month for 3 months. If the counseling firm finds that it is spending more time than estimated on the account, it has the choice of cutting back the number of hours during the next month or asking the client for permission to raise the established budget.

Most large public relations firms have sophisticated cost-accounting systems to keep track of hours and supplies spent on an account. Even use of the telephones and photocopying machines is programmed to produce a computer printout showing what calls or copying should be billed to what account number. As previously mentioned, anyone who works on the client account is required to keep detailed time sheets that are computer-tabulated on a weekly basis. This gives the counseling firm's management the ability to determine the status and profitability of an account at any given moment.

How Estimates Are Made A number of variables are considered when a public relations firm estimates the cost of a program. These may include the size and duration, geographical locations involved, the number of personnel to be assigned to the project, and even the nature of the client. A major variable, of course, is billing the use of the firm's personnel to a client at the proper hourly rate.

The hourly billing rate of an employee depends on his or her experience, title, and salary level. An account executive who earns $32,000 annually would be making $20 per hour, based on an average work year of 1600 hours after deducting vacation, holidays, illness, and personal time off. The firm's management must also include such overhead expenses as office space, equipment, utilities, phone, insurance benefits, and pension plans. Another factor is the percentage of profit after all the bills are paid. In general, public relations firms try to operate on a profit level of between 18 and 22 percent.

Usually a public relations firm bills clients at three to five times a staff person's base hourly salary. The account executive in the example just cited would cost a client between $60 and $100 per hour. At this rate, the account executive should generate between $96,000 and $160,000 of billable income for the firm on an annual basis. Meeting these standards of productivity and profitability is an important criterion for a person's career advancement in the firm. The principals of a counseling firm, because of their much higher salaries, often command $150 to $500 an hour depending on the size and capabilities of the firm.

Large public relations firms have also developed guidelines for the allocation of staff time to a client. In a typical $100,000 program, the director or president of the firm would generate $5,000 of the fee income, while the vice president in charge of a group would bill $15,000. The account supervisor would bill $30,000, and the account executives producing the materials for the client would bill $50,000 for services.

The primary income of a public relations firm comes from the selling of staff time, but some additional income results from mark-ups on all production costs, such as printing, photography, and artwork that the firm facilitates and supervises. The standard in the trade is between 15 and 20 percent of costs. Out-of-pocket expenses are billed to clients at net cost.

PEANUT BUTTER: A GOOEY SUCCESS STORY

Would you believe a peanut butter fan club, or a reunion of peanut butter lovers at Opryland in Tennessee? These are two of the creative ideas that Ketchum Public Relations used on behalf of its client, the Peanut Advisory Board, to boost the sales of peanut butter.

Background Consumption of peanuts and peanut butter in the United States was declining, and the 20,000 peanut growers in Georgia, Alabama, and Florida were becoming concerned. The positioning of peanut butter traditionally had been on consumption by children, but the nuclear family of the 1980s was having few or no children. Yet, the "big three"—Jif, Skippy, and Peter Pan—were still spending $75 million in advertising directed at "mom and the kids."

The Plan Ketchum researched the problem and found U.S. Dept. of Agriculture statistics showing that adults consume one-half of the 700 million pounds of peanut butter sold each year. The decision was made to reposition peanut butter for a new audience, aged 28 to 40. They were the largest, fastest-growing population group, the one with the most discretionary income.

Communications Strategy In an early public relations effort, a food-page publicity campaign was aimed at getting chefs to develop recipes praising the taste of Southeast Asian satays dipped in peanut butter sauce. The results were less than spectacular, so the idea was advanced of creating an Adults-Only Peanut Butter Lovers Fan Club (AOPBLFC). This would move the product from the food page to the feature page, but there was one problem. The Peanut Advisory Board couldn't afford a celebrity spokesperson. Ketchum solved the problem by making peanut butter–loving celebrities honorary members of the fan club and publicizing their names in news releases.

Media coverage of the fan club's celebrity members got the general public interested, and the Peanut Advisory Board responded with membership certificates, bumper stickers, and refrigerator magnets. A newsletter, *Spread the News,* was sent to the 5,000 persons who joined in the first year. By the third year, the fan club had 25,000 members.

Additional national media coverage was generated by staging a fan club "reunion" at Opryland in Nashville. The site was chosen because 70 percent of the U.S. population lives within 1000 miles. To publicize the reunion, news releases were sent to 600 travel editors and 450 food editors nationwide. Soupy Sales, the comic, became the celebrity spokesperson for the fan club, and went on a media tour.

Results Reunion attendance at Opryland was almost 2,000. Print and broadcast placements included *USA Today, Newsday,* and ABC-TV's "Good Morning America." Fan club membership eventually grew to 60,000. And, most important, peanut butter consumption rose 6 percent, the biggest increase in two decades. During 1989, consumption increased 15 percent, the first double-digit growth since the 1960s.

Billing on the Basis of Placement As already noted, the industry standard is for public relations firms, like law and management consulting firms, to charge clients an amount based on the number of hours spent on a project.

A few firms, however, charge on the basis of actual media placements. A California organization, Primetime, has a price list for various media. Typical charges are $42,800 for placing a piece on CBS-TV's "60 Minutes," $21,135 for a story in *People* magazine, and $11,875 for an article in the New York *Times*.

The owner of Primetime, Reed Trencher, says he charges clients only for actual placements because companies were getting tired of public relations firms charging high hourly fees and coming up with few actual media placements. He told *Newsweek,* "We found a growing segment of companies that wanted to only pay for results, not promises."

Although Trencher's approach seems on first glance to be somewhat logical, there are a number of complications. Does a client pay for a placement if the article also contains negative information or material about competitors? Does the client pay for multiple placements of the same story—which could easily add up to $100,000 or more? Payment for actual placements also stirs up media hostility. Primetime's approach implies that the media can be "delivered"—that the firm's employees have special access to editors. This is an inference that journalists strongly resent. Payment for direct placement also reinforces the idea that publicity is just "free advertising" or, as *Newsweek* noted, "advertising with journalistic gloss."

These gray areas, according to the *Columbia Journalism Review,* cause disputes between Trencher and clients. A Houston recording company was charged $1,000 for a one-line mention in the *Wall Street Journal* and $14,089 for one paragraph in *People,* and the case went into arbitration. Another point of contention is the $10,000 start-up fee that Primetime charges clients.

Jack O'Dwyer, publisher of an industry newsletter, sums up the attitude of most public relations professionals. He told the *Columbia Journalism Review,* "PR people don't like publicity to be sold by the pound. They feel it is immoral, illogical. It puts a price tag on media copy, which is not supposed to be for sale."

Joseph F. Awad, director of public relations for Reynolds Metals Company in Richmond, Virginia, thinks the contingency-payment arrangement "focuses attention on publicity almost as a value in itself, and away from the practice of public relations."

Professional public relations firms also avoid working on commission. In other words, firms do not make arrangements with clients for a percentage of the sales that might result from product publicity efforts, for two reasons:

1. Committing staff time and resources is risky because of numerous variables and unpredictable developments. Even with outstanding publicity a product may fail because it is overpriced or inferior to competing products. A counseling firm once developed an excellent campaign for an airline, but the pilots went on strike shortly after the campaign began.

2. A vested interest by the public relations firm in the success of a product or event can lead to overzealous and even unethical tactics in order to get favorable publicity.

Public relations firms are in the business of counseling management and providing specialized communication services to help clients achieve stated objectives. They are not simply publicity agents who are "hired guns" for anyone who wants to use their services. An ethical firm works only with clients who have legitimate objectives that contribute to public discussion of issues or inform the public about products and services. (See Chapter 6.)

CASE PROBLEM

You will graduate from college in several months and plan a career in public relations. After several interviews, you receive two job offers. One is with a large paint manufacturer in the state capital, 100 miles away. The public relations staff numbers about 20, and it is customary for beginning staff members to start in employee relations. Later, with more experience, you might be assigned to product press relations, investor relations, or community affairs.

The second job offer is from a small local public relations firm in which you would be an assistant account executive on several current accounts, including a resort hotel and a dry-cleaning chain. The jobs pay about the same, but the corporation offers better overall employee benefits.

What factors would you consider before choosing either job? What job would you take? Explain your reasons.

QUESTIONS FOR REVIEW AND DISCUSSION

1. How have the role and function of public relations departments changed in recent years?

2. In what ways do the structure and external environment of a corporation affect the role and influence of the public relations department?

3. What three types of service does management expect from a public relations department?

4. What kinds of names are commonly given to a corporate public relations department?

5. What is the difference between a line and a staff function? To which function does public relations belong, and why?

6. Why is a compulsory-advisory role within an organization a good one for a public relations department to have?

7. What are two advantages and disadvantages of working in a corporate public relations department?

8. In your opinion, should public relations or human resources be responsible for employee communications?

9. Public relations firms offer many services to their clients. List and describe five of these.

10. What are the three largest public relations firms in the world?

11. In your opinion, is it a good idea for the advertising, public relations, and marketing functions of a corporation to be handled by a single mega-agency offering a "total communications network"? Why or why not?

12. How does the account team of a public relations firm operate?

13. What are some reasons why a company hires a public relations firm? What "complaints" do companies have about public relations firms?

14. What are the standard methods used by a public relations firm to charge for its services?

15. What is your opinion of Primetime's approach to charging clients only for placement of articles?

SUGGESTED READINGS

Alter, Jonathan, and Abramson, Pamela. "Is This Article Worth $19,260?" *Newsweek,* April 20, 1987, p. 77. Charging fees on basis of media placement.

Barnett, Chris. "Pro-Bono PR Scores a Global Coup." *Communication World,* January 1991, pp. 34–37. How a San Francisco public relations firm handled Gorbachev's visit to that city.

Dilenschneider, Robert L. *Power and Influence: Mastering the Art of Persuasion.* New York: Prentice Hall, 1990. A personal account by the president of America's largest public relations firm.

Goodell, Jeffrey. "What Hill & Knowlton Can Do for You." New York *Times* magazine, September 9, 1990, pp. 44, 74–75, 102, 103. Profile of public relations firm.

Grunig, James E. "IABC Study Shows CEOs Value PR." *Communication World,* August 1990, pp. 5–6.

Grunig, Larissa A. "Horizontal Structure in Public Relations: An Exploratory Study of Departmental Differentiation." Chapter 10 of *Public Relations Research Annual,* edited by James Grunig and Larissa Grunig, Volume 1, Hillsdale, NJ: Lawrence Erlbaum Associates, 1989, pp. 175–196.

Grunig, Larissa A. "Power in the Public Relations Department." Chapter 5 of *Public Relations Research Annual,* edited by James Grunig and Larissa Grunig, Volume 2, Hillsdale, NJ: Lawrence Erlbaum Associates, 1990, pp. 115–156.

Josephs, Ray. ''Japan Booms with Public Relations Ventures.'' *Public Relations Journal,* December 1990, pp. 18–25. American firms forge links with Japanese counterparts.

Kelly, Kate. ''How to Figure Your Fees.'' *Public Relations Journal,* April 1987, p. 29.

Nager, Norman R., and Truitt, Richard H. *Strategic Public Relations Counseling.* New York: Longman, 1987.

Reagan, Joey, and others. ''A Factor Analysis of Broom and Smith's Public Relations Roles Scale.'' *Journalism Quarterly,* Spring 1990, pp. 177–183.

Reisman, Joan. ''Taking on the World.'' *Public Relations Journal,* March 1990, pp. 18–24. Global outreach of public relations firms.

Ritchie, Eugene, and Spector, Shelley. ''Making a Marriage Last: What Qualities Strengthen Client–Firm Bonds?'' *Public Relations Journal,* October 1990, pp. 16–21.

Ryan, Michael. ''Organizational Constraints on Corporate Public Relations Practitioners.'' *Journalism Quarterly,* Summer–Fall 1987, pp. 473–482.

''Shandwick Is Top PR Firm with $180 Million in Fees.'' *O'Dwyer PR Services* magazine, May 1990, pp. 1, 8. Profiles of top 25 firms.

Wilmot, Richard E. ''How to Build Credibility with Senior Management.'' *Communication World,* June 1989, pp. 32–37.

CHAPTER

5

The Individual in Public Relations

Earlier chapters have examined public relations as an institution; this chapter will alter the perspective and look at the field from a personal point of view: Where does the individual fit into public relations work? The pages that follow explain the mission of the public relations practitioner and discuss the talents and attitudes necessary for success in the field.

This chapter resembles an orientation tour. It opens the doors of public relations offices and shows what goes on inside. Students sit down at desks, figuratively, and learn answers to questions that every potential worker has about career opportunities, satisfactions, and rewards.

What should a newcomer expect to encounter on the job—what kind of assignments, what kind of pay, what kind of people? What career paths can the public relations practitioner follow, and toward what ultimate goals?

The importance of writing skill, research ability, and planning are emphasized. So is the need for creativity in finding solutions to problems.

THE PUBLIC RELATIONS ROLE

HOW PUBLIC RELATIONS DIFFERS FROM JOURNALISM

Everyone entering public relations should understand its purpose and the role of the individual in carrying out that purpose. Although they may need many of the same skills as news reporters—writing ability, skill at synthesizing large amounts of information, interviewing ability—public relations practitioners have an entirely different mission. The goal of reporters is to uncover the facts, to the fullest extent possible, and to keep watch on society's institutions. Ideally, reporters practice objectivity and have no causes to promote or protect.

Public relations representatives, on the other hand, are by definition advocates. Their mission is to help their employer or client accomplish organizational goals and objectives. They do this by informing and educating the public, as reporters do, but the objective is to influence the public in a favorable way. Public relations people do as much listening as communicating, and they often implement preventative strategies. If they know that their employers or clients are vulnerable to criticism for certain policies and decisions, they suggest ways to remove the vulnerability by changing the policy or positioning a decision in a more favorable light.

A CHANGING FOCUS IN PUBLIC RELATIONS

Traditionally, it was held widely that public relations practitioners should if possible have experience as reporters, to polish their writing skills and to learn firsthand how the media function. In an earlier era, a large percentage of public relations people did have newspaper or broadcast experience. This is no longer true for several reasons, however.

The field of public relations has broadened far beyond working with the mass media. Writing skill and knowledge of the media are vital, but so is training in management, logistics, and planning—skills not usually acquired on a reporter's beat. In fact, former newspaper reporters often fail at public relations because they don't perceive the work as more than writing news releases and don't understand the multiple special publics a public relations program should reach. Some former reporters also have trouble conforming as corporation-oriented team players who must use comprehensive communication strategies.

Another factor limiting the number of graduates who acquire reporting experience before beginning public relations careers is the limited number of newspaper jobs. There are more corporations and institutions with public relations departments than there are daily and weekly newspapers. Movement of well-educated graduates direct from the classroom into public relations jobs is well accepted today, and a *PR Reporter* survey showed that there are now just as many practitioners in the field without newspaper experience as there are with such experience.

Part of the reason for this, no doubt, is the major growth of public relations sequences and programs at the undergraduate level in American universities. Professor Paul Peterson of Ohio State University in a recent study found almost 10,000 majors in public relations. Actually, Peterson's survey probably underestimates the number of students planning careers in public relations since an unknown number of journalism majors also go into public relations, as well as students who study public relations in departments of speech communication and business. Increasing numbers of these students go directly into public relations careers after graduation.

Many graduates choose public relations because they find the work at times to be stimulating and challenging, providing variety along with the routine. As the fictional hero in *Dazzle* by Elinor Klein and Dora Landey, a paperback novel about a public relations man, states: ''As far as I know, it is the only profession left with infinite possibilities for learning everything from cereal to senators. . . . It allows me to keep in touch with all worlds and give up none.'' One day the young practitioner may prepare a news release; the next, work on a slide presentation; and the following, organize a conference. On a typical day, the practitioner may answer press inquiries, compile lists for mailing and for media contacts, escort visitors, read proof, write a brochure, scan incoming publications, help produce displays, select photographs, or compile questionnaires.

PERSONAL QUALIFICATIONS AND ATTITUDES

ATTRIBUTES FOR SUCCESS

Any attempt to define a single public relations type of personality is pointless, because the field is so diverse that it needs people of differing personalities. Some practitioners deal with clients and the public in person on a frequent basis; others work primarily at desks, planning, writing, and researching. Many do both.

A few basic personal attributes are evident in all successful practitioners, however, no matter what their specific assignments. These include:

1. Ability with words, written or spoken
2. Analytical skill, to identify and define problems
3. Creative ability, to develop fresh, effective solutions to problems
4. An instinct for persuasion

Bill Cantor, writing in the Public Relations Student Society of America's *Forum,* emphasizes the importance of curiosity and persistence.

The public relations professional should have an inquiring mind, should want to learn everything possible about the product, service, client or organization, and the competition.

Because public relations is not an exact science, frequently the public relations person must try a number of approaches in order to solve a problem, some of which might not work. If and when they don't work, the professional does not regard them as personal blunders, but as learning experiences. Problems are solved by persistence and intelligence.

A former public relations executive of a large oil corporation, Donald Sweeney, was asked his opinion about the attributes needed for success in public relations. He responded:

Unfortunately too many people think that a pleasing personality is the number one (and, often, only) qualification for public relations work. Except for a few jobs with a high increment of representational skills (read ''glad hand''), personality has nothing to do with public relations work or success therein. I don't mean that boors and misfits should be preferred, but normal people with normal personalities who have the bundle of skills that often make good writers (information-gathering, analysis, idea formulation, idea presentation, articulateness, a will to persuade, a will to win) are the people I used to look for when I was hiring PR people.

I used to ask applicants a key question at the end of a long interview: ''Why do you want to work in public relations?'' Many would answer, ''Because I like people.'' This was always a knockout factor with me; I'd offer to send their resumes to the sales department where liking people was a plus, explaining that PR people have to be strictly objective about people to succeed.

Sweeney's outlook was that of corporate operations. Another public relations executive, who for many years directed Hollywood motion picture and television publicity programs, Ralph "Casey" Shawhan, answered the same question somewhat differently. His work involved promotion of shows and of personalities, many of whom are notoriously egocentric and unstable. (Entertainment publicity constitutes a minor segment of the public relations field.)

"Publicists must like the work and the people they are promoting, and be able to get along with them," Shawhan said. "No matter how good they are as writers and as creators of ideas, they will fail if they aren't congenial."

PUBLIC RELATIONS PERSONALITY CHECKLIST

This checklist, based on careful evaluation, can measure the effectiveness of your personality in terms of the public relations profession.

Rate each item "yes" or "no." Each "yes" counts for 4 points. A "no" doesn't count. Anything below 60 is a poor score. A score between 60 and 80 suggests you should analyze your weak areas and take steps to correct them. Scores above 80 indicate an effective public relations personality.

_____ Good sense of humor
_____ Positive and optimistic
_____ Friendly, meet people easily
_____ Can keep a conversation going with anybody
_____ Take frustration and rejection in stride
_____ Able to persuade others easily
_____ Well-groomed, businesslike appearance
_____ Flair for showmanship
_____ Strong creative urge
_____ Considerate and tactful
_____ Adept in use of words
_____ Able to gain management's confidence
_____ Enjoy being with people
_____ Enjoy listening
_____ Enjoy helping other people resolve problems
_____ Curious about many things
_____ Enjoy reading in diverse areas
_____ Determined to complete projects
_____ High energy level
_____ Can cope with sudden emergencies
_____ See mistakes as learning experiences
_____ Factual and objective
_____ Respect other people's viewpoints
_____ Perceptive and sensitive
_____ Quickly absorb and retain information

Source: PRSSA Forum, Spring 1990.

These two views do not conflict; they merely emphasize the fact that public relations work has varying needs. Practitioners working extensively with clients and the public obviously need more "people" skills. Persons who make careers in the field eventually gravitate to the area they find most attractive.

FOUR ESSENTIAL ABILITIES

Those who plan careers in public relations should develop four basic abilities, no matter what area of work they enter. These are writing skill, research ability, planning expertise, and problem-solving ability.

1. *Writing skill*. The ability to put information and ideas onto paper clearly and concisely is essential. Good grammar and good spelling are vital, not only to convey thoughts precisely but to make a favorable impression on those who receive written material. Misspelled words and sloppy sentence structure look amateurish. The importance of writing skill is emphasized in a career advice column in *Working Woman:* "I changed careers, choosing public relations as having the best potential, but found it difficult to persuade employers that my *writing and interpersonal skills* were sufficient for an entry-level job in the profession."

2. *Research ability*. Arguments for causes must have factual support instead of generalities. A person must have the persistence and ability to gather information from a variety of sources, as well as to conduct original research by designing and implementing opinion polls or audits. Too many public relations programs fail because the organization does not do its homework by assessing audience needs and perceptions. Skillful use of computer databases for acquiring information is an important element of research work, as is the ability to interpret survey results.

3. *Planning expertise*. A public relations program involves a number of communication tools and activities that must be carefully planned and coordinated. A person needs to be a good planner to make certain that materials are distributed in a timely manner, events occur without problems, and budgets are not exceeded. Public relations people must be highly organized, detail-oriented, able to see the big picture.

4. *Problem-solving ability*. Innovative ideas and fresh approaches are needed to solve complex problems or to make a public relations program unique and memorable. Although many public relations people plod along and continue to handle new situations in a routine, unimaginative way, their results are rarely the kind that merit increased salaries and promotions. If a public relations person shows top management how to solve problems creatively, he or she becomes a key part of the organization. Technicians who just do what they are told, however, can be easily replaced.

Three typical help-wanted advertisements illustrate how a public relations career may develop. The first is for an entry-level position of a routine nature, the second for a middle-level position requiring a few years of experience, and the third for a high-level director who does strategic planning, directs a staff, and serves as the institution's spokesperson.

SKILLS FOR THE 1990s

What kind of public relations staff person is needed in the 1990s? AT&T has compiled a list of skills and personal characteristics that it looks for in potential employees:

Professional Experience/Acquired Skills

- Polished, versatile communications skills
  —at the core, public relations writing
  —interpersonal (oral and aural skills, including public speaking)
  —visual (including print and electronic media)
- Strategic PR thinking, problem solving, planning
  —results orientation
- Providing PR counsel and support to management
  —special emphasis on marketing, finance, international business, employee relations, constituency and governmental relations
- Understanding, working effectively with mass media
- Understanding, effectively using organizational communications
- Enthusiasm for and ability to explain technological change
- PR evaluation; survey research
- Special events management
- Managing, supervising and developing subordinates in a creative professional environment
- External focus, involvement with outside publics and process of social change
- Understanding corporate social responsibility and relationships to governmental and nonprofit sectors.

Desired Personal Characteristics

- Intellectual curiosity
- Results orientation
- Creativity
- Flexibility
- Energy
- Initiative
- Integrity
- Ability to meet deadlines
- Broad interests (e.g., with regard to political, social, economic issues)
- Foreign language fluency

Source: AT&T.

STAFF AIDE

Credit union seeks public relations aide to write and edit monthly newsletter, design and write brochure, and plan a variety of promotions for each quarter. Successful applicant must maintain rapport with members through publications as well as telephone and personal contact and assist various departments with public relations/promotion activities. Degree in public relations or journalism required. Candidate should be a self-starter with initiative to work independently, be able to work under pressure to meet deadlines, and accept constructive criticism without being offended.

PUBLIC RELATIONS DIRECTOR

Acute care hospital is seeking a PR director with excellent communication skills including public speaking, writing/journalism, photography, and computer training. Duties include publications, news releases, publicity generation, media placement, and media relations. In addition, event planning and implementation plus community networking. Requires bachelor's or master's degree in public relations and previous hospital experience.

FIGURE 5.1
An example of the challenging jobs open to experienced public relations practitioners is described in this advertisement from *Public Relations Journal,* January 1990, p. 381.

PUBLIC RELATIONS REPRESENTATIVE, SENIOR

Our Public Relations Department has recently been charged with expanding its community relations role and is therefore recruiting a seasoned Public Relations professional.

Qualified candidates will have no less than seven years corporate or organizational public relations experience. Additionally, the chosen candidate will possess verifiable skills in special events and programs creation, development and implementation, governmental and community relations, and charitable and educational programs.

To be considered for this challenging and rewarding role, please submit, in confidence, a resume with salary history (necessary to be considered) to:

Walt Disney World Co.
Professional Staffing
P.O Box 10,090 MKLD03
Lake Buena Vista, FL 32830

ROLE

The university seeks an individual to create, direct, and manage a comprehensive and integrated public affairs program in support of the university's mission and goals on a national, regional, and community level. This entails developing communication and public affairs strategies and programs in conjunction with the president and other officers and academic leaders.

Serving as the principal spokesperson for the university, specific responsibilities include directing the dissemination of information within the university itself, to the media and to the many publics involved with the university, promoting special events, enhancing the university's visibility and identifying areas within the community that could benefit from university resources and facilities.

Systematic research shows that there is a hierarchy of roles in public relations practice. In several studies, Professors Glen Broom and David Dozier of San Diego State University have found four empirically grounded organizational roles. They describe the four roles as follows:

Communication Managers. Practitioners playing this role are perceived by others as the organization's public relations experts. They make communication policy decisions and are held accountable by others and themselves for the success or failure of communication programs. They follow a systematic planning process.

QUALITIES FOR A SUCCESSFUL CAREER

Art Stevens, president of Lobsenz-Stevens Inc. in New York City and author of *The Persuasion Explosion,* has formulated what it takes to become successful in public relations. The individual . . .

1. Must be an excellent writer capable of writing client reports, effective article themes to editors, news releases, captions, annual reports, feature stories, and the like. His or her writing must require little editing and supervision.

2. Must be able to do short- and long-range planning, conceive and execute a full public relations plan for each account, and adhere strictly to deadlines.

3. Must be innovative and imaginative, not bound by trite, traditional ideas. Must be willing to keep an open mind to new ideas, to researching better ways.

4. Must be well informed about a client's business and continue to keep abreast of all developments in business and government that have an effect on the client's or company's business. Must function as a counselor as well as a communicator.

5. Must be results-oriented, whether the task is the placement of major stories about a client in important publications or the successful execution of a special event. Must be a doer, a self-starter. Must know what follow-up means, and have a solid respect for timetables and deadlines.

6. Must be a thorough "pro," skilled in all the techniques used in the practice of public relations: writing and distribution of news releases, producing press kits, running press conferences, and so on. Must be familiar with feature writers, magazine contributors, and hot current subjects being written about.

Communication Liaisons. Practitioners playing this role represent the organization at public meetings and create opportunities for management to hear the views of priority publics. Predominantly communication facilitators, these practitioners also identify alternative solutions to organizational problems. Similar to communication managers in many respects, communication liaisons do not make policy decisions and are not held accountable for program success or failure.

Media Relations Specialists. Practitioners playing this role actively seek to place messages about the organization in the mass media. At the same time, they keep others in the organization informed of what is being said about the organization (and about issues important to the organization) in the media. They do not make policy, nor are they accountable for program outcomes.

Communication Technicians. Practitioners playing this role are responsible for producing communication products, implementing decisions made by others. They take photographs, assemble graphics; write brochures, pamphlets and news releases; and handle all aspects of production. They do not participate in policy decision-making, nor are they responsible for outcomes.

The San Diego research indicates that practitioners, as well as employers, rate the communication manager at the top of the hierarchy in terms of prestige and salary levels. Although this hierarchy of roles can serve as a career ladder for aspiring public

7. Must know how to create publicity by conceiving a meaningful idea and carrying it through to its conclusion. Must know how to create sundry ideas where none are evident and must know where to take them.

8. Must know what it takes to establish and maintain acquaintanceship with key media people, since editorial contact is one of the primary functions of the public relations professional. The public relations professional must know how to deal with the media and understand their need for quick and responsive answers.

9. Must be able to learn and grow as new situations and client needs arise. Must draw upon prior experience in the public relations field to move into new situations effortlessly and effectively.

10. Must be a good manager, capable of organizing and arranging his or her workload for maximum results. Must be capable of carrying many assignments at the same time, and be in control of each one.

11. Finally, the public relations professional must not be a yes man/woman. Public relations has outgrown the caricature of second-class professionalism by producing individuals who speak their minds confidently to top management of major corporations and make valuable recommendations to these executives. So long as the public relations professional earns the respect and confidence of the chief executive officer, public relations will grow as a profession and will contribute to the broad communications goal of companies and institutions across the United States.

Source: Newsletter of the PRSA Counselors Academy.

relations professionals, many practitioners continue to play lower-level organizational roles (technician or media relations specialist) even after years of professional experience.

NEEDED: AN UNDERSTANDING OF ECONOMICS

In preparing themselves for public relations careers, students should obtain as solid a grounding in economics as possible. Once they are employed as professionals, they should study the financial aspects of their employers or clients. More and more, public relations involves distribution and interpretation of financial information. To handle this material well, the practitioner first must understand it.

After a few years of work, some public relations people return to the classroom to earn advanced degrees. The Master of Business Administration degree, commonly called the MBA, probably is the most frequently sought, but the list of master's and Ph.D. degrees held by public relations specialists ranges over many fields.

Students who plan to do corporate public relations work should remember the fundamental fact about American business: every company was created to earn a profit for those who risked their money to start it. Businesses can continue to exist only as long as they are profitable. The task of public relations in the business world is to help companies prosper. Unfortunately, many college students believe that American business makes excessive profits. This belief arises from a lack of comprehension of free enterprise economics. Typical of this general attitude is a survey of public relations majors in 18 universities nationwide. Professor Richard Piland of Miami University (Ohio) analyzed the responses of 1052 public relations majors to a survey questionnaire. He found a disturbing misconception about the size of profits. He reported:

> The estimated average after-tax profit on one dollar of sales was 31.7 cents, considerably higher than the actual figure of 4.8 cents. In fact, only one in five students had profit estimates within 5 cents of the actual average. More than half of the sample estimated company profits to be at least 25 cents above the actual figure. Tied to this exaggerated concept of business profits was the belief expressed by 38 percent of the respondents that most companies could easily raise wages without raising prices.

PROFESSIONAL SUPPORT SERVICES

ORGANIZATIONS AND SOCIETIES

Public relations groups at the local, state, national, and international levels provide an important channel of communication for practitioners in all areas of the profession. Some of the better known organizations include the Council for the Advancement and Support of Education (CASE), the National Investor Relations Institute (NIRI), and the International Public Relations Association (IPRA).

The largest national group is the Public Relations Society of America, with about 15,000 members and 101 chapters in 1990. PRSA was organized in 1948 with the merger of two groups, the National Association of Public Relations Counsel and the

American Council on Public Relations, and in 1951 was joined by the American Public Relations Association. The society has 14 special interest sections, a national professional development and awards program, and publishes the monthly magazine *Public Relations Journal*. PRSA also operates an Information Center, which provides answers to members' research requests from its extensive library and from the Nexis and Dialog databases. The society distributes issue papers that help recipients plan strategies. It is the parent organization of the Public Relations Student Society of America (discussed in the next section).

The second largest organization of communication and public relations professionals is the International Association of Business Communicators (IABC), with about 12,000 members in more than 35 countries. About 9,900 belong to the 107 chapters found in the United States and another 1,800 members are in Canada. The remaining 500 members, or about 4 percent of the total, are foreign-based, with the United Kingdom and Hong Kong having the largest chapters. Although its membership has diversified somewhat in recent years, a large percentage of IABC members are in-

FIGURE 5.2
Shown here are the logos of the Public Relations Society of America (PRSA), the Public Relations Student Society of America (PRSSA), the International Association of Business Communicators (IABC), and the International Public Relations Association (IPRA).

volved in employee communications. Two-thirds of the respondents in a recent Profile study, for example, said employees were their primary audience. The organization publishes the monthly magazine *Communication World*.

PRSA and IABC investigated the possibility of merging during the late 1980s but decided against doing so. They continue to cooperate on a number of issues, such as ethics and professionalism.

INTERNSHIPS

Internships are extremely popular in the communications industry, and a student whose resume includes practical work experience along with an academic record has an important advantage. Obtaining an internship offered by a public relations firm, company department, or charitable agency is among the best ways to get this desired experience. The intern, in most cases, earns academic credit and gets firsthand knowledge of work in the professional field.

Although internships offer an advantage in getting a first job, the practice by some companies of using unpaid interns has drawn increasing criticism because it puts downward pressure on wages in fields where internships proliferate. The contention is that when students or recent graduates work for nothing, aspiring professionals will accept low beginning salaries. A trend is growing among colleges and universities, and employers as well, to advocate paid internships. The brightest students are insisting on payment for their work, and employers find that students are more productive when treated like actual employees.

Another way for students to get exposure and experience is through membership in the Public Relations Student Society of America (PRSSA). The society has chapters at about 175 universities and a national membership of 6,000. Many students participate in a national case study competition or carry out projects on local campuses as part of a corporate collegiate program. Many chapters also have student-run firms that implement programs for local and campus organizations. A university must offer five courses in public relations before a PRSSA chapter can be established on its campus.

A DIVERSIFIED WORKFORCE

Because the field is relatively small and expanding swiftly, public relations work in the United States is less controlled by the white ''old boy network'' than some media and other fields have been historically. Fewer vestiges of the attitude that ''this is a man's job'' exist in public relations than in other communications industries.

Similarly, opportunities for minority men and women in general public relations work are increasing. In addition, growth of the black and Latino segments of the U.S. population in particular creates a need for practitioners who understand and can respond to the special desires of these audiences.

Even beyond this, as public relations increasingly becomes an international business, with constant communication between U.S. offices and firms in other countries, there is need for persons with personal knowledge of other countries, language skills, and sensitivity to the customs and attitudes of others.

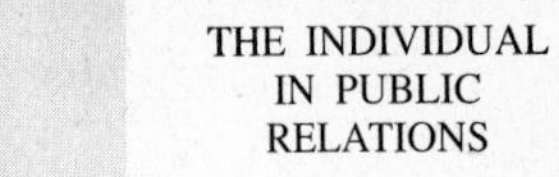

Denise A. Gray, a rising national leader in public relations, is external communications director at AT&T Bell Laboratories. She leads a staff of 30 and oversees public relations programs supporting AT&T's worldwide research and development activity. A former national president of Women in Communications, Gray was instrumental in setting up PRSA's Minority Scholarship Program. She is a life member of the NAACP and active in voluntary organizations.

More than half the public relations practitioners in the United States are women. As more and more young women entered the field during the 1980s, the percentage of female workers rose swiftly. In February, 1987, the U.S. Bureau of Labor Statistics for the first time showed women in the majority, at 51.7 percent. The percentage continues to rise, in part because such a large percentage of public relations graduates are female. The number of female practitioners has grown similarly in other countries.

Statistical surveys have shown that the percentages of women workers are much higher in the lower and middle levels of public relations work than in the top command positions. A recent *PR Reporter* survey showed that women represent nearly 77 percent of practitioners under age 24 and 66 percent of those age 30 to 34, but at age 40 and up men predominate. This has led to charges of a ''glass ceiling'' that subtly prevents women from obtaining the highest positions of authority in the field.

Others, both women and men, deny that such a restraint exists. They point to numerous women holding top positions in their firms and departments. High-level positions go to persons who are prepared by experience to hold them, they point out, and as the younger women who entered the field in the 1970s and 1980s become senior in experience, more will achieve the highest positions. The trend is inevitable, if uneven.

More disturbing is evidence that, as a whole, women receive lower salaries for public relations work than men do. Obviously this discrepancy results in part from the high percentage of less experienced women in the lower and mid-level positions. The problem is more deep-seated than that, however. The *PR Reporter* survey showed that at almost every level of experience, men are better paid than women. A PRSA task force national survey in early 1991 also found salary differences beginning at about the sixth year of employment ($40,000 for men and $35,000 for women). The gap was found in every region of the United States. The report noted, however, that the gap seems to be narrowing. Women, on the average, had received higher raises than men in the previous year (7 percent as opposed to 6 percent).

This group of high-ranking executives exemplifies the rise of women to senior positions in public relations at large corporations and counseling firms. From left to right, top row: Lynda J. Stewart, ABC, Director of Communications and Employee Relations, Cox Enterprises, Inc.; Sharon A. Paul, ABC, Vice President of Corporate and Public Affairs, Abitibi-Price, Inc.; Joyce Hergenhan, Vice President of Corporate Public Relations, General Electric; Marilyn Laurie, Senior Vice President of Public Relations and Employee Information, AT&T. From left to right, bottom row: Karen Bachman, Vice President of Communications, Honeywell, Inc.; Ann H. Barkelew, APR, Vice President of Corporate Public Relations, Dayton-Hudson Corporation; Rosalee A. Roberts, Vice President, Bozell Public Relations, and 1992 president of the Public Relations Society of America. [Photo of Ann H. Barkelew copyright © 1990, Gene Garrett Studio]

Complex social and economic explanations for this discrepancy are advanced, many of them involving conflicting pressures on a woman's time by job demands and child-bearing.

Optimists believe that equality will be achieved eventually. Pessimists worry that the large number of women in the field will result in a "velvet ghetto" with lower prestige and pay than in fields requiring comparable education and skill. Their argument tends to overlook the fact that other fields such as law, accounting, and marketing are also seeing large growth in their percentage of female workers without having such a problem.

CAREER ROUTES FOR MINORITIES

In 1934 Joseph Varney Baker became the first black public relations practitioner to gain nationwide prominence by obtaining accounts with major corporations for his firm in New York City. About a half-century later, in 1980, Inez Kaiser became the first black female to open a public relations firm with national accounts.

Both of these individuals stand out, quite frankly, because the public relations field has been dominated by whites for most of its history. Thus far the field has failed to include black, Asian, and Native American practitioners in numbers anywhere near their representation in the total U.S. population. This unfortunate shortcoming is not exclusive to public relations; the same situation exists in newspapers and in some other media fields. By the early 1990s, the nonwhite minority population in the United States was nearly 50 million, 20 percent of the U.S. total. This multiethnic population, especially the Latino portion of it, continues a strong growth at a rate of about five times that of the general population. Yet ethnic groups as a whole represent only an estimated 13 percent of journalism school enrollments.

Bureau of Labor Statistics in 1987 showed minorities forming only 7.3 percent of the public relations workforce, up from 5 percent in 1980, while minority representation in the U.S. workforce as a whole in 1987 was 21 percent.

Various explanations have been offered. Among them are inadequate school counseling to steer minority students toward public relations careers; a fear among some young people, usually unfounded, that they will not be accepted by coworkers; a dislike of being paraded as "token" minorities and assigned only to minority clients; and in some instances actual discrimination by public relations offices and/or clients.

As the 1990s progress, the situation is improving. Wise employers recognize that diversity of backgrounds makes their staffs more creative and sensitive. The upsurge of young minority adults in the U.S. population provides a deeper pool of talent from which to draw. As growing numbers of well-educated members of ethnic groups find public relations jobs, their fear of "tokenism" diminishes and their accomplishments gain them advancement.

Some minority men and women take the route into "mainstream" departments and firms. Their traditional complaint has been that they have been restricted to lower-level jobs, primarily working on minority accounts. Others join local and regional minority-owned firms. These firms, usually small, earn much of their income by representing minority clients or working in the minority marketplace on behalf of large general firms such as fast-food companies and financial institutions.

Substantial evidence exists to suggests that practitioners from ethnic groups will play a much-expanded role in the mainstream of public relations by the year 2000.

WHAT KINDS OF SALARIES?

Public relations work pays well. This is true from the entry level to the top, where a few senior executives receive between $300,000 and $400,000 in various forms of compensation. The annual cash compensation (base and bonus) in 1988 for chief information officers of Fortune 500 companies who responded to a survey made by Heidrick and Struggles was $162,000. In the graduation-time hunt for employment, holders of college degrees find that beginning public relations jobs pay higher average salaries than those in advertising, newspapers, and broadcasting, as the following figures (from the Dow Jones Newspaper Fund) show:

	1988	1987	1986	1985
Public relations	$18,356	$16,744	$15,300	$14,560
Advertising agencies	16,380	15,028	14,700	13,780
Newspapers	16,120	13,900	13,900	13,520
Broadcasting	15,236	12,792	12,600	11,180

Members of the PRSA received a median salary of $44,250 in 1990, according to a *Public Relations Journal* survey. The IABC, which has members in more than 35 countries, found in its 1989 Profile that the median salary of its members worldwide, when translated into U.S. currency, was $47,400. The typical IABC communicator was a 39-year-old woman who had been in the business for ten years.

The discrepancy between the salaries of men and women, discussed earlier, was evident in the *Public Relations Journal* survey. The men's median salary was $53,637, the women's only $35,933. Among practitioners under age 35, the male median was 24 percent higher than the female median, and above that age the men's advantage rose to 35 percent. Median salary for men over 35 was $59,150, for women, $43,829.

In terms of experience, men in the field from one to four years reported a median salary of $31,993 and women $25,398. At the other end of the career ladder, the median for men with more than twenty years' experience was $68,963 and for women $55,898.

The financial rewards of a successful public relations career are many. However, they are not the only consideration for job satisfaction; other factors must be present. Larry Marshall, president of Larry Marshall Consultants, Inc., of New York, an executive search organization, reported in a study of the public relations field that in recruiting professionals he had found them looking for what he called the ''Five C's'' in a job: career growth, creativity, challenge, commitment, and compensation.

The box titled ''Public Relations Salaries'' shows median salaries in several areas of public relations practice.

PUBLIC RELATIONS SALARIES

	Median	%Men	%Women
Industrial/manufacturing	$58,169	69	31
Public relations firms	50,377	57	43
Utilities	49,446	36	64
Scientific/technical	45,200	58	42
Financial/insurance	43,937	52	48
Media/communications	42,089	50	50
Miscellaneous services	41,485	49	51
Associations/foundations	40,958	48	52
Government	40,622	56	44
Solo practitioner	39,803	54	46
Health care	38,620	31	69
Advertising agency	38,608	54	46
Transportation/hotels/resorts/ entertainment	36,853	39	61
Education	31,415	54	46
Religious/charitable	31,289	36	64

Source: Public Relations Journal survey of members, 1990.

CASE PROBLEM

Staff members of public relations firms have skills in problem solving and planning. Because of this, a new Chinese restaurant in town has retained a local public relations firm to plan and publicize its grand opening.

The restaurant, costing $1.1 million, is decorated in authentic Chinese style, and many of its furnishings are antiques from various Chinese dynasties. The immediate goal is to have a unique and successful grand opening that will generate news coverage. The long-term goal is to position the restaurant as the premier Chinese restaurant in the area.

Outline some ideas that show your creative problem-solving and planning ability.

QUESTIONS FOR REVIEW AND DISCUSSION

1. In what ways does a job in public relations differ from news reporting?
2. Why do some former newspaper reporters fail in public relations work?

3. Those who plan careers in public relations should develop four basic abilities. What are they?

4. What kinds of jobs are available in public relations?

5. What basic economic fact should students who enter corporate public relations work always keep in mind?

6. Glen Broom and David Dozier say there is a hierarchy of roles in public relations. What are they?

7. What is the largest national organization of public relations professionals? The second largest?

8. Why is it important for a student to complete an internship while in college?

9. Do you think the increasing numbers of women in the public relations field will cause the field to have lower status and salaries? Why or why not?

10. What are three other factors in addition to compensation that public relations practitioners consider when looking for a job?

SUGGESTED READINGS

"Annual Survey of the Profession: Salaries and Demographics." *PR Reporter,* October 1, 1990, pp. 1–6.

Belz, Andrew, and others. "Using Role Theory to Study Cross Perceptions of Journalists and Public Relations Practitioners." Chapter 7 of *Public Relations Research Annual,* edited by James Grunig and Larissa Grunig, Volume 1, Hillsdale, NJ: Lawrence Erlbaum Associates, 1989, pp. 125–140.

Cantera, Ron. "Flacks vs. Hacks." *Editor & Publisher,* January 13, 1990, p. 48. Differences between working in journalism and public relations.

Condino, Joan. "The Young and the Restless." *Public Relations Journal,* June 1987, pp. 18–22. Recent college graduates making careers in public relations.

"Education in Public Relations." *Public Relations Review,* Spring 1989. Entire issue devoted to topics about the teaching of public relations.

Jacobson, David, and Tortorello, Nicholas. "Salary Survey." *Public Relations Journal,* June 1991, pp. 14–21. National survey of PRSA members.

Kern-Foxworth, Marilyn. "African-American Achievements in Public Relations." *Public Relations Journal,* February 1991, pp. 18–19.

Kern-Foxworth, Marilyn. "Minorities: The Shape of Things to Come." *Public Relations Journal,* August 1989, pp. 14–22. Minorities in the public relations field.

Lipman, Joanne. "PR's Linda Robinson Emerges at Forefront of Image-Building Art." *Wall Street Journal,* December 5, 1988, p. 1.

Olson, Laury Masher. "Job Satisfaction of Journalists and PR Personnel." *Public Relations Review,* Winter 1989, pp. 37–45.

Paul, Celia, and Sanger, Ann W. "Checklist: Charting Your Career Goals." *Public Relations Journal,* June 1987, pp. 31–32.

Post, Linda C. "View from the Top: Women Executives in Communication." *Communication World,* February 1987, pp. 17–19.

Schuler, Joseph F. *"Trivet! Kak u Tebya?* As Global Economy Heats Up, Demand for Multilingual Practitioner Grows." *Public Relations Journal,* November 1990, pp. 10, 16.

Wakefield, Gay, and Cottone, Laura. "Knowledge and Skills Required by Public Relations Employers." *Public Relations Review,* Fall 1987, pp. 24–32.

Winkleman, Michael. "The Paper Chase." *Public Relations Journal,* April 1987, pp. 16–18. Pros and cons of getting an MBA degree.

"Writing Remains Essential Practitioner Skill, Survey Affirms." *Public Relations Journal,* March 1989, pp. 11–12.

CHAPTER

6

Ethics and Professionalism

Sound ethical conduct and a high level of professionalism are important components of public relations. In the wake of Watergate and the business- and government-related scandals of the 1980s, including the near-collapse of the savings and loan industry, the American public is skeptical of institutions and demands higher ethical practices of business firms and organizations than it did in the past. These accelerating changes in public attitudes are reflected in legislation, in court decisions, in the views of professional commentators upon public affairs, and in public opinion as expressed in the news media.

These demands place a premium upon stellar performance by public relations specialists as they advise management executives about the probable effects of company and institutional decisions. Of equal importance to practitioners is the role of ethics in their own lives. In an effort to establish benchmarks of responsible conduct, they have enacted codes of ethics that are basic to the professionalism that they claim. Credibility, after all, is their chief stock in trade.

In this chapter we examine the role of ethics in public relations and the standards that two of the field's organizations expect their members to uphold. We explore what constitutes professionalism, whether public relations practitioners should be licensed, and the values of accreditation in the field. Two case studies demonstrate some of the ethical problems involved.

DEFINITION

Ethics refers to the value system by which a person determines what is right or wrong, fair or unfair, just or unjust. It is expressed through moral behavior in specific situations. An individual's conduct is measured not only against his or her conscience but also against some norm of acceptability that has been societally, professionally, or organizationally determined. The difficulty in ascertaining whether an act is ethical lies in the fact that individuals have different standards and perceptions of what is "right" and "wrong." Often the situation is not black or white, but falls into the gray area.

A person's philosophical orientation can also determine how he or she acts in a specific situation. Philosophers say the three basic value orientations are (1) absolutist, (2) existentialist, and (3) situationalist. The absolutist believes every decision is either "right" or "wrong," regardless of the consequences. The existentialist, whose choices are made without a prescribed value system, decides on the basis of immediate rational choice. The situationalist's decisions are based on what would cause the least harm or most good.

Most people, depending on the actual situation, probably choose a course of action somewhere along the continuum of the three types. They make decisions on the building blocks of truth-telling, promise-keeping, loyalty, and commitment.

Public relations professionals have the added dilemma of making decisions that satisfy (1) the public interest, (2) the employer, (3) the professional organization's code of ethics, and (4) their personal values. In the ideal world, the four would not conflict. In reality, however, they often do.

CODES OF ETHICS

Most professional organizations and many businesses have codes of ethics. These documents, also called *codes of professional conduct,* are supposed to set acceptable norms of behavior for working professionals and employees. The Public Relations Society of America and the International Association of Business Communicators both have such codes for their members, to be discussed in the following pages. The PRSA code is emphasized because of its age (dating back to 1950) and its enforcement process, unique among communications organizations.

THE PRSA CODE OF PROFESSIONAL STANDARDS

When the Public Relations Society of America was founded in 1948, one of its first concerns, according to the late Rea W. Smith, former executive vice president, was "the development of an ethical code so that (1) its members would have behavioral guidelines, (2) managements would have a clear understanding of standards, and (3) professionals in public relations would be distinguished from shady promoters and ballyhoo advance men who, unfortunately, had been quick to appropriate the words 'public relations' to describe their operations."

The PRSA Code of Professional Standards for the Practice of Public Relations was adopted in 1950 and strengthened by revisions in 1959, 1963, 1977, 1983, and 1988. The PRSA Assembly approved the latest revision in order (1) to make the language clearer and more understandable—hence easier to apply and to follow and (2) to help advance the unification of the public relations profession—part of PRSA's mission. No substantive changes were made.

The 1988 revision was based on the Code of the North American Public Relations Council (NAPRC), an organization of 13 member groups, including PRSA. At the time of the revision 8 of the 13 had revised their own codes in accordance with the NAPRC code, actions considered important steps toward unification. See the current PRSA "Declaration of Principles" and "Code of Professional Standards for the Practice of Public Relations," reprinted here.

PRSA'S DECLARATION OF PRINCIPLES

Members of the Public Relations Society of America base their professional principles on the fundamental value and dignity of the individual, holding that the free exercise of human rights, especially freedom of speech, freedom of assembly, and freedom of the press, is essential to the practice of public relations.

In serving the interests of clients and employers, we dedicate ourselves to the goals of better communication, understanding, and cooperation among the diverse individuals, groups, and institutions of society, and of equal opportunity of employment in the public relations profession.

We pledge:

- To conduct ourselves professionally, with truth, accuracy, fairness, and responsibility to the public;
- To improve our individual competence and advance the knowledge and proficiency of the profession through continuing research and education;
- And to adhere to the articles of the Code of Professional Standards for the Practice of Public Relations as adopted by the governing Assembly of the Society.

PRSA'S CODE ENFORCEMENT

The PRSA has a Board of Ethical and Professional Standards to receive, initiate, and review complaints about members. If a complaint has merit, the case is sent to district-level grievance boards charged with gathering testimony and making a recommendation to the board.

The findings are reviewed and a final decision made by the society's board of directors. PRSA may *expel, suspend, censure,* or *reprimand* a member if he or she is found in violation of the code. If a person is expelled from PRSA—the highest sanction—it simply means he or she cannot be a member. PRSA has no legal authority to prohibit an expelled member from continuing to practice public relations.

The threat of condemnation by one's professional peers, however, is a strong incentive for following the code. The by-laws do permit public announcement of actions taken against a member, but this usually is done through insertion of a short item in the society's internal newsletters, and no general news release is made.

The PRSA can discipline only its own members; it has no legal right to condemn nonmembers for incompetent practice. Since only about 10 percent of the estimated 157,000 public relations people in the United States are members of PRSA, code

ETHICAL DILEMMAS IN PUBLIC RELATIONS PRACTICE

How would you respond to the following situations? Consider your answers. Then, turn the page to see how your responses correspond with interpretations of the PRSA Code.

1. The company president asks you to write a news release claiming that a new product is four times better than the competition and that it represents a "revolutionary" breakthrough in technology.

2. You're a student intern at a public relations firm. One of your assignments is to call corporations and say you're a student doing a class project. You would like to know what kinds of outside public relations services would be most helpful to the company.

3. An American company wants to increase its visibility and market share in Eastern Europe. As director of public relations, you invite a group of German business editors to visit the firm's headquarters with all expenses paid.

4. Your company, in order to improve the quality and media acceptance of news releases, hires the local daily's business editor on a retainer fee for periodic advice and counsel.

5. Your company, as part of its Christmas tradition, gives journalists who regularly cover it an expensive gift. Last year, it was a weekend at a local resort.

6. You are asked by your employer to establish a "citizens' task force" for the purpose of writing state legislators opposing an environmental bill that negatively affects the company.

7. Your public relations firm is competing for an account with two other firms. As a sales point, you say, "We can get you coverage in the *Wall Street Journal*."

8. You're looking for a job in public relations, and a tobacco company offers you the highest salary.

9. You work for a public relations firm. A printing company representative contacts you with the following proposal: If you refer clients that result in new business, the representative will pay you a $250 "finder's fee."

enforcement provisions possibly are less important than the existence of the code itself, which is widely accepted by members and nonmembers as a guideline for professional behavior.

As Donald B. McCammond, a former ethics board chairman, once said, "The board of ethics is more interested in compliance with the code than in recrimination and headlines."

Types of complaints A compilation by the Foundation for Public Relations Research and Education (now called the Institute for Public Relations Research & Education) found that in a 33-year period the ethics board received or initiated 165 complaints about code violations by PRSA members. Of that total, the board determined that 65 percent merited investigation.

ANSWERS TO ETHICAL DILEMMAS IN PUBLIC RELATIONS PRACTICE

1. Making extravagant claims about a product, which cannot be substantiated, should be avoided. Article 4 says a member shall adhere to the highest standards of truth and accuracy. Article 5 also says that a member shall not knowingly disseminate false and misleading information.

2. Although you're a student, you are acting as an agent of the public relations firm. Consequently, you are not representing yourself with honesty and integrity (Article 2), and you are serving the undisclosed interest (Article 8) of the public relations firm that is seeking the information for marketing and direct mail purposes.

3. Inviting German editors to headquarters, all expenses paid, is permissible under Article 6, which is concerned about corrupting the channels of communication. It can be argued that the visit has legitimate news value, and it furthers press understanding of the company's operations. Article 6 would be violated, however, if the all-expense-paid trip were simply a pleasant holiday.

4. Hiring an editor to be a consultant violates Article 6 about the corruption of communication channels because there is a strong indication that such an arrangement is designed to gain preferential or guaranteed news coverage. Article 6, however, would not necessarily be violated if there were full public disclosure and the editor's employer approved.

5. Article 6 does not forbid gifts of nominal value to the media, especially if the gift is a sample of the company's product. Major gifts, however, raise serious questions about expectations of favorable media coverage in return—and thus could corrupt the channels of communication.

6. The establishment of ''citizen task forces'' violates Article 8, especially if the intent is to portray the group as independent or unbiased—yet serving the undisclosed interest of the company organizing and funding its activities. This is not in accord with the public interest (Article 1), nor is the practitioner dealing fairly with the public (Article 3).

7. Promising an employer or client that you can get coverage in a specific publication is a violation of Article 9, which says a member shall not guarantee the achievement of specified results beyond the member's direct control. A person can guarantee the quality of work, but not the decisions of editors.

8. The decision to work for a tobacco company is a personal choice. Article 11, however, says that a member should not place himself or herself in a position where the member's personal interest is in conflict with an employer or client. Therefore, if you oppose smoking and believe it is hazardous to health, it would be difficult to fulfill your obligations to your employer.

9. Accepting a ''finder's fee'' from a printing representative violates Article 12, which states that such fees should not be accepted unless the employer or client is told and gives consent. Accepting a ''finder's fee'' places the practitioner in a conflict-of-interest situation (Article 10) because he or she may not act in the best interests of the client or employer.

Many cases involve several articles of the code. The articles most frequently cited in complaints were, in descending order of frequency:

- Article 3: Fair dealing with clients, employers, and the public
- Article 5: Intentional communication of false and misleading information
- Article 1: Conducting professional life in accordance with the public interest
- Article 4: Adherence to standards of accuracy and truth
- Article 6: Engaging in practices that corrupt the channels of communication or processes of government

Eventually, 32 of the 165 complaints were forwarded to judicial panels, and ten individuals ultimately were disciplined by the society. Two were expelled, two suspended, three censured, and three reprimanded. In the remaining 22 cases, the charges were dismissed for lack of evidence or the member resigned while the case was in progress.

Critics complain that ten disciplinary cases in 33 years doesn't speak particularly well for code enforcement. Others, more positive, see the scarcity of "convictions" as evidence of high ethical standards among PRSA members.

The Harrison Case The proceedings of PRSA's Board of Ethics, according to the society's bylaws, are confidential, in order to protect the rights of those bringing complaints and of those against whom complaints are filed. Although this provision protects the society from possible lawsuits regarding libel and slander, criticism has been made that the proceedings are so secret that society members, as well as the public, aren't even informed when a complaint is filed.

A stricture also is imposed that society members cannot publicly disclose proceedings of the ethics board, as Summerlyne S. Harrison, a vice president of a Washington, D.C., public relations firm, discovered. She publicly criticized a board decision that dismissed her complaint against four PRSA-member executives. She had charged that the executives violated the code by advising William Casey, late head of the CIA, how the Reagan administration could get greater support for its policies in Central America.

Harrison was cited by PRSA for improperly disclosing confidential proceedings of the ethics board and failing to reply promptly to a board inquiry about the matter. At that point Harrison voluntarily resigned from the society and the case was closed.

Jack O'Dwyer's Newsletter, which covers the public relations industry, criticized PRSA for its treatment of Harrison. The newsletter reported that respondents to a fax poll felt justice had not been served, and that a majority believe PRSA members do not surrender the right publicly to discuss ethics charges against members when they join the society.

PRSA President Jerry Dalton said the society doesn't deprive members of free speech, nor does it abridge a member's right to comment on any matter. Harrison, he added, was charged only with violating the confidential proceedings of the ethics board by informing the press that the case had been dismissed. PRSA's procedure is to make a public announcement only if the board of directors votes to expel, suspend, censure, or reprimand a member. A news release also is prepared if a member voluntarily resigns while ethics charges are pending. Harrison was the subject of such a release.

PRSA'S CODE OF PROFESSIONAL STANDARDS FOR THE PRACTICE OF PUBLIC RELATIONS

These articles have been adopted by the Public Relations Society of America to promote and maintain high standards of public service and ethical conduct among its members.

1. A member shall conduct his or her professional life in accord with the *public interest*.

2. A member shall exemplify high standards of *honesty and integrity* while carrying out dual obligations to a client or employer and to the democratic process.

3. A member shall *deal fairly* with the public, with past or present clients or employers, and with fellow practitioners, giving due respect to the ideal of free inquiry and to the opinions of others.

4. A member shall adhere to the highest standards of *accuracy and truth,* avoiding extravagant claims or unfair comparisons and giving credit for ideas and words borrowed from others.

5. A member shall not knowingly disseminate *false or misleading information* and shall act promptly to correct erroneous communications for which he or she is responsible.

6. A member shall not engage in any practice which has the purpose of *corrupting* the integrity of channels of communications or the processes of government.

7. A member shall be prepared to *identify publicly* the name of the client or employer on whose behalf any public communication is made.

8. A member shall not use any individual or organization professing to serve or represent an announced cause, or professing to be independent or unbiased, but actually serving another or *undisclosed interest*.

Although PRSA's confidential procedures do guard against false and malicious charges, they also tend to have a chilling effect on robust discussion of what constitutes ethical and professional practice. Some practitioners suggest that PRSA could be more open, and that standards of the profession could be more sharply defined by publicly disclosing the disposition of all cases considered by the board of ethics.

The critics must remember, however, that PRSA is a voluntary membership society, and the organization doesn't have a legal mandate to be a court of law, which can subpoena witnesses, order the presentation of evidence, or even fine individuals for refusing to cooperate. On the other hand, the optimists often underestimate the perception among many practitioners that it is "unprofessional" to question or criticize the activities of fellow members in the "club."

For example, when some members criticized the public relations department of Firestone Tire Company for disseminating false and misleading information about the safety of the tiremaker's radial tires, they themselves were criticized as being "unprofessional" by people such as Denny Griswold, owner and editor of *PR News*.

Some PRSA members contend that Article 14—stating that a member shall not intentionally damage the professional reputation or practice of another practitioner—means that one should remain silent about the performance of his or her peers. PRSA's

9. A member shall not *guarantee the achievement* of specified results beyond the member's direct control.

10. A member shall *not represent conflicting* or competing interests without the express consent of those concerned, given after a full disclosure of the facts.

11. A member shall not place himself or herself in a position where the member's *personal interest is or may be in conflict* with an obligation to an employer or client, or others, without full disclosure of such interests to all involved.

12. A member shall *not accept fees, commissions, gifts or any other consideration* from anyone except clients or employers for whom services are performed without their express consent, given after full disclosure of the facts.

13. A member shall scrupulously safeguard the *confidences and privacy rights* of present, former, and prospective clients or employers.

14. A member shall not intentionally *damage the professional reputation* or practice of another practitioner.

15. If a member has evidence that another member has been guilty of unethical, illegal, or unfair practices, including those in violation of this Code, the member is obligated to present the information promptly to the proper authorities of the Society for action in accordance with the procedure set forth in Article XII of the Bylaws.

16. A member called as a witness in a proceeding for enforcement of this Code is obligated to appear, unless excused for sufficient reason by the judicial panel.

17. A member shall, as soon as possible, sever relations with any organization or individual if such relationship requires conduct contrary to the articles of this Code.

interpretation carries no such connotation, however. It simply says that a practitioner should not solicit clients by demeaning the quality or ability of the competition. In sum, the concept of "professionalism" means that there should be a healthy, frank discussion of contemporary practice.

An example of how the board of ethics is most effective occurred when a PRSA member scheduled a press conference and several speeches for an "independent" British scientist who had tested a new medical product. A reporter discovered that the scientist was, in fact, an employee of the manufacturer. An inquiry from the board resulted in an immediate response from the member, who enclosed a letter to the client resigning from the account while citing Article 17. The client wanted to communicate false and misleading information, which is contrary to the code.

OTHER CODES

The PRSA code of professional standards, despite some flaws of enforcement, is unique in the communications field in having a highly structured grievance procedure and a history of actually censuring or expelling members of the organization.

SECRECY IN PUBLIC RELATIONS

Should public relations counselors and firms be *required* to make public the names of clients for whom they work?

Article 7 of the PRSA code states only that, "A member shall be prepared to identify the name of the client or employer on whose behalf any public communication is made."

Jack O'Dwyer's Newsletter, in a fax poll, asked professionals whether they favor establishment of a system of mandatory client disclosure, patterned on the rules of the United Kingdom's Public Relations Consultants Association.

The newsletter reported that 70 corporate public relations respondents voted only 36–34 in favor of allowing confidentiality. Sixty-three percent of public relations counselors (115 of 185 responding) voted in favor of the statement, "PR firms should not have to reveal clients."

A sister publication, *Jack O'Dwyer's PR Services Report,* summed up the responses in its May 1990 issue as follows:

> Those in favor of confidentiality argued that certain relationships and projects require secrecy and others said there is an inalienable "right to privacy" that is as sacred as freedom of speech.
>
> However, the pro-disclosure supporters maintained that account secrecy gives "sinister" overtones to the PR field, enables PR firms to hide conflicts, and makes it hard for clients to judge the work of PR firms.

What do *you* think?

The International Association of Business Communicators (IABC) has the ability to suspend members for up to one year after the third violation (see next section), but professional advertising and journalism groups have so far declined to undertake the disciplining of their individual members. Organizations such as the Business/Professional Advertising Association, the American Society of Newspaper Editors (ASNE), and the Society of Professional Journalists (SPJ) have canons or codes of professional conduct, but their function primarily is informational and educational—enunciating standards of conduct rather than enforcing them.

SPJ, for example, took this approach in 1987 after a lengthy and bitter controversy about a statement in its code that, "Journalists should actively try to prevent violation of these standards. . . ." Convention delegates voted to eliminate the clause, primarily because of fears that enacting any punishment would open the society to costly lawsuits, concerns about First Amendment rights of journalists, and the difficulty of establishing a workable method of enforcement. The SPJ code now states in part that, "This society shall, by programs of education and other means, encourage individual journalists to adhere to these tenets. . . ."

SPJ thus followed the lead of ASNE. In the 1920s that organization considered expelling, suspending, or censuring its members for ethical violations. In 1932 ASNE amended its canons to permit such action, but no effort to censure its members has been undertaken.

IABC's Code of Ethics The International Association of Business Communicators adopted a code of standards in 1976, superseded by a code of ethics approved in 1985. The IABC code contains only 7 provisions, as compared with 14 in the PRSA code. Like the PRSA code, IABC encourages its members to (1) be truthful and accurate, (2) obey the law, (3) treat employer or client information with confidentiality, and (4) uphold the organization's standards. The code also encourages members to get permission before using printed materials from other organizations.

IABC places primary emphasis on information and education about the code rather than actual enforcement. An ethics committee answers inquiries from members and works with the national professional development committee to assure that ethics is discussed in chapter, district, and national meetings. For example, IABC bylaws require that at least one article about ethics shall appear annually in the organization's magazine, *Communication World,* and at least one session on ethics be conducted at the international conference. IABC, as well as PRSA, also distributes copies of the code to all members and includes a pledge to support the code in all membership application forms.

Sanctions against a member found in violation of the code primarily consist of warnings that IABC considers to be ''informative and educational.'' It is only after the third warning that, if the individual shows no serious commitment to improvement and the situation is a ''flagrant'' violation, the IABC executive board can suspend a member for up to one year.

IABC headquarters receives inquiries every month about the code, mostly involving questions about copyright, plagiarism, and invasion of privacy. An example is an inquiry whether it is all right to use a published article, with minor changes, without getting permission. Between 1985 and 1990, however, only two formal complaints were filed. One involved a case of possible embezzlement of funds from a chapter treasury, which was turned over to the police, and the other a case of plagiarism, which was resolved by talking to the individual. To date, no member has been suspended because of code violations.

In general, legal counsel for membership organizations such as IABC, ASNE, and SPJ caution against establishing quasilegal mechanisms to discipline members, primarily because of possible lawsuit. A member censured or expelled by such an organization, for example, might sue, claiming defamation and libel, or that the organization's censure deprived him or her of getting a job in the communications field. Also, it is expensive for an organization to ''prosecute'' ethics cases. Reportedly, PRSA spent more than $100,000 on staff time and legal counsel to investigate allegations of ethics violations by Tony Franco, a case discussed at the end of this chapter.

PROFESSIONALISM, LICENSING, AND ACCREDITATION

PROFESSIONALISM

Among public relations practitioners there are considerable differences of opinion about whether public relations is a craft, a skill, or a developing profession. Certainly, at its present level, public relations does not qualify as a profession in the same sense that medicine and law do. Public relations does not have prescribed standards of educa-

IABC'S CODE OF ETHICS

Communication and Information Dissemination

1. Communication professionals will uphold the credibility and dignity of their profession by encouraging the practice of honest, candid and timely communication.

The highest standards of professionalism will be upheld in all communication. Communicators should encourage frequent communication and messages that are honest in their content, candid, accurate and appropriate to the needs of the organization and its audiences.

2. Professional communicators will not use any information that has been generated or appropriately acquired by a business for another business without permission. Further, communicators should attempt to identify the source of information to be used.

When one is changing employers, information developed at the previous position will not be used without permission from that employer. Acts of plagiarism and copyright infringement are illegal acts; material in the public domain should have its source attributed, if possible. If an organization grants permission to use its information and requests public acknowledgement, it will be made in a place appropriate to the material used. The material will be used only for the purpose for which permission was granted.

Standards of Conduct

3. Communication professionals will abide by the spirit and letter of all laws and regulations governing their professional activities.

All international, national and local laws and regulations must be observed, with particular attention to those pertaining to communication, such as copyright law. Industry and organizational regulations will also be observed.

4. Communication professionals will not condone any illegal or unethical act related to their professional activity, their organization and its business or the public environment in which it operates.

tional preparation, a mandatory period of apprenticeship, or state laws that govern admission.

Adding to the confusion about professionalism is the difficulty of ascertaining what constitutes public relations practice. John F. Budd, Jr., a veteran counselor, wrote in *Public Relations Quarterly:* "We *act* as publicists, yet we *talk* of counseling. We *perform* as technologists in communication but we *aspire* to be decision-makers dealing in policy."

On the other hand, there is an increasing body of literature about public relations—including this text and many others in the field. PRSA has compiled a Body of Knowledge abstract that contains more than 1000 references, available on computer disk or hard copy. Substantial progress also is being made in developing theories of public relations, conducting research, and publishing scholarly journals.

It is the personal responsibility of professional communicators to act honestly, fairly and with integrity at all times in all professional activities. Looking the other way while others act illegally tacitly condones such acts whether or not the communicator has committed them. The communicator should speak with the individual involved, his or her supervisor or appropriate authorities—depending on the context of the situation and one's own ethical judgment.

Confidentiality/Disclosure

5. Communication professionals will respect the confidentiality and right-to-privacy of all individuals, employers, clients and customers.

Communicators must determine the ethical balance between right-to-privacy and need-to-know. Unless the situation involves illegal or grossly unethical acts, confidences should be maintained. If there is a conflict between right-to-privacy and need-to-know, a communicator should first talk with the source and negotiate the need for the information to be communicated.

6. Communication professionals will not use any confidential information gained as a result of professional activity for personal benefit or for that of others.

Confidential information cannot be used to give inside advantage to stock transactions, gain favors from outsiders, assist a competing company for whom one is going to work, assist companies in developing a marketing advantage, achieve a publishing advantage or otherwise act to the detriment of an organization. Such information must remain confidential during and after one's employment period.

Professionalism

7. Communication professionals should uphold IABC's standards for ethical conduct in all professional activity, and should use IABC and its designation of accreditation (ABC) only for purposes that are authorized and fairly represent the organization and its professional standards.

IABC recognizes the need for professional integrity within any organization, including the association. Members should acknowledge that their actions reflect on themselves, their organizations and their professions.

There is also the idea, advanced by many professionals and PRSA itself, that the most important thing is for the individual to *act like a professional* in the field. This means that a practitioner should have:

1. A sense of independence.
2. A sense of responsibility to society and the public interest.
3. Manifest concern for the competence and honor of the profession as a whole.
4. A higher loyalty to the standards of the profession and fellow professionals than to the employer of the moment. The reference point in all public relations activity must be the standards of the profession and not those of the client or the employer.

Unfortunately, a major barrier to professionalism is the attitude that many practitioners themselves have toward their work. As James Grunig and Todd Hunt state in their text *Managing Public Relations,* practitioners tend to hold more "careerist" values than professional values. In other words, they place higher importance on job security, prestige in the organization, salary level, and recognition from superiors than on the values listed above. For example, 47 percent of the respondents in a survey of IABC members gave a neutral or highly negative answer when asked if they would quit their jobs rather than act against their ethical values. And 55 percent considered it "somewhat ethical" to present oneself misleadingly as the only means of achieving an objective. Almost all agreed, however, that ethics is an important matter, worthy of further study.

On another level, many practitioners are limited in their professionalism by what might be termed a "technician mentality." These people narrowly define professionalism as the ability to do a competent job of executing the mechanics of communicating (preparing news releases, brochures, newsletters, etc.) even if the information provided by management or a client is in bad taste, is misleading, lacks documentation, or is just plain wrong.

The *Wall Street Journal* several years ago highlighted the pitfalls of the technician mentality. The story described how Jartran, Inc., used the services of the Daniel J. Edelman, Inc., public relations firm to distribute a press packet to the media. The packet included a letter offering information about wheels falling off trucks owned by U-Haul, its archrival. When the newspaper reporter asked about the ethics of this approach, an Edelman junior account executive was quoted as saying, "It was their idea. We're merely the PR firm that represents them."

In other words, readers may get the impression that the public relations expertise of a firm is available to the highest bidder, regardless of professional values, fair play, and ultimately, the public interest. When public relations firms and departments take no responsibility for what is communicated—only *how* it is communicated in terms of techniques—they reinforce the perception that public relations is more flackery than profession.

Some practitioners defend the technician mentality, however, arguing that public relations people are like lawyers in the court of public opinion. Everyone is entitled to his or her viewpoint and, whether the public relations person agrees or not, the client or employer has a right to be heard. Thus, a public relations representative is a paid advocate, just as a lawyer is. The only flaw in this argument is that public relations people are not lawyers, nor are they in a court of law where judicial concepts determine the role of defendant and plaintiff. In addition, lawyers have been known to turn down clients or resign from a case because they doubted the client's story.

In Chapter 13, which concerns legal aspects of public relations, it is pointed out that courts increasingly are holding public relations firms accountable for information disseminated on behalf of a client. Thus, it is no longer acceptable to say, "The client told me to do it."

LICENSING

Proposals that public relations practitioners be licensed were discussed before PRSA was founded. One proponent, Edward L. Bernays, who was instrumental in formulating the modern concept of public relations (see Chapter 3), believes that licensing would protect the profession and the public from incompetent, shoddy opportunists who do not have the knowledge, talent, or ethics required.

The problem is stated by PRSA's task force on demonstrating professionalism:

> Pick up any metropolitan newspaper and scan the employment ads. Under the "public relations" classification, you are likely to find opportunities for door-to-door salespersons, receptionists, used-car salesmen, singles bar hostesses and others of less savory reputation. The front pages of the newspapers are full of stories about former government employees peddling influence and calling it public relations.

Thus, under the licensing approach, only those individuals who pass rigid examinations and tests of personal integrity could call themselves "public relations" counselors. Those not licensed would have to call themselves "publicists" or adopt some other designation.

Several arguments for mandatory licensing and registration with legal sanctions exist:

1. It would define the practice of public relations.
2. It would establish uniform educational curricula.
3. It would set uniform ethical and professional standards.
4. It would provide for decertification of violators of ethical standards.
5. It would protect the consumer of public relations services (clients and employers) from impostors and charlatans.
6. It would protect qualified practitioners from unfair competition from the unethical and unqualified.
7. It would raise the credibility of public relations practitioners.
8. Since licensing would not control anyone's right to deal with the media, government, or public, or to speak out in any way, no infringement of First Amendment rights would be involved.

Several arguments against licensing and in favor of continued reliance on a voluntary approach to public relations ethics also exist:

1. Any licensing in the communications field is an infringement on the First Amendment.
2. It is difficult to define public relations.
3. Too much emphasis would be placed on education.
4. Voluntary accreditation is sufficient to establish standards.
5. Civil and criminal laws already exist to deal with malpractice.
6. Legislatures show little or no interest in licensing public relations since the health and welfare of the general public are not at stake.

7. Licensing would be a state function, and public relations people often work on a national and international basis.

8. Licensing assures only minimum competence and professional standards; it doesn't necessarily assure high ethical behavior.

9. The credibility and status of an occupation are not necessarily assured through licensing. Attorneys, for example, don't particularly enjoy high public status and prestige because they are licensed. Nor do licensed practical nurses.

10. The machinery required for government to license and police all public relations practitioners in this country would be elaborate and very costly to the American taxpayer.

A PRSA study group on licensing and registration bluntly reported:

> There is an almost universal disdain for licensing and a sharp dislike for any type of government oversight of public relations practice. It is our judgment . . . that the ethical code and sense of public and professional morality that must be maintained by public relations professionals cannot be delegated to government. The process of morality, while personal, is democratic and cannot be legislated. It can best be sustained through peer-imposed discipline based on a common code of ethics and consistently maintained levels of professional excellence in practice.

ACCREDITATION

The major effort to improve standards and professionalism in public relations has been related to establishing accreditation programs. PRSA, for example, began its accreditation program in 1965.

To become an accredited member of the society, with the designation *APR,* a person must have at least five years' experience in public relations practice or teaching, must have two sponsors who will testify as to integrity and ability, and must pass a one-day written examination and an oral exam as well. To date, about a third of PRSA's 15,000 members have earned the *APR* designation.

Since *APR* is trademarked by PRSA, a person is prohibited from using *APR* if he or she isn't a current member of the society.

In 1989 the PRSA Assembly adopted a requirement that, in order to maintain accreditation, *APR*s must accumulate ten points every three years in the areas of education, professionalism, or service. The system went into effect in 1991. PRSA is the only group of U.S. professional communicators to have such a requirement.

In 1990 PRSA established a College of Fellows in order to recognize accredited members who for 20 years or more have demonstrated superior capability as practitioners, whose personal and professional qualities have served as role models for other practitioners, and who have advanced the state of public relations. Eighty-five of the society's approximately 15,000 members were the first Fellows elected.

In recent years the society has also launched an information campaign to make the general public and potential employers aware of what the *APR* designation means. In this way, it is hoped that such a "seal of approval" will separate public relations professionals from those less qualified. It is a slow process, however, because many senior public relations practitioners do not feel the need to prove themselves through a ''test.'' Another major obstacle is that few employers require accreditation as a prerequisite for top-level positions in public relations.

The International Association of Business Communicators also has an accreditation program for its membership. A member may use the designation *ABC* (*Accredited Business Communicator*) after submitting a portfolio for evaluation and passing written and oral examinations. At present, fewer than 5 percent of IABC's 12,000 members have an *ABC* designation.

OTHER STEPS TOWARD PROFESSIONALISM

PRSA, IABC, and the Public Relations Division of the Association for Education in Journalism and Mass Communication (AEJMC) have worked to improve and standardize the curricula for programs of public relations at the bachelor's and master's degree level. The 1987 Commission on Undergraduate Public Relations Education set the new standard that a public relations sequence should have a minimum of five core courses covering the following public relation topics: (1) principles and theory, (2) writing and publicity techniques, (3) research for planning and evaluation, (4) case studies on strategy and implementation, and (5) supervised internship. This core curriculum has been endorsed by PRSA, IABC, the Public Relations Division of AEJMC, and the public relations section of the International Communication Association.

The educational and professional community generally agrees that preparation for public relations work requires a specialized course of study with strong emphasis on a broad liberal arts education coupled with a minor in economics or a business area. Highly traditional schools and departments of journalism, however, continue to insist that a journalism curriculum is the best preparation for a public relations career.

The Institute for Public Relations Research & Education and the IABC Foundation also work to expand the body of knowledge about public relations. Both advance professionalism through sponsorship of books and monographs, symposiums, scholarships, and grants for research studies. A major project of the IABC Foundation, for example, has been a six-year, $400,000 study to investigate ''Excellence in Public Relations and Communication Management'' through a series of surveys and the testing of organizational communication models. Early findings of the project were discussed in Chapter 4.

In 1990 PRSA established its own foundation to fund a number of special projects. One is a $50,000 National Minority Scholarship program to encourage more minority students to select public relations as a career. The foundation also funds the Body of Knowledge project, previously described in this chapter.

ETHICS IN INDIVIDUAL PRACTICE

Despite codes of professional practice and formalized accreditation, ethics in public relations boils down to deeply troubling questions for the individual practitioner: Will I lie for my employer? Will I rig a doorprize drawing so a favorite client can win? Will I deceive in order to gain information about another agency's clients? Will I cover up a hazardous condition? Will I issue a news release presenting only half the truth? Will I seek to bribe a reporter or a legislator? Will I withhold some information in a news conference, and provide it only if a reporter asks a specific question? Will I quit my job rather than cooperate in a questionable activity? In other words, to what extent, if any, will I compromise my personal beliefs?

These and similar questions plague the lives of many public relations people, although a number hold such strong personal beliefs and/or work for such highly principled employers that they seldom need to compromise their personal values. If employers make a suggestion that involves questionable ethics, the public relations person often can talk them out of the idea by citing the possible consequences of such an action—adverse media publicity, for example.

''To thine own self be true,'' advised New York public relations executive Chester Burger at an IABC conference. A fellow panelist, Canadian politician and radio commentator Stephen Lewis, commented: ''There is a tremendous jaundice on the part of the public about the way things are communicated. People have elevated superficiality to an art form. Look at the substance of what you have to convey, and the honesty used in conveying it.'' With the audience contributing suggestions, the panelists formulated the following list of commendable practices:

- Be honest at all times.
- Convey a sense of business ethics based on your own standards and those of society.
- Respect the integrity and position of your opponents and audiences.
- Develop trust by emphasizing substance over triviality.
- Present all sides of an issue.
- Strive for a balance between loyalty to the organization and duty to the public.
- Don't sacrifice long-term objectives for short-term gains.

Adherence to professional standards of conduct—being truly independent—is the chief measure of a public relations person. Faced with such personal problems as a mortgage and children to educate, practitioners may be strongly tempted to become yes men (or yes women) and decline to express their views forcefully to an employer, or to resign. J. Kenneth Clark, vice president of corporate communications, Duke Power Company, Charlotte, North Carolina, gave the following advice to an IABC audience:

> If the boss says newspapers are no damn good, the yes man agrees.
>
> If the boss says to tell a reporter ''no comment,'' the yes man agrees.
>
> If the boss says the company's employees get a paycheck and don't really need to be informed about anything else, the yes man agrees.
>
> If the boss says the public has no right to pry into what's going on inside a company—even though that company is publicly held and is dependent upon public support and public sales—the yes man nods his head agreeably and starts work on the corporate version of a Berlin Wall.
>
> The fate of the yes man is as inevitable as it is painful. Although your boss may think you're the greatest guy in the world for a while, you're going to lose your internal credibility because you never really state your professional opinions. And you're talking to a person who dotes on strong opinions and does not think highly of people who fail to offer them.

Allen H. Center, a professor at San Diego State University and a long-time corporate public relations executive, has written: ''Public relations has emerged more as an echo of an employer's standards and interests than that of a professional discipline applied to the employer's problems.'' Yet many a practitioner has resigned rather than submit to a compromising situation.

Told that his job at a company was ''to turn excrement into applesauce'' (the official used a less elegant word than *excrement*), one public relations man resigned. He pointed out later that ''the attitude exemplified two things—the reality of the company at the top level, where policy is made, and the perception at that level of the role of public relations.''

In some cases practitioners have been arbitrarily fired for refusing to write news releases that are false and misleading. This happened to an accredited PRSA member in the San Francisco Bay area. The company president wanted him, among other things, to write and send a news release giving a list of company clients when, in fact, none of the companies had signed a contract for services. When the practitioner refused, on the grounds that the PRSA code would be violated, he was fired. In turn, the practitioner sued the company for unlawful dismissal and received almost $100,000 in an out-of-court settlement.

Tommy Ross, pioneer public relations practitioner and partner of Ivy Lee before founding T. J. Ross and Associates, once told a *Fortune* magazine interviewer: ''Unless you are willing to resign an account or a job over a matter of principle, it is no use to call yourself a member of the world's newest profession—for you are already a member of the world's oldest.''

Thus, it can be readily seen that ethics in public relations really begins with the individual—and is directly related to his or her own value system as well as to the good of society. Although it is important to show loyalty to an employer, practitioners must never allow a client or an employer to rob them of their sense of self-esteem.

ETHICAL DEALINGS WITH NEWS MEDIA

The most practical consideration facing a public relations specialist in his or her dealings with the news media is that anything less than total honesty will destroy credibility and, with it, the practitioner's usefulness to an employer. The news media depend on public relations sources for much of the information they convey to readers and listeners. Although a number of public relations releases are used simply as tips on which to develop stories, many reporters and editors know that they can rely on the accuracy and thoroughness of much public relations copy and use it with little change.

Achieving trust is the aim of all practitioners, and it can be achieved only through highly professional and ethical performance. It is for this reason that providing junkets with doubtful news value, extravagant parties, expensive gifts, and personal favors for media representatives should never be done. On occasion, an unethical journalist will ask favors, but the public relations professional will decline such requests tactfully.

Newspeople and public relations executives alike questioned the propriety of Coca-Cola USA's sending sample cans of Coke Classic stuffed with $5 bills to 200 consumer and trade reporters and editors. The attention-getting gimmick was part of the company's ''Magic Summer '90'' promotion in which 750,000 cans of the soft drink were to be distributed nationwide containing up to $200 cash and prize vouchers for trips and tickets to vacation and entertainment destinations. The cans were devised so that the cash or a voucher would pop up when what looked like an ordinary container was opened.

When some cans malfunctioned and a few purchasers drank the slightly noxious liquid, Coca-Cola USA launched an advertising campaign urging consumers to "take a good look" and not to drink the liquid. It then cancelled the promotion. The public relations newsletter *Bulldog Reporter* quoted a number of newspeople and public relations executives who, for the most part, pointed out that the sending of cash to news sources raised the question of a conflict of interest whether a bribe was intended or not. (Ethical aspects of media relations are discussed further in Chapter 23.)

FIGURE 6.1
Magazines and newsletters edited for public relations professionals—among them *Bulldog Reporter*—provide a forum for discussion of ethical issues. Also shown here are the *Public Relations Review,* the *Public Relations Journal, Communication World, International Public Relations, PR Reporter, PR News, Jack O'Dwyer's Newsletter,* and *Communication Briefings.*

AUTOS: SHADES OF GRAY

Although it is fairly obvious that expensive gifts and bribes are unethical by almost anybody's standard of professionalism, the most difficult ethical situations are those that are neither black nor white, but differing shades of gray.

Relationships between automotive journalists and car manufacturers are questionable, according to an article in the *Wall Street Journal*. It is not unusual, for example, for an editor at *Car and Driver* to write reviews for autos made by a manufacturing firm that also employs the journalist as a consultant. As the article writer says, "Welcome to the world of automotive enthusiast journalism where the barriers that separate advertisers from journalists are porous enough for paychecks to pass through."

PRSA's Article 6 forbids "corrupting the channels of communication" by placing journalists on the payroll, but this stricture doesn't seem to mean much in the world of "buff" magazines such as *Car and Driver, Motor Trend,* and *Road & Track*. The journalists say they are professionals and would never let their consulting relationships interfere with their writing independence, but the public is left wondering about the integrity of such statements. At the same time, if hiring editors to be consultants is standard operating procedure, how does the public relations person for an auto company reconcile this "reality" with the standards of his or her profession? Ethical issues in the travel industry are discussed in Chapter 20. Some other aspects of public relations–news media ethical relationships are examined in "The Press Party" section of Chapter 23.

BUSINESS, GOVERNMENT, AND ETHICS

Public relations executives and lobbyists were heavily embroiled in the top-level business and government scandals of the 1980s involving Wall Street securities firms, defense industries, the savings and loan industry, and the Iran–Contra affair. Ironically, the revelations followed a period when hundreds of business firms adopted codes of ethics and required employees to attend ethics seminars and sign annual affidavits that they were following company policy. The Ethics Resource Center reported that, whereas only three of every four of the 1500 largest corporations had written codes of ethics in 1984, by 1990 virtually all had them. Companies conducting extensive ethics training programs for employees included Martin Marietta, McDonnell Douglas, and General Dynamics.

According to the Ethics Resource Center, the following matters are addressed most often in the codes of business corporations:

- A general statement of company philosophy and commitment to ethical conduct
- Compliance with all applicable laws and regulations
- Prohibition of bribery and kickbacks
- Conflicts of interest
- Gifts, gratuities, and entertainment

- Confidential and proprietary information
- Accurate books, records, and financial reports
- Proper use of corporate assets
- Proper relationships with dealers, agents, suppliers, competitors, customers, and government representatives
- Honesty in communication
- Political activities and relationships with foreign governments
- Social responsibility of the company
- Industrial integrity and adherence to high standards of personal morality

Said Don Bates, APR, president of the Bates Company, in a speech at Northern Illinois University: ''Often, the public relations practitioner drafts the code to begin with, assisted by top management and corporate counsel. Regardless, he [or she] has a crucial role in promoting its existence and significance to employees, suppliers, and others.''

ONE CORPORATION'S CODE OF ETHICS

Public relations practitioners, in addition to adhering to the standards of professional conduct for PRSA or IABC, must be aware of ethics guidelines established by employers. FMC Corporation, for example, has a code of ethics in pamphlet form that is distributed to all employees. An example of its content is the following:

Conflict of Interest All business decisions should be made in the best interest of FMC. Conflicts can arise in many situations. They occur most often in cases where an employee, or members of his or her immediate family, could obtain some personal benefit at the expense of the company or its stockholders. FMC's Business Conduct Guidelines require all employees to refrain from certain activities or to obtain approval from an appropriate manager before engaging in others. These activities incude:

1. Conducting FMC business personally or with relatives.
2. Holding a significant financial interest in any FMC suppliers, contractors, customers, competitors, merger targets or acquisition targets.
3. Moonlighting without permission that affects job performance, or for a business that deals or competes with FMC.
4. Accepting improper gifts, loans or preferential treatment from suppliers, contractors, customers, or competitors. (Gifts of nominal value may be given and received on customary occasions.)
5. Benefiting unfairly from the use or disposition of company property.
6. Taking advantage of inside information not yet available to the public to trade in FMC securities.

GUIDELINES FOR FAIR DEALING

Ketchum Public Relations has established guidelines for its employees on how to deal fairly with clients.

The code deals with (1) truth and accuracy in communications, (2) confidential information, (3) purchasing, (4) gifts and excessive entertainment and other payments, (5) industry groups, (6) union agreements, (7) suppliers to the agency and clients, (8) services for competitors, (9) use of inside information, and (10) misuse of business opportunities.

"We will deal with clients in a fair and businesslike fashion, providing unbiased, professional recommendations to move their business ahead," the code promises.

"We will safeguard their proprietary information and help protect their financial assets."

Many other public relations firms have similar codes.

ETHICS AND LAWS CONCERNING FINANCIAL NEWS

Public relations personnel working for publicly held companies have not only an ethical but also a legal obligation to promptly release news about dividends, earnings, new products, mergers, and any other developments that might affect security values or influence investment decisions of stockholders or the public. As noted on the preceding pages, news must not be delayed so that insiders can derive financial benefit. The Securities and Exchange Commission (SEC), described in Chapter 13, strictly enforces these requirements.

Corporations are also prohibited from using "hype" in connection with the sale of new securities or from being overly optimistic about the financial health of the companies. Public relations staff members and outside counsel increasingly are being held responsible by the SEC, and they also run the risk of violating PRSA's guidelines for financial public relations. These tell practitioners to find out for themselves if management gives them questionable information to disseminate. The rule states: "Where members have any reason to doubt that projections have an adequate basis in fact, they shall satisfy themselves as to the adequacy of the projections prior to disseminating them." Practitioners are put on notice that they can't simply plead, "This is what management told me to say."

A more troublesome ethical dilemma is how and when to release information regarding mergers and acquisitions. Such negotiations between companies are very sensitive; untimely release of information may adversely affect a company's bargaining position. Secrecy of negotiations is essential in business but, at the same time, the SEC requires public release of information. The problem is what and how much to disclose at any given time. If negotiations are just starting, for example, is it all right to be evasive so investors don't misinterpret the information? The SEC definition of "material information" is somewhat elastic and subject to a number of court interpretations.

Public relations personnel also must be well aware of Federal Trade Commission (FCC) regulations regarding the promotion of a product or service. A company can get into trouble for such things as unsubstantiated claims, fraudulent testimonials, deceptive pricing, surveys that are not really independent, and rigged contests. Again, the public relations professional has the responsibility to ascertain the facts rather than to take the word of the marketing or advertising director. The credibility of the company and the public relations practitioner is at stake.

The Food and Drug Administration (FDA) also has a list of regulations concerning the promotion and advertising of medicines and drugs.

CASE STUDY 1: HILL & KNOWLTON'S ANTIABORTION CAMPAIGN

A lively controversy with multiple ethical aspects erupted in 1990 when Hill & Knowlton, the nation's largest public relations firm, agreed to conduct an antiabortion campaign for U.S. Roman Catholic bishops. The bishops also hired the Worthlin Group, a leading Republican polling operation that served Ronald Reagan in his campaign for the White House and during his presidency. The aim of the bishops' campaign, expected to cost $3–$5 million over a three-to-five-year period, was to persuade both Catholics and non-Catholics to oppose abortion.

Many Hill & Knowlton employees publicly criticized the decision; two resigned, and the firm lost at least one client. President Robert L. Dilenschneider said any employee could refrain from working on the account with impunity.

"Some organizations have lost sight of fundamental values, such as the sanctity of human life, or they have tried to convince America that the main issue in the abortion debate is the right to choose rather than, as it really is, what is being chosen," said Cardinal John J. O'Connor, archbishop of New York and chairman of the Committee for Pro-Life Activities of the U.S. Catholic Conference. Noting that abortion-rights groups have hired pollsters and media advisers to help them, O'Connor added: "Given the stakes—life itself—we can do no less."

Critics branded the campaign as a waste of church resources and a violation of the constitutional separation of church and state. Charged Kate Michelman, president of the National Abortion Rights Action League: "They're not just trying to deliver a message, they're trying to interject their religious and moral views into politics." Added Frank Greer, president of the organization's public relations agency: "The bishops are using their PR firm to try to change public policy—something they shouldn't be able to do as long as the Catholic Church keeps its tax-exempt status." As for wasting church resources, the bishops said funds would be sought from private sources.

Jerry Dalton, PRSA president, said in a letter to the New York *Times* that the bishops have a First Amendment right to use public relations counsel to help them shape arguments against abortion.

"However controversial or unpopular a cause, advocates—or opponents—have the right to seek professional PR counsel to help them shape and communicate persuasive arguments," Dalton wrote. "That's what the First Amendment is all about." Other corporate executives, interviewed by the *Public Relations Journal,* echoed Dalton's opinion.

A former priest, Eugene Kennedy, professor of psychology at Loyola University, wrote in the New York *Times* that the bishops had chosen a strategy "that is manipulative at best and numbingly amoral at worst."

''Good shepherds do not invite wolves to help them tend flocks. . . . You call in PR operatives when the truth won't do. . . . Humans cannot be manipulated into moral positions.''

A story in *National Catholic Reporter* titled ''What Does H&K Sell?'' provided the answer: ''Anything the customer is prepared to pay for.''

Dilenschneider responded to both attacks: ''We do not shy away from controversy but we will not misrepresent a client's position. And if cash were the determinant for representation of a client, we would certainly not have turned away, as we have, representation of Muammar al-Qaddafi, General Noriega, Ferdinand Marcos, South Africa (in its previous posture), Guatemala, and the Colombian drug lords.''

In a letter to the New York *Times,* Dilenschneider wrote that Hill & Knowlton has a long record of representing those whom others shun, sometimes at personal risk, as in the civil rights struggle in the 1960s. He added: ''We have been involved in efforts to raise awareness on acquired immune deficiency syndrome and the environment; to

Pickets march outside the Hill & Knowlton office in New York to protest the public relations firm's decision to conduct an antiabortion campaign for U.S. Roman Catholic bishops. (Kalfus, © New York Post)

free Soviet Jews; to get passports for Hong Kong residents; to implement the United States immigration amnesty program; to arrange Andrei Sakharov's visit to the United States; to aid Covenant House in an hour of need; and to improve the health of an entire community. None of these were without controversy.''

Other criticisms of the firm's acceptance of the Catholic account included the following:

1. The firm violated Article 10 of the PRSA code: ''A member shall not represent conflicting or competing interests without the express consent of those concerned, given after a full disclosure of the facts.'' The *Bulldog Reporter* newsletter raised the issue, pointing out that among Hill & Knowlton's hundreds of clients are the Church of Scientology; DNS, a gene-splicing bioengineering firm; Wyeth-Ayerst, makers of contraceptive devices; and Playboy Enterprises, which supports abortion rights. The newsletter said representatives of the Bishops Committee in both New York and Washington said they were unaware of Hill & Knowlton's ties to Playboy.

Asked about a possible conflict of interest, according to the newsletter Dilenschneider replied: ''We will not resign any business we currently have.'' Another H&K executive said the firm's work for Playboy dealt with First Amendment rights.

2. Hill & Knowlton responded slowly in handling the firm's internal communications problem. Staff members complained that they first heard of H&K's agreeing to work for the bishops from newspaper reports. No backup spokesperson was appointed to respond to innumerable press inquiries after the story broke, according to some accounts.

Robert L. Dilenschneider, president of Hill & Knowlton.

3. The firm should not accept "an assignment whose ultimate goal is to limit our fundamental rights," according to a petition signed by 160 staff members in the company's New York office. Davia Tenin, vice president for marketing at the Wertheim Schroder investment banking firm, said the decision "says to me that it is going to sacrifice women's rights for the pocketbook."

4. Acceptance of the account reinforced with some people the image of public relations professionals as being simply "hired guns" (the accusation of Frances Kissling, president of Catholics for a Free Choice). Other published statements included the stereotypical charge that "PR people don't care whose side they are on so long as the pay is good" and Kennedy's statement, "You call in public relations operatives when the truth won't do. That's why PR—the very letters evoke subtle maneuvers and manipulation of opinion—has become, in business and in politics, the substitute for genuine moral and ethical sense." An article in the June 1990 issue of *Public Relations Journal* (*PRJ*) was titled, "Has the Field's Image Been Affected?"

The "Briefings" column in the same issue quoted numerous public relations executives as expressing concern over their future acceptance of controversial accounts, in view of possible employee dissent and the increasing tendency of the media to publicize the "behind the scenes" workings of public relations. Said Ronald Watt, president of Watt, Roop & Co. in Cleveland: "I think the '90s will be a time when firms are faced with the option of either handling these hot accounts or not handling them." A number of firms were reported to be holding ethics conferences with employees or beginning to interview them about the causes they advocate. Some have established policies such as Burson-Marsteller's stance of not becoming involved in religious or political issues.

PRJ quoted David Mona, president of Mona Meyer & McGrath in Minneapolis, as declaring that firms must protect themselves by devising crisis plans well before making a decision to take on a controversial client. "What this means," he said, "is we may have to blow the dust off our crisis communications books and see that we practice what we preach."

The Hill & Knowlton controversy raises a number of questions for discussion. Some of them involve ethics, while others are operational in nature:

- Should Hill & Knowlton have accepted the Catholic bishops' account, or should it have adopted Burson-Marsteller's policy of not handling religious or political accounts?
- Do the bishops have a constitutional right to use a public relations firm to develop new strategies?
- Was the principle of separation of church and state violated?
- Did Hill & Knowlton violate an article of the PRSA Code of Professional Standards for the Practice of Public Relations?
- Did the firm follow the precepts of a public relations communications crisis plan?
- Should public relations practitioners be required to work on a controversial account if they do not wish to do so?

- Should Hill & Knowlton have anticipated the attacks on public relations that followed the announcement of its decision?
- Does Hill & Knowlton have a good record of acceptance or nonacceptance of controversial accounts?
- Will the campaign succeed in shifting the focus of debate from women's rights (prochoice) back to what is being chosen (possibly abortion)?

CASE STUDY 2: THE FRANCO AFFAIR

The public relations profession was jolted in late 1986 when it was disclosed that Anthony ''Tony'' M. Franco, then national president of the Public Relations Society of America, had been charged by the Securities and Exchange Commission with insider trading.

In a civil action suit, the SEC alleged that Franco had violated Section 10(b) and rule 10b-5 of the Securities Exchange Act of 1934, which prohibits use of inside information to buy or sell shares of stock in a company. The act also requires insiders to make immediate public disclosure of any information that materially affects the price of a stock.

Franco, chairman and chief executive officer of his own public relations firm in Detroit, Anthony M. Franco, Inc., was charged with using confidential information from a client, Crowley, Milner and Company, in 1985. The company had hired Franco to prepare a news release about its proposed acquisition by Oakland Holding Company with a stock offer of $50 per share.

The SEC suit charged that Franco used this confidential information, before any public disclosure was made, to have his broker purchase 3000 shares of Crowley, then listed on the American Stock Exchange at $41 a share. The purchase of so many shares, on a stock relatively inactive on the market, triggered the American Stock Exchange to inform the Crowley company that Franco was the purchaser.

According to the SEC complaint, Franco denied he was responsible for the trade. Later that day, however, Franco allegedly telephoned his broker and directed him to rescind the trade. Franco did not deny that the stock purchase had been made, but maintained that his broker had acted without his authorization, and the purchase of the stock a day before public announcement of an acquisition was an unfortunate coincidence.

The SEC notified Franco that it was investigating the incident, which resulted in Franco's being named a defendant in a civil suit filed in the U.S. District Court for the District of Columbia. On January 1, 1986, Franco became the new national president of PRSA.

The Franco case became public knowledge on August 27, 1986, when the *Wall Street Journal* and the Associated Press carried the news that Franco had signed a consent decree with the SEC. In a consent decree, the defendant neither denies nor admits any of the allegations but promises to obey the law in the future.

The knowledge that Franco had signed a consent decree generated a storm of criticism in the public relations community. Many practitioners saw it, in the words of several, as a real "tragedy," "a terrible stigma for PR people," and "a stupid mistake by someone who is supposed to stand for everything that is right about PR."

The board of directors of the large Chicago PRSA chapter immediately called for Franco's resignation as president of PRSA. Charles Werle, chapter president, said: "Regardless of the legal ramifications of the SEC consent decree, our decision was based on the fact that Franco accepted the national presidency of PRSA knowing that there was a possibility of a damaging SEC action involving him personally that could reflect negatively on PRSA during his term of office. Withholding such information could easily be interpreted as a violation of the PRSA code of ethics."

On August 28, Franco did resign. He said that his resignation was in the best interest of PRSA and that the widespread criticism of his actions made it impossible to do his job effectively. He did, however, retain his membership and requested a hearing before the PRSA Board of Ethics.

The PRSA ethics board finally met on September 19 to hear testimony from Franco and his lawyer. On October 4, the society's board of directors met to hear the recommendations of the ethics board and to determine what disciplinary actions, if any, to take. While the board of directors was in executive session, Franco sent word that he was resigning his membership, effective immediately. Since the society can discipline only members, Franco had removed himself from PRSA code enforcement procedures. Code violations being considered by the board at the moment of Franco's resignation from membership were:

- A member shall deal fairly with clients, employers, fellow practitioners, and the public.
- A member shall safeguard confidences of present and former clients, as well as others who have disclosed confidences to a member in the context of communications relating to an anticipated professional relationship.
- A member shall not intentionally communicate false or misleading information, and is obligated to use care to avoid communicating false or misleading information.

In the aftermath of the Franco affair, PRSA initiated new rules and regulations. Candidates for national office are now required to sign a disclosure statement that they are not involved in anything that might reflect adversely on the society. And new by-laws now permit the society to continue investigating a code violation for up to 90 days after a member has resigned membership. A member can also be temporarily suspended from membership if he or she has been named a defendant in a criminal case.

CASE PROBLEM

Prism Computer Corporation, a manufacturer of personal computers, has developed a new laser printer that is cheaper and more efficient than those produced by competitors. Although prototype models have been built, actual production of the new printer has been stalled up to three months by manufacturing problems.

Despite these difficulties, Prism's top management believes it is important from a marketing standpoint to announce that the new laser printer is now available. Consequently, they ask you as the product information specialist to write and distribute a new product release about the laser printer and its features.

You are told that no mention should be made in the news release that the product won't be available for another three months. What would you do in this situation? Does the situation violate professional ethics in any way? Why or why not?

QUESTIONS FOR REVIEW AND DISCUSSION

1. Sound ethical practice is essential in public relations work. What is meant by *ethics,* and how is it that two individuals can disagree about what constitutes an ethical dilemma?

2. What do you consider the most important points in the PRSA and IABC codes? How do the standards serve the interest of (1) the organizations' members and (2) the public? Can you find any loopholes that might hinder full-fledged enforcement?

3. What are some of the principal problems involved in enforcing the codes?

4. What does the PRSA code say about giving gifts and free trips to representatives of the media? Is it all right to buy drinks or dinner for a news reporter?

5. Under what circumstances should public relations practitioners (1) criticize each other and (2) not criticize each other?

6. To what four standards should a practitioner adhere in acting like a professional?

7. Should public relations practitioners be licensed? What are some of the reasons pro and con?

8. What special ethical and legal obligations are involved in the handling of financial news? What agencies enforce the legal requirements?

9. What portion of the PRSA code, if any, did Hill & Knowlton violate when it accepted the Catholic bishops' antiabortion account?

10. Review the Tony Franco case study. Do you think Franco should have been expelled from PRSA? Why or why not?

SUGGESTED READINGS

Bivins, Thomas H. "A Theory-Based Approach to Public Relations Ethics." *Journalism Educator,* Winter 1991, pp. 39–41.

Heger, Kyle. "One Communicator's Gold Star Is Another's Scarlet Letter." *Communication World,* September 1989, pp. 34–36. Ethics and professional practice.

Jackson, Pat. "Demonstrating Professionalism." *Public Relations Journal,* October 1988, pp. 27–31. Special report on PRSA's efforts to upgrade professionalism.

Jurgensen, John H., and Lukaszewski, James. "Ethics: Content Before Conduct." *Public Relations Journal,* March 1988, pp. 47–48.

Kennedy, Eugene. "Catholic Bishops' Big PR Blunder." New York *Times,* April 19, 1990. Op-ed article on editorial page.

Lesly, Philip, and others. "Licensing Public Relations." *Public Relations Review,* Winter 1986. Entire issue devoted to the pros and cons of licensing.

McCauley, Kevin. "H&K Keeps Pro-Life Account Despite Heavy Opposition." *O'Dwyer's PR Services* magazine, June 1990, pp. 1,8, 31–35.

Pollock, John C. "Business Ethics Affects the Bottom Line." *Communication World,* July–August 1989, pp. 48–49.

Pratt, Catherine, and Rentner, Terry Lynn. "What's Really Being Taught About Ethical Behavior?" *Public Relations Review,* Spring 1989, pp. 53–66. Teaching ethics in public relations courses.

"Public Relations Body of Knowledge." *Public Relations Review,* Spring 1988. Entire issue devoted to a bibliography of information in the field.

Ruddell, Tom, and Pettegrew, Lloyd. "The Best Companies Have and Heed Codes/Creeds." *Communication World,* September 1988, pp. 30–31.

Seligman, Mac. "Travel Writers' Expenses: Who Should Pay?" *Public Relations Journal,* May 1990, pp. 27–28, 34.

Stevenson, Peter M. "Hill and Knowlton's Big PR Problem." *Manhattan, Inc.,* July 1990, pp. 61–68. Controversy over taking prolife account.

White, Joseph. "Car Magazine Writers Sometimes Moonlight for Firms They Review." *Wall Street Journal,* May 15, 1990, p. 1. Ethics of magazine writers working as consultants to auto-manufacturing firms.

Wylie, Frank W. "Communicating for Ethical Change." *Communication World,* December 1990, pp. 10–11.

Wylie, Frank W., and Langham, Barbara D. "Ethics: Where Do You Stand? *Communication World,* May 1989, pp. 21–25. A self-test.

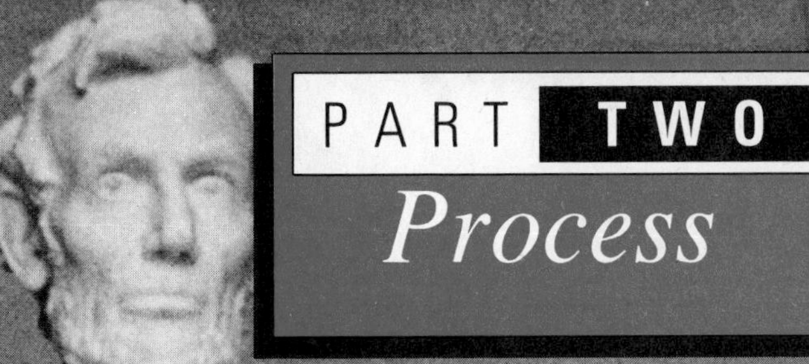
PART TWO
Process

EQUAL RIGHTS
FOR ALL SPECIES
SAVE THE RAINFOREST
EARTH FIRST!

CHAPTER

Research

Effective public relations is a process, and this chapter is about the essential first step—research. Walter K. Lindenmann, senior vice president and director of research for Ketchum Public Relations, New York, says there is "a growing recognition by a wide majority of PR professionals that research is and can be a necessary and integral part of the public relations planning, program development, and evaluation process."

Professors Glen Broom and David Dozier of San Diego State University, in their book *Using Research in Public Relations,* quote public relations executives on the value of research. Among them is Blair C. Jackson, senior vice president of Rogers & Cowan, Inc., in New York:

> The most compelling reason for using research is to make sure that your program is the best it can be—that what you are doing is as "right on" as it can be. You will be confident that you are addressing the right audiences, that you are using the right messages, and that you are focusing on the right perceptions or attitudes. Evaluation research will tell you whether or not it works.

This chapter examines the role of research in public relations and the kinds of research methods utilized. Two general types—informal and scientific sampling—are discussed. The text stresses the importance of systematic research and gives suggestions for questionnaire design and scientific sampling. It provides a case study on the use of psychographic research in public relations strategies.

THE NEED FOR RESEARCH

Research is a form of listening. Broom and Dozier say simply, "Research is the controlled, objective, and systematic gathering of information for the purpose of describing and understanding.'' Before any public relations program can be undertaken, information must be gathered, data collected, and interpretation done. Only by performing this first step in the public relations process can an organization begin to map out policy decisions and strategies for effective communication programs.

WHAT RESEARCH CAN ACCOMPLISH

Research, or fact-gathering, can accomplish a number of objectives:

1. Help probe basic attitudes of groups so that pertinent messages can be structured.
2. Measure true opinions of various groups. A vocal minority may not represent the group's genuine feelings or beliefs.
3. Identify opinion leaders who can influence target publics.
4. Reduce costs by concentrating on valid objectives and key audiences.
5. Help pretest messages and proposed communication channels on a pilot basis before implementing an entire program.
6. Help determine the timing of a public relations program to take advantage of current public interests and concerns.
7. Achieve two-way communication. Feedback from audiences can fine-tune messages and choice of media.
8. Reveal trouble spots and public concerns before they become page-one news. Problems seldom just happen; they often begin as minor nuisances and then develop into full-scale explosions.
9. Achieve credibility with top management. Executives want facts, not guesses and hunches. Public relations practitioners get more support from top management if they can provide evidence to back up their recommendations.

WHY RESEARCH IS NECESSARY

Research is necessary in today's complex society for several reasons. One is the increasing fragmentation of audiences into groups that have specific interests and concerns. One research firm, for example, has classified 240,000 neighborhoods in the United States into 40 different lifestyle groups. To communicate effectively, it is necessary to have a detailed knowledge of audiences. A practitioner who understands these audiences—their attitudes, hopes, fears, concerns, frustrations—will be better able to formulate messages that appeal specifically to them. In addition, self-interest is a strong motivating force. If communication can be tailored to the self-interest of audiences, there is a much greater chance of reaching them.

A second reason is the increasing isolation of top management from personal contact with the public. Top management and those in specialized professions tend to associate only with each other. Rarely does an executive, for example, get a chance to exchange views with an assembly-line worker or talk with customers in a department store. Systematic and periodic research about customers and clients can help bridge this gap and give executives vital feedback.

Third, research can prevent organizations from wasting time, effort, and money in attacking problems that don't really exist. Several years ago, for example, American companies spent millions of dollars on advertising and public relations campaigns to make sure that Americans understood the benefits of the free-enterprise system. Survey research showed, however, that the American public was thoroughly sold on capitalism as an economic system; citizens were just unhappy with inflation and the overabundance of shoddy goods in the marketplace.

A great deal of money and energy also is spent on public relations programs that do not interest the public. More than a few companies continue to flood the media with information about personnel changes or sophisticated new machines in which the general public is not interested. Systematic monitoring of materials and their use (or nonuse) would eliminate many expensive brochures and the shotgun method of distributing them. Bottom-line considerations require that all communications activity be cost-effective.

Fourth, research can provide the facts upon which a public relations program is based. A good example is an extensive communications audit that Turnbull Fox Phillips public relations firm in Brisbane, Australia, did for the University of Queensland. The audit had several facets. One part consisted of extensive interviews with campus administrators, key faculty opinion leaders, student leaders, and members of the university's public information unit. Interviews with community leaders and heads of large corporations in Queensland formed the second portion. The third part was a

Surveys of public opinion, often taken by researchers on the street or in shopping malls, help public relations practitioners define target audiences they wish to reach and to shape their messages. (Forsyth, Monkmeyer Press)

content analysis of news releases, the resulting media coverage, and university newsletters and brochures. Armed with this comprehensive research, Turnbull Fox Phillips recommended extensive restructuring of the university's public relations efforts and outreach to the community.

Fifth, surveys can generate publicity through dissemination of results. Ketchum Public Relations based an entire public relations program for Miller Brewing Company on a national survey of women in sports. The survey, done in conjunction with the Women's Sports Foundation, was titled "The Miller Lite Report on Women in Sports," and generated 850 published or broadcast stories. This helped position Miller Lite beer as a product for the 21–25 female age group. Sales went up 3 percent over the previous year.

INFORMAL RESEARCH METHODS

Research does not consist necessarily of formal methods such as scientific surveys and statistical tabulations. In fact, a survey of 250 public relations executives conducted by Lindenmann found that almost three-fourths of the respondents believed that most current public relations research is casual and informal, perhaps done over a cup of coffee, rather than scientific and precise.

The type of research needed, therefore, really depends on the subject and the situation. Time and budget are important considerations, as well as the perceived importance of the situation. Consequently, many questions should be asked before formulating a research design.

1. What is the problem?
2. What kind of information is needed?
3. How will the results of the research be used?
4. What specific public (or publics) should be researched?
5. What research techniques should be used (literature review, mail, telephone, personal interviews)?
6. Should there be open-ended (essay) or closed (multiple-choice) questions?
7. Should the organization do the research or hire an outside consultant?
8. How will the research data be analyzed, reported, and applied?
9. How soon are the results needed?
10. How much will it cost?

These questions will help the public relations practitioner determine the extent and nature of the research that is needed. Informal research may be all that is required, and there are a number of approaches. The box here shows some research methods and their characteristics.

Research Tools and Their Characteristics

Research Tools: Traditional/Modern	Scientific Validity	Turnaround Time	Cost	News Value
1. Focus group/blue ribbon panel of experts	Very little	Relatively fast	Moderate	Elastic depending on research topiç
2. Magazine insert poll (client-sponsored)	Little	Slow	Inexpensive	Limited (one magazine's readers)
3. Omnibus survey	Snapshot probe (even though national random sample)	Fast	Inexpensive	Broad (because national)
4. Case study/ thematic case study (systematic selection, reputation sample, running theme)	Little, but rich in illustrations	Slow	Moderately expensive	Broad (because rich)
5. Intercept technique/on-site computerized survey at meetings	Face validity	Instant	Very inexpensive	Multiple: on-site, off-site (handouts)
6. National poll/ national survey study	Impeccable	Slow	Expensive	Abundance of multipliers
■ Panel of experts pretest				
■ Narrative interpretation-accessibility				

Source: Courtesy of John C. Pollock, president, New World Decisions, Kendall Park, NJ

ORGANIZATIONAL MATERIALS

All pertinent data relating to the problem or project at hand should be collected. The material may include business records, marketing studies, policy statements, summaries of objectives, market projections, annual financial reports, speeches by key executives, reports on past public relations efforts, pamphlets, newsletters, and news releases.

PERSONAL CONTACTS

Much information can be gained from talking to people informally. Public relations practitioners exchange ideas about successful programs, and they contact experts in industries of interest to them. Organizations often employ outside public relations counsel because of their extensive contacts. The French cognac industry, for example, used the services of Hill & Knowlton to pinpoint 400 American and European "allies" in business, government, and media who would help persuade Congress to abandon the idea of a 200 percent tariff on imported cognac.

NEWS ARTICLES

Content analysis of newspapers, popular magazines, and trade publications often discloses the way that an organization is being portrayed in the media. Faneuil Hall Marketplace in Boston stepped up its public relations activities after it was found that the number of travel articles about it had decreased. A tenth-anniversary celebration of the Marketplace helped generate increased coverage. Monitoring of publications also provides information about trends and issues affecting an industry. A file on relevant current issues is the first step in issues management.

REGIONAL AND NATIONAL POLLS

It is often not necessary for a public relations person to conduct a poll because public attitudes on various issues may have already been assessed by regional and national polling firms. Corporations, for example, have duly noted national polls showing widespread public concern for the quality of the environment and have attempted to change their marketing strategies accordingly. The results of these surveys regularly appear in the news media. When reading the results of a poll in the newspaper, however, the public relations person should assess the information by ascertaining (1) who paid for the poll, (2) when it was taken, (3) how the interviews were obtained, (4) how the questions were worded, (5) who was interviewed, and (6) how large the sample was.

TRADE GROUPS

Local, regional, and national trade groups, including professional societies, should be contacted. Many organizations maintain reference libraries and conduct periodic surveys and studies that are available to those interested. When Brigham Young University was preparing its Ramses II Egyptian exhibit, ideas for reaching potential out-of-state audiences came from surveys already done by the Utah Ski Association and the Utah Travel Commission.

LIBRARY RESEARCH

Reference books, other scholarly publications, and books and journals about particular subjects should be consulted. Old Stone Bank of Providence, Rhode Island, and its public relations counsel, for example, did research in the Library of Congress to develop a community relations program that promoted literacy and reading by children. Government documents, particularly the *Statistical Abstract of the United States,* and other publications based on the 1990 census can provide a wealth of demographic data.

ON-LINE DATABASES

Closely aligned to library research, and increasingly used by public relations people, are on-line databases accessible 24 hours a day. In fact, in the Lindenmann survey, literature searches and computer information retrieval were the most frequently cited research techniques.

Tim Turner, director of marketing and sales for Dow Jones Information Services, wrote in *IABC*'s *Communication World:*

> Communication professionals are increasingly turning to the computer to assist them in tracking and managing the voluminous information about their companies and their competitors as well as general trends in industry and the economy. . . . Executives frequently turn to on-line databases for instantaneous coverage of the news as well as in-depth historical searches for background and trend information.

More information about databases is provided in Chapter 21.

ADVISORY PANELS, IDEA JURIES

Many organizations form advisory boards to generate recommendations and provide ideas about issues facing the organization. Most nonprofit groups have citizen advisory boards to provide feedback on how the agency is doing in terms of public support. A public relations advisory board usually consists of outstanding public relations professionals in the community.

MAIL AND TELEPHONE ANALYSIS

Letters and telephone calls from consumers or clients often provide good feedback about problems with the organization's policies and services. A pattern of letters and telephone calls pointing out a defect in a product or the quality of service is evidence that something should be done.

FOCUS GROUPS

Focus groups, popular in advertising, are used with increasing regularity in public relations. Basically, the organization or an outside consultant assembles 8 to 15 people representing the characteristics of the target audience, such as employees, consumers, or residents of a community. A trained facilitator uses nondirective interviewing techniques that encourage group members to talk freely about a topic. An employee group might be asked to express its feelings about the quality and credibility of company publications. Or a consumer group might discuss its expectations for a particular product.

For example, the U.S. Office of Disease Prevention and Health Promotion conducted 12 focus groups with senior citizens to determine how receptive they were to health-related information, and to ascertain the kinds of information that older people wanted. The National Pasta Association also used focus groups to determine the image of pasta among consumers before designing a public relations program to increase consumption.

June 1990

ALPHA LIST

of sources available in NEXIS®
and related services

Ad Day
Advanced Manufacturing Technology
Advantage*
Advertising Age®
ADWEEK
Aerospace America
Aerospace Daily®
AI Expert*
Air Force Magazine
Air Transport World*
Airports®
Alaska Business Monthly*
Alaska Journal of Commerce*
ALERT[1]
—Archive
—Update
Almanac of American Politics, The
American Banker
American Family Physician
American Federationist*
American Hospital Formulary Service Drug Information 1987, The

Arthritis & Rheumatism
Asahi News Service
Asia Pacific Business*
Asian Wall Street Journal Weekly**
Associated Banks of Europe Corporation
Associated Press, The (AP)
—Campaign News
—Candidate Biographies
—News
Atlanta Business Chronicle*
Atlantic, The*
Austin Business Journal*
Automation*
Automotive Engineering*
Automotive Industries*
Automotive Marketing*
Automotive News®
AutoWeek®
Aviation Daily®
Aviation Week & Space Technology

Boston Globe, The
Boulder County Business Report*
British Journal of Surgery
Broadcasting*
Bulletin on the Rheumatic Diseases
Business & Commercial Aviation*
Business America*
Business Asia***
Business Atlanta*
Business China***
Business Digest of Southeastern Massachusetts*
Business Digest of Southern Maine*
Business Digest of the Cape & Islands*
Business Eastern Europe***
Business Europe***
Business First-Buffalo*
Business First-Columbus*
Business First-Louisville*
Business for Central New Jersey*
Business Insurance®

San Francisco Business Times*
San Francisco Chronicle, The
Sarasota Magazine*
Saskatchewan Business*
Saturday Evening Post*
Scientific American*
Screen Finance
Seattle Business*
Seattle Times, The
Securities Regulation & Law Report
Securities Week
Seminars in Arthritis & Rheumatism
Seminars in Hematology

Technology Review*
Telecommunications*
Telephony*
Texas Secretary of State Corporate Information
Texas Secretary of State Sales and Use Tax
Texas Secretary of State Uniform Commercial Code
Time
Times and The Sunday Times, The
Toledo Business Journal*
Transportation & Distribution*

Wall Street Journal**
Ward's Auto World*
Washington Business Journal*
Washington Monthly*
Washington Post, The
Washington Post Biographical Stories, The
Washington Quarterly, The
Washington Times, The
Weekly of Business Aviation,™ The
Westchester County Business Journal, The*
Which Computer?*

FIGURE 7.1
This small sample indicates the extent and variety of database sources available to users of Nexis® and related services.

COPY TESTING

It is important that the target audience thoroughly understand the message. Consequently, several representatives of the target audience should read or view the material in draft form before it is mass-produced and distributed. A brochure about employee medical benefits or pension plans, for example, should be pretested with rank-and-file employees for comprehension. Executives and lawyers who must approve copy may understand the material, but a worker with an eighth-grade education might find it difficult to follow.

COMMUNICATION AUDITS

Many organizations periodically check what employees are reading in the company newsletter or magazine. Another form of communication audit is to have employees complete a questionnaire on topics they would like covered in company publications. Communication audits also can be done among editors of general-circulation and trade publications to determine if they are receiving information pertinent to their needs.

FORMAL RESEARCH: SAMPLING

The informal approaches to research methods just mentioned can provide good insight to public relations staff members and help them formulate effective programs. Practitioners must be sure, however, that the feedback is representative, so that decisions are made on the basis of information that is typical of general trends or majority views.

The number of people interviewed is a crucial factor. If not enough people are questioned, the results of the survey may be *skewed,* or distorted. When public relations practitioners want more dependable, systematic responses, they often utilize scientific sampling methods. These methods are based on established procedures that make it more likely that the results will be meaningful and useful.

THE PROBABILITY SAMPLE

For best results, a *probability sample* is taken. This means that everyone in the targeted audience (called the *universe*) has an equal chance of being selected for the survey. This method contrasts with a nonprobability sample, in which everyone does not have an equal chance to be selected.

A nonprobability survey, for example, might consist of interviews with employees in the company cafeteria between 11:30 A.M. and noon. The interviewer using this time period, however, will miss completely employees from a division who have their lunch from noon to 12:30 P.M. The interviewer also will miss employees who work another shift. In other words, *any* survey of employees in the cafeteria between 11:30 A.M. and noon would be a nonprobability sample—not every employee in the organization would have an equal chance of being selected.

The survey would be more scientific if the interviewer remained in the cafeteria during the entire lunch period. Yet the results may continue to be skewed if a large number of employees did not use the cafeteria that day but ate lunch in nearby restaurants or brought their lunches from home and ate at their workplaces.

The best way to ensure that every employee has a chance of being surveyed is to select names from a master list of employees. The selection can be made by using a table of random numbers or simply drawing a number from a hat. If the number were 25, the researcher would then interview every twenty-fifth person on the master list.

THE QUOTA SAMPLE

Another common method to ensure representation is to draw a sample that matches the characteristics of the audience. This is called *quota sampling*. Human resources departments, for example, usually have breakdowns of employees by job classification, and it is relatively easy to proportion a sample accordingly. If 32 percent of the employees work on the assembly line, for instance, then 32 percent of the sample should be assembly-line workers. A quota sample can be drawn on any number of demographic factors—age, sex, religion, education, race, income—depending upon the purpose of the survey.

THE SIZE OF THE SAMPLE

In any probability study, there is always the question of sample size. National polling firms usually sample 1200 to 2000 persons and get a highly accurate idea of what the U.S. adult population is thinking. The average national poll samples 1500 people, and the margin of error is within three percentage points 95 percent of the time. In other words, 19 out of 20 times that the same questionnaire is administered, the results should be within the same three percentage points and reflect the whole population accurately.

The three-percentage-point variance in poll results is important in predicting the outcome of an election. If 48 percent of the voters say they will support Candidate A and 52 percent endorse Candidate B, the election is too close to call. What the three-point variance means is that Candidate A may actually receive 45 to 51 percent of the vote. Candidate B, on the other hand, may gather 49 to 55 percent of the vote. This means that, given the statistical accuracy of polls, either candidate could win.

In public relations the primary purpose of poll data is to get indications of attitudes and opinions, not to predict elections. Therefore, it is not usually necessary or practical to do a scientific sampling of 1500 people. A sample of 250 to 500 will give relatively accurate data—with a 5 or 6 percent variance—that will help determine general public attitudes and opinions. A sample of about 100 people, accurately drawn according to probability guidelines, will include about a 10 percent margin of error.

This percentage of error would be acceptable if a public relations person, for example, asked employees what they want to read in the company magazine. Sixty percent may indicate that they would like to see more news about opportunities for promotion. If only 100 employees were properly surveyed, it really doesn't matter if the actual percentage is 50 or 70 percent. The large percentage, in either case, would be sufficient to justify an increase in news stories about advancement opportunities.

This is also true in ascertaining community attitudes. If a survey of 100 or fewer citizens indicates that only 25 percent believe the organization is a good community citizen, it really doesn't matter whether the result is 15 or 40 percent. The main point is that the organization must take immediate steps to improve its image.

PURPOSIVE SAMPLING

Probability sampling, with the size of the sample varied as needed for accuracy, offers the most valid data to a public relations researcher. Nonprobability sampling, however, may be better for certain kinds of research. One kind of nonprobability research is called *purposive sampling*.

In use of this method, the people interviewed are selected because they are opinion leaders. Fund-raising firms, for example, conduct purposive sampling before advising a hospital, school, or other nonprofit organization on the potential success of a capital fund drive.

Crucial to the success of any major fund drive seeking $500,000 or more is the support of key community leaders and wealthy individuals, because about 90 percent of these funds come from 10 percent of the population. It is therefore necessary to interview influential people in a community to get their reactions to the proposed drive and, most important, to secure their financial support. In such a situation, interviewing the average homemaker or the man or woman in the street will not generate the type of information or the financial support needed to determine the feasibility of the project.

In one use of purposive sampling, the Greater Durham, North Carolina, Chamber of Commerce contacted 50 "movers and shakers" in the community to determine support for an extensive image-building and economic development program. (For a detailed discussion of fund-raising, see Chapter 18.)

QUESTIONNAIRE DESIGN

Although correct sampling is important in gaining accurate results, pollsters generally acknowledge that sampling error may be far less important than the errors that result from poor question selection.

BIAS IN QUESTIONS

The wording of questions on a questionnaire is a time-consuming process; every attempt should be made to ensure that a question does not bias the respondent's answer. There is a difference between one question, "Is it a good idea to limit handguns?" and another, "Do you think registration of handguns will curtail crime?" On first glance, they seem to be asking the same thing. On closer examination, however, one can realize that a respondent could easily answer "yes" to the first question and "no" to the second.

The first question asks if the limiting of handguns is a good idea. The second asks if people think it will curtail crime. A third question that might elicit a different response would be, "Do you think laws curtailing the use of handguns would work?" Thus, the questions emphasize three different aspects of the problem. The first stresses the value of an idea, the second explores a possible effect, and the third examines the practicality of a proposed solution. Research shows that people often think something is a good idea, but do not think it would work. Another related problem is how respondents might interpret the words *limit* and *curtail*. To some, they may refer to a total ban on handguns, while others may think the words suggest that all guns should be kept away from people with criminal records.

Questionnaires also should avoid loaded and leading questions. An example of a loaded question is one from the Gun Owners of California, "Do you believe that federal and state governments have a right to confiscate firearms from law-abiding citizens?'' The question is doubly skewed because most respondents would not endorse ''confiscation'' of anything from ''law-abiding citizens.''

A leading question results when a behavioral context is set up. A prolife group may easily bias the results with this: ''Many people believe in the sanctity of human life. Do you think abortion should be illegal?'' Or an employee questionnaire may contain this somewhat leading item: ''*Fortune* magazine reported that this company has a great reputation for technological innovation. Do you agree with this assessment?''

DOUBLE-BARRELED QUESTIONS

Questions can also be double-barreled by including two concepts in the same question. A double-barreled question might be, ''Do you favor stricter laws about the ownership of handguns and hunting rifles?'' This question poses a problem for the individual who favors stricter laws concerning handguns but who believes such laws should not affect the use of rifles by hunters.

"COURTESY BIAS"

Some survey questionnaires do not generate accurate answers because respondents choose the ''correct'' answer instead of the one that accurately reflects their feelings. Those conducting employee surveys often fall into this trap by posing such questions as ''How much of each employee newsletter do you read?'' or ''How well do you like the column by the general manager?'' Employees may never read the publication or may think the manager's column is ridiculous, but they know the ''correct'' answer should be that they read the ''entire issue'' and that the column is ''excellent.''

Less of this *courtesy bias* is obtained if the respondents are reasonably assured that their answers are confidential, that there is a mechanism for questionnaires to be filled out in such a way that no one (including the surveyor) will know who completed which questionnaire. Because employees usually consider the public relations department a part of management, many companies seeking candid feedback from employees hire an outside research firm to interview employees or process questionnaires. In any case, a survey of employee attitudes should guarantee anonymity to the respondent.

THE ANSWER CATEGORIES

Answer categories can skew a questionnaire. It is important that answer choices are provided to cover a range of opinions. A national polling organization several years ago asked the question ''How much confidence do you have in business corporations?'' but provided only the following answer categories: (*a*) a great deal, (*b*) only some, and (*c*) none at all. A large gap exists between ''a great deal'' and the next category, ''only some.'' Such categories invariably skew the results to show very little confidence in business. A better list of answers might have been (*a*) a great deal, (*b*) quite a lot, (*c*) some, (*d*) very little, and (*e*) none. Perhaps an even better approach would be to provide the answer categories (*a*) above average, (*b*) average, and (*c*) below average. The psychological distance between the three choices is equal, and there is less room for respondent interpretation of what "quite a lot" means.

In general, "yes-or-no" questions are not very good for examining respondents' perceptions and attitudes. A "yes" or "no" answer provides little feedback on the strength or weakness of a respondent's opinion. A question such as "Do you agree with the company's policy of requiring drug testing for all new employees?" can be answered by "yes" or "no," but more useful information would be obtained by setting up a Likert-type scale—(*a*) Strongly agree, (*b*) Agree, (*c*) Undecided, (*d*) Disagree, (*e*) Strongly disagree. These types of answers enable the surveyor to probe the depth of feeling among respondents, and may serve as guidelines for management in making major changes or just fine-tuning the existing policy.

Another way of designing a numerical scale in order to pinpoint a respondent's beliefs or attitudes is to use, for example, a 5-point scale. Such a scale might look like this:

Question: How would you evaluate the company's efforts to keep you informed about job benefits? Please circle one of the following numbers ("1" being a low rating and "5" being a high rating).

Answer: 1 2 3 4 5

The advantage of numerical scales is that medians and means can be easily calculated. In the example above, the average from all respondents might be 4.25, which indicates that employees think the company does keep them informed about job benefits but that there is still room for communication improvement.

Another way to get at perceptions is to use the *semantic differential technique*. Essentially, this is a list of bipolar words; the respondent places a mark along a continuum. A semantic scale might look like this:

Question: How would you evaluate the company magazine on the following criteria?

Unbiased	____	____	____	____	____	Biased
Trustworthy	____	____	____	____	____	Untrustworthy
Valuable	____	____	____	____	____	Worthless
Fair	____	____	____	____	____	Unfair
Interesting	____	____	____	____	____	Uninteresting

QUESTIONNAIRE GUIDELINES

Here are some general guidelines for the construction of questionnaires:

1. Decide what kinds of information are needed and in what detail.
2. State the objectives of the survey in writing.
3. Decide which group will receive the questionnaire.

PROFESSIONAL AND ETHICAL GUIDELINES FOR THE CONDUCT AND REPORTING OF PUBLIC OPINION RESEARCH

The American Association for Public Opinion Research (AAPOR) has established a code of professional ethics for the conduct and reporting of public opinion research. The following is a selection of guidelines from the code that are particularly relevant to public relations personnel.

Conduct of Research

1. Exercise due care in gathering and processing data, taking all reasonable steps to assure the accuracy of results.

2. Use only research tools which are well suited to the research at hand.

3. Do not make interpretations of research results that are inconsistent with the data available.

4. Do not mislead survey respondents or use methods which abuse, coerce, or humiliate them.

5. Respect the confidentiality of respondents and do not disclose the names for nonresearch purposes.

Release of Survey Research Findings in News Releases or Other Publicity Materials

1. Identify who sponsored the survey.

2. Give exact wording of the questions asked.

3. Define the population actually sampled.

4. Give size of sample. For mail surveys, this should include the number of questionnaires mailed out and the number returned.

5. Tell what allowance should be made for sampling error.

6. Tell what results are based on parts of the sample, rather than on the whole sample.

7. Indicate whether interviewing was done personally, by telephone, or mail; at home or on street corners.

8. Give time of the interviewing in relation to relevant events.

Source: Adapted from the code of professional ethics and practices, American Association for Public Opinion Research, Box 17, Princeton, NJ 08540.

4. Decide on the size of the sample.

5. State the purpose of the survey and guarantee anonymity.

6. Use closed-end (multiple-choice) answers as much as possible. Respondents find it easier and less time-consuming to check answers than to compose them in an open-end (essay) questionnaire.

7. Design the questionnaire so that it is easy to read; use simple-to-understand sentences and an orderly format.

8. Make the questionnaire 25 questions or fewer. Long questionnaires ''put off'' people and reduce the number of responses.

9. Pretest questions for understanding and possible bias. Representatives of the proposed sampling group should read the questionnaire and make comments for possible improvement.

10. Use categories when asking questions about education, age, and income. People are more willing to answer when a category is used. For example: What category best describes your age? (*a*) Under 25, (*b*) 26 to 40, (*c*) 41 to 55, and (*d*) 56 or above.

11. Provide space at the end of the questionnaire for respondents' comments and observations. This allows them to provide additional information or elaboration that may not have been covered in the main body of the questionnaire.

WAYS OF REACHING RESPONDENTS

MAIL QUESTIONNAIRES

Questionnaires may be used in a variety of settings. They may be handed out at a manufacturing plant, at a county fair, or even in a bank lobby. Most survey questionnaires, however, are mailed to respondents. There are several reasons for this:

1. Because the researchers have better control as to who receives the questionnaire, they can make sure the survey is representative.

2. Large geographical areas can be covered economically.

3. It is less expensive to administer them than to hire an interviewer to conduct personal interviews.

4. Large numbers of people can be included at minimal cost.

Mail questionnaires have some disadvantages. The biggest is a low response rate. A mail questionnaire by a commercial firm to the general public usually produces a response rate of 1 to 2 percent. If the survey concerns issues affecting the general public, the response rate might be 5 to 20 percent. A much better response rate would be generated, however, if the questionnaire were mailed by an organization to its members. In this case, the response rate may be 30 to 80 percent. The more closely people identify with the organization and the questions, the better the response.

The response rate to a mail questionnaire can be increased, say the experts, if all the guidelines of questionnaire construction are followed. In addition, a researcher should keep the following suggestions in mind:

1. Include a stamped, self-addressed return envelope and a personally signed letter explaining the importance of participation.

2. Mail questionnaires by first-class mail. Some research shows that placing special issue stamps on the envelope attracts greater interest than simply using a postage meter.

3. Mail a reminder postcard three or four days later.

4. Do a second mailing (either to nonrespondents or to the entire sample) two or three weeks after the first mailing. Again, enclose a stamped, self-addressed return envelope and a cover letter explaining the crucial need for the recipient's participation.

A number of commercial firms are now enclosing token amounts of money with the questionnaire to generate a higher response rate. *Aviation Week,* for example, tucks a dollar in the envelope with the questionnaire. *Newsweek* promises to make a charitable donation in the subscriber's name if he or she returns the survey form. Other groups, if the questionnaire is short, enclose a quarter or a 50-cent piece.

Sending a dollar bill usually guarantees at least a 50 percent response, states an official of Erdos & Morgan, a New York market research firm. According to an article in the *Wall Street Journal,* enclosing money makes people feel guilty if they don't respond.

TELEPHONE SURVEYS

Surveys by telephone, particularly if the survey is locally based, are extensively used by research firms. The telephone survey has several advantages:

1. There is an immediate response or nonresponse. A researcher doesn't have to wait several weeks for responses to arrive by mail.

2. A telephone call is personal. It is effective communication, and it is much cheaper than a personal interview.

3. A phone call is less intrusive than going door-to-door and interviewing people. Surveys show that many people are willing to talk on the phone for up to 45 minutes but will not stand at a door for more than 5 or 10 minutes and are less willing to admit strangers to their homes.

4. The response rate, if the survey is properly composed and phone interviewers trained, can reach 80 to 90 percent.

One major disadvantage of phone interviews is the difficulty in getting access to everyone's telephone number. In some cities, up to a third of households have unlisted telephone numbers. Although researchers can utilize a "reverse" telephone book that lists numbers according to street address, this method is not as effective as actually knowing who is being called. Another disadvantage is the negative connotation of a phone interview because so many salespeople have attempted to sell goods by posing as researchers.

PERSONAL INTERVIEWS

The personal interview is the most expensive form of research because it requires trained staff and travel. If travel within a city is involved, a trained interviewer often can interview only eight or ten people a day—and salaries and transportation costs make it expensive. There is also the need for considerable advance work in arranging interviews and appointments and, as previously pointed out, researchers encounter reluctance by residents to admit strangers to their homes.

Personal interviews, on the other hand, can be cost-effective and can generate a wealth of information if the setting is controlled. Many research firms conduct personal interviews at national conventions or trade shows, where there is a concentration of people with similar interests. An equipment company, for example, may hire a research firm to interview potential customers at a national trade show.

CASE STUDY: TURKEY GROUP USES PSYCHOGRAPHICS

This chapter has emphasized that research can take many forms and serve a variety of public relations purposes. A relatively new form of research is called *psychographics,* which is an attempt to classify people by lifestyle, attitudes, and beliefs. The Values and Lifestyle Program, popularly known as VALS, was developed by SRI International, a think tank in Menlo Park, California, during the mid-1970s.

The usefulness of VALS as a research tool is demonstrated by the way in which Burson-Marsteller applied it to structure an effective program for the National Turkey Foundation. The problem was quite simple: how to encourage turkey consumption throughout the year instead of just at Thanksgiving and Christmas.

Research indicated that Sustainers and Survivors, whom VALS identifies as low-income, poorly educated, and often elderly, ate at erratic hours, consumed inexpensive, starchy foods, and seldom ate out. Belongers, on the other hand, were highly family-oriented and served food in traditional ways. Achievers, according to the VALS typology, were more innovative and willing to try out new foods.

Burson-Marsteller tailored a strategy for each group. For the Survivors and Sustainers, the message stressed bargain cuts of turkey that could be stretched into a full meal. The message for Belongers, who were highly traditional, focused on cuts that signaled turkey—like drumsticks. Achievers, who were better educated and at higher income levels, received the message about gourmet cuts and new, innovative recipes.

By segmenting the consumer public into various VALS lifestyles, Burson-Marsteller was able to select the appropriate media for specific story ideas. An article placed in *True Experience,* a publication reaching the demographic characteristics of Survivors and Sustainers, was headlined "A Terrific Budget Stretching Meal." *Better Homes and Gardens* was used to reach the Belongers with such articles as "streamlined summer classics" and barbecued turkey on the Fourth of July. Articles for Achievers in *Food and Wine* magazine and *Gourmet* included recipes for turkey salad and turkey tetrazzini.

By identifying and appealing specifically to the three groups, Burson-Marsteller succeeded in expanding the turkey market to a full year.

CASE PROBLEM

Krupp Manufacturing Corporation is located in a midwestern city of 500,000 people. Its 6000 employees make it one of the largest employers in the country, and the company has been in its present location for the past 50 years. Despite this record, management believes that the company doesn't have a strong identity and visibility in the community.

The director of public relations is asked to prepare a new public relations plan for the coming fiscal year. She recommends that the company first do research to determine exactly what its image is in the community.

If you were the public relations director, what informal methods of research would you use? What more formal research methods could be used? What kinds of information about the company's image should be researched?

QUESTIONS FOR REVIEW AND DISCUSSION

1. What kinds of objectives can be accomplished through public relations research?
2. Name four reasons why public relations personnel should use research in today's complex society.
3. How can survey research data be used as a publicity tool?
4. What questions should you ask yourself before formulating a research study?
5. Name at least seven informal research methods.
6. What is the difference between probability and nonprobability samples?
7. What percentage margin of error is associated with various size samples? What size samples are usually adequate for public relations research?
8. Name at least three pitfalls of questionnaire design that should be avoided.
9. Name at least five guidelines that should be followed when designing a survey questionnaire.
10. Compile a list of pros and cons of mail questionnaires, telephone interviews, and personal interviews.

SUGGESTED READINGS

Brody, E.W., and Stone, Gerald. *Public Relations Research.* New York: Praeger, 1989. Concepts and techniques.

Broom, Glen, and Dozier, David. *Using Public Relations Research.* Englewood Cliffs, NJ: Prentice Hall, 1990. Research concepts and techniques.

Davidson, Jeffrey P. ''Everything You Ever Needed to Know About Anything: Precision Targeting Your Customer.'' *Communication World,* May–June 1990, pp. 147–151. Databases and directories available.

Grunig, Larissa A. ''Using Focus Group Research in Public Relations.'' *Public Relations Review,* Summer 1990, pp. 36–49.

Hiebert, Ray E., editor. *Precision Public Relations.* New York: Longman, 1988. Section 3, ''Researching the Problem,'' pp. 109–170.

Nassar, David. ''How to Run a Focus Group.'' *Public Relations Journal,* March 1988, pp. 33–34.

Pavlik, John, and others. ''Using Readership Research to Study Employee Views.'' *Public Relations Review,* Summer 1990, pp. 50–60.

Rosser, Connie, and others. ''Using Research to Predict Learning from a PR Campaign.'' *Public Relations Review,* Summer 1990, pp. 61–77.

Ryan, Michael, and Martinson, David L. ''Social Science Research, Professionalism and Public Relations Practitioners.'' *Journalism Quarterly,* Summer 1990, pp. 377–390.

Stoltz, Eric, and Torobin, Jack. ''Public Relations by the Numbers.'' *American Demographics,* January 1991, pp. 42–46. Research methods.

Turner, Tim L. ''On-Line Databases: The Professional Edge.'' *Communication World,* October 1989, pp. 34–37. Includes directory of database providers.

Walker, Albert. ''Anatomy of the Communications Audit.'' *Communication World,* September 1988, pp. 19–22.

Winkleman, Michael. ''Their Aim Is True.'' *Public Relations Journal,* August 1987, pp. 18–19, 22, 23, 39. Segmentation research.

CHAPTER

Planning the Action

Chapter 7 examined the goals and methods of research, a fundamental step in the public relations process. The second phase—planning a program—embodies the results of the research effort.

A public relations program should not be a hit-or-miss action. When a problem arises, it is foolish to throw money at it haphazardly, in hope of hitting the target. Rather, a successful campaign consists of a series of basic steps. Chapter 8 takes a close look at this well-established procedure.

The process begins with a definition of the problem and ends with an assessment of the results. The steps follow each other in logical progression so that waste is avoided. Setting the objectives of a campaign before the problem has been clearly defined, for example, can lead to muddled results.

In the first step the practitioner applies the research techniques explained in Chapter 7. Similarly, each element that follows evolves from the step taken just before it. The procedure offers guidance for both the beginner and the experienced practitioner in setting up a well-conducted campaign.

THE MBO APPROACH

The concept of *management by objectives (MBO)* increasingly is being applied to public relations planning. Once the situation has been researched (previous chapter), it is now necessary to plan a program of action. Norman R. Nager and T. Harrell Allen, in their book *Public Relations Management by Objectives* (Longman), discuss nine basic MBO steps, whether a practitioner is writing a single news release or putting together a multi-faceted communications program. The steps, adapted from their book, are as follows:

1. *Client/employer objectives*. What is the purpose of the communication, and how does it help promote or achieve the objectives of the organization? Specific objectives such as "to position the product as the leading one in the market" are more meaningful than "to make people aware of the product."

2. *Audience/publics*. Who exactly should be reached with the message, and how can that audience help achieve the organization's objectives? What are the characteristics of the audience, and how can demographic information be used to structure the message?

3. *Audience objectives*. What is it that the audience wants to know, and how can the message be tailored to audience self-interest?

4. *Media channels*. What is the appropriate channel for reaching the audience, and how can multiple channels (news media, brochures, special events, direct mail, etc.) reinforce the message among key publics?

5. *Media channel objectives*. What is the media gatekeeper looking for in a news angle, and why would a particular publication be interested in the information?

6. *Sources and questions*. What primary and secondary sources of information are required to provide a factual base for the message? What experts should be interviewed? What database searches should be conducted?

7. *Communication strategies*. What environmental factors will affect the dissemination and acceptance of the message? Are the target publics hostile or favorably disposed to the essence of the message? What other events or pieces of information negate or reinforce the message?

8. *Essence of message*. What is the planned communications impact on the audience? Is the message designed merely to inform, or is it designed to change attitudes and behavioral patterns? Are organizational expectations realistic?

9. *Nonverbal support*. How can photographs, graphs, films, artwork, and so forth clarify and add interest to the written message?

Nager and Allen make the case that MBO techniques can do much to help a public relations person work through a systematic process of determining exactly what must be done and why. MBO provides focus and direction for producing effective program plans and public relations materials. In the pages that follow, additional discussion is provided about defining the problem, setting objectives, selecting audiences, choosing communication strategies, establishing time lines, and assessing the results.

THE STEPS IN DETAIL

DEFINE THE PROBLEM

The initial step in formulating a public relations program is to determine the nature of the problem the practitioner is called upon to solve.

In corporate life, recognition of public relations problems sometimes is more difficult than might be assumed. All too frequently a chief executive, deeply immersed in the immediate pressures of making the company return a satisfactory profit, is unaware that a public relations problem exists in the organization—a problem that in the long run may seriously threaten the very profitability for which the chief executive is striving.

Using sensitive antennae developed to detect the moods of both the public and employees, a company's public relations director and/or a counseling firm should recognize a problem as it develops. Then the specialist must demonstrate to top management that a problem is emerging that requires prompt attention. Unless this attention-calling function is carried out successfully, the necessary funds for attacking the problem will not be forthcoming from management.

If an unexpected crisis occurs, the problem is urgently and painfully evident to everyone. When seven persons in Chicago died after taking capsules of Tylenol laced with cyanide, top management at Johnson & Johnson, makers of the headache remedy, instantly recognized a public relations crisis. The question was not "Should we do something?" but "What can we do right now?" (A detailed discussion of the Tylenol crisis appears in Chapter 14.)

When no dramatic event occurs to raise a danger flag, a public relations problem may be less readily recognized. The problem may be insidious, sneaking up over a long time or concealed beneath the surface of routine corporate or organizational life.

So numerous and so varied are the problems addressed by public relations practitioners that listing them all is impossible. They may be grouped, however, into three general categories. Each must be approached in a different way.

1. *Overcoming a negative perception of an organization or product.* Usually such perceptions develop slowly. A specific occurrence may jar management into recognizing the unfavorable trend and precipitate action. Here are a few examples of negative perceptions:

   a. Resistance by the public to company products on the basis of price, quality, or company behavior—for example, a word-of-mouth assertion that a local manufacturing company is damaging the environment by secretly dumping toxic waste material in nearby hills
   b. Belief expressed by security analysts that a manufacturing company's production equipment has become outdated, making the firm lose ground competitively
   c. Evidence that employees believe their company lacks concern for their interests
   d. Complaints from patients about what they perceive as excessively high hospital bills
   e. A decline in membership of a professional association

2. *Conducting a specific one-time project.* On most public relations assignments in this category the practitioner starts from a neutral position. No obvious negative perceptions exist to be overcome. If they do exist, they will come to light later in the program. Conversely, latent support for the program probably exists but has not been developed. The specialist given such an assignment is in the same position as a baseball hitter stepping up to the plate: no balls or strikes have yet been called on the batter. To make a hit, the batter must study the pitcher's movements and "stuff"—that is,

define the problem being faced. Here are typical problems in the one-time project category that a public relations specialist must define and attempt to solve:

a. Organize a citizens' campaign demanding that the city council adopt an ordinance banning smoking in public buildings and restaurants.
b. Introduce a new product.
c. Conduct a fund drive for a hospital expansion.
d. Enlist employee input and support for a major revision of company medical benefits.
e. Obtain shareholder approval for acquisition of another company.

3. *Developing or expanding a continuing program.* Much public relations work is of an ongoing nature—the necessity to create or maintain a favorable situation. Although lacking the urgency of a crisis or the clearly drawn needs of a one-time project, this work is vital. It also contains the inherent danger of slipping into stagnant routine and losing effectiveness. The practitioner should watch for fresh techniques, especially the rapidly expanding use of computer technology, and should review the entire program periodically to determine whether it needs redefining. The following are common examples of continuing program objectives:

a. Maintain community confidence that a company is a good corporate citizen with a sense of social responsibility.
b. Satisfy employees that the company is a good place to work. Retention of trained employees is a constant management problem.
c. Convince householders that their city's recycling program is achieving significant results and encourage them to increase their contributions to it.
d. Raise funds on an annual basis to keep human welfare programs like those of the American Red Cross or American Heart Association functioning.
e. Supply the media with a steady flow of newsworthy information about the employer and answer their requests promptly and openly.

To summarize, a public relations program usually is designed to correct a negative situation, achieve a well-defined, one-time objective, or maintain and improve an existing positive situation.

SET OBJECTIVES

To conduct successful campaigns, practitioners should ask, "Precisely what do we wish to accomplish?" The more specifically they answer that question, the better is the prospect for success and the greater the potential for measuring results. A vague goal such as, "To get publicity for our new product," is relatively meaningless. The objective might be better stated: "To make people aware of our new product and induce them to buy it." The significant target is the number of units sold, not the size of the press clipping file.

It is particularly important that public relations objectives complement and reinforce the organization's objectives. Professor David Dozier of San Diego State University expressed the point well in a *Public Relations Review* article, saying: "The prudent and strategic selection of public relations goals and objectives linked to organizational survival and growth serves to justify the public relations program as a viable management activity.''

The Two Types of Objectives Objectives are of two types—*informational* and *motivational*.

An *informational objective* may be to tell people about an event, introduce a product, or seek to enhance the perception of a company. One difficulty with informational campaigns occurs in measuring how well the objective has been achieved, because public awareness is somewhat abstract and difficult to quantify.

Although difficult to accomplish, *motivational objectives* are easier to measure. They should be stated as succinctly as possible, such as, ''Increase attendance at this year's concert by 25 percent,'' ''Convince voters to approve the bond issue for the new municipal stadium,'' or ''Improve the employees' understanding of the company's retirement program.'' (Evaluation of public relations campaigns is discussed in Chapter 10.)

GOALS, OBJECTIVES, AND STRATEGIES

Confusion sometimes arises concerning the actual meaning of these three words, widely used in public relations programming. A practical illustration can be found in the campaign to revive interest in the Six Flags Great Adventure theme park in New Jersey and promote its giant new roller coaster.

Goal Gain widespread media coverage of the park to increase slumping attendance by emphasizing fun and safety.

Objectives

- Create a positive image of the park to overcome public worry about injuries suffered by park visitors.
- Introduce the spectacular new roller coaster, ''The Great American Scream Machine.''

Strategies

- Bozell PR, hired for $150,000 to conduct the campaign, held a fun/educational kickoff event in nearby Philadelphia to highlight safety improvements at the park. This included musicians, live safari animals, performers, and a video of the new coaster. Take-away informational packets and souvenirs were distributed.
- A comprehensive publicity kit and video were sent to the media.
- A grand opening of the Great American Scream Machine was held.

The grand opening received coverage by network news programs, newspapers such as the New York *Times* and *USA Today*, and magazines including *Fortune* and *Money*. More than 100 stories ran in regional media.

Park attendance increased 20 percent. More than 1.3 million individuals rode on the Great American Scream Machine. The campaign won a 1990 PRSA Silver Anvil award.

If well planned and conducted, public relations projects can accomplish much, but they cannot achieve impractical goals. Objectives must be realistic. They should be placed high, so participants must stretch to reach them, but not at an impossible level. If a goal is unattainable, despite determined and ingenious efforts to achieve it, the failure may cause frustration and disenchantment among those who work on a campaign. This creates a negative attitude toward future projects. If a public fund-raising goal is impossibly high and the drive fails by a wide margin, the campaign force is embarrassed, and public support for the project may dwindle.

Budget Considerations In setting objectives, practitioners must consider the amount of money available. Budget and achievement are not always directly related, of course. Under some circumstances a small budget judiciously spent may attain remarkable success. Nevertheless, large expenditures increase the prospect of success because they make possible the use of more extensive methods and staff. If the cost of a campaign exceeds the value of its objective, however, the effort cannot be called a success. When a charitable organization spends so much to conduct a fund drive that operating costs absorb an excessive portion of the donations, it is properly open to public criticism. (A discussion of fund-raising appears in Chapter 18.) No matter how much money is spent and how much effort is made, a program cannot succeed if the product is poor or the objective unacceptable to the audience.

A management decision must be made, either to establish a large objective or a set of objectives and supply sufficient funds to permit success, or to allot a limited amount of money and set an objective attainable with such a sum. The public relations specialist should supply top management with well-informed opinions about what its money might achieve.

The Time Factor Time is another factor to be considered in setting an objective. The amount of time to be spent on a campaign depends on its purpose and its nature. Some programs should be quick, hard-driving, and completed within a relatively brief, specified period. Other projects—for instance, publicity for an event such as an exhibition—have a built-in time limit; by the close of the show they have either succeeded or failed. When a project is designed to correct a negative perception or to develop public acceptance of a new concept, a long period of time may be required. *Negative attitudes change slowly*. There is no quick fix for an unfavorable public perception. Objectives for such projects should be determined with this in mind; one-, two-, and three-year goals may be appropriate. Interim measurements of progress can be made, but everyone involved in creating the program must recognize the need for patience.

The Written Statement Before planning a program, the practitioner should state its objective, or objectives, in writing. This helps to focus individual thinking and to prevent later misunderstanding with management. Depending on the complexity of the program, the goal can be summarized in two or three sentences, perhaps in one.

Take the case of a small women's college in financial trouble because its enrollment has fallen. It could achieve financial security by admitting men, but its student body and faculty want it to remain all-female. It decides, therefore, to mount a major campaign among alumnae for contributions. Its objective might be summarized as follows:

Conduct a $75 million endowment campaign among alumnae to preserve the college's 100-year tradition of providing its female student body with a unique academic and social atmosphere

DEFINE THE AUDIENCES

Once the objective has been set, the practitioner should define the audience or audiences at which the campaign will be aimed. Precisely whom is the campaign intended to inform or motivate? The purpose of specifying an audience is simply to avoid wasted effort and dollars. Some campaigns can be aimed at the general public. Other campaigns should be directed at a smaller, more focused audience. Spending large sums of money to educate the public at large on issues in which it has no stake is nonproductive. Targeting the message to the appropriate audience is more likely to produce significant results.

Public relations programs fall into three general categories, aimed at these groups: (1) *a broad general audience,* (2) *an external target audience,* and (3) *an internal audience.*

Entire Public In a broad-based project aimed at the *entire public,* the practitioner seeks to register as many impressions as possible on as many individuals as possible. The American Cancer Society, for example, uses a number of methods to warn every person it can reach about the seven danger signs of cancer. The more often that individuals read or hear about those signs, the more likely they are to check their bodies for symptoms. On a local level, sponsors of a citywide July 4 ethnic festival in a midwestern city, trying to attract as many people as possible to the event, spread the word through newspaper stories, radio and television shows, publicity photographs in newspapers of exotic foods to be sold, club meeting announcements, personal solicitation of ethnic groups to operate booths, and as many other methods as they had the time and money to employ.

External Target Audience In a campaign aimed at an external *target audience,* selection of public relations methods is more restricted. Impressions made upon individuals not concerned with an issue are wasted. Broadside use of radio and television, in particular, might be of scant value—if, indeed, the practitioners could convince news directors and program directors to use their material.

How is a target audience campaign conducted? As an example, consider the campaign run by motorcycle enthusiasts seeking repeal of a state law that requires them to wear helmets while riding. The issue is of minimal interest to the general public. The campaign must be aimed at two special audiences—state legislators, who will vote on the repeal proposal, and motorcycle users, whose opinions pro and con will influence their decision. Since the issue is nonpartisan and involves no expenditure of state money, two common concerns of legislators—party loyalty and the budget—are not involved.

Sharp differences of opinion exist among motorcyclists as to the wisdom of the repeal effort. Those who favor repeal maintain that the government has no right to tell them as citizens how they should dress—an emotional argument—and that helmets impair their peripheral vision—a physical one. They agree that the use of helmets reduces the danger of head injuries but argue that they should have freedom of choice about wearing them. Supporters of the law contend that helmets save lives and that the government has a duty to protect those motorcyclists who would be foolhardy enough to ride bareheaded unless forbidden by law.

The perimeters of the two target audiences are easily defined. There is a known number of legislators, approximately 100. The names and addresses of registered motorcycle owners and licensed riders can be obtained from the Department of Motor Vehicles. Motorcycle sales agencies, equipment stores, and repair shops are natural channels of repeal communication. So are motorcycle clubs.

The proponents of repeal ask club members to write to their legislators, using sample letters provided for them. Clubs are urged to adopt formal resolutions to be sent to the legislature. Repeal advocates testify before legislative committee hearings on the bill and hold face-to-face discussions with individual legislators, pressing their cause. They distribute pamphlets and information sheets urging repeal. They hand out stickers with a catchy repeal slogan to their members and place piles of them in motorcycle shops for free distribution. They submit feature stories favoring repeal to motorcycle publications and request supporting editorials.

Safety organizations and motorcyclists who want the helmet law retained also mount a campaign, but with less fervor and money. They cite instances in which a motorcyclist's life was saved by a helmet and show the legislators graphs depicting the rise in motorcycle fatalities in states that have repealed the helmet law. However, their arguments are overpowered by the pile of letters, petitions, and resolutions favoring repeal that arrive on legislators' desks. Convinced that a majority of motorcyclists desire repeal, the legislators shrug, "If they want to risk their necks, let them," and pass the bill repealing the law.

The general public, meanwhile, hears little about the dispute, except for a few news stories by legislative reporters, a smattering of letters to newspaper editors, and passing glimpses of stickers. Its awareness of the intense, tightly focused public relations campaign is almost nonexistent. Its concern about the outcome is negligible.

Internal Audience The third type of campaign is aimed at an *internal audience*. This might be the employees of a company or members of a professional organization. This kind of campaign also relies upon specific types of public relations tools.

If a company plans to revise the stock-purchase plan it offers to employees, for instance, management should explain the changes and the reasons for them to employees. Failure to do so may produce confusion, rumors, and suspicious grumbling that management is attempting a trick that will harm employees financially. It is axiomatic that in any large group some people will resist change and suspect the motives for it. Although the issue is of intense concern to employees, the general public probably knows (or cares) nothing about it and has no influence in shaping the outcome. Thus distribution of the company's message to the public is pointless.

To tell its story to employees, management uses brochures illustrated with simple graphs and charts explaining how the revised plan will operate and how it will benefit the workforce. These are distributed at in-plant meetings or mailed to employees' homes. Top management officials address groups of employees, give audiovisual presentations, and answer questions. One issue of the employee magazine concentrates on the plan. If the company's plants are situated in several cities, the chief executive officer may use a videoconference to address the staffs of all the plants simultaneously.

Or, the top official may make a videotape, copies of which are distributed systemwide. These actions constitute an intensive internal communications project, yet the only information the public may learn about it is from a news story on the financial pages reporting the proposal.

That is how public relations programs are planned for carefully analyzed audiences. A good program is designed to fit the need as carefully as a tailor measures a customer for an expensive suit.

PLAN THE PROGRAM

As indicated in the discussion of the ways in which audiences should be defined and addressed, a practitioner has numerous options available when planning the program. A list is provided of principal ways in which public relations messages can be delivered. Subsequent chapters will examine each of these three methods in detail: written tactics (Chapter 22), spoken tactics (Chapter 23), and visual tactics (Chapter 24).

Written Methods

- News releases
- Factsheets
- Newspaper and magazine feature articles
- Newsletters
- Brochures and handbooks
- Company periodicals
- Annual reports
- Corporate advertising
- Books
- Facsimile releases
- Electronic bulletin boards

Visual Methods

- Television newscasts
- Television appearances
- Videotapes
- Motion pictures
- Slides and filmstrips
- Transparencies
- Still photographs

- Teleconferencing
- Charts and graphs
- Other graphics (cartoons, paintings, logos)
- Billboards
- Video news releases

Spoken Methods

- Face-to-face discussions
- Speeches
- Radio newscasts
- News conferences
- Press parties
- Interviews, printed and broadcast
- Meetings
- Word-of-mouth (the "grapevine")
- Audiotapes

The three types of methods truly provide a smorgasbord from which to choose! In most cases, an integrated program using several of these methods in a coordinated manner is best. Under certain circumstances, however, the practitioner might find it desirable or necessary to use only a single carefully chosen medium.

EXECUTE THE PROGRAM

Conducting a public relations project requires preparation time, efficient administration, and sufficient trained personnel. Temporary additions to the staff may be needed, along with the services of outside specialists.

An example of a well-run program occurred in Minnesota, where a civic organization named Our Fair Carousel raised $1 million to save the picturesque, 75-year-old Minnesota State Fair carousel, which was to have been sold horse-by-horse at a New York auction.

The civic group pledged to repay the City of St. Paul for a $1.3 million emergency loan it obtained to keep the carousel. It generated concern for the carousel by several techniques: telephone interviews with opinion leaders; a newsletter distributed in Minnesota and to members of the National Carousel Association; displays of carousel horses; and media publicity stressing nostalgia and the economic value of the carousel.

During a yearlong drive, Our Fair Carousel raised $1 million from individuals and foundations, plus a $500,000 pledge from a corporation that agreed to prepare a new site for the carousel and provide a $350,000 interest-free loan to repay the balance of the city's loan. Our Fair Carousel received a 1990 PRSA Silver Anvil award for this public service.

PREPARING A PROGRAM PLAN

Writing a plan for a public relations activity is nothing more than preparing a blueprint of what is to be done and how it will be accomplished. By preparing such a plan, either as a brief outline or an extensive document, the practitioner can make sure that all elements have been properly considered and that everybody involved knows what the procedure is. Ketchum Public Relations, San Francisco, uses the following outline in preparing program plans for clients:

1. *Define the problem.* Valid objectives cannot be set without a clear understanding of the problem. To understand the problem, (1) discuss it with the client to find what the public relations effort is expected to accomplish, (2) do some initial research, and (3) evaluate ideas in the broader perspective of the client's long-term goals.

2. *Identify objectives.* Once the problem is understood, it should be easy to define the objective. A stated objective should be evaluated by asking, (1) Does it really solve the problem? (2) is it realistic and achievable? and (3) can success be measured in terms meaningful to the client?

3. *Identify audience.* Identify, as precisely as possible, the group of people who comprise the primary audience for the message. If there are several groups, list them according to what group would be most important in achieving the client's primary objectives.

4. *Develop strategy.* The strategy describes how, in concept, the objective is to be achieved. Strategy is a plan of action that provides guidelines and themes for the overall effort. There is usually one, and often several, strategies for each target audience. Strategies may be broad or narrow, depending on the objective and the audience.

5. *Specify tactics.* This is the body of the plan that describes, in sequence, the specific activities proposed to achieve each objective. In selecting communication tools—news releases, brochures, radio announcements, videotapes, special events, etc.—make sure the communication tools are appropriate for the designated audience.

6. *Develop calendar.* It is important to have a timetable, usually in chart form, that shows the start and completion of each project within the framework of the total program. Using a calendar enables practitioners to make sure that projects—such as brochures, slide presentations, newsletters, and invitations—are ready when they are needed.

7. *Ascertain budget.* How much will it cost to implement the public relations plan? Outline, in sequence, the exact costs of all activities. Budgets should include such details as postage, car mileage, labor to stuff envelopes, typesetting, office supplies, telephone, etc. About 10 percent of the budget should be allocated for contingencies.

8. *Specify evaluation procedures.* Determine what criteria will be used to evaluate the success of the public relations program. Evaluation criteria should be realistic, credible, specific, and in line with client expectations. When determining objectives, make sure that each of them can be adequately evaluated at the end of the program.

When a crisis arises, a program in response must be executed quickly. Having a contingency plan ready for use in a foreseeable crisis speeds the response time, but some crises take unexpected forms. In most projects, however, crisis urgency is not involved. Sufficient time usually is available to prepare the materials and make the physical arrangements before the kickoff date. A program that starts, then bogs down because necessary materials are not ready or speakers are not available, is headed for failure.

The director and staff of a campaign must take several steps in order to execute the program efficiently:

- Create a program calendar and maintain a checklist of progress. This prevents the possibility of deadlines being missed or of some aspects being overlooked.
- Write the printed material and scripts.
- Obtain management approval of program material.
- Order the printing, after obtaining price bids and having specialists prepare attractive layouts.
- Write the speeches to be delivered. These may include the ''pattern'' speech, a basic presentation that various speakers may adapt appropriately to fit individual situations.
- Train the speakers and brief them thoroughly.
- Arrange meeting dates and places, and schedule speakers.
- Make contact with editors to propose feature stories in newspapers and magazines and supporting editorials if the campaign objective justifies them.
- Offer articulate representatives for appearances on radio and television shows.
- Send out invitations to news conferences, press parties, and meetings.

The press tour checklist used by Hewlett-Packard Company managers in planning introductions of major new products, reproduced on the following pages, shows the meticulous detail with which a major corporation prepares a public relations program.

ASSESS THE RESULTS

Every public relations campaign is an educational experience for those who conduct it as well as for those to whom it is directed. Assessment of the program's results, like the fact-finding step taken before it is planned, should be a time for candor and self-examination.

The results of some projects are easily determined. A fund drive either meets its announced goal or it does not. A campaign for passage of certain legislation either succeeds or fails. The crowds attending a state fair can be counted at the turnstiles. However, measuring the effectiveness of campaigns with more abstract goals, such as reversing a negative perception, is more difficult because no obvious statistics are available as benchmarks.

In summary, many resources are needed to design a public relations plan for a company or a client. These resources—public relations, marketing, editorial, financial, and research—draw from a large set of tools, some of which are shown in Figure 8.2. Turning a public relations idea into an effective program involves following a well-structured pattern. The practitioner moves logically, first defining the problem, then

FIGURE 8.1
A timetable for the Koosh Kins public relations program conducted by Ketchum Public Relations, San Francisco, showing the steps to be taken week by week over a four-month period.

KOOSH KINS TIMETABLE 1990

ACTIVITY DESCRIPTION	SEPTEMBER				OCTOBER					NOVEMBER				DEC.
	3	10	17	24	1	8	15	22	29	5	12	19	26	3
PRESS KIT DEVELOPMENT														
-- Develop releases/kit contents	XXX	XXX	XXX	XXX										
-- Meet with designer	XXX	XXX												
-- Issue for client approval	XXX	XXX	XXX	XXX										
-- Execution/printing/production				XXX										
NEW YORK EDITOR TRIP (short leads)														
-- Revise/review mailing lists					XXX	XXX								
-- Reproduce press materials/photos					XXX	XXX								
-- Draft pitch letter						XXX	XXX							
-- Book meetings							XXX	XXX	XXX	XXX				
-- Production/Execution											XXX			
-- Follow up												XXX	XXX	
TOP 40 NEWSPAPER/SYNDICATE MAILING														
-- Revise/review mailing lists	XXX	XXX												
-- Develop creative mailing concepts	XXX	XXX												
-- Customize/update press materials					XXX	XXX								
-- Issue for client approval		XXX	XXX											
-- Reproduce photos			XXX	XXX										
-- Draft pitch letter			XXX											
-- Production/execution					XXX	XXX	XXX							
-- Follow up								XXX	XXX	XXX	XXX	XXX	XXX	XXX
TOP 20 MARKETS/NATIONAL TV MORNING SHOWS														
-- Revise/review mailing lists						XXX	XXX							
-- Customize/update press materials							XXX	XXX						
-- Develop personalized mailing							XXX	XXX						
-- Issue for client approval								XXX						
-- Draft pitch letter								XXX	XXX					
-- Production/execution									XXX	XXX				
-- Follow up											XXX	XXX	XXX	XXX
4th QUARTER MEDIA OPPORTUNITIES/INQUIRIES	XXX	XXX	XXX	XXX	XXX	XXX	XXX	XXX	XXX	XXX	XXX	XXX	XXX	XXX
SUNDAY SUPPLEMENTS														
-- Develop media list				XXX	XXX	XXX								
-- Coordinate mailing list				XXX	XXX	XXX								
-- Follow-up phone calls							XXX	XXX						

2622K p. 1

progressing through subsequent steps that include setting an objective, identifying the audiences to be reached, planning the program, creating a timetable and budget, and executing the program. When carried out efficiently, these steps should produce a cohesive, workable public relations program that obtains results.

FIGURE 8.2
Some of the tools needed to design a public relations plan are shown here. (Courtesy of Regis McKenna, Inc., Palo Alto, California.)

PUBLIC RELATIONS PROGRAMMING REQUIRES MANY TOOLS

Many resources are needed to design a public relations plan for a company or a client. These resources—public relations, marketing, editorial, financial, and research—draw from a large set of tools.

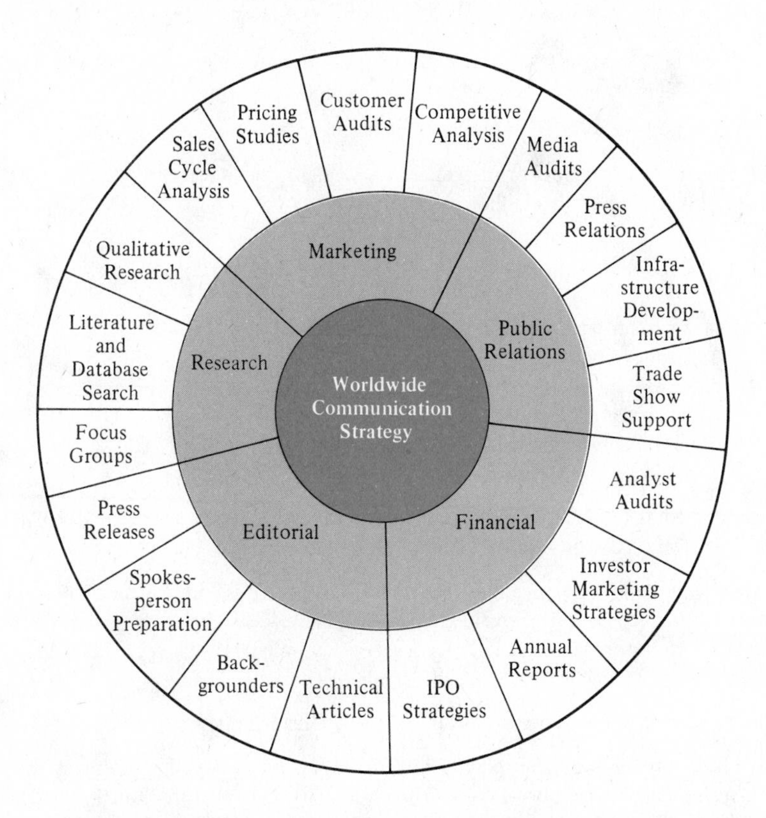

Source: Courtesy of Regis McKenna, Inc., Palo Alto, California.

HEWLETT-PACKARD PRESS TOUR CHECKLIST

Stage 1 Four months ahead of release date:

- Establish objectives of tour: emphasis on engineering, market positioning, new family of products, addition to present family, new product line, etc.
- Establish need for tour. Prepare estimate of cost: airfare, hotel, rental cars, equipment shipment, other expenses.
- Set tour-start date. Last visit to a bi-weekly should be at least 45 days before street date of that pub. If you're doing monthlies, then 60 days.
- DO NOT schedule a press tour in the week of a major trade show. TRY NOT to schedule the week before or after a major trade show or close to any major holiday.
- Check availability of working product and supporting equipment for tour dates. Best bet: take along a backup main unit for breakdowns.
- If product is easy to set up and move, visit trade journals directly. If not, plan to invite editors to centrally located hotel. Avoid using HP sales offices.
- Determine makeup of press-tour crew (marketing, engineering, PR), but keep number to minimum.
- Set press-release data (first publication) based on best-magazine street date.
- If product is of interest to market analysts, then schedule them. Analyst meetings typically are longer than editor calls.

Stage 2 Three months ahead of press-release date:

- Develop written pitch for editor/market-analyst telephone calls.
  — Will editor honor embargo?
  — Major feature of new product/system.
  — Establish date, time and place.
  — Lunch or dinner (with most valuable editors).
  — If any journal has exclusive, tell other editors up front.
- Plan schedule (order of cities). Don't forget Toronto, Canada. Don't fly into Chicago or JFK-New York on Sunday evening. They're zoos.
- Sites with the most publications: New York City, Long Island, Boston, Philadelphia, Chicago and Cleveland. Plan at least two days in New York area. Hayden/VNU Publications in Hasbrouck Heights, NJ, is about 20 minutes west of Manhattan. CMP Publications (Long Island) is about 45 minutes east.
- Most market analysts are in Boston area and Silicon Valley.
- Phone your most-valuable publications (MVP) in each city first. Contact editorial manager/managing editor who is familiar with the publication's editorial schedule and what editor covers your products.
- Editors within McGraw-Hill and Cahners consider each other to be competitors, prefer separate meetings. You may wish to treat CMP the same way.

- When visiting the Eastern office of a publication, be sure the West Coast editor gets a press kit before leaving. Copy the West Coast editor on all correspondence with Eastern office.
- Make hotel, airline and rental-car reservations. Reserve room/suite at hotel if meeting there. If going to publisher, be sure the editor knows you want a meeting room. Also don't be afraid to ask for audio-visual equipment for backup.
- Avoid shuttle flights between New York, Boston and Philadelphia. It may be more practical to take the train or drive as it lessens the chances of lost equipment on the airlines and delays in line. Some shuttles have no luggage check-in. In winter, train is more comfortable and safer than driving, cheaper than the airlines.
- After lining up MVPs, contact the other trade journals for the trip.
- Develop standard confirmation letter that can be modified for each editor.
- Reconfirm that editor will observe embargo date.
- Repeat model or product name, date, time and location of visit. If at trade journal, indicate early arrival for setup.
- Hotel arrangements (if meeting editors there): darkened room for slides; rental audio-visual; sign in lobby, name of catering/meeting manager; refreshments (Danish, coffee, juice for first session; coffee, soft drinks, water for other sessions).
- Prepare extra color transparencies of product so individual editors may have exclusive photos to use. These custom transparencies should be 4 × 5, if possible.

Stage 3 Three weeks ahead of tour start:

- Prepare complete agenda including summary page and timing for each day (see Samples 9-11).
  - Airline, flight, etc., for each day.
  - Rental-car confirmation. Rent nine-passenger wagon or van for large load of equipment.
  - Directions to hotel from airport, from hotel to each publication or from publication to publication; travel time between each.
  - Hotel address, telephone. Names of catering or meeting manager. Reservation number for rooms.
  - Special section for each journal: name, address, telephone of each publication; title of editors expected; masthead showing staff; description of journal reader (from Standard Rate & Data); any articles from previous journal issues of interest, etc. Allow 30 or more minutes for setup at each stop.
  - Special arrangements with key editors: lunches, dinners.
  - Home phones of tour people and PR contact at home division.
- Prepare overhead and 35mm slides, videotape. Use videotape only if hardware is not ready. Editors prefer executive interview to videotapes.
- Dry run all speakers and visuals at least twice. Look for misspellings, use of product nicknames, inconsistencies among speakers. Prepare Q&A for the trip. Have backup main speaker in case of illness.

Continued

HEWLETT-PACKARD PRESS TOUR CHECKLIST *(Continued)*

- Allow time before leaving to fix slides. Print hardcopy of all slides for editor handouts.
- Prepare information package to give to each journal: hardcopies of overheads; press releases; photos; brochures; backgrounders; latest HP quarterly financial release; HP annual report (if fresh); HP catalog (if just published). Ship last half of tour by FedExp or parcel post. Carry first few packages on plane. Special color transparencies should be carried in separate envelope. Allow only one to be selected by each publication unless you can afford more.

Stage 4 Seven days ahead of tour start:

- Practice packing and unpacking products. Label each box with its contents or obtain carrying cases. They're easier to repack.
- Phone each journal to confirm appointment. Check names of attendees.
- Publish complete agenda and summaries. Make enough copies for each tour-team member plus extras for secretaries of each member. Provide special comments about each journal as required (doesn't use color, wants technical article, etc.).
- For leader of tour, make special book with chapters on each publication: personal quirks of editors, editorial calendars for six months, clips of recent articles on HP, responses to generic questions about HP—financial, Spectrum, RISC, etc.
- Remind HP people to take HP badges for easy identification by editors. Wear business attire.
- Tour PR leader should have plenty of credit in credit-card account. Enough cash should be taken to handle quick transactions plus tips to move equipment from car to hotel or office of publication.
- If going to Canada, prepare all paperwork before leaving. Also allow time for clearing customs going in and out of Toronto. Photos and printed materials may not be admissible. Check in advance with our host office in Canada.
- Carry the following items for the tour: two or more rolls of packing tape; small pocket knife for opening boxes and cutting tape; two-to-three prong plug converter; heavy-duty power cords with three or four outlets.

Stage 5 Departure of tour:

- Secretary calls each editor/market-analyst to confirm HP visit THE DAY BEFORE HP crew arrives (on Friday for Monday, on Monday for Tuesday, etc.).

Stage 6 On the road—at hotel or at magazine/market-analyst:

- PR check with desk clerk on arrival to see that room is set up, shades can be lowered, equipment requested is available.
- Early a.m., PR check with desk clerk, concierge and telephone operators to let them know HP is here.
- Sign in lobby with room number.
- Sign outside or on door of meeting room.
- Early a.m., check catering for refreshments, timing of refills, afternoon soft drinks, etc.
- During morning, PR reconfirm next flights, make notes of special discussions with editors for letter following tour.
- Keep detailed notes for follow-up.
- Don't run in and out of room during interviews.
- Listen to editor comments.
- Take notes for managers.

Stage 7 Week following tour:

- Write letter to main editor contact at each publication and send a copy to other editors at the same site. Personalize your thanks, ask if editor needs additional information or photographs.
- Do all editorial follow-up.

Stage 8 Four weeks following tour:

- Create book with all printed data, letters, schedules from the tour to be used as a reference for the next tour of your division/group.

CASE PROBLEM 1

Alpha Corporation's large manufacturing facility in Knoxville employs 15,000 people. The corporation's manufacturing facilities in five other Tennessee towns employ another 3,000 people. Recent research shows little public awareness of the company's contributions to the state economy and its charitable activities in the communities where it operates.

Top management decides that this situation must be corrected. One decision is to produce a brochure that will create more awareness of the corporation among key publics. You are assigned to write the brochure.

Before writing anything, use the MBO guidelines at the beginning of the chapter (adapted from the Nager-Allen text) to outline the brochure's objectives in the context of the nine guidelines mentioned.

CASE PROBLEM 2

The Wonderlawn Company, a client of your public relations firm, has developed an exciting garden tool, the Laserzapper, whose laser beams destroy weeds in lawns without damaging the grass. It plans both to introduce the product nationally with heavy media coverage and to develop a marketing program focused on the peak potential sales periods of the year.

The Laserzapper helps the environment because it uses no poisonous chemicals. The user walks around the lawn, holding the three-foot-long wand horizontally and waist-high while its laser beams flash down on the weeds.

Although the Laserzapper will be offered first to home gardeners, Wonderlawn sees future uses in agriculture to control weeds in fields.

Using the eight-point method described in this chapter, prepare a public relations program for introducing the Laserzapper. Develop a set of public relations objectives, identify groups of potential purchasers, decide which promotional techniques will be most effective, create a timetable, develop a defensive strategy against anticipated attacks from the chemical companies, and write a catchy promotional slogan.

QUESTIONS FOR REVIEW AND DISCUSSION

1. Name the first step in every successful public relations program.

2. Negative perceptions often develop about an organization. What are some danger signals for which a public relations director should watch?

3. List three examples of specific one-time projects a public relations specialist might be asked to conduct.

4. If assigned to research the reasons why a certain brand of bicycle sells poorly, what important questions would you ask?

5. Describe how you would try to determine why the number of volunteer workers at a hospital is decreasing and list ways to recruit new volunteers.

6. Why should the goal of a public fund drive be set at an attainable level?

7. Public relations objectives should be stated in writing. Prepare a one-sentence statement of objectives for a campaign to convince local residents that the local factory of a national company is a good community citizen.

8. What public relations methods are often used to reach an internal audience?

9. List five visual methods for delivering public relations messages.

10. A program calendar is a basic tool in a public campaign. Why is it so important?

SUGGESTED READINGS

Hiebert, Ray E., editor. *Precision Public Relations*. New York: Longman, 1988. Section 4, "Planning the Process," pp. 171–216.

Nager, Norman R., and Allen, T. Harrell. *Public Relations Management by Objectives*. New York: Longman, 1983.

Pavlik, John. "Audience Complexity as a Component of Campaign Planning." *Public Relations Review,* Summer 1988, pp. 12–21.

Pearson, Ron. "Public Relations Writing Methods by Objectives." *Public Relations Review,* Summer 1987, pp. 14–26.

Pollare, Frank L. "Surviving the Budgeting Game." *Public Relations Journal,* March 1990, pp. 29–30.

Reid, Sheryll. "How to Develop a Strategic Plan." *Public Relations Journal,* August 1987, p. 31.

Simmons, Robert E. *Communication Campaign Management*. New York: Longman, 1990.

CHAPTER

Communication

The third step in the public relations process, after appropriate research and planning, is communication.

In a public relations program plan, as pointed out in Chapter 8, communication is the *implementation of a decision*. In other words, communication is the process and means by which public relations objectives are achieved. It may take the form of news releases, press conferences, special events, brochures, speeches, bumper stickers, newsletters, parades, posters, and the like. In a program plan, this stage is referred to as *strategies and tactics,* but it is also known as *outbound communication*.

The goal of the communication process, of course, is to inform, persuade, and motivate people. To be an effective communicator, a person must have a thorough knowledge of what constitutes communication and of how people receive messages. Also needed are an understanding of the way people adopt new ideas, and an awareness of the ever-present barriers that limit effective communication.

This chapter explores these concepts and offers guidelines on the construction and dissemination of messages. Additional aspects of communication, from a persuasion standpoint, are discussed in Chapter 11.

THE NATURE OF COMMUNICATION

THE NEED FOR A COMMON GROUND

Communication is the act of transmitting information, ideas, and attitudes from one person to another. Communication can take place, however, only if the speaker and the listener (called *the sender* and *the receiver*) have a common understanding of the symbols being used.

Words are the most common symbols. The degree to which two people understand each other is heavily dependent upon their common knowledge of word symbols. Anyone who has traveled abroad can readily attest to the observation that very little communication occurs between two people who speak different languages. Even signs translated into English for tourists often lead to some confusing and amusing messages. An advertisement for a Hong Kong dentist, for example, said, "Teeth extracted by the latest Methodists." Gestures often provide a form of simple communication, but every traveler has his or her favorite stories of frustration and amusing misinterpretations.

Even if the sender and receiver speak the same language and live in the same country, the effectiveness of the communication depends on such factors as education, social class, regional differences, nationality, and cultural background.

Public relations specialists in employee communications are finding that communication in the workplace is a much more complex problem than it used to be. The number of white males, who traditionally dominated the workforce, will be reduced by 39 percent by the year 2000 in the United States. New entries into the workforce will be 85 percent white women, immigrants, blacks, Latinos, and Asians. For many of these new workers, English will be a second language.

A multicultural workforce will require communicators to be better informed about cultural differences and conflicting values in order to find common ground and build bridges between the various groups. At the same time, a major task will be to communicate in clear and simple terms. Studies show that one in eight employees reads at no better than the fourth-grade level, and one in five at the eighth-grade level or less.

FEEDBACK

An important aspect of communication is the opportunity for *feedback,* or response from the listener to the speaker. Although early communication models assumed that messages were simply "injected" into listeners under what was commonly known as the "hypodermic needle theory," researchers soon realized that feedback was just as important as the message itself. Feedback tells the sender whether he or she is being understood. Questions, for example, can clarify meaning for the listener and also alert the sender that alternative words and examples should be used.

Most communication models now show feedback as an integral part of the process. Social scientist David K. Berlo's model has four components—sender/source (encoder), message, channel, and receiver (decoder)—with a feedback line between the sender and the receiver.

Mass media researcher Wilbur Schramm's early models (see Figure 9.1) started with a simple communication model (top), but he later expanded the process to include the concept of "shared experience" (middle diagram). In other words, little or no communication is achieved unless the sender and the receiver share a common language and even an overlapping cultural or educational background. The importance of "shared experience" becomes apparent when a highly technical news release about a new computer chip causes the local business editor to shake his or her head in bewilderment.

Schramm's third model (bottom) incorporates the idea of continuous feedback. Both the sender and receiver continually encode, interpret, decode, transmit, and receive information. This loop process also is integral in all models showing the public

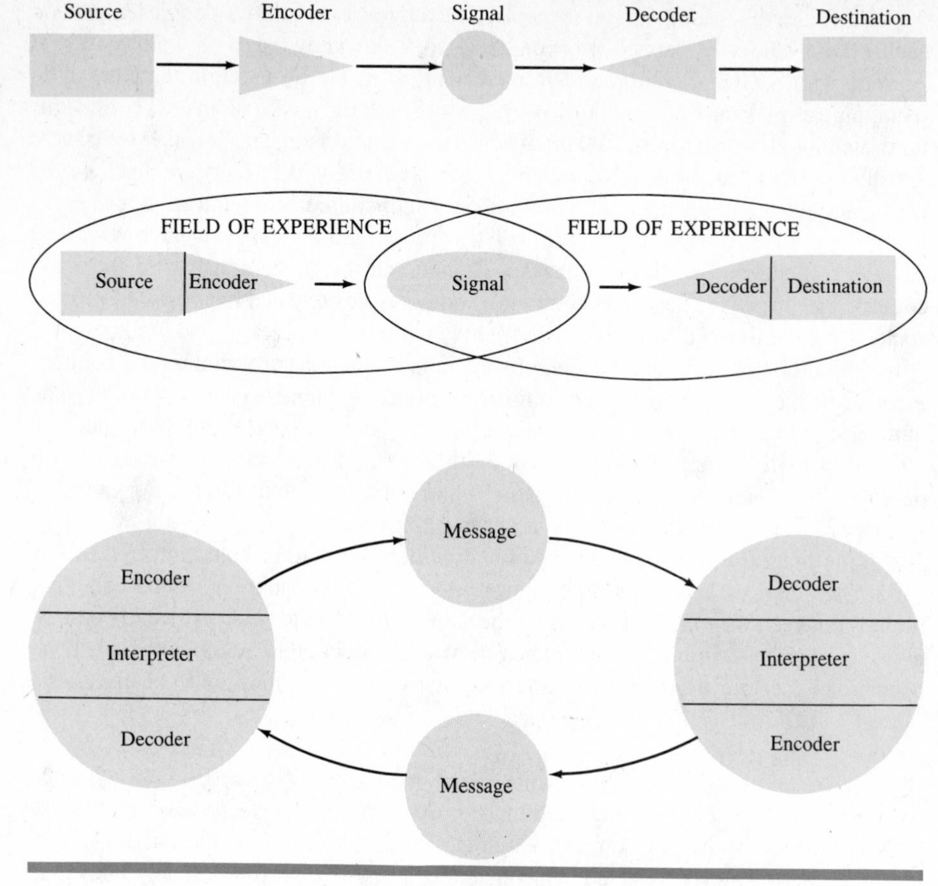

FIGURE 9.1
Three of Wilbur Schramm's communication models, with the latter two showing the importance of "shared experience" and the feedback loop process. (from Wilbur Schramm (Ed.), *The Process and Effects of Mass Communication,* Urbana: University of Illinois Press, 1954. Copyright © 1954 by the University of Illinois. Reprinted with permission.)

relations process of research, planning, communication, and evaluation. (You'll remember the diagram in Chapter 1 that shows public relations as a cyclical process.) Communication to internal and external audiences produces feedback that is taken into consideration during research, the first step, and evaluation, the fourth step. In this way, the structure and dissemination of messages are continually refined for maximum effectiveness.

Generally, *interpersonal communication* (two or more people talking together) is the most effective form of communication. It is effective because the message is fortified by gestures, facial expressions, intimacy, tone of voice, and the opportunity for instant feedback. If the listener asks a question or looks puzzled, the speaker has an instant cue and can rephrase the information or amplify a point.

This is also true of small-group meetings, but the barriers of effective communication tend to mount as one advances to large-group meetings and, ultimately, the mass media. In other words, mass media can multiply an audience many times over, but the psychological as well as the physical distance between the sender and the receiver is considerably lengthened. This causes less effective communication because the audience is no longer intimately involved with the speaker. No immediate feedback is possible, and the message can undergo distortion as it passes through media gatekeepers.

THE ROLE OF THE SENSES

The five senses—sight, hearing, smell, touch, and taste—play a vital role in communication. Television and film or videotape, for example, are the most effective of the mass media because the audience's senses of both sight and hearing can be engaged. In addition, there are the attractions of color and movement. Radio, on the other hand, relies on only one sense, that of hearing. Print media, although capable of communicating a large amount of information, rely only on sight.

Individuals learn through all five senses, but psychologists estimate that 83 percent of learning is accomplished through sight. Hearing accounts for 11 percent of learning, while only 3 percent of total information is gained from smell. Two percent of learning comes from the sense of touch and only 1 percent is through taste. Fifty percent of what individuals retain consists of what they see and hear.

These figures have obvious implications for the public relations practitioner. Any communication strategy should, if possible, include vehicles of communication that combine sound and sight. This is why it is a good idea for speakers to use graphs, charts, overhead transparencies, and slides to supplement their talks. It also means that a variety of communication tools—news releases, slide presentations, videotapes, billboards, newsletters, radio announcements, TV clips, and so on—should be used to communicate a message to selected audiences. This practice not only assists learning and retention but also provides repetition of the message in a variety of forms that facilitate audience understanding.

THE EFFECTS OF COMMUNICATION

AVOID THE WASTED MESSAGE

Sociologist Harold Lasswell, in the 1940s, defined the act of communication as "Who says what, in which channel, to whom, with what effect."

Although in public relations much emphasis is given to the formation and dissemination of messages, all this effort is wasted if the message has no effect on the intended audience. It is therefore important for a student of public relations to understand fully the axiom of Walt Seifert, professor emeritus of public relations at Ohio State University. He says, "Dissemination does not equal publication, and publication does not equal absorption and action." In other words, "All who receive it won't publish it, and all who read or hear won't understand or act upon it."

Seifert, as well as social psychologists, recognizes that the majority of the audience—at any given time—is passive and not particularly interested in the message or in adopting the idea. Polling specialist Elmo Roper, in his analysis of how messages are received, says that only 5 to 10 percent of the population is "politically active." Others are politically "inert," adopting ideas only after opinion leaders (the politically active) have evaluated and adopted them.

Roper's hypothesis is a variation of sociologist Paul Lazarsfeld's two-step flow theory of communication. He postulated that people rely on interpersonal communication with friends and opinion leaders in making decisions or adopting new ideas. Messages in the mass media, therefore, have limited influence in changing attitudes or opinions. The two-step flow idea is discussed more fully in Chapter 11.

A BEHAVIORAL COMMUNICATION MODEL

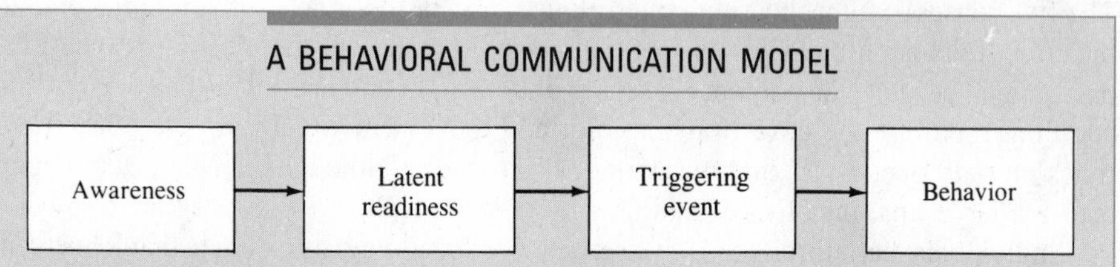

The above behavioral communication model, suggests *PR Reporter,* is better than traditional communication models because it forces practitioners to think in terms of what behaviors they are trying to motivate in target publics, rather than what information is being communicated. The process is described as follows:

1. ***Awareness.*** Salience or relevance is the key to reaching awareness. The purpose of communication here is to create awareness, which is the start of any behavioral process.

2. ***Latent readiness.*** Either positive or negative readiness to behave in a certain way starts to form, often subconsciously (latently). People get ready to act by accumulating and developing experience, information, word-of-mouth, beliefs, opinions, and emotions.

3. ***Triggering event.*** The triggering event step gives people a chance to act on their latent readiness. Triggering events may be an election day, a store sale, distribution of a company's annual report, or even a news release announcing a new product or service. Public relations people should build triggering events into their planning: this moves the emphasis from communication to behavior motivation.

4. ***Behavior.*** Although the ultimate goal is to motivate people to buy something or act in a certain way, they may adopt intermediate behaviors such as requesting more literature, visiting a showroom, or trying the product or idea experimentally.

HOW NEW IDEAS AND PRODUCTS ARE ADOPTED

What all this research suggests, of course, is the concept that ideas (and their adoption) penetrate the public very slowly. A public relations person may disseminate messages efficiently, but the effect on the intended audience is dependent on other processes at work.

The Five-Stage Adoption Process One key process in understanding the public is the way people adopt new ideas or accept new products. The adoption process idea suggests five stages:

1. *Awareness*. A person becomes aware of an idea or a new product, often by means of an advertisement or a news story.

2. *Interest*. The person seeks more information about the idea or the product, perhaps by ordering a brochure, picking up a pamphlet, or reading an in-depth article in a newspaper or magazine.

3. *Evaluation*. The person evaluates the idea or the product on the basis of how it meets specific needs and wants. Feedback from friends is part of the process.

4. *Trial*. The person tries the product or the idea on an experimental basis, by using a sample, witnessing a demonstration, or making qualifying statements, such as, ''I read . . . '' or ''Senator Smith says . . . ''

5. *Adoption*. The individual begins to use the product on a regular basis or integrates the idea into his or her belief system. The ''Senator Smith says . . . '' becomes ''I think . . . '' if peers provide support and reinforcement of the idea.

It is important to realize that a person does not necessarily go through all five steps in connection with any given idea or product. The process may be terminated after any one of the steps. In fact, the process is like a large funnel. Although many are made aware of an idea or a product, only a few will ultimately complete the adoption process.

The Time Factor Another aspect that confuses people is the amount of time it takes to adopt a new idea or product. Depending on the individual and the situation, the entire adoption process can take place almost instantly if the result is of minor consequence or requires low-level commitment. Buying a new brand of soft drink or a bar of soap is relatively inexpensive and often done on impulse. On the other hand, deciding to take a new job or vote for a particular candidate may involve an adoption process that takes several weeks or months.

Research also shows that some people are ''early adopters'' and others ''late adopters,'' depending upon personality traits and the risk involved. A wealthy person can afford to be more innovative and experimental than a person who is barely able to afford food and housing. Much of the research about ''adopters'' has come out of research in the 1930s about introducing new kinds of hybrid seed corn. Researchers found that individuals with large farms were much more willing to experiment with new types of hybrid seed corn than farmers with small plots of land who couldn't afford to take the risk.

How Decisions Are Influenced Of particular interest to public relations people is the primary source of information at each step in the adoption process. Mass media vehicles such as advertising, short news articles, feature stories, and radio and television news announcements are most influential at the *awareness* stage of the adoption process. A news article or a television announcement makes people aware of an idea, event, or new product. They also are made aware through such vehicles as direct mail, office memos, and simple brochures.

Individuals at the *interest* stage also rely on mass media vehicles, but they are actively seeking information and pay attention to longer, in-depth articles. They rely more on detailed brochures, specialized publications, small-group seminars, and meetings to provide details. At the *evaluation, trial,* and *adoption* stages, group norms and opinions are the most influential. Feedback, negative or positive, from friends and peers may determine adoption. If a person's friends generally disapprove of the candidate, the movie, or the automobile brand, it is unlikely that the individual will complete the adoption process even if he or she is highly sold on the idea. If a person does make a commitment, mass media vehicles become reinforcing mechanisms. Studies show, for example, that owners of a new car are the most avid readers of that car's advertising.

THE PUBLIC RELATIONS OBJECTIVES

All of this gives perspective on exactly what a public relations person can hope to accomplish. James Grunig, professor of public relations at the University of Maryland, has organized a typology of possible objectives for an information campaign:

1. *Message exposure*. Public relations personnel provide materials to the mass media and disseminate other messages through controlled media such as newsletters and brochures. Intended audiences are exposed to the message in various forms.

2. *Accurate dissemination of the message*. The intended audience acknowledges the message and retains all or part of it.

3. *Acceptance of the message*. Based on its view of reality, the audience not only retains the message but accepts it as valid.

4. *Attitude change*. The audience not only believes the message but makes a verbal or mental commitment to change behavior as a result of the message.

5. *Change in overt behavior*. Members of the audience actually change their current behavior or begin a new behavior.

Grunig says that most public relations experts usually aim at the first two objectives—exposure to the message and accurate dissemination. The last three objectives—acceptance of the message, attitude change, and changes in overt behavior—are difficult to accomplish unless the audience is already highly interested and predisposed to accept the message in the first place. The first two objectives are also much easier to evaluate than attitude change.

PASSIVE AND ACTIVE AUDIENCES

A professional communicator, says Grunig, can better tailor messages and select appropriate communication channels if he or she understands the mental state of the intended audience. Grunig's model divides the audience into two modes—those who actively seek information and those who passively process information. As might be expected, it is much easier to accomplish communication objectives if the intended audience is actively seeking information. It wants to receive the message and will listen to or read it. The passive information processor, as explained earlier, is not seeking information and generally will do little to understand it.

Grunig goes on to say that the effective communicator will acknowledge the existence of both audiences, and structure messages accordingly. Passive audiences, for example, can be made aware of a message only through brief encounters—with the billboard glanced at on the way to work, the radio announcement heard in the car, the television advertisement broadcast before the show begins, and information available in a doctor's waiting room—in other words, with communication channels that can be utilized while the audience is doing little else.

In addition, passive audiences need messages that have style and creativity. The person must be lured, by photos, illustrations, and catchy slogans, into processing information. Press agentry, the dramatic picture, and even the use of ''beefcake'' or ''cheesecake'' models can make passive audiences aware of the message. The objec-

EFFECTIVE COMMUNICATIONS

Philip Lesly, president of the Philip Lesly Company, outlined some guidelines for effective communications. Lesly made his remarks during a lecture, sponsored by the Ball Corporation, at Ball State University. His points are summarized here.

- Approach everything from the viewpoint of the audience's interest—what is on their minds, what is in it for them.
- Give the audience a sense of involvement in the communication process and in what is going on. Get them involved and you get their interest.
- Make the subject matter part of the atmosphere the audience lives with—what they talk about, what they hear from others. That means getting the material adopted in their channels of communication.
- Communicate with people, not at them. Communication that approaches the audience as a target makes people put their defenses up against it.
- Localize—get the message conveyed as close to the individual's own milieu as possible.
- Use a number of channels of communications, not just one or two. The impact is far greater when it reaches people in a number of different forms.
- Maintain consistency—so what is said on the subject is the same no matter which audience it's directed to or what the context is. Still, tailor-make each message for the specific audience as much as possible.
- Don't propagandize but make sure that you make your point. When a communicator draws conclusions in his [or her] summation of information, it is more effective than depending on the audience to draw its own conclusions.
- Maintain credibility—which is essential for all of these points to be effective.

tives of the communication, therefore, are simply exposure to and accurate dissemination of the message. Changes in attitude or overt behavior rarely occur among passive audiences.

A communicator's approach to audiences actively seeking information may be different. These people are already at the *interest* stage of the adoption process and seek supplemental information. At any given time, of course, the intended audience has passive and active information-seekers in it. It is important, therefore, that multiple messages and a variety of communication channels be used in a full-fledged information campaign.

Two approaches can help the public relations practitioner determine appropriate strategies. First, research into audience attitudes can give insight into the extent of group interest in or apathy toward a new product or idea. Second, more efficient communication can be achieved if the intended audience is segmented as much as possible. If research shows that the audience is passive about the product or idea, the strategy calls for communication tools that include (1) billboards, (2) radio and television announcements, (3) posters, (4) catchy slogans, (5) dramatic pictures, (6) bumper stickers, (7) buttons, and (8) special events that emphasize entertainment. On the other hand, more sophisticated messages should be planned for those who have passed the *awareness* stage and are seeking more information. These tools might include (1) brochures, (2) in-depth newspaper and magazine articles, (3) slide presentations, (4) videotape demonstrations, (5) 30-minute movies, (6) symposiums and conferences, (7) major speeches before key groups, and (8) display booths at trade shows.

This book contains a number of case histories about public relations programs. The reader should note the diverse messages and media used in most of the campaigns to reach both passive and active audiences.

THE PROCESS OF COMMUNICATION

Communication among individuals, groups, or organizational entities is a complex process involving a number of variables: source credibility, message context, and symbols, acronyms, and slogans.

SOURCE CREDIBILITY

One key variable, discussed more fully in Chapter 11, is *source credibility*. Do members of the audience perceive the source as knowledgeable and expert on the subject? Do they perceive the source as honest and objective or just representing a vested interest? Audiences, for example, ascribe lower credibility to an advertisement than to the same information contained in a news article. The perception is that news articles, selected by media gatekeepers, are more credible. Source credibility is the main reason that organizations use respected experts or celebrities as representatives to convey their messages.

CONTEXT OF THE MESSAGE

A second variable is the *context* of the message. It has already been pointed out that action (performance) speaks louder than a stack of news releases. A bank may spend thousands of dollars on a promotion campaign with the slogan, "Your friendly bank—where service and courtesy count," but the effort is wasted if employees are not trained to be friendly and courteous. An industrial firm can position itself as deeply concerned about chemical wastes, but all the executive speeches in the world mean nothing if the company makes headlines after dumping toxic wastes into the local river.

SYMBOLS, ACRONYMS, AND SLOGANS

Clarity and simplicity of message constitute another important variable. This is why symbols, acronyms, and slogans are used in public relations campaigns. Each is a form of shorthand that quickly conceptualizes ideas and travels through extended lines of communication.

The world is full of symbols, such as the Christian cross, the Star of David, and the crusading sword of the American Cancer Society. Corporate symbols such as the Mercedes Benz star, the General Electric logo, the Chase Manhattan octagon, and the multicolored apple of Apple Computer are known throughout the world. On a national level, one of the most successful symbols ever used by the U.S. government is Smokey the Bear, who has reminded several generations of Americans about the danger of forest fires.

A symbol should be unique, memorable, widely recognized, and appropriate.

FIGURE 9.2
Smokey the Bear has become so well known as a symbol of the fight against forest fires that this poster delivers its message effectively by implication.

FIGURE 9.3
The Apple Computer logo has achieved widespread instant recognition by visual impact alone, without any lettering.

Organizations spend millions annually on searching for unique symbols that convey the essence of what they are or hope to be. Additional millions are spent on publicizing the symbols and creating meaning for them. The Mercedes star means nothing without the context of a reputation for precision engineering, fine craftsmanship, and expensive automobiles. The symbol is a simple, graphic way of saying all this.

Acronyms also are shorthand for conveying information. An acronym is a word formed from the initial letters of other words. The Group Against Smokers' Pollution goes by the acronym *GASP*. Juvenile Opportunities in Business becomes *JOB*. The National Organization of Women has the acronym *NOW,* which says a great deal about its political priorities.

In many cases, the acronym—because it is short and simple—becomes the common name. Thus, the mass media continually use the term *AIDS* instead of "acquired immune deficiency syndrome." And *UNESCO* is easier to write and say than *United Nations Educational, Scientific and Cultural Organization*. *SWAT* is less cumbersome than *special weapons and tactics team*.

Public relations personnel, when involved in naming an organization, committee, or special event, should consider a title that provides a good acronym, especially if the official name is quite long. The acronym may succinctly convey what the organization does (such as *JOB*), or it may simply be easy to say and memorable (such as *NATO*).

Slogans have been part of the American scene since "No Taxation Without Representation" and "Don't Tread on Me" were used during the American Revolution. Corporations also use slogans, which are often trademarked (see Chapter 13). Massive advertising and promotion have made "Don't Leave Home Without It" readily identified with American Express. "The Ultimate Driving Machine" is strongly identified with BMW.

FITTING THE LANGUAGE TO THE AUDIENCE

Public relations personnel should be alert for more than occupational and bureaucratic words. Words and media channels used by college-educated, white-collar professionals often are quite different from those used by people with less education.

The Illinois Public Health Department had the right idea when it commissioned a song in rap-music style as one way to reach low-income, poorly educated groups about the dangers of AIDS. The words and music of the "Condom Rag," however, were offensive to elected officials, who squelched the song.

This example poses the classic dilemma for the expert communicator.

Company executives or elected officials, who are not the target audience for the message, often control its content. The State Bar of California, for example, has its consumer brochures approved by committees of lawyers. It is hardly surprising, then, that the low-income, poorly educated citizens for whom the brochures were intended find them hard to understand. One solution is to copy-test all public relations materials on the target audience. This helps convince management that what it likes isn't necessarily what the audience wants or understands.

WRITING FOR CLARITY

A communicator should pretest messages on the intended audience. Do members of this audience understand what is being said? Do they have difficulty with word meanings? Can simple, one-syllable words be substituted for multisyllable ones? Are the writing level and sentence structure appropriate to the audience's educational level? These questions need to be answered, and they often are not when experts within an organization write, approve, and send messages without considering the target audience.

AVOID JARGON

One source of blocked communication is technical and bureaucratic jargon. When delivered to a general audience, it is called *semantic noise* by social scientists. Jargon interferes with the message and impedes the receiver's ability to comprehend it. (The study of words and how they are used and interpreted is called *semantics*.) Thus, the vice president of engineering may understand perfectly a product news release that means nothing to the general public. A good example of a useless news release is the following, which was actually sent to business editors of daily newspapers. This is how it began:

> Versatec, a Xerox Company, has introduced the Graphics Network Processor-SNA (Model 451). The processor, operating as a 377x RJE station, sends and receives EBCDIC or binary data in IBM System Network Architecture (SNA) networks using Synchronous Data Link Control (SDLC) protocol. . . .

Another news release that raised the ire of business editors began:

> NCR Corporation's SCSI Technology Group today announced a new dual-channel synchronous SCSI host adapter for Multibus which provides the Multibus user with two independent SCSI-to-Multibus channels on one standard Multibus card.

No wonder that media gatekeepers complain bitterly about the poorly written, jargon-ridden news releases that often blanket their desks! The major problem seems to be that public relations personnel in too many organizations have abdicated their professional responsibility to distribute messages that are clear, simply stated, and devoid

Keep It Simple

Strike three.
Get your hand off my knee.
You're overdrawn.
Your horse won.
Yes.
No.
You have the account.
Walk.
Don't walk.
Mother's dead.
Basic events
require simple language.
Idiosyncratically euphuistic
eccentricities are the
promulgators of
triturable obfuscation.
What did you do last night?
Enter into a meaningful
romantic involvement
or
fall in love?
What did you have for
breakfast this morning?
The upper part of a hog's
hind leg with two oval
bodies encased in a shell
laid by a female bird
or
ham and eggs?
David Belasco, the great
American theatrical producer,
once said, "If you can't
write your idea on the
back of my calling
card,
you don't have a clear idea."

FIGURE 9.4
This advertisement reads like modern poetry, but in fact it is a vital meassage, prepared by a major manufacturing company to strengthen its institutional image. (Courtesy of United Technologies Corporation.)

of jargon. (The difference between being a counselor and a technician is discussed in Chapter 6.)

AVOID CLICHÉS AND HYPE WORDS

Highly charged words with connotative meanings can pose problems, and overuse of clichés and hype words can seriously undermine the credibility of the message.

The *Wall Street Journal,* for example, mocked the business of high-tech public relations with a story titled ''High-Tech Hype Reaches New Heights.'' A reporter analyzed 201 news releases and compiled a ''Hype Hit Parade'' that included the 11 most overused and ineffective words:

leading
enhanced
unique
significant
solution
integrated
powerful
innovative
advanced
high performance
sophisticated

Similar surveys have uncovered overused words in business and public relations. A New York firm, John Rost Associates, complied a list of words and phrases used excessively in business letters and reports. The list includes: *agenda, proactive, interface, networking, finalize, done deals, impact, bottom-line, vis-à-vis, world class, state-of-the-art, user-friendly, competitive edge, know-how, win-win, breakthrough, fast track, hands-on input, dialogue,* and *no-brainer.*

A survey of corporate annual reports also reveals the constant use of certain words. Robert K. Otterbourg, president of a company that does annual reports for corporations, says the most overused words include *challenge, opportunity, fundamental achievements, pioneering efforts,* and *state-of-the-art.*

*Miscommunication caused when one party uses jargon not understood by the other is a common difficulty. This cartoon exemplifies the bewilderment of a listener exposed to such specialized "in" talk. (*Public Relations Journal*)*

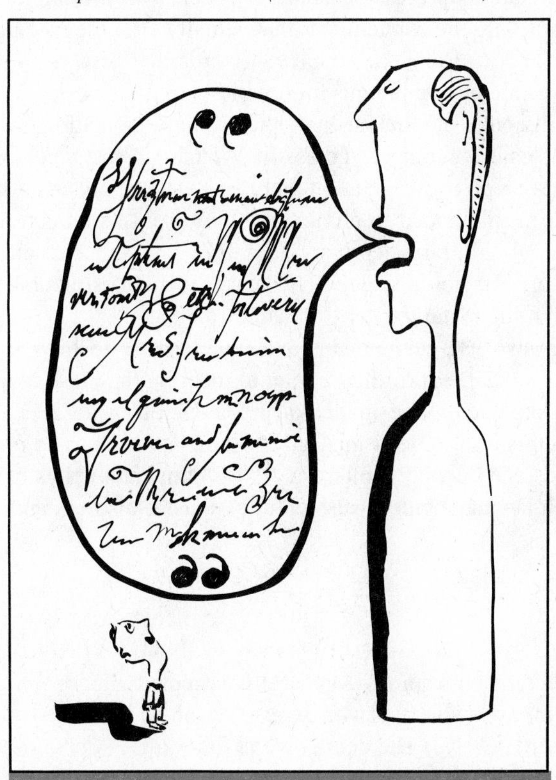

When words are overused, their special meaning becomes devalued. As the *Wall Street Journal* implies, if every product is "unique" and "sophisticated," the words simply become meaningless hype that impresses neither the media gatekeeper nor the public.

AVOID EUPHEMISMS

A euphemism, according to *Webster's New World Dictionary,* is "the use of a less expressive or direct word or phrase for one considered distasteful or offensive."

Public relations personnel should use positive, favorable words to convey a message, but they have an ethical responsibility not to use words that hide information or mislead. Probably little danger exists in substituting positive words such as *alcohol misuse* for *alcohol abuse,* which has a negative connotation. Nor is it improper to say that someone *has a disability* rather than use the more negative word *handicapped.*

In today's society, some euphemisms cause more amusement than concern. Stockbrokers, after the stock market crash of 1987 (referred to on Wall Street as "a major technical correction"), are now called "account executives" and "financial consultants." Car mechanics are "automotive internists" and grocery store checkout clerks "associate scanning professionals." Used luxury cars are "preowned," and people are no longer fired but "selected out" and "dehired."

Such inflated language is found in many kinds of writing, to the point of looking silly, but public relations professionals should keep it to a minimum.

More dangerous are the euphemisms that actually alter the meaning or impact of a precise word. Writers call this *doublespeak*—words that pretend to communicate but really don't. Governments are famous for doublespeak. For example, in World War II, Winston Churchill spoke of "dehousing" the civilian population of Germany, which really meant full-scale bombing of cities. In Vietnam, "resource control programs" were really efforts to poison vegetation and the water supply. And in the 1980s, the U.S. State Department decided to eliminate *killing* from its human rights reports and call it "unlawful or arbitrary deprivation of life." In the Persian Gulf war, U.S. military briefing officers described civilian casualties and destruction caused by bombs that missed their military targets as "collateral damage."

Corporations also use euphemisms and doublespeak to hide unfavorable news. One airline, in its annual report, didn't want to mention the crash of a plane with lives lost, so it called the event "the involuntary conversion of a 727."

Use of euphemisms to hide or mislead obviously is contrary to professional public relations standards and the public interest. As William Lutz writes in *Public Relations Quarterly,* "Such language breeds suspicion, cynicism, distrust, and, ultimately, hostility."

BEWARE OF NEGATIVE CONNOTATIONS

Words have *denotative* meanings—generally accepted dictionary definitions—and *connotative* meanings—what the word means to an individual or a group. A good example is the word *scheme.* The denotative definition is "a plan of work or action." The connotative definition, to most Americans, is something that is underhanded and dishonest. It is acceptable to have a "scheme" in England but it is better to have a "program" in the United States.

Many other words have strong negative connotations for the majority of Americans. They include *socialist, communist, propaganda,* and *terrorist*. Of course, the difference between a "terrorist" and a "freedom fighter" depends on which side the person using the term supports. In Central America, for example, President Reagan called the Contra insurgents in Nicaragua freedom fighters, while supporters of the Nicaraguan government denounced them as terrorist rebels. In more recent conflicts, the United States called foreigners stranded in Iraq "hostages" while the Iraq government called them "guests," "restrictees," and, finally, "detainees."

The use of adjectives to describe individuals also can conjure up positive or negative connotations. Newspapers often color the reader's perception by describing someone as "philanthropist John Jones" or "industrialist Dick Smith." By the same token, reporters often create negative impressions by writing "Mafia figure Joe Casey" or "corporate raider John Morlan." Adjectives used to describe President Saddam Hussein of Iraq have included "madman," "strongman," "Hitler-like," and "fanatic."

AVOID DISCRIMINATORY LANGUAGE

In today's world, effective communication also means *nondiscriminatory* communication. Public relations personnel should double-check every message to eliminate undesirable gender, racial, and ethnic connotations.

This cartoon illustrates the difficulty of delivering information to diverse audiences, an issue in cross-cultural communication. A word that conjures up a certain mental picture for one recipient may create a quite different picture for another. (Regis McKenna, Inc.)

In regard to gender, it is unnecessary to write about something as being *man-made* when a word like *synthetic* or *artificial* is just as good. Companies no longer have *manpower* but *employees, personnel,* and *workers*. Most civic organizations have *chairpersons* now, and cities have *fire fighters* instead of *firemen,* and *police officers* instead of *policemen*. Airlines, of course, have *flight attendants* instead of *stewardesses*. Although much progress has been made in desexing language, some changes remain awkward. For example, the terms *businessperson* and *congressperson* are resisted by many writers as being too stilted.

Careless writing and editing, or lack of sensitivity, also can cause a company trouble. The city of San Francisco, feeling the pressure of its powerful gay lobby, threatened to cancel a $500,000 contract with General Motors for vehicles after it was learned that a GM internal video contained a reference to a foreign competitor's product as ''that little faggot truck.''

In a letter of apology to the city, GM explained that the ''faggot'' reference was unintentional and made by a customer being interviewed for the video on why he preferred Chevrolet products to foreign models. The company also added a new directive to its antidiscrimination policy: ''Abuse of the dignity of anyone through slurs or other derogatory or objectionable conduct, including that based on sexual orientation, is offensive employee behavior. . . .''

Writers also should be careful about descriptive phrases for women. *Bulldog Reporter,* a West Coast public relations newsletter, has given several ''fireplug'' awards to public relations firms for the way they have described women in news releases. One Chicago firm, for example, spoke of a company president: ''A tall, attractive blonde who could easily turn heads on Main Street is instead turning heads on Wall Street.''

In *Bulldog*'s opinion, the prize for capitalizing on racist, sexist stereotypes goes to a Los Angeles public relations firm's news release about the appointment of a female to head a Japanese company's consumer electronics division. It said, in part, ''Demure, naturally pretty and conservative in her dress and manner, Miho Suda could easily pass as a college student.'' *Bulldog* saw this kind of writing as ''a desperate and ignorant pitch that completely overlooked Ms. Suda's qualifications and achievements. It practically positions her as the corporate geisha.''

Nor is it appropriate in professional settings to say that a woman is the wife of someone also well known. A female vice president of a public relations firm in San Francisco, for example, cried foul when a local newsletter described her as the wife of a prominent journalist. The newsletter editor apologized in the next issue.

Messages should avoid any ethnic designations. It is unacceptable to say, for example, ''Juan Hernandez, a Latino, is employed. . . .'' Persons using any racial reference should always ask whether the same sentence would sound awkward if the word *white* or *Anglo-Saxon* were substituted for *black, Latino, Asian,* and so on. (Chapter 13 discusses the possible legal consequences of racial slurs.)

BARRIERS TO COMMUNICATION

Despite the communicator's best efforts, a number of barriers may impede effective communication. A major obstacle is that no message is received in its pure form. The receiver may magnify, modify, misinterpret, or even ignore it. This is called *self-selection* and *self-perception*. As previously discussed, each person interprets messages through a complex array of social structures and belief systems.

Barriers also exist because the sender and the receiver, as discussed earlier, lack common backgrounds and shared levels of experience. There are many kinds of barriers:

- Divergent backgrounds of participants
- Differences in education
- Differences in interest about the message
- Differences in intelligence level
- Lack of mutual respect
- Differences in age, gender, race, and class
- Differences in language skills
- Lack of skill on the part of the communicator
- Lack of skill on the part of the listener
- Lack of background information

Messages also undergo distortion as they are sent through long lines of communication. Paul Lazarsfeld, for example, says that a message undergoes sharpening and leveling as it is received, interpreted, summarized, and passed on to others. Other social scientists call this *message entropy*—a natural tendency for a message to dissipate (lose information) as it is disseminated.

A two-page news release often is published only as a one-paragraph story in the local daily. A complex social issue, because of perceived audience interest and media space requirements, is often portrayed in simplistic terms without any of the nuances that made it a complex issue in the first place.

The pollster George Gallup has compiled a list of seven regulators that, he says, restrict the absorption of new information or ideas:

1. *Complexity of the idea.* The more complex the idea, the less likely people will be to understand it and take action. Bankers, for example, say that the regulations for opening Individual Retirement Accounts (IRAs) are so complex that many Americans have not taken advantage of them.

2. *Difference from accustomed patterns.* People do not accept new ideas or products if they are radically different from what they know. Cable television companies are finding penetration of the market much slower than originally projected because, among other reasons, people are not accustomed to the idea of paying for television programming.

3. *Competition with prevailing ideas.* New ideas must compete in the marketplace with already accepted ideas. Tobacco companies have slowed the enactment of anti-

smoking laws capitalizing on the prevailing idea that such laws restrict individual freedom and generate more government bureaucracy.

THE DECLINE OF MESSAGE UNDERSTANDING

Messages tend to disintegrate as they pass through various levels of an organizational structure. E. Scannell, author of *Communication for Leadership* (McGraw-Hill, 1970), developed the following chart. It shows, in numerical terms, how much of the original message remains as it travels down the corporate hierarchy:

100 percent	Top management's understanding
66 percent	Vice president's understanding
56 percent	General supervisor's understanding
40 percent	Plant manager's understanding
30 percent	Foreman's understanding
20 percent	Production line worker's understanding

Message entropy, coupled with various barriers to effective communication, is a problem that every professional communicator must overcome.

4. *Necessity for demonstration and proof*. Ideas are more readily accepted if they can be demonstrated and proved. Achieving public support for additional taxes to fund local schools is difficult because it cannot be clearly demonstrated that the quality of teaching and learning would correspondingly improve.

5. *Strength of vested interests*. Vested interests may be strong enough to block innovative concepts. Unions, for example, have been highly successful in forestalling the use of robots in manufacturing plants. Millions of hunters and sports enthusiasts effectively prevent major gun control legislation.

6. *Failure to meet a felt need*. Supporters of a plan to build a large baseball stadium in one California city had trouble selling the idea to voters who felt their tax money should go to something more tangible than "improving the quality of life."

7. *Frequency of reminders*. An idea or a product succeeds only if the public is constantly reminded of it. Advertising and public relations campaigns for a new product may cost millions of dollars and continue over a period of months. The Coca-Cola Company spent $12 million in six months to introduce Diet Coke.

A CHECKLIST

The professional communicator considers a host of variables when planning a message on behalf of an employer or client.

Patrick Jackson, editor of *PR Reporter* and past national president of the Public

Relations Society of America, says communicators should ask several questions about the communication:

1. Is it appropriate?
   a. For the sender?
   b. For the recipient?
2. Is it meaningful?
   a. Does it stick to the subject?
   b. Is it geared to the recipient's interest, not the sender's?
3. Is it memorable?
   a. In phraseology or metaphor?
   b. Through the use of visual or aural devices?
4. Is it understandable?
   a. In both denotative and connotative language?
   b. Graphically or aurally?
5. Is it believable?
   a. Does the audience trust the spokesperson?
   b. Does the communication exhibit expertise in the subject matter?

"Many a wrongly directed or unnecessary communication has been corrected or dropped by using a screen like this," Jackson says. And after all, that is what effective communication is all about.

CASE PROBLEM

Extensive information campaigns are being mounted throughout the world to inform people about the dangers of acquired immune deficiency syndrome (AIDS). Information specialists must utilize a variety of communication tools and messages to create public awareness.

In your estimation, is the general public passive, or is it actively seeking information about AIDS? Depending upon the answer you give, what communication tools and messages do you believe would be most effective in reaching the public? If the public is made aware of the AIDS danger, do you believe that information campaigns will be able to change audience attitudes and behavior? Why or why not?

QUESTIONS FOR REVIEW AND DISCUSSION

1. Why is interpersonal communication the most effective form of communication?

2. Name some reasons why public relations personnel should use a variety of communication vehicles to reach an intended audience.

3. Name and describe the five stages of the process by which new ideas are adopted or new products accepted.

4. What is the role of the mass media in the adoption process? the role of friends and peer groups?

5. What communication methods would you use to reach passive audiences? active information-seeking audiences?

6. What makes a good symbol? a good slogan?

7. How do clichés, hype words, euphemisms, and negative connotations block communication effectiveness?

8. Analyze the *PR Reporter* behavioral communication model. Is it more useful for public relations people than traditional communication models? Why or why not?

9. What guidelines are suggested to avoid discriminatory communication and stereotyping?

10. What are six barriers to effective communication?

11. George Gallup says seven regulators inhibit the absorption of new ideas. Can you name and describe them?

12. In what ways to you think a multicultural workforce will affect employee communications?

SUGGESTED READINGS

Alexander, Pamela. "Avoiding High-Tech Hype." *Public Relations Journal,* March 1989, pp. 9–10.

Allen, Gray. "Valuing Cultural Diversity: Industry Woos a New Work Force." *Communication World,* May 1991, pp. 14–17.

"Are Communicators the Cause or the Solution to the Environmental Dilemma?" *Communication World,* February 1991, pp. 13–25. Various perspectives on the role of public relations spokespersons in the debate about the environment.

Armstrong, John. "Goodbye to the Golden Era of Mass Communication." *Communication World,* May–June 1990, pp. 135–139. The growth of specialized media channels.

"Behavioral Model Replacing Communication Model as Basic Theoretical Underpinning of PR Practice." *PR Reporter,* July 30, 1990, pp. 1–3.

DeFleur, Melvin, and Ball-Rokeach, Sandra. *Theories of Mass Communication.* 5th ed. New York: Longman, 1989. Chapter 9 on "Mass Communications and the Construction of Meaning."

DeVito, Joseph. *Messages: Building Interpersonal Communication Skills.* New York: HarperCollins, 1990.

Hiebert, Ray E., Editor. *Precision Public Relations*. New York: Longman, 1988. Section 5 on "Communicating the Idea," pp. 217–264.

Lutz, William. "Doublespeak." *Public Relations Quarterly,* Winter 1989–90, pp. 25–30.

Miller, Michael. "High-Tech Hype Reaches New Heights." *Wall Street Journal,* January 12, 1989, p. B1.

Parnell, Myrtle, and Vanderkloot, Jo. "How to Build Cross-Cultural Bridges." *Communication World,* July–August 1989, pp. 40–42.

Ward, John R. "Without Listening, There Is No Communication." *Communication World,* July 1990, pp. 20–22.

Williams, Mary V. "Will Diversity = Equality for Multicultural Communicators?" *Communication World,* February 1991, pp. 27–30.

CHAPTER

10

Evaluation

After performing research, the planning and action steps, and then the communication itself, the public relations practitioner must take the final step—evaluation. It is the measurement of results against the established objectives set during the planning process discussed in Chapter 8.

Evaluation is well described by Professor James Bissland of Bowling Green State University. He defines it as "the systematic assessment of a program and its results. It is a means for practitioners to offer accountability to clients—and to themselves."

Results and accountability also are the themes of Professors Glen Broom and David Dozier of San Diego State University. In their text *Using Research in Public Relations,* they state, "Your program is intended to cause observable impact—to change or maintain something about a situation. So, after the program, you use research to measure and document program effects."

Professor Frank Wylie of California State University, Long Beach, summarizes: "We are talking about an orderly evaluation of our progress in attaining the specific objectives of our public relations plan. We are learning what we did right, what we did wrong, how much progress we've made and, most importantly, how can we do it better next time."

The desire to do a better job next time is a major reason for evaluating public relations efforts, but another equally important reason is the widespread adoption of the management-by-objectives system by clients and employers of public relations personnel. They want to know if the money, time, and effort expended on public relations are well spent and contribute to the realization of organizational objectives—whether it is attendance at an open house, product sales, or increased awareness of the organization's community contributions.

This chapter examines the most widely used methods for evaluating a public relations campaign, including measurement of production, distribution, message exposure, message accuracy, audience acceptance, attitude change, and audience action. The merits and shortcomings of the techniques are discussed to provide students with a means of determining the usefulness of a particular approach. We stress the fact that sheer numbers of press clippings, for example, do not necessarily indicate how well a message is getting across to the audience.

OBJECTIVES: A PREREQUISITE FOR EVALUATION

Before any public relations program can be properly evaluated, it is important first to have a clearly established set of objectives. This should be part of the program plan (discussed in Chapter 8), but some points need reviewing because measurement of programs without goals is extremely difficult.

Ketchum Public Relations, in a monograph on public relations programming, points out that a public relations person and management should jointly agree on the criteria that will be used to evaluate the success of attaining objectives. The criteria should be as follows:

1. Realistic (achievable)
2. Credible (the achievement was the result of public relations activity)
3. Specific (avoidance of vague promises)
4. Acceptable (in line with the client's expectations regarding public relations)

Objectives and evaluation criteria must be compatible. If an objective is *informational,* measurement techniques must show how successfully information was communicated to target audiences. Such techniques go under the rubric of "dissemination of message," but they do not measure the effect on attitudes or overt behavior.

On the other hand, *motivational* objectives are more difficult to accomplish. If the objective is to increase sales, it is important to show that public relations efforts caused the increase rather than advertising, lower competitive prices, or other variables. Or, if the objective is to change attitudes, research should be done both before and after the public relations activity, to measure differences in attitude.

In any event, a practitioner should carefully set up objectives in the program plan that can be measured in some way to evaluate the success of public relations activity. The Ketchum Public Relations monograph simply states: "Write the most precise, most results-oriented objectives you can that are realistic, credible, measurable, and compatible with the client's demands on public relations."

CURRENT STATUS OF MEASUREMENT AND EVALUATION

In the past decade, public relations professionals have made considerable progress in evaluation research and the ability to tell clients and employers what has been accomplished. More sophisticated techniques are being used, including computerized news-clip analysis, survey sampling, and attempts to correlate efforts directly with sales.

A large percentage of practitioners, however, still count news clips by the inch or use what Dozier calls a ''seat-of-the-pants'' approach to ''pseudo-evaluation.''

He criticizes public relations managers for simply compiling ''clip-file statistics'' and citing only the amount of media coverage that a particular program or event generated. This is the publicist's approach to evaluation, and, Dozier points out, ''The outcome of a successful public relations program is not a hefty stack of news releases that fatten the practitioner's clip file. . . . Communication is important only in the *effects* it achieves among publics.''

The emphasis on media coverage as an evaluation method is reinforced by a comparative analysis of winning programs in PRSA's national awards program. Bissland found that 79 percent of the winning programs in 1988–1989 used media coverage as an evaluation criterion.

In comparing the 1980–1981 entries with the 1988–1989 winners, however, Bissland did find increased use of other evaluation methods to supplement media coverage. For example, a trend developed for more documentation of (1) actual audiences reached, (2) audience feedback, (3) behavioral science measurements, (4) inferred achievement, and (5) substantiated achievement.

The trend coincided with a decline in such evaluation measures as (1) messages produced, (2) contacts from media, and (3) praise from the employer or client.

Clearly, there is a trend toward greater use of more systematic evaluation mea-

FIGURE 10.1
An analysis of clippings received by Hewlett-Packard concerning the different categories of its work shows the total in each category and how many were positive, negative, and neutral in tone. (Copyright © 1989 The Delahaye Group, Inc.)

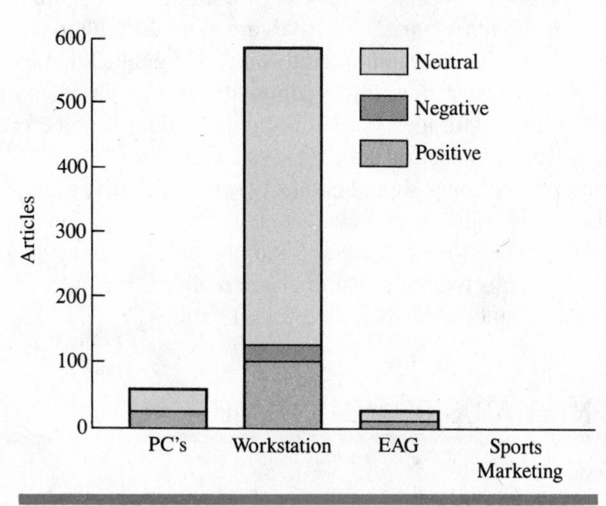

sures. Some reasons that have influenced this trend are (1) more expertise by public relations practitioners who have studied social science research methods as part of their public relations majors in college, (2) more sophisticated computer software programs, (3) the constant pressure of proving to top management that public relations achieves meaningful results, and (4) the need for solid data to make public relations programs more cost-effective.

Despite advances in evaluation techniques, the fact remains that public relations activity is not an exact science and is extremely difficult to measure. As Walter Lindenmann wrote in the *Public Relations Journal*:

> The hunt for the best research techniques has yielded the cold, hard truth that public relations programs are not easy to measure. The campaigns themselves encompass a wide range of variables, including sources, messages, audiences, and the media. In addition, totally isolating the effect of a public relations program from other factors that influence people's opinions and behaviors is nearly impossible.

Not surprisingly, Lindenmann notes, public relations personnel are developing a mix of methods—many borrowed from advertising and marketing—to provide more complete evaluations. On the basic level, the following checklist contains the most important evaluating questions a practitioner should ask.

1. Was the activity or program adequately planned?
2. Did recipients of the message understand it?
3. How could the program strategy have been more effective?
4. Were all primary and secondary audiences reached?
5. Was the desired organizational objective achieved?
6. What unforeseen circumstances affected the success of the program or activity?
7. Did the program or activity fall within the budget set for it?
8. What steps can be taken to improve the success of similar future activities?

MEASUREMENT OF PRODUCTION

One elementary form of evaluation is simply to count how many news releases, feature stories, photos, letters, and the like are produced in a given period of time.

This kind of evaluation is supposed to give management an idea of a staff's productivity. Public relations professionals, however, do not believe that this evaluation is very meaningful because it emphasizes quantity instead of quality. It may be more cost-effective to write fewer news releases and spend more time on the few that really are newsworthy. It may, for example, be more important for a staff person to spend five weeks working on an article for the *Wall Street Journal* or *Fortune* than to write 29 routine personnel releases.

Another side of the production approach is to specify what the public relations person should accomplish in obtaining media coverage. One state trade association evaluated its director of media relations on the expectation that (1) four feature stories would be run in any of the 11 largest newspapers in the state and (2) news releases would be used by at least 20 newspapers, including 5 or more among the 50 largest.

Such evaluation criteria not only are unrealistic but almost impossible to guarantee because media gatekeepers—not the public relations person—make such decisions. Management may argue, however, that such placement goals provide incentive to the public relations staff and are tangible criteria in employee performance evaluation.

AN EVALUATION SAMPLER

Public relations programs are evaluated in more ways than by counting press clippings. Here are some samples from programs that received PRSA Silver Anvil Awards in 1990:

- *Geneva Steel Company, Utah:* The company decided to show its economic impact on the community by paying its employees with $2 bills. Focus groups of community residents four months later showed a high retention rate of the event and its message.
- *Pacific Gas & Electric, San Francisco:* The utility sought to determine community attitudes about the quality of its communications during and just after the earthquake of October 1989. Polls of customers showed that the public's already high opinion of the company was improved. (See Chapter 14.)
- *MSD Agvet, New Jersey:* An extensive campaign to alert dog owners to the dangers of heartworm disease and the existence of a new once-a-month preventive pill resulted in a 27 percent increase in veterinary prescriptions and a 7 percent increase in market share.
- *Atlanta Police Department, Georgia:* An information and recruitment campaign netted 80 new officers. A tracking study showed that 25 percent of the recruits directly resulted from the advertising and public relations campaign.
- *Troy School District, Michigan:* After the defeat of two bond issues to build a new high school, the community passed a third bond issue by a 2–1 margin after a public information campaign.

MEASUREMENT OF DISTRIBUTION

Closely allied to the production of publicity materials is their distribution. Thus a public relations department might report, for instance, that a total of 756 news releases were sent to 819 daily newspapers, 250 weeklies, and 137 trade magazines within one year, or that 110,000 copies of the annual report were distributed to stockholders, security analysts, and business editors. Although such figures may be useful in evaluating how widely a particular piece of publicity was distributed, they do not answer the question of readership or, more important, of attitude change.

MEASUREMENT OF MESSAGE EXPOSURE

The most widely practiced form of evaluating public relations programs is the compilation of press clippings and radio-television mentions. Public relations firms and company departments working primarily on a local basis often have a secretary or intern clip the area newspapers. Large companies with regional, national, or even international outreach usually hire clipping services to scan large numbers of publications. It also is possible to have "electronic" clipping services monitor and tape major radio and television programs on a contractual basis. Burrelle's, for example, monitors nearly 400 local TV stations in 150 cities.

Manning, Selvage & Lee and the Atlanta-based Matlock & Associates used news clips as one measure of their program to publicize the reopening of Underground Atlanta, a specialty marketplace in the downtown area. According to their report, "Underground Atlanta received more than 500 national and local print stories and 300 television segments." And Paul Werth Associates of Columbus, Ohio, assessed its efforts on behalf of the Ohio Department of Health by saying, "More than 2,000 column inches of positive coverage appeared in over 60 newspapers across the state."

This kind of compilation measures the media's acceptance of the story, and shows that the client got extensive media coverage. It also shows that the project accomplished the first stage of the adoption process by making people aware of Underground Atlanta. The statistics, however, do not disclose how many people actually read the stories and, more important, how many absorbed or acted on the information. Media exposure statistics also fail to provide information on whether the news stories caused people to have a more favorable attitude or to act on the information. Other techniques are needed for this kind of evaluation, as is discussed later in this chapter.

GROSS IMPRESSIONS

The way to determine the number of people who may have been exposed to a message is to compile statistics on *gross impressions*—that is, the potential audience reached by a periodical or by a broadcast program.

If, for example, a story about the company appears in the local daily with a circulation of 130,000, the gross impressions figure is 130,000. The evaluation of the Underground Atlanta campaign noted, "The total impressions for the 12-month period, excluding radio coverage, was 200,000,000."

A radio report to management by the public relations department might be designed in the following manner:

Radio	Placements		Gross Impressions		Total Gross Impressions
KGO-AM	6	×	109,000	=	654,000
KCBS-AM	1	×	60,000	=	60,000
KYA	2	×	30,000	=	60,000
KMEL-FM	10	×	35,000	=	350,000
Grand Total:					1,124,000

Gross impressions tabulations commonly are used in advertising to illustrate the penetration of a particular message. The number of gross impressions, however, shows only that the company's message appeared in 130,000 copies of the newspaper, or that a radio announcement potentially reached 109,000 people. It is improbable that all newspaper purchasers or listeners actually received the message.

DOLLAR VALUE

The numbers game is also played by calculating *dollar value*—converting publicity stories in the regular news columns or on the air into equivalent advertising costs. For example, if a five-inch article about the company appeared in a publication that charges $100 per column inch for advertising, a public relations person might report to management that the article was worth $500 to the company. Indeed, one major electronics firm estimated that it had received $158,644 worth of exposure in a single year because of press mentions about the company and its products.

Other examples received PRSA's 1990 Silver Anvil awards:

- *Six Flags Great Adventure, New Jersey*. "The placements reached millions in the target audience and were valued at nearly $350,000."
- *General Aviation Task Force, Alexandria, Virginia:* "Tracked media coverage valued at $5.5 million through clipping services and follow-up calls to media contacts. The agency estimates that for every dollar spent, the client netted $15 worth of coverage."
- *Governor's Chesapeake Bay Communications Office, Maryland:* "The Party on the Bay's estimated publicity value (based on advertising rates) was more than $107,905 in newspaper and television news coverage."

Although such results graphically illustrate an important dimension of publicity and quickly show top management the value of publicity efforts, the technique is a bit like comparing apples and oranges. Advertising copy is directly controlled by the company or institution and can be oriented to specific objectives. News mentions, on the other hand, are determined by media gatekeepers and can be negative, neutral, or favorable. A company purchasing advertising can also control the size and placement of the message in key publications that reach the desired audience. News and features, in contrast, may appear in any number of publications and may be edited to the point that key corporate messages are deleted.

It also becomes a question of what is being measured. Should the article be counted in comparable advertising rates if it is negative? It is doubtful that a company making headlines for closing a plant without notice has garnered thousands of dollars of "free advertising." It is also questionable whether a 15-inch article that mentioned the company only once among six other firms is comparable to 15 column-inches of advertising space. And the numbers game doesn't show that a 4-inch article in the *Wall Street Journal* was more valuable in reaching key publics than the 20-inch article in the Cedar Rapids (Iowa) *Gazette*.

On the other hand, there is an argument that a news story is worth more than a comparable advertisement. James B. Strenski notes, in *Public Relations Quarterly:*

This value equivalency rate for the publicity is actually a conservative figure. It reflects only the cost of the space or air-time. It has no direct one-to-one relationship with the actual value or exposure. It could easily be argued, for example, that the value of the publicity exposure is, in fact, far greater than the equivalent advertising value due to the higher credibility inherent in news and feature exposure.

One final note: the equating of publicity with advertising rates for comparable space does not engender good media relations. The technique reinforces the opinion of many media gatekeepers that all news releases are just attempts to get ''free advertising.''

COST PER PERSON

Another way to evaluate exposure to the message is to find out how much it costs to reach each member of the audience—the *cost per person*.

The technique is commonly used in advertising in order to place costs in perspective. Although a 30-second commercial during a Super Bowl football game telecast may cost $700,000, advertisers feel it is well worth the price because an audience of more than 100 million people is reached. The advertiser has communicated a message to an audience for about seven-tenths of a cent each—a relatively good bargain even if several million viewers take the opportunity to visit the refrigerator while the commercial is playing.

Cost effectiveness, as this technique is known, is used widely in public relations to evaluate collateral materials such as films, brochures, and newsletters. A film produced by Ford Motor Company, for example, may cost $50,000 but may reach 150,000 school children during its distribution period. It thus costs Ford 33 cents to reach each child. Cost effectiveness, of course, is increased if the film is shown to additional children.

Determining the cost effectiveness of public relations materials is very important, and it can help professionals control the price of message exposure. A division of a large corporation had only 500 employees but the monthly magazine cost $3500 to produce and distribute—at $7 per employee. The division quickly decided on a newspaper format that cost only $2 per employee to produce and distribute.

SYSTEMATIC TRACKING

As noted earlier, press clippings are often measured by sheer bulk. Systematic tracking, however, can determine (1) exactly which news releases are most utilized by which periodicals, (2) whether releases are being used by the news media in key market area, and (3) whether the coverage is negative or positive.

A content analysis may show that 40 percent of a company's news releases consist of management and personnel stories, but that these releases account for only 5 percent of the stories published about the company. In contrast, stories about new product developments may constitute only 10 percent of the news releases but amount to 70 percent of the press and broadcast coverage. Given these data, public relations personnel likely will decide to send out fewer personnel stories and more product development articles.

A systematic tracking also can show which publications and broadcast media are using a company's news releases. If only half the publications on a company's mailing list have a record of ever having used company-provided material, it could be wise and cost-effective to cull the mailing list. After such a systematic tracking, Ampex Corporation found that it could reduce its mailing list from 447 publications to 358. Another company might do research to find out why certain publications don't use its material. This research might show that the news releases are too technical or that a certain publication doesn't cover the company's particular industry. Given this information, the company can make adjustments accordingly.

News releases, of course, have value only if they reach appropriate audiences in key market areas. A manufacturer of an expensive consumer product is more interested in having media placements and broadcast mentions in affluent urban areas than in rural areas with smaller populations and less disposable income.

The tone of coverage also is important. Is the media coverage neutral, positive, or negative? Are the product's key attributes and selling points included in the story? Has the television talk-show host or the magazine writer mentioned the brand name? *Sunset* magazine, for example, has a policy against using brand names in articles.

Companies and public relations firms increasingly are doing content analysis of clippings to determine market penetration, tone of coverage, and mention of key copy points. Ketchum Public Relations has developed a computer tracking model that analyzes the amount of media exposure a company gets in the top 120 U.S. markets and even computes a publicity value index, assessing the worth of publicity. PR Data Systems of Wilton, Connecticut, a pioneer in computer analysis of press clippings, has a similar program. Computer profiles can help a company tell exactly what is being published and in what markets. If the profile doesn't match the needs of the company's marketing and sales strategy, the public relations strategy needs restructuring.

REQUESTS AND "800" NUMBERS

Another measure of media exposure is provided by evaluating requests and the use of "800" numbers. Many trade and specialized magazines have cards on which readers can request more information about a specific product by circling a number. If the information is disseminated in a newsletter or brochure, a self-addressed postcard often is enclosed so that more information may be requested. Another method is to telephone people who request information and ask how they heard about the product or service.

A story in a newspaper frequently carries the name and address of the company so readers may request more information. This is often done in the travel and food sections of a newspaper. On broadcast media a product representative may give a demonstration and then tell listeners or viewers how they may receive a book of recipes or other information. The California Prune Board, for example, got 7000 requests for a booklet on exercise and nutrition after its representative appeared on a number of television shows.

A toll-free 800 telephone number also can be used to track the success of a public relations program. The Illinois Department of Public Aid, through the services of Public Communications, Inc., launched a child support enforcement campaign employing news releases, media interviews, bus cards, and billboards to publicize an 800 number that parents could call for assistance in collecting delinquent child support payments. Calls to the number averaged 500 a week at the time of the publicity campaign; the result was that applications for child support enforcement more than doubled from 353 per month to 721 after the campaign was initiated.

AUDIENCE ATTENDANCE

Counting *audience attendance* is a relatively simple way of evaluating the number of people exposed to a message. Publicity about the reopening of Underground Atlanta, for example, motivated more than 1 million people to attend the grand reopening weekend. And publicity during the first month resulted in almost 3 million visitors, against projections of 1 to 2 million.

Poor attendance at a meeting or event can indicate inadequate publicity and promotion. Another major cause is lack of public interest, even when people are aware that a meeting or event is taking place. Low attendance usually results in considerable finger-pointing; thus an objective critique of exactly what happened is good policy in order to avoid future embarrassment.

PILOT TESTS AND SPLIT MESSAGES

Evaluation is important even before a public relations effort is launched. If exposure to a message is to be maximized, it is wise to pretest it with a sample group from the targeted audience. Do its members easily understand the message? Do they accept the message? Does the message motivate them to adopt a new idea or product?

A variation of pretesting is the *pilot test*. Before going national with a public relations message, companies often test the message and key copy points in selected cities to learn how the media accept the message and how the public reacts. This approach is quite common in product marketing because it limits the costs and enables the company to revamp or fine-tune the message for maximum exposure. It also allows the company to switch channels of dissemination if original media channels are not exposing the message to the proper audiences.

The *split-message approach* is common in direct mail publicity campaigns. Two or three different appeals may be prepared by a charitable organization and sent to different audiences. The response rate is then monitored (perhaps the amount of donations is totaled) to learn what message and graphics seemed to be the most effective.

A variation of the split message can even be done in community relations. A company may select two comparable communities and target one of them for an extensive community relations program while the second community remains untouched. After one year, a survey will indicate if the residents of the targeted community have improved their opinions of the company. These results should be compared to those found in a follow-up survey in the community where nothing special was done.

MEASUREMENT OF MESSAGE ACCURACY

The computer analysis of press clippings, which many large public relations firms and corporations now do routinely, is a valuable way to make sure that key copy points are being included in published stories or broadcast items. A company may wish to emphasize in all its publicity materials that it manufactures high-quality kitchen appliances and is a well-established firm with the largest share of the market. Analysis may show that 70 percent of the media stories mention the high quality of the products but that only 20 percent mention or give the impression that the company has the largest share of the market. This kind of evaluation helps the company restructure its news releases so that the percentage of the market is given more emphasis.

MEETING OBJECTIVES

One way to determine whether the media are conveying the key copy points accurately is to measure the *meeting of objectives*—how well the message supports the organization's objectives. If the objective of an organization is to raise $50,000 for charitable purposes, raise sales by 25 percent, get a political candidate elected, or change the attitudes of Americans about oil companies, effective evaluation must be based on achievement of these goals.

Ketchum Public Relations, for example, won a Silver Anvil award from the Public Relations Society of America by showing that its extensive publicity campaign for the California Prune Board resulted in a sales gain of 4 percent for the year (with no advertising involved) after more than five years of declining sales.

Ketchum's objective was to increase prune sales. The strategy was to generate positive awareness among women from 25 to 49 years of age through a campaign with the theme "Prunes . . . Just Plum Good." By using a credible representative and introducing prunes as a health snack food, Ketchum attained its objective by making sure that its publicity and key copy points were accurately disseminated by the media.

AUDIENCE SURVEYS

The other approach to determining the accuracy of the message is to ascertain the knowledge base of potential audiences through *audience surveys*. This can be done in a variety of ways (Chapter 7 outlined such methods as focus groups, random personal or telephone interviews, and the more formalized use of a written questionnaire).

The objective here is to measure comprehension, not necessarily to learn whether the audience agrees or disagrees with the message or plans to do anything about it. Multiple-choice items on a questionnaire may simply ask the person to match concepts and images with a specific organization. For example, Mobil Corporation wants to be positioned as a strong supporter of the arts and the Public Broadcasting Service. A multiple-choice question may ask:

What company sponsors "Masterpiece Theatre" on public television?

a. General Electric

b. Texaco Oil Company

c. Mobil Corporation

d. Chrysler Corporation

e. Chevron Corporation

If the majority of respondents select Mobil as the correct answer, the idea is supported that this particular message has been adequately understood.

Another way of measuring audience comprehension is the day-after recall. Under this method, participants are asked to view a specific television program; then they are called the next day to learn which messages they remembered.

Ketchum Public Relations, on behalf of the California Prune Board, used this technique to determine if a 15-city media tour was conveying the message that prunes are a high-fiber food source. Forty women in Detroit considered likely to watch daytime television shows were asked to view a particular program on which a Prune Board spokesperson would appear. The day after the program, Ketchum asked the women questions about the show, including their knowledge of the fiber content of prunes.

Ninety-three percent of the women remembered the Prune Board spokesperson and 65 percent, on an unaided basis, named prunes as a source of high fiber.

MEASUREMENT OF AUDIENCE ACCEPTANCE

So far, techniques of measuring audience exposure and accurate dissemination of the message have been discussed. It is important, however, for the public relations person also to know if the target audience has accepted the message. Does the recipient agree with the information?

Audience acceptance of a message concerns the formation of attitudes rather than the acceptance of factual information. A person may easily identify Mobil Corporation as the sponsor of "Masterpiece Theatre" on public television but may or may not agree that Mobil is a company that practices a high degree of social responsibility—the real message that Mobil wants to communicate through such sponsorship.

Again, surveys or interviews can be used to discover whether audiences agree or disagree with opinion statements. As noted in Chapter 7, the most commonly used is a Likert scale, in which respondents can indicate the extent of their agreement with an opinion statement. For example:

Mobil makes significant contributions to the arts in America and is a socially responsible company.

_____ Strongly agree (5)
_____ Agree (4)
_____ Undecided (3)
_____ Disagree (2)
_____ Strongly disagree (1)

Depending on the results of such a survey, Mobil may decide that more public relations efforts are needed in order to gain acceptance of its message among the American public. Or, if people do agree with the statement, only reinforcement of the message is needed.

On a more informal basis acceptance of the message can also be determined by noting what critics of business continue to write or talk about, proposed legislation restricting profit levels of companies, the nature of letters to the editor in magazines and newspapers, and the results of national opinion polls conducted by Gallup or Harris.

MEASUREMENT OF ATTITUDE CHANGE

Public relations efforts designed to change a person's perceptions and opinions are even more difficult to evaluate than determining acceptance of the message.

A major technique to determine attitude change is the *benchmark study*. Basically, it is a measurement of audience attitudes before, during, and after a public relations campaign. This kind of study graphically shows the percentage difference in attitudes as a result of increased information and publicity. There are, of course, a number of possible intervening variables that may account for changes in attitude, but statistical analysis of variance can help pinpoint to what degree the attitude change is attributable to public relations efforts.

Mobil, General Electric, AT&T, and other Fortune 500 companies regularly utilize benchmark surveys to measure the effectiveness of public relations campaigns. Surveys before and after specific campaigns document to a great extent the impact of public relations efforts. Continuing surveys, for example, show that Mobil's sponsorship of "Masterpiece Theatre" on PBS has gained the company a reputation among opinion leaders for corporate leadership and social responsibility.

Dow Chemical Company's effort to improve its corporate image also was tracked among key audiences during an extensive public relations campaign, and favorable attitudes continually increased throughout the program. The major advantage of continuous tracking is the ability to fine-tune and adjust the program as it proceeds. Dow's program is discussed in Chapter 14.

MEASUREMENT OF AUDIENCE ACTION

The ultimate objective of any public relations effort is to make something happen. This takes us back to the beginning portion of the chapter which pointed out that the purpose of public relations activity is to advance organizational objectives.

The objective of the amateur theater group is not to get media publicity; the objective is to sell tickets. The objective of an environmental organization like Greenpeace is not to get editorials written in favor of whales, but to motivate the public (1) to write elected officials, (2) to send donations for its preservation efforts, and (3) to get protective legislation passed. The objective of a company is to sell its products, and the creation of goodwill through public relations is one method to accomplish this objective.

Thus it can be seen that public relations efforts are ultimately evaluated on how they help the organization achieve its objectives. The evidence may be as follows:

1. The increase in number or amount of donations to a charitable agency
2. Sales of the product or service

3. The number of letters written to members of Congress about a public issue
4. The election of a candidate
5. The defeat or passage of proposed legislation
6. Attendance at a conference or symposium

Other changes in behavior can be ascertained through surveys to determine if people have altered their personal patterns. Have they quit smoking? Have they decided to get an annual physical checkup? Have they reduced their alcohol consumption? Are they driving more carefully? How people answer often depends on the public relations efforts of organizations and groups interested in such matters.

Change can also be tracked by informal or formal observation of audience behavior. In recent years, utilities have launched extensive information campaigns about energy conservation. The success of such efforts can partly be noted in the reduced energy consumption per household, as shown on individual bills, or by observing thermostat settings during a door-to-door survey. In some ways, observation is more valid than survey data. People may state on a survey questionnaire that they have a commitment to energy conservation, but their actual behavior—leaving lights on and keeping the thermostat up—may negate their good intentions.

MEASUREMENT OF SUPPLEMENTAL ACTIVITIES

COMMUNICATION AUDIT

The entire communication activity of an organization should be evaluated at least once a year to make sure that every primary and secondary public is receiving appropriate messages.

David Hilton-Barber, past president of the Public Relations Institute of South Africa, has written:

> The most important reasons for an audit are to help establish communication goals and objectives, to evaluate long-term programs, to identify strengths and weaknesses, and to point up any areas which require increased activity.
>
> . . . A communications audit can be useful at any time, but is especially appropriate when a company changes direction—changes product/service emphasis, goes public, merges or acquires—or when there is a change in management. The audit is also useful when management senses that something is wrong with its communications efforts and wants to find out what it is—or when a communications function is being created or restructured.

A communication audit, as an assessment of an organization's entire communication program, could include the following:

1. Analysis of all communication activities—newsletters, memos, policy statements, brochures, annual reports, position papers, mailing lists, media contacts, personnel forms, graphics, logos, advertising, receptionist contacts, waiting lounges for visitors, and so on
2. Informal interviews with rank-and-file employees and middle management and top executives

3. Informal interviews with community leaders, media gatekeepers, consumers, distributors, and other influential persons in the industry

A number of research techniques, as outlined in Chapter 7, can be utilized during a communication audit—including mail and telephone surveys, focus groups, and so forth. The important point is that the communications of an organization should be analyzed from every possible angle, with the input of as many publics as possible. Security analysts may have something to say about the quality of the company's financial information; municipal leaders are best qualified to evaluate the company's efforts in community relations. Consumers, if given a chance, will make suggestions about quality of sales personnel and product instruction booklets.

The box here shows how a company can evaluate the effectiveness of its public relations messages. The questions it asks force a practitioner to assess a program critically to determine how well it worked.

After an audit is completed, a written set of recommendations should be made to top management suggesting better ways to communicate effectively.

MEETINGS AND EVENTS

It has already been pointed out that meetings can be evaluated to some degree by the level of attendance. Such data provide information about the number of people exposed to a message, but still don't answer the more crucial question of what they thought about the meeting.

Public relations people often get an informal sense of an audience's attitudes by its behavior. A standing ovation, spontaneous applause, complimentary remarks as people leave, and even the expressions on people's faces provide clues as to how a meeting was received. On the other hand, if people are not responsive, if they ask questions about subjects supposedly explained, if they express doubts or antagonism, the meeting can be considered only partly successful.

Public relations practitioners use a number of information methods to evaluate the success of a meeting, but they also employ more systematic methods. The most common technique is an evaluation sheet that participants fill out at the end of the meeting.

A simple form asking people to rate such items as location, costs, facilities, and program on a 1-to-5 scale (one being the best) can be used. Other forms may ask people to rate aspects of a conference or meeting as (1) Excellent, (2) Good, (3) Average, and (4) Could be better.

Evaluation forms also can ask how people heard about the program and what suggestions they would make for future meetings.

The systematic gathering of such information enables meeting planners to pinpoint problem areas and to recognize which aspects of the program went especially well. A better meeting then can be planned next time. The evaluation thus is not just an analysis of a past event but the start of planning for future activities.

NEWSLETTERS

Editors of newsletters should evaluate readership annually. Such an evaluation can help ascertain (1) reader perceptions, (2) the degree to which stories are balanced, (3) the kinds of stories that have high reader interest, (4) additional topics that should

COMMUNICATIONS AUDIT FOR AN AUDIENCE OF DAILY NEWSPAPER FOOD EDITORS

	INDEPENDENT VARIABLES				
DEPENDENT VARIABLES	**Source (Who)**	**Message (What)**	**Audience (To Whom)**	**Channel (How)**	**Destination (Intended Effect)**
Output **Exposure (Presentation)**	Company's public relations department	Product is nutritious and tasty	Food editors, 50 largest U.S. dailies	Press releases and deskside briefings leading to news and feature articles	Pay attention to key messages; understand them; pass them along to readers
Outcomes **Attention (Receptivity)**	To whom else are editors listening?	What messages are editors receiving?	Are editors directing their messages to female readers?	Are female readers paying attention?	Are editors and female readers paying attention?
Comprehension (Awareness/ understandability)	How credible are editors' information sources?	What do editors understand about the product?	Do female readers understand messages from food editors?	Do female readers understand what is in articles?	Do both understand what the company is saying?
Yielding (Change of opinion/ attitude)	How have the editors' views toward the company changed?	How have editors' attitudes toward the messages changed?	Are female readers changing their opinions as a result of the publicity?	Do their views change based on what's in the food pages?	Is there opinion or attitude change—if so, in what direction, what magnitude, etc?
Retention (Are they retaining messages?)	What do editors remember about sources?	What do editors recall about the messages?	Are female readers retaining the key messages?	Do they retain what's in the food pages?	What's the overall retention level?
Action (Behavior change)	To whom are editors turning for more information?	Are the editors passing along the desired messages?	Are these female readers buying the product or writing the company for recipes?	What actions do women take based on the food-page publicity?	What's happening as a result of the publicity efforts?

Source: Walter Lindenmann, ''Beyond the Clipbook,'' in *Public Relations Journal,* December 1988.

be covered, (5) credibility of the publication, and (6) the extent to which it is meeting organizational objectives.

Systematic evaluation, it should be emphasized, it not based on whether all the copies are distributed or picked up. This information doesn't tell the editor what the audience actually read, retained, or acted upon. A newsletter, newspaper, or even a brochure can be evaluated in a number of ways. The methods include (1) content analysis, (2) readership interest surveys, (3) readership recall of articles actually read, (4) application of readability formulas, and (5) use of advisory boards.

Content Analysis From a representative sample of past issues, stories may be categorized under general headings such as (1) management announcements, (2) new product developments, (3) new personnel and retirements, (4) features about employees, (5) corporate finances, (6) news of departments and divisions, and (7) job-related information.

Such a systematic analysis will show what percentage of the publication is devoted to each category. It may be found that one division rarely is covered in the employee newsletter or that management pronouncements tend to dominate the entire publication. Given the content-analysis findings, editors may wish to shift the content somewhat.

Readership Interest Surveys The purpose of these surveys is to get feedback about the types of stories employees are most interested in reading.

The most common method is simply to provide a long list of generic story topics and have employees rate each as (1) Important, (2) Somewhat important, or (3) Not important. The International Association of Business Communicators (IABC) conducted such a survey on behalf of several dozen companies and found that readers were not very interested in "personals" about other employees (birthdays, anniversaries, and the like).

A readership interest survey becomes even more valuable when it is compared with the content analysis of a publication. Substantial differences signal a possible need for changes in the editorial content.

Article Recall The best kind of readership survey occurs when trained interviewers ask a sampling of employees what they have read in the latest issue of the publication.

Employees are shown the publication page by page and asked to indicate which articles they have read. As a check on the tendency of employees to report that they have read everything, interviewers also ask them (1) how much of each article they have read and (2) what the articles were about. The results are then content-analyzed to determine which kinds of articles have the most readership.

A variation of the readership recall technique involves individual evaluation of selected articles for accuracy and clarity. For example, an article about a new production process may be sent before or after publication to the head of production for evaluation. On a form with a rating scale of Excellent, Good, Fair, and Deficient, the person may be asked to evaluate the article on the basis of such factors as (1) technical data provided, (2) organization, (3) length, (4) clarity of technical points, and (5) quality of illustrations.

Readability It is important to ensure that employees understand the story even if it concerns technical data. Although the source of the article—a scientist or an engineer—thoroughly understands the multisyllabic words, workers on the assembly line may find the material over their heads. The use of jargon also creeps into publications unless there is constant monitoring. For effective communication, of course, it is necessary to write at the educational level of the organization's employees. (For a further discussion of jargon and word choice, see ''Writing for Clarity'' in Chapter 9.)

Readability can be assessed by using such common formulas as those of Rudolf Flesch and Robert Gunning, or the Cloze procedure. Basically these methods allow a researcher to determine the comprehension level of copy by determining the average length of sentences and the number of multisyllabic words used. Some methods also include the number of personal pronouns. In general, material is more readable if the sentences are simple and short, and there are many one- or two-syllable words.

One solution to the problem of producing a publication suitable for disparate groups is to prepare several periodicals or brochures. Scientists and engineers may get one newsletter and assembly-line workers another.

Advisory Boards Periodic feedback and evaluation can be provided by organizing an employee advisory board that meets several times a year to discuss the direction and content of the publication. This is a useful technique because it expands the editor's feedback network and elicits comments that employees might be hesitant to tell the editor face-to-face.

A variation of the advisory board method is periodically to invite a sampling of employees to meet to discuss the publication. This approach is more systematic than just soliciting comments from employees in the hallway or cafeteria.

CASE PROBLEM

The Etak Navigator is the world's first practical vehicle navigation system. The easy-mounted viewing screen displays electronic road maps that provide a continuous, automatic pinpointing of your location, with your destination marked by a flashing star.

Etak and its partner, General Motors, say this revolutionary product will eliminate the need for cumbersome maps and the fear of getting lost in large urban areas like Los Angeles.

Your public relations firm is retained to introduce the Etak Navigator to the media through a news conference, a press kit, news releases, and interviews on broadcast talk shows.

What methods would you use to evaluate the effectiveness of your public relations efforts on behalf of this ''user-friendly'' twenty-first-century product that is available today?

QUESTIONS FOR REVIEW AND DISCUSSION

1. What is the role of stated objectives in evaluating public relations programs? What is the difference between informational and motivational objectives?

2. What primary method of evaluation do public relations people use? Is there any evidence that other methods are increasingly being used?

3. What are some general types of evaluation questions that a person should ask about a program?

4. Name four ways that publicity activity is evaluated. What, if any, are the drawbacks to each one?

5. Do you think news stories about a product or service should be evaluated in terms of comparable advertising costs? Why or why not?

6. What are the advantages of systematic tracking and content analysis of news clippings?

7. How are pilot tests and split messages used to determine suitability of a message?

8. How does measurement of message accuracy differ from measurement of audience acceptance of the message?

9. How are benchmark studies used in evaluation of public relations programs?

10. What is a communication audit?

11. What methods of evaluation can be done for a company newsletter or magazine?

SUGGESTED READINGS

Bissland, James. "Accountability Gap: Evaluation Practices Show Improvement." *Public Relations Review,* Summer 1990, pp. 25–35.

Broom, Glen, and Dozier, David. *Using Research in Public Relations.* Englewood Cliffs, NJ: Prentice Hall, 1990. Chapter 4, "Using Research to Evaluate Programs," pp. 71–88.

Dozier, David. "Planning Evaluation in PR Practice." *Public Relations Review,* Summer 1985, pp. 17–24.

Hiebert, Ray E., Editor. *Precision Public Relations.* New York: Longman, 1988. Section 6, "Evaluating the Results," pp. 265–323.

Jeffers, Dennis W. "Using Public Relations Theory to Evaluate Specialized Magazines as Communication Channels." Chapter 6 of *Public Relations Research Annual,* edited by James Grunig and Larissa Grunig, Volume 1. Hillsdale, NJ: Lawrence Erlbaum Associates, 1989, pp. 115–124.

Leahigh, Alan K. "Marketing Communications: If You Can't Count It, Does It Count?" *Public Relations Quarterly,* Winter 1985, pp. 23–27.

Lesly, Philip. "Multiple Measurements of Public Relations." *Public Relations Review,* Summer 1986, pp. 3–8.

Lindenmann, Walter. "Beyond the Clipbook." *Public Relations Journal,* December 1988, pp. 22–26.

Lindenmann, Walter. "Research, Evaluation and Measurement: A National Perspective." *Public Relations Review,* Summer 1990, pp. 3–16.

Piekos, Jennie, and Einsiedel, Edna. "Roles and Program Evaluation: Techniques Among Canadian Public Relations Practitioners." Chapter 4 of *Public Relations Research Annual,* edited by James Grunig and Larissa Grunig, Volume 2. Hillsdale, NJ: Lawrence Erlbaum Associates, 1990, pp. 95–114.

Tortorello, Nicholas, and Dowgiallo, Ed. "Evaluating the Impact of Public Relations." *Public Relations Journal,* November 1990, pp. 34, 36–37.

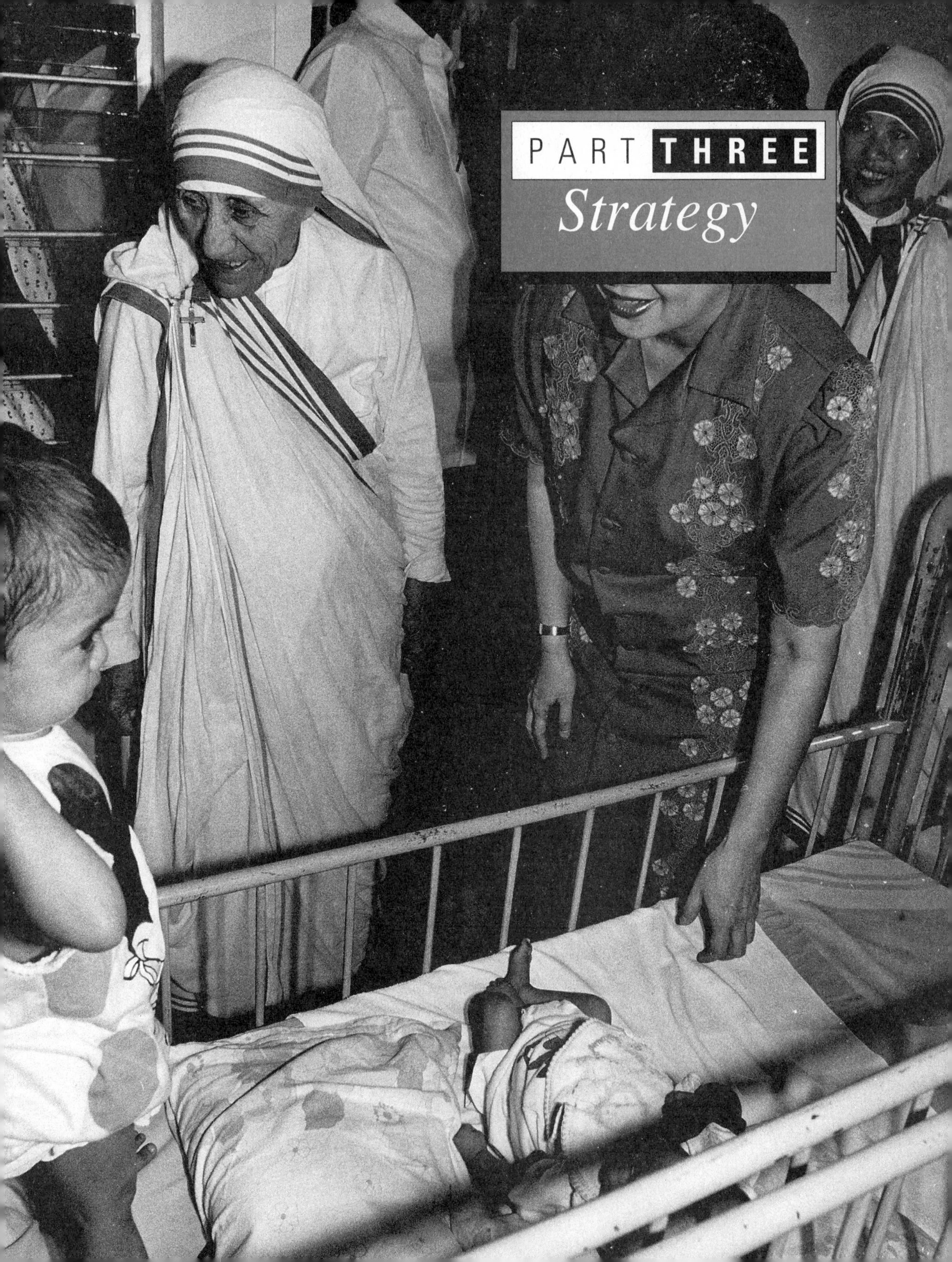

PART THREE
Strategy

CHAPTER

Public Opinion and Persuasion

''The public be damned'' was the comment attributed to railroad tycoon William Vanderbilt in the 1880s. Earlier in the century, Sir Robert Peel wrote: ''Public opinion is a compound of folly, weakness, prejudice, wrong feeling, right feeling, obstinacy, and newspaper paragraphs.''

Neither thought much of public opinion, but it has emerged as a powerful force in the late twentieth century. Cutlip, Center, and Broom, authors of *Effective Public Relations,* for example, have written: ''The power of public opinion must be faced, understood, and dealt with. It provides the psychological environment in which organizations prosper or perish.''

Public relations personnel in particular should know what constitutes public opinion and how this major force is formed. They are constantly engaged in interpreting shifts in public opinion and at the same time attempting to influence it through persuasive communications. They are active participants in the marketplace of ideas. As such, public relations people are an essential part of freedom of inquiry and expression that leads to democratic decision-making.

In its examination of public opinion, the chapter discusses the role of opinion leaders, both formal and informal. It outlines the methods that practitioners use in gauging public opinion. Factors in persuasion, including source credibility, audience analysis, and appeal to self-interest, are detailed. Also covered are clarity of message, timing and context, audience participation, suggestions for action, content and structure of messages, and persuasive speaking. The chapter ends with a review of ethical guidelines for those who use persuasion on behalf of an employer or client.

WHAT IS PUBLIC OPINION?

Americans talk about public opinion as if it were a monolithic entity overshadowing the entire landscape. Editorial cartoonists, in contrast, humanize it in the form of John Q. or Jane Publics, characters who symbolize what people think about any given issue. The reality is that public opinion is somewhat elusive and extremely difficult to measure at any given moment.

In fact, to continue the metaphor, public opinion is a number of monoliths and John and Jane Q. Publics all existing at the same time. Few issues create unanimity of thought among the population, and public opinion on any issue is split in several directions. It may also come as a surprise to note that only a small number of people, at any given time, take part in public opinion formation on a specific issue.

There are two reasons for this. First, psychologists have found that the public tends to be passive. Few issues generate an opinion or feeling on the part of an entire citizenry. It is often assumed that a small, vocal group represents the attitude of the public when, in reality, it is more accurate to say that the majority of the people—because the issue doesn't interest or affect them—are apathetic. Thus, "public" opposition to nuclear power plants is really the view of a small, but significant, number of Americans who are concerned about the issue.

Second, one issue may engage the attention of one part of the population, while another arouses the interest of another segment. Parents in a community, for example, may form public opinion on the need for improved secondary education, while senior citizens constitute the bulk of public opinion on the need for increased Social Security benefits.

These two examples illustrate the most common definition of public opinion: "Public opinion is the sum of individual opinions on an issue *affecting* those individuals." Another popular definition states: "Public opinion is a collection of views held by persons *interested* in the subject." Thus a person unaffected by or uninterested in (and perhaps unaware of) an issue does not contribute to public opinion on the subject.

Inherent in these definitions is the concept of *self-interest*. The following statements appear in the literature of public opinion:

1. Public opinion is the collective expression of opinion of many individuals bound into a group by common aims, aspirations, needs, and ideals.

2. People who are interested or who have a vested or *self-interest* in an issue—or who can be affected by the outcome of the issue—form public opinion on that particular item.

3. Psychologically, opinion basically is determined by *self-interest*. Events, words, or any other stimuli affect opinion only insofar as their relationship to *self-interest* or a general concern is apparent.

4. Opinion does not remain aroused for any long period of time unless people feel their *self-interest* is acutely involved or unless opinion—aroused by words—is sustained by events.

5. Once *self-interest* is involved, opinion is not easily changed.

How practitioners utilize the concept of self-interest in focusing their message to fit the audience is discussed under "Appeal to Self-Interest," later in this chapter.

The literature also emphasizes the importance of *events* in the formation of public opinion. Social scientists, for example, have made the following generalizations:

1. Opinion is highly sensitive to *events* that have an impact on the public at large or a particular segment of the public.

2. By and large, public opinion does not anticipate *events*. It only reacts to them.

3. *Events* trigger formation of public opinion. Unless people are aware of an issue, they are not likely to be concerned or have an opinion. Awareness and discussion lead to crystallizing of opinions and often a consensus among the public.

4. *Events* of unusual magnitude are likely to swing public opinion temporarily from one extreme to another. Opinion does not stabilize until the implication of the event is seen with some perspective.

An example of an event that triggered formation of public opinion—and caused people to swing from apathy to outrage—was the Exxon oil spill in Alaska. During the first month after the spill, media coverage was intense, and polls showed rapid growth in the public's support for environmental causes. Memberships in environmental organizations soared; there were many calls for legislation to prevent future spills. As the months went by and media coverage thinned, polls showed that Americans had considerably moderated their initial feelings. However, public opinion experts believe that the event set in motion political forces that in the long run will lead to tougher environmental legislation. (Exxon is discussed in detail in Chapter 14.)

It also has been found that people have more opinions and are able to form opinions more easily with respect to goals than with the methods necessary to reach those goals. Thus there is fairly strong public opinion, according to polls, in favor of improving the quality of the nation's schools. There is not much agreement, however, on how this goal should be accomplished. One group advocates higher salaries for "master" teachers, while another equally vocal group endorses substantial tax increases for school operations. A third group thinks more rigorous standards will solve the problem. All three groups, plus assorted other ones with still other solutions, make up public opinion on the subject.

OPINION LEADERS AS CATALYSTS

Public opinion on an issue may have its roots in self-interest or in events, but the primary catalyst is public discussion. Only in this way does opinion begin to crystallize, and pollsters can measure it.

Serving as catalysts for the formation of public opinion are people who are knowledgeable and articulate about specific issues. They are called *opinion leaders*. Sociologists describe them as (1) highly interested in the subject or issue, (2) better informed on the issue than the average person, (3) avid consumers of mass media, (4) early adopters of new ideas, and (5) good organizers who can get other people to take action.

TYPES OF LEADERS

Sociologists traditionally have defined two types of leaders. First are the *formal opinion leaders,* so called because of their positions as elected officials, presidents of companies, or heads of membership groups. Often news reporters ask them for statements when a specific issue relates to their areas of responsibility or concern. People in formal leadership positions also are called *power leaders*.

Second are the *informal opinion leaders,* who have clout with peers because of some special characteristic. They may be *role models* who are admired and emulated, or opinion leaders because they can exert peer pressure on others to go along with something. *Cheerleaders* boost morale and action among peers; *celebrities* can be influential because they attract attention and make people aware of a topic. In general, informal opinion leaders exert considerable influence on their peer groups by being highly informed, articulate, and credible on particular issues. Teenagers, for example, are influential with their parents when it comes to buying a personal computer, a new car, or even a television set. In many cases, they are more knowledgeable than their parents about innovations in technology.

THE FLOW OF OPINION

Many public relations campaigns, particularly those in the public affairs area, concentrate on identifying and reaching key opinion leaders who are pivotal to the success or failure of an idea or project. Sociologists Daniel Katz and Paul Lazarsfeld in the 1940s discovered the importance of opinion leaders during a study of how people chose candidates in an election. They found that the mass media had minimal influence on electoral choices, but voters did rely on person-to-person communication with formal and informal opinion leaders.

These findings became known as the *two-step flow theory of communication*. Although later research confirmed that it really was a multiple-step flow, the basic idea remained intact. Public opinion is really formed by the views of people who have taken the time to sift information, evaluate it, and form an opinion that is expressed to others.

The *multiple-step flow model* is graphically illustrated by a series of concentric circles. In the epicenter of action are opinion-makers. They derive large amounts of information from the mass media and other sources, and share that information with people in the adjoining concentric circle, who are labeled the ''attentive public.'' These latter are interested in the issue but rely on opinion leaders to provide synthesized information and interpretation. The outer ring consists of the ''inattentive public.'' They are unaware of or uninterested in the issue and remain outside the opinion-formation process. The multiple-step flow theory, however, means that some will eventually become interested in, or at least aware of, the issue.

THE MEDIA'S ROLE

The mass media, of course, pervade all three concentric circles, but only opinion leaders actively use the information. An opinion leader on local politics, for example, avidly reads stories and editorial comment about the affairs of the city, while a member of the inattentive public may skip such reading in favor of the sports page. It should be noted, however, that the devoted sports-page reader may be an informal opinion leader among his or her friends about who is the best player in the league.

Lazarsfeld and Katz's point is that the influence of the mass media is exaggerated. It is now generally accepted that the mass media serve the primary role of *agenda-setters*. They tell the public, through selection of stories and headlines, what to think about—but not what to think. For opinion leaders they are an information source but not (except for editorial comment) a source of ready-made opinions. Social scientist Joseph Klapper coined the name for this phenomenon—the "limited effects" model of mass media. He postulated, "Mass media ordinarily does not serve as a necessary and sufficient cause for audience effects, but rather functions among and through a nexus of mediating factors and influences."

Although this understanding of mass media influence is generally valid, other research indicates that there are some exceptions. When people have no prior information or attitude disposition regarding a subject, the mass media do play a role in telling people what to think. Psychologist Carl Hovland says people tend to change their perceptions if the information and opinion provided (by mass media or other sources) are not ego-involving or contradictory to previous experiences. Thus a person who doesn't know much about the state budget tends to accept the newspaper's headline "School Officials Call Budget a Disaster."

Opinion-makers tend to get their information not only from the mass media but from other highly specialized sources. The opinion leader on environmental problems, for example, reads various newsletters, government reports, and specialized magazines. He or she also attends meetings and conventions during which environmental topics are discussed.

Chapter 9, concerning the process of communication, has already pointed out that the mass media are most influential in making people aware of an issue or topic. Motivating and influencing people comprise a more complex process that requires thorough knowledge of formal and informal opinion leaders as receivers of communication and conduits of persuasion.

PUBLIC OPINION AND PUBLIC RELATIONS

Understanding public opinion and how it is formed is fundamental to public relations. Such knowledge enables the practitioner to (1) effectively monitor shifts in public opinion, (2) pinpoint formal and informal opinion leaders who should be reached with specific messages, and (3) understand that dissemination of information through the mass media can only create awareness, not tell people what to think.

Public relations people use a number of methods to monitor public opinion. They include the following:

1. *Personal contacts*. Friends, business associates, consultants, opinion leaders, customers, and employees.

2. *Media reports*. News stories, letters to the editor, op-ed (opposite the editorial page) articles, and editorials.

3. *Field reports*. Questions, inquiries, complaints, suggestions, and compliments expressed by salespeople and customers.

4. *Letters and telephone calls*. The tracking and monitoring of patterns that might indicate necessary changes in policies—communication messages.

5. *Advisory committees*. Citizen committees to provide feedback on proposed policies, ideas, and public relations programming.

6. *Staff meetings*. An opportunity to share knowledge gleaned from experience and informal research.

7. *Polling/sampling*. Systematic research on public attitudes and interests (see Chapter 7).

Failure to monitor public attitudes and consult opinion leaders can cause a number of problems for an organization.

The California battle against the invasion of the Mediterranean fruit fly is a good example. State and federal officials finally decided that aerial spraying of malathion over urban areas was necessary to eradicate the pest. Permission to spray, however, required the consent of 14 city councils in the San Francisco Bay area.

Medfly officials, without any monitoring of public concerns about spraying or even consulting with the key opinion leaders in government and citizen organizations, simply went to scheduled city council meetings and made a request. This caught city officials off-guard and without adequate background information. On the other hand, environmentalists, highly organized, testified against aerial spraying. Given the situation, each city council promptly voted against the request.

The ultimate result was a delay of several months while Medfly officials went back to square one and started the tedious process of building support for aerial spraying. The project lost valuable time simply because officials had failed to do their homework about the necessity of preselling aerial spraying to civic and community leaders before requesting permission. Background briefing sessions would have gone a long way in allaying public fears and answering the charges of environmental groups. Once key opinion leaders understood the necessity of aerial spraying, the two-step flow process was instrumental in getting community support.

A contrast to the Medfly failure is the success of an electronics company that was successful in building a plant in a small Oregon community after other firms had failed to get city approval. The key to success was the effort by the company's public relations staff to contact local opinion leaders and civic officials before final plans were announced. Discussion of the company's projected plans gave local opinion leaders an opportunity to make suggestions and also to participate in the decision-making process. As a result they announced support of the new plant to their followers. This illustrates another aspect of public opinion. *People who participate in solving a problem are more likely to support the implementation of the solution.*

PERSUASION: PERVASIVE IN OUR LIVES

It is difficult to imagine any human activity in which persuasion does not exist. The process involves everybody from children convincing parents that bedtime should be

THE LIFE CYCLE OF PUBLIC OPINION

Public opinion and persuasion are important catalysts in the formation of a public issue and its ultimate resolution. The natural evolution of an issue involves five stages:

Definition of the issue. Activist and special-interest groups raise an issue, perhaps a protest against scenic areas being threatened by logging or strip mining. These groups have no formal power but serve as "agenda stimuli" for the media that cover controversy and conflict. Visual opportunities for television coverage occur when activists hold rallies and demonstrations.

Involvement of opinion leaders. Through media coverage, the issue is put on the public agenda and people become aware of it. Opinion leaders begin to discuss the issue and perhaps see it as symbolic of broader environmental issues.

Public awareness. As public awareness grows, the issue becomes a matter of public discussion and debate, with extensive media coverage. Complexity of the issue is simplified by the media into a "them vs. us" issue. Suggested solutions tend to be at either end of the spectrum.

Government/regulatory involvement. Public consensus begins to build for a resolution as government/regulatory involvement occurs. Large groups identify with some side of the issue. Demand grows for government to act.

Resolution. The resolution stage begins as people with power and authority (elected officials) draft legislation or interpret existing rules and regulations to make a statement. A decision is made to protect the scenic areas, or to reach a compromise with advocates of development. If some groups are unhappy with the outcome, however, the cycle may repeat itself.

delayed a half hour to a salesperson who makes a living persuading people to buy a product. Friends persuade each other when debating what movie to see. Employees try to persuade bosses that they deserve a raise.

The study of persuasion was central to the education of the Greeks. Aristotle was the first to set down the ideas of *ethos, logos,* and *pathos,* which roughly translate as "source credibility," "logical argument," and "emotional appeal."

DEFINITIONS OF PERSUASION

Winston Brembeck and William Howell, two communication experts, have described *persuasion* as "communication to influence choices." A longer description is "any communication, intended or not, that causes a change in a receiver's attitude, belief, or action." Another definition is "a process that changes attitudes, beliefs, opinions, or behaviors."

STRATEGY

USES OF PERSUASION

The strategies of persuasion are used daily by public relations practitioners because their job is to engage in purposive communication—with the objective of influencing people in some way.

Persuasion is used to (1) change or neutralize hostile opinions, (2) crystallize latent opinions and positive attitudes, and (3) conserve favorable opinions.

The most difficult persuasion task is to turn hostile opinions into favorable ones. There is much truth to the adage "Don't confuse me with the facts; my mind is made up." Once people have decided, for instance, that oil companies are making excessive profits or that a nonprofit agency is wasting public donations, they tend to ignore or disbelieve any contradictory information. Everyone, as Walter Lippmann has described, has pictures in his or her head based on an individual perception of reality. People generalize from personal experience and what peers tell them. For example, if a person has an encounter with a rude clerk, the inclination is to generalize that the entire department store chain is not very good. The self-perception of the audience is a barrier to communication that will be discussed later in this chapter.

The task of persuasion is much easier if the message is compatible with a person's general disposition toward a subject. If a person tends to identify Toyota as a company with a good reputation, he or she may express this feeling by purchasing one of its cars. Nonprofit agencies usually crystallize the public's latent inclination to aid the less fortunate by asking for a donation. Both examples illustrate the reason that organizations strive to have a good reputation—it is translated into sales and donations. The concept of message channeling will be discussed in more detail later in the chapter.

The easiest form of persuasion is communication that reinforces favorable opinions. Public relations people, by providing a steady stream of reinforcing messages, keep the reservoir of goodwill in sound condition. More than one organization has survived a major problem because public esteem for the organization tended to minimize current difficulties. Continual efforts to maintain the reservoir of goodwill is called *preventive public relations*—the most effective of all.

FACTORS IN PERSUASIVE COMMUNICATION

A number of factors are involved in persuasive communication, and the public relations practitioner should be knowledgeable about each one. The following is a brief discussion of (1) audience analysis, (2) source credibility, (3) appeal to self-interest, (4) clarity of message, (5) timing and context, (6) audience participation, (7) suggestions for action, (8) content and structure of messages, and (9) persuasive speaking.

AUDIENCE ANALYSIS

Recycling programs in the United States had a slow start in the 1980s because the public was resistant. People were accustomed to throwing away used newspapers, bottles, and cans without a thought about the social and economic consequences. In an affluent, disposability-oriented society, convenience was king.

Gasoline prices and the facts of life

Last week in this space we let numbers do our talking. The numbers showed what most people already knew—that the prices Mobil charged our dealers and distributors for gasoline went up between July 3 and August 7. The numbers also showed what many people hadn't considered—that the increases didn't add up to anywhere near the higher prices we paid third parties for the crude oil and gasoline we bought during that period.

Since that time, we have assured the President of the United States that we would "continue to show restraint" and that "in this time of crisis Mobil will do its fair share." We have kept our word.

Even so, the pricing mechanism seems to represent a great mystery even for those who should (and probably do) know better. As a result, demagogic cries of "gouging" and "rip-off" continue to fill the airwaves and the public print. And we keep trying to set the record straight.

The economic facts of life are really quite straightforward, even in a business as complex as ours. When business costs rise, prices have to rise, or eventually the business will cease to exist. We pinpointed some dates in last week's message, but the fact is that our costs were rising even before Iraq began rattling its saber, and we weren't passing those costs along as quickly as we normally would have because competition was so keen.

Another fact of life involves time frames. The one we discussed last week was highlighted by a brewing crisis in the Middle East. But markets constantly go up and down, for factors other than crises. And the downturns occur without fanfare, and certainly without any expressions of concern for the businesses involved. Between August and December last year, for example, crude prices went up, but pump prices fell, because demand couldn't absorb enough product.

For an ongoing business, prices during any arbitrary time frame tell an incomplete story—witness the heating oil price spike caused by the brutal cold of last December, when what went up came down as the weather turned warm.

Even so, we sympathize with our customers who find themselves paying more for reasons well beyond anyone's control. Fortunately, this nation has some political cards to play in response to today's political crisis. Several oil-producing nations already have indicated a willingness to increase their production, and thereby minimize the impact on world markets of the loss of Iraqi and Kuwaiti crude. And many of the nations of the world have strategic petroleum reserves which can be used as necessary.

If other producing countries can't make up the shortfall, then these SPRs are available to add stability to the situation.

America needs unity and determination right now, and it needs to follow up with a rational dialogue on a sensible national energy policy.

Mobil®

FIGURE 11.1
Mobil Corporation has achieved wide public attention with its persuasive advertisements on issues, often sharply worded. This typical one appeared shortly after the beginning of the Persian Gulf crisis in 1990. (©1990 Mobil Corporation)

This public attitude toward recycling illustrates two key points about persuasion. First, people are good at reacting to events and situations but not at anticipating them. Second, any message or suggested action must be compatible with group values and beliefs. Recycling was not really adopted until the public realized that (1) forests were disappearing and metals were not a renewable resource, (2) collection of litter was costing taxpayers millions of dollars, and (3) landfills were becoming mountains of ugly trash. Recycling suddenly became more salient because it was in people's economic and environmental self-interest.

Knowledge of group attitudes and beliefs is, therefore, an essential part of persuasion because it helps the communicator to tailor messages that are salient, answer a felt need, and provide a logical course of action. Polling and census data, as well as pretesting of messages, can accomplish a great deal in structuring a message that builds upon group attitudes.

Tapping a group's attitudes is called *channeling*. It is the technique of recognizing a general audience belief and then suggesting a specific course of action. One common channeling tactic is the appeal to patriotism by politicians. Lyndon Johnson called on all patriotic Americans to "support our boys" in Vietnam; Ronald Reagan urged support for his defense policies because, he said, America is the "hope of the free world"; George Bush declared that nothing less than "our way of life" was at stake in the standoff with Saddam Hussein of Iraq.

Environmental groups such as the Wilderness Society or the Sierra Club channel messages that capitalize on the public's concern for the quality of life. If a person wants to preserve forests and mountains for his or her children (and who doesn't?), isn't it worth a $20 membership?

There are numerous other examples of how organizations tailor messages to group beliefs. The public has a distaste for exploitation, so unions talk about "workers as pawns of big business." Pro-gun organizations capitalize on the public's concern about crime and the need to protect one's family. The California Raisin Board took advantage of the craze for physical fitness by depicting its product as a nutritious snack for the jogger.

SOURCE CREDIBILITY

A message is more believable to the intended audience if the source has *credibility*. This was Aristotle's concept of *ethos,* and it explains why organizations use a variety of spokespeople, depending upon the message and the audience.

The California Strawberry Advisory Board, for example, arranges for a home economist to appear on television talk shows to discuss nutrition and to demonstrate easy-to-follow strawberry recipes. The audience for these programs, primarily homemakers, not only identifies with the representative but perceives her as highly credible. By the same token, a manufacturer of sunscreen lotion uses a professor of pharmacology who is past president of the State Pharmacy Board to discuss the scientific merits of sunscreen versus suntan lotions. And, of course, Lee Iacocca has been the chief speaker in Chrysler Corporation advertisements because he is both articulate and chairman of the company.

The Three Factors Source credibility is based upon three factors. One is *expertise*. Is the person perceived by the audience as being an expert on the subject? Companies, for instance, use engineers and scientists to answer news conference questions about how an engineering process works or whether a chemical waste dump is dangerous to human life.

The second component is *sincerity*. Does the person come across as believing what he or she is saying? Bill Cosby may not be an expert on all the products he endorses, but he does get high ratings for sincerity.

The third component is even more elusive. It is *charisma*. Is the individual attractive, self-assured, and articulate, projecting an image of competence and leadership? All contribute to source credibility.

Public relations personnel are well aware of the need for providing the right person for an audience. They know that reporters prefer to talk with the person in the organization who is most directly involved in or knowledgeable about the subject. It may be the chief executive officer or the head of the research laboratory. It is also a good idea to use, say, a physicist or a biologist to address an audience of scientists, or a corporate treasurer to speak to a group of security analysts, because the audiences will accord them more credibility.

Celebrities who project sincerity and charisma make endorsements for the primary purpose of calling consumers' attention to a product. Michael Jackson, Madonna, Bo Jackson, Cosby, and many other athletes, singers, and movie stars frequently endorse products. The sponsor's purpose is to associate the person's popularity with the product.

Even Marla Maples, an instant celebrity because of her affair with real-estate tycoon Donald Trump, became an endorser of No Excuses jeans (see Chapter 20). Her predecessor as No Excuses endorser was Donna Rice, who became widely known after her involvement with presidential candidate Gary Hart. Using celebrity endorsements is called *transfer,* mentioned later in this chapter as a propaganda device.

Use of celebrities, however, is not without some credibility problems. One is the rising clutter of endorsements, to the point that the public can't remember who endorses which product. This is particularly true in the athletic shoe business, in which Nike, L.A. Gear, and Reebok use numbers of sports figures. A second problem is overexposure of a celebrity who endorses many products, such as Cosby. With overexposure, credibility with the public tends to go down, especially when news stories report how much money the celebrity is paid for the endorsements.

The third problem occurs when conflicting messages come from the celebrity. Actress Cybill Shepherd, who starred in commercials for beef, caused considerable anguish in the cattle industry when she was quoted in a magazine that she rarely ate beef. In another case, Bruce Willis appeared in ads for Seagram's wine coolers as *National Enquirer* headlines alleged that he had sought help for an alcohol problem.

Problems with celebrities have caused many companies to use cartoon figures as a way to attract audience interest. McDonald's uses ''The Little Mermaid,'' and a battery company has its ''Energizer bunny.'' Disney characters are popular, and the California Raisin Board struck paydirt with its California Raisins. As one advertising agency executive says, ''They're much more controllable than a real, live celebrity.'' And like live celebrities, people dressed in costume representing the cartoon character

"LUMINARIES" HELP LAUNCH APPLE'S MACINTOSH

"Ninety percent of the world's views are controlled by the 10 percent who are opinion makers," says Regis McKenna, whose public relations firm handled product publicity for the introduction of Apple Computer's Macintosh.

As part of the overall strategy, Apple executives and staff from Regis McKenna, Inc., spent many months giving background briefings to key groups within the electronics industry—software designers, distributors, and computer dealers—before making any public announcement about the computer.

In addition, McKenna made sure that the "luminaries," or key opinion leaders in the electronics industry, knew about the Macintosh and its capabilities. He explains: "There are probably no more than 20 or 30 people in any one industry who have major impact on trends, standards, and a company's image or character."

McKenna also realizes that journalists rely on opinion leaders to provide objective judgments about the merits of a new product and the way it compares with the competition. Thus the strategy was to ensure that opinion leaders in the industry were cultivated and informed about the Macintosh before the media picked up the story and began interviewing their sources in the electronics field. Positive statements from such sources provided important third-party endorsement for the new product.

can go on media tours and attend special events. A troupe of California dancing raisins has made several national media tours.

APPEAL TO SELF-INTEREST

Self-interest was described during earlier discussion about the formation of public opinion. People get involved in issues or pay attention to messages that appeal to their psychic or economic needs.

The public relations person, when structuring an angle for a news release, brochure, or slide presentation, must think, first and foremost, about the nature of the audience and what it wants to know.

Publicity for a personal computer can serve as an example. A news release to the trade press serving the computer industry might focus on the technical proficiency of the equipment. The audience, of course, consists of engineers and computer programmers interested in the hardware. A brochure prepared for the public, however, may emphasize how the computer can (1) help people keep track of personal finances, (2) assist youngsters in becoming better students, (3) fit into a small space, and (4) offer good value. Consumers are less interested in technical details than in how the personal computer can make life easier for them.

Charitable organizations don't sell products, but they do need volunteers and donations. This is accomplished by careful structuring of messages that appeal to self-interest. This is not to say that altruism is dead. Thousands of people give freely of their time and money to charitable organizations, but they do receive something in return or they would not do it. The "something in return" may be (1) self-esteem,

(2) the opportunity to make a contribution to society, (3) recognition from peers and the community, (4) a sense of belonging, (5) ego gratification, or even (6) a tax deduction. Public relations people understand psychic needs and rewards, and that is why there is constant recognition of volunteers in newsletters and award banquets. (Further discussion of volunteerism appears in Chapter 18.)

Sociologist Harold Lasswell says people are motivated by eight basic appeals. They are power, respect, well-being, affection, wealth, skill, enlightenment, and physical and mental vitality. Psychologist Abraham Maslow, in turn, says any appeal to self-interest must be based on a *hierarchy of needs*. The first and lowest level involves basic needs such as food, water, shelter, and even transportation to and from work. The second level consists of security needs. People need to feel secure in their jobs, safe in their homes, and confident about their retirement. At the third level are "belonging" needs—people seek association with others. This is why individuals join organizations. Depending on the person's need in this area, he or she may join only one club or up to 10 or 12.

"Love" needs comprise the fourth level in the hierarchy. Humans have a need to be wanted and loved—fulfilling the desire for self-esteem. At the fifth and highest level in Maslow's hierarchy are self-actualization needs. Once the first four needs are met, Maslow says, people are free to achieve maximum personal potential; for example, through traveling extensively or perhaps becoming experts on orchids.

Maslow's hierarchy helps explain why some public information campaigns have difficulty getting the message across to people who are classified in the VALS lifestyle categories (see Chapter 7) as "survivors" and "sustainers." Efforts to inform minorities and low-income groups about AIDS provide an example of this problem. For these groups, the potential danger of AIDS is less compelling than the day-to-day problems of poverty and satisfying the basic needs of food and shelter.

The challenge for public relations personnel, as creators of persuasive messages, is how to tailor information to fill or reduce a need. More than one social scientist has said that success in persuasion largely depends on the ability to assess audience needs and self-interests accurately.

CLARITY OF MESSAGE

Many messages fail because the audience finds the message unnecessarily complex in content or language. The most persuasive messages are direct, are simply expressed, and contain only one primary idea. Peter Drucker, a management expert, once said, "An innovation, to be effective, has to be simple and it has to be focused. It should do only one thing, otherwise it confuses." The same can be said for the content of any message.

Public relations personnel should always ask two questions: "What do I want the audience to do with the message?" and "Will the audience understand the message?" Although persuasion theory says people retain information better and form stronger opinions when they are asked to draw their own conclusions, this doesn't negate the importance of explicitly stating what action an audience should take. Is it to buy the product, visit a showroom, write a member of Congress, make a $10 donation, or what?

If an explicit request for action is not part of the message, members of the audience may not understand what is expected of them. Public relations firms, when making a presentation to a potential client, always ask for the account at the end of the presentation.

TIMING AND CONTEXT

A message is more persuasive if environmental factors support the message or if the message is received within the context of other messages and situations with which the individual is familiar. These factors are called timing and context.

Information from a utility on how to conserve energy is more salient if the consumer has just received the January heating bill. A pamphlet on a new stock offering is more effective if it accompanies an investor's dividend check. A citizen's group lobbying for a stoplight gets more attention if a major accident has just occurred at the intersection.

Political candidates are highly aware of public concerns and avidly read polls to find out what issues are most salient with voters. If the polls indicate that high interest rates and high-quality secondary education are key issues, the candidate begins to use these issues—and to offer his or her proposals—in the campaign.

Timing and context also play an important role in achieving publicity in the mass media. Public relations personnel, as pointed out earlier, should read newspapers and watch television news programs to find out what media gatekeepers consider newsworthy. A manufacturer of a locking device for computer files got extensive media coverage about its product simply because it followed a rash of news stories about thieves' gaining access to bank accounts through computers. Media gatekeepers, ordinarily uninterested in security devices for computers, found the product newsworthy within the context of actual news events.

The value of information and its newsworthiness are based on timing and context. Public relations professionals disseminate information at the time it is most highly valued.

AUDIENCE PARTICIPATION

A change in attitude or reinforcement of beliefs is enhanced by *audience involvement and participation*.

A company, for example, may have employees discuss productivity in a quality-control circle. Management may already have figured out what is needed, but if workers are involved in the problem-solving, they often come up with the same solution or even a better one. And, from a persuasion standpoint, the employees are more committed to making the solution work because it came from them—not as a policy or order handed down by higher management.

Participation can also take the form of samples. Many companies distribute product samples so the consumer can conveniently try them without expense. A consumer who samples the product and makes a judgment about its quality is more likely to purchase it.

Activist groups use participation as a way of helping people actualize their beliefs.

Not only do rallies and demonstrations give people a sense of belonging, but the act of participation reinforces their beliefs. Asking people to do something—conserve energy, collect donations, or picket—activates a form of self-persuasion and commitment.

SUGGESTIONS FOR ACTION

A principle of persuasion is that people endorse ideas only if they are accompanied by a proposed action from the sponsor.

Recommendations for action must be clear. Public relations practitioners must not only ask people to conserve energy, for instance, but also furnish detailed data and ideas on how to do it.

A campaign conducted by Pacific Gas & Electric Company provides an example. The utility inaugurated a Zero Interest Program (ZIP) to offer customers a way to implement energy-saving ideas. The program involved several components:

- *Energy kit.* A telephone hotline was established and widely publicized so interested customers could order an energy kit detailing what the average homeowner could do to reduce energy use.
- *Service bureau.* The company, at no charge, sent representatives to homes to check the efficiency of water heaters and furnaces, measure the amount of insulation, and check doors and windows for drafts.
- *ZIP program.* The cost of making a home more energy-efficient was funded by zero-interest loans to any qualified customer.

CONTENT AND STRUCTURE OF MESSAGES

A number of techniques can make a message more persuasive. Writers throughout history have emphasized some information, while downplaying or omitting other pieces of information. Thus they addressed both the *content and structure of messages*.

Expert communicators continue to use a number of devices, including (1) drama, (2) statistics, (3) surveys and polls, (4) examples, (5) testimonials, (6) mass media endorsements, and (7) emotional appeals.

Drama Because everyone likes a good story, the first task of a communicator is to get audience attention. This is often accomplished by graphically illustrating an event or situation. Newspapers often dramatize a story to get reader interest in an issue. Thus we read about the family evicted from its home as part of a story on the increase in bankruptcies; the old man who is starving because of red tape in the welfare office; or the worker who is now disabled because of toxic waste. In newsrooms, this is called *humanizing an issue*.

Dramatizing is also used in public relations. Relief organizations, in particular, attempt to galvanize public concern and donations through drama as shown in Figures 11.2 and 11.3. The UNICEF fund-raising letter's description of a child dying of malnutrition, like the stark black-and-white photographs used by other relief organizations, creates powerful imagery, emotion, and drama.

STRANDED!

Over 80,000 men, women and children are now stranded in the desert "no-man's land" between Iraq and Jordan. Most of them are poor laborers from Bangladesh, India, Pakistan & Sri Lanka, who were working to send money back to their families. They now face unbelievable hardships — burning heat by day and frigid cold at night. And the children suffer most.

Help us rush life-sustaining aid — food, water, blankets, tents — by sending your contribution today.

Send to:

SAVE THE CHILDREN®
MIDDLE EAST EMERGENCY
P.O. BOX 975
WESTPORT, CT 06881

THANK YOU FOR YOUR SUPPORT!

Annual report available on request.
Your contributions are U.S. tax deductible and will directly benefit Save The Children.

FIGURE 11.2
Strong emotional appeals such as this advertisement for funds in the New York *Times* (September 9, 1990) achieve best results when they portray the plight of victims in ways easy for readers to visualize. (Courtesy of Save the Children)

A more mundane use of dramatizing is the so-called *application story*, sent to the trade press. This is sometimes called the *case study technique*, in which a manufacturer prepares an article on how an individual or a company is using the product. Apple Computer, for example, provides a number of application stories about the unique ways in which its product is being used.

Statistics It is often said that people are awed by *statistics*. Use of numbers and statistics can convey objectivity, bigness, and importance in a credible way. Volvo, seeking to position itself as one of Europe's leading companies, publicizes the fact that it has 79,000 employees worldwide and sales of $15 billion. Rockport shoes says it uses 12 "technologies" to make its product. A writer, however, should use numbers and statistics sparingly. A news release crammed with them tends to be boring and turns off the potential reader.

Surveys and Polls Airlines and auto manufacturers, in particular, use the results of *surveys and polls* to show that they are first in "customer satisfaction," "service," and even "leg room" or "cargo space." The most credible surveys are those conducted by independent research organizations, but readers still should read the fine

United States Committee for

unicef

United Nations Children's Fund

Dear Friend:

In the ten seconds it took you to open and begin to read this letter, three children died from the effects of malnutrition somewhere in the world.

No statistic can express what it's like to see even one child die that way ... to see a mother sitting hour after hour, leaning her child's body against her own ... to watch the small, feeble head movements that expend all the energy a youngster has left ... to see the panic in a dying tot's innocent eyes ... and then to know in a moment that life is gone.

But I'm not writing this letter simply to describe an all-too-common tragedy.

> I'm writing because, after decades of hard work, UNICEF -- the United Nations Children's Fund -- has identified four simple, low-cost techniques which, if applied, have the potential to cut the yearly child mortality rate in half.

These methods don't depend on solving large-scale problems like increasing food supply or cleaning up contaminated water. They can be put into effect before a single additional bushel of wheat is grown, or before a single new well is dug.

They do depend on what you decide to do by the time you finish reading this letter. You see, putting these simple techniques to work requires the support of UNICEF's projects by people around the world. In our country, it means helping the U.S. Committee for UNICEF contribute to that vital work.

FIGURE 11.3
Successful persuasion by direct mail depends heavily on an eye-catching opening that persuades the recipient to read on, rather than toss the letter aside. Letters such as this UNICEF appeal often stir the reader's sense of guilt, then suggest how the reader can contribute to ease the problem.

print to see what is being compared and rated. Is an American-made auto, for example, being compared only with other U.S. cars or with foreign cars as well? Also, there is the selected publicizing of results. An airline may be highly rated in ''cabin service'' but be at the bottom of the list for ''on-time arrivals and departures.''

Examples A statement of opinion can be more persuasive if some *examples* are given. A school board often can get support for a bond issue by citing examples of how the present facilities are inadequate for student needs. Environmental groups give examples of how other communities have successfully established greenbelts when requesting a local city council to do the same. Auto manufacturers often attest to the durability of their vehicles by citing their performance on a test track or in a cross-country road race.

Testimonials A form of source credibility, *testimonials* can be either explicit or implied. A campaign to curtail alcohol and drug abuse may feature a pop singer as a spokesperson, or have a young woman talk about being paralyzed and disfigured as the victim of a drunk driver. Implied testimonials also can be effective. Proclamations by mayors and governors establishing ''Red Cross Day'' or ''Library Week'' are implied testimonials. The testimonial as a propaganda device is discussed later in the chapter.

Endorsements *Endorsements* can be made by individuals, organizations, or media outlets. In addition to endorsements by celebrities, as discussed earlier, products and services benefit from endorsements by experts. A well-known medical specialist may publicly state that a particular brand of exercise equipment is best for general conditioning. Organizations such as the American Dental Association and the National Safety Council also endorse products and services.

Media endorsements come through editorials and surveys that rate products and services. Daily newspapers regularly endorse political candidates and community ef-

KEYS TO PERSUASION: MULTIPLE TOOLS AND LONG-TERM ACTIVITY

The public's attitudes and behavior can be changed through information campaigns if multiple tools of communication are utilized over a long period of time.

Stanford University conducted a five-year information campaign to improve the health of people living in Monterey and Salinas by bombarding them with health promotion messages. Messages were delivered through newspapers, radio, television, pamphlets, classes, contests, on-the-job education, advice stuffed in grocery bags, tips for school children, and a weekly medical column. During the campaign, researchers estimate that every adult was hit with a campaign message about twice a week.

After five years, surveys showed that citizens of these two cities had a 13 percent drop in smoking, and changes in blood pressure and cholesterol were better than those found in two control cities not exposed to the information campaign. The researchers estimate that the information campaign saved hundreds of people from dying of heart attacks and cancer. Monterey County is estimated to have saved $38 million in medical costs, while the information campaign only cost $340,000 per year.

Research studies show that most public information campaigns fail because they are short-term and generally only use public service advertising. Mass media campaigns only succeed if they (1) address an issue of ongoing public concern, (2) incorporate multiple tools of communication, (3) utilize the principles of behavior change, and (4) continue long enough to achieve total saturation of the messages.

forts such as the United Way campaign. Another type of endorsement is a newspaper or magazine survey or ranking of the best restaurants, shopping malls, bookstores, and so on in an area. Manufacturers constantly tout the fact that one of their models was named "car of the year" or "best-in-class" by *Car and Driver* or other car buff magazines.

Emotional Appeals *Emotional appeals* have been used throughout history, and the 1990s are no exception. The Greenpeace organization, for example, sends out literature that constitutes strong emotional appeal to save harp seals. The cover of a direct mail brochure shows a baby harp seal—all fuzzy, with large liquid eyes—and the headline "Kiss This Baby Good-Bye." Inside, seal behavior is portrayed so the reader can identify the seal's fate with that of a human infant. Here is an excerpt:

> At that tender and vulnerable age, with his mother at his side, he wiggles forward, waggling his whole backside. He goes to meet, in a curious, friendly, playful way, the first human being he has ever seen and is—by the same human—clubbed in the head and skinned on the spot—sometimes while he is still alive.

Such material, distributed in thousands of bulk mail letters, has been extremely successful in creating a groundswell of demand that the harvesting of seals be forbidden. In response to the public outcry against the killing of seals, the European Community banned sealskin imports. The annual harvest of seals dropped from nearly 200,000 to less than 15,000.

Emotional appeals can do much to galvanize the public into action, but they can also backfire. Such appeals raise ego defenses, and people don't like to be told that in some way they are responsible. A description of suffering makes many people uncomfortable, and, rather than take action, they may tune out the message. A relief organization runs full-page advertisements in magazines with the headline "You Can Help Maria Get Enough to Eat . . . Or You Can Turn the Page." Researchers say that most people, their ego defenses raised, turn the page and mentally refuse to acknowledge that they even saw the ad. In sum, emotional appeals that attempt to lay a guilt trip on the audience are not very successful.

Strong fear arousals also can cause people to tune out, especially if they feel that they can't do anything about the problem anyway. Research indicates, however, that a moderate fear arousal, accompanied by a relatively easy solution, is effective. A moderate fear arousal is: "What would happen if your child were thrown through the windshield in an accident?" The message concludes with the suggestion that a baby, for protection and safety, should be placed in a secured infant seat.

Psychologists say the most effective emotional appeal is one coupled with facts and figures. The emotional appeal attracts audience interest, but logical arguments also are needed.

PERSUASIVE SPEAKING

Psychologists have found that successful speakers (and salespeople) use several persuasion techniques:

1. *Yes–yes*. Start with points with which the audience agrees, to develop a pattern of "yes" answers. Getting agreement to a basic premise often means that the receiver will agree to the logically developed conclusion.

2. *Structured choice*. Give structured choices that require the audience to choose between A and B. Political candidates or cause-oriented organizations often use this technique. "Do you want four more years of inflation, or a new beginning?" "Will you work for wilderness preservation, or allow industrial exploitation?"

3. *Partial commitment*. Get a commitment for some action on the part of the receiver. This leaves the door open for commitment to other parts of the proposal at a later date. "You don't need to decide on the new insurance plan now, but please attend the employee orientation program on Thursday."

4. *Ask for more/settle for less*. Submit a complete public relations program to management, but be prepared to compromise by dropping certain parts of the program. It has become almost a cliché that a department asks for a larger budget than it expects to receive. Or, to put it another way, the entire sales field is built on the notion of setting prices that can be marked down.

A persuasive speech can either be one-sided or give several sides of an issue, depending on the audience. A series of studies by social scientist Carl Hovland and his associates determined that one-sided speeches were most effective with persons favorable to the message, while two-sided speeches were most effective with audiences that might be opposed to the message.

By mentioning all sides of the argument, the speaker accomplishes three objectives. First, he or she is perceived as having objectivity. This translates into increased credibility and makes the audience less suspicious of motives. Second, by giving all sides, the speaker is treating the audience as mature, intelligent adults. Third, including counterarguments allows the speaker to control how these arguments are structured. It also deflates opponents in the audience who might challenge the speaker by saying, "But you didn't consider. . . ."

Panel discussions and debates present other problems. Psychologists say the last person on a panel to talk probably will be most effective in changing audience attitudes—or at least be longer remembered by the audience. But it has also been shown that the first speaker sets the standard and tone for the remainder of the discussion. Being first or last is better positioning than being between two presentations.

PROPAGANDA

No discussion of persuasion would be complete without mentioning propaganda and its techniques.

Webster's New World Dictionary defines *propaganda* as "The systematic, widespread promotion of a certain set of ideas, doctrines, etc. to further one's own cause." Its roots go back to the 17th century when the Roman Catholic Church set up the *congregatio de propaganda* (congregation for propagating the faith), but the word has taken on extremely negative connotations in the 20th century.

In World Wars I and II, propaganda was associated with the information activities of the enemy. Germany and Japan were sending out "propaganda," while the U.S. and its allies were disseminating "truth." Today, propaganda has the connotation of falsehood, lies, deceit, and duplicity, which opposing groups and governments accuse each other of using.

Closely associated with propaganda is a newer word, *disinformation*. During the Cold War, both the Soviet KGB and the United States's CIA, secret agencies, regularly planted negative, and often untrue, information about each other's nation in media outlets around the world. More recently, the Iraqi government started a disinformation campaign after U.S. troops were dispatched to the Middle East to protect Saudi Arabia and its oil fields from possible invasion. The Baghdad press began alleging that American soldiers, thousands of them supposedly with AIDS and addicted to drugs, were importing 5000 Egyptian prostitutes to Saudi Arabia. In addition, U.S. troops were said to be shooting Saudis who protested the "occupation" and were dumping nuclear wastes in the desert. These propaganda efforts were aimed at deep-seated fears in the Moslem nations of Western secularism, decadence, and a pro-Israel Zionist conspiracy.

Meanwhile, the media in Egypt and other nations reported that scores of Iraqi senior military officers were executed by Baghdad for refusing to take part in the invasion of Kuwait. Foreign correspondents on the scene, however, had trouble verifying the story and surmised that it was part of a disinformation campaign by Egypt and its allies, including the United States.

Some have argued that propaganda, in the broadest sense of the word, also includes the advertising and public relations activity of such diverse entities as Exxon and the Sierra Club. Social scientists, however, say that the word should be used only to denote activity that sells a belief system or constitutes political or ideological dogma. Advertising and public relations, for commercial purposes, are not propaganda in themselves but could contain elements of propaganda if there were an attempt to mislead an audience by concealing (1) the source of information, (2) the source's goal, (3) the other side of the story, and (4) the consequences if the message were adopted.

PROPAGANDA TECHNIQUES

A number of techniques also used in propaganda are used today by many commercial and political organizations. The most common are the following:

1. *Plain folks*. An approach often used by individuals to show humble beginnings and empathy with the average citizen. President Bush, for example, likes to remind people of his early days as a Texas oil field worker trying to support his young family.

2. *Testimonial*. A frequently used device to achieve credibility, as discussed earlier. A well-known expert or popular celebrity gives testimony about the value of a product or the wisdom of a decision.

3. *Bandwagon*. The implication or direct statement that everyone wants the product

or that the idea has overwhelming support. ''Millions of Americans support a ban on abortion'' or ''Every leading expert believes. . . .''

4. *Card-stacking*. The selection of facts and data to build an overwhelming case on one side of the issue, while concealing the other side. The advertising industry, for example, says a ban on beer advertising would lead to enormous reductions in network sports programming, and a ban on cigarette advertising would kill several hundred magazines. The timber industry says 30,000 jobs will be lost if the environmentalists are successful in protecting the spotted owl.

5. *Transfer*. The technique of associating the person, product, or organization with something that has high or low credibility, depending on the intention of the message. Rolex watches are associated with high performance athletes, or a product used by NASA astronauts is associated with high reliability. On the negative side, opponents of a politician may attempt to link the person with drug lords or individuals reputed to be corrupt.

6. *Glittering generalities*. The technique of associating a cause, product, or idea with favorable abstractions such as freedom, justice, democracy, and the American way. Las Vegas bills itself as ''The American Way to Play,'' and American oil companies argue for off-shore drilling to keep ''America energy-independent.''

7. *Name-calling*. The use of terms, charged with negative meanings, such as *kook, fellow traveler, radical,* or *right-winger*. The Rev. Donald Wildmon, head of the American Family Association, attacked the National Endowment for the Arts (NEA) for sponsoring ''godless, perverted artists'' and spending tax money to promote ''bigoted, anti-Christian and obscene art.'' Opponents of Saddam Hussein call him *killer, bloodthirsty tyrant, autocrat, dictator,* and *a new Hitler*.

A WORD ABOUT ETHICS

A student of public relations should be aware of these techniques, if only to ensure that he or she doesn't intentionally use them in such a way as to deceive and mislead the public. Ethical responsibilities exist in any form of persuasive communication; guidelines are discussed at the end of the chapter.

PERSUASION AND MANIPULATION

On previous pages are discussions of a number of ways in which an individual can formulate persuasive messages. The ability to use this persuasive language often leads to charges that public relations people have great power to manipulate—a loaded word.

In reality, persuasion as on overwhelming influence is greatly exaggerated. Persuasion is not an exact science, and there is no sure-fire way to predict that people will be persuaded to act on a message, or even accept it. If persuasion techniques were as refined as the critics say, everyone might be driving the same car, using the same soap, and voting for the same political candidate.

Four factors limit the effectiveness of any persuasive message. They are (1) lack of message penetration, (2) competing messages, (3) self-selection, and (4) self-perception.

LACK OF MESSAGE PENETRATION

Diffusion of messages, despite modern communications technologies, is not pervasive. Not everyone, of course, listens to the same television programs or reads the same newspaper and magazines. Not everyone receives the same mail or attends the same meetings. Everyone the communicator wants to reach will not be in the audience eventually reached. There is also the problem of the distortion of messages as they pass through media gatekeepers.

A SAMPLER ON PERSUASION

A number of research studies have contributed to a basic understanding of persuasion concepts. Here are some basic ideas from the text *Public Communication Campaigns,* edited by Ronald E. Rice and William J. Paisley (Sage, 1982):

- Positive appeals generally are more effective than negative appeals for retention of the message and actual compliance.
- Radio and television messages tend to be more persuasive than print but, if the message is complex, better comprehension is achieved through print media.
- Strong emotional appeals and fear arousal are most effective when the audience has minimal concern about or interest in the topic.
- High fear appeals are only effective when a readily available action can be taken to eliminate the threat.
- Logical appeals, using facts and figures, are better for highly-educated, sophisticated audiences than strong emotional appeals.
- Altruistic need, like self-interest, can be a strong motivator. Men are willing to get a physical check-up more to protect their families than themselves.
- A celebrity or an attractive model is most effective when the audience has low involvement, the theme is simple, and the more personalized broadcast channels are used. An exciting spokesperson attracts attention to a message that would otherwise be ignored.

COMPETING MESSAGES

Earlier in the century, before much was known about the complex process of communication, it was believed that people received information directly without any intervening variable. This was called the *hypodermic needle theory of communication.* Today communication experts realize that no message is received in a vacuum. Messages are filtered through a receiver's entire social structure and belief system. Nationality, race, religion, gender, cultural patterns, family, and friends are some of the variables that filter messages. In addition, people receive countless competing and conflicting messages daily.

Social scientists say a person is rewarded for conforming to the standards of the group. Consequently, people are cautious about adopting new ideas or opinions without first testing them on their peers.

THE FORMULA FOR WRITING THAT SELLS AND PERSUADES

James F. Fox, owner of his own public relations firm in New York City, says persuasive writing begins with determining the audience's attitudes and identifying with them. The formula for persuasive writing, he says, is this:

1. Get attention.
2. Show a need.
3. Satisfy that need.
4. Point out benefits.
5. Request action.

Source: PR Reporter, November 18, 1985.

SELF-SELECTION

The people most wanted in an audience are often the least likely to be there. As any minister attests, sinners don't go to church on a regular basis. Vehement supporters of a cause frequently ignore information provided by the other side. Asking a friend which magazines he or she subscribes to may reveal a good deal about that person's interests and political philosophy. In sum, people seek out information that is compatible with and reinforces their current dispositions and attitudes.

SELF-PERCEPTION

Self-perception is the channel through which messages are interpreted. People will perceive the same information differently, depending upon predispositions and already-formulated opinions. Carl Rogers, a psychotherapist, says: "The greatest barrier to human communications is the tendency to form snap judgments about a person or what he or she is saying and then tune out." Thus, depending on a person's views, an action by a company may be considered a "great contribution to the community" or "a self-serving gimmick." A good example of how self-perceptions influence messages is the divided public opinion concerning Oliver North's testimony to Congress on the Iran-Contra scandal. Many who saw the hearings perceived North as a "true patriot" who served his country admirably. An equal number of Americans saw a person who was a liar and went beyond the law to involve the U.S. government in highly questionable activities.

PERSUASION AND ETHICS

The strategies and tactics of persuasion, like all knowledge, can be used to subvert or benefit the public interest. Bill Moyers, host for a Public Broadcasting Service program on the early beginnings of public relations (''A Walk Through the Twentieth Century''), wondered, in a concluding comment on the program, about the persuasive power of public relations. He said:

> And where has public relations led us? To a world where just about everybody uses it and defends it. The people in the business say their aim is to inform as much as to persuade. And persuasion is no dirty word, they insist; it's the sound of democracy and free enterprise in action. That's a point. But it is hard to recognize Adam Smith's ''rational buyers'' or Jefferson's ''enlightened voters'' in a public bombarded with contrived events to make someone's point. Who's pulling the string and why? It's one thing when funny people in bathing suits celebrate Equal Potato Chips Week, another when the answer to some government breach of law, or violation of human rights, is a highly paid media consultant. Something else too when the remedy for shoddy merchandise is a new corporate logo or a press conference featuring a blizzard of facts from hired experts. In a world where the rich and powerful can hire more and better persuaders, who has the last word? So the challenge for those who use public relations is one of ethics. . . .

THE ETHICS OF PERSUASION

Public relations people by definition are advocates of clients and employers. The emphasis is on persuasive communication to influence a particular public in some way. At the same time, as Chapter 6 pointed out, public relations practitioners must conduct their activities in an ethical manner.

The use of persuasive techniques, therefore, calls for some additional guidelines. Professor Richard L. Johannesen of Northern Illinois University, writing in *Persuasion,* a text by Charles Larson, lists the following ethical criteria for using persuasive devices that should be kept in mind by every public relations professional:

1. Do not use false, fabricated, misrepresented, distorted, or irrelevant evidence to support arguments or claims.

2. Do not intentionally use specious, unsupported, or illogical reasoning.

3. Do not represent yourself as informed or as an ''expert'' on a subject when you are not.

4. Do not use irrelevant appeals to divert attention or scrutiny from the issue at hand. Among the appeals that commonly serve such a purpose are ''smear'' attacks on an

opponent's character, appeals to hatred and bigotry, innuendo, and "God" or "devil" terms that cause intense but unreflective positive or negative reactions.

5. Do not ask your audience to link your idea or proposal to emotion-laden values, motives, or goals to which it actually is not related.

6. Do not deceive your audience by concealing your real purpose, your self-interest, the group you represent, or your position as an advocate of a viewpoint.

7. Do not distort, hide, or misrepresent the number, scope, intensity, or undesirable features of consequences.

8. Do not use emotional appeals that lack a supporting basis of evidence or reasoning or that would not be accepted if the audience had time and opportunity to examine the subject itself.

9. Do not oversimplify complex situations into simplistic, two-valued, either/or, polar views or choices.

10. Do not pretend certainty when tentativeness and degrees of probability would be more accurate.

11. Do not advocate something in which you do not believe yourself.

CASE PROBLEM

The state of New Jersey has a "Green Acres" program to acquire land for state forests, parks, game reserves, and beaches. Since 1980, the state's voters have approved bond proposals totaling $540 million to acquire "Green Acres" for preservation. This year, the voters are being asked to approve another $135 million in bonds to purchase more land for open space and to protect the shoreline from erosion.

Although voters in the past have been supportive, the state commissioner of environmental protection is somewhat nervous about the outcome of the vote because the state's economy has been weak for several years. Taxpayers are in a rebellious mood. Many local governments oppose the bond issue because they think state purchase of additional land from private owners will cause a loss of local tax revenues.

Given this environment, you are asked to write a persuasive direct mail letter on behalf of the commissioner that will be sent to every taxpayer in the state. As you keep in mind basic persuasion principles, what would you write? In the right margin of your draft letter, note the persuasion concepts being utilized.

QUESTIONS FOR REVIEW AND DISCUSSION

1. Public opinion is highly influenced by self-interest and events. What are these concepts?

2. What is the importance of opinion leaders in the formation of public opinion?

3. What is the role of mass media in opinion formation?

4. Can you name several ways in which public relations people monitor public opinion?

5. What are the stages of public opinion in the life cycle of an issue?

6. Name the three objectives of persuasion in public relations work. What objective is the most difficult to accomplish?

7. Can you name and describe the nine factors involved in persuasive communication?

8. What are three factors involved in source credibility?

9. What are the pros and cons of using celebrities for product endorsements?

10. What are the levels of Maslow's hierarchy of needs? Why is it important for public relations people to understand the basic needs of people?

11. Why is audience involvement and participation important in persuasion?

12. What kinds of techniques can a person use to write persuasive messages?

13. Name several propaganda techniques. Should they be used by public relations people?

14. What are some ethical responsibilities of a person who uses persuasion techniques to influence others?

SUGGESTED READINGS

Davids, Meryl. "Recent Research in Psychology." *Public Relations Journal,* June 1988, pp. 15–19. Short briefs on the psychology of persuasion.

Hiebert, Ray E., Editor. *Precision Public Relations.* New York: Longman, 1988. Section 2, "Influencing Public Opinion," pp. 67–108.

Ignatius, David. "How Britain Persuaded U.S. To Join Anti-Nazi Struggle." Manchester *Guardian Weekly,* September 24, 1989, p. 18.

"In '89 More than Before, Public Relations Will Be Expected to Affect Behavior." *PR Reporter,* January 2, 1989, p. 1.

"Mind Watch: Group Dynamics." *Public Relations Journal,* January 1989, pp. 8–11.

Nagy, Alex. "Word Wars at Home: U.S. Response to World War II Propaganda." *Journalism Quarterly,* Spring 1990, pp. 207–213.

"Oversupply of Celebrity Hawkers Could Trip Up Sneaker Makers." *Wall Street Journal,* May 23, 1990, p. B8.

Pollay, Richard W. "Propaganda, Puffing and the Public Interest." *Public Relations Review,* Fall 1990, pp. 39–54. Hill and Knowlton's work for the tobacco industry in the 1950s.

Sciolino, Elaine. "Iraq's Propaganda May Seem Crude, But It's Effective." New York *Times,* September 16, 1990, p. E3.

Severin, Werner, and Tankard, James. *Communication Theories.* New York: Longman, 1988.

"When It's Commercial Time, TV Viewers Prefer Cartoons to Celebrities Any Day." *Wall Street Journal,* February 16, 1990, p. B1.

CHAPTER

12

The Audience and How to Reach It

So far in this book we have examined what public relations is, the types of work it involves, and some of the ethical and technical problems practitioners encounter. We will look now at both the characteristics of the audience to whom public relations messages are addressed and the media channels through which the messages are delivered.

Selection of the most effective ways to communicate in a public relations program is a crucial part of strategy. Just as a general seeks the most advantageous terrain for battle, the director of a public relations campaign must decide which media are most suitable for reaching the desired audiences and attaining the objective.

This chapter explains how the organized media in our society operate, the special attributes of each, and the ways in which practitioners can use the various channels.

Like a highway map, the chapter shows major routes leading to the various audiences that public relations seeks to address. Later chapters will examine in detail how to tailor messages to these audiences once they have been reached.

THE NATURE OF THE PUBLIC RELATIONS AUDIENCE

If the audience on which public relations practitioners focus their messages were a monolithic whole, their work would be far easier—and far less stimulating. The audience, in fact, is just the opposite: a complex intermingling of groups with diverse cultural, ethnic, religious, and economic attributes whose interests coincide at times and conflict at others.

For the public relations professional, knowledge of these shifting audience dynamics is essential. A successful campaign must be aimed at those segments of the mass audience which are most desirable for its particular purpose and must employ those media most effective in reaching them. Some of these segments are easily identifiable and reachable, a category that Zoe McCathrin of Kent State University calls "prepackaged publics." These are well-organized groups whose members have banded together in a common interest; they constitute ready-made targets for practitioners who have projects of concern to them. Examples of such prepackaged publics are business people in Rotary Clubs, animal lovers in the Humane Society, and educationally involved members of the Parent-Teachers Association.

Diversity is the most significant aspect of the mass audience. This is particularly true in the United States. Its historical image as a beckoning land of opportunity has drawn numbers of immigrants from around the world for more than two centuries. They have brought a bubbling mixture of personal values, habits, and perceptions that are absorbed slowly, and often reluctantly, into the pattern of the United States.

Similar mixtures are found increasingly in many other countries as global air transportation, the growth of international trade, and instant communication break down once-rigid national frontiers.

Especially on the East and West Coasts of the United States, and along the southern border, foreign-born residents cluster together. The recent heavy influx of Asians and Latinos, along with the growing population of blacks—some of whom prefer to be called African-Americans to identify their heritage—is bringing a striking change in the makeup of the total U.S. population, and of its workforce in particular.

MULTIETHNIC EMPHASIS NEEDED

The great diversity in the United States has led, among other things, to a proliferation of Spanish-language radio and television stations and black radio stations.

It is essential that public relations programs be designed with this trend in mind. The field must be multiethnic in thinking and practice, a description that will require staffs to be more strongly multiethnic in personnel than they are today.

Every segment of the population is a potential target for public relations programs. When the average U.S. citizen thinks of Los Angeles, Hollywood comes to mind. So should Koreatown, a bustling Asian neighborhood nearby with its own media. Miami's image originally was as a winter resort; now a very large percentage of its residents come from Latin America with Latino traditions that differ widely from those of northern "snowbirds."

Diversity enriches any society. Intercultural contacts broaden mutual understanding and stimulate fresh thinking in politics, art, education, and commerce. At the same time, however, racial differences often create friction, especially in crowded urban areas where rival groups competing at the poverty level take out their frustrations in physical confrontation. Here creative public relations efforts could help to improve community life.

nia, New York, and Florida. Black stations also have substantial audiences, primarily in urban centers.

Newspapers and magazines aimed at Latinos and blacks also are important targets for public relations efforts. Some Spanish-language newspapers, such as *La Opinion* in Los Angeles—with more than 100,000 audited circulation—are powerful voices. So are black newspapers such as the Chicago *Defender* and the Atlanta *Daily World*. *Ebony* and *Jet* are the best-known magazines for the black audience.

Seniors Marketing experts generally define this group as including individuals more than 50 years old. By the year 2000, seniors are expected to represent nearly 38 percent of all adults in the United States and control more than 75 percent of its wealth. Thus public relations material aimed at their interests will be very important. Especially after

Public Relations
150 Alhambra Circle
Coral Gables, FL 33134
305-529-4504

News from
TEXACO

LA GIRA LATINOAMERICANA TEXACO DE LA SINFONICA DEL NUEVO MUNDO

A INICIARSE EL 4 DE AGOSTO EN LA ARGENTINA

La Sinfónica del Nuevo Mundo Actuará en
Buenos Aires y Montevideo

CORAL GABLES -- El Teatro Colón en Buenos Aires y el Teatro Solís en Montevideo, dos de los salones de concierto de mayor renombre en todo el mundo, se encontrarán colmados de la música de la Sinfónica del Nuevo Mundo durante la Gira Texaco que dicha orquesta realizará por la América Latina.

La Sinfónica del Nuevo Mundo tocará en tres conciertos, vendidos ya a capacidad, en el Teatro Colón, recientemente renovado, antes de volar a Montevideo, donde tocará para un público numeroso en el Teatro Solís.

Gracias en parte a una generosa donación de la Fundación Filantrópica Texaco, la orquesta partirá en su gira hacia la Argentina el 1 de agosto.

FIGURE 12.1
To reach ethnic audiences in the United States and audiences in other countries, some organizations distribute news releases in languages other than English. This Texaco release in Spanish is an example. (Courtesy of Bruce Rubin Associates, Inc.)

retirement, many older citizens travel extensively. They are concerned, too, about health and finances.

MEDIA RELATIONS

Before examining the print, electronic, and film media individually, we need to look at the basic relationship between the media and public relations practitioners. Unless public relations people understand this sometimes sensitive interplay, they cannot be fully effective.

Editors and reporters on the one hand, and public relations people on the other, need each other. The media must have material and ideas from public relations sources, and practitioners must have the media as a place to display their stories.

Public relations people need to remember several things about editors and reporters:

1. They are busy. When you approach them with a story idea, either verbally or on paper, make your sales pitch succinctly and objectively.

2. Editors pride themselves on making their own decisions about what stories to run and how to run them. That is their job. Excessive hype of a story often turns them against it. An aggressive demand that editors *must* run a story will make them bristle and will lead to rejection.

3. Able editors and competent public relations people respect each other and work well together. If editors discover, however, that they have been misled or fed false information, they will never again fully trust the offending practitioner and will look negatively on future submissions from that source.

Practitioners also need to remember several things about themselves when dealing with the media:

1. Your job is important in keeping the public informed. You are performing a service, not asking a favor, when you submit a story idea or a news release.

2. You should assume that your story will be judged on its merits, as seen by the editor, and should not demean yourself by begging an editor to use it.

3. Your role continues after the story or idea has been accepted. You cannot control the tone of the story that appears, but you can influence it by providing favorable story angles and additional information. A public relations person's helpful, pleasant personality does influence most writers, at least subtly.

THE PRINT MEDIA

NEWSPAPERS

Every edition of a newspaper contains hundreds of news stories and pieces of information, in much greater number than the largest news staff can gather by itself. More than most readers realize, and many editors care to admit, newspapers depend upon information brought to them voluntarily.

The *Columbia Journalism Review* noted, for example, that in one edition the *Wall Street Journal* had obtained 45 percent of its 188 news items from news releases. Because of its specialized nature, the *Journal's* use of news releases may be higher than that of general-interest daily newspapers. Public relations generates about 50 percent of the stories in New York City newspapers, according to Albert Scardino, press secretary for Mayor David L. Dinkins.

Approximately 1625 daily newspapers and 7600 weekly newspapers are published in the United States. Most cities today have only one daily newspaper, although competition between two newspapers, or more, exists in the metropolitan centers and in a few smaller cities. While some metropolitan newspapers have circulations of more than a million copies a day, approximately two-thirds of the daily newspapers have circulations of 20,000 or less.

Newspapers published for distribution in the late afternoon, called evening or P.M. papers, outnumber morning (A.M.) papers approximately three to one. Especially in larger cities, however, a substantial trend toward morning publication is in progress. Some cities have 24-hour newspapers; these publish several editions around the clock. Knowledge of a newspaper's hours of publication and the deadlines it enforces for submission of copy is essential for everyone who supplies material to the paper.

Approximately three-quarters of American daily newspapers are owned by newspaper groups. The publishers and editors of a group-owned newspaper have broad local autonomy but must adhere to certain operating standards and procedures laid down by the group headquarters.

A Commercial Institution In dealing with a newspaper, public relations people should remember that it is a commercial institution, created to earn a profit as a purveyor of news and advertising. Although newspapers often are so deeply rooted in a community that they seem like public institutions, they are not. Their publishers and editors as a whole seek to serve the public interest, and often succeed admirably in doing so. Like any other business, however, a newspaper that does not earn a profit soon disappears. Therefore, in the long run and sometimes in the short run as well, management decisions about what appears in a newspaper must be made with the balance sheet in mind.

Newspapers receive about 70 percent of their income from advertising and about 30 percent from circulation sales. They cannot afford to publish press releases that are nothing more than commercial advertising; to do so would cut into their largest source of income. To be published, a release submitted to a newspaper must contain information that an editor regards as news of interest to a substantial number of readers.

Since newspapers are protected by the First Amendment to the Constitution, they cannot be forced to publish any material, including news releases, nor need they receive permission from the government or anyone else to publish whatever they desire. Editors resist pressure on them to suppress material they consider to be newsworthy and, conversely, to print material they believe to be unnewsworthy. However, the definitions of newsworthiness are abstract and fluctuating. What one newspaper considers to be news, another will not.

MEDIA DIRECTORIES

Accurate, up-to-date mailing lists and files of personal contacts are essential in public relations programs. Media directories are a primary source in preparing such lists.

Numerous directories exist, some of them quite specialized. The following major ones are widely used:

- *Gale's Directory of Publications and Broadcast Media* (Detroit: Gale Research, Inc.). Lists newspapers, magazines, journals, related publications, and radio and television stations. Annual.
- *Broadcasting/Cablecasting Yearbook* (Washington: Broadcast Publications, Inc.). Lists radio and television stations and cable TV systems.
- *Editor & Publisher International Year Book* (New York: *Editor & Publisher*). Detailed information about newspapers, their associations, and agencies that serve them.
- *SRDS Special Issues* (Wilmette, IL: Standard Rate & Data Service). Six issues a year provide editorial profiles of more than 5000 major print media.
- *Working Press of the Nation* (Chicago: National Research Bureau). Lists more than 30,000 publicity outlets in the print and electronic media.
- *Bacon's PR and Media Information Systems* (Chicago). Covers magazines, newspapers, radio, and television.

Several firms offer mailing lists designed to reach target audiences. They handle distribution of a client's news releases by mail, wire, or satellite. Among the major ones are PR Newswire, (New York), Business Wire (New York), Media Distribution Services (New York), Burrelle's Information Services (Livingston, NJ), and North American Precis Syndicate, Inc. (New York).

Nevertheless, editors do not enjoy the unfettered privilege of publishing whatever they desire. Two severe limitations hang over their decisions:

1. *The laws of libel and invasion of privacy.* Publication of material that, if challenged in court, is ruled to be libelous or an unreasonable invasion of privacy can cost a newspaper extremely heavy judgments and legal expenses. The newspaper management is legally responsible for everything a newspaper publishes, including material submitted by outsiders. Even letters to the editor are covered by the law of libel.

2. *The interests and desires of their readers.* If a newspaper fails to publish news and features that readers find to be valuable or entertaining, its circulation will dwindle and it will perish. Alert editors, therefore, are receptive to fresh ideas. They recognize the need for community service and look for ways in which their newspapers can perform this function. Their doors are open to public relations representatives who supply ideas and information that help the papers to please and inform their readers and to carry out the newspapers' social responsibility.

Organization of a Newspaper Those who work with newspapers in any aspect of public relations should know how a newspaper staff is organized, so they can take story ideas or policy problems to the proper person. In the usual table of organization, the publisher is the director of all financial, mechanical, and administrative operations. Frequently the publisher also has ultimate responsibility for news and editorial matters; in many instances he or she carries the title of editor and publisher.

The editor heads the news and editorial department. The associate editor conducts the editorial and commentary pages and deals with the public concerning their content. The managing editor is the head of news operations, to whom the city editor and the editors of sections such as sports, business, entertainment, and family living answer. Some newspapers have an executive editor above the managing editor. The city editor directs the local news staff of reporters. Some members of the city staff cover beats such as police and city hall; others are on general assignment, meaning that they are sent to cover any type of story the city editor deems to be potentially newsworthy. (Submission of news releases to editors is discussed in Chapter 22.)

Weekly newspapers have a different focus from that of daily newspapers, and much smaller staffs. The weekly concentrates exclusively on its own community. Its target zone may be no more than one segment of a metropolitan area. Weekly editors need the help of much volunteered material. Although weekly newspapers often are overlooked in public relations programs, they can be effective outlets for those who study how to meet their needs. The circulation for each weekly newspaper may be small because of its limited distribution area, but the intensity of readership is high and story exposure is good.

Large daily newspapers, to demonstrate editorial independence, often have a rule against publishing a news release exactly as received. Relatively few weekly newspapers have the staffs to enforce such a policy.

THREE CARDINAL RULES FOR NEWS RELEASES TO NEWSPAPERS

A news release submitted to a newspaper should . . .

1. Contain information that is newsworthy in that newspaper's circulation area.

2. Be addressed to the city editor if it is of general interest, or to the appropriate section editor if it contains special-interest material such as sports news.

3. Be delivered to the newspaper well in advance of the desired publication date, to provide time for processing.

PUBLIC RELATIONS OPPORTUNITIES IN NEWSPAPERS

Material for a newspaper should be submitted either as a news release ready for publication or as a factsheet from which a reporter can develop a feature story or interview. When an invitation to a news conference is sent to a newspaper, it should include a factsheet containing basic information. Frequently, the reporter to whom an editor assigns a news release for processing rewrites and expands it, developing additional story angles and background. When a public relations representative presents an important story idea in factsheet form rather than as a news release for publication, a personal conversation with the appropriate editor, if it can be arranged, helps to sell the concept and expand its potential. *Such personal calls on editors should last no longer than is necessary to explain the idea adequately*. Although some practitioners make a follow-up phone call shortly after the factsheet has arrived, this practice irritates many editors. They dislike being interrupted. (Preparations of news releases and factsheets is discussed in Chapter 22).

Emphasizing contemporary living styles, newspapers often publish special sections on home improvement, fashion and beauty, business, sports, and recreation. This trend creates additional opportunities for practitioners, because editors seek story ideas and well-developed releases for these sections.

A public relations representative wishing to discuss a large-scale project such as a communitywide fund drive should do so by appointment with the managing editor or city editor after the deadline hour has passed. A cooperative plan of publicity can be developed at such a session. A newspaper is more likely to give a major project sympathetic treatment if its editors receive background information before the first stories break. This allows them time to think about the ramifications of the project and plan coverage.

At times, an organization's representative or other individual needs to discuss a policy issue with the newspaper management—a complaint against perceived mistreatment by the newspaper, for example, or an attempt to obtain editorial support. Usually this is done by appointment with the editor or associate editor or, in the case of a news story, with the managing editor. Often problems arise from misunderstanding rather than from intent.

To cite an actual example, in a city with three hospitals, directors of the smallest institution believed that the city's newspaper was ignoring it. They were upset because no story had been published about enlargement of the hospital's outpatient treatment facilities. When a director discussed the problem with the newspaper's associate editor, however, the fact emerged that the hospital administrator had failed to notify the paper about the construction. He had assumed wrongly that the editors knew about it.

The lesson here is clear: when you have news to announce, tell the media; don't wait for them to come to you.

CREATING NEWS EVENTS

Some news stories *happen*. Other stories must be *created*. Successful public relations practitioners must do more than produce competent, accurate news releases about routine occurrences in the affairs of their clients or employers. They must use ingenuity and organizing ability to create events that attract coverage in the news media. Historian Daniel Boorstin calls these projects "pseudoevents." This extra dimension of creativity is the difference between acting to make news and merely reacting to news that happens. We are not speaking here of feeding phony stories to the media or doing anything else unethical. We are talking about causing something to occur. A good example is Light's Golden Jubilee, which was organized by Edward Bernays (see Chapter 3).

Simple ideas can have rewarding payoffs. The Warner-Lambert Company, which makes antacid tablets, recently received national television and front-page newspaper coverage with a created event, its National Rolaids Heartburn Index. This index indicated which of 198 U.S. population areas consume the most antacids. Eureka, California, had the dubious honor of winning first place. El Paso, Texas, residents used the fewest.

This offbeat event was based on company sales figures. Yet it grabbed attention because so many Americans take antacids for upset stomachs. The company backed up its statistics with analysis from a sociologist. At a kickoff press conference in New York, Warner-Lambert presented a Heartburn Capital plaque to the mayor of Eureka. He said he takes antacids daily. Edelman Public Relations worked with the company on the project.

Every one of the events in the accompanying list represents a legitimate news story that the local newspaper and other media might cover. But these stories exist only because a public relations adviser convinced the company to sponsor or conduct them. Once this decision is made, the practitioner must produce a flow of news releases with fresh angles, as well as use other techniques to build public interest.

Openings of stores and shopping centers, as well as groundbreakings, happen so frequently that the ingenuity of public relations representatives is challenged. Newspapers are weary of the traditional, rigidly posed group of men in dark business suits and incongruous hardhats lined up behind one man with a shovel. The same is true of ribbon-cuttings. Some newspapers refuse to publish these photographic clichés. However, fresh approaches can be found, especially if a little humor is employed.

In one small Southwestern town, a long-retired movie cowboy, who had won additional fame in early television Westerns, was a prominent resident. When a new shopping area was to be opened, he was invited to appear in a cowboy costume on a horse and cut the ribbon. Things didn't work out that way. His horse had died. He had grown too heavy to get into his cowboy pants. But clever thinking saved the situation for the community sponsors. The actor arrived at the scene in an automobile, wearing his cowboy hat and shirt. The gun he carried was a cap pistol. The broad red ribbon strung across the street had secretly been cut almost through the middle by the public relations specialist in charge.

At a signal, the rotund cowboy fired his toy pistol at the ribbon. At the popping sound, a slight tug by the ribbon-holders sent the red strand fluttering. Cameras clicked and everyone laughed. Although born of a practitioner's desperation, the tongue-in-cheek travesty drew more publicity than a routine ribbon-cutting would have done.

MAGAZINES

Magazines differ markedly from newspapers in content, time frame, and methods of operation. Therefore, they present different opportunities and problems to the public relations practitioner. In contrast to the daily newspaper with its hurry-up deadlines, magazines are published weekly, monthly, or sometimes quarterly. Because these publications usually deal with subjects in greater depth than newspapers do, magazine editors may allot months for the development of an article. Those who seek to supply

TRUCKLOAD OF BROCCOLI FOR BUSH

Quick thinking by a group of packers and growers at a vegetable packing shed in Guadalupe, California, created an entertaining news event that held international attention for a week.

One Monday morning, a packing executive mentioned to the group at work a little TV news story that President Bush had banned broccoli from the menu on Air Force One, his private plane, because he disliked the rugged green vegetable.

"Let's send him a case of broccoli," someone said. "No, let's send a whole truckload so they'll really notice it," another replied.

The next evening a big rig carrying nearly 10 tons of broccoli hit the road on a 3000-mile haul to Washington, D.C. Growers told the media what was happening. They hoped to give some cases to the White House and planned to donate the remainder to Washington food charities.

Would the anti-broccoli president accept the gift? Humorous speculation kept the story going.

On Friday the White House staff phoned to say that Mrs. Bush would receive the broccoli donation on the White House lawn on Monday morning. As cameras rolled and reporters sniffed the homely but wholesome vegetable, Mrs. Bush was presented with three cases of broccoli, a broccoli bouquet, and a recipe book. The TV networks featured the story tongue-in-cheek. Back at the packing shed, orders for broccoli rolled in.

"We could have spent $50,000 on ads in trade journals and not had anything like the impact we're getting," a packing house executive said. Thinking big and acting quickly made the idea succeed.

Barbara Bush, representing her husband, holds up her hands in mock surrender when presented with boxes of broccoli. California growers won national attention by sending a truckload of the vegetable to the White House after President Bush banned broccoli from Air Force One because he dislikes it. (Reuters/Bettmann)

FIGURE 12.2
The fiftieth anniversary celebration of the Golden Gate Bridge opening in San Francisco drew 800,000 people for a morning "bridge walk" in 1987 and another huge crowd for nighttime illumination and fireworks. The Pacific Gas and Electric Company contributed half the cost of the bridge lighting. (Photo by Ted Tsoi, courtesy of Pacific Gas and Electric Company.)

subject ideas or ready-to-publish material to them must plan much further ahead than is necessary with newspapers. Ideas for Christmas season stories, for example, should be submitted by July.

A newspaper is designed for family reading, with something for men, women, and children; its material is aimed at an audience of varying educational and economic levels. Its editors fire buckshot, to hit the reading interests of as many persons as possible. Magazine editors, on the other hand, in most instances aim carefully at special-interest audiences. They fire rifle bullets at limited, well-defined readership groups.

The more than 11,000 periodicals published in the United States may be classified in several ways. For purposes of this discussion, periodicals are grouped into two

THIRTY-TWO WAYS TO CREATE NEWS FOR YOUR ORGANIZATION

1. Tie in with news events of the day.

2. Work with another publicity person.

3. Tie in with a newspaper or other medium on a mutual project.

4. Conduct a poll or survey.

5. Issue a report.

6. Arrange an interview with a celebrity.

7. Take part in a controversy.

8. Arrange for a testimonial.

9. Arrange for a speech.

10. Make an analysis or prediction.

11. Form and announce names for committees.

12. Hold an election.

13. Announce an appointment.

14. Celebrate an anniversary.

15. Issue a summary of facts.

16. Tie in with a holiday.

17. Make a trip.

18. Make an award.

19. Hold a contest.

20. Pass a resolution.

21. Appear before public bodies.

22. Stage a special event.

23. Write a letter.

24. Release a letter you have received.

25. Adapt national reports and surveys for local use.

26. Stage a debate.

27. Tie into a well-known week or day.

28. Honor an institution.

29. Organize a tour.

30. Inspect a project.

31. Issue a commendation.

32. Issue a protest.

broad categories, those for the public at large and those for specific audiences. Each is in turn broken down into several subdivisions.

Periodicals for the Public at Large Among the types in this category are the following:

General Interest. Only a few national magazines with across-the-board appeal exist today. Prominent among them are *Reader's Digest,* enormously successful worldwide; *People,* which capitalizes on the contemporary interest in personalities; and *National Geographic.*

News Magazines. High-circulation weekly news magazines report and interpret the news, adding background that daily newspapers lack time to develop. The biggest periodicals of this type are *Time, Newsweek,* and *U.S. News & World Report.*

Women's Interest. Magazines designed for women have a very large audience. They publish articles about fashions and beauty, cooking, home decorating, self-improvement, work and leisure, and personal relationships. Prominent in this group are *Ladies' Home Journal, Cosmopolitan, Working Woman, Better Homes and Gardens, Good Housekeeping, House and Garden,* and *Family Circle*.

Men's Interest. Growing participation of women in athletics has increased female readership of traditionally male sports magazines. *Sports Illustrated* and *Field and Stream* are perhaps the best known of these magazines. With their emphasis on sex, *Playboy* and *Penthouse* aim primarily at the male audience but also draw substantial female readership.

The Senior Market. *Modern Maturity*, published by the American Association of Retired Persons (AARP), has the largest magazine circulation in the United States, more than 21 million. Maturity News Service sells feature stories of particular interest to older readers. Many monthly publications for seniors, usually distributed free in places where retirees live (such as mobile-home parks) are excellent outlets for public relations material at the local level. In general, older citizens read magazines and newspapers more than young people do; retirees in particular are heavy watchers of television as well.

The categories of magazines just listed offer public relations opportunities that pay large rewards in readership when successful. They are difficult markets to hit, however, except by highly experienced specialists well acquainted with the magazines' operating methods. Far more abundant opportunities for placing public relations material exist with the other periodicals, those aimed at more specific audiences.

Periodicals for Specific Audiences The specific-interest group includes a wide array of publications, including the following:

Special-Audience Magazines. Hundreds of these prosper because they are carefully edited on single themes. Each attracts an audience with strong interest in its particular topic; this audience in turn draws advertisers whose products are especially relevant to these readers. A glance at the magazine rack in a supermarket gives an indication of the diversity of special-interest magazines—only an indication, however, because such periodicals are far too numerous for over-the-counter sale. Many are distributed primarily by subscription.

A few examples include *Dog World, Backpacker, Stereo Review, Car Craft, Skin Diver, Surfing, Photography, Ski,* and *Hot Rod*. Broader in appeal than many of these are magazines about business, including *Fortune, Business Week, Forbes,* and *Barron's*.

Trade Journals Each of the special-audience magazines listed above appeals to a portion of the public that cares about its particular topic mostly as a hobby or a sport. Trade journals, on the other hand, are designed for persons who read them for business and professional reasons, not recreational ones. While virtually unknown to the public, these periodicals are vital channels of communication within various industries and professions. In their pages, readers learn about the activities of their competitors, new products and trends in their field of work, and the movement of individuals from one job to another. Often trade journals have the same intimacy in their respective fields as weekly newspapers do in their communities.

The following small sampling of trade journals indicates the extremely specialized nature of their contents: *American Christmas Tree Journal, Mini-Micro Systems, Fleet Owner, The Indian Trader, Insulation Outlook, Progressive Grocer, Wire Journal.*

Placement of material in trade journals is an essential assignment for many public relations representatives. A story about a new product published in an appropriate trade journal may be more valuable to the manufacturer of that product than a story about it in a large newspaper, because the information reaches a target audience containing potential purchasers. Products and specialized services offered by companies often are not publicized to a general audience, because it neither needs nor cares about them. If a manufacturer of coin-operated machines has a new product ready for release, for example, its public relations representative should concentrate on placing announcement stories in such trade journals as *American Coin-Op, Coinamatic Age, Play Meter Magazine,* and *Vending Times.*

Practitioners handling specialized products or services should scrutinize pertinent trade journals, to be certain that they are supplying these publications with effective news releases, story ideas, and illustrations. A one-year analysis of these journals will show how well a client and its competitors fared. With this analysis in hand, the publicist might find it desirable to submit more stories about large orders received by the client, for example, or stories about unusual uses of a product.

FIGURE 12.3
Food producers and manufacturers focus much of their public relations effort on food sections of newspapers and magazines, and on homemaking programs on television. News releases usually are accompanied by luscious photographs of the food, as in this material from the California Strawberry Advisory Board prepared by Ketchum Public Relations, San Francisco.

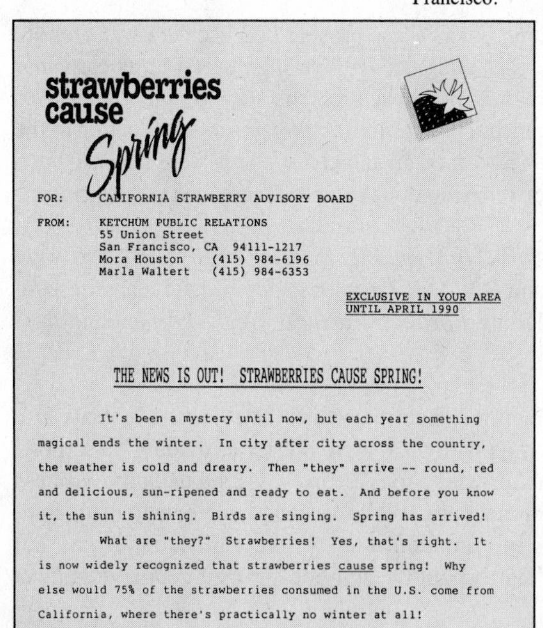

strawberries cause Spring

FOR: CALIFORNIA STRAWBERRY ADVISORY BOARD

FROM: KETCHUM PUBLIC RELATIONS
55 Union Street
San Francisco, CA 94111-1217
Mora Houston (415) 984-6196
Marla Waltert (415) 984-6353

EXCLUSIVE IN YOUR AREA
UNTIL APRIL 1990

THE NEWS IS OUT! STRAWBERRIES CAUSE SPRING!

It's been a mystery until now, but each year something magical ends the winter. In city after city across the country, the weather is cold and dreary. Then "they" arrive -- round, red and delicious, sun-ripened and ready to eat. And before you know it, the sun is shining. Birds are singing. Spring has arrived!

What are "they?" Strawberries! Yes, that's right. It is now widely recognized that strawberries cause spring! Why else would 75% of the strawberries consumed in the U.S. come from California, where there's practically no winter at all!

Company and Organizational Magazines There are two types of company and organizational magazine:

1. *Internal,* designed for and distributed primarily to employees, retirees, influential outsiders who may have some interest in the organization, and often stockholders of the firm. (These are discussed in Chapter 22.)

2. *External,* distributed to selected portions of the public. Published by companies and organizations to promote public appreciation of the sponsor, and to form a psychological tie between sponsor and recipient, these usually are circulated among customers, stockholders, and users of the sponsor's services. The editorial content appearing in such external periodicals has general appeal—articles on travel, personalities, self-help, food, and the like—plus material about the issuing company. The magazines that airline travelers find in the seat pockets in front of them, such as *American Way* (American Airlines) and *TWA Ambassador* (Trans World Airlines), are prime examples of this group. Such external magazines offer a good target for the public relations specialist. Their audiences tend to be relatively affluent.

PUBLIC RELATIONS OPPORTUNITIES IN MAGAZINES

A study of the annual *Writer's Market* and the monthly periodicals *Writer's Digest* and *The Writer* will provide abundant information about individual magazines and the kind of material each publishes. Every magazine has its special formula.

Operating with much smaller staffs than newspapers have, magazines are heavily dependent on material submitted from outside their offices. Some, especially the smaller ones, are almost entirely staff-written. The staffs create ideas and cover some stories; they also process public relations material submitted to them. The more carefully the submitted material is tailored to the particular periodical's audience and written in a style preferred by the editor, the more likely it is to be published, with or without rewriting by the staff. Many magazines purchase part, or almost all, of their material from free-lance writers on a fee basis. An editor may buy a submitted article for publication if it fits the magazine's formula, or the editor may commission a writer to develop an idea into an article along specified lines.

Editors are always looking for ideas. Many magazine articles had their origins in suggestions submitted by public relations practitioners. An article in a women's magazine on preventing sunburn, for example, may have resulted from a letter and a press kit sent to an editor by a sunscreen manufacturer or by the manufacturer's public relations firm.

A public relations practitioner has four principal approaches for getting material into a periodical:

1. Submit a story idea that would promote the practitioner's cause either directly or subtly, and urge the editor to have a writer, free-lance or staff, develop the story on assignment.

2. Send a written query to the editor outlining an article idea and offering to submit the article in publishable form if the editor approves the idea.

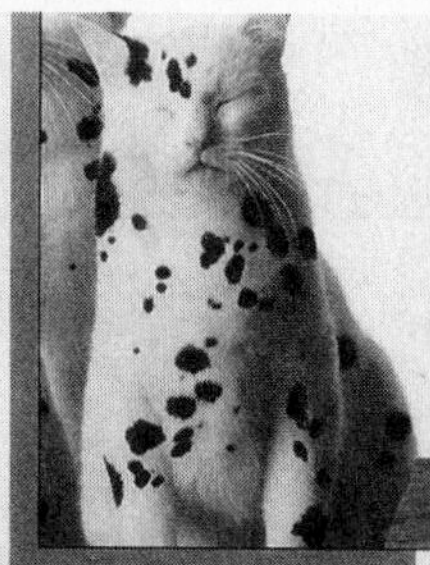

FIGURE 12.4
Trade magazines are an important channel for reaching special audiences. Most fields of business, industry, and professional endeavor have magazines in which trends, new products, and company changes are among the topics covered. This is the cover of a typically attractive, well-edited trade magazine.

3. Submit a completed article, written either by the practitioner or by an independent writer under contract, and hope that the editor will accept it for publication. In this and the two previously mentioned instances, however, the editor should be made fully aware of the source of the suggestion or article. As pointed out in Chapter 6, allowing a free-lance writer to place what presumably is an "independent" article is a violation of Article 9 of the PRSA Code of Professional Standards, which forbids using third parties who are purported to be independent but serve the special interests of the employer or client.

4. For trade journals and other periodicals that use such material, submit news releases in ready-to-publish form.

The size and nature of each magazine determines its content. Most common is a formula of several major articles, one or two short articles, and special departments. These may be personal commentary, a compilation of news items in a specific category (short items about new products in a trade journal, for example), or chit-chat about personalities. Special departments offer excellent public relations opportunities. A favorable item in one of them need not be long to be effective.

When a magazine has a by-lined columnist and the publicist has material suitable for that column, it may be sent directly to the columnist. The risk is that if the columnist rejects the item, he or she may throw it in the wastebasket when in fact it might be usable elsewhere in the magazine. When there is doubt, it is safer to submit such material to the editor. Examination of a magazine's masthead will show the name of the proper editor to address.

BOOKS

Because their writing and publication is a time-consuming process, often involving years from the conception of an idea until appearance of the volume, books are not popularly recognized as public relations tools. Yet they can be. A book, especially a hardcover one, has stature in the minds of readers. They read it with respect and give attention to the message it carries.

Books are promulgators of ideas. As channels of communication, they reach thoughtful audiences, including opinion leaders. Often publication of a book starts a trend or focuses national discussion on an issue.

The standard method of book publishing is for an author and publisher to sign a contract describing the material the author will deliver to the publisher and the conditions under which the publisher will issue and sell the book. The publisher pays the cost of production and marketing. The author receives a royalty fee on each copy sold, perhaps 10 to 15 percent of the retail price. Publishers often make advance payments to authors against the royalties their books are expected to earn.

A book published in hardcover often requires a year from acceptance of the manuscript to publication. Thus, a public relations effort made through publication of a hardcover book must be long range in nature and aimed at the broad-stroke influencing of public opinion. The hardcover book is not the tool for stirring up a new hula-hoop fad or publicizing a video game.

The tremendous growth of paperback publishing has opened new avenues for use of books as public relations vehicles. Hundreds of titles ranging from classical literature to how-to-do-it books on gardening, plumbing, and sex are on sale. An examination of nonfiction titles on the paperback shelves will show the range of opportunity that exists to promote products, ideological movements, personalities, and fads.

The traditional royalty system of hardcover books is also used for paperback books, but various forms of fee payments to authors are employed as well.

Literary agents have an influential role in the creation of books. An agent represents the author in dealings with publishers, urging a publishing house to accept a manuscript and negotiating contracts that include provisions for subsidiary rights, film rights, and other sources of income. For this assistance, the agent ordinarily receives 10 percent of the author's income from the literary property involved. Unless he or she is well acquainted with the publishing industry, a public relations representative seeking to publicize a client's cause through publication of a book is well advised to work through an agent rather than make a personal round of publishing houses. Competent agents know the financial angles and offer shrewd editorial advice as well.

Although the fact is seldom mentioned publicly, companies and nonprofit organizations sometimes pay subsidies to both hardcover and paperback publishers to help defray production costs of a book they wish to see published. The subsidy may take the form of a guarantee to purchase a specific number of copies. A corporation, for example, might wish to commemorate its centennial with a company history or to publicize its chief executive officer in a book, and may desire the prestige of a prominent publishing house behind it. Yet sales experience indicates that the book will not sell enough copies for the publisher to break even. So a quiet subsidy arrangement is made. A handsome book results; it receives favorable reviews, the corporation gains prestige, the publisher makes some money, and the public's fund of knowledge is increased. The book must be an honest one, however, not a blatant ''puff'' job. It must report the bad with the good. If not, everyone involved loses respect instead of gaining it.

The idea for a beautifully illustrated book on New England, to cite an example, might come from a state travel agency, which approaches the publisher either directly or through an author. The state agency pays part of the publisher's cost, knowing that the book will draw visitors to the area.

Another recently developed form of subsidized book has been created by Whittle Publications L. P. Books in the series are underwritten by major advertisers and cover important business and social topics. Each book contains full-page color advertisements for the sponsor's service or product interspersed throughout the text. Copies are sent free to managers and policymakers in business and the public sector.

Typical of such subsidized books published by Whittle is *Life After Television* by George Gilder, which contains 18 full-page advertisements for Federal Express.

PUBLIC RELATIONS OPPORTUNITIES IN BOOKS

As indicated above, books as public relations tools, both hardcover and paperback, usually are best suited to promote ideas and create a favorable state of mind. Political movements often are publicized through books by proponents. On a more mundane level, every book published about gardening indirectly helps the sale of garden tools. Although a specific brand of tools is not mentioned in such a book, it benefits from the book's existence. The manufacturer's public relations representative can help the company's cause by assisting the author in assembling material for the book. Public relations efforts need not be overt to be effective. Also, public relations benefits may occur without being planned. The cookbook *The Complete Dairy Foods Cookbook,* by E. Annie Proues and Lew Nichols, inevitably helped promote use of dairy products, while *The Joy of Chocolate,* by Judith Olney, must have made chocolate manufacturers happy.

From the point of view of publishers, publicity for books and their authors is an important public relations function. The public relations departments of publishing houses use news releases, prepublication endorsements, interviews, and other standard techniques to create awareness of a forthcoming book. If the book lends itself to heavy promotion and the author is articulate, the writer may be taken on a tour of major cities for an intensive series of radio and television appearances and newspaper interviews, plus autographing parties in bookstores.

THE SPOKEN MEDIA

RADIO

Speed and mobility are the special attributes that make radio unique among the major media of communication. If urgency justifies such action, messages can be placed on the air by radio almost instantly upon their receipt at a radio station. They need not be delayed by the time-consuming production processes of print. Since radio programming is more loosely structured than television programming, interruption of a program for an urgent announcement can be done with less internal decision-making. Although most public relations material does not involve such urgency, moments of crisis do occur when quick on-the-air action helps a company or other organization get information to the public swiftly.

Radio benefits, too, from its ability to go almost anywhere. Reporters working from mobile trucks can be broadcasting from the scene of a large fire within minutes after it has been discovered. They can hurry from a press conference to a luncheon speech, carrying only a small amount of equipment. A disc jockey can broadcast an afternoon program from a table in a neighborhood shopping center. Flexibility is ever-present.

So is flexibility among listeners. Radios in automobiles reach captive audiences, enhancing the popularity of drive-time disc jockeys. The tiny transistor or mini earphone-type radio brings programs to mail carriers on their routes, carpenters on construction sites, homeowners pulling weeds in their gardens.

Approximately 10,000 radio stations are on the air in the United States, ranging from low-powered outlets operated by a handful of staff members to large metropolitan stations audible for hundreds of miles. Slightly less than half of these stations are of the amplitude modulation (AM) type; the others use frequency modulation (FM), which has shorter range but generally clearer reception. Some AM stations aim at general audiences, using middle-of-the-road music, while others appeal to special listener interests. FM stations, with restricted listening areas, usually seek target audiences. Both AM and FM stations attempt to develop distinctive ''sounds'' by specializing in one kind of music or talk format. A public relations practitioner should study each station's format and submit material suitable to it. There is little sense in sending information about senior citizen recreational programs to the news director of a hard-rock station with an audience primarily of teenagers.

A radio station operates under license, renewable every seven years, from the Federal Communications Commission. After several decades of strict FCC regulation, the radio industry was partially deregulated in 1981, thus obtaining greater flexibility in programming. No longer must a station devote part of its air time to nonentertainment programming or restrict the number of minutes in each hour devoted to commercials. Even with these restrictions removed, a station may encounter license renewal trouble if it cannot demonstrate reasonably well under challenge that it operates in the public interest, necessity, and convenience. All programs are subject to the laws of libel.

PUBLIC RELATIONS OPPORTUNITIES IN RADIO

Commercial radio is highly promotional in nature and provides innumerable opportunities for public relations specialists to further their causes. Radio programs may be divided into two general categories, news programs and entertainment shows. A station's news director is responsible for the former, the program director for the latter. At least seven possible targets exist in radio for a public relations practitioner:

1. *Newscasts.* Many stations have frequent newscasts, of which the five-minute variety is the most common. If the station has a network affiliation, some newscasts it carries are national in content. Of much more interest to the public relations practitioner are the local newscasts. These have abundant public relations potential. News releases sent to a radio station should cover the same newsworthy topics as those sent to a newspaper; they should follow identical rules of accuracy and timeliness. The practitioner cannot expect to hear extended versions of these releases on the air. Brevity is fundamental on radio. A story that runs 400 words in a newspaper may be told in 75 words or fewer on radio. Lengthy news releases for radio stations are unnecessary, indeed unwise, unless portions of them are clearly identified as background information, in case the news director chooses to develop a story at greater length in a special feature broadcast.

2. *Community calendars.* Stations broadcast a daily program called the "Community Bulletin Board" or a similar title. This listing of coming events is an excellent place to circulate information about a program the practitioner is handling.

3. *Actualities.* Radio news directors brighten their newscasts by including *actualities.* These are brief reports from scenes of action, either live or on tape. Public relations representatives may supply stations with actualities to be used on newscasts. If a high executive of a practitioner's client speaks at a luncheon, a brief taped highlight from that speech, if sent to a radio station, may find a place on a local newscast. So might a taped highlight from the dedication ceremony for a manufacturing plant. Radio stations tend to have small news staffs and cannot cover as many events as they desire. They welcome assistance if it is provided in an objective manner.

4. *Talk shows*. Another goal for public relations efforts is the radio talk show, on which a moderator and guests discuss issues. Placement of a client on a talk show provides exposure for the individual and for the cause being espoused. Talk shows may be news-oriented, such as a discussion of a controversial issue, and produced by the news director. Or they may be entertainment-oriented, controlled by the program director and handled by a staff producer. Midmorning homemaker hours have numerous spots for guest appearances.

5. *Editorials*. More powerful radio stations, in particular, broadcast daily editorials, comparable to newspaper editorials. Usually these are delivered by the station manager. Public relations specialists may be able to persuade a station to carry an editorial of endorsement for their cause. They should stay alert, too, for editorials that condemn a cause they espouse. The representative should request equal time on the air for a rebuttal, usually given by a leading executive of the organization or cause under attack. Hundreds of smaller stations, however, do not carry editorials.

6. *Disc jockey shows*. On the entertainment side, disc jockeys in their programs of music and chit-chat frequently air material provided by public relations sources. The DJs conduct on-the-air contests and promotions, give away tickets to shows, discuss coming local events, offer trivia quizzes—whatever they can think of to make their programs distinctive and lively. A disc jockey talking on the air several hours a day devours large amounts of material. After studying a program's style, an able practitioner can supply items and ideas that the DJ welcomes, and thus promote the causes of public relations clients.

7. *Community events*. At times, radio stations sponsor community events such as outdoor concerts or long-distance runs. Repeated mention of such an event on the air for days or weeks usually turns out large crowds. Here, too, is an opportunity for the public relations person, either to convince a station to sponsor such an event or to develop tie-ins with it.

A close relationship exists between radio stations and the recording industry. Recording companies depend on the stations to play their new releases; the stations in turn use those companies as the primary source for the music they play. This relationship has created a highly specialized form of public relations work by representatives of the record companies.

TELEVISION

Our lives feel the impact of television more than that of any other communications medium. Approximately 1400 television stations are in operation, projecting over-the-air visual programming. According to estimates provided by the A. C. Nielson Company, the major rating firm for national programming, more than 88 million American households own television sets. According to Nielsen statistics, the average American family watches television a little more than 7 hours a day.

Little wonder that public relations specialists look upon television as an enormous arena in which to tell their stories!

The fundamental factor that differentiates television from the other media and gives it such pervasive impact is the visual element. Producers of entertainment shows, newscasts, and commercials regard movement on the screen as essential. Something must happen to hold the viewer's attention. Persons talking on the screen for more than a brief time without movement, or at least a change of camera angle, are belittled as "talking heads."

Because of this visual impact, television emphasizes personality. Entertainment programs are built around stars. Only on television do news reporters achieve "star quality." When public relations people plan material for television, they should remember the importance of visual impact and personality.

Television shows live and die by their ratings. A scorecard mentality dominates the selection of programs and program content, especially on the networks. The viewing habits of a few thousand Americans, recorded by the Nielson, Arbitron, and other rating services, determine what programs all TV watchers can see. The explanation is money. Networks and local stations determine the prices they charge to show commercials by the estimated size of the audience watching a program when the commercial is shown. Thus the larger the audience, the higher the price for commercial time and the higher the profit. Even nonprofit television stations keep a close watch on the size of their audiences, because their income in part comes from the grants corporations give them to show certain programs.

A tremendous battle for admission to the home viewer's screen has developed among cable TV, video, and the traditional over-the-air stations and networks. In the mid-1970s, the three basic commercial networks were viewed by 92 percent of the audience during prime-time evening hours. This figure had fallen into the low 60 percent range in the early 1990s and continued to fall as the total television audience was fragmented.

This turmoil opened enormous new programming potential and a consequent increase in public relations opportunities. When a cable system offers up to 100 channels, as some are technically capable of doing, the demand for program material is voracious.

Although most television stations are on the air for 18 hours or more a day, only a few hours of programming originate in their studios—mostly newscasts, local talk shows, and midmorning homemaker programs with a host or hostess and guests. Much of the day's programming consists of network "feeds," if the station has a network affiliation. Development of satellite transmission (discussed in Chapter 21) has created numerous smaller networks that provide entertainment, news, and sports shows, giving independent stations new sources of programming.

Cable Television Because television networks and individual stations, especially those in major cities, gear their programming to large audiences, public relations practitioners have difficulty in obtaining air time for projects lacking mass appeal. Cable television, however, often presents valuable opportunities.

Approximately 54 million U.S. households were wired for cable TV by 1990. However, the number of viewers for a cable channel usually is relatively small, because the total TV audience is fragmented among the numerous competing channels. On the plus side, the public relations specialist faces fewer editing and management barriers in getting a program or short segment broadcast.

The Cable Communications Policy Act of 1984 gives local authorities the right to demand that cable systems to which they grant operating franchises include an *access channel* for public, educational, or government programming. These so-called PEG channels carry programs of a special-interest nature. Such programs do not contain advertising. Public relations directors for cultural, social, and other nonprofit agencies—and even for commercial interests—can use them effectively to promote public-service causes by creating interesting programs.

Some cable systems also produce *local origination* (LO) programming. LO programs may carry advertising. They offer an outlet for public relations material that provides substantial information without being obviously commercial in tone. Video news releases of various lengths are a good possibility for local origination programs.

PUBLIC RELATIONS OPPORTUNITIES IN TELEVISION

The possibilities for the public relations specialist to use television are so numerous that they are worth examining on two levels, network and local.

The Network Level There are six principal methods commonly used:

1. *Guest appearances on news and talk shows*. Placement of clients on such programs as the ''Tonight'' and ''Today'' shows allows them to give plugs to new products, books, films, and plays, and to advocate their causes. For entertainment personalities in particular, these interviews provide a setting in which to display their skills. National leaders are interviewed in depth on the Sunday discussion panel shows such as ''Meet the Press.'' Guests on network interview shows must be articulate and poised, so they won't freeze up before the camera. Consequently, they are carefully screened by show production staffs before being granted an appearance. Nationally syndicated talk programs such as the ''Phil Donahue Show,'' the ''Oprah Winfrey Show,'' and the ''Arsenio Hall Show,'' which are sold to individual stations, provide excellent showcases.

   Public relations people wishing to place guests on these programs should apply to the producers of the shows.

2. *News releases and story proposals to network news departments*. This process is identical to that followed with radio stations. If a story or an idea is accepted, the assignment editor gives it to a reporter for visual development. Letters like the one in Figure 12.5 often are sent directly to popular TV personalities, suggesting stories for them to do. When a client is criticized in a controversial news situation or editorial, a representative should submit the client's response and urge that it be used on the air. If the response is submitted in concise videotape form, the likelihood of a quick airing is increased.

3. *Video news releases,* commonly called VNRs. These are ready-to-broadcast tapes for use in news programs. News programs will use VNRs in some form if they are well done and avoid delivering an obvious commercial message. (VNRs are discussed in Chapter 24.)

4. *Program ideas*. The representative of an important cause may propose to a network that it build an episode in a dramatic or situation comedy series around this cause.

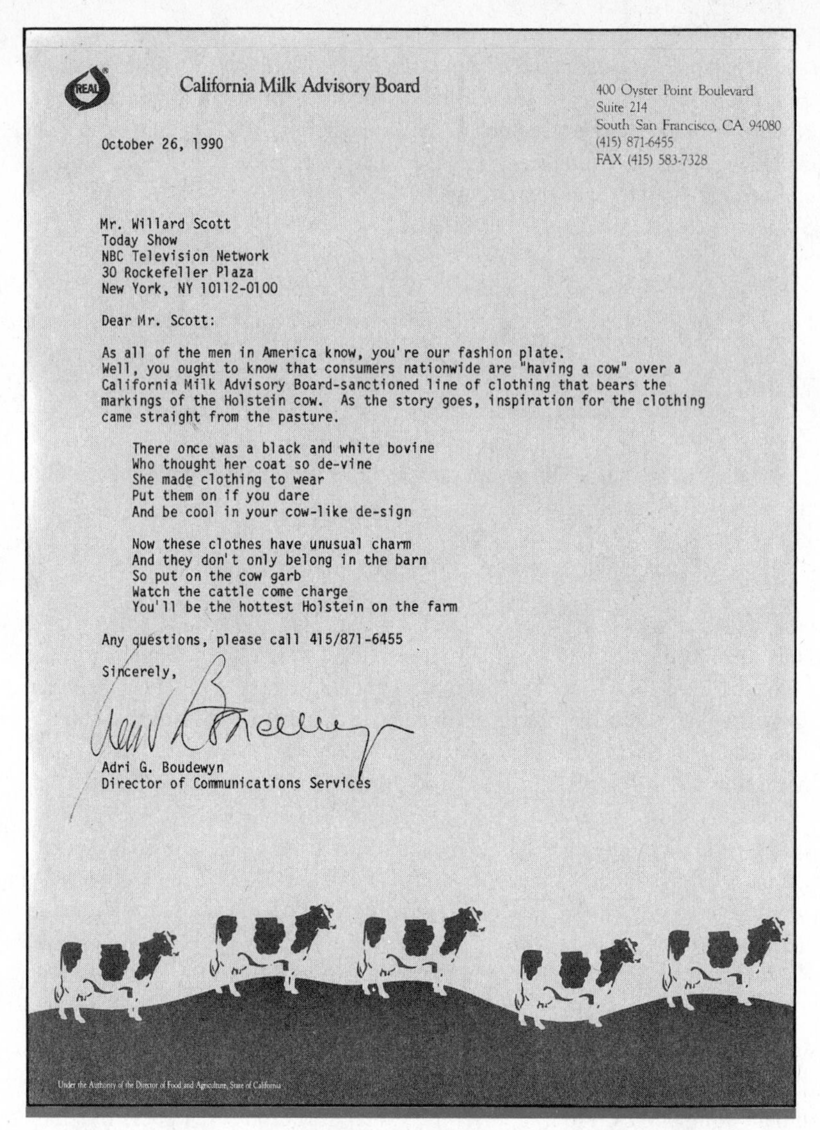

California Milk Advisory Board

400 Oyster Point Boulevard
Suite 214
South San Francisco, CA 94080
(415) 871-6455
FAX (415) 583-7328

October 26, 1990

Mr. Willard Scott
Today Show
NBC Television Network
30 Rockefeller Plaza
New York, NY 10112-0100

Dear Mr. Scott:

As all of the men in America know, you're our fashion plate. Well, you ought to know that consumers nationwide are "having a cow" over a California Milk Advisory Board-sanctioned line of clothing that bears the markings of the Holstein cow. As the story goes, inspiration for the clothing came straight from the pasture.

There once was a black and white bovine
Who thought her coat so de-vine
She made clothing to wear
Put them on if you dare
And be cool in your cow-like de-sign

Now these clothes have unusual charm
And they don't only belong in the barn
So put on the cow garb
Watch the cattle come charge
You'll be the hottest Holstein on the farm

Any questions, please call 415/871-6455

Sincerely,

Adri G. Boudewyn
Director of Communications Services

Under the Authority of the Director of Food and Agriculture, State of California

FIGURE 12.5
Pitch letters to broadcasters and editors, intended to stimulate their interest in a story idea, are an essential public relations tool. They often are written cleverly to catch the recipient's attention in a crowded mailbag, as is this one to a prominent national television figure known for doing offbeat things on the air.

The public relations person can assist the program producer by supplying technical information. Such programs do not make overt sales pitches for the treatment organizations, but the message is inherent in the story line.

Activist groups apply considerable pressure on television producers and the networks to include social issues such as environmental cleanups, drunk driving, and

AIDS in their program scripts. Characters in situation comedies or dramas quite frequently take strong advocacy positions in the plot line, thus delivering a message to viewers. A case in point: the character Joey Harris in the NBC comedy "My Two Dads" was sent to jail in one episode for dumping sludge from a polluted beach into the toilets at an oil company's office.

5. *Silent publicity.* There are almost subliminal impacts in entertainment programs that quietly publicize a representative's cause. In a private detective show, for example, the star may be shown chasing the villain through an airport terminal past a TWA sign. Or the automobiles used by the lead characters may be Ford products exclusively. Sometimes a program's credits include a mention such as, "Transportation provided by American Airlines." Another way to generate silent publicity, especially valuable for the tourist industry, is to convince network show producers to shoot their programs in a client's city or region, showing the scenery there. The network series "Miami Vice," "The Streets of San Francisco," and "Cheers" (set in Boston) provided those localities with immeasurable publicity.

6. *Public service commercials.* Announcements for important nonprofit causes are run occasionally by stations nationwide as public relations gestures. The Advertising Council often prepares materials for national nonprofit organizations as a public service.

The Local Station Level The methods listed for network public relations apply just as effectively on the local level—indeed, even more so in some instances, because competition for time on local stations often is less intense. The more intimate nature of local programming increases public relations opportunities. Even a diaper-changing contest at a shopping mall can gain air time.

HOW TO PLACE A CLIENT ON A TV TALK SHOW

Television stations are looking for interesting, articulate guests for their talk shows. The larger the station, the more stringent are its requirements for accepting a guest. This summary of needs and procedures for "AM/San Francisco," the morning show on KGO-TV, the ABC network outlet in San Francisco, is typical of those for metropolitan stations. The information is from an article published in *Bulldog,* a West Coast public relations newsletter.

The station wants guests "who will provide information that will help our viewers to save money and save time, helpful hints around the house, consumer-type things." The station also uses guests from the business community who can comment on money, taxes, the stock market, and similar topics.

KGO-TV defines the audience for this show as primarily nonworking women, 18 to 49, married, with at least one child. The show also attracts working viewers before they leave for their jobs.

Segments on the one-hour show run from 6 to 10 minutes. The usual pattern is to open with a celebrity-entertainer, then offer two segments on consumer topics. Segments 4, 5, and 6 cover "more serious subjects."

The production staff normally will consider for appearance only those who have appeared on television previously. Usually it asks to see a video clip of a prior TV appearance; an effective clip is an important way to gain acceptance.

"TV is a visual medium and a lot of our audience isn't just sitting there watching. They're folding clothes or ironing, so we need a voice that will grab their attention."

The public relations practitioner should submit a brief written query to the show's producer—"a 1-page letter getting straight to the basics: whom you're offering, what their experience is, exactly what their topic would be, what shows they've been on previously, a bio (biographical statement) and all other information available on the person, as well as clippings, copies of articles on the person or topic."

Staff members try to answer queries in about a week, perhaps sooner. The show is booked at least a week in advance but sometimes has last-minute openings.

There are four most frequently used techniques:

1. *Guest appearances on local talk shows*. Visiting experts in such fields as homemaking crafts, sponsored by companies and trade associations, demonstrate their skills for moderator and audience. National public relations firms send such clients around well-established circuits of local television and radio shows in each city they visit.

2. *Protest demonstrations*. Filmed demonstrations are such a staple on some television stations in large cities as to be a visual cliché. A group supporting or opposing a cause notifies a station that it will march at a certain time and place. Carrying placards, the marchers parade before the camera and a representative is shown explaining their cause. Such protesting drew international attention during the 1990 global AIDS conference in San Francisco, when marchers aggressively demanded faster progress in research for a cure for the disease. Although, for fairness, stations should put on an advocate for the other side in the same sequence, some stations neglect this responsibility, and so the marching group's point of view dominates. Many group demonstrations are so much alike, however, that their impact is minimized. Stations use them primarily because they involve movement.

3. *Videotapes for news shows*. Smaller TV stations, in particular, lack enough staff to cover all potentially newsworthy events in their areas. Practitioners can fill the gaps by delivering videotapes of events they handle, for inclusion in newscasts. Excerpts from a local speech by a prominent client may be incorporated in an evening news show. Arrival or departure at the local airport of a client in the news might be used, too, if the person says something newsworthy on camera.

4. *General-interest films*. Local cable channels sometimes will show films of 15- or 20-minute duration produced by corporations in which the direct commercial message is nonexistent or muted. The purpose of such films is to strengthen a company's image as a good community citizen. Films explaining large civic programs by nonprofit organizations also may be used.

MOTION PICTURES

Mention of motion pictures brings to mind, first and inevitably, the commercial entertainment film turned out by that nebulous place called Hollywood. From a public relations point of view, possibilities for influencing the content of commercial motion pictures for client purposes are relatively limited. Practitioners who know their way through the labyrinth of Hollywood financing and production can make deals for silent publicity through use of brand-name merchandise; and in a broad sense, causes sometimes get a helping hand from the thrust of a plotline, perhaps inadvertently.

Some producers charge from $10,000 to $60,000 for a commercial mention in their films, depending on the amount of exposure. General Motors arranged for a prominent appearance of the Chevrolet Lumina model in the Tom Cruise racing film, *Days of Thunder,* and in return promoted the film in its dealer showrooms.

Public relations counselors and corporate departments serve occasionally as advisers on films that involve their areas of expertise. Filmmakers seek this advice to prevent embarrassing technical errors on the screen and to protect themselves from inadvertently angering a group that might retaliate by denouncing the picture. In terms of specific public relations results similar to those obtainable from the other mass media, however, commercial films are a minor channel.

SPONSORED FILMS

In other forms, the motion picture is an important public relations tool.

Corporations and nonprofit organizations use motion pictures for internal purposes as part of audiovisual programs to train and inform their employees, or for external purposes to inform and influence the public and the financial community. Some films are effective for both internal and external audiences.

Levi Strauss & Co., for example, created an outstanding film for internal use. The company hired eminent photographers and filmmakers, along with broadcast news crews, to work with 38 employee photographers in shooting 120 hours of videotape during a single day at its 58 locations in 20 countries. The results were edited down to a half-hour program titled "A Day in the Life of Levi Strauss."

The artistically distinctive presentation—part of the company's employee orientation program—is being shown to all 22,000 Levi Strauss employees worldwide. Its purpose is to bolster their pride in the company and to demonstrate that it is a special place to work.

A second significant use of the motion picture in public relations is directly promotional. Although avoiding frontal-attack sales messages such as those in television commercials, these films seek to whet the interest of audience members who are potential purchasers of the sponsor's product or contributors to the sponsor's cause. For example, a travel agency shows members of an invited audience a film about a Caribbean cruise. Colorful photography with voice-over narration depicts the scenery cruise passengers will see. Shipboard activities, including a few humorous touches, are shown. So are the luxurious accommodations and the enormous buffet tables from which travelers select their meals (no passenger ever is seasick in such films, of course).

Similarly, a university president at a dinner meeting of alumni shows a film of the campus as it is today. The film is a carefully contrived balance of nostalgia and progress, with scenes of football games and students at work in the new science building. Having rekindled alumni interest in the old school, the film closes with a recital of

FIGURE 12.6
Preparations are made for shooting a dramatic sequence in the Levi Strauss corporate film *Quality Never Goes Out of Style* at Old Tucson, Arizona. (Produced by Furman Films, directed by Will Furman, for Levi Strauss & Co.)

the university's plans and aspirations. Usually these include the need for a new building, the funds for which the alumni are invited to contribute.

Motion pictures of the types just described often are made on 16-millimeter film. Others are made on videotape and a few on 8-millimeter film.

A discussion of filmmaking appears in Chapter 24.

CASE PROBLEM

Cygna Labs, a medium-sized pharmaceutical firm located in Salt Lake City, has developed a sunscreen lotion. The product, Sun-Cure, joins a number of similar products on store shelves. Independent laboratory testing shows that Sun-Cure is particularly effective in blocking UVB rays, which cause burning and even premature aging of the skin. It is a good product and gets high ratings from dermatologists.

Unfortunately, the public still shows confusion about the differences between sunscreens and suntan lotions, as well as the merits of competing brands. Your public relations firm is retained to develop a product publicity program for Sun-Cure that would reach daily newspapers, selected magazines, radio, and television. What communication strategies would you develop for getting coverage in each medium?

QUESTIONS FOR REVIEW AND DISCUSSION

1. On what basis do newspaper editors select the news releases they publish?

2. When a public relations practitioner desires to challenge and/or respond to a daily newspaper editorial, to whom should the material be addressed?

3. A good public relations person knows how to create news events. Why is this important?

4. What significant differences between magazines and newspapers must a public relations practitioner keep in mind when submitting material to them?

5. Why are special-audience magazines and trade journals such important targets for many public relations people?

6. For what purpose can books be used effectively as public relations outlets?

7. What two special attributes make radio distinctive among the major media of mass communication?

8. Do local radio newscasts have a good potential as an outlet for news releases? If so, why?

9. Ratings determine which television programs survive and which die. Why do ratings have such power?

10. How should public relations representatives go about trying to place their clients on television interview shows?

SUGGESTED READINGS

Caruba, Alan. ''Media Musical Chairs: A Guide to Media Directories Worth Owning.'' *Communication World,* July–August 1988, pp. 49–51.

Claudill, James. ''Working with Editorial Boards.'' *Public Relations Journal,* March 1989, pp. 31–32.

DuPont, Stephen. ''The Personal Touch: A Guide to Media Relations Angling.'' *Communication World,* January 1990, pp. 20–22.

Evans, Fred J. *Managing the Media: Proactive Strategy for Better Business–Press Relations.* New York: Quorum Books, 1987.

Fischer, Rick. ''Media Lists: Let Your Computer Do the Searching.'' *Public Relations Quarterly,* Summer 1990, pp. 15–21.

Fry, Susan L. ''Reaching Hispanic Publics with Special Events.'' *Public Relations Journal,* February 1991, pp. 12–13, 30.

Hart, Mark. ''Getting Exposure Using Radio Promotions.'' *Public Relations Journal,* July 1990, pp. 27–28.

Holland, James R. ''Reaching Older Audiences: Aging America Presents Communications Challenges and Opportunities.'' *Public Relations Journal,* May 1991, pp. 14–15, 20–21.

Kaufman, Joanne. ''Hello, Can You Be a Talk Show Guest?'' New York *Times,* May 31, 1987, p. 25. The role of bookers in getting celebrities on talk shows.

Kneale, Dennis. ''Cable Television Channels Emerge as Important Sources of Programs.'' *Wall Street Journal*, March 16, 1988, p. 29.

Sabolik, Mary. ''Print Media Placement Strategies for the New Segmentation.'' *Public Relations Journal,* November 1989, pp. 15–19.

Schwartz, Donald, and Glynn, Carroll. ''Selecting Channels for Institutional Public Relations.'' *Public Relations Review,* Winter 1989, pp, 24–36.

Smolowe, Jill. ''Read This!!!!'' *Time,* November 26, 1990, pp. 62–67, 70. Cover story on the proliferation of direct (junk) mail in American society.

Stevenson, Richard. ''And Now a Message from an Advocacy Group.'' New York *Times*, May 27, 1990, p. 21H. How groups lobby TV producers to get messages in scripts.

Trufelman, Lloyd. ''How to Plug In to Cable TV.'' *Public Relations Journal*, September 1988, pp. 43–44.

CHAPTER

13

Public Relations and the Law

The public relations professional, in order to do his or her job well, must be familiar with laws and government regulations that affect the content and distribution of messages.

A practitioner, for example, can be held liable (along with the organization's officers) for such malpractices as (1) using an employee's picture in a sales brochure without proper authorization, (2) writing a news release that makes false claims about a product, (3) implying that a labor union leader is associated with organized crime, (4) using a copyrighted article or cartoon without permission, or even (5) failing to take precautions to avoid injury to a participant at a special event.

The impact of what public relations people do or say is magnified many times because they are considered the official representatives of an organization. A practitioner's words are interpreted as reflecting management's viewpoint. And the courts have long held that public relations materials and advertising are subject to legal action if they are misleading, untruthful, or libelous.

This chapter provides a brief overview of legal concepts that must be kept in mind as members of a public relations staff go about their work. It covers the areas of (1) libel and slander, (2) employee rights, (3) photo releases, (4) ownership of ideas, (5) copyright, (6) trademarks, (7) the Federal Trade Commission (FTC) and the Securities and Exchange Commission (SEC), (8) corporate free speech, (9) meeting rooms, plant tours, and open houses, and (10) relationship with legal counsel.

A SAMPLING OF LEGAL PROBLEMS

The law and its many ramifications are somewhat abstract to the average person. Many people may have difficulty imagining exactly how public relations personnel can run afoul of the law, or generate a suit, by simply communicating information.

To bring things down to earth, and to make this chapter more meaningful, we provide here a sampling of recent government regulatory agency cases and lawsuits that involved public relations materials and the work of practitioners.

- The vice president of public affairs for Beneficial Corporation and her two brothers were charged with insider trading after trading stock the day before a public announcement about the company's finances.
- Lotus Development Corporation filed a lawsuit against a Boston advertising agency alleging that the firm tried to solicit new business from Microsoft Corporation by offering to share Lotus trade secrets.
- An $875,000 libel judgment was levied against a chemical industry newsletter that published a letter of reprimand given a cancer researcher without checking its accuracy.
- The North Carolina attorney general's office launched an investigation of a BellSouth Corporation subsidiary, alleging that the corporation coerced employees to write misleading letters to the state utilities commission.
- A Seattle developer who planned to launch thousands of balloons at a shopping center opening spent a large amount fighting a lawsuit filed by an environmental group.
- An artist sued American Family Association (AFA) for copyright infringement after the association used portions of his work in a mass mailing.
- Anheuser-Busch won a trademark infringement suit against an insecticide manufacturer that took the slogan ''Where There's Life, There's Bud'' and converted it to ''Where There's Life, There's Bugs.''
- Anthony M. Franco, owner of Detroit's largest public relations firm, signed an SEC consent decree after being charged with using inside information from a client to purchase stock (see Chapter 6).
- The SEC suspended stock sales of ATI, Inc., after the company made the misleading claim in a news release that one of its disinfectants was ''newly developed'' and was able to kill one kind of herpes virus.
- The Department of Justice began proceedings against the public relations firm of Gray & Co. for violating the Foreign Agents Registration Act by not clearly identifying a video news release produced on behalf of Morocco.
- Michael Deaver, who started a Washington lobbying and public affairs firm after

leaving the White House staff, was convicted for violation of the Ethics in Government Act, which bars influence peddling (see Chapters 6 and 15).

- The Jos. Schlitz Brewing Company and its public relations firm were sued for $3.5 million by three former executives of the company who maintained that a news release had libeled them.
- The United Way of America was sued for $100,000 by an 81-year-old man featured on a campaign poster. He charged that his picture had been used without permission.
- A news release by Getty Oil about an impending merger with Pennzoil became a significant document in the court case charging Texaco with illegally interfering with Pennzoil's move to purchase Getty. The result was a $3 billion judgment against Texaco.
- United Features Syndicate sued a New York senator for copyright and trademark infringement when he used the famous cartoon character Snoopy on campaign literature.
- Shandwick, the British-based public relations firm, sued the former president of an acquired firm for violating an agreement by starting a competing firm and taking two clients with him.

These examples provide some idea of the legal pitfalls that a public relations person may encounter in preparing materials for a client or employer. In many cases the suits are eventually dismissed or settled out of court, but the organization still pays dearly for the adverse publicity generated and the expense of defending itself.

Public relations personnel and firms must also be aware that they can be held legally liable if they provide advice or tacitly support an illegal activity of a client or employer. This area of liability is called *conspiracy*. A public relations person can be named as a co-conspirator with other company officials if he or she . . .

1. Participates in an illegal action such as bribing a government official or covering up information of vital interest to the public health and safety.
2. Counsels and guides the policy behind an illegal action.
3. Takes a major personal part in the illegal action.
4. Helps establish a ''front group'' whereby the connection to the public relations firm or its client is kept hidden.
5. Cooperates in any other way to further an illegal action.

LIBEL AND SLANDER

Public relations professionals should be thoroughly familiar with the concepts of libel and defamation. Such knowledge is crucial if an organization's internal and external communications are to meet legal and regulatory standards with a minimum of legal complications. At the same time, a knowledgeable public relations staff can help monitor the media and other sources to spot potentially libelous statements about the client or employer.

Defamation is a published or spoken false statement that damages a person's reputation. A written defamation constitutes *libel* and an oral defamation, *slander*. Because a person may be injured as greatly in a radio or television broadcast as in a printed publication, the courts have come to treat broadcast defamation as libel.

LAWSUITS AGAINST A COMPANY

There isn't much investigative reporting in public relations work, but libel and slander suits are filed against company officials when they send out news releases or make false statements that injure someone's reputation. More than one executive has been sorry that he or she lost control during a news conference and called the leaders of a labor union "a bunch of crooks and compulsive liars." Suits have also been filed for calling a news reporter "a pimp for all environmental groups" or charging that a dissident stockholder is "a closet communist."

Although news releases rarely are involved in libel suits, a 1987 ruling supports the idea that a company can use the same standards of defense as does a media organization that prints the story. The ruling was made by a justice of the New York Supreme Court, who dismissed a $20 million libel suit against J. Walter Thompson advertising agency. The case involved a former employee who claimed she was libeled by a news release from the firm announcing that she had been dismissed because of financial irregularities in the department she headed. The New York justice ruled that the plaintiff had not proved a "preponderance of evidence that the publisher acted in a grossly irresponsible manner without due consideration for the standard of information gathering and dissemination ordinarily followed by responsible parties."

The situation just described is the major reason why organizations often say an employee left for "personal reasons" instead of spelling out the exact circumstances. To say otherwise, unless the person is convicted in a court of law, is to invite charges of libel and damage to a person's professional reputation.

Other kinds of employee lawsuits are discussed later in this chapter.

LAWSUITS FILED BY A COMPANY

Most libel suits are directed against newspapers, magazines, and broadcast media when an individual feels that a false statement has damaged his or her reputation. Traditionally, before winning a libel case, a person or organization had to prove that a statement was false, defamatory, and published with knowledge of its falseness. In a growing number of cases, however, individuals and public figures are suing on grounds that an article created a false impression, even if each statement taken separately was true.

Thus, if a newspaper runs a series of articles about a company executive or the company itself tending to imply that the company has done something illegal, there may be grounds for a lawsuit. Wayne Newton, the singer, won a $5.3 million judgment against NBC News for a report creating the impression that he had received financial assistance from organized crime figures to purchase a hotel. Among other things, he cited the reporters' failure to include the fact that he had received a bank loan to finance the purchase. The damage award later was overturned unanimously by the U.S. Circuit Court of Appeals.

Although the legal department often decides if legal action is required against an alleged libel, public relations staffs often counsel, and calm down, company executives and clients who feel they have been libeled. For example, a company executive may feel that a newspaper reporter has falsely attributed quotes to him or her. The Ninth U.S. Circuit Court of Appeals ruled in a 1989 libel case, however, that journalists may fabricate quotes if they reflect the essence of what was said. The case involved Jeffrey Masson, former director of the Sigmund Freud Archives, who claimed that a *New Yorker* writer dreamed up quotations which she falsely attributed to him. Many journalists spoke strongly against the idea that fabricated quotations are permissible, and the case was appealed to the Supreme Court.

Executives also are often incensed when an environmental group includes their corporation on its annual list of "dirty dozen" polluters or on similar lists. A corporate reputation can be damaged, but the defamation is difficult to prove in a court of law. The company must show beyond all doubt that the damaging words were not true, and that the statements actually caused a drop in sales and/or public esteem.

On the other hand, Procter & Gamble won a dozen lawsuits against individuals who were spreading false rumors that the company's logo expressed Satanic symbolism and that the company was in league with the devil. The individuals, including a minister and a school teacher, were charged with defaming the company. (See Chapter 23.)

For the most part, however, corporations and organizations are subject to the legal concept of *fair comment and criticism*. This is the same defense used by theater and music critics when they lambaste a play or concert. The term means that companies and individuals who voluntarily display their wares to the public for sale or consumption are subject to "fair comment," whether good or bad. Thus, an individual or corporation criticizing another corporate entity for shoddy products or poor service usually is protected, provided it is done with honest purpose and lack of malicious intent.

A utility in Indiana once tried to sue a citizen who wrote a letter to a newspaper criticizing the utility for seeking a rate hike. The judge threw the suit out of court, stating that the rate increase was a "matter of public interest and concern" even if the letter writer didn't have all the facts straight.

Fair comment and criticism, however, often doesn't cover a major dispute between two corporations. Home Shopping Network, Inc. of Florida, for example, filed a $1.5 billion lawsuit against GTE maintaining that the telephone company cut off or "lost" millions of callers. GTE responded with a countersuit accusing the video order firm with business libel and slander.

THE "PUBLIC FIGURE" CONCEPT

The other concept that public relations personnel should know about, from the standpoint of answering press inquiries, is what constitutes a *public figure*. Does the press, for example, have a right to publish information about the activities of the company's chief executive officer? Does a newspaper have a right to make judgments about the management decisions of a company executive? Can an executive who is the subject of such a newspaper article sue for invasion of privacy? The answers tend to vary somewhat depending upon how the courts continue to define "public figure." Recent court decisions are somewhat contradictory on the matter.

Such persons as political candidates, government officeholders, actors, athletes, and business celebrities like Donald Trump or Lee Iacocca usually are considered public figures and thus have trouble winning suits for libel, slander, and invasion of privacy. On the other hand, a corporate executive who has not sought the limelight is more likely to be considered a private citizen, with better odds for winning such a suit. The U.S. Supreme Court, however, in 1986 ruled that private individuals who sue for libel must prove, not simply claim, that a news account was false.

Public relations counselors have an obligation to keep up with the changing standard of what constitutes a public figure. They must also advise top executives that some of their immunity to press criticism and investigative reporting dissipates if they voluntarily step into debates on controversial issues. Immunity also is lessened if the company is involved in a major news event, such as the crash of a DC-10 or the Tylenol poisonings.

RIGHTS OF EMPLOYEES

EMPLOYEE COMMUNICATIONS

The concepts of libel, defamation, and invasion of privacy must be kept in mind as public relations personnel write and edit materials that involve employees.

It is no longer true, if it ever was, that an organization has an unlimited right to publicize the activities of its employees. In fact, Morton J. Simon, a Philadelphia lawyer and author of *Public Relations Law* (1969), said, "It should not be assumed that a person's status as an employee waives his right to privacy." Simon correctly points out that a company newsletter or magazine does not enjoy the same First Amendment protection that the news media enjoy when they claim "newsworthiness" and "public interest." A number of court cases, he says, show that company newsletters are considered commercial tools of trade.

This distinction does not impede the effectiveness of newsletters, but it does indicate that they should try to keep employee stories organization-oriented. Indeed, most lawsuits and complaints are generated by "personals columns" that may invade privacy by telling everyone that Joe Doaks honeymooned in Hawaii or that Mary Worth is now a great-grandmother. This information in itself may not constitute an invasion of privacy, but it is often compounded into possible defamation by "cutesy" editorial asides that are in poor taste. If there is any chance that the person will be embarrassed by what is printed, it is a good policy not to make the statement.

To avoid any embarrassment and possible lawsuits, many organizations have abandoned the "personals" column in their publications. Others continue the columns but require that all copy must be submitted in writing by the persons involved. Another method is to have those named initial the copy before it is sent to the printer. A more vexing legal thicket concerns the advent of computer bulletin boards in various companies. To avoid messages that may be libelous, the company should scan all messages on a daily basis and remove those that are offensive.

An employee publication must be careful to avoid stereotypical or racial comments. An employee can file a lawsuit or a complaint to the Equal Employment Opportunity Commission based on the way he or she is portrayed. For example, it would be poor practice to do a feature story about the organization's only black manager and write, "John, a black with amazing leadership abilities, is going places." This implies that blacks generally lack leadership abilities. Women are also stereotyped. A woman in the accounting department with an MBA degree doesn't like being described as "a beautiful redhead with laughing eyes who hides her petite figure behind a charcoal-gray business suit. . . ."

In sum, one should avoid anything that might subject an employee to ridicule by fellow employees. It is expensive and unpleasant for an organization to deal with a lawsuit of any kind, even one with no merit.

Here are some guidelines to remember when writing about employee activities:

1. Keep the focus on organization-related activities.
2. Have employees submit "personals" in writing.
3. Double-check all information for accuracy.
4. Ask, "Will this embarrass anyone or cause someone to be the butt of jokes?"
5. Have employees initial a draft copy of the story in which they are named.
6. Don't rely on second-hand information; confirm the facts with the person involved.
7. When photographing or writing about employees, tell them what the purpose of the photo or story is and how it will be used.
8. Have employees sign a blanket release that the organization may publicize their work activity in newsletters and news releases.

ADVERTISING CONSIDERATIONS

The information just given applies to employee newsletters and news releases. If an employee's photograph or comments are used in an advertisement or sales brochure, however, it is essential that a signed release be on file. As an added precaution it is better to give some financial compensation to make a more binding legal agreement. Jack Daniel Distillery, for example, pays employees $1 for posing in its advertisements.

Chemical Bank of New York unfortunately learned this lesson the hard way. The bank used pictures of 39 employees in various advertisements designed to "humanize" the bank's image, but the employees maintained that no one had requested permission to use their photos in advertisements. Another problem was that the pictures had been taken up to five years before they began appearing in the series of advertisements.

An attorney for the employees, who sued for $600,000 in damages, said, "The bank took the individuality of these employees and used that individuality to make a profit.'' The judge agreed and ruled that the bank had violated New York's privacy law. The action is called *misappropriation of personality*. Jerry Della Femina, an advertising executive, succinctly makes the point: get permission. ''If I used my mother in an ad,'' he said, ''I'd get her permission—and I almost trust her 100 percent.''

Written permission should also be obtained if the employee's photograph is to appear in sales brochures or even in the corporate annual report. (In the case of outsiders, the same rule applies. If, for example, a corporation wants to show customers dining in one of its chain restaurants, permission must be given in writing.) To avoid any possible lawsuits, many companies use professional models as ''customers.'' This avoids the problem of a person's agreeing orally at the time of the photo session but having second thoughts several months later when the picture is published. When a child appears in such a photo, it is essential that the parents sign a release.

PRESS INQUIRIES

Because press inquiries have the potential of invading an employee's right of privacy, public relations personnel should follow basic guidelines as to what information will be provided in the employee's behalf.

In general, employers should give a news reporter only basic information. This may include (1) confirmation that the person is an employee, (2) the person's title and job description, and (3) date of beginning employment, or, if applicable, date of termination.

Unless it is specified by law or permission is given by the employee, a public relations person should avoid providing information about an employee's (1) salary, (2) home address, (3) marital status, (4) number of children, (5) organizational memberships, and (6) job performance.

If a reporter does seek any of this information, because of the nature of the story, several methods may be followed.

First, a public relations person can volunteer to contact the employee and have the person speak directly with the reporter. What the employee chooses to tell the reporter is not then a company's responsibility. Second, many organizations do provide additional information to a reporter if it is included on an optional biographical sheet that the employee has filled out. In most cases, the form clearly states that the organization may use any of the information in answering press inquiries or writing its own news releases. A typical biographical form may have sections in which the employee can list his or her (1) honors and awards, (2) professional memberships, (3) marital status and names of any children, (4) previous employers, (5) educational background, and (6) hobbies or interests. This sheet should not be confused with the person's official employment application, which must remain confidential.

If an organization uses biographical sheets, it is important that they be dated and kept current. A sheet compiled by an employee five years previously may be hopelessly out of date. This is also true of *file photographs* taken at the time of a person's employment (see the section ''Photo Releases'').

INFORMATION ABOUT EMPLOYEE BENEFITS

Recently enacted federal and state legislation makes it easier for employees to know what benefits they are entitled to: For one thing, regulations require that pension and insurance plans be written in such a way that employees can understand them. The rationale is that an employee should not be deprived of benefits simply because no one in the organization explained them in basic English. Suits can be filed against employers who have not complied with the law. Furthermore, employers must post information about health and safety regulations, workers' compensation guidelines, and so on. Increasing legislative pressure has developed for companies to give employees advance warning of a plant closing. Public relations practitioners are often involved when such situations arise. In 1988, a congressional bill requiring employers to give 60 days' notice of plant closings and mass layoffs became law without the signature of President Reagan, who opposed the measure.

EMPLOYEE FREEDOM OF SPEECH

Public relations executives, as well as high-level managers, must work to ensure that employees are not arbitrarily denied promotion or fired simply because they have criticized the organization. Employees, as citizens, have a right to express a point of view. Thus, many employee newsletters now carry "letters to the editor" from employees who question company policy. This not only breeds a healthy atmosphere of two-way communication but makes employee publications more credible.

Unfortunately too many executives still perceive employee questions and criticism as "disloyalty." Public relations personnel can do much to dispel this perception by educating managers about employee rights. A number of state and federal laws already protect the job rights of "whistle-blowers," and this area is rapidly expanding to prevent employees from being dismissed just because they express views not popular with the boss.

On another level, companies have a legal right to prevent employees and former staff members from disclosing confidential information and trade secrets obtained on the job. A case in point arose when Carl Byoir & Associates, a public relations firm, filed a lawsuit against a former employee who wrote a book about Home Box Office after working on the account. The firm contended that the employee violated an employment contract stipulating that all information provided by a client would be considered confidential, not to be disclosed publicly. The case was settled out of court by an agreement that gave the firm the right to review the manuscript before publication.

PHOTO RELEASES

A public relations department should have a central photographic file containing readily available information: (1) source of the picture and date taken, (2) copyright information, and (3) signed releases from subjects in photos.

Such information will ensure the proper use of photos and substantially reduce the threat of lawsuits. A notation of the date taken, for example, will help eliminate the use of pictures that are no longer appropriate for news releases or company brochures. It is embarrassing to publish a picture of a person who died three years ago, or to show in a new brochure a picture of a manufacturing facility that was sold last year.

Permission statements indicate whether the photo may be used in company brochures and advertising or whether it is strictly a file photo for use in the employee magazine. The copyrighting of a picture by a free-lance photographer may mean that the organization cannot use it again unless the photographer gives permission or receives payment. A photo release is important if a person protests that his or her picture was used without permission.

Ordinarily a public relations practitioner doesn't need to worry about getting a signed release if the person gives "implied consent" by posing for the picture and is told how it will be used. This is particularly true for "news" pictures to be published in internal newsletters or for materials accompanying a news release.

If it is not known in what specific ways the photo will ultimately be used, however, the best solution is to get a written release. Public relations personnel often accompany a photographer to (1) ensure that the names of all persons in a picture are properly recorded and (2) to have each sign a release.

Here is a Lockheed release form:

> The undersigned, having previously consented to being photographed, does hereby authorize Lockheed Aircraft Corporation and Lockheed Missiles & Space Company, Inc., to use and reproduce the said photograph and copy for Lockheed publicity and promotional purposes.

OWNERSHIP OF IDEAS

The word *idea* conveys many meanings; ownership often is difficult to prove unless the "idea" is expressed in some tangible form. Organizations, however, solicit ideas and also receive a number of unsolicited ones. Because of this, public relations staffs need to know some basic legal concepts about the handling and ownership of ideas.

Employee Ideas Many organizations regularly encourage employees to submit ideas on how to conserve energy, make the workplace safer, or even produce a better product. More thought must be given to the process, however, than simply installing suggestion boxes. The organization must clearly spell out the conditions under which an idea will be accepted and the extent of compensation that will be paid for an implemented idea. This information is best conveyed on the suggestion forms that the employee uses to present his or her idea.

If cash awards are to be made for good ideas, it is best to specify the maximum amount that will be paid. This tends to limit the organization's liability, but court cases can still result if an employee is not given a reasonable amount for an idea that saves a company millions of dollars.

Solicited Proposals Public relations firms and advertising agencies often are asked by an organization to present proposals for communications programs. And, in a competitive situation, a winning proposal is selected. What is less clear, however, is whether the organization can implement any of the ideas proposed by the losing firms. The courts have generally ruled that if the idea is original and in concrete form (the slogan of an advertising campaign, for example, or a novel idea for a sponsored event), there is an implied contract that the company should provide reasonable compensation. To protect themselves further, a number of public relations firms are now copyrighting their proposals. (Copyright protection is discussed in the next section.)

Unsolicited Public Ideas Businesses often receive unsolicited advice on how to develop new products or improve existing ones, and the public relations department is frequently responsible for keeping track of these suggestions. It is important, then, to establish policies for handling submitted ideas.

Some companies totally reject all unsolicited ideas and have the public relations department return the communication with a polite letter. Others will consider an idea if the sender signs a release form that (1) the company is the sole arbiter of how much the idea is worth, (2) no compensation whatsoever will be given, or (3) a specific maximum amount (perhaps $100 to $500) will be awarded if the idea is used. The latter, however, may not prevent a lawsuit if the value of the idea is worth more than a token amount of money.

The worth of an idea, of course, is determined by how detailed and specific it is. A scribbled note suggesting that the company have a scholarship program for minority students is less valuable, obviously, than a detailed plan outlining how such a program would be set up and funded.

USE OF COPYRIGHT

Should a news release be copyrighted? How about a corporate annual report? Can a *New Yorker* cartoon be used in the company magazine without permission? What about reprinting an article from *Fortune* magazine and distributing it to the company's sales staff? Are government reports copyrighted? What constitutes copyright infringement?

These are some of the bothersome questions that a public relations professional should be able to answer. Knowledge of copyright law is important from two perspectives: (1) what organizational materials should be copyrighted and (2) how correctly to utilize the copyrighted materials of others.

Before going into these areas, however, it is important to know what copyright means. In very simple terms, *copyright* means protection of a creative work from unauthorized use. A section of the U.S. copyright law of 1978 states: "Copyright protection subsists . . . in the original works of authorship fixed in any tangible medium of expression now known or later developed." The word *authorship* is defined in seven categories: (1) literary works; (2) musical works; (3) dramatic works; (4) pantomimes and choreographic works; (5) pictorial, graphic, or sculptural works; (6) motion pictures; and (7) sound recordings. The word *fixed* means that the work is sufficiently permanent or stable to permit it to be perceived, reproduced, or otherwise communicated.

The shield of copyright protection was reduced somewhat in 1991 when the Supreme Court ruled unanimously that directories, computer databases, and other compilations of facts may be copied and republished unless they display "some minimum degree of creativity." The court stated, "Raw facts may be copied at will."

Thus a copyright does not protect ideas, but only the specific ways in which those ideas are expressed. An idea for promoting a product, for example, cannot be copyrighted—but brochures, drawings, news features, animated cartoons, display booths, photographs, recordings, videotapes, corporate symbols, slogans, and the like that express a particular idea can be copyrighted.

Because much money, effort, time, and creative talent are spent on organizational materials, copyright protection is important. By copyrighting materials, a company can prevent competitors from capitalizing on its creative work or producing a facsimile brochure that tends to mislead the public. A manufacturer of personal computers would be in serious legal difficulties if it began distributing sales brochures that tended to look just like ones from Apple Computer. (The concept of trademark infringement [such as copying the Apple logo with slight changes] will be discussed in the section titled "Trademarks.")

The 1978 law, in a major change from the previous one, presumes that material produced in some tangible form is copyrighted from the moment it is created. This is particularly true if the material bears a copyright notice. One of the following methods may be employed:

1. Using the letter "c" in a circle (©), followed by the word *copyright*.
2. Citing the year of copyright and the name of the owner.

This presumption of copyright is often sufficient to discourage unauthorized use, and the writer or creator of the material has some legal protection if he or she can prove that the material was created before another person claims it.

A more formal step, providing full legal protection, is official registration of the copyrighted work within three months after creation. This is done by depositing two copies of the manuscript (it is not necessary that it has been published), recording, or artwork with the Copyright Office, Library of Congress, Washington, DC 20559. Copyright registration forms are available from U.S. post offices. Registration is not a condition of copyright protection, but it is a prerequisite to an infringement action against unauthorized use by others.

Copyright protection of a work lasts for the life of the author plus 50 years, and no longer. Material copyrighted by a business or organization is protected for 75 years from the time the material is published. When a public relations writer creates materials as part of regular employment for an organization, the employer owns the material and has right of copyright. In legal terms, this situation is known as "work made for hire."

PHOTOGRAPHY AND ARTWORK

The copyright law makes it clear that free-lance and commercial photographers retain ownership of the image in a picture unless they specifically agree, in writing, to surrender that right. In other words, these photographers own all negatives, and they can negotiate with a business regarding the use of a picture.

In a further extension of this right, the duplication of copyrighted photos also is illegal. This was established in a 1990 U.S. Federal District Court case in which the Professional Photographers of America (PP of A) sued a nationwide photofinishing firm for ignoring copyright notices on pictures sent for additional copies.

Free-lance photographers generally charge for a picture on the basis of its use. If it is used only once, perhaps for an employee newsletter, the fee is low. If, however, the company wants to use the picture in the corporate annual report or on the company calendar, the fee may be considerably higher. Consequently it is important for a public relations person to tell the photographer exactly how the picture will be used. Arrangements and fees then can be determined for (1) one-time use, (2) unlimited use, or (3) the payment of royalties every time the picture is used.

In practice there is much slippage in honoring a photographer's copyright—either because the client is unfamiliar with the copyright law or the photographer doesn't pursue the letter of the law. Nevertheless, responsible public relations practitioners strive to give adequate compensation and recognition for a photographer's creative work.

The guidelines discussed for photography also apply to created artwork and even variations of a famous theme. Saul Steinberg, who created the famous ''New Yorker's View of the World'' for the *New Yorker* magazine in 1976, successfully sued Columbia Pictures for using a facsimile of the copyrighted artwork to promote the film *Moscow on the Hudson*. The judge ruled that a promotional poster for the movie ''meticulously imitated'' Steinberg's artwork and violated copyright law. In other words, slightly changing a copyrighted photo or a piece of artwork can be considered a violation of copyright if the intent is to capitalize on widespread recognition of the original work.

RIGHTS OF FREE-LANCE WRITERS

Although the rights of free-lance photographers have been established for some years, it was only recently that free-lance writers gained more control over the ownership of their work.

In the now famous Reid Case (*Community for Creative Nonviolence* vs. *Reid*), the U.S. Supreme Court in 1989 ruled that writers retained ownership of their work and that purchasers of it simply gained a ''license'' to reproduce the copyrighted work.

Prior to this ruling, the common practice was to assume that commissioned articles were ''work for hire'' and the purchaser owned the copyright. In other words, a magazine could reproduce the article in any number of ways and even sell it to another publication without the writer's permission.

Under the new interpretation, ownership of a writer's work is subject to negotiation and contractual agreement. Writers may agree to assign all copyright rights to the work they have been hired to do, or they may give permission only for a specific one-time use.

Public relations firms and corporate public relations departments are responsible for ensuring compliance with the copyright law. This means that all agreements with a free-lance writer must be in writing, and the use of the material must be clearly stated. Ideally, public relations personnel should negotiate multiple rights and even complete ownership of the copyright.

On another level, public relations firms often operate as free-lance agents by supplying clients with written materials such as news releases, newsletters, and brochures. Although the public relations firm is the copyright owner, such ownership also entails legal liability for the accuracy of the materials.

FAIR USE VERSUS INFRINGEMENT

Public relations people are in the business of gathering information from a variety of sources, so it is important to know where *fair use* ends and *infringement* begins.

Fair use means that part of a copyrighted article may be quoted directly, but the quoted material must be brief in relation to the length of the original article. It may be, for example, only one paragraph in a 750-word article and up to 300 words in a long article or in a book. Complete attribution of the source must be given regardless of the length of the quoted copy.

It is important to note, however, that fair use has distinct limitations when the material is to appear in a format outside the traditional scope of scholarship and critical review or analysis. If part of a copyright article is to be used by a corporate entity directly to influence sales and profits, permission is required. Thus the use of a selected quotation from an outside source in a sales brochure should be cleared with the source, whereas its use in a company magazine as part of a feature article does not require permission.

The extent of use is significant. Photocopying a *Business Week* article for distribution to 10 persons in a department could be considered fair use, but photocopying 250 for the entire sales staff likely would be considered unfair use and copyright infringement. *Business Week* might contend that the company, by reprinting the article in quantity, had violated copyright (all magazines and newspapers are copyrighted) and deprived the magazine of potential income. Quantity reprints should be ordered directly from the publisher.

Government documents (city, county, state, and federal) are in the public domain and cannot be copyrighted. Public relations personnel can freely use quotations and statistics from a government document, but care must be exercised to ensure that the material is in context and not misleading. The most common problem occurs when an organization uses a government report as a form of endorsement for its services or products. An airline, for example, might cite a government study showing that it provides the most service to customers, but neglect to state the basis of comparison or other factors.

Copyright infringement also extends to videotaping television documentaries or news programs. The Supreme Court has ruled that it is ''fair use'' to make a videotape of a television show for later personal viewing, but a public relations staff must get permission from the television producer if widespread use of the videotape is planned. Adolph A. Coors Company paid $40,000 to CBS-TV for the right to show a videotape throughout the country of a ''60 Minutes'' segment about the company.

Titles of books or plays cannot be copyrighted, but the principle of unfair competition is in effect. Lawyers counsel that a public relations staff should not copy anything if the intent is to capitalize on or take advantage of its current renown. The key to a suit is whether an organization in some way is obtaining commercial advantage by implying that a service or product has the endorsement of or is closely allied with the literary property.

COPYRIGHT GUIDELINES

A number of points have been discussed about copyright. A public relations person should keep the following in mind:

1. Ideas cannot be copyrighted, but the expression of those ideas can be.

2. Major public relations materials (brochures, annual reports, videotapes, motion pictures, position papers, and the like) should be copyrighted if only to prevent unauthorized use by competitors.

3. Although there is a concept of *fair use,* any copyrighted material intended directly to advance the sales and profits of an organization should not be used unless permission is given.

4. Copyrighted material should not be taken out of context, particularly if it implies endorsement of the organization's services or products.

5. Quantity reprints of an article should be ordered from the publisher.

6. Permission is required to use segments of television programs or motion pictures.

7. Permission must be obtained to use segments of popular songs (written verses or sound recordings) from a recording company.

8. The purchaser should tell photographers how photos will be used.

9. Permission is always required to reprint cartoons and cartoon characters. Cartoons in magazines are copyrighted, as well as characters such as Snoopy and Donald Duck.

TRADEMARKS

What do Coca-Cola, IBM, Sony, Porsche, and McDonald's have in common? Their names are registered trademarks protected by law and should be capitalized any time they are used.

This section will discuss trademarks and the role that a public relations department plays in (1) selecting trademarks, (2) safeguarding their use, and (3) avoiding improper use of other registered trademarks. It also will briefly explain the significance of generic names.

According to the Trademark Law Revision Act of 1988, a *trademark* is ''any word, name, symbol, or device, or any combination thereof, (1) used by a person, or (2) which a person has a bona fide intention to use in commerce and applies to register on the principal register established by the Act, to identify and distinguish his or her goods . . . .'' Or, to put it more simply, a trademark is ''a name, symbol, or other device identifying a product, officially registered and legally restricted to the use of the owner or manufacturer'' *(American Heritage Dictionary).*

SELECTING TRADEMARKS

To protect a trademark by law, a company registers its name, logo (identifying symbol), and product names. The registered trademark symbol is a superscript, small capital ''R'' in a circle—®. ''Registered in U.S. Patent and Trademark Office'' and ''Reg. U.S. Pat. Off.'' also may be used. A ''TM'' in small capital letters indicates a trademark that isn't registered. It represents a company's common-law claim to a right of trademark, or a trademark for which registration is pending.

A service mark is like a trademark, but it designates a service rather than a product, or is a logo. An ''SM'' in small capitals in a circle—℠—is the symbol for a registered service mark. If registration is pending, the ''SM'' should be used without the circle.

Businesses and industrial firms spend millions of dollars each year in the search for a distinctive name, slogan, or logo that can be used to symbolize the company in the minds of the American consumer. Research indicates that 53 percent of Americans claim brand quality takes precedence over price considerations so, quite literally, a famous trademark is worth millions of dollars. Additional millions are spent advertising and publicizing the trademark (see Figure 13.1).

SAFEGUARDING TRADEMARKS

A public relations practitioner must be thoroughly familiar with the registered trademarks of his or her employer so that the trademarks can be used correctly in news releases, brochures, background kits, videotapes, and so on. A registered trademark name, for example, is always capitalized. Failure to do so in company materials can lead to a loss of trademark status; if so, the word becomes generic, available for anyone's use.

The public relations department and legal counsel work to safeguard an organization's trademarks in several ways. They are:

1. Ensuring that company trademarks are capitalized in all organizational literature and graphics.

2. Ensuring that any graphics of the logo or phrases (''Reach Out and Touch Someone'') indicate that they are trademarked by using, ®, TM, ℠, or SM next to the logo or phrase.

3. Distributing trademark manuals and brochures to editors and reporters and placing advertisements in trade publications, designating names to be capitalized.

4. Educating employees as to what the company's trademarks are and how to use them correctly.

5. Monitoring publications—newspapers, trade magazines, newsletters—to ensure that trademarks are capitalized. If not, a gentle reminder is sent.

6. Monitoring publications to ensure that other organizations are not infringing on a registered trademark. If they are, the legal department pursues the situation with letters and threats of injunctions or lawsuits.

7. Placing advertisements in journalism magazines and reviews reminding readers of trademark names. Johnson & Johnson does this for Band-Aids, Xerox reminds the press that there is no such thing as a ''xerox''—only a Xerox copier—and Coca-Cola is adamant that *Coke* is always capitalized.

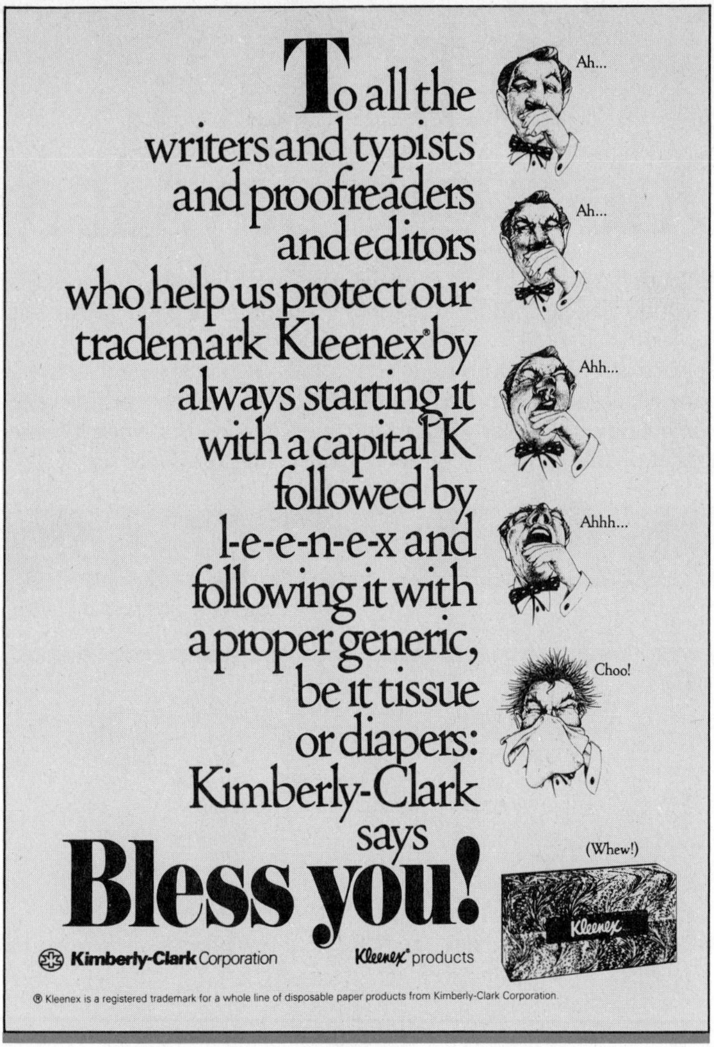

FIGURE 13.1
Protection of trademark requires corporate diligence. Some companies deliver warning messages through advertisements in trade magazines. In this advertisement, Kimberly-Clark uses a light touch to deliver a serious message.

8. Making sure the trademark is actually being used. A 1988 revision of the Trademark Act no longer permits an organization to hold a name in reserve.

Although the print media usually capitalize the first letter of a trademarked name, editors are less willing to go along with the idea that a company's official name should be spelled in all capital letters or some variation; for example, BellSouth is a trademarked name that editors routinely spell as Bell South or Bellsouth. And Toys ''R'' Us

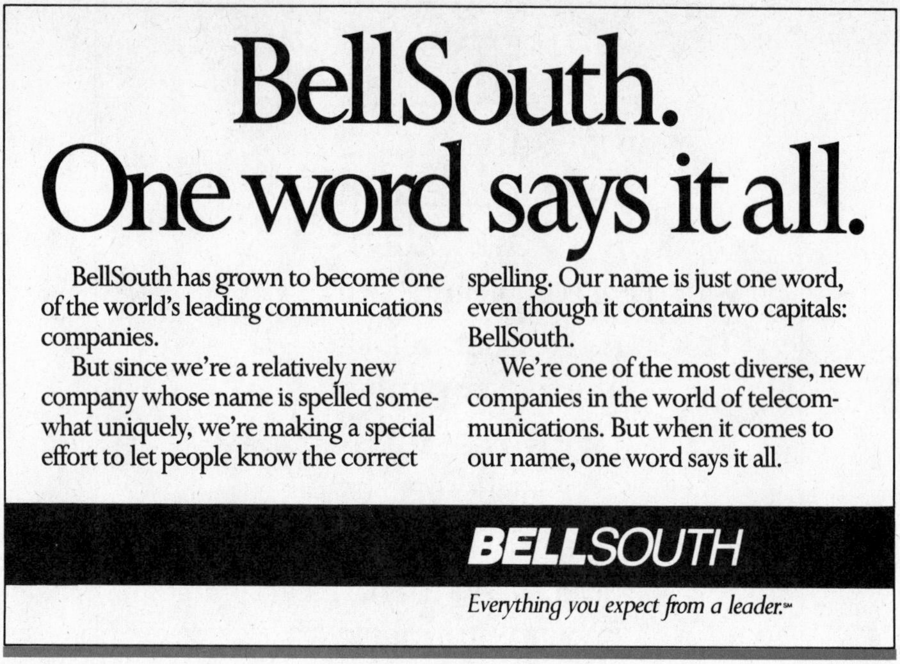

BellSouth.
One word says it all.

BellSouth has grown to become one of the world's leading communications companies.

But since we're a relatively new company whose name is spelled somewhat uniquely, we're making a special effort to let people know the correct spelling. Our name is just one word, even though it contains two capitals: BellSouth.

We're one of the most diverse, new companies in the world of telecommunications. But when it comes to our name, one word says it all.

BELLSOUTH

*Everything you expect from a leader.*SM

FIGURE 13.2
Having adopted an unusual trademark by running two words together and capitalizing both, BellSouth published this advertisement in the *Washington Journalism Review* to alert editors and writers to the correct spelling. (Reprinted with permission of BellSouth Corporation)

is actually trademarked with a backward ''R,'' but few typesetting devices have such a letter.

AVOIDING IMPROPER USE OF OTHER REGISTERED TRADEMARKS

Public relations personnel often work with the legal department and outside design consultants to come up with names, slogans, and logos for an organization. The first step is to conduct a brainstorming session for ideas, but the second step is to research a potential trademark to be sure it isn't already being used. This is usually done by specialty trademark search firms that make extensive use of the computer.

Today, when there are thousands of businesses and organizations, finding a name trademark not already in use is extremely difficult. The task is even more frustrating if a company wants to use a trademark on an international level.

It is not uncommon for a company to start with 150 possible names and, after a trademark search, be left with only two or three possible designations. The other choice a company has is to purchase rights to a name. First Interstate Bank, in 11 western states, had to pay a small, rural Vermont bank $1 million because that bank

news release

INTEL CORPORATION
3065 Bowers Avenue
P.O. Box 58065
Santa Clara, CA 95052-8065

CONTACT: Paula Zimmerman
(609) 936-7615

FOR IMMEDIATE RELEASE

AUTHORING SYSTEM DEVELOPED
FOR INTEL'S DVI TECHNOLOGY

LAS VEGAS, Nev., November 13, 1989 -- Intel Corporation's Princeton Operation today announced a new software authoring package designed exclusively for Intel's DVI™ Technology called Authology*: MultiMedia. The program was created by CEIT Systems, Inc., a developer of software tools for multimedia and interactive video authoring, located in San Jose, California.

Authology: MultiMedia authoring software enables DVI

Page 4
Intel/IU-631

*DVI is a trademark of Intel Corporations.
*Authology is a registered trademark of CEIT Systems, Inc.
*Comdex is a registered trademark of Interface Group, Inc.
*Lumena is a trademark of Time Arts, Inc.

FIGURE 13.3
This news release contains trademarked names, so the Intel Corporation, which issued it, lists the registered trademarks at the end of the release. This common practice helps to protect the trademarks and emphasizes to media recipients that the names should be capitalized.

owned the name First Inter-State Bank. By purchasing the name, the bank's holding corporation now has its name registered in all 50 states.

The complexity of finding new names, coupled with the attempt of many to capitalize on an already known trade name, has invariably spawned a number of lawsuits claiming trademark infringement. Here are some examples:

- Kellogg Company charged that General Mills' Oatmeal Raisin Crisp cereal infringed on its Apple Raisin Crisp trademark.
- Warner Bros. and DC Comics got an injunction against a California shop for selling Batman skate boards without paying a licensing fee for the use of the caped crusader's likeness.
- Miller Brewing Company filed a suit against a group of Texas doctors for trademark infringement after the group began selling T-shirts with the logo "Killer Lite: We're selling a drug."
- The maker of an Italian gun known as the Beretta filed a trademark infringement suit against General Motors over its Beretta automobile. The court ruled, however, that the suit had no basis since it wasn't likely anyone would confuse the two products.
- An Illinois hair-styling salon won a $2.1 million suit against L'Oreal after the manufacturer named one of its hair dyes Zazu. The hair salon was already marketing a product by the same name.
- The U.S. Olympic Committee filed suit against the March of Dimes for trademark infringement because the charity sponsored the "Reading Olympics," which rewarded children for reading books. Under federal statute, no one can use the word "Olympic" or related words and symbols without the U.S. Olympic Committee's consent. The March of Dimes, to avoid a lengthy court battle, changed the name of its program to "Reading Champions."

In all these cases organizations filed lawsuits charging that their registered trademarks were being improperly exploited for commercial or organizational purposes. Some guidelines used by courts to determine if there has been trademark infringement are as follows:

1. Has the defendant used a name as a way of capitalizing on the reputation of another organization's trademark—and does the defendant benefit from the original organization's investment in popularizing its trademark?

2. Is there an intent (real or otherwise) to create confusion in the public mind? Is there an intent to imply a connection between the defendant's product and the item identified by trademark?

3. How similar are the two organizations? Are they providing the same kinds of products or services?

4. Has the original organization actively protected the trademark by publicizing it—and by actually continuing to use it in connection with its products or services?

5. Is the trademark unique? A company with a trademark that merely describes a common product might be in trouble.

MISAPPROPRIATION OF PERSONALITY

A form of trademark infringement also can result from the use of ''sound-alikes'' and ''look-alikes'' of well-known figures in company materials and advertising campaigns. Bette Midler, for example, won a $400,000 judgment against Young & Rubicam after the advertising agency used another singer to imitate her singing style and rendition of the song ''Do You Wanna Dance?'' for a Ford auto commercial.

The court ruled, ''When a distinctive voice of a professional singer is widely known and is deliberately imitated in order to sell a product, the sellers have appropriated what is not theirs.''

Companies and advertising firms also have gotten into legal trouble for using ''look-alikes'' of famous personalities to sell goods. Woody Allen has used federal and state laws to stop ads featuring actors who resembled him. But protection is not just for the living. Deceased celebrities also are protected—be they Marilyn Monroe, James Dean, W.C. Fields, the Marx Brothers, and even Albert Einstein.

In order to use the likenesses of these famous people, the company or the advertising agency must get permission and pay a licensing fee to an agent who represents the families, movie studios, or estates of the deceased.

Licensing fees also are being collected by colleges and universities for use of their logos and names on everything from beer mugs to sweatshirts. UCLA, for example, estimates its trademark revenue at about $800,000 annually.

Conclusion: don't use a famous cartoon figure, picture of a deceased celebrity, movie stills, a ''sound-alike'' or ''look-alike,'' or a college coat of arms in publicity and advertising materials unless permission and a licensing fee have been negotiated.

GENERIC NAMES

Every company wants to publicize its trademarks to the point that they become household names, but there is a danger in doing so. A U.S. court of appeals has stated: ''When the public takes unto itself a trade name word and substitutes it for the commodity, the manufacturer loses the exclusive right to the name.''

Some trade names that have become generic include *aspirin, cellophane, thermos, escalator, corn flakes, yo-yo,* and *mimeograph*. This essentially means that any company can use these names to describe a product.

When a trade name becomes generic, the company suffers a tremendous loss; that is why corporations zealously guard the trademark from incorrect use. Coca-Cola, it is said, has a battery of 200 lawyers constantly monitoring how restaurants and the media use the name *Coke*. If a person orders a Coke in a restaurant and is served another kind of cola, Coca-Cola lawyers immediately file suit. Xerox spends several hundred thousand dollars annually making sure the public understands that *Xerox copy* and *photocopy* are not interchangeable words.

FEDERAL TRADE COMMISSION

It is well known that the Federal Trade Commission (FTC) has jurisdiction over advertisements to determine that they are not deceptive or misleading, but public relations personnel should know that the commission also has jurisdiction over product news releases and product photography.

In the eyes of the FTC both advertisements and product publicity materials are vehicles of commercial trade—and therefore subject to regulation. Thus, a company cannot claim ''freedom of speech'' when the FTC moves to curb news releases that are misleading or making deceptive claims.

The FTC, for example, filed an administrative complaint against Campbell Soup Company for claiming that its soups were low in fat and cholesterol and thus helpful in fighting heart disease. The agency charged that the claim was deceptive because publicity and advertisements didn't disclose that the soups also were high in sodium, a fact that increases the risk of heart disease. In an earlier case, Campbell Soup got into trouble with the FTC for adding marbles to the bottom of bowls of its vegetable soup so it would look chunkier in product publicity photographs.

Although the FTC kept a somewhat low profile during the laissez-faire Reagan years, the agency has taken a more active stance in the 1990s, especially in regard to health claims for products. Traditionally, the agency filed a complaint against the manufacturer of the product. Recent cases, however, show a tendency to prosecute advertising agencies and production companies that script and produce the commercials.

In general, the FTC monitors advertising and publicity by assigning one of the following labels to material it considers misleading:

1. Unsubstantiated claims
2. Ambiguous claims
3. Fraudulent testimonials
4. Puffery and exaggerated claims
5. Deceptive demonstrations
6. Deceptive pricing
7. Defamation of the competition
8. Fraudulent contests
9. Misuse of the word *free*
10. ''Bait and switch'' tactics

Public relations practitioners must be cognizant of these guidelines when writing product publicity. It is also their responsibility, says the FTC, to avoid claims that cannot be substantiated by competent and reliable evidence.

The following guidelines should be taken into account when writing product publicity materials:

1. Make sure the information in the release is accurate and can be substantiated.

2. Don't make flat statements that are difficult to prove. Stick to the facts. Don't "hype" the product or service by using flowery, nonspecific adjectives.

3. Make sure that celebrities who endorse a product actually use it. They should not say anything about the product's properties that cannot be substantiated.

4. Don't use testimonials from satisfied consumers for publicity purposes unless the individuals give written permission.

5. Watch the language. Don't say "independent research study" when the research was done by the organization's staff.

6. If government findings are quoted, provide proper context. Government agencies do not endorse products.

7. Describe tests and surveys in sufficient detail so the consumer understands what was tested and under what conditions.

8. Describe prizes and awards accurately.

9. Remember that a product is not "new" if only the packaging has been changed or the product is more than six months old.

Companies found in violation of FTC guidelines usually are given the opportunity to sign a consent decree. This means that the company admits no wrongdoing but agrees to change its advertising and publicity claims.

Companies also may be fined by the FTC or ordered to engage in corrective advertising and publicity. Listerine makers and Firestone Tire Company in recent years have been ordered to do corrective advertising. If a product is defective and a hazard to public health, the FTC can order a product recall.

SECURITIES AND EXCHANGE COMMISSION

The megamergers of the 1980s, coupled with insider trading scandals on Wall Street, made the Securities and Exchange Commission (SEC) practically household words in the business world. This federal agency closely monitors the financial affairs of publicly traded companies and protects the interests of stockholders and potential investors.

SEC guidelines on public disclosure and insider trading are particularly relevant to corporate public relations staff members who play a key role in meeting disclosure requirements. The distribution of misleading information or failure to make a timely disclosure of material information may be the basis of liability under the SEC code. A company may even be liable if it satisfies regulations by getting the information out, but decreases the likelihood of use in the media by presenting crucial information in a vague manner or by burying it deep in the news release.

The role of public relations personnel is made even more difficult by SEC Rule 10b–5, which doesn't precisely state when the material information should be disclosed. An early release may be misleading if the news does not develop as expected. A late release invites insider trading and other abuses.

It is no wonder that specialists in investor and financial relations are highly paid. They must not only be fully aware of SEC regulations and the laws of other governmental agencies, but they must constantly monitor new interpretations and court decisions that can affect their clients and employers. Equipped with such knowledge, these experts must make judgments every day on the release of information.

The SEC has three basic guidelines:

1. Full information must be given on anything that might materially affect the company's stock.

2. Timely disclosure is essential. A company must act promptly to dispel or confirm rumors that result in unusual market activity or market variations.

3. Insider trading is illegal. Company officials, including public relations staffs and outside counsel, cannot use inside information to buy and sell company stock. (See the Anthony M. Franco case in Chapter 6.)

Through the years there have been a number of cases in which companies have been heavily fined for not adhering to these guidelines. The major case setting the pattern for illegal insider trading occurred in 1965 involving Texas Gulf Sulphur. Company executives used inside information about an ore strike in Canada to buy up stock while at the same time issuing a news release tending to deny that a rich strike had been found.

Other situations since then have included the following:

- *Pig 'n Whistle (1971).* This administrative proceeding established the concept that a company's public relations counsel can be named as a defendant if news releases contain false and misleading information. The court ruled that public relations firms must take prudent caution to ascertain the accuracy of information given them for release by either a client or an employer.

- *Memorex Corporation (1975).* The corporation had to pay $3.6 million in an out-of-court settlement with persons who purchased the company's stock. The company was charged with artificially inflating the price of stock by issuing incorrect and misleading statements and news releases about the earnings of a subsidiary.

- *Bache & Co. (1976).* The brokerage firm was ordered to return $900,000 to customers who bought shares of an insurance company shortly before the company announced an unexpectedly large loss. The brokerage firm in turn sued the insurance company, maintaining that the vice president of investor relations had given analysts misleading and distorted information.

- *Staffin* v. *Greenberg (1982)*. A public disclosure must not only be accurate but also sufficiently complete so as not to be misleading. There is no obligation to disclose every material fact, but the information released must be complete enough so as not to mislead.

- *Apple Computer Inc. (1984)*. A group of stockholders filed a lawsuit against company executives, claiming that they sold 2.1 million shares of stock and received proceeds of $84.1 million by making ''positive public statements'' about the expected success of the Lisa when the executives knew about slow sales and production difficulties.

These examples should make it clear that public relations staff and counsel are responsible for the full, accurate, and prompt disclosure of financial data. A public relations person is often privy to information affecting the price of stock before the press and the public know about it.

Most corporations have developed policies to handle financial rumors and also to adhere to SEC and other regulatory guidelines. For example, to avoid any hint of possible insider trading, many corporations have a policy that earnings reports are released to the media before company executives and employees are informed. Harvey L. Pitt, a corporate legal counsel with a Washington, D.C., law firm, recommends that corporate public relations departments establish guidelines. He suggests the following:

- Sensitivity to corporate confidences.
- Logging all media inquiries and the type of information provided.
- Using code words for sensitive corporate transactions to avoid leaks.
- Maintaining a continually updated binder containing company press statements and news articles that result.
- Limiting corporate spokespersons on financial matters to only one or two people.

CORPORATE FREE SPEECH

FTC and SEC regulations, coupled with Supreme Court decisions, have made it quite clear that commercial speech (advertising and product publicity) is not fully protected by the First Amendment. Commercial speech can be regulated and even restricted if standards of disclosure, truth, and accuracy are violated. A more difficult question is whether advertising of a legal consumer product can be banned on the basis of health considerations. This major legal battle will be fought in the 1990s as numerous public groups continue to seek the banning of cigarette advertising.

On another level, however, the Supreme Court has upheld the right of corporations to express their views on matters of public policy and interest.

A series of court cases has supported the concept of corporate free speech. Some landmark cases are as follows:

- *First National Bank of Boston (1978).* The Supreme Court struck down a Massachusetts law that prohibited corporations from publicizing their views on issues subject to the ballot box. The ruling essentially gave corporations the same status as an individual under the First Amendment.
- *Consolidated Edison (1980).* The Supreme Court ruled that a New York Public Utilities Commission regulation prohibiting utilities from making statements on matters of public policy and controversy was unconstitutional.

SEC DISCLOSURE REQUIREMENTS

The Securities and Exchange Commission (SEC) requires public relations personnel to disclose the following information about a company in a timely fashion:

- Dividends or their deletion
- Annual and quarterly earnings
- Preliminary, but unaudited, interim earnings
- Annual reports
- Stock splits
- Mergers or takeovers
- Major management changes
- Major product developments
- Expansion plans
- Change of business purpose
- Defaults
- Proxy materials
- Disposition of major assets
- Purchase of own stock
- Announcements of major contracts or orders

To be avoided are the following:

- Unrealistic sales and earnings reports
- Glowing descriptions of products in the experimental stage
- Announcements of possible mergers or takeovers that are only in the speculation stage
- Junkets for business reporters or offers of stock to financial analysts and columnists
- Omission of unfavorable news and developments
- Leaking of information to selected outsiders and financial columnists

- *Pacific Gas & Electric (1986)*. The Supreme Court ruled that the California Public Utilities Commission could not require PG&E to include messages from activist consumer groups in its mailings to customers. The utility argued that inclusion of such messages impaired the company's right to communicate its own messages.

Although corporations can speak out on public issues in the context of First Amendment rights, a 1990 decision by the Supreme Court seems to indicate that this "free speech" right doesn't extend to endorsement of political candidates.

In a 6–3 decision in *Austin* v. *Michigan Chamber of Commerce,* the Court said a Michigan law that prohibits corporations from buying newspaper advertisements on behalf of a political candidate did not violate the chamber's right to free speech. The Michigan legislation, which applies to all incorporated bodies (even the Sierra Club and the American Civil Liberties Union) is part of a campaign finance law.

MEETING ROOMS, PLANT TOURS, AND OPEN HOUSES

What is the responsibility of a firm if meeting rooms are made available to community groups? What about the legal ramifications of having plant tours or a community open house?

These are not idle questions to the public relations staff, who are often responsible for such activities. Providing a meeting room or having an open house is part of community relations. Plant tours also involve the public, and specialized audiences as well.

MEETING ROOMS

Every firm or organization that makes a meeting room available to community groups should have an established policy in writing that specifies what types of groups qualify. Some companies specify that only nonprofit groups associated with the United Way may use facilities. Other firms allow religious organizations, hobby clubs, and senior citizen groups if an employee of the company sponsors them.

Groups should submit a written request and perhaps sign a standard form that outlines their responsibilities in using the room. The standard form might clearly state that the company in no way officially endorses the activities of the group. Furthermore, standard agreement forms enable the organization to keep track of which groups have booked the room for which date. Also, from a legal standpoint, the company is less liable if the community group has formally requested such use.

Here are some other points to remember:

1. The room must be clean and well maintained so that there are no safety hazards such as worn rugs, frayed electrical cords, or flimsy chairs.

2. Instructions on how to operate the coffee maker or other electrical equipment must be clearly posted.

3. An employee of the company should be on the premises during the meeting in case of emergency.

4. Parking lots must be well lighted and easily accessible.

5. Icy sidewalks and other possible danger areas must be made safe before the meeting.

It is only good community relations to ensure that a community meeting room creates goodwill for the company, not antagonisms or even possible lawsuits because of negligence.

PLANT TOURS

Plant tours should not be undertaken lightly. They require detailed planning by the public relations staff to guarantee the safety and comfort of visitors. Consideration must be given to such factors as (1) logistics, (2) possible work disruptions as groups pass through the plant, (3) safety, and (4) amount of staffing required.

A well-marked tour route is essential; it is equally important to have trained escort staff and tour guides. Guides should be well versed in company history and operations, and their comments should be somewhat standardized to make sure that key facts are conveyed. In addition, guides should be trained in first aid and thoroughly briefed on what to do in case of an accident or heart attack. At the beginning the guide should outline to the visitors what they will see, the amount of walking involved, the time required, and the number of stairs. This warning tells visitors with heart conditions or other physical handicaps what they can expect.

Such precautions will generate good will and limit the company's liability. It should be noted, however, that a plaintiff can still collect if negligence on the part of the company can be proved.

OPEN HOUSES

Many of the points about plant tours are applicable to open houses. The additional problem is having large numbers of people on the plant site at the same time. Moffett Field in California, for example, was host to 300,000 people on a Sunday when a Blue Angels precision-flying team performed. Such an event calls for special logistical planning by the public relations staff, possibly including the following measures:

1. Hiring off-duty police to direct traffic
2. Chartering shuttle buses
3. Arranging to have paramedics and an ambulance on site
4. Renting portable toilets
5. Briefing employee volunteers who will be stationed throughout the facility
6. Providing for additional parking space

7. Contracting with catering firms for food
8. Supplying special rest areas for those who get fatigued
9. Providing a central location for lost-and-found children
10. Providing maps of the facility and a schedule of events
11. Building and staffing displays and exhibits
12. Hiring entertainment groups
13. Providing special permits for vendors selling souvenirs
14. Making alternative arrangements in case of adverse weather
15. Providing for extra liability insurance

Each special event or open house has its own requirements. It is the responsibility of the public relations staff to ascertain exactly what is needed and to make appropriate plans. To do less is poor public relations and may result in legal problems.

PUBLIC RELATIONS AND LEGAL COUNSEL

Public relations and legal counsel are often at odds, as is pointed out in Chapter 4, but this is not an ideal situation.

A better relationship consists of a strong rapport between the two staffs so that their individual stores of expertise can complement each other. Public relations personnel are not lawyers, and they often need assistance in choosing the proper course of action about a matter that has clear legal ramifications. On the other hand, lawyers need to understand how important the court of public opinion is in determining the future of an organization. Respect and credibility must be maintained by both sides.

A number of steps can be taken by a company or organization to ensure that the public relations and legal staffs have a cordial, mutually supportive relationship:

1. The public relations and legal staffs should report to the same top executive, who can effectively listen to the viewpoints of both sides and decide on a course of action.

2. The organization should draft a clearly defined statement of responsibilities for each staff and its relationship to the other. Neither should dominate.

3. Both functions should be represented on key committees.

4. Public relations personnel and legal staff should get to know each other personally so a trusting relationship can be built.

5. Periodic consultations should be held during which materials and programs are reviewed.

6. The legal staff, as part of its duties, should brief public relations personnel on

impending developments in litigation, so press inquiries can be answered in an appropriate manner.

7. Arrangements should be made for both staffs to forestall public relations and legal problems in connection with proxy battles; unfriendly takeover attempts; possible antitrust, consumer, and environmental legal action; and labor unrest.

Admittedly, the list is idealistic. As laws and government regulations become more complex, however, it is essential that public relations and legal counsel work as equal partners in achieving organizational objectives.

CASE PROBLEM

Russian River Vineyards is a large winery located near Healdsburg, north of San Francisco. As director of public relations for the winery, you are charged with increasing public awareness of the vineyard's wines and instituting an employee and community relations program.

Some of your ideas include (1) public tours through the winery, (2) a grape harvest festival every fall at which local musicians would perform and local artists would display their works, (3) advertisements quoting a government study about the high percentage of varietal grapes in Russian River wines, (4) photocopying magazine articles that mention the winery favorably and mailing them to wine consumers, (5) a ''folksy'' newsletter for employees of the winery, (6) employment of a free-lance photographer to take pictures of employees and winery guests for possible use in future product publicity, and (7) release of an ''independent'' survey quoting wine experts about the quality of the vineyard's products.

Each of these activities involves an understanding of the law and various governmental regulations. What legal aspects should be considered in each project?

QUESTIONS FOR REVIEW AND DISCUSSION

1. What are the five situations in which a public relations person, as the representative of an organization, can be named a co-conspirator with other company officials?

2. In what ways do libel and slander considerations affect the work of a public relations person?

3. What is the concept of *fair comment and privilege,* and what are the limitations?

4. What are some guidelines to follow in employee communications to avoid lawsuits?

5. What are some guidelines to follow if a news reporter inquires about an employee?

6. What is the concept of *implied consent* in the taking of photographs?

7. What legal precautions should an organization take if it actively solicits suggestions from employees and the public?

8. What are the basic guidelines of the 1978 copyright law about which public relations personnel should be familiar?

9. What constitutes "fair use" and "infringement" of copyrighted materials?

10. Why is it important for public relations personnel to know about trademarks?

11. Name at least five guidelines of the Federal Trade Commission that affect the way products can be publicized.

12. In what ways does the Securities and Exchange Commission regulate financial public relations activity? What kinds of information must be disclosed in a timely fashion?

13. What are some guidelines to remember if an organization is having an open house or a tour of a manufacturing facility?

14. Do corporations have the right of free speech regarding issues of public concern?

15. What should be the relationship between the public relations and legal staffs of an organization?

SUGGESTED READINGS

Brynes, Sondra J. "Privacy vs. Publicity: Flip Sides of the Same Coin." *Public Relations Review,* Winter 1990, pp. 29–35.

Brynes, Sondra J. "Private Matters." *Public Relations Journal,* August 1987, pp. 7–9. Invasion of privacy.

Collins, Erik L., and Cornet, Robert J. "Public Relations and Libel Law." *Public Relations Review,* Winter 1990, pp. 36–47.

Davids, Meryl. "How Now, IR?" *Public Relations Journal,* April 1989, pp. 15–19. SEC disclosure requirements.

Durant, Sandra, and Isaacs, Audrey. "Law, Loyalty, and Communication." *Communication World,* October 1987, pp. 30–31. Laws affecting employee communications.

Ecker, Charles R. "Paying the Piper." *Public Relations Journal,* March 1988, pp. 18–19. Using copyrighted music.

Gartner, Michael. "If Corporations Are Silenced in Political Debate, Who's Next?" *Wall Street Journal,* April 5, 1990, p. A23.

Grassmuck, Karen. "Colleges Fight Bootleggers as Sales Boom for Goods That

Bear Logos and Emblems.'' *Chronicle of Higher Education,* February 21, 1990, pp. A32, 36.

Joffe, Bruce H. ''Law, Ethics and Public Relations Writers.'' *Public Relations Journal,* July 1989, pp. 38–39, 40. Contracting with free-lance writers.

Lipman, Joanne. ''Firms' Outings Pose Liability Dilemma.'' *Wall Street Journal,* September 14, 1988, p. 35.

Lipman, Joanne. ''FTC Zaps Infomercials.'' *Wall Street Journal,* June 19, 1990, p. B1.

Marcus, Amy D. ''False Impressions Can Spur Libel Suits, Even if News Media Get the Facts Right.'' *Wall Street Journal,* May 15, 1990, p. B1.

Mattman, Jurg W. ''Checklist: Securing and Insuring Special Events.'' *Public Relations Journal,* March 1987, p. 30.

Pratt, Catherine A. ''First Amendment Protection for Public Relations Expression: The Application and Limitations of the Commercial and Corporate Speech Models.'' Chapter 9 of *Public Relations Research Annual,* edited by James Grunig and Larissa Grunig, Volume 2. Hillsdale, NJ: Lawrence Erlbaum Associates, 1990, pp. 205–218.

Rubin, Maureen. ''Avoid Truthful, But Incomplete Press Releases.'' *Public Relations Journal,* March 1991, pp. 26–27. Liability in news releases.

Rubin, Maureen. ''Rethinking the Anonymous Source Dilemma.'' *Public Relations Journal,* November 1988, pp. 12–15, 54. Possible liability of news media for revealing sources of information.

Rubin, Maureen. ''VNRs: Re-examining 'Unrestricted' Use.'' *Public Relations Journal,* October 1989, pp. 58–59. Station use of video news releases and legal aspects of editing them.

Rubin, Maureen. ''Threat to Corporate Image Advertising Left Unresolved.'' *Public Relations Journal,* September 1990, pp. 37–39. Corporate advertising and First Amendment rights.

Schmitt, Richard. ''Singers Get Green Light to Sue Imitators.'' *Wall Street Journal,* August 19, 1988, p. 19. Misappropriation of personality.

''Trademarks and the Press.'' *Editor & Publisher,* December 2, 1989, pp. 1–20. Special annual supplement about copyright and trademarks.

Walsh, Frank. *Public Relations and the Law.* New York: Institute for Public Relations Research and Education, 1988.

PART FOUR
Application

CHAPTER

Corporations

All areas of endeavor in which public relations practitioners are engaged share basic operating methods. Yet each has its special needs and emphasis. The largest of these areas, in which approximately half of all professionals are involved, is public relations for corporations.

In corporate work, the task of public relations personnel is to interpret the goals, methods, products, and services of commerce and industry to the public and simultaneously to help their employers operate in a socially responsible manner. Such practitioners indeed function as bridges. On one side are managements whose legitimate profit-motivated goals suffer at times from their own insensitivity to the public's wishes and perceptions. On the other side, part of the public misunderstands the role of business in a free, competitive society and looks at corporations—especially the large ones—suspiciously.

Corporate responsibility for protecting the global environment has emerged in the 1990s as a challenging aspect of public relations practice. This chapter explores environmental problems companies face and attitudes they need to develop. Case studies of good and bad performances provide specific examples.

A closely related topic is the corporate approach to consumerism. Other subjects examined are the human factor in business, the business-media relationship, the handling of crises, and issues management—the process whereby companies take the initiative in becoming involved in matters of public concern. The chapter explains how corporations have handled difficult situations—with blunder and counterattack, or with openness and concern for the public welfare. We also discuss employer-employee relations.

THE CORPORATE ROLE

This is an era of giantism in American and, indeed, world business. International conglomerates control subsidiary companies that often produce a grab bag of seemingly unrelated products and services under the same corporate banner. These conglomerates must deal with government at many levels. Their operations affect the environment, control the employment of thousands, and have an impact on the financial and social well-being of millions. Truly, they have a compelling influence on contemporary life.

Bigness brings remoteness. The popular phrase "the faceless corporation" may be a cliché, but it represents a genuine distrust in the public mind—a distrust often based on lack of knowledge about a corporation rather than on actual unfavorable experiences.

When an oil company pays more than $13 billion to buy out a competitor, as Standard Oil of California did to purchase the Gulf Corporation, the scope of the deal exceeds the comprehension of most citizens. They feel uneasy about the vast economic power of such a huge enterprise and suspect that it wields enormous backstage political influence. Beyond these broad, vague concerns they also see such a combination in short-range personal perspective: "Will this force me to pay more for a gallon of gasoline?"

Since a corporation's impact on society is felt at so many levels, those who plan and conduct its public relations face a complex task. Even relatively small corporations need public relations programs that show them conducting their affairs, both external and internal, in a socially responsible manner.

Figure 14.1 presents, in schematic form, the way one company—General Electric—categorizes the various concerns it must take into consideration at every step of executive decision-making.

THE HUMAN FACTOR

THE PUBLIC PERCEPTION

The fundamental, irreplaceable element of every business is people—those who produce goods and services, those who consume them, and those inside and outside the companies whose lives and attitudes are influenced by how the companies act. What corporations *do* is not enough. The public's perception of their conduct also matters. A corporation may operate in a completely legal, technically sound, and financially efficient manner yet find itself viewed by segments of the public as cold, greedy, and heedless of cherished social values. The public relations practitioner's job is to see that this does not happen. The practitioner must work within the company to foster constructive, socially aware behavior, and outside the company to convince the public that the firm is a worthy, caring corporate citizen.

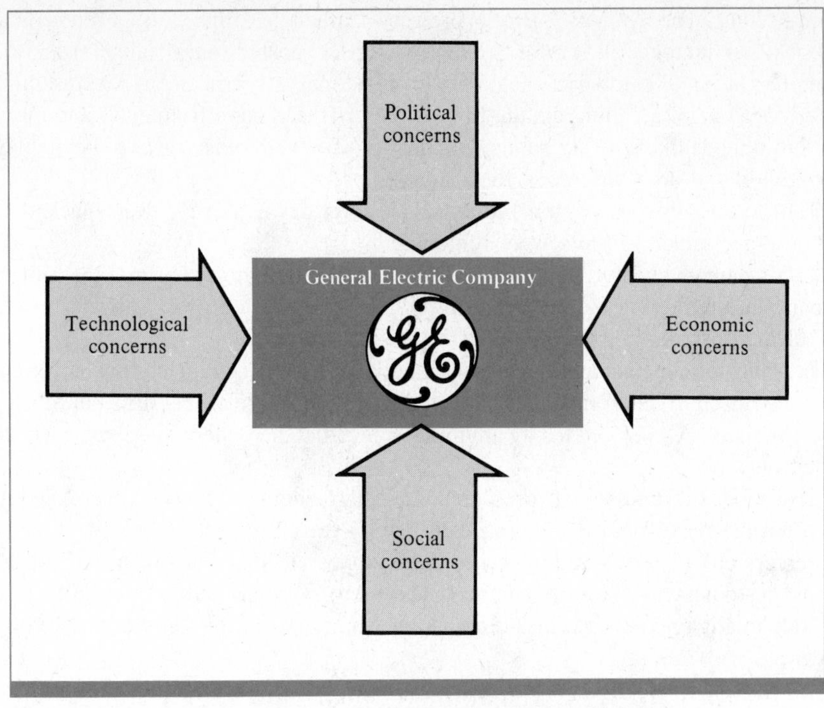

FIGURE 14.1
General Electric Company sees four factors that must be taken into consideration whenever a management decision is made. (1) Political—How do government regulations and other pressures affect the decision? (2) Technological—Do we have the engineering know-how to accomplish the goal? (3) Social—What is our responsibility to society? (4) Economic—Will we make a profit?

WHAT CAN HAPPEN WHEN BUSINESSES OVERLOOK THE HUMAN FACTOR

Businesses sometimes fail to recognize the human factor. They become so engrossed in computer technology, cash-flow charts, and management techniques that they overlook personal sensitivities. In a public relations blunder, the U.S. Bank of Washington in Spokane did exactly that, to its regret. A man in shabby clothes parked his pickup truck in the bank's parking lot, cashed a check, then asked the teller to validate his 60-cent parking ticket. She refused, claiming that cashing a check wasn't a transaction, as required for validation. When the man protested, she called a supervisor, who looked distastefully at the ragged character and also refused.

"Fine," the man replied. "You don't need me and I don't need you." Whereupon he closed his account and took the $1 million he had on deposit to a competing bank down the street.

When a corporation lets itself be perceived as a bully, especially against a child, its stature suffers. The Anheuser-Busch brewery learned just that. Lisa French won a contest at her junior high school in Georgia for her poster against alcohol and drug abuse. Her design featured a skeleton, a tombstone, a beer can, a dog resembling Spuds MacKenzie (a canine featured in Anheuser-Busch advertisements) and the slogan ''Drinking is like shaking hands with death.'' The prize poster was to be displayed on neighborhood area billboards for a month.

The poster went up on ten billboards. Within days, the dog was blacked out. Shortly thereafter the posters were removed.

Lisa's parents charged that an Anheuser-Busch distributor pressured the billboard company into removing the posters. The mother said that a brewery official had told her that the posters were offensive to the alcohol industry.

Learning of the incident, the Associated Press (AP) sought comment from the Anheuser-Busch division manager, the company's public relations firm, and the billboard company. All refused to say anything, a fact that the widely distributed AP story pointed out.

Lisa received a lesson in pressures against freedom of speech, and Anheuser-Busch got an embarrassing, self-inflicted black eye.

Perception! In these examples, the bank appeared to be snobbish and prone to judging customers by their appearance. The brewery came across as willing to use corporate might against a 12-year-old girl for expressing an opinion that differed from its own.

The lesson is clear: before a company takes an action affecting the public, its management should attempt to view the move through the eyes of others. Providing management with these outside perceptions is the job of the public relations specialists. Their antennae must be sensitive to changes in public attitudes.

A contrast to these incidents: when thunderstorms knocked out electric service for a prolonged period during a July heat wave, the Baltimore Gas & Electric Company gave 7000 customers free dry ice to preserve their perishable foods. The result was a perception that the company cared about its customers.

Similarly, corporate managements should pay heed to how their actions are perceived by their employees. If employees believe that management is treating them unfairly, their work suffers and internal tensions develop.

That is exactly what happened recently when General Motors announced that its 380,000 United Auto Workers union employees would receive no profit-sharing payments. Shortly thereafter it became known that GM executives would share a $169 million bonus. Incensed hourly employees at the GM plant in Saginaw, Michigan, donated pennies and dimes to a fund for corporate chairman Roger Smith, sarcastically earmarked to help him pay his living expenses. The leader of the campaign explained, ''It's a symbolic gesture to show we're getting the shaft and we're tired of it.'' Carried nationally by the Associated Press, the story showed the corporate management in a bad light at the very moment Smith was sending a letter to one million shareholders in response to other criticisms of the corporation's performance.

Episodes such as this led Michael Moore to produce the 1989 documentary motion picture, *Roger & Me,* a bitter but humorous attack on Smith and General Motors for callous attitudes. Although some critics complained that the filmmaker altered time sequences, *Roger & Me* was widely acclaimed and drew a large audience. Clearly it damaged GM's corporate image.

COMPUTERS VERSUS HUMANS

As computer wizardry multiplies and increasingly ingenious automated voice equipment comes into service, companies are tempted to substitute this technology for human contact with customers. This should be done with extreme caution. Unwise use of electronic response may alienate the very people the company needs to please. A dissatisfied customer who telephones to protest a billing error or shipping mistake resents being answered by a recording. Similarly, complaining letter-writers dislike receiving a computerized form-letter reply. Nor are customers placated by the cliché answer, "It was a computer error." They know that mistakes on computers result from errors committed by operators of the machines. Here is an area in which corporate public relations practitioners should exercise influence with management to maintain the human touch.

COURTESY PAYS

Too many corporations ignore opportunities to bind customers to them with small gestures such as thank-you letters. Although easily offended if they believe they are taken for granted, customers are impressed if someone in a supposedly remote corporation writes a note of appreciation.

Responding to customer inquiries and complaints is not only good public relations but good business. *Esquire* magazine carried the following item:

> In a rare follow-up on complaints and inquiries from customers, Coca-Cola discovered that more than 30 percent of those who said they felt their complaints had not been resolved satisfactorily no longer buy company products and that 17 percent of those whose inquiries were satisfied buy more Coca-Cola products now. A company spokesperson reflected, "This study demonstrates that forward-looking management can turn the corporate response system into a high performance profit center."

CONSUMERISM

The day when business could operate successfully on the Latin precept of *caveat emptor*—"Let the buyer beware"—is long gone. In today's society, sellers are expected to deliver goods and services of safe, acceptable quality on honest terms, without misleading claims and deceptive financing practices. Consumers have rights protected by the federal government and enjoy the assistance of government and private agencies in enforcing those rights. Consumerism is a significant and growing force in the conduct of business. The manner in which public relations practitioners help to guide a company in handling the pressures of consumerism strongly affects the public's attitude toward that company.

DEVELOPMENT OF THE CONSUMER MOVEMENT

The consumer movement developed during the past three decades because far too often business firms were caught either cheating their customers or carelessly giving them inferior products, then making it difficult for them to obtain adjustments. Public trust in business diminished. When the firm of Yankelovich, Skelly and White took a poll in 1967 to measure public trust, the result showed confidence in business at about 70 percent. In a similar poll 14 years later, public confidence had plummeted to 19 percent. The troubles encountered by consumers contributed to this precipitous decline, which paralleled a loss of approval of most public institutions during that period.

Indicative of the public resentment was the creation in newspapers of ''Action Line'' columns, whose editors publish complaints from badly treated customers and try to solve their problems. In many instances a telephone call from ''Action Line'' to an offending business, with the implied threat of bad publicity, obtains results that the frustrated customer has been unable to achieve directly. Some television stations have similar consumer-service programs.

The high priest of the consumer movement during its growth stages was Ralph Nader, a youthful attorney in Washington, D.C. His book *Unsafe at Any Speed,* published in 1965, was a searing indictment of automobile safety standards. Nader organized study groups that published generally critical reports on other industries and dwelt heavily upon corporate responsibility to consumers.

Rising consumer protests coincided with a period of rapid expansion in the ''watchdog'' role of government. The power of federal regulatory agencies over business expanded in numerous directions. The Food and Drug Administration determines what medications can be sold to the public. The Federal Trade Commission regulates truth in advertising, and the Securities and Exchange Commission controls the financial conduct of corporations (see Chapter 13). The National Highway Traffic Safety Administration sets standards for automobile manufacture. The Consumer Product Safety Commission examines other manufactured goods. Other federal and state agencies have consumer-oriented policing powers in their domains.

CONSUMERISM TODAY

Although Ronald Reagan's efforts as president to limit government regulation of business reduced government's role in several fields during the 1980s, public demand for government protection of consumers remained strong. In a study taken by Louis Harris and Associates, strong sentiment was expressed favoring continued government regulation of safety, health, and truth in advertising, although opposition was voiced to regulation as a general concept.

As citizens have frustrating experiences in obtaining good service and quality, and as they learn about the conviction of many companies and their executives for various forms of cheating, the momentum of consumerism multiplies. Nader said recently, ''The '90s will make the '60s pale into insignificance in terms of the reform drive to clean up the fraud, waste, abuse, and crimes of many corporations.''

USE OF BOYCOTTS

The *boycott*—refusal to buy the products or services of an offending company—is a widely used tool of the consumer movement, aimed at firms for many different reasons.

FIGURE 14.2

News headlines illustrate how closely the actions and policies of corporations are watched by the public, and the types of situations in which their public relations representatives are involved.

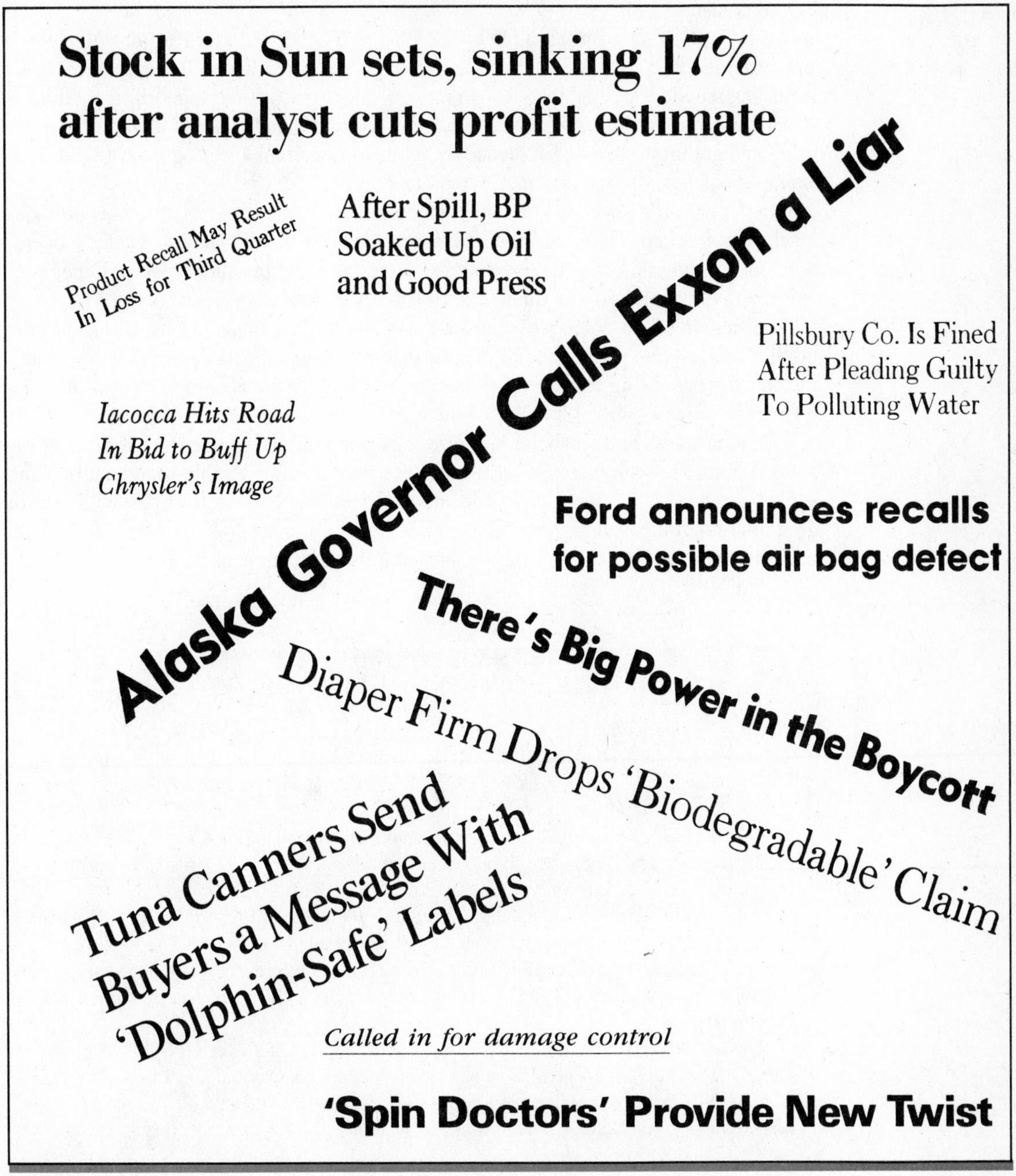

Stock in Sun sets, sinking 17% after analyst cuts profit estimate

Product Recall May Result In Loss for Third Quarter

After Spill, BP Soaked Up Oil and Good Press

Alaska Governor Calls Exxon a Liar

Pillsbury Co. Is Fined After Pleading Guilty To Polluting Water

Iacocca Hits Road In Bid to Buff Up Chrysler's Image

Ford announces recalls for possible air bag defect

There's Big Power in the Boycott

Diaper Firm Drops 'Biodegradable' Claim

Tuna Canners Send Buyers a Message With 'Dolphin-Safe' Labels

Called in for damage control

'Spin Doctors' Provide New Twist

At one period in the early 1990s, Nike athletic shoes were being boycotted by Operation PUSH, which demanded that Nike, Inc., appoint a black member to its board of directors and create additional nonwhite department heads. At the same time, the Miller Brewing Company's beers and the Philip Morris conglomerate's Marlboro cigarettes were under boycott by AIDS activist groups. These organizations demanded that the corporations halt financial support for Senator Jesse Helms, an opponent of homosexuals.

A boycott against Burger King by the Christian Leadership for Responsible Television was ended in late 1990 after the fast-food chain published half-page advertisements nationwide stating that it "wishes to go on record as supporting traditional American values on television." The boycott operators had claimed that the company promoted gratuitous sex and violence by sponsoring certain TV programs. (Additional examples of boycotts appear in Chapter 17.)

In the private sector, the nationwide network of Better Business Bureaus provides machinery through which wronged consumers may seek satisfaction. Nader's operations in Washington continue to publicize defective products and services. Other consumer organizations do similar work. *Consumer Reports* is widely read.

Formation of the Society of Consumer Affairs Professionals in Business (SOCAB) provides an avenue for exchange of information among specialists in the field and a method for increasing corporate awareness of what can be accomplished in building goodwill.

Thus business and financial organizations function under extensive legal controls and unofficial pressures designed to give the public safe, reliable merchandise, and honest services. Whether a company meets the demands of consumers willingly or grudgingly—volunteering corrective action when the need is evident or fighting against having to do so—influences the public's perception of it.

PHONES DON'T RING; AT&T APOLOGIZES

AT&T boasts about the reliability of its long-distance telephone service—calls it the most sophisticated and dependable in the world. So when the system suffered a nationwide breakdown for nine hours in early 1990, the giant company was embattled and embarrassed, to put it mildly.

Realizing how vulnerable it was to consumer condemnation, AT&T chose to face the problem head-on and apologize. It published full-page newspaper advertisements containing an open letter to customers from Chairman Robert E. Allen.

"We didn't live up to our standards of quality and we didn't live up to yours," Allen wrote. "It's as simple as that. And that's not acceptable to us. Or to you."

In compensation, AT&T offered its patrons a full day of reduced-price phone calls on the approaching Valentine's Day. Discounts ranged up to 30 percent depending on the time of day.

The result: much favorable comment and 124 million calls over AT&T lines on the chosen day. That was 14 percent more than on Valentine's Day the previous year. Open admission of error and clever choice of the traditional lovers' day for the make-good helped the company turn a potential public relations disaster into a victory.

PUBLIC ANGER GETS RESULTS

Public anger against a company can develop quickly. When R.J. Reynolds began to test-market a new cigarette aimed at blacks, called Uptown, criticism was vehement for both health and racial reasons. Antismoking groups pointed out that blacks historically have suffered higher rates of cancer than other groups. Dr. Louis W. Sullivan, Health and Human Services Secretary, accused R.J. Reynolds of "promoting a culture of cancer." It retorted that he was promoting paternalism.

Within days the company cancelled the test-marketing, not with an apology but with a grumbling statement that the brand had received "unfair and biased attention" and that the criticism was "a further erosion of the free enterprise system."

Unfortunately, companies with clean records and constructive consumer programs tend to be lumped with the bad ones in the public's mind. Their public relations representatives must work diligently and ingeniously to make the public aware of this commendable performance. The challenge to these practitioners is to remain watchful for any company action that would blemish a good record.

PRODUCT RECALLS

Recall of a defective product from its purchasers is the most visible, and frequently very expensive, form of corporate response to consumer pressure. Millions of automobiles have been called back for correction of defects that might endanger the safety of riders. Some recalls by the automakers are preventive and voluntary. Others have been done by agreement between manufacturer and the federal government. In certain instances, however, car makers have strenuously opposed government recall demands. Reaching the owners of defective automobiles is relatively easy, because of the state car registration laws. When other types of products are involved, especially those often purchased as gifts, the problem is more difficult.

Experience has shown that if a manufacturer recalls a defective product voluntarily, in a gracious manner that offers the owner suitable compensation, the company may generate enough goodwill to overcome the negative implications of the recall.

The worldwide recall of Perrier, the bubbly French bottled water, is a striking example of the financial loss and image problems such an action can create.

Perrier management in early 1990 ordered distributors everywhere to recall 160 million bottles of the popular drink, which long had been advertised as "naturally sparkling," after traces of benzene (a cancer-causing agent) were found in a few bottles. Almost three months later, after the source of contamination had been found and eliminated, Perrier water was returned to store shelves with a heavy advertising and public relations campaign. Nonetheless, the company suffered considerably from the episode.

Benzene traces were discovered first in the United States. Ronald V. Davis, head of Perrier's American branch, immediately ordered a nationwide recall of all bottles. Company headquarters in Paris said the contamination apparently had been caused by a worker cleaning the production line on which bottles for export to America were filled. Within days, however, tests in Denmark and the Netherlands revealed benzene in bottles there as well. At that time the worldwide recall was issued.

Perrier headquarters then changed its story a bit. Under heavy media questioning, officials said that the benzene traces entered the water because workers had failed to change charcoal filters in the bottling plant. Why the charcoal filters, people asked. That question led to disclosure that Perrier water does not emerge from the company's spring full of sparkling bubbles, as company promotion had always indicated. Instead, the fizz is added later by pumping carbon dioxide gas from the spring into the water through filters.

When Perrier bottles returned to the market, the labels carried the words *Nouvelle Production* (New Production). The U.S. Food and Drug Administration, reacting to the disclosure about production methods, ordered Perrier to remove the words "naturally sparkling" from the labels. Since carbonated gas is inserted into the water, it ruled, the carbonation is artificial.

How much this episode will harm Perrier sales in the long run is uncertain. In the short term, Davis said the recall had cost the American branch about $30 million in direct expenses, plus lost sales. One year after the recall was announced, Perrier had regained only 60 percent of the market share it held before the benzene was discovered.

CORPORATIONS AND THE ENVIRONMENT

An upsurge in public concern about protecting the environment forces corporations to face an issue that is emotionally charged, often costly to solve, and potentially damaging to those companies that fail to do their part in the cleanup. The public relations role in the environmental battle obviously is crucial.

Evidence that the public wants action, although recognizing that this might cost it money, is strong. In a survey of national opinion leaders by the Ford Motor Company, more than 90 percent of the respondents said the environment will be the public's top priority of the 1990s.

Distrust of corporate attitudes toward the environment also is evident. When a *Business Week*/Harris Poll in 1989 asked how far respondents thought a company would go to make a profit, 47 percent believed a company would be willing to harm the environment and 38 percent said it would endanger public health.

This is a considerable burden of unfavorable opinion to overcome. Too many corporation executives have dragged their feet, not yet recognizing the depth of public desire. Their public relations representatives have an internal selling job to do in convincing top management that environmental inaction will harm their companies in the long run.

Alice Rivlin, a Brookings Institute economist who is in the unusual position of being chairman of the Wilderness Society governing council and a director of Union Carbide, summarized the problem many companies face:

> It's sometimes difficult for companies to be as environmentally responsible as they'd like to be, because it's costly in the short run. That's part of the general problem of short-term focus in American companies. But I think if they take a long-range view, especially with the rising concern about the environment in the general public, it's clear that long-term profitability will be aided by environmental responsibility.

4 SEARS, ROEBUCK & CO., CHICAGO, ILL. CATALOGUE No. 117.

FACTORIES IN VARIOUS STATES WHICH WE OWN IN THEIR ENTIRETY, IN PART, OR OF WHICH WE CONTROL THE PRODUCT.

The Safe Plant at Newark, Ohio.

The Great Stove Foundry at Newark, Ohio.

The Plumbing Goods Factory in Wisconsin.

The Modern Wall Paper Mill in Chicago.

The Agricultural Implement Factory in Wisconsin.

The Upholstered Furniture Factory in Chicago.

The Wire Fence Mill at Knightstown, Indiana.

The Big Furniture Factory at Binghamton, New York.

The Great Organ Factory at Louisville, Kentucky.

The Big Paint Factory in Chicago.

The Saw Factory in Michigan.

The Enormous Vehicle Factory at Evansville, Indiana.

The Camera Factory at Rochester, Minnesota.

The Great Gun Factory at Meriden, Connecticut.

THESE very small illustrations will give you but a very faint idea of the combined strength and capital represented in these enormous factories. Among them are factories that cover acres and acres of ground. For example, the stove plant is the largest stove foundry in the world. Many of the other factories are among the largest in the world.

IN addition to these factories we own in their entirety, in a large part, or control the output of many other factories, included in which might be mentioned another cream separator factory in New York, furniture factories, factories for the manufacture of clothing, wearing apparel, millinery, hardware, etc. The factories we illustrate are but a few of the vast number in which we wield a controlling influence.

The Cream Separator Plant in Iowa.

The Modern Shoe Factory at Littleton, New Hampshire.

FOR example, in the manufacture of wall paper which we make in our own mill, from the raw paper stock to the finished wall paper in all shades, grades and colorings, in order to make absolutely certain that we own our wall paper at the lowest possible cost, we go to the very bottom of the source of supply. We contract with the manufacturer of raw hanging paper stock, who owns thousands of acres of standing timber, who can make our paper stock with the smallest loss of time or expense, who can deliver this raw wall paper stock to our mill under positively ideal conditions, thus forging the last link in the chain of conditions necessary to produce high grade wall paper at our marvelously low prices, all of which is plainly shown in our free Wall Paper Sample Book illustrated on another page of this catalogue.

IN addition to the factory connections which we have mentioned, and illustrated, we might go on and tell you of many other connections, arrangements and advantages by means of which we have effected wonderful economy for our customers on such items as Sewing Machines, Harness, Saddles, Horse Clippers, Sheep Shearing Machines, Watches, Jewelry, Silverware, Clocks, Musical Instruments, Hardware, Washing Machines, Cement Block Machines, Doors, Sash, Blinds, Mill Work, Bicycles, Electrical Goods, Photographic Goods, Cutlery, Sporting Goods, Graphophones, Crockery, Carpets, Rugs, Curtains, Blankets, Furnishing Goods, Notions and thousands of other items mentioned in this Big Catalogue. To get the right quality and the right cost on these thousands of items, we have gone to the very bottom of the sources of supply, of manufacture, of raw materials; we have investigated every point in connection with the manufacture and marketing of merchandise that possibly could be of benefit to our customers; and every advantage that could be gained by the investment of capital or the employment of experts has been secured for only one purpose, for only one reason—**to give you a better quality in any given article than you could get elsewhere, to give you a much lower price than you could secure from any other dealer.**

FIGURE 14.3
Smoke pouring from their smokestacks once was advertised by companies as a sign of prosperity. Today it is condemned for polluting the atmosphere. This page from the 1908 Sears Roebuck catalogue illustrates what a radical change has occurred.

ACTIVIST ORGANIZATIONS

Public opinion is led by environmental activist organizations skilled in protest actions and in litigation. Their attitude toward corporations in most cases is distrustful, frequently vehemently antagonistic. (These organizations are examined in Chapter 17.) Trying to establish a dialogue with these critics, in the hope of at least creating some understanding and perhaps certain common goals, is part of the corporate public relations challenge.

Stockholders who introduce resolutions at annual meetings demanding corporate environmental action form another aspect of the problem.

AREAS OF ENVIRONMENTAL CONCERN

Companies face differing problems, of course, depending on what they produce, and the areas of public concern are many. A survey by NEXIS News Monitor of 80,000 news stories about the environment during a five-year period in the late 1980s provides an indication of the major issues and the degree of attention they received.

Pesticide use drew the most attention, 29 percent of the news stories. This was followed by toxic waste, 19 percent; acid rain, 16 percent; nuclear waste, 13 percent; oil spills, 8 percent. The ozone layer, greenhouse effect, radon, and chemical dumping followed with 5 percent or less each.

WHAT COMPANIES CAN DO

Public relations specialists in environmental work recommend that as a first step a company should take a ''green audit'' (''green'' having become a symbolic word for being environmentally clean). This audit involves a detailed investigation of every aspect of the business for its impact on the environment. An audit by a qualified outsider may be more objective than a self-examination.

Next, management should develop a long-range clean-up program. Some environmental faults may be overcome quickly and cheaply, while more fundamental ones could involve heavy expense and retooling. This may require the company to raise the prices of its products to remain profitable. Willingness to spend the money and take the risk is what Alice Rivlin was talking about. Jobs may also be at jeopardy as a result of some environmental decisions, a painful personnel problem.

Public relations practitioners should tell the public not only what a company has accomplished but also its long-range plans for cleanup. Realistic people recognize that complex solutions take time. Providing them with evidence that improvement is in progress will strengthen their perception of the company as a good corporate citizen.

Environmental improvements a company claims should be genuine, however, not window-dressing of dubious validity. Some companies try to exploit the environmental movement to grab a marketing advantage. Pointing at them, Attorney General Hubert Humphrey, III, of Minnesota commented, ''The selling of the environment could make the oat-bran craze look like a Sunday School picnic.'' Claims by some firms that their products are biodegradable, photodegradable, or ''ozone friendly'' have been shown to be invalid or exaggerations of questionable research. When this happens, the company's reputation is damaged.

A FEW EXAMPLES

Some things, big and small, that corporations have done to improve the environment as a result of public pressure:

- AT&T said it would substitute biodegradable cardboard for plastic foam packaging for telephones and answering machines.
- Some companies have signed the "Valdez Principles," a code of conduct for protecting the environment, drawn up by environmental groups.
- Procter & Gamble began selling several of its products in bottles made of recycled plastic.
- A California wine and food company packs its shipments in popcorn instead of plastic foam because popcorn is naturally biodegradable.
- Recycled products, especially paper, have been put on the market by numerous companies. When they use recycled paper, many firms state that fact on their printed materials.
- McDonald's decided to prepare its french fries in vegetable oil instead of fat as a good health measure, and to replace its plastic foam sandwich boxes with paper-based wrapping. Later it announced plans to eliminate at least 80 percent of its garbage by such methods as using smaller paper napkins, recycling behind-the-counter cardboard boxes, and eliminating plastic cutlery wrappers wherever permitted by local health laws.

MARKETING PUBLIC RELATIONS

The tools and techniques of public relations are used extensively to support the marketing and sales objectives of a business. This is called "marketing communications" or "marketing public relations." Personnel who work in this area usually serve in or are closely affiliated with the marketing department.

Intel, for example, has product public relations specialists who report to a marketing vice president instead of the vice president of corporate communications. At Hewlett-Packard, the public relations department has a section called Product Press Relations. General Motors, in 1990, tied its public relations to marketing by creating a new department of "Communications and Marketing."

Thomas L. Harris, former vice chairman of Golin/Harris Communications in New York, in his book *A Marketer's Guide to Public Relations,* says that corporate public relations and marketing public relations will be more highly defined within business organizations. Corporate public relations, he states, will remain a management function supporting overall corporate objectives, while marketing public relations will be a marketing management function.

Harris defines marketing public relations as "the process of planning, executing and evaluating programs that encourage purchase and consumer satisfaction through

COMPANIES PLEDGE "DOLPHIN-SAFE" TUNA

Environmentalists achieved a widely publicized victory when the three largest canners of tuna announced that henceforth they would buy only tuna caught by methods that do not endanger dolphins.

The H. J. Heinz Company announced its decision in early 1990; its two chief competitors followed within hours. So did a large pet food company. This ended a 14-year campaign by the Humane Society of the United States to stop the netting of the playful, intelligent dolphins, which often became entangled in fishing boats' nets and drowned.

A crusade by schoolchildren pressured the tuna companies. So did such actions as having characters in movies and comic strips refuse to eat tuna sandwiches. Some restaurants took tuna off their menus.

While environmentalists celebrated, members of the American Tuna Boat Association feared their livelihoods would be destroyed. They predicted that foreign boats, operating without such restrictions, would harvest most of the tuna and sell the fish to U.S. customers.

credible communication of information and impressions that identify companies and their products with the needs, wants, concerns, and interests of consumers.''

The objectives of marketing public relations, often called *marcom* in industry jargon, are accomplished in several ways.

Product Publicity The cost and clutter of advertising and sales promotion have mounted dramatically, and companies have found that product publicity is a cost-effective way of reaching potential consumers. Products, if presented properly, can be newsworthy and catch the eyes of reporters and editors. Life Savers, for example, generated many news articles about the introduction of Life Saver Holes, pellet candies that represented the ''holes'' in its regular product.

Other forms of product publicity are found on the food, auto, real estate, business, travel, and sports pages of newspapers as news and feature stories. These cover the development and launching of new products, and even new uses for established products. Radio and television talk shows and consumer programs also contain large amounts of product publicity.

Joan Aho Ryan and George H. Lemmond, writing in the *Public Relations Journal,* make the case for product publicity: ''Cynical consumers, zapping commercials and ignoring print ads, are more receptive to the editorial message. The 'third party endorsement' allows advertisers to sell a new product while enveloping the commercial message in a credible environment.''

Information Bureaus Several companies operate information bureaus that help position their products in the marketplace. Quaker's Gatorade has its Sports Science Institute, Reebok has an Aerobic Information Bureau, and Nutri/System operates a Health and Fitness Information Bureau. One primary function of these ''information bureaus'' is the distribution of news releases and press kits that report research results and give consumer tips on keeping healthy and fit. Of course, the sponsor of the research and the source of the "tips" are mentioned in the resulting news stories.

Polls Bearing a Brand Name Another form of product publicity that gets good media coverage is polls. The Chlor-Trimeton Allergy Season Index has measured pollen counts since 1984. Philip Morris Company publicized its Merit brand cigarettes by publishing the Merit Report, a public opinion poll on a wide variety of topics. Even the Gallup Poll, which newspapers use regularly, is a product publicity technique for the company to promote its polling services to business and industry.

Public Relations Tours Company executives can do much to promote products by giving speeches and news conferences. Perhaps the most effective CEO in this respect is Lee Iacocca of Chrysler Corporation, who is the company's top salesman. Early in 1990, he made a six-city tour to promote Chrysler's new products and to tell people that the automaker had recovered from an earlier recession. He took his message to 12,000 invited opinion-makers and gave numerous news interviews.

School Promotions Companies try to instill brand loyalty early by sponsoring special programs in schools. AT&T has an Adventure Club, which includes student newsletters, classroom posters, and teaching guides designed to foster understanding of communications and build AT&T awareness among first-graders. Coca-Cola's Minute Maid unit enhanced the wholesome image of its juice products by sponsoring a literacy program. More than 3.7 million elementary-school children were encouraged to read a book a week during summer vacation and track their progress on a chart provided by the unit. Product coupons were provided with the chart. Nike, Inc., sent one million high school students free textbook covers bearing the company's name.

Parent and consumer groups are less than happy about school children being the target of corporate marketing programs, but officials in financially strapped school districts often welcome business support if the program isn't too commercial and serves a legitimate educational function.

Cause-Related Marketing Companies in highly competitive fields often strive to differentiate themselves by supporting causes that appeal to various market segments. American Express, for example, promised its customers that if they used its credit card for purchases, 1 percent of the bill would be given to the Statue of Liberty restoration campaign. Visa and MasterCard have used the same technique with the Sierra Club and other conservation groups.

Another approach is to underwrite events and information campaigns. Reebok International Ltd. supplied $10 million for a "Human Rights Now!" concert tour, which helped focus the world's attention on human rights abuses. Johnson & Johnson's Personal Products Company underwrote a $1 million campaign to educate the public about the sensitive issue of domestic violence.

Although cause-related marketing doesn't necessarily improve product sales, public relations professionals call it an effective way to communicate a company's values and corporate philosophy. From a marketing perspective, support of a popular cause can foster brand loyalty by consumers who believe in that cause.

Companies usually avoid controversial causes that could lead to a possible boycott by consumers.

Corporate Sponsorships An estimated 3500 or more companies are spending between $2 and 3 billion annually on sponsorships of all kinds. Growth averaged about 30 to 40 percent during the past decade, and a continued stampede to corporate sponsorship seems likely during the 1990s.

The popularity of sponsored events is due to several reasons. They give companies high visibility among key audiences that can afford and would be interested in a particular product or service. Event sponsorship also generates news coverage, brings out audiences, provides a focal point for marketing efforts and sales campaigns, and often is more cost-effective than an advertising campaign. The tobacco industry became an early leader in sponsorship primarily because its advertising on radio and television was banned by U.S. law.

Sporting Events Sporting events are extremely popular and are well funded by corporations. The Orange Bowl is now officially the Federal Express Orange Bowl and the Sun Bowl is the John Hancock Sun Bowl, although the media have resisted using these official titles. In fact, by 1990 a dozen of the 19 annual college football bowl games had title sponsors.

Companies attempting to reach specialized audiences sponsor many sports. Volvo, the Swedish auto maker, and Grundig of West Germany have sponsored the Track and Field Federation of East Germany; the Japanese manufacturer Toshiba is a sponsor of the Tour de France bicycle race. Chrysler Plymouth Division sponsors the U.S. Pro Ski Tour and provides $1 million in prizes. The Kemper Insurance Group has sponsored the Professional Golf Association for more than 20 years.

Manufacturers of products for affluent customers tailor their sponsorships accordingly. Range Rover, the British maker of expensive four-wheel-drive vehicles, underwrites equestrian events and yachting races. Lexus, the luxury car division of Toyota, sponsors polo championships because, an official said, ''Involvement in this event allows us to position the Lexus product line in the proper demographic segment.''

On an international level, the 1992 Summer Olympic Games in Barcelona, Spain, are expected to attract scores of multinational corporations. Involvement in the Olym-

AVON RUNS AROUND THE WORLD

Avon Cosmetics, anxious to reach women its house-to-house salesforce may not see, decided to sponsor a running program. In a single year it conducted 54 races for women in 27 countries, among them France, Brazil, Japan, and Thailand.

The company chose to promote running because the sport is compatible with the self-made-woman image Avon promotes. Also, the events generated community involvement with the use of volunteer race workers.

In evaluating the program, Avon found that the races strengthened its image in the United States and increased awareness of its beauty products in countries where it is less well known.

BEER, CIGARETTE SPONSORSHIPS UNDER ATTACK

Legislators in the United States and other nations are beginning to introduce laws that would ban beer and cigarette advertising, as well as sponsorship of sporting events.

Safety and health groups say that beer companies spend $50 million annually on sponsorships of motor sports races that link beer and fast cars in the minds of racing fans. They contend that such sponsorships encourage drunk driving and auto deaths among impressionable teenagers. The Beer Institute counters that 98 percent of racing enthusiasts are over age 21 and there is no scientific evidence that sponsorship of motor sports promotes drunk driving.

Events such as the Virginia Slims Tennis Tournament, the Winston Cup auto race, and the Camel Supercross motorcycle race are under attack for aligning cigarette smoking with sports. Antismoking advocates say that such sponsorships send a wrong message to young people and make smoking look glamorous. Critics also argue that television coverage of these events is a ''back-door tactic'' by the tobacco industry to circumvent a 20-year-old television ad ban. For example, during television coverage of the 1989 Marlboro Grand Prix, the Marlboro logo was shown 49 percent of the time.

Health and Human Services Secretary Louis W. Sullivan increased the pressure in 1991 by urging sports fans and promoters to boycott sports events sponsored by tobacco companies.

The tobacco industry counters that sponsorship of events isn't advertising, just promotion of a company and its legal products. Any ban on advertising or sponsorship of events, the industry says, violates the First Amendment of the Constitution.

Whatever the merits, pro and con, of the issues involved, the dispute is shaping up as a major public relations headache for the beer and tobacco industries.

pics is an effective way of reaching a worldwide audience, but some marketing experts wonder if the numerous sponsorships create so much clutter that audiences tune out most of the messages. Still, promotion and advertising before and after the event place a company in a special niche as an ''Olympic sponsor.'' (Sports publicity is discussed further in Chapter 20.)

Art and Music General Motors GMC Division, interested in selling pickups, sponsored a 15-city country and western tour featuring Randy Travis and Tammy Wynette. Toyota underwrote performances of the Dallas Opera and the Miami City Ballet. Ford Motor Company, seeking to enhance its image among the affluent and well-educated, sponsored an exhibition of impressionistic paintings in Pittsburgh.

THE BUSINESS-MEDIA RELATIONSHIP

Reporting by the media is a basic source of public information about the performance and objectives of business. Too frequently it generates misunderstanding and irritation between these two essential segments of society, a situation for which both sides are partially responsible. The trouble arises most frequently when a corporation becomes involved in a communications crisis.

Many business executives regard media stories about them and their companies as inaccurate, incomplete, and biased. In a recent survey, 35.8 percent of the 150 chief executive officers of major corporations participating called media coverage of their businesses "unfair." On the positive side, 42 percent said that coverage was "fair to business."

According to the survey, conducted for Public Relations Exchange, Inc., of Pittsburgh, the CEOs rated network TV news coverage as the "most unfair" to business and business dailies such as the *Wall Street Journal* as the fairest.

In reply to the criticism, editors and reporters say that often they cannot publish or broadcast thorough, even-handed stories about business because many company executives, uncooperative and wary, erect barricades against them. They complain, too, that some business leaders don't understand the concept of objectivity and assume that any story involving unfavorable news about their company is intentionally biased.

Public relations practitioners serving business stand in the middle. They must interpret their companies to the media, while showing their chief executive officers and other high officials how open, friendly press relations can serve their interests.

A RESEARCH STUDY OF THE RELATIONSHIP

Concerned about the misconceptions and distrust, the American Management Association commissioned a research study by David Finn, an eminent public relations counselor, the results of which were published in a booklet titled "The Business-Media Relationship." Its findings and recommendations are a valuable guide to all practitioners in the business field.

Finn conducted a series of detailed surveys. These are key findings as stated in the study:

> AMA's surveys of public relations executives found that 73 percent believe reporters don't accurately research their topics, 62 percent believe reporters play on public emotion, and 72 percent see anti-business feelings and public sentiment as being on the side of the media. Most public relations executives (76 percent) consider the main problem of business reporting to be not necessarily bias but inaccuracies due to sloppiness.
>
> AMA's companion survey of journalists found that 64 percent agreed that reporters don't accurately research their subjects, 58 percent attributed inaccuracies to sloppiness rather than bias, and 58 percent volunteered that media presentation is more important than factual reporting.
>
> A majority of journalists (60 percent) feel that business executives are defensive and don't give reporters the chance to question them. A full 61 percent believe business people are not honest with their own public relations departments, and 36 percent think they often lie to reporters.*

*Reprinted, by permission of the publisher, from *The Business-Media Relationship: Countering Misconception and Distrust,* an AMA Research Study, by David Finn, pp. 10–13. © 1981 American Management Association, New York. All rights reserved.

Finn offers this set of recommendations to executives and reporters for achieving better reporting of business:

For Executives

- Arrange for direct contact between senior executives and reporters. Keep in touch with PR specialists and journalists on a continuing basis—not just when crises erupt. Do not, however, try to win favor of a reporter by giving confidences off the record or by offering gifts.
- Provide means for executives to learn details of media practices, such as the need to attract readers and the importance of meeting deadlines.
- Allow for the possibility that reporters may not be well acquainted with business practices, management techniques, economic principles, or the terminology of your industry.
- Be well prepared on expected topics before meeting reporters. Where controversial issues are expected, consider drilling with colleagues beforehand; e.g., have them ask the twenty or so most likely questions to be sure pertinent facts and explanations are at hand.
- Study and practice specific techniques—e.g., using short sentences, repeating key phrases, avoiding "no comment" answers—that help to get ideas across in interviews.
- Provide handouts or special memos to summarize key points, especially when complicated issues or financial data are involved.
- Don't try to squelch a story by bringing pressure on higher-ups in the media.
- Be aware of public concerns when commenting on issues involving corporate interests.
- Have a third person present at interviews to listen objectively to what is said and to call inadvertent inaccuracies or oversights to the principal executive's attention.
- Maintain a continuing good relationship between legal and PR counsel so that there will be a thoughtful balance between legal exposure and the amount of information volunteered.
- Don't argue with a negative report in the media. To do so is to keep the issue before the public more than may be warranted.
- In the event of a damaging story or series, make a long-range plan for constructive future actions.

For Reporters

- Prepare for interviews by such means as studying pertinent company statements, position papers, and annual reports.

- Become familiar with the fundamentals of finance, accounting, economics, and management practices.
- Be aware of legitimate constraints—privacy laws, SEC rules, impending lawsuits, the value of certain facts to competitors—that limit the ability of executives to divulge certain information.
- Be open with business executives. Be receptive to presentation materials and to the business point of view.
- Be careful not to make the selling of news more important than the news itself.
- Make certain that headlines reflect the content of the story. An effective, responsible story can be damaged by a misleading heading. [This is outside a reporter's realm, since copyeditors write headlines.]
- Discourage off-the-record remarks by business executives.
- Understand that business reactions to extensive, well-researched stories cannot always be immediate.
- When possible, check quotes with source, in order to permit review.
- When necessary, explain deadlines, off-the-record requirements, and other journalistic restrictions to executives.
- Take advantage of business's willingness to review financial information.
- Be wary of quoting disgruntled ex-employees exclusively.

In keeping with these guidelines, a corporate public relations department should serve as a door-opener for reporters within the corporation, as well as handle routine inquiries and provide background material. The public relations practitioners should make company executives realize that reporters are not automatically enemies out to get them.

CRISIS PUBLIC RELATIONS

The most challenging test of public relations skill in corporate life arises in times of crisis. When an unexpected development involving a company embarrasses the organization or frightens the public—even in the worst instance creating the threat of death—the company's credibility and decency come under intense scrutiny. With the news media in hard pursuit of the facts, executives and public relations experts must act under severe pressure.

In a crisis, the first instinct of some companies is to ''stonewall it'': deny that a crisis exists, refuse to answer media questions, and resist involvement by appropriate government agencies. By behaving in this manner, managements suggest a ''public-be-damned'' attitude that harms their images severely.

A second course, followed by some, is to ''manage'' the news about the crisis by releasing partial, often inaccurate, and delayed information while concealing especially unfavorable facts. If these facts slip out anyway, as they frequently do through insider ''leaks'' and government inquiries, disclosure of a company's cover-up attempt shatters its credibility.

THE BEST COURSE TO FOLLOW

The third and best course is an open communication policy. The company keeps the media fully and promptly informed of the facts while providing background information to put the facts into perspective. A story candidly told, while perhaps embarrassing in its immediate impact, is less damaging than a cover-up version that generates rumors and suspicions much worse than reality.

Chairman Harold Burson of Burson-Marsteller strongly advocates such openness. Writing in *Management Review,* he states:

> Burson-Marsteller's experience has taught us that however severe the crisis, however painful the task, it is in a company's best interest to tell what it knows and doesn't know quickly, responsibly, and with sensitivity to the people affected. By taking the offensive and addressing the concerns, real and imagined, of key audiences, a company is more likely to be viewed as a responsible and responsive citizen rather than a recalcitrant or indifferent monolith.

Because crises may develop without warning, every corporation needs a well-prepared policy of emergency action. The plan should include advance selection of a qualified representative who will issue consistent, truthful information with an awareness of media deadlines. A management committee that meets frequently to assess the situation as it develops is an excellent way to identify and satisfy the public's concerns.

Other elements of an emergency plan should include these measures:

- A manual of operations, distributed to all management personnel. The manual lists procedures to be followed in such emergencies as an earthquake, oil spill, product tampering, or other possibilities peculiar to the particular corporation.
- Arrangements for media facilities at a central location with telephones, typewriters, and electronic hookups.
- Selection and training of employees to handle the surge of telephone calls any emergency creates.
- Plans for notifying families of injured or dead workers.
- Arrangements with local hospitals and ambulances for handling casualties.

THREE MILE ISLAND

The classic case of public relations confusion in a life-and-death situation occurred when the Three Mile Island nuclear power plant near Harrisburg, Pennsylvania, suffered a series of breakdowns in its No. 2 reactor cooling system in 1979. A critical situation developed. A potentially disastrous melt-down of the reactor and a devastating explosion of hydrogen gas, with high loss of life from radiation, became a possibility.

During the weeklong crisis, the public received a baffling mixture of contradictory statements from Metropolitan Edison Company, the plant's owner; the Nuclear Regulatory Commission (NRC); and companies that had built portions of the nuclear system. Metropolitan Edison tended to issue statements minimizing the danger, while government representatives spoke in more alarming terms. The plant owners did not always keep the NRC and the public informed about their actions during the crisis—at a time when the nation, shaken by the realization of nuclear plant vulnerability and the fear of deadly release of radioactive material, deserved the fullest possible information. During several crucial moments public relations representatives of the company seemed ill-informed about what was happening.

At one point a Metropolitan Edison vice president told a news conference, "I don't know why we need to tell you every step we take. We certainly feel a responsibility for people who live around our plant, and we need to get on with our job." The rather brusque tone of this statement added to the generally poor impression made by the company's handling of the news.

CASE STUDIES: PUBLIC RELATIONS CRISIS—A CONTRAST

When a corporation finds itself caught in a major crisis that threatens its reputation, its management and public relations department are put under severe stress. The way in which they handle the bad news demonstrates company philosophy and their state of preparedness. One company reacts with candor, open communication, and obvious concern for the public good. Another company tries to ride out the storm by brushing aside media and public questions, belligerently denying the existence of trouble, and creating the impression that it puts self-interest above public safety and welfare.

The forthright company emerges stronger in the public eye than before the crisis. The cover-up company harms its reputation so badly that it is damaged for years to come.

Two leading corporations—Johnson & Johnson, health product manufacturers, and the Exxon Corporation—endured major crises. The former, as the victim of an unknown criminal, earned praise for its handling of the problem. The other suffered a public relations disaster and was seen by the public as a "villain." Studies of these two cases, and a third showing how British Petroleum handled an oil spill in a positive way, illustrate what a difference public relations performance can make.

THE WRONG WAY: EXXON'S ALASKA OIL SPILL

Riding low in the water with its load of crude oil from the Alaska pipeline, the huge tanker Exxon Valdez plowed south from the port of Valdez, Alaska, in a drizzle shortly after midnight of March 24, 1989. Suddenly it ran onto a reef, split open, and spilled masses of oil into the sea.

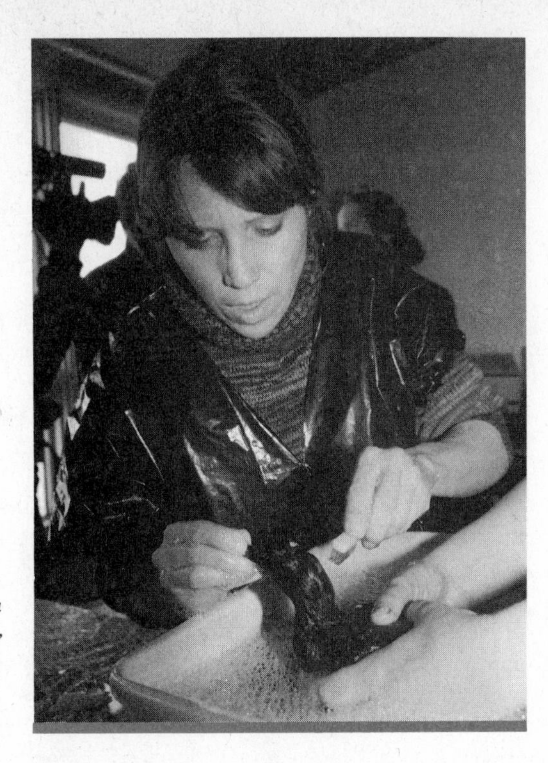

Using a toothbrush and soapy water, Dr. Jessica Porter cleans the oil off a sea bird at the animal rescue center in Valdez, Alaska, in March 1989. Thousands of birds were covered with oil that leaked from the tanker Exxon Valdez *in an environmental disaster. (Reuters/Bettmann)*

Thus began one of history's worst environmental accidents—and a public relations performance so bungled that the public perceived the Exxon Corporation as a cold, uncaring company more concerned about escaping responsibility than about the damage it had caused.

The Facts Shortly after the Exxon Valdez sailed from the terminal into Prince William Sound, Captain Joseph J. Hazelwood turned over command of the vessel to Third Mate Gregory Cousins, who was not legally licensed to pilot a ship in those waters. Concerned about floating ice, the captain instructed Cousins to steer the ship out of the normal southbound shipping channel to a certain point, then turn back into its normal course. The return was not made in time and the ship hit Bligh Reef, where rocks tore eight holes in its bottom.

Nearly 11 million tons of oil—240,000 barrels—spread across the remote, austerely scenic sound, fouling some 1100 miles of shoreline. Immense numbers of fish died, and Alaska's fishing industry was critically damaged. More than 30,000 dead birds and about 1,000 dead sea otters were counted.

By the end of summer, 1989, Exxon had spent more than $1 billion on cleanup work, yet the job was far from finished, and the company's reputation had suffered an extreme blow. The company fired Captain Hazelwood, who faced criminal charges for allegedly drinking shortly before he sailed and operating a ship while intoxicated.

Exxon's Public Relations Actions During the hours just after the accident, as the public began to comprehend the enormity of the spill, Lawrence G. Rawl, Exxon's chairman, made two public relations mistakes that he later regretted.

- He elected to stay at New York headquarters rather than fly to the oil spill scene and take charge of the cleanup in person. Instead, he sent lower-level officials. This was widely interpreted as indifference on his part.
- He decided that all information about the spill and cleanup efforts should be released at Valdez, on the scene. This remote port of 3000 people had only limited telephone lines and other facilities, so reporters who flew to Alaska had trouble getting out their stories. Exxon officials in New York refused to talk for nearly a week, creating an impression that Exxon was not seriously concerned and was trying to restrict coverage.

Rawl himself made no public comment until six days after the accident and didn't meet reporters until April 18. Three weeks had passed after the spill before he went to Alaska.

Ten days after the spill, Exxon published a full-page newspaper advertisement in the form of an open letter from Rawl. In it he said, "I want to tell you how sorry I am that this accident took place." He failed to state, however, that Exxon accepted responsibility for the spill, an omission that was widely noticed.

Quarrel with Alaska and U.S. Coast Guard Soon after this, Exxon got into a public quarrel with the state of Alaska and U.S. Coast Guard officials over delays in the cleanup effort, and tried to shift the blame for this from itself to them. This led Governor Steve Cowper to accuse Exxon of making false statements.

Exxon claimed that it could have minimized the damage had it been permitted to use chemical dispersants quickly after the spill, but was prevented from doing so by the state and the Coast Guard. State officials called this claim false; they said that Exxon had not sought permission for general use of dispersants. Cowper called the Exxon assertion a "systematic effort to mislead the public." State officials said Exxon had not mentioned its claim about dispersants until a week after the accident.

The *Wall Street Journal* pointed out that this claim was similar to one made by Amoco, another oil giant, when its Amoco Cadiz spilled oil off the French coast. Exxon's claim about dispersants apparently was a legal maneuver for use in defense of anticipated lawsuits, but it added to the public image of a belligerent, uncooperative company.

Public Reaction Response by the public to these events was strongly against Exxon, both for letting the spill occur and for the way it handled the cleanup. More than 18,000 customers mailed their credit cards back to the company. Talk of a boycott was heard; an Exxon statement called such action unjust. Late-night TV talk-show hosts aimed their barbs at Exxon. Congressional committees did the same. Company officials were summoned to the White House and told that cleanup efforts were inadequate. Corporate profits fell, and stockholders gave Rawl a bad time at the annual meeting.

Headlines such as "Alaska Governor Calls Exxon a Liar," "Angry Response to

Exxon's Edict,'' and ''Oil Spill Panelists Lambaste Exxon'' put nasty scars on the company's image.

Suspicions of the company's intentions increased when its executives made a seemingly small but significant change in the official line.

In the early weeks, Exxon officials said that the company would ''clean up'' the oil-soaked beaches by September 15. By midsummer, however, they told Congress that the company would ''treat'' the beaches, a less emphatic pledge. Chided for this linguistic retreat, Exxon President William D. Stevens replied that ''cleanup is very much in the eye of the beholder.''

Blunt Memo Becomes Public In late July, an internal corporate memo signed by the general manager of the cleanup reached the press, and the company was in even worse trouble. The memo stated that Exxon would halt cleanup activities at the end of the summer, no matter what state and federal governments wanted it to do. Cleanup equipment would be fully demobilized.

''These are not negotiable points,'' the memo stated. ''No commitment should be made to any private or government party on timing of demobilization, for wintertime activity or for 1990 activity.''

This was a direct slap at the Alaskan government, which had asked Exxon to maintain an emergency force during the winter and to resume work the following spring.

An irate congressional committee responded to the memo by calling a hearing. Some of Exxon's major stockholders, such as the New York City government, expressed concern about the company's attitude. Reaction was so intense that in the end Exxon had to retreat. It arranged for emergency crews to be available during the violent Alaskan winter, and resumed cleanup for five months in 1990 after clearing its program with the Coast Guard. Rawl paid a call on Governor Cowper to assure him that Exxon was not abandoning Alaska.

Aftermath Years must pass before the full impact of the oil spill on the Alaskan habitat is determined. More than 36,000 migratory birds and many other species of wildlife are known to have died. Financially, Exxon was hit heavily. In order to settle a federal lawsuit, it agreed in 1991 to pay a $100 million criminal fine plus $900,000 in damages to be used for restoration of natural resources. This $1 billion settlement was in addition to the $2 billion Exxon said it had spent in cleanup work. The agreement collapsed in 1991, however, when a federal judge ruled that the $100 million fine was too small. A long criminal trial appeared certain unless a more costly settlement could be negotiated. Captain Hazelwood was acquitted of charges that he operated the ship while intoxicated but was convicted of a misdemeanor, negligent discharge of oil. The Exxon Valdez has been repaired and renamed the Exxon Mediterranean; it will sail only in foreign waters.

Lessons of the Exxon Case Careful study shows four major shortcomings in Exxon's public relations operation during the oil spill:

1. Failure of the company's top official to establish clear public command of the problem from the start, by going to the scene.

2. Failure to provide an open flow of information to the media, with ample facilities for its distribution.

3. Creation of an adversarial relationship with state and federal governments. This led to a perception that the company was belligerent and uncooperative.

4. Failure to have an adequate crisis plan ready to handle such an oil spill emergency. The company had publicly belittled the possibility of an Alaskan oil spill and became complacent.

In an interview with *Fortune,* Rawl conceded some of these points. ''From a public relations standpoint, it probably would have been better had I gone up there,'' he said. Asked if he should have been more visible early in the crisis, he replied, ''In hindsight it would have helped.''

When invited to give advice to other chief executive officers on handling such a crisis, he answered, ''You'd better prethink which way you are going to jump from a public affairs standpoint before you have any kind of problem. You ought to always have a public affairs plan, even though it's kind of hard to force yourself to think in terms of a chemical plant blowing up or spilling all that oil in Prince William Sound.''

Few companies have ever had such a costly lesson in public relations.

THE RIGHT WAY: HANDLING AN OIL SPILL PROPERLY

A few months after the Exxon disaster, the American Trader, a tanker leased by British Petroleum (BP), apparently ruptured by its own anchor, spilled oil two miles off the Southern California coast. Approximately 400,000 gallons of oil poured into the Pacific and threatened to flow onto popular beaches.

BP, aware of Exxon's mistakes, reacted quickly and with considerable ingenuity. Not only did it organize an efficient cleanup operation, but it kept the media fully informed.

The BP chairman, James Ross, flew to the scene immediately and took charge. Public relations representatives with hand-held cellular phones were stationed at every point along the beaches where cleanup forces functioned to gather and dispense information, favorable or unfavorable to the company.

Private public relations specialists were flown down from San Francisco to reinforce the BP staff.

BP officials appeared on local and national TV programs. The company provided underwater photos of holes in the tanker's hull. Media headquarters equipped with a large battery of phones were set up next to the cleanup command center.

The results were detailed, positive news coverage and virtually no complaint from media or public. Cleanup efforts and favorable tides held oil-spill damage on the beaches to a low level. BP emerged from the accident with its credibility strengthened.

THE RIGHT WAY: THE TYLENOL CYANIDE DEATHS

Johnson & Johnson had reason to be pleased with its pain-reliever product, Tylenol. Medically endorsed and vigorously publicized, the packaged aspirin-free medication was sold over the counter in pharmacies, groceries, and other stores in substantially greater amounts than its competitors. With $400 million in annual sales, Tylenol controlled 37 percent of the market and earned handsome profits. Manufacture of Tylenol was done by a Johnson & Johnson subsidiary, McNeil Consumer Products Company.

A Sudden Crisis Then, one morning, the telephone rang in the office of Lawrence G. Foster, Johnson & Johnson's vice president for public relations in New Brunswick, New Jersey. The news that phone call brought was startling. A staff member of the Chicago *Sun-Times* reported that cyanide contained in Extra-Strength Tylenol capsules apparently had caused the deaths of some individuals in that city. The reporter requested information about the manufacture of the medication.

Eventually doctors determined that seven persons in Chicago had been killed by cyanide contained in Tylenol capsules. The news created fear in millions of other Tylenol users.

As news of the mysterious poison deaths spread during early October, 1982, millions of Americans with Tylenol on their medicine shelves wondered, "If I take a capsule, will it kill me?"

The corporate crisis caused by the frightening news was unpredictable and intense, with the company's reputation and financial well-being at stake. Events of the next ten days subjected top management and the public relations department of Johnson & Johnson to an extreme test of communication skills and company philosophy—one that won the corporation high marks for the way it conducted itself.

The unanswered questions about the incident were bewildering. Had the poison been placed in the capsules during the manufacturing process, either by error or on purpose? Had a killer slipped the cyanide into Tylenol bottles during shipping or on store shelves? If the poison had been inserted intentionally, why? Did the killer have a grudge against Johnson & Johnson or against certain stores? Or was the poisoner a random killer proud of the power to destroy unknown humans? How many of the millions of Tylenol bottles on store shelves contained the fatal poison?

Johnson & Johnson was as mystified as the public was. Management sensed immediately that it faced an overpowering demand from the public for guidance and protection.

As public relations director, Foster plunged into the baffling case with two strong assets: a plan for emergency action and a written set of corporate principles to guide him.

He sent an associate to Chicago aboard a company jet to collect first-hand information. He set up a large bank of telephones to handle the mass of media inquiries he knew would come. To answer the phones, he brought to headquarters 50 public relations staff members from the corporation's subsidiaries. This quick action enabled reporters to reach the company without frustrating delays.

Open Policy Without hesitation, during the first hours of the crisis, top management put into operation an open information policy. This was in keeping with the long-established written corporate credo, which declared that the company's first responsibility is to "those who use our products and services." The credo stated, "In a business society, every act of business has social consequences and may arouse public interest. Every time business hires, builds, sells, or buys, it is acting for the . . . people as well as for itself, and it must be prepared to accept full responsibility."

The company's most urgent task was to get Tylenol capsules off store shelves and out of purchasers' homes. It halted Tylenol production, stopped distribution, and recalled supplies from retailers. To recover the capsules from consumers' homes, the company issued coupons with which consumers could exchange containers of capsules for an equal amount of Tylenol tablets, which were not subject to cyanide tampering. Later, the company announced a toll-free number individuals could telephone to request a $2.50 coupon for purchase of safe replacement Tylenol. Altogether, the company recalled 22 million bottles of Tylenol capsules.

The public relations department was besieged with inquiries from the media—1411 telephone calls during the first ten days, a figure that rose to 2500 before the story died down. Johnson & Johnson received 120,000 clippings of news stories about the crisis from its clipping service.

A seven-member management committee, of which the public relations director was a member, met twice daily at the height of the crisis to evaluate the situation. To unify management's response to the public, the president of the McNeil subsidiary served as the principal spokesman.

From the first, the company cooperated fully with federal investigators, never waiting for them to pressure it to act. It offered a $100,000 reward for capture of the perpetrator.

After testing 8 million recalled capsules, investigators determined that the cyanide had not entered the fatal capsules during the manufacturing process, but on the store shelves. In fact, the exhaustive and costly testing found only eight tampered-with bottles, in which 75 capsules contained cyanide.

While conducting the recall and debating a future course, Johnson & Johnson took numerous public opinion surveys. These showed, among other things, that because of the intensive news coverage more than 90 percent of the public knew after the first week not to take Tylenol capsules. By the second week, more than 90 percent knew that Johnson & Johnson was not to blame. Another survey indicated that 35 percent of those who had Tylenol capsules in their homes threw them away.

Although the company was absolved of blame, the image of Tylenol was so critically damaged that its share of the market dropped from 37 percent to a mere 6 percent within days after the news broke. Numerous marketing experts asserted that Tylenol as a brand name was dead; that if the company decided to resume selling such a medication, it must change the brand name and image. Johnson & Johnson took a severe financial beating during the recall period—an after-tax loss of $50 million for the recall and testing, as well as development of a new tamper-resistant package.

Ignoring the doomsayers, Johnson & Johnson decided to gamble on restoring Tylenol to public acceptance. Much of the public appeared to know that the product was safe and the tampering had been an isolated incident.

Recovery Campaign Thus began the second phase of the Tylenol story, the comeback campaign.

To prevent a recurrence, Johnson & Johnson designed a tamper-resistant container for Tylenol capsules. It strongly endorsed federal legislation making tampering a felony and regulations requiring tamper-resistant packaging for a wide range of over-the-counter drugs. The company was the first to get such packaging onto store shelves.

Company representatives visited the offices of more than 160 members of Congress to gain support for the regulations and legislation.

The public phase of Tylenol's recovery campaign opened with a 30-city video teleconference from New York six weeks after the deaths occurred. Twenty-five hundred mailgram invitations were sent out; more than 500 media representatives attended. Two-way audio arrangements were made at Philadelphia, Chicago, Los Angeles, and Washington so that reporters there could ask questions of company executives in New York. Reporters in the other 25 cities could hear the questions and answers.

During the 90-minute teleconference, James E. Burke, chief executive officer, and other company officials spoke, the new packaging was shown, and the audience heard a videotaped statement by the head of the Food and Drug Administration. Samples of the safety packaging were distributed.

To induce the public to overcome its lingering psychological resistance, Burke announced two attractive offers. Former users who had thrown away their capsules were invited to call a toll-free number and request a free bottle in the new packaging. No proof of previous ownership was required. Advertisements in Sunday newspapers with 40 million combined circulation contained coupons entitling the bearer to a $2.50 discount on the purchase of any Tylenol product. This permitted consumers to obtain smaller Tylenol packages free. The headline of the advertisement was "Thank you, America."

The company also sent about 50 million capsules to physicians for free distribution to their patients, thus in effect demonstrating medical confidence in the safety of the product.

Use of the toll-free numbers by the public to obtain information and free bottles was immense; more than 325,000 calls were made.

Burke also used the teleconference to thank the news media for the fair, responsible way in which they reported the cyanide deaths—the kind of public compliments reporters and editors rarely hear.

Johnson & Johnson followed up the teleconference with an intensive advertising and marketing campaign. Restoration of public confidence was so successful that six months after the death story broke, Tylenol had recaptured about 32 of the 37 percent of the market it had previously held, despite vigorous advertising efforts by its competitors.

A Second Crisis In early 1986, three and one-half years after their stressful experience, one could almost hear Johnson & Johnson's leaders exclaim, "No, not again!" when another death occurred from cyanide in Tylenol capsules. This time the victim was a 23-year-old woman in Westchester County, New York.

Again the company put its crisis plan into operation with a telephone hotline, press conferences, and a warning for customers not to take capsules from the affected lot number. Stores and customers were asked to return products from this lot. The company's quick determination that this death was an isolated incident was generally accepted.

When further search found another Tylenol bottle containing five capsules of cyanide in a nearby store, the company urged stores to withdraw all Tylenol capsules and urged customers to return capsules for exchange or refund. Finally, Johnson & Johnson announced that it no longer would sell Tylenol capsules direct to consumers and would offer the seemingly tamper-proof caplets instead.

By mid-1991, no arrests had been made in either Tylenol case. The company had recovered its sales position so well that it reported Tylenol to be "by far the leading over-the-counter pain reliever in the country."

The Lessons of the Tylenol Story Open communication was one key to Johnson & Johnson's success. The other key was the company's adherence to its longtime policy that the safety of its customers comes first.

Several specific steps were especially helpful. Establishment of additional telephone lines and expansion of the public relations staff gave reporters quick access to company representatives. Selection of a skillful principal spokesman provided the firm's statements with consistency. The company's close cooperation with government investigators encouraged public confidence.

Another less tangible but significant factor was evident in Johnson & Johnson's previous record of friendly dealing with the media. When the crunch came, Johnson & Johnson benefited from its adherence to a longtime constructive relationship with the media.

ISSUES MANAGEMENT

Corporations do not exist in a vacuum. They are an integral part of society, and what they do, or don't do, affects a broad range of publics and institutions. In today's world, the success of a corporation involves more than producing goods and services at a profit. A corporation's policies and actions are shaped and developed in reaction to political, economic, social, and technological forces as previously shown in Figure 14.1 (the GE diagram).

A corporation must consider numerous publics and institutions in developing its policies and strategies. Among these are the general public, media, activist groups, government officials, regulatory agencies, and local, state, and national laws. Any one of these can have a major effect on the future and success of the corporation. Corporations also operate in an environment where *social responsibility* is not only expected but required.

The interaction of corporations with various elements of society has led to the emergence of *issues management* as an important part of effective public relations and strategic corporate planning. Essentially, issues management is a proactive and systematic approach to identifying issues and concerns that currently face a corporation or that will emerge in the next 12 to 36 months. Issues management and corporate policymaking require sophisticated understanding of the various publics and pressures that affect decisions. Figure 14.4 shows the interactive nature of the process.

Ideally, strategic planning allows a corporation to analyze issues, formulate policy, and take action before the emerging issues become subjects of newspaper headlines and part of the public agenda. In reality, many companies have the difficult task of managing an issue after it has reached the public debate stage.

Beer and tobacco companies, as mentioned elsewhere in the chapter, must contend

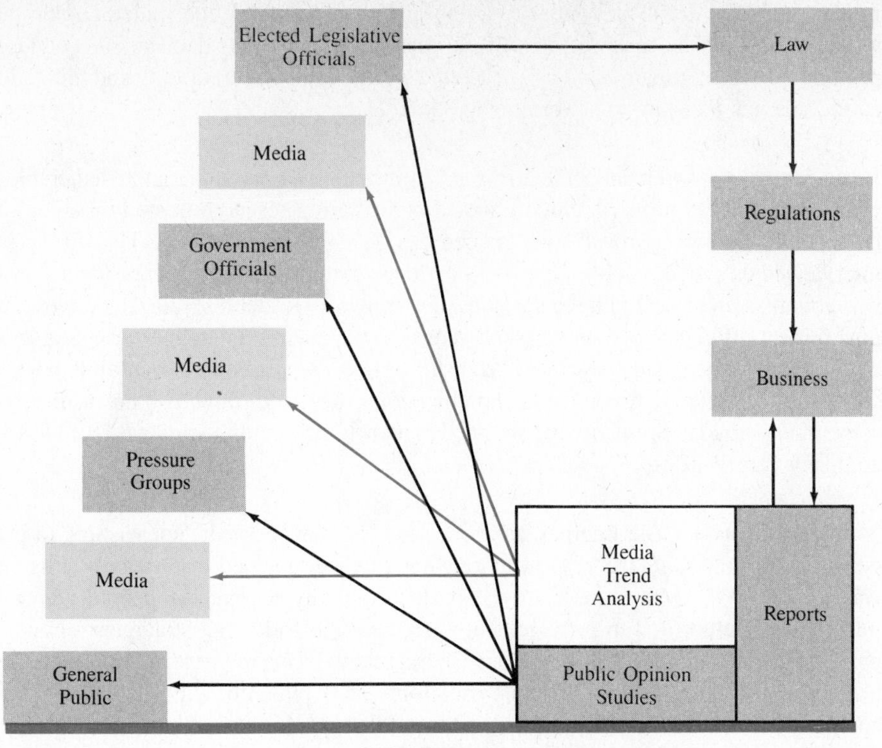

FIGURE 14.4
This model shows the interactive nature of the public policy process model. (''Issues'' by Raymond P. Ewing, *Public Relations Journal,* June 1980.)

with the public debate on the banning of advertising and sponsored events. Timber companies in the Pacific Northwest are under siege for destroying the habitat of such endangered species as the spotted owl.

Public relations counselors W. Howard Chase and Barrie L. Jones were among the first practitioners to specialize in issues management. They define the process as (1) identification of the issues, (2) systematic analysis, (3) strategy options, (4) action plan, and (5) evaluation of results. PPG Industries perceives the process along the same lines but identifies the steps as (1) issue identification, (2) impact assessment, (3) position formulation, (4) action-plan development and implementation, and (5) communications. Inherent in either process, however, is the idea that issues management involves input from all levels of the corporation and must have the complete commitment of top management.

Perhaps the best way to illustrate issues management is to show how Dow Chemical Company used the concept to improve its credibility and reputation among key publics.

Issue Identification Dow Chemical, as the second-largest chemical manufacturer in America, was a major supplier of Agent Orange to the U.S. government during the war in Vietnam. The defoliant contained a tiny amount of a by-product called Dioxin that was later alleged to cause a form of cancer. Complaints and damage suits focused primarily on the company, and Dow suffered a critical loss of credibility and reputation as the charges and lawsuits were being settled.

Issue Analysis Top management formed an internal task force that included employees from public relations, public affairs, and marketing research to study the company's public policy approach and to identify Dow's key audiences. The task force interviewed employees and managers to get their opinions, and an independent survey was commissioned to obtain the attitudes of community leaders, media executives, and government officials. They were asked about Dow's environmental performance, concern for employees, and corporate citizenship. The survey findings, according to Richard Long, director of corporate communications, depicted Dow as "an insular and sometimes arrogant company that shunned compromise—a reputation which a modern company can ill afford."

Strategy Options The internal task force and top management, not wishing to perpetuate the negative image of Dow among key publics, decided that the best objective was to "make Dow a more highly regarded company among the people who can influence its future." Top management agreed on the following strategies: (1) company "practices" must change before "perceptions" can improve, (2) communications must improve with public interest groups, (3) philanthropic efforts would be coordinated with public affairs to reach key audiences, (4) new substantive and symbolic programs would be created to show Dow's changed policies, and (5) a long-range approach to public policy would be implemented, because company reputations are not formed overnight.

Action Plan The tactics for accomplishing Dow's strategies included the following:

- To improve media relations, a 24-hour-a-day toll-free 800 number was established and advertised in journalism periodicals to let newspeople know that Dow was accessible to answer any inquiries.
- Every executive who might have media contacts was taught the concepts of effective media relations and how to field reporters' questions.
- Dow, assisted by other corporations, established and funded a science-writing center at the University of Missouri School of Journalism. It features science-writing courses for working journalists and a reference library to help reporters become better informed about the chemical industry.
- Dow scientists are sent regularly to various cities for interviews with local media on such topics as environmental standards, hazardous waste management, and chemical plant safety.
- Dow has established coalitions with such groups as the League of Women Voters and the National Resources Defense Council to communicate the dangers of hazardous household wastes and ways to preserve the environment.

- An extensive speakers' program has been established in which Dow executives talk to civic and environmental groups.
- Local plant managers in 65 locations across the United States have been given resources and advice from corporate headquarters on how to conduct plant tours and organize volunteer efforts.
- "Public interest reports," published by Dow about a number of economic and political issues, are regularly mailed to 60,000 opinion leaders.
- Dow contributes more than $1 million annually to a national education program that publicizes the importance of organ transplants and the need for organ donors.
- A national nonproduct advertising campaign focuses on the benefits of Dow's research and the ways company employees work to benefit other people.

Evaluation After two years of effort, an independent survey showed highly favorable attitudes toward Dow on the part of customers, scientists, and employees. There also was a 60 percent gain in favorable media opinion, and the *Washington Journalism Review* found that Dow's public relations efforts were better than those of any other chemical company on the Fortune 500 list.

FINANCIAL INFORMATION

At a time when corporate takeovers, Wall Street insider trading scandals, and junk bond bankruptcies make headlines almost daily, the role of investor relations is essential in corporate operations. This falls within the general scope of public relations.

The men and women who handle investor relations work are specialists. In large corporations they may function as a separate unit, in smaller companies as part of the public relations department. No matter how the organization chart is designed, cooperation between the general public relations function and this special field should be close. A good public image strengthens a company's financial position, and the other way around.

The two primary targets for a company's financial information are (1) its stockholders and (2) the financial analysts who advise brokers and bankers on the current and probable future financial health of a company. Since large blocks of stock often are held by a single investor, such as a pension fund, special attention must be paid to those investors, as well as to the growing number of foreign stockholders. (Corporate annual reports are discussed in Chapters 13 and 22.)

Annual meetings of corporations commonly are routine and dull, with everything going precisely as management has arranged it. Proxy votes obtained in advance assure management solid control of the voting. Managements often present slide- and videotaped shows to illustrate their achievements, serve light refreshments, and in general try to create an atmosphere of competence and geniality. Behind the scenes, many hours of public relations department work have been spent in planning the meetings.

At times abrasive moments of controversy may arise if stockholders challenge management policies. This is done through antimanagement resolutions that must be

WORKING WITH ACTIVIST GROUPS

Issues management today involves working with special-interest groups that concern themselves with public policy. There are an estimated 2500 consumer and public interest groups in the United States. Mary Ann Pires, a counselor specializing in public affairs and issues management, suggests in *Public Relations Journal* some approaches to dealing with activist groups:

- Absorb all available "second-hand" information about how activist groups operate and work to influence the public agenda.
- Identify mutually beneficial relationships between the corporation and special-interest groups. Analyze your issues from their standpoint.
- Be honest and don't mislead, patronize, or attempt to "cash in" on the relationship that has been built. Activists have their own networks and the word will spread.
- Establish realistic goals. Don't expect the activist group to change its agenda and goals overnight.
- Agree on specific agendas. Select discussion topics on which there can be possible cooperation and conflict resolution. Support the group by offering in-kind services such as printing, meeting facilities, and access to computer databases.
- Consider financial support of the group. But remember, consumer and public interest groups are not "for sale," and a check guarantees nothing.

put to a vote of all stockholders. During the 1990s many of these concern the environment, demanding that the company do something the activists advocate or stop doing something they dislike. During the 1980s resolutions frequently demanded that companies quit doing business in South Africa because of apartheid.

Many resolutions, especially those by environmentalists, seek changes in corporate advertising policy. Both Bristol-Meyers and Gerber Products were confronted by proposals that they stop advertising their baby formula products directly to parents on grounds that the advertising encourages mothers to stop breast-feeding.

Although antimanagement resolutions rarely pass, they obtain publicity and at times gather enough votes to influence management thinking. Sometimes managements negotiate compromises with advocacy groups in exchange for withdrawal of their resolutions.

Financial Analysts Discussion of a company's condition and prospects with financial analysts is important because the advice they give to traders influences the price of a company's stock. In addition to periodic formal presentations to groups of analysts, investor relations people send them a steady flow of information by computer, fax, and even video.

Investor relations work has no room for publicity hype and verbal sleight-of-hand. Financial analysts are experts, and their questions are searching. When a company's chief executive officer makes a presentation, the public relations department is called on to help him prepare. An effective presentation showing a solid growth pattern and sound financing may win "buy" recommendations and make the stock price rise, thus increasing the company's value.

EMPLOYEE COMMUNICATIONS

The employees of a company form a crucial audience for its public relations department. The department, often working with or within the human resources department, must concentrate on communicating with employees just as vigorously as it does on delivering the corporate story to the outside world. A workforce that respects its management, has pride in its products, and believes that it is being treated fairly is a key factor in corporate success.

In these days of corporate turmoil, with companies being bought and sold almost casually and mass layoffs resulting from cost-cutting moves, unrest and uncertainty among employees create a greater need than ever for effective employee communications. Surveys indicate a dropoff in employees' loyalty to their companies, based in part on their belief that remote corporate managements feel no loyalty to them.

Job security and financial protection against illness are two principal concerns among employees. As much as the facts justify, they need to be reassured on these points. Stimulation of company loyalty helps to stabilize the workforce, an important need of management.

Company magazines, brochures, newsletters, and policy manuals written for employees, such as the one shown in Figure 14.5, are a fundamental form of internal communication. These are discussed in detail in Chapter 22.

Much employee communication work is relatively standard—distribution of information about working conditions, retirement benefits, new company products, changes in management and supervisory personnel, and corporate plans for expansion or alterations in operating procedures. *The better informed employees are, the less likely they are to spread erroneous and possibly damaging misinformation.* Gossip flourishes in an information vacuum. The company grapevine always exists, because humans like to talk and speculate, but a flow of accurate information from management can make the company grapevine a positive rather than a negative force.

HEALTH AND SOCIAL ISSUES

Communication with employees involves much more than the nuts and bolts items just described. Critical health and social issues are involved, in which the company must steer a cautious course.

The skyrocketing cost of health insurance for employees has become a heavy and still growing burden on employers, who hunt ways to control it. Yet with personal medical and hospital bills so high, employees regard medical insurance for themselves and their families as an extremely important part of their employee benefits. Company attempts to trim health benefits encounter fervent resistance.

Circle K, which operates convenience stores nationwide, found that out when,

The DRAGONSLAYER

A Newsletter For the Citizens of A Magical Domain

Vol. 1 No. 1

DRAGONSLAYER

BY ORDER OF GOOD KING JERRY

IS RECOGNIZED AS A GRAND KNIGHT
OF A MAGICAL DOMAIN

ADVANCED MICRO DEVICES 1987

About the Dragonslayer

This is the inau
issue of The
gonslayer, a monthly news
designed to chronicle the
plishments of Dragonslay
gonbusters, Swordmaker
finalists.

The Dragonslayers Ca
was conceived by **Jerry**
as a means of inspiring
warding extraordinary ef
service to customers by
performers. An equally in
goal is to restore the spiri
that has characterized AM
past and to set the compan
from other electronics firms
Hopefully, an increase in mo
will create by-products—like i
creases in productivity—that w
hasten the company's return to profitability with benefits to all employees.

The Dragonslayers Program will last through December. Each month, the Royal Council of Dragonslayers, which consists of **Jerry Sanders, Tony Holbrook, John East, Rich Previte, Jim Downey** and **George Scalise,** will select two winners from the categories of VIGOR, RIGOR and NIMBLE. These winners will be designated Grand Knights and each will receive a medallion and $1,000. Four Dragonbusters will be named, and these employees will receive T-shirts and checks for $500. New product design teams will also be honored as Swordmakers. For more information on categories, eligibility and nomination procedures, contact **David K. Mulder** at 43785.

Kneeling with bows and arrows are the Grand Knights NIMBLE Ken Pope and Gale Olson. Nimble finalists included (left to right) Anne Friend, Kevin Wenck, Melinda Bradshaw, Richard Kittler and (inset) Ernest Sierra.

responsive when dealing with last-minute requests. Gale was also
ked to act as temporary depart-
t manager because of her su-
sor's leave of absence. She
assumed her new respon-
while meeting commit-
d maintaining the
ess of the department.

pe, Programmable Logic
PLP) marketing man-
amed Grand Knight
r his innovative ap-
esponding to PLP ap-
uestions from field
engineers (FAEs). He
distributes a monthly
called the "FAE
at answers questions
sses the concerns of
e newsletter allows
respond more quickly to
r inquiries and problems.

continued on page 8

New Team Category

A new Dragonslayers Team category has been added to the Dragonslayers Program.

Teams, which should consist of six people or less, will be nominated by vice presidents. The Royal Council of Dragonslayers will select the team they feel has achieved the most extraordinary accomplishment. Each month, the winning team will equally divide $2,000 and each member will receive a Dragonslayer plaque. Only employees eligible for Dragonslayers awards—which include RIGOR, VIGOR and NIMBLE categories—are eligible for team awards.

For more information on the Dragonslayers Team category, call **David K. Mulder** at 43785.

FIGURE 14.5
Advanced Micro Devices used a ''Dragonslayer'' theme to build employee morale and reward workers for increased productivity. As ''King Jerry,'' the president of the California electronics company, Jerry Sanders, awarded employees such titles as ''Dragonslayer,'' ''Dragonbuster,'' and ''Swordmaker'' for outstanding achievements. Some titles carried cash awards. All company publications used the theme of mythical comic book heroes in text and graphics. (Courtesy of Advanced Micro Devices, Sunnyvale, California.)

with little preparation, it denied new employees coverage for illnesses and accidents related to ''personal life-style decisions.''

This meant no coverage for new employees if they became ill with acquired immune deficiency syndrome (AIDS) or had drug or alcohol problems. Circle K was accused, among other things, of making a thinly veiled attack on homosexuality. The dispute was covered on national television and the front pages. Reaction was so severe that Circle K suspended implementation of the plan.

Management efforts to identify and halt use of drugs on the job is a tricky social issue. How much on-the-job drug testing, if any, should a company do? When does a company's right to maintain strong, safe production levels intrude upon the individual rights of employees? Decisions on such questions must be made by top management, but the manner in which they are communicated to employees heavily influences how the workforce accepts them.

Still another aspect of behavior by employees involves smoking. Evidence that exposure to smoke from others may injure nonsmokers has increased pressure for

"STONEWALLING" CAN BE COSTLY

As the Christmas shopping season approached, the management of the large University Park mall at the northeast edge of South Bend, Indiana, refused to let the municipal bus line run a holiday shopping service to the mall. The bus company manager informed his board that the mall managers had told him the shuttle would bring mostly ''downtowners'' and ''West Siders,'' whom they called ''undesirable.''

A local TV news show broke the story on a Wednesday evening, and the next day the South Bend *Tribune* covered it extensively.

A surge of anger hit the city. Everyone knew that the downtown has a heavy black population and the West Side is predominantly Polish. The refusal had strong racial and ethnic connotations.

Mall managers refused to talk to the media, referring them to the mall's owners, the Edward J. DeBartolo Corporation in Youngstown, Ohio. For three days DeBartolo headquarters ignored calls from the media. This brush-off increased public displeasure.

The postal clerks union proposed boycotting the mall. So did letter writers in the newspaper. Shopkeepers in the mall, facing a loss of business, protested. A Polish city councilman held a news conference demanding an apology.

After three days the corporation issued a vague statement about a possible misunderstanding. Then on Monday, the fifth day, it published a full-page ad in the newspaper, in which it apologized for ''any misunderstanding'' and claimed that the refusal was based solely on limited bus parking space.

This ad didn't even mention any offensive statements. The evasion increased community irritation. Eight of the nine city council members and the acting mayor called for dismissal of the mall managers.

Finally, on the seventh day of the furor, the corporation held a news conference in South Bend at which it distributed a release announcing that the two mall managers involved had been relieved of their duties.

Officially, the episode was closed, but the bad taste lingered in the community. A serious initial mistake that could have been mitigated by a quick public apology was made much worse by the corporation's foolish decision to stonewall.

no-smoking rules in company work and recreation areas. Yet some smokers vehemently insist that they have rights, too. Once management has decided the extent of a no-smoking policy on company property, public relations has the task of "selling" it to employees.

Sexual harassment in the workplace worries both employees and management, the latter for legal as well as ethical reasons. The U.S. Supreme Court ruled in *Monitor Savings Bank* v. *Vinson* (1986) that a company may be held liable in sexual harassment suits even if management is unaware of the problem and has a general policy against discrimination.

One major corporation, the DuPont Company, meets the problem of sexual harassment thus, as reported in *Public Relations Journal:* a travel safety seminar for female employees, a personal safety program that includes a rape-prevention workshop, a managers' workshop to define their role in helping employees who have been assaulted, legal assistance, liability coverage, and public relations assistance in handling publicity that might result from a rape trial. The company promotes the program in internal publications, on the company news hotline, and in monthly safety meetings.

With so many mothers working and the cost of private day care so high, should companies provide day-care facilities? Some companies do. To what extent should a company offer general education programs beyond direct job-training education? Is there a danger that companies, in trying to keep employees happy, will do too much and assume a big brother role that causes resentment?

Medicine Chest Checklist

It's a healthy idea to make it a habit to check out your medicine cabinet regularly to see that it has all you may need—and to get rid of outdated medications. Here are a few things you should be sure to have:

- A tweezer.
- Adhesive bandages in several sizes.
- Antidiarrhea medication, such as Diasorb®.
- Antiseptic skin cleanser.
- Sterile cotton.
- Aspirin.
- Aspirin substitute.
- Non-prescription cold medication such as aspirin-free Coricidin 'D'® Tablets.
- Rubbing Alcohol.
- A laxative.
- Antacid.

Also, be sure your medicine chest is not accessible to young children.

FIGURE 14.6
Camera-ready stories that contain useful information and include mention of the sponsoring firm's products are sent free to newspapers, especially weeklies, as a marketing device. This example was distributed by the North American Precis Syndicate for a manufacturer of over-the-counter medicines mentioned in it.

Employee attitudes toward these and similar issues should be closely considered by managements as they make decisions. The public relations department's role in gathering employee opinion, and in providing employees with management's thinking, thus becomes vital.

CASE PROBLEM

Drug abuse increasingly is a problem in the workplace. Although no one knows exact figures about the percentage of employees who might be popping pills, using cocaine, or even abusing alcohol, evidence exists that drugs in the workplace are causing problems in employee morale, absenteeism, and loss of productivity.

The president of Zebra Company, a manufacturer of computer software, decides to create an employee awareness program that will (1) inform employees about the health dangers of drug abuse and (2) encourage them to seek company-funded counseling. The issue, however, is sensitive and has the potential of alienating employees if the wrong approach is taken.

As director of public relations for the company, you are asked to present a public relations plan at the next meeting of the company's officers. What message themes and communications strategies would you recommend?

WHEN AN EARTHQUAKE STRIKES . . .

Pacific Gas & Electric Company knew what to do when the huge earthquake struck the San Francisco Bay area in October, 1989, because four months earlier it had conducted an all-day emergency response drill. It had a clearly defined objective: to restore service quickly and safely and *to communicate effectively with the company's many publics.*

The company did exactly that, so well that it earned public praise and a Gold Anvil award for Emergency Public Relations from the Public Relations Society of America.

Immediately after the quake it activated an emergency response center at its San Francisco headquarters. During the next week the center handled about 3400 media queries worldwide. The news department communicated with almost all the 565 media outlets in the PG&E service area. The company placed four full-page advertisements in daily newspapers and one in weekly newspapers, reporting on recovery efforts.

PG&E also sent special letters to its 106,000 shareholders, telephoned 140 security analysts, held editorial background meetings at major newspapers, and communicated with its 26,000 employees by hotline phone, special issues of employee publications, and video programs.

Planning and vigorous execution to well-defined audiences paid off. So successful were these efforts that signs appeared in the windows of stores and homes in the stricken areas, "PG&E, we love you."

THERE WHEN YOU NEED US.

Oakland. Hollister. Santa Cruz. San Francisco. Watsonville. Whenever there was trouble in the recent earthquake emergency, PG&E people were there to help.

Above are just a few of PG&E's 26,000 employees, but they symbolize the energy and spirit of all of them. Within minutes of the October 17th earthquake, PG&Eers were on the job, overcoming the damage of the earthquake, doing what had to be done: assessing the status of our system, responding to thousands of customer calls, taking action to restore service and performing all the support functions needed to back up the line workers.

The quake caused as many as 1 million customers to lose power. Within 48 hours all but 12,000 of those customers had their electric service restored. Soon thereafter power was available throughout the system. During the emergency more than 150,000 customers lost or turned off their gas. Within a week every pilot light was relit except in a few places where safety prevented us from doing so.

Yes, it's our job to respond to crises. But never before have our employees done it with more dedication or professionalism. I'm extremely proud of all of them. I salute them every one.

PG&E
At your service.

Richard A. Clarke
Chairman of the Board

An Advertisement prepared by
McCANN ERICKSON SAN FRANCISCO

PG&E won praise for its frequent comprehensive reports to the public about its efforts to restore gas and electric service after the San Francisco earthquake in 1989. This advertisement appeared in the San Francisco Chronicle *and other newspapers.*

QUESTIONS FOR REVIEW AND DISCUSSION

1. Why is the public's perception of a corporation so important to its success?

2. What caused the growth of the consumer movement between 1960 and 1980 in the United States? Who was its best-known leader?

3. Explain the double role of public relations practitioners in the relationship between companies and the news media.

4. As a corporate public relations director, what actions might you recommend to top management in order to establish your company's public image as an environmentally responsible organization?

5. How do corporate public relations and marketing public relations differ? How does marketing public relations function?

6. What are some measures corporate executives can take to achieve better reporting of business?

7. Do you approve or disapprove of having tobacco and beer companies promote sporting events in the social environment of the 1990s? Why?

8. On the basis of the "right" and "wrong" case studies in this chapter, what steps would you want your company to take if it became involved in an unexpected crisis involving the public?

9. Describe four publicity methods a company can use to increase public awareness of its identity and products.

10. What is "issues management"? Describe the five steps in the process.

11. Name Exxon's public relations mistakes in the controversy over the Alaskan oil spill.

SUGGESTED READINGS

"Assessing the Damage: Practitioner Perspectives of the Valdez." *Public Relations Journal,* October 1989, pp. 40–45.

Cantor, Bill. "Minority Hiring Shows Problems in Corporate America." *Communication World,* July–August 1990, pp. 22–25. Employee relations.

Cline, Allen. "Drugs in the Workplace: An Emerging PR Issue." *Communication World,* April 1987, pp. 26–28.

Davids, Meryl. "How Now, PR?" *Public Relations Journal,* April 1989, pp. 15–19. Investor relations.

Dyer, Samuel Coad; Miller, M. Mark; and Boone, Jeff. "Wire Service Coverage of the Exxon Valdez Crisis." *Public Relations Review,* Spring 1991, pp. 27–36.

Fisher, Lynn, and Briggs, William. "Communicating with Employees During a Time of Tragedy." *Communication World,* February 1989, pp. 32–35.

Foehrenbach, Julie, and Goldfarb, Steve. ''Employee Communication in the '90s.'' *Communication World,* May–June 1990, pp. 101–106.

Freedman, Alix, and King, Thomas. ''Perrier's Strategy in the Wake of Recall: Will It Leave Brand in Rough Waters?'' *Wall Street Journal,* February 12, 1990, p. B1.

Hainsworth, Brad. ''How Corporations Define Issue Management.'' *Public Relations Review,* Winter 1988, pp. 18–30.

Hayes, Arthur, and Pereira, Joseph. ''Facing a Boycott, Many Companies Bend.'' *Wall Street Journal,* November 8, 1990, p. B1.

Heath, Robert L. ''Corporate Issues Management: Theoretical Underpinnings and Research Foundations.'' Chapter 2 of *Public Relations Research Annual,* edited by James Grunig and Larissa Grunig, Volume 2. Hillsdale, NJ: Lawrence Erlbaum Associates, 1990, pp. 29–66.

Heath, Robert L., and Nelson, Richard. *Issues Management*. Newbury Park, CA: Sage Publications, 1986.

''Issues Management in Public Relations.'' *Public Relations Review,* Spring 1990, pp. 1–62. Series of articles on issues management.

''It's a Whole New World of Internal Communication.'' *Communication World,* December 1990, pp. 13–55. Special issue devoted to employee communications.

Lipman, Joanne. ''Critics Use New Soapbox to Assail Ads for Infant Formulas, Tobacco.'' *Wall Street Journal,* March 15, 1990, p. B6. Stockholder resolutions.

McCathrin, Zoe. ''Beyond Employee Publications: Making the Personal Connection.'' *Public Relations Journal,* July 1989, pp. 14–20.

McGoon, Cliff. ''Still Searching for Excellence.'' *Communication World,* October 1989, pp. 20–22. Results of research showing what types of organizations have excellent public relations.

O'Connor, James. V. ''Building Internal Communications.'' *Public Relations Journal,* June 1989, pp. 29–33.

Pinsdorf, Marion K. *Communicating When Your Company Is Under Siege*. Lexington, MA: Lexington Books, 1987.

Pinsdorf, Marion K. ''Flying Different Skies: How Cultures Respond to Airline Disasters.'' *Public Relations Review,* Spring 1991, pp. 37–56.

''Public Relations and Marketing.'' *Public Relations Quarterly,* Spring 1991, pp. 9–47. Series of articles on the relationship between the two fields.

Ramirez, Anthony. ''From Coffee to Tobacco, Boycotts Are a Growth Industry.'' New York *Times*, June 3, 1990, p. E1.

Saunders, Martha. ''Eastern's Employee Communication Crisis: A Case Study.'' *Public Relations Review,* Summer 1988, pp. 33–44.

Sen, Falguni, and Egelhoff, William G. ''Six Years and Counting: Learning from Crisis Management at Bhopal.'' *Public Relations Review,* Spring 1991, pp. 69–84.

Small, William J. ''Exxon Valdez: How to Spend Billions and Still Get a Black Eye.'' *Public Relations Review,* Spring 1991, pp. 9–26.

Smith, Alvie L. ''Bridging the Gap Between Employees and Management.'' *Public Relations Journal,* November 1990, p. 20–21, 41.

Smith, Alvie L. ''Bridging the Gap Between Employees and Management.'' *Public Relations Journal,* November 1990, pp. 20–21, 41.

Taylor, Anne Marie. ''CEOs in the Slammer.'' *Communication World,* May–June, 1990, pp. 157–162. Crisis public relations.

Theus, Kathryn T. ''Organizational Response to Media Reporting.'' *Public Relations Review,* Winter 1988, pp. 45–57. Media relations.

Tortorella, Albert J. ''Crisis Communication: If It Had a Precedent, It Wouldn't Be a Crisis.'' *Communication World,* June 1989, pp. 42–45.

Troy, Kathryn. ''Internal Communication Restructures for the '90s.'' *Communication World,* February 1989, pp. 28–31.

Webster, Philip J. ''Strategic Corporate Public Relations: What's the Bottom Line?'' *Public Relations Journal,* February 1990, pp. 18–21.

Williams, Louis C. ''Hottest Communication Topics Are Improving Quality and Customer Satisfaction.'' *Communication World,* August 1990, pp. 35–37.

Woodyard, Chris. ''After Spill, BP Soaked Up Oil and Good Press.'' Los Angeles *Times,* February 20, 1990, pp. BF1, 10.

CHAPTER

15

Public Affairs and Government

The term *public affairs* increasingly is used to describe a specialty area of public relations that deals with community relations and government affairs.

Although some companies incorrectly use the term as a euphemism for the full range of their public relations activities, it should be more narrowly defined as ''corporate citizenship.'' Activities included in the term range from a donation to a local charity to the monitoring of social and political issues and lobbying for passage of favorable legislation. James H. Dowling, president of Burson-Marsteller, elaborates on the concept of public affairs thus: ''PA includes government relations, constituency relations, crisis preparedness and crisis management, issue management, and risk communications, which interact in a creative and innovative manner with our other counseling and communications capabilities for maximum possible effect.''

On the other hand, ''public affairs'' is used in a much broader context by state legislatures, Congress, and various government agencies. The term is employed, as will be explained in this chapter, as a euphemism for the public relations activities of government to inform citizens about programs and policies. All military bases, for example, have a public affairs officer who regularly mails hometown news releases, arranges tours and special events, and answers inquiries from the taxpaying public.

This chapter describes public affairs activities from the standpoint of business and industry and explains how public affairs is used in government information efforts. In both cases, public affairs plays a vital role in a democratic society.

BUSINESS PUBLIC AFFAIRS

"Corporate citizenship" is a basic tenet of American business and industry for two reasons.

First, many business leaders have realized that the only way to combat the tide of government regulation is to take the initiative and voluntarily exercise a sense of social responsibility. A great many company managers now recognize that if they don't treat employees fairly, give consumers quality products, and make efforts to solve some of society's problems, then government—reacting to public pressure—will saddle business with more regulations.

Indeed, history shows that business has been regulated in direct proportion to its social abuses. The so-called robber barons of the late nineteenth century exploited labor and resources, generating considerable regulation of railway, utility, oil, and other companies (see Chapter 3). In more recent times industry's failure to solve many of the environmental problems caused by manufacturing gave rise to increased government regulation, including creation of the Environmental Protection Agency. And the disposition of many companies to lay off workers with insufficient notice led to legislation passed by Congress in 1988 requiring firms to give 60 days' notice of plant closings and mass layoffs.

The second reason for the rise of corporate citizenship and the emphasis on public affairs is realization by business and industry that they can survive and prosper only in a sound society. Thus it is to the advantage of business to help find solutions to a number of societal problems. Such assistance not only improves the quality of life but creates a reservoir of public support.

With this thought in mind, companies in recent years have undertaken a number of projects under the rubric of public affairs. Examples abound:

- Levi Strauss & Co. made an education video, "Talk about AIDS," for distribution nationally by the San Francisco AIDS Foundation.
- AT&T is a major benefactor of nonprofit theater. In the past five years, it has supported 26 projects at 19 nonprofit theaters in 12 cities.
- Texaco sponsors the annual Texaco Star National Academic Challenge at Rice University, in which more than 600 students nationwide compete on 78 high-school teams for scholarships and personal computers. The winning team's school receives a $45,000 scholarship fund.
- International Paper Co. pledged ten million Southern pine seedlings for use in federal and state planting programs.
- The Carnation Company sent musical kits to inner-city schools titled "The Many Sides of Black Music." Each kit contained an album of five records and a lesson guide for teachers.

- Ralston-Purina pays high-school youths in St. Louis to work for volunteer agencies during the summer.
- U.S. West, the telephone company serving Minneapolis, donated and maintained all communications equipment when Mikhail Gorbachev visited the city. Hundreds of phones were needed just to serve the needs of the 4000 reporters and technical media people who covered the event.
- Pacific Gas & Electric of San Francisco published and distributed a paperback book on ways in which citizens could preserve and safeguard the environment.

Such endeavors are just the tip of the iceberg, however. Corporate public affairs specialists are engaged in a wide range of projects that foster cooperation and interaction at the community and various government levels. A survey of corporations by the Public Affairs Research Group of the Boston University School of Management, for example, indicated that the top four activities of corporate public affairs departments are (1) community relations; (2) government relations, including grassroots lobbying and political action committees; (3) corporate contributions; and (4) media relations.

To put it another way, corporate public affairs usually includes government relations, lobbying, community relations, and philanthropy. The following sections describe in detail the role corporations and trade associations play in all these areas. In the first two—government relations and lobbying—other types of organizations, including labor unions and public interest groups, are also actively involved.

GOVERNMENT RELATIONS

THE ROLE OF PUBLIC AFFAIRS SPECIALISTS

In the field of government relations, practitioners have a number of functions: they gather information, disseminate management's views, cooperate with government on projects of mutual benefit, and motivate employees to participate in the political process.

As the eyes and ears of a business or industry, corporate public affairs specialists spend a great deal of time processing information. Because what happens in Washington or at the state and local level may have a great impact on business, corporations constantly monitor the activities of many government units. Monitoring may consist of simply keeping track of proposed legislation or of finding out what issues may be coming up for debate and possible vote. Such intelligence-gathering enables a corporation or an industry to plan ahead and, if necessary, adjust policies or provide information that may influence the nature of government decision-making.

The value of good information is explained by Warren Bennis, author of *On Becoming a Leader*. In a New York *Times* article, he wrote, "In a world of growing complexity, leaders are increasingly dependent on their subordinates for good information, whether the leaders want to hear it or not. Followers who tell the truth and leaders who listen to it are an unbeatable combination."

Public affairs specialists are responsible for communicating an organization's

ETHICAL GUIDELINES FOR BUSINESS PUBLIC AFFAIRS PROFESSIONALS

A. The Public Affairs Professional maintains professional relationships based on honesty and reliable information, and therefore:

1. Represents accurately his or her organization's policies on economic and political matters to government, employees, shareholders, community interests, and others.

2. Serves always as a source of reliable information, discussing the varied aspects of complex public issues within the context and constraints of the advocacy role.

3. Recognizes diverse viewpoints within the public policy process, knowing that disagreement on issues is both inevitable and healthy.

B. The Public Affairs Professional seeks to protect the integrity of the public policy process and the political system, and therefore:

1. Publicly acknowledges his or her role as a legitimate participant in the public policy process and discloses whatever work-related information the law requires.

2. Knows, respects and abides by federal and state laws that apply to lobbying and related public affairs activities.

3. Knows and respects the laws governing campaign finance and other political activities, and abides by the letter and intent of those laws.

C. The Public Affairs Professional understands the interrelation of business interests with the larger public interests, and therefore:

1. Endeavors to ensure that responsible and diverse external interests and views concerning the needs of society are considered within the corporate decision-making process.

2. Bears the responsibility for management review of public policies which may bring corporate interests into conflict with other interests.

3. Acknowledges dual obligations—to advocate the interests of his or her employer, and to preserve the openness and integrity of the democratic process.

4. Presents to his or her employer an accurate assessment of the political and social realities that may affect corporate operations.

Source: Public Affairs Council, a Washington-based organization of public affairs executives for major corporations.

viewpoint to elected officials and regulatory agencies—either informally, through an office visit to a government official, or formally, through testimony at a public hearing. Public affairs specialists also convey management's viewpoints by writing letters, position papers, and speeches. They may use issue advertising, plant tours, and employee publications to make sure that several publics—employees, taxpayers, elected officials, government employees—know how the company or industry stands on a particular issue.

Indeed, public affairs and public policy seem to go hand in hand today as corporations become more interested in issues management and grassroots coalition-building (issues management is discussed in Chapter 14). A New York *Times* writer emphasized the importance of having a presence in Washington, through either a public relations firm that represents the company or the company's own staff:

> Public relations executives can rightly point out that, with the cacophony of interests clamoring for attention in Washington, there is a role for professional advice on how to insure that one's message is heard. With the expanding role of Congress and the increasing complexity of government, this probably is true now more than ever. There are undoubtedly times that public relations firms can help journalists, politicians and clients.

Probably the most active presence in Washington and many state capitals is the trade association that represents a particular industry. The Boston University survey previously mentioned showed that 67 percent of the responding companies monitored government activity in Washington through their trade associations. Second on the list were frequent trips to Washington by senior executives of a company, with 58 percent of the respondents saying they engaged in this activity. Almost 45 percent of the responding firms reported that they also had a company office in the nation's capital.

This high interest in public affairs paralleled the growth of government regulation and scrutiny in the 1970s as most major companies responded by expanding the number of their personnel in Washington or in state capitals.

Corporations have also cooperated with government on a number of projects. For example, an association of business and civic leaders in New York City formed the Youth Employment Task Force, which worked with government agencies to create 14,000 summer jobs for young people. On another level AT&T loaned its computers to the state of New Jersey to compile the results of a statewide survey on education.

The public affairs specialist frequently considers company employees a significant public. It is important that employees regularly receive information regarding the company's position on economic and political issues that could have an impact on the organization in some way. Because of this, many corporations provide educational programs to encourage employees to participate in the political process and community service.

Many companies regularly conduct a "candidate's day" at their plants so that employees can meet aspirants for local, state, and national office. Others, such as United Life Insurance of Indianapolis, pay the postage if employees wish to write to their elected representative. And AT&T allows employees to take a leave of absence to run for office. Corporations such as Chrysler and Lockheed also have found employees to be a potent lobbying force when government aid was needed to bail the companies out of financial difficulty.

Organized programs to encourage worker involvement in community service operate in more than 500 companies. Such programs create higher corporate visibility in a community and generate local goodwill. Some companies maintain local skill banks of employees for community groups, and many now honor outstanding employee volunteers with cash awards to their favorite social service groups.

TRACKING LEGISLATION BY COMPUTER

An important part of governmental relations is monitoring all legislation that can possibly affect the employer or client.

Literally thousands of bills and regulatory proposals are introduced each year at the federal level, and the 50 states consider more than 200,000 bills every year. Online tracking services are now widely used to monitor this mass of pending legislation.

Online services enable a public affairs specialist to

1. Identify by subject matter any bill introduced in Congress
2. Track a bill from introduction through the committee process and amendments to floor votes
3. Review the voting records of lawmakers on specific bills in committees
4. Monitor committee and subcommittee activities

One tracking service offers a vote forecast service that purports to predict the likelihood of a bill being enacted.

By such systematic tracking, corporations and other groups also can spot national trends. This form of research is crucial to effective public affairs planning.

LOBBYING

Public relations and public affairs specialists who spend most of their time influencing the outcome of legislation are commonly called lobbyists. *Webster's New World Dictionary* defines a *lobbyist* as "a person acting for a special interest group, who tries to influence the voting on legislation or the decisions of government administrators."

The *Public Relations Journal* reports:

> Today, there are approximately 11,000 men and women in Washington, D.C. who are registered representatives of more than 10,000 corporations, trade associations, labor unions and various special interest groups. The interests that are represented include virtually the entire spectrum of U.S. business, educational, religious, local, national, and international pursuits.

Lobbyists also can be found in every state capital and in city halls of large cities. California, the most populous state, has 843 registered lobbyists who represent about 1600 special interests—business and trade associations, local governments, and social advocacy groups.

Registered lobbyists represent only a small percentage of those who work in the field, however. A large number of public relations specialists who support lobbying activity by handling grass-roots campaigns, building coalitions, and disseminating information to the media are not formally registered (one example is the National Trust for Historic Preservation, whose restoration campaign is illustrated in Figure 15.1).

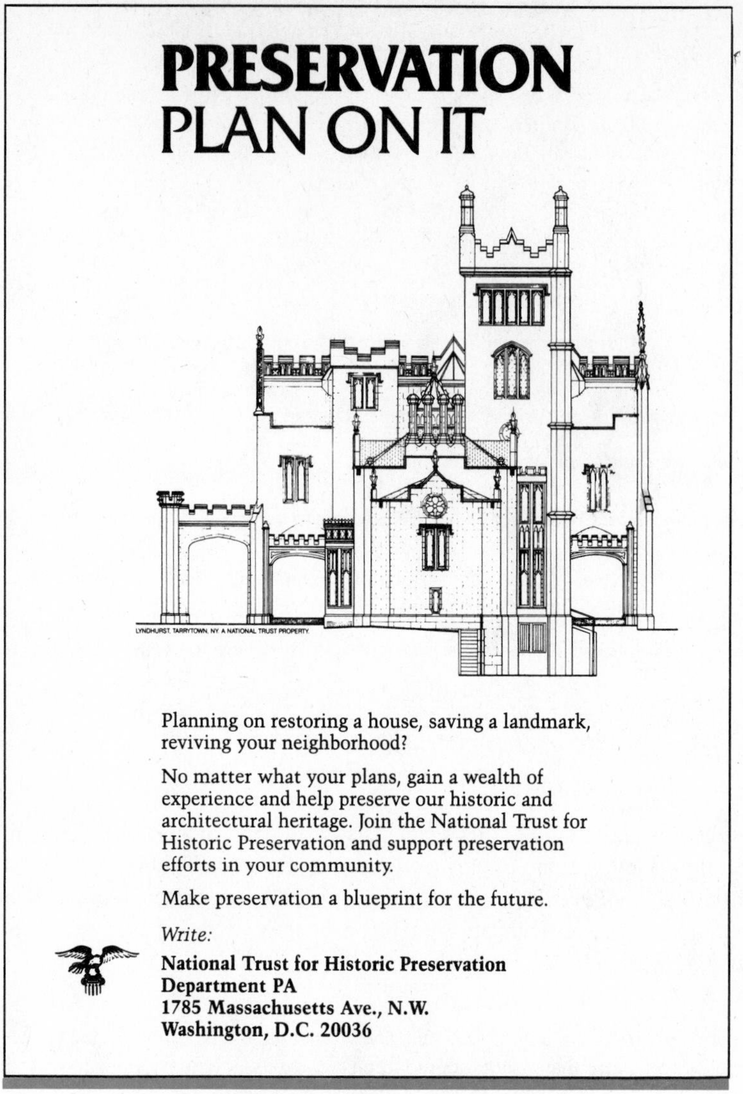

PRESERVATION
PLAN ON IT

LYNDHURST, TARRYTOWN, NY A NATIONAL TRUST PROPERTY

Planning on restoring a house, saving a landmark, reviving your neighborhood?

No matter what your plans, gain a wealth of experience and help preserve our historic and architectural heritage. Join the National Trust for Historic Preservation and support preservation efforts in your community.

Make preservation a blueprint for the future.

Write:

National Trust for Historic Preservation
Department PA
1785 Massachusetts Ave., N.W.
Washington, D.C. 20036

FIGURE 15.1
Preserving landmarks and restoring buildings is a growing concern in the United States, for which the National Trust for Historic Preservation is a focal point. This advertisement arouses public interest and solicits memberships.

Hill & Knowlton, the largest public relations–lobbying firm in Washington with $20 million in annual revenues, is an example. Only a few of its large staff, usually key executives, are registered lobbyists.

Although the public visualizes a lobbyist as a fast-talking person twisting an elected official's arm to get special concessions, the reality is quite different. Today's lobbyist may be a quiet-spoken, well-educated man or woman armed with statistics and

Do you have a tough legislative battle ahead?

Grassroots support can help you win!

For you to win a tough legislative battle, it is not enough to just tell elected officials their voters care about an issue. You must prove they care.

Bonner & Associates specializes in producing effective grassroots support.

We have achieved a winning track record on behalf of Fortune 500 corporations, trade associations and coalitions, in Washington and state capitals.

To help you win at the federal and state levels, Bonner & Associates' unique grassroots system proves you have in-depth constituent support by:

- Personally educating and recruiting the precise number of on-record constituent supporters (10-10,000 per targeted legislator) you feel you need to win.
- Enlisting constituents who have no direct vested interest but who strongly and actively support your position.
- Organizing local coalitions of groups which politically count with their legislators to show your position has potent broad-based support.
- Arranging face-to-face meetings between constituent supporters and legislators which prove support is deeply felt and goes far beyond any slick mail campaign.
- Generating on very short notice (24 hours) effective grassroots contacts for critical amendments and floor votes.

Bonner & Associates' **unique "pay for results only"** policy ensures you get the most for your investment.

Call today and find out how Bonner & Associates can help you win at the federal and state levels.

Bonner & Associates

1625 K Street N.W. Suite 300 • Washington, D.C. 20006 • 202-463-8880

FIGURE 15.2

Stimulating public opinion for or against a pending piece of legislation is a specialized form of public affairs work. This advertisement by a Washington, D.C., consulting firm lists ways in which the company generates grassroots response to impress lawmakers. (Courtesy of Bonner & Associates)

research reports. Lobbyists work for such diverse groups as the Sierra Club, Mothers Against Drunk Driving, National Association of Social Workers, American Civil Liberties Union, United Farm Workers, IBM, and General Motors, and they may be involved in awakening grass-roots support.

Lobbying, quite literally, is an activity in which widely diverse organizations engage as an exercise of free speech and representation in a democratic society. (Figure 15.2 shows how one lobbying firm operates.)

LOBBYING AND THE "PUBLIC INTEREST"

Organizations that lobby, by definition, represent special interests. Environmentalists and other activist coalitions often call themselves "public interest groups," but this description depends on who defines "public interest." In many disputes, each rival group argues legitimately that the higher "public interest" is served by its position on pending legislation.

A classic conflict is the debate between saving jobs and improving the environment. A coalition of environmental groups constantly lobbies Congress for tougher legislation to clean up industrial pollution. At the same time, however, the United Mine Workers Union claims that proposed legislation would mean loss of 25,000 jobs by forced closing of most coke ovens by the year 2020. Says a union official, "We would be exporting pollution and the jobs" because companies would buy coke abroad.

The controversy over preserving the habitat of a rare bird, the spotted owl, also involves the environment vs. jobs. The timber industry of the Pacific Northwest claims 30,000 jobs will be lost if logging operations are prohibited. Is it in the "public interest," the companies ask, to throw thousands of people out of work?

The "public interest" also comes into question when higher costs for consumers are threatened. The beer industry, for example, fought an increase in the federal excise tax on beer, claiming that 80 million drinkers would be penalized. Industry advocates called the tax unfair to working people and claimed that drinkers would pay more excise tax on beer than on a diamond necklace if the legislation passed.

LOBBYING—MORE THAN ACCESS

The clash between competing interests must be weighed by legislators and regulatory agency personnel before a vote is taken or a decision made. Lobbyists, as *Time* magazine puts it, "do serve a useful purpose by showing busy legislators the virtues and pitfalls of complex legislation."

Robert Gray, head of Hill & Knowlton's Washington office and a public affairs expert and lobbyist for 25 years, adds, "Lobbying is no longer a booze and buddies business. It's presenting honest facts and convincing Congress that your side has more merit than the other." He rejects lobbying as being simply "influence peddling" and button-holing top administration officials. In an opposite-editorial page article in the New York *Times,* he explained:

> Access is an earned, essential raw material for the lobbying process but vastly overrated as a finished product all by itself. No dam ever was built, no publicly funded program saved, no vacancy filled—and surely no lobbyist's success assured—solely on the basis of access. . . . Credibility is earned over the years, not conferred by having been 'the former director of almost everything that matters.' . . .
>
> After all, people whose job requires what we now call access are really conduits through which clashing attitudes reach decision-makers. A state legislature anxious to meet the challenge of toxic-waste disposal ought to hear the views of environmentalists as well as those of industry. When voting on foreign aid, Congress ought to know the positions of other governments on key issues affecting America's national interest. Access aids the process because it enlarges the discussion.

THE PROBLEM OF "INFLUENCE PEDDLING"

Although Gray makes the case for lobbying as a legitimate activity, deep public suspicion still exists about former legislators and officials who capitalize on their connections and charge large fees for doing what is commonly described as "influence peddling."

Indeed, the roster of registered lobbyists in Washington includes a virtual "who's who" of former legislators and government officials.

Richard Allen, former head of the National Security Council in President Reagan's White House, bills himself as an expert on U.S. trade policy and charges $540,000 for his services. Anne Wexler, former assistant to President Carter, is president of a lobbying firm specializing in energy issues. The late Senator John Tower of Texas earned $750,000 as a consultant to the defense industry in the first two years after he left the Senate. Revelations about his "consulting" connections were the primary reason that he was not confirmed as President Bush's Secretary of Defense.

Influence peddling came into sharp public focus in 1985 when Michael Deaver quit his job as White House deputy chief of staff for Reagan and promptly became a public affairs consultant. In short order, he had a list of corporations and foreign governments as clients, including a $1 million contract with South Korean interests. *Time* magazine placed Deaver on the cover of its March 3, 1986, edition to illustrate an extensive story about influence peddling in Washington. This turned out to be his downfall. Although he claimed to be doing "strategic planning," Deaver was indicted by a special prosecutor for conflict of interest, perjury, and violation of the Ethics in Government Act. Found guilty, he was ordered to pay a $100,000 fine and do 1500 hours of community work.

Another Reagan friend and former White House aide, Lyn Nofziger, also was found guilty of illegal lobbying in 1988. He was sentenced to 90 days in jail and a $30,000 fine.

The Ethics in Government Act, which forbids government officials from actively lobbying their former agencies for one year after leaving office, is what got Deaver and Nofziger in trouble. Critics say, however, that "influence peddling" is still rampant because Congress has so far failed to pass such a law for former legislators.

THE USUAL PROCESS OF LOBBYING

While Tower and Deaver made headlines, other lobbyists went quietly about their business of developing "cases for support" and persuading decision-makers that their clients' viewpoints deserved serious consideration.

Although lobbyists describe their work as "strategic planning," "comprehensive communication program design," and "image enhancement campaigns" in brochures, these terms translate into a wide range of down-to-earth practical activities. Peter Carlson, in an extensive Washington *Post* article, "The Image Makers," described the activities of lobbyists and public relations people as follows:

> They send out press releases and audio press releases and video press releases. They teach their clients how to appear on television without looking foolish and how to appear before congressional committees without looking foolish. They write speeches and brochures and congressional

testimony. They ghostwrite editorials and op-ed pieces and then try to persuade newspaper editors to run them. They lobby Congress and they run grass-roots campaigns to persuade constituents to bombard Congress with letters. They stage press conferences and other media events. And they serve as the Washington equivalent of matchmakers, introducing their clients to the movers and shakers of government and the media.

Perhaps the best way to show what lobbyists and public relations firms such as Hill & Knowlton do is to give some examples:

American Council of Life Insurance Wanting to preserve tax breaks benefiting the insurance industry in a new tax bill, the American Council of Life Insurance the following sponsored activities:

- Thirty-second television spots that depicted a bird nibbling away on a loaf of bread. A homemaker is quoted saying, "We shouldn't have to pay taxes for protecting our family."
- A film titled "The Worst Little Horror Story in Taxes," shown to life insurance agents throughout the country. It encouraged them to write their elected representatives.
- A direct mail campaign in which seven million preprinted, postage-paid cards were mailed to Congress from insurance policyholders.

The campaign was successful. The insurance lobby was able to restore about $80 billion in tax breaks cut out by the Treasury Department.

The Road Information Program (TRIP) Congress was considering raising taxes on gasoline and using the funds for offsetting the federal deficit. TRIP, a nonprofit highway industry coalition, opposed any taxes that would not go directly to the maintenance and repair of the nation's highway system. TRIP and its public relations counsel, Ketchum Public Relations, conducted numerous activities:

- Carried out extensive research to document the need for gasoline taxes to repair roads
- Organized coalitions of legislators, state transportation departments, transportation industry executives, farm/agricultural leaders, citizen groups, and state auto associations
- Conducted regional briefings for the media and key opinion leaders
- Produced press kits, video news releases, audiocassettes, and pamphlets with the theme "No Deficit Gas Tax"
- Arranged for influential individuals, including former Federal Highway Administration (FHWA) administrators, to write op-ed articles for the consumer and trade press
- Delivered to members of Congress reams of documents containing examples of media coverage of and editorial opposition to a deficit gas tax

- Convinced members of Congress to oppose publicly the deficit gas tax through a signed resolution

As a result of this activity, the National Economic Commission, which had introduced the idea of a deficit gas tax, dropped the recommendation in its final report to President Bush.

LOBBYING FOR FOREIGN GOVERNMENTS AND POLITICAL FIGURES

Foreign governments and their various industries also are represented by lobbyists. To cite one example, Japanese companies and government agencies are now spending about $350 million annually on lobbying and public relations activity in the United States.

A great deal of the lobbying on behalf of Japan centers on trade issues and the threat of protectionist legislation. Lobbyists work hard to convince legislators and the American people that Japanese business and investment contribute to the American economy.

After his release from long imprisonment in South Africa, Nelson Mandela toured the United States to raise support and money for his fight against apartheid. His tour was conducted by an American public relations firm. (UPI/Bettmann)

On occasion, even revolutionaries hire Washington public relations firms to get support. Jonas Savimbi, the Angolan insurgent leader, employed the public relations firm of Black, Manafort, Stone & Kelly to persuade Americans that he had a noble cause worth U.S. economic and military aid. Savimbi was coached in the art of television interviews and on how to answer questions on Capitol Hill. By the time he left town, he was considered a "freedom fighter" and given assurances of American support against the Marxist government of Angola. (A detailed discussion of representing foreign governments in the United States appears in Chapter 16.)

A CHECKLIST FOR LOBBYISTS

A checklist for an effective lobbyist, according to the late David Evans, founder of a public relations firm in Salt Lake City, includes the following questions:

- Is the client's or the company's position defensible? If not, what must be done to make the position acceptable?
- Do both the client or the company and the lobbyist have credibility? Are both trusted as reliable and reputable sources of information, arguments, and statistics?
- Have the key people been identified? Who are the people most likely to influence decisions?
- To what extent is the general public affected? Are the public impacts reasonable and acceptable?
- Has a strategy, including timing, been clarified? Does the plan include the necessary elements for both offense and defense?
- What can the opposition do? Have they answered the same basic questions we are asking? What is their strategy and plan?

"The accuracy and thoroughness with which these few questions are answered can spell the difference in victory or defeat for the legislative lobbyist," Evans said.

In summary, lobbying is an important part of the public affairs function. An intimate knowledge of the issues and governmental procedures, and the ability to communicate effectively the organization's viewpoint, are required.

POLITICAL ACTION COMMITTEES

A specialized area of public affairs and lobbying is the organization and administration of *political action committees,* commonly known as PACs. Corporations, trade groups, professional societies, and labor unions use this mechanism to support candidates for public office.

PACs, regulated by the Federal Election Commission, were designed to put a limit on the amount of money an organization or business could give to a single candidate and to make public the sources of gifts to various candidates. The law limits an individual PAC to a maximum contribution of $10,000 to a single candidate—$5,000 for a primary contest and another $5,000 for the general election.

This doesn't sound like much, but a corporation with multiple plant sites and operations may have a score of individual PACs. Each local of a national labor union may have its own PAC. At last count, more than 4500 PACs existed; in 1989 alone, they raised $171 million and spent $132 million supporting political candidates at local, state, and national levels. The Teamsters' union led the field by raising $5.4 million. The American Medical Association was a distant second with $2.9 million.

This money comes from employees or members of organizations. Corporations encourage employees (particularly managers) to contribute through payroll deduction or by writing an annual check. Blue-collar workers usually contribute through their unions. Professionals such as architects, nurses, doctors, and lawyers use PACs organized by their societies.

PACs are becoming a major way of funding politics, particularly at the federal level. The 432 members of the House received $31.6 million from PACs in 1989, and senators $17.7 million. The average Democratic House incumbent obtained $81,380 from PACs, the average Republican $61,122.

Averages, however, don't indicate the fact that the majority of PAC funds is received by members of key legislative committees. For example, the 42 members of the House Energy and Commerce Committee, which has wide jurisdiction over business, collected $4.3 million. Ways and Means Committee members, who write the nation's tax laws, received $3.8 million.

Individuals in key positions also receive considerable PAC money from special interests. Democratic Senator John D. Rockefeller IV of West Virginia was the top Senate PAC recipient in 1989–1990 with $886,142 in contributions from special interests in energy, insurance, and hospitals. Republican Senator Phil Gramm of Texas was second with $879,547 from energy, finance, and real estate interests. In the House, Representative Glen Browder of Alabama, a Democrat, was the top PAC recipient with $444,105, which accounted for 63 percent of his total campaign contributions.

Because PACs have become so important, they have stirred up controversy. Many citizens' groups believe that vested interests exercise undue influence on legislation and elected representatives by making substantial political contributions. One major criticism is that incumbents serving on key legislative committees get 90 percent of the funds, thus perpetuating the status quo. Defenders call the threat overrated; they say PACs simply give individual employees and union members a chance to participate in the political process. In addition, PAC contributions to a legislator do not guarantee a vote, or even a promise of help. The contributions, supporters say, help ensure that a group will be able to present its case on an issue to members and their staffs. Legislators often receive donations from competing interest groups; this also dilutes the financial clout of a particular interest.

A notable example is pending legislation on product liability. A coalition of chemical, auto, pharmaceutical, and insurance companies wants federal legislation to limit the rights of plaintiffs in lawsuits over allegedly defective products. Opposing them is a coalition of attorney groups, led by trial lawyers, who are spending six-figure sums to defeat any restrictions that would endanger their contingency fees in product liability cases. Because each side is contributing substantial sums of PAC money to key legislators, the proposed bill is known in Washington as a "cash cow" for a number of legislators, and there is a reluctance to bring the bill to a vote.

Executive directors of corporate PACs are not completely happy with the system.

They complain that elected officials continually pressure them for contributions by inviting them to countless "fund-raisers." A former legislative aide, quoted in the *Washington Monthly,* thinks the potential for corruption is very great. He said, "If you're a legislator, it has got to cross your mind; a rent control bill is coming up and it's important to the real estate brokers, landowners, and developers. So you call ten PACs the day before the vote and invite them to a fund-raiser.

HONORARIUMS: TALK ISN'T CHEAP

Legislators also fatten their campaign funds by receiving speaking fees. The Tobacco Institute, funded by tobacco companies, paid $123,400 in one year to 85 representatives and eight senators. The National Association of Broadcasters, funded by the broadcasting industry, gave $113,500 to 39 representatives and 15 senators.

Common Cause reported that, in one recent year, House and Senate members received a total of $1.4 million in speaking fees. Most of these honorariums go to legislators with committee assignments most closely aligned with the group's legislative interests. For example, Common Cause said 11 military contractors paid a total of $457,387 to members of Congress; 67 percent of the funds went to members of the House and Senate Armed Services Committees. However, a ban on honorariums for House members began in 1991; senators voted a similar ban for themselves. Both houses raised their salaries as an offset.

COMMUNITY RELATIONS

Not all public affairs activity takes place in Washington or the state capital. An important part consists of community relations, particularly in those towns and cities in which the company maintains an office or a manufacturing facility.

Because a corporation relies heavily on local governments for construction permits, changes in zoning laws, and even tax concessions, it is important that there be a good working relationship among the corporation, city hall, and the various community groups.

Public affairs specialists serve primarily in a liaison capacity, and, like their counterparts at the national level, they continually monitor emerging issues that may affect the corporation. These specialists are the eyes and ears of corporate management in a community, but they also spend much time interpreting the organization to the community. Telephone companies, for example, encourage executives to join civic clubs.

Corporate citizenship at the local level takes a number of forms. Syntex Corporation in Palo Alto, California, maintains an art gallery for the community. Allis-Chalmers provides construction equipment to help build nonprofit youth and community centers. Merrill Lynch supports local productions of operas and other fine arts events. First Interstate Bank of California conducts free financial planning seminars for older citizens.

Community relations specialists also are necessary when a community is concerned about a problem. Mobil Corporation's oil refinery in Torrance, California, faced such a problem when local politicians proposed a ban on a key chemical the company used to produce high-grade gasoline.

Local officials and residents were worried about safety after hearing media reports of chemical spills in other communities. The Mobil facility met all safety standards, but that fact obviously had not made an impact on area residents. An innovative community relations program was necessary. One approach was to have Mobil employees invite residents to their homes to discuss the safety issue. Some sessions were videotaped, and a 30-minute program showing them was broadcast on Torrance's cable outlet at 7:30 P.M. on four consecutive nights prior to the city election on the proposed ban.

Viewership was strengthened by a promotional campaign, including newspaper ads and mailings to tell residents about the program. The proposed ban was voted down, 3–1. Mobil research found that about one-third of those who voted were aware of the cable program. Mobil also reached other community members with an open house to explain its safety measures.

THE JAPANESE CONNECTION

Japanese-owned firms in American communities are becoming increasingly involved in community relations as part of good citizenship. They are reacting to polls that show 25 percent of the U.S. population have a "generally negative" feeling toward Japan and its economic clout. Other polls have found that 60 percent of American respondents view the Japanese as least trustworthy of all foreigners.

Alarmed by these polls, the Japanese Chamber of Commerce and Industry of New York, representing 320 top Japanese firms operating in the United States, has launched a drive to involve companies in more community relations efforts. To this end, the chamber hired Burson-Marsteller to produce a community relations handbook for local managers.

In many ways, the problem is cross-cultural. In Japan, companies think they are contributing to the community by creating jobs and paying taxes. Tsutomu Karino, executive director of the Japanese Chamber of Commerce and Industry, told *O'Dwyer's PR Services Report,* "It is a different way in the U.S.; a corporation plays two roles. It produces a product or service with the goal of making money and is also supposed to support community activities. . . . Americans expect more from their employers."

Corporate contributions also are handled differently in Japan. The new handbook states, "Despite a natural reticence that most Japanese have about 'tooting their own horn,' it is important in American society to take credit for good works accomplished. This is not bragging; it is a matter of getting deserved credit."

The handbook also encourages Japanese firms in the United States to do the following:

- Send news of your company's achievements to local newspapers.
- Include mention of your community involvement program in company publications distributed externally.
- Periodically survey employees about their interests and participation.

Members of Congress smash a Japanese radio, made by Toshiba, on the Capitol grounds in a symbolic protest against a Toshiba subsidiary's sale of strategic submarine technology to the Soviet Union. Left to right: Rep. Don Ritter, R-Pa.; Rep. Helen Bentley, R-Md.; and Rep. Elton Gallegly, R-Calif. (UPI/Bettmann)

- Link philanthropy to involvement; create a fund to contribute to the organizations your employees work for.
- Create corporate volunteer pins, caps, T-shirts, and emblems to be used in all volunteer activities.

The ideas seem to be catching on. Hitachi America Ltd. in Tarrytown, New York, funds a $20,000 college scholarship, finances a teacher-exchange program with Japan, and operates a local homework hotline to help high-school students. Fujitsu-America, Inc., in Santa Clara, California, is the primary sponsor of the Cable Car Classic Basketball Tournament, a national invitational hosted by the University of Santa Clara.

CORPORATE PHILANTHROPY

Another area of public affairs, which often overlaps community relations, is corporate philanthropy.

In 1989, American companies and their foundations contributed $5 billion to charitable organizations, according to statistics compiled by the American Association of Fund-Raising Counsel. This amount represented 4.4 percent of the $114.7 billion given to charitable organizations during the year (see Chapter 18.) Although no breakdown of categories is provided by the AAFRC, a Conference Board report based on recent figures and a survey of more than 400 major firms shows that corporate contributions were distributed in the following ways: education, 38.3 percent; health and human services, 29.2 percent; civic and community activities, 16.5 percent; culture and art, 11.1 percent; and other, 4.9 percent.

The Conference Board also reported that 1.96 percent of pretax net income was the average for major corporations, despite the fact that they can legally deduct up to 10 percent of their taxable income for charitable gifts. Studies show that 50 percent of all corporate philanthropy comes from just 1 percent of American corporations.

The rationale for giving has been summarized by Frank Saunders, vice president for corporate relations of Philip Morris, Inc. He stated:

> Corporate executives speak of putting something back into the community, improving the quality of life for employees, attracting prospective employees, practicing corporate citizenship—what boils down to enlightened self-interest. Business doesn't get anything tangible or real that you can put in your pocket and walk away with. This is a way that corporations make friends.

There are any number of worthwhile causes competing for the corporate philanthropic dollar, and it is not unusual for a major corporation to receive more than 5000 requests annually. Consequently, most corporations formulate specific policies regarding the kinds of charitable organizations they will support. Computer companies such as IBM, Hewlett-Packard, Apple, and Texas Instruments usually give cash and equipment to science and engineering programs of colleges and universities. Hewlett-Packard Company, for example, gave $5 million each to Carnegie-Mellon University and Brigham Young University. Nationwide Insurance Company, more concerned with health, gave $1.5 million to the Children's Hospital Foundation.

With trade competition straining relations between the United States and Japan, the Japanese have decided that philanthropy is a good way to promote goodwill and cultural understanding. Japanese companies have endowed 13 chairs at the Massachusetts Institute of Technology and have given cash to other American universities.

Corporations also loan executives to charitable groups, donate land and facilities, and give shares of stock.

Although corporate philanthropy is an integral part of public affairs, it does have its limitations. Contributions can help generate a reservoir of public support, but they are not a substitute for corporate performance in other areas.

David Finn, chairman of the public relations firm of Ruder & Finn (now Ruder, Finn & Rotman), once said in a speech at Columbia University:

> The practical risk of being dishonest or deceptive in [public affairs] programs can be considerable. A consumer advocate who believes that nonreturnable containers should be banned for environmental reasons is not likely to change his mind because a major company in one of these industries subsidizes a series of marvelous films on the history of civilization or a related subject. If the advocate believes that such an expenditure is made in the hope of changing his mind, he is likely to be more vigorous than ever in his attack on the company.

Corporate philanthropy, despite the company's performance, also can come under attack from special interest groups. General Mills, through its foundation, gave an $18,000 grant to Planned Parenthood of Minnesota and immediately was condemned by prolife groups.

The foundation received more than 10,000 protest letters criticizing the grant, and critics accused General Mills of supporting an abortion clinic. The foundation tried to explain politely that it doesn't take a stand for or against abortion and it doesn't make grants that would pay for abortions.

If a corporation's contributions do come under fire, there are several steps it can take:

- Have the company's chief executive write opinion articles for the local newspaper.
- Return all calls and answer letters from concerned citizens.
- Publicly correct opponents when they misstate the company's policies.
- Hold meetings with leaders of adversary groups.

There also is another solution, which AT&T took when it was criticized for funding Planned Parenthood. It decided to make no more grants to the organization.

Further discussion of corporate giving appears in Chapter 18.

PUBLIC AFFAIRS IN GOVERNMENT

Since the time of the ancient Egyptians 5000 years ago, governments have always engaged in what is known in the twentieth century as public information, public relations, and public affairs.

The Rosetta Stone, discovered by Napoleon's troops and used by scholars as the key to understanding Egyptian hieroglyphics, turned out to be a publicity release for the reign of Ptolemy V. Julius Caesar was known in his day as a master of staged events in which his army's entrances into Rome after successful battles were highly orchestrated.

There has always been a need for government communications, if for no other reason than to inform citizens of the services available and the manner in which they may be used. In a democracy public information is crucial if citizens are to make intelligent judgments about the policies and activities of their elected representatives. Through information it is hoped that citizens will have the necessary background to participate fully in the formation of government policies.

In the United States today, there is an increasingly strong trend toward the organized dissemination of government information. The employment of government information officers, despite efforts to reduce the federal bureaucracy, keeps expanding. Several factors have led to the growth of the government information effort. Among them are the following:

1. *Increasing urban population*. The nation now has more than 250 million people, and the traditional New England "town hall" meeting plan in which townspeople made decisions is no longer feasible, except in very small communities. Thus more systematic lines of communication must be established to reach residents in a metropolitan area where multicultural diversity is common.

2. *Increasing complexity of society*. The cliché that today's society is more complex than it was 20 years ago means that government is more complex as well. There has been a proliferation of specialized agencies along with thousands of laws and regulations. Ordinary citizens increasingly find it difficult to understand what the law is, let alone to know the proper agency to which an inquiry can be directed.

3. *Increasing mobility*. City and county populations are constantly changing, and newcomers must be regularly informed about local laws and regulations, including property taxes and even something as mundane as the days of garbage pickups.

4. *Increasing citizen demands*. Sociologists call this "the age of entitlement"; citizens are demanding more services than ever from their local, state, and national governments. At the same time, there is considerable public resistance to higher taxes to pay for these services.

5. *Increasing public scrutiny*. People today are scrutinizing the costs and programs of government more than ever. There is considerable public debate on how to spend limited resources, and special interest groups are more active and vocal than in previous years. In addition, citizens now have greater access to the deliberations of government bodies through state and federal freedom of information, or "sunshine," laws.

All these factors contribute to the trend whereby government units are providing extensive public information in order to develop public understanding of programs and policies. Commonplace today are news releases, news conferences, reports, information bulletins, posters, special events, exhibits, broadcast public service announcements, brochures, and even paid advertising by government bodies.

The objectives of government information efforts have been summarized by William Ragan, former director of public affairs for the United States Civil Service Commission:

1. Inform the public about the public's business. In other words, communicate the work of government agencies.

2. Improve the effectiveness of agency operations through appropriate public information techniques. In other words, explain agency programs so that citizens understand and can take actions necessary to benefit from them.

NASA STRUGGLES TO RESTORE CREDIBILITY

On January 28, 1986, the National Aeronautics and Space Administration lost a quarter-century of excellent media relations and high public credibility when the space shuttle *Challenger* exploded shortly after lift-off, killing all seven astronauts aboard.

NASA violated the rules of crisis communications by waiting five hours to confirm the disaster, even though millions saw live coverage of it on television. This not only violated NASA's own guidelines for releasing information within 20 minutes of an incident but also infuriated the press, which accused the space agency of "stonewalling" and engaging in a cover-up. In subsequent days the media portrayed NASA as reluctant to release quality control and engineering records. Much of the salvage operation, lifting debris from the Atlantic Ocean, was done in secrecy, and at one point NASA enforced a flat ban on the release of any details about the recovery operation despite intense public interest.

An article in the *Wall Street Journal* (February 14, 1986) expressed the view of the press and many public relations professionals: "The agency's muddled handling of the *Challenger* explosion has turned a major human and technological loss into a public relations fiasco that could damage the agency's prestige and credibility for years."

What went wrong? NASA failed to follow its emergency communications plan. Several reasons are given why it failed to communicate in an open, candid manner.

First, there was a vacuum of leadership at the top levels. William Graham, acting administrator, had been on the job only a week and was not at Cape Canaveral during the launch. Shirley Green, public affairs director of NASA, had been in her job only three weeks. She was two levels removed from top management and had not yet developed a good working relationship with the agency's administrators. She was not able to get any of them to face the press and was unwilling to do so herself, according to Robert Irvine, author of *When You Are the Headline: Managing a Major News Story* (Dow Jones–Irwin).

A second reason why NASA failed the test in crisis communication was

3. Provide feedback to government administrators so that programs and policies can be modified, amended, or continued.

4. Advise management on how best to communicate a decision or a program to the widest number of citizens.

5. Serve as an ombudsman. Represent the public and listen to its representatives. Make sure that individual problems of the taxpayer are satisfactorily solved.

6. Educate administrators and bureaucrats about the role of the mass media and how to work with media representatives.

"PUBLIC INFORMATION" VERSUS "PUBLIC RELATIONS"

Although many of the objectives described by Ragan would be considered appropriate goals in almost any field of public relations, in government such activities are never referred to as "public relations." Instead, various euphemisms are used. The most common titles are (1) public information officer, (2) director of public affairs, (3) press secretary, and (4) administrative aide.

summed up in the same *Wall Street Journal* article: ". . . after years of preoccupation with promoting the shuttle program and after 24 successful flights, the agency was clearly caught off-guard." In other words, the shuttle program had been so successful that the agency became lackadaisical.

In the aftermath of the *Challenger* disaster, NASA began working on policies and actions to regain credibility. Some of the steps taken include:

- Revision of the contingency plan for emergencies to have trained, designated spokespersons with science and engineering backgrounds immediately available to the press. (During the *Challenger* emergency, the agency's public affairs staff was overwhelmed by a flood of media inquiries.)
- Communication of two key messages: (1) NASA, overall, has a stellar record of successes, and (2) the national space program must proceed despite the *Challenger* disaster.
- Improved employee communications including the use of biweekly satellite broadcasts, supplemented with newsletters, to all NASA facilities.
- Increased traveling exhibits and astronaut appearances to inform the public about the work of NASA.
- Incorporation of communication strategies as part of regular drills testing potential engineering problems with a shuttle launch.

Three lessons emerge from the *Challenger* disaster that any corporation or government agency can learn: (1) a crisis communication plan is only as good as management's willingness to implement it, (2) public relations personnel must be given the "green light" by management to communicate quickly and truthfully, and (3) delays in providing pertinent information lead only to rumor, loss of credibility, and press hostility.

In addition, government agencies do not have departments of public relations. Instead, the FBI has an External Affairs Division; the Interstate Commerce Commission has an Office of Communications and Consumer Affairs; and the Environmental Protection Agency has an Office of Public Awareness. The military services usually have Offices of Public Affairs.

Such euphemisms serve to reconcile two essentially contradictory facts: (1) the government needs to inform its citizens and (2) it is against the law to use appropriated money for the employment of "publicity experts."

Congress, as early as 1913, saw a potential danger in executive branch agencies' spending taxpayer dollars to sway the American public to support programs of various administrations. Consequently, the Gillett Amendment (Section 3107 of Title V of the United States Code) was passed; it stated, "Appropriated funds may not be used to pay a publicity expert unless specifically appropriated for that purpose." The law was reinforced in 1919 with prohibition of the use of any appropriations for services, messages, or publications designed to influence a member of Congress. Another law that year required executive agencies to utilize the U.S. Government Printing Office so that publications could be more closely monitored than in the past. Restrictions also prohibit executive departments from mailing any material to the public without a specific request.

Congress clearly was attempting to limit the authority of the executive branch to spend taxpayer money on public relations efforts to gain support for pet projects of the president. Some presidents chafed at this, but others thought it was entirely proper that the government should not be in the business of propagandizing the taxpayers. President Eisenhower, for example, ordered all executive branch agencies to dispense with field office information activity. The only problem was the great number of public and press requests for information. Consequently, information offices lost their titles but continued their dissemination functions under such titles as "technical liaison officers" for the Corps of Engineers and "assistant to the director" in the Bureau of Reclamation.

In 1972, alarmed by Richard Nixon's expansion of the White House communications staff, Congress reaffirmed prior legislation by stating that no part of any appropriation bill could be used for publicity or propaganda purposes designed to support or defeat legislation before Congress.

Although most citizens would agree that government should not use tax money to persuade the public of the merits or demerits of a particular bill or program, there is a thin line between merely providing information and using information as a lobbying tool.

If a public affairs officer for the Pentagon testifies about the number of surface-to-air missiles deployed by Iran or Libya, does this constitute information or an attempt to influence congressional appropriations? Or, to use another example, is a speech by the secretary of the interior about America's large coal reserves on federal land information or an attempt to lobby for the opening of wilderness areas to mining?

While ascertaining the difference between "public relations" and "public information" may be an interesting semantic game, the fact remains that the terms *public relations* and *publicity* are seldom used by a government agency—not even by the National Aeronautics and Space Administration, which is mandated by law to provide the American public with full information about its program.

SCOPE OF FEDERAL GOVERNMENT INFORMATION

The U.S. government often is said to be the world's premier collector of information. It is also maintained, without much counterargument, that the federal government is one of the world's great disseminators of information (see Figure 15.3).

Ascertaining the exact size of the government's "public information" efforts, however, is rather like counting jelly beans in a large jar. Then-Senator William Proxmire asked the General Accounting Office (GAO) in 1986 to come up with some estimates.

The GAO, noting that federal agencies do not uniformly define "public affairs," estimated that $337 million was spent on "public affairs" and another $100 million on "congressional affairs." An estimated $1.9 billion went into a catch-all category, "public affairs-related activities." Total estimated expenditures thus are more than $2.3 billion. And that figure includes only federal agencies. The massive amounts spent by Congress and its members were not even estimated.

An estimated 10,000 to 12,000 federal employees are engaged in what can be called "public relations" work. The Department of Defense, for example, has about 1,000 public affairs officers.

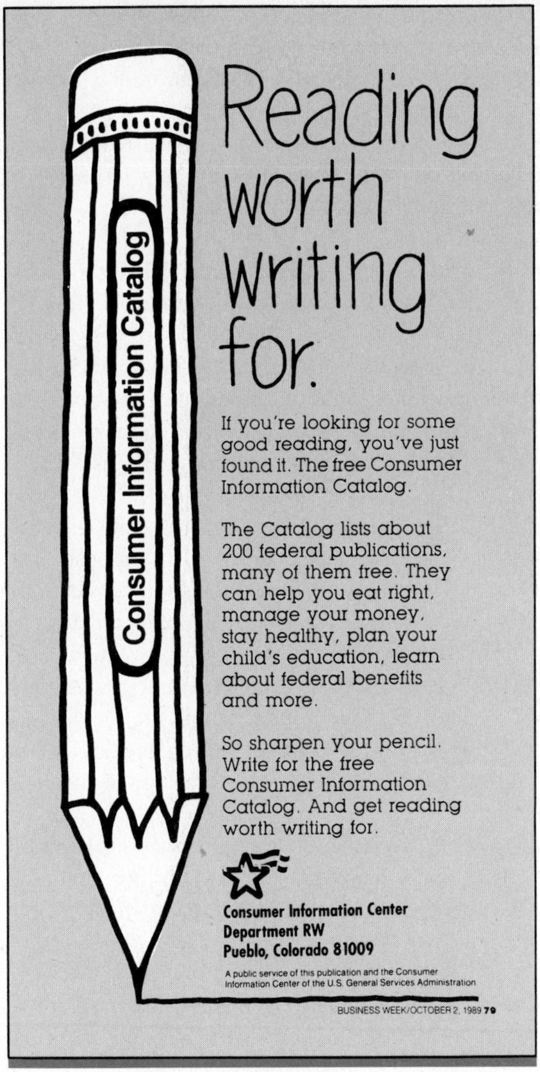

Consumer Information Catalog

Reading worth writing for.

If you're looking for some good reading, you've just found it. The free Consumer Information Catalog.

The Catalog lists about 200 federal publications, many of them free. They can help you eat right, manage your money, stay healthy, plan your child's education, learn about federal benefits and more.

So sharpen your pencil. Write for the free Consumer Information Catalog. And get reading worth writing for.

Consumer Information Center
Department RW
Pueblo, Colorado 81009

A public service of this publication and the Consumer Information Center of the U.S. General Services Administration

BUSINESS WEEK/OCTOBER 2, 1989 **79**

FIGURE 15.3
The U.S. government publishes huge amounts of consumer information, much of it free, and promotes its distribution with advertisements. This example appeared in *Business Week*.

The size and scope of governmental information efforts are given in other ways. At last count, there were about 12,000 government publications ranging from a monthly law enforcement magazine published by the FBI to a Department of Agriculture pamphlet titled, "Making Pickles and Relishes at Home." The armed services have so many magazines, newsletters, and pamphlets that, says one media reporter, it would take a truck to deliver everything on the list. Another writer, probably on a slow news day, estimated that the federal government's production of everything from news releases to magazines would fill four Washington Monuments every year.

This mass of paper, of course, does not include the films and videos the government produces every year. The government's output makes the efforts of Hollywood studios puny by comparison, but few government films are blockbusters. Most are produced by the Department of Defense and used in training. Other films and videos are shown primarily to school and civic groups.

Advertising is another governmental activity. Federal agencies spent several hundred million dollars a year on public service advertising, primarily to promote military recruitment, government health services, and the U.S. Postal Service.

Government Agencies Public information specialists and public affairs officers, as they are known, engage in tasks common to any public relations department and also work on special programs and projects. One of the longest-running public relations efforts has been the FBI's legendary list of the ten most wanted fugitives. Initiated in 1950, the list immediately captured the imagination of the public and the media. The media regularly report who is on the list. In addition to making the FBI highly visible as America's premier law enforcement organization, the list has led to the apprehension of 377 fugitives.

More recently, the U.S. Census Bureau budgeted more than $5 million for public relations activities to promote the 1990 census. The purpose was to make citizens aware of the census and to enlist their cooperation in the collection of information. In 1987, the Immigration and Naturalization Service budgeted $10.7 million to explain the new Immigration Reform and Control Act to employers and a multilingual, multiethnic pool of illegal immigrants. The Internal Revenue Service conducted an intensive campaign in 1988 to help taxpayers understand the new income tax law (see Figure 15.4). And the U.S. Postal Service, noting the loss of business to private carriers, launched an internal communications campaign to dispel its poor image as a service organization.

Federal agencies also use the services of public relations firms. The Environmental Protection Agency (EPA) signed a three-year, $4 million contract with one firm to communicate new regulatory information to companies responsible for underground storage of chemicals.

Congressional Efforts Although the expenses of Congress are not included in the GAO study, one report in 1985 estimated that the House spent $68 million and the Senate $43 million on a barrage of news releases, newsletters, recordings, brochures, taped radio interviews, and videotapes, so that individual members could inform constituents about the operations of Congress. Critics complain that most of the materials are designed for self-promotion and have little value, but the legislators say that voters have a right to know what is being done in their behalf. Unquestionably, the franking privilege (free postage) is abused by some members of Congress. The late Senator John Heinz (R) of Pennsylvania, for example, sent out 15 million pieces of mail financed by taxpayers in one election year.

Cabinet-level Efforts Members of the cabinet engage in various public relations activities. One of the more active cabinet members in President Reagan's second administration was Secretary of Education William J. Bennett. He used his position as a platform to promote educational reform and, through the public affairs office of the department, issued a flow of news releases, pamphlets, and position statements. The public affairs staff kept newspaper and broadcast coverage going for months after

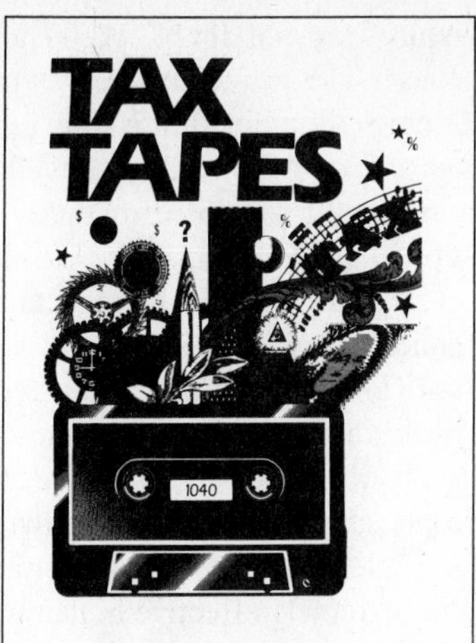

A cassette is available with simple, step-by-step instructions to help you complete your federal income tax forms: 1040EZ; 1040A and Schedule 1; 1040, Schedules A, B and W and special tips, including tips for self-employed and the military.

Ask your librarian for further information.

FIGURE 15.4
The Internal Revenue Service provides tapes containing step-by-step information on completing federal income tax forms. Public libraries provide information about obtaining the tapes, and the IRS publicizes the program on bookmarks it gives away at libraries.

Bennett issued a booklet, "Schools Without Drugs." Bennett's combative attitude and quickness to make controversial statements made him "good copy," and department news releases got widespread attention.

Attorney General Edwin Meese also received extensive media attention, much of it critical. Opponents called for his resignation on grounds of conflict of interest and incompetence. Meese fired his chief public affairs officer, Terry Eastland, in 1988 for allegedly failing to generate positive media coverage. Eastland pointed out in a published letter that he had a duty to be more than a mouthpiece for Meese. He wrote, "My view of the Office of Public Affairs is that it has an obligation to serve not only the attorney general, but also the Department of Justice and the American people."

White House Efforts At the apex of government public relations efforts is the White House. The president receives more media attention than all the federal agencies and Congress combined. It is duly reported when the president plays golf or signs a piece of legislation. All presidents have taken advantage of the intense media interest to implement public relations strategies that would improve their popularity, generate citizen support for programs, and explain embarrassing policy decisions.

Ronald Reagan, by most accounts, was a master at utilizing public relations techniques and was so successful at maintaining his popularity despite scandals like the Iran-Contra affair that critics dubbed him the "Teflon president." Although the arms-for-hostages deal with Iran and the secret funneling of money to the Contras in Nicaragua badly tarnished his image, he did regain a degree of public respect by accepting responsibility and admitting that he had made a mistake.

Television plays an important part in the imagery of the presidency, and Reagan was extremely effective in that medium. Critics complained that his acting background led Reagan to think that the world was one giant movie set and he had the leading role. The manner in which the public relations capability of the federal government was utilized to make the president's four-hour visit to Grenada a major media event illus-

THE MILITARY VS. THE PRESS

American involvement in the Persian Gulf war often pitted government public affairs officers (PAOs) against reporters, who demanded more access and accused the military of filtering news to polish its image.

One Washington reporter wrote, "Despite frequent military briefings, non-stop television coverage, and a flood of newspaper words and pictures, Americans still don't know very much about how the Persian Gulf war is going."

He referred to military restrictions that barred reporters from traveling to the war zone on the Kuwait-Iraq border except with a military escort, formation of press pools, and military review of reporters' stories before distribution.

The military, however, defended the restrictions as necessary to insure security and protect the lives of American troops. "There is no censorship," a PAO for the Pentagon told one press briefing. "You don't want information reported that would jeopardize an operation or endanger lives." He said that military escorts and pool reporting (groups of about 15 reporters representing the more than 1000 journalists assigned to the Gulf war) were simply "intended to facilitate movement, insure safety, and protect operational security."

In polls during the war, the American public seemed to agree. By about a 75–25 margin, voters were unsympathic with press complaints about censorship and thought the Pentagon was doing a good job of releasing information.

The tug-of-war between the military and the press was nothing new, according to Liz Trotta, a former NBC and CBS news correspondent. In the *Wall Street Journal* she wrote, "Media executives insist they understand why 'sensitive strategies' must not be revealed, yet they demand the facts—names, numbers, places and plans—all of which collides with that admirable summary of the military attitude offered by a British intelligence chief during World War I: 'Say what you like, old man. But don't mention any places or people.'"

trates the Reagan administration's technique. The U.S. Information Agency (discussed in Chapter 16) distributed thousands of red, white, and blue posters with the president's portrait and urged the island's population to attend the rally. The stage for the president's talk was built by the U.S. Agency for International Development; other governmental agencies installed phone lines and satellite equipment for the 150 news reporters and television crews covering the event. The result was extensive television news coverage of President Reagan receiving the cheers of Grenada citizens for sending troops to rescue them from Cuban domination and communism.

President Bush is no Ronald Reagan as a public relations figure, but he projects enthusiasm in his job. Like presidents before him, he takes advantage of "photo opportunities" and frequently gives news interviews to get his points across to the American people.

In keeping with his self-proclaimed title as the "environmental president," Bush plants trees on his many visits around the country. Environmentalists call it a "public relations gimmick," but White House staffers think it is symbolic of his interest in cleaning up America. Of course, tree planting photographs show a vigorous and active President. Bush has quipped to reporters that he's been so busy "planting trees all over the country that I might have to open a branch office."

Advance People The White House staff includes individuals called *advance people* who are responsible for making certain that everything goes smoothly on a presidential trip. They confirm that the man who heads the receiving line isn't a convicted felon and that the sound system works. They make arrangements for the press, organize the cheering crowds, select the best photographic and television possibilities, arrange the banners and seating in auditoriums, and plan the schedule down to the last minute.

Advance people are detail-oriented and good at handling logistics. Peggy Noonan, a speech writer for Presidents Reagan and Bush, wrote in the *Wall Street Journal* that you can always spot the advance person: "a certain jut-jawed intensity, an addiction to jogging and junk food, and a desire to carry on three conversations at the same time on the car phone, the cellular phone, and the radio."

Media Concern The combined public relations activities of government agencies, Congress, and the executive branch cause suspicion and concern in many quarters. James Reston, an observer of the Washington scene for the New York *Times* for many years, has often written columns calling for less "federal P.R." At the start of the Bush Administration in early 1989, Reston wrote:

> Every four years, it is suggested in this corner that the new Administration could double the efficiency of its public relations operations by cutting the Federal P.R. budget in half. . . . the growth of honest Government "flacks" and propaganda fakes has far outdistanced the public demands for their services, and it's not clear why Nancy Reagan had a bigger personal staff in the White House than Franklin D. Roosevelt had at the height of the New Deal. In fact, the title "public relations" is itself misleading for many of these officials are engaged more in political aggrandizement of their masters than in the education of the public.

Although Reston is rightfully concerned about manipulation of information by government, particularly at the White House level, there apparently is less to fear from

President Bush and Mayor William Hudnut shovel dirt onto a freshly planted elm tree in downtown Indianapolis. Bush dedicated the tree to Ryan White, an Indiana youth whose losing fight against AIDS won national sympathy. (UPI/Bettmann)

information and press officers of federal agencies. Stephen Hess, a senior fellow at the Brookings Institution in Washington, D.C., conducted a year-long study of government public information officers and concluded that they didn't manage, manipulate, or control the news. In his book, *The Government/Press Connection,* he wrote:

> The hypothetical time sheet of the press officers I observed might have the following allocation: responding to reporters' inquiries, 50%; keeping informed and working on agency business, 25%; and initiating materials and events, 25%. . . . I observed no press officer, outside of the White House, who spent most of his time staging events or initiating material as innocuous as handouts. . . . The typical government agency initiates very few events, especially when compared with the daily menu of congressional hearings. . . . There is one significant exception to the modest behavior, however; the White House is expected to put on a daily show.

STATE INFORMATION SERVICES

Every state provides organized public information services. In California, for example, there are 250 information officers in about 70 state agencies. Here are some examples of their activities:

- The Department of Health launched a $28.6 million antismoking advertising campaign paid for from cigarette tax revenues.
- The AIDS Education Campaign operates a hotline giving information about the disease and conducts an advertising campaign (see Figure 15.5).
- The Department of Health Services distributed news releases about outbreaks of rabies and black plague—two communicable diseases that could cause epidemics.
- The Solid Waste Management Board conducted an extensive information program on the theme "Untrash California," designed to make citizens aware of littering and the need to recycle materials.
- The Department of Commerce launched a $6.5 million campaign to lure business and tourists to California. Part of the effort was a 28-page brochure that described the state, according to one newspaper writer, as "the largest, the greatest, the richest—the place to achieve success."
- The Office of Traffic Safety and private agencies launched a $1.5 million program to promote a new seat-belt law using music videos, billboards, brochures, and road signs.

Most states spend a good deal of money to stimulate business and tourism. Arizona funds the monthly magazine *Arizona Highways,* while other states, including Vermont, Florida, and North Carolina, place advertising in publications such as *Time* asking readers to send for four-color brochures. (Chapter 20 discusses tourism in more detail.)

MUNICIPAL INFORMATION SERVICES

Large cities employ information specialists to disseminate news and general information from numerous municipal departments. Such agencies may include the airport, transit district, redevelopment office, convention and visitor's bureau, police department, fire department, city council, and the mayor's office. Cities also employ information specialists to generate tourism and lure and retain business. Baltimore advertises itself with a 90-foot replica of a nineteenth-century clipper ship. St. Louis invested in a replica of Lindbergh's *Spirit of St. Louis* aircraft, and flight crews and publicity people barnstormed 102 cities to hail the city as a destination for tourists and a good business site.

The City of San Francisco and the Golden Gate Bridge and Highway District, with citizen groups, sponsored the 50th-anniversary celebration of the Golden Gate Bridge. Lack of civic planning, however, stranded thousands of people when no city buses showed up.

Municipal information services also are manifested in a number of smaller ways. The city librarian publicizes a list of current best-sellers; an airport administrator sets

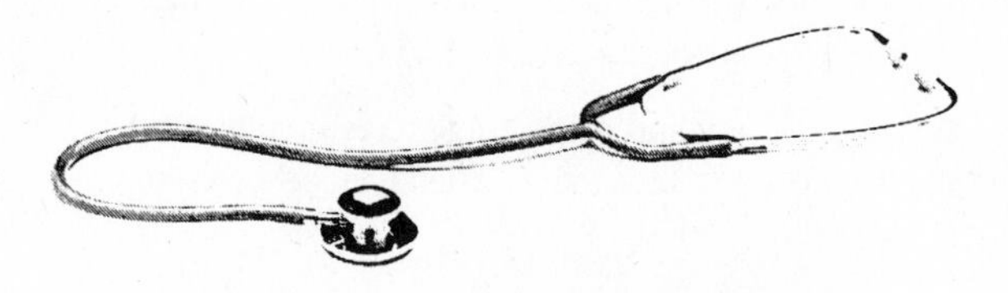

FIGURE 15.5
State governments frequently conduct public relations programs to promote health, safe driving, and similar public issues. This advertisement is one of a series sponsored by the State of California AIDS education campaign.

up an exhibit showing the future growth needs of the airport; and a local film council works with community leaders in an effort to lure movie production companies for location shots.

City council members and administrators also pay attention to public relations strategies. They engage in such activities as the following:

- Conducting city council meetings at night to increase attendance
- Consulting with citizens before policy is formulated

- Holding neighborhood meetings
- Appearing on radio and TV talk shows, particularly those that allow audience call-ins
- Implementing information and complaint telephone lines and publicizing the numbers
- Using citizen advisory committees

The importance of public information and public relations at the municipal level is best described by the International City Management Association:

> Public relations is one of many important variables which affect the ability of an administrator to accomplish program objectives. It involves cooperation between the agency (its personnel, decisions and programs) and the attitudes and desires of persons and groups in the agency's external environment. It imposes on administrators the necessity for dealing with public relations as an inherent and continuing element in the managerial process. The administrator must be mindful of public relations considerations at every stage of the administrative process, from making the decision to the final point of its execution.

CRITICISMS OF GOVERNMENT INFORMATION SERVICES

Although the need for government to inform citizens and publicize programs is generally accepted in principle, many legislators and members of news media still express skepticism about the activity, as mentioned earlier in this chapter.

In 1987, for example, Rep. John Bryant (D) of Texas was so irate that the Dallas Housing Authority had hired a public relations firm that he introduced a bill in the House of Representatives to forbid public housing agencies from spending government funds on any public relations activity. The housing authority had hired a local firm on a six-month contract to help improve the authority's communications with the community and other local agencies as a result of a scandal surrounding the city's subsidized housing. The proposed bill died for lack of congressional support.

The most severe media criticism is reserved for the often amateurish efforts of legislators. *Bulldog Reporter* awarded a ''fireplug award'' to members of the California legislature who used state funds to issue personal tirades against one another. The Senate majority leader issued a news release about another senator titled, ''Carpetbagger Richardson Advised to Stay South.'' In another release, a senator called another legislator a ''north coast liberal that has protected the interests of commercial marijuana growers.''

The abuse of news releases by legislators, coupled with snide newspaper headlines, rankles dedicated public information officers (PIOs) who work very hard to keep the public informed of government programs and how they can help the average citizen. One PIO complains: ''I'm not a flack, and I resent getting stereotyped as one. It makes me wonder about the objectivity and fairness of the media, which depend on me for much of their information.'' His complaint is echoed by an information officer for a California agency who said that she was tired of those who complain about information officers. She added: ''I'd like to see the press find out what's going on in state government without us. The press would be frustrated. People are not going to be informed unless you have people like us bending over backward for them.''

Indeed, a degree of press hostility toward government information efforts seems to stem from resentment of the fact that reporters must rely heavily on them. The reason is that there are simply not enough press representatives in Washington to cover adequately the hundreds of federal offices. Although the White House, Congress, and even the Pentagon probably have more than enough reporters covering their activities, a news service reporter still may be assigned to cover three or four cabinet-level agencies that have staffs in the thousands and budgets in the billions. Even a White House correspondent must rely on news releases most of the time rather than chat with the president or senior staff aides.

The result is a major dependency on the handouts of federal agencies. One text, *Media: An Introductory Analysis of American Mass Communications* by Peter M. Sandman, David M. Rubin, and David B. Sachsman, puts it bluntly: ''If a newspaper were to quit relying on press releases, but continued covering news it now covers, it would need at least two or three times as many reporters.'' One study shows that 22 percent of all news emanating from Washington during a certain period was traced to handouts from executive agencies.

These handouts and news releases supplied to the media have been called ''information subsidies'' by Professor Judy VanSlyke Turk of the University of South Carolina at Columbia. She found in a survey of Louisiana state agencies during an eight-week period that PIOs disseminated a total of 444 ''information subsidies'' to the eight Louisiana daily newspapers. A content analysis of these newspapers showed they used 225, or 51 percent, of them. She continued in *Journalism Monographs* (December 1986): ''Use of these 225 handouts resulted in the publication of 183 separate news stories, or 48 percent of all 383 stories the newspapers published about the six agencies during the eight-week period.''

And although there is much congressional and media criticism of the government's extensive publications, these are defended on the basis of cost efficiency. A deputy director of the Department of Agriculture publications branch, for example, reported that his office alone receives about 350,000 inquiries a year. Two-thirds of the requests, he says, can be answered with pamphlets that cost between half a cent and 12 cents each, whereas individual responses could cost up to $20 each when personnel costs are included. In other words, the sheer volume of public requests requires a large array of printed materials.

An Associated Press reporter acknowledged in a story that government information does have value. He wrote:

> While some of the money and manpower goes for self-promotion, by far the greater amount is committed to an indispensable function of a democratic government—informing the people.
>
> What good would it serve for the Consumer Product Safety Commission to recall a faulty kerosene heater and not go to the expense of alerting the public to its action? An informed citizenry needs the government to distribute its economic statistics, announce its antitrust suits, tell about the health of the president, give crop forecasts.

Indeed, public affairs officers in government contend that their work is vital because the best-planned programs will do little good if the public does not know about them.

The Department of Housing and Urban Development, for example, wanted to inform the public about a graduated payment mortgage program. To this end, the department produced three public service announcements (PSAs) for television and a press kit for all print media, and distributed eight million brochures to lenders and bankers. The total cost of the program, $256,000, was thought to be inexpensive compared to the estimated $5 million that advertising experts consider necessary to introduce a new product nationally.

In sum, defenders of government information efforts argue two points. First, if billions are spent on government programs, it makes sense to spend some money on publicizing those programs so that citizens can take advantage of them. Second, it is often more cost-efficient to publicize a cause than to pay for the problems that might result if no campaign had been waged. A good example is the promotion of Smokey the Bear, perhaps the most recognized symbol in America. The government information campaign about preventing forest fires has helped preserve woodlands, and it has been much more cost-effective than fighting forest fires. By the same token, a county antilitter campaign to make the public more conscious of trash might be more cost-effective than setting up crews to police roadways.

PUBLIC RELATIONS AND POLITICAL CANDIDATES

This chapter so far has dealt with business public affairs and government information efforts. Another area of widespread public relations activity is in behalf of political candidates.

American political public relations is a multimillion-dollar industry; it has come a long way since the first distribution of campaign literature on a massive scale in the 1880 presidential elections. It now consists of computer-generated letters and telephone calls tailored to specific audiences, extensive use of radio and television advertising, and staged events designed to give a candidate visibility. It also involves speech-writing, press kits, and news releases.

An estimated 2000 to 5000 firms are involved in the political ''industry'' at some level, and about 50,000 people are employed. Larry J. Sabato, professor of government at the University of Virginia and author of *The Rise of Political Consultants,* estimates that approximately $100 million of the estimated $1.8 billion spent annually on party and elective politics finds its way to political consultants who do everything from media relations to direct mail, fund-raising, polling, position papers, scheduling, and overall strategic planning.

The computer age has made it possible for some political consultants to specialize in mailing lists that can segment the American voter up to 28,000 different ways. The technique, called *geodemographic clustering,* uses ZIP codes and other audience characteristics to aim candidate appeals at increasingly narrow demographic groups. One company, for example, discovered that 90 percent of Volvo owners are wealthy liberals, while 80 percent of Jaguar owners are conservatives with incomes above $50,000. Knowing this allows a national candidate to tailor a specific message to every Volvo and Jaguar owner in the United States.

Political consultants have been called the ''mercenaries of American politics,'' and many critics charge that they use slick, empty "Madison Avenue techniques" to sell politicians and policies like soap. They lament that the voting public becomes a victim of created and often distorted candidate images and that the important issues are never debated.

The critics raise several legitimate concerns, but political candidates say they need all the help they can get to generate public awareness. Political campaigning is very sophisticated and very expensive. The 1990 campaign for the California governorship, in which Pete Wilson narrowly defeated Dianne Feinstein, cost the two candidates a combined total of $40 million.

In addition to consultants, candidates have their own paid staffs and volunteers. Almost all state and national candidates have press secretaries responsible for preparing news releases, briefing the media, and making sure that reporters are provided transportation and hotel rooms. Major candidates also have advance people whose specialty is attention to logistical detail. These people are responsible for arranging the details of a rally, a factory tour, or a visit to the children's ward of a hospital. They work with local citizen groups to assure a noisy, cheering reception for the candidate, decide who will share the platform with the candidate, and schedule every minute with military precision.

Volunteer workers often work with paid staff on many of these activities and, if the candidate is elected, may be asked to become a staff member in the state capital or Washington. Jody Powell began as a volunteer on Jimmy Carter's campaign and became the president's press secretary.

There are several ethical guidelines for people working in political public relations. Here are some of them, as formulated by the Public Relations Society of America:

1. It is the responsibility of professionals practicing political public relations to be conversant with the various local, state, and federal statutes governing such activities and to adhere to them strictly. This includes laws and regulations governing lobbying, political contributions, disclosure, elections, libel, slander, and the like.

2. Members shall represent clients or employers in good faith, and while partisan advocacy on behalf of a candidate or public issue is expected, members shall act in accord with the public interest and adhere to truth and accuracy and to generally accepted standards of good taste.

3. Members shall not issue descriptive material or any advertising or publicity information or participate in the preparation or use thereof which is not signed by responsible persons or is false, misleading, or unlabeled as to its source, and are obligated to use care to avoid dissemination of any such material.

4. In avoiding practices which might tend to corrupt the processes of government, members shall not make undisclosed gifts of cash or other valuables which are designed to influence specific decisions of voters, legislators, or public officials.

5. Members shall not, through the use of information known to be false or misleading, conveyed directly or through a third party, intentionally injure the public reputation of an opposing candidate.

APPLES AND ALAR: A PUBLIC RELATIONS BATTLE

Public relations firms often find themselves on opposite sides in campaigns to influence legislators and the public, as in the battle over Alar and apples (examined in Chapter 2). Ralph Nader and the Natural Resources Defense Council (NRDC), a Washington-based environmental group, had lobbied for an immediate ban on Alar, contending that it created a danger of cancer. The issue never caught fire, however, until NRDC hired the public relations firm of David Fenton.

Fenton's assignment was to publicize an NRDC study called "Intolerable Risk: Pesticides in Our Children's Food." The report alleged that apples sprayed with Alar represented a risk to children. He kept the report secret until the CBS show "60 Minutes" could break the story to 40 million viewers. Using the show as a form of third-party endorsement, NRDC released the report the next morning at 13 simultaneous news conferences around the country. The result was enormous publicity.

A week later, Fenton scored another publicity coup by having actress Meryl Streep announce at a Washington news conference the formation of an NRDC spinoff group, "Mothers and Others for Pesticide Limits." She appeared before a congressional committee and gave 16 satellite TV interviews across the nation. The Hollywood angle attracted the "Today," "Donahue," and "Entertainment Tonight" television programs, as well as *People* magazine.

According to Peter Carlson's article in the Washington *Post,* Fenton summarized his strategy this way: "Our goal was to create so many repetitions of NRDC's message that average American consumers could not avoid hearing it. The idea was for the story to achieve a life of its own."

Meanwhile, Hill & Knowlton, representing the apple industry, was galvanized into action. The firm rounded up scientists and doctors who declared that apples were safe. Their testimonials were spread by printed, video, and audio news releases. Full-page ads appeared in newspapers across the country. Luncheons were held to brief House and Senate staffers. Federal agencies responsible for food safety were lobbied to defend the beleaguered apple, which they did. They announced jointly that apples were safe to eat and that Alar was not an "imminent hazard" to children.

All this rebuttal was published in the media, but the damage had been done. "NRDC and their hired PR counsel did a superb job of playing the news media like a Stradivarius," said Jack Bonner, owner of a Washington public relations firm. Public relations had killed Alar.

CASE PROBLEM

Foreign-made bicycles now constitute 70 percent of bicycle sales in the United States, and this worries the American Association of Bicycle Manufacturers. To survive, the domestic industry needs import quotas.

Obtaining quotas is an uphill battle, however, for several reasons. First, bicycle manufacturing in the United States, even in the best of times, is not a major industry employing thousands of people. Second, the administration in Washington is not sympathetic to "protectionist" legislation. Third, some consumer groups believe that restricting foreign imports will cause consumers to pay more for bicycles.

On the other side, jobs of Americans making bicycles are being jeopardized, and the United States has an alarming $150 billion trade deficit. Your public relations firm is retained to develop the case for setting quotas on foreign bicycles and creating a strategy to persuade legislators to vote for such restrictions. What would you recommend?

QUESTIONS FOR REVIEW AND DISCUSSION

1. Give two reasons why companies should engage in corporate citizenship.
2. Name the four major activities of a corporate public affairs department.
3. Explain how a political action committee (PAC) works. What are the pros and cons?
4. Discuss lobbying as part of the democratic process. What kinds of groups engage in lobbying?
5. In what ways can corporate philanthropy be beneficial to the company?
6. List ten ethical guidelines for corporate public affairs specialists.
7. What societal and environmental factors have led to the growth of government information programs?
8. What are the objectives of government information efforts? What are the criticisms of such activities?
9. In what way is the press dependent on government information programs?
10. List at least five guidelines for the conduct of political public relations.
11. What kinds of services do political consultants provide candidates?

SUGGESTED READINGS

Abrahmson, Jill, and Jackson, Brooks. ''Debate over PAC Money Hits Close to Home as Lawmakers Tackle Campaign Finance Bill.'' *Wall Street Journal,* March 7, 1990, p. A20.

Alexander, Suzanne. ''Japanese Firms Embark on Program of Lavish Giving to American Charities.'' *Wall Street Journal,* May 23, 1991, pp. B1, 4.

Babcock, Charles, and Marin, Richard. "Following the Path of Self-Interest: Do PACs Find the Candidates or Vice Versa?" Washington *Post* National Weekly Edition, June 25, 1990, p. 14.

Berke, Richard L. "Study Confirms Interest Groups' Pattern of Giving." New York *Times,* September 16, 1990, p. Y18. Campaign finances.

Browne, Malcolm W. "The Military vs. The Press." New York *Times* Magazine, March 3, 1991, pp. 27–31, 44–45.

Carlson, Peter. "The Image Makers." Washington *Post* magazine, February 11, 1990, pp. 12–17, 30–35. Lobbying and public relations in Washington, D.C.

Childers, Linda. "Credibility of Public Relations at the NRC (Nuclear Regulatory Commission)." Chapter 5 of *Public Relations Research Annual,* edited by James Grunig and Larissa Grunig, Volume 1, Hillsdale, NJ: Lawrence Erlbaum Associates, 1989, pp. 97–114.

Cosco, Joseph. "Bringing Illegal Aliens Out of the Shadows." *Public Relations Journal,* October 1988, pp. 17–20. Immigration and Naturalization Service public information campaign.

Cutlip, Scott. "Public Relations in the Government." *Precision Public Relations,* edited by Ray E. Hiebert. New York: Longman, 1988, pp. 30–57.

Dennis, Lloyd. "Public Affairs: Deja Vu All Over Again." *Public Relations Journal,* April 1990, pp. 14–17.

Gibson, Richard. "Brewers Gird to Head Off Tax Increase." *Wall Street Journal,* July 7, 1990, p. B1. Lobbying and public relations campaign.

"The Gorbachev Visit: Lessons and Themes in Media Relations." *Public Relations Journal,* August 1990, pp. 9–12.

Gray, Robert. "Lobbying for Special Interests." *Experts in Action,* edited by Bill Cantor. New York: Longman, 1989, pp. 139–148.

Harris, William. "How AT&T Tosses a Lifeline to the Arts." New York *Times,* May 27, 1990, Section 2, p. 1. Corporate philanthropy.

Levy, Reynold, and Oviatt, Frank. "Corporate Philanthropy." *Experts in Action,* edited by Bill Cantor. New York: Longman, 1989, pp. 126–138.

Lowengard, Mary. "Community Relations: New Approaches to Building Consensus." *Public Relations Journal,* October 1989, pp. 24–30.

Mack, Charles S. *Lobbying and Government Relations.* Westport, CT: Quorum Books, 1990.

McAvoy, James. "Tactics for the Military in the Media War." *Wall Street Journal,* February 7, 1991, p. A14. Media relations in the Gulf War.

Noonan, Peggy. "Advancing Gorbachev." *Wall Street Journal,* June 1, 1990, p. A14. Logistics and media relations for the Soviet president's trip to U.S. cities.

Phair, Judith. "The Battle for Support: Pro and Anti NEA Forces Wage Grass-Roots Campaigns." *Public Relations Journal,* August 1990, pp. 18–23, 34–36. National Endowment for the Arts controversy about censorship.

Seib, Gerald. "Will George Bush Ever See a Gimmick as Lovely as a Tree?" *Wall Street Journal,* May 1, 1990, p. 1.

Shapiro, Walter. "Is Washington in Japan's Pockets?" *Time,* October 1, 1990, pp. 106–107. Lobbying by Japanese companies.

Shell, Adam. "Military PAOs direct 'Theater of War.'" *Public Relations Journal,* March 1991, pp. 9, 15.

Steward, Hal D. "A Public Relations Plan for the U.S. Military in the Middle East." *Public Relations Quarterly,* Winter 1990–1991, pp. 7–10.

Streitmatter, Rodger. "The Rise and Triumph of the White House Photo Opportunity." *Journalism Quarterly,* Winter 1988, pp. 981–985.

Vandervoort, Susan S. "Big Green Brother Is Watching: New Directions in Environmental Public Affairs Challenges Business." *Public Relations Journal,* April 1991, pp. 14–19, 26.

Wise, Jim. "Tracking Legislation." *Public Relations Journal,* September 1990, pp. 43–44. Online databases.

CHAPTER

16

International Public Relations

Public relations on an international scale and within individual countries is a post–World War II phenomenon. The practice is spreading rapidly as international trade and tourism increase, more nations seek industrial and technological development, and governments strive for greater visibility and influence in the world community.

International acquisitions and mergers of giant public relations, advertising, and marketing firms characterized the 1980s, introducing a new age of global marketing fueled by satellite television, computer networks, and other new communications technologies.

Corporations that operate in other countries do so in a kaleidoscope of laws, languages, and value systems often markedly different from those of their home countries. In such circumstances public relations can make the critical difference between success and failure. So it is also with governments and industries that seek to influence publics in other countries: professional public relations counseling becomes a necessity.

This chapter examines the phenomenon and identifies many of the methods employed and the problems encountered by those who engage in international public relations.

A DEFINITION

International public relations may be defined as the planned and organized effort of a company, institution, or government to establish mutually beneficial relations with the publics of other nations. These publics, in turn, may be defined as the various groups of people who are affected by, or who can affect, the operations of a particular firm, institution, or government. Each public is united by a common interest vis-à-vis the entity seeking acceptance of its products or programs.

International public relations also may be viewed from the standpoint of its practice in individual countries. Although public relations is commonly regarded as a concept developed in the United States at the beginning of the twentieth century, some of its elements, such as countering unfavorable public attitudes by means of disclosure of operations through publicity and annual reports, were practiced by railroad companies and at least one share-holding corporation in Germany as far back as the mid-nineteenth century, to mention only one such country. (See Chapter 3.)

Even so, it is largely American techniques that have been adapted to national and regional public relations practices throughout the world, including many totalitarian nations. Today, although in some languages there is no term comparable to *public relations,* the practice has spread to more than 100 countries. This is primarily the result of worldwide technological, social, economic, and political changes and the growing understanding that public relations is an essential component of advertising, marketing, and diplomacy.

INTERNATIONAL CORPORATE PUBLIC RELATIONS

THE NEW AGE OF GLOBAL MARKETING

For decades hundreds of corporations based in the United States have been engaged in international business operations including marketing, advertising, and public relations. These activities swelled to unprecedented proportions during the 1980s, largely because of new communications technologies, development of 24-hour financial markets almost worldwide, the lowering of trade barriers, growth of sophisticated foreign competition in traditionally ''American'' markets, and shrinking cultural differences bringing the ''global village'' ever closer to reality.

Today almost one-third of all U.S. corporate profits are generated through international business. In the case of Coca-Cola, probably the best-known brand name in the world, international sales account for 80 percent of the company's operating profit.

At the same time, overseas investors are moving into American industry. It is not uncommon for 15 to 20 percent of a U.S. company's stock to be held abroad. The United Kingdom, for example, has a direct foreign investment in the United States of $122.8 billion, followed by the Japanese with a total direct investment of $60.1 billion, according to the U.S. Department of Commerce. In third place is the Netherlands, with a $55.7 billion investment.

The worldwide explosion in advertising that began more than two decades ago has been marked by the formation of huge multinational advertising conglomerates and, during the 1980s, by the rise of mega-agencies such as Britain's Saatchi & Saatchi Company and the WPP Group. Saatchi & Saatchi's acquisitions included Ted Bates Worldwide, then America's third largest agency. The WPP Group's U.S. acquisitions included the J. Walter Thompson Company, Hill & Knowlton, and the Ogilvy PR group. In 1989 WPP, a holding company that owns a number of mostly independently operating marketing, advertising, and public relations firms, became the world's largest marketing operation, with 21,000 employees serving more than 5,000 clients in 50 countries.

Public relations is an essential ingredient in the global megamarketing mix being created. (Chapter 4 examines the outreach of U.S. public relations firms abroad through their own offices, full or partial ownership of foreign companies, and affiliations with foreign public relations companies.)

"Everyone realizes now that they have to be part of an international structure, because the big agencies are getting bigger and the small ones are disappearing," said Edward M. Stanton, chief executive of MSL Worldwide, public relations arm of the D'Arcy Benton & Bowles advertising agency.

The fact that advertising agencies own six of the top ten U.S. public relations firms points up the overall objective of the marketing conglomerates: to develop on a global scale seamlessly blended operations involving public relations, creative advertising campaigns, direct mail, special events (often in sports), special promotions or sweepstakes, in-store merchandising, sponsored publications, and other such efforts.

Fueling the new age of global marketing are satellite television, computer networks, electronic mail, fax, fiber optics, cellular telephone systems, and emerging technologies such as integrated services digital networks (ISDN) allowing users to send voice, data, graphics, and video over existing copper cables. For example, Hill & Knowlton has its own satellite transmission facilities, and the General Electric Company has formed an international telecommunications network enabling employees to communicate worldwide, using voice, video, and computer data, by simply dialing seven digits on a telephone. Using three satellite systems, Cable News Network (CNN) is viewed by more than 200 million people in about 95 countries. A number of newspapers and magazines are reaching millions with international editions. *Reader's Digest,* to cite one instance, distributes about 11.5 million copies abroad—almost 40 national editions in more than a dozen languages, and the *Wall Street Journal* has both Asian and European editions.

David Miln, business development director of Saatchi & Saatchi, declared in 1989 that it is now possible "to produce the same product, in the same packaging, with the same name, at the same price, wherever you want within the world markets, in the cheapest place probably, and, if there are enough people out there who want it—terrific. But first come finding the need and branding the product."

Differences in language, laws, and cultural mores among the countries (to be discussed shortly) pose serious problems for such a marketing program. As Richard D. O'Connor, chief executive of Lintas: Campbell-Ewald Company, has pointed out, middle-sized agencies, understanding the consumer character and differences of the regions in which they operate, are able to plan and execute a wide range of market-specific programs. Smaller agencies, he emphasized, will continue to play a key role in breaking new ground and setting trends.

Another problem lies in the need for both managers and employees to learn to think and act in global terms as quickly as possible. Claudio Belli, head of Hill & Knowlton International, predicts that "we will see public relations firms investing in training and development programs as they never have before." Already, Burson-Marsteller, with offices in many countries, has been spending more than $1 million a

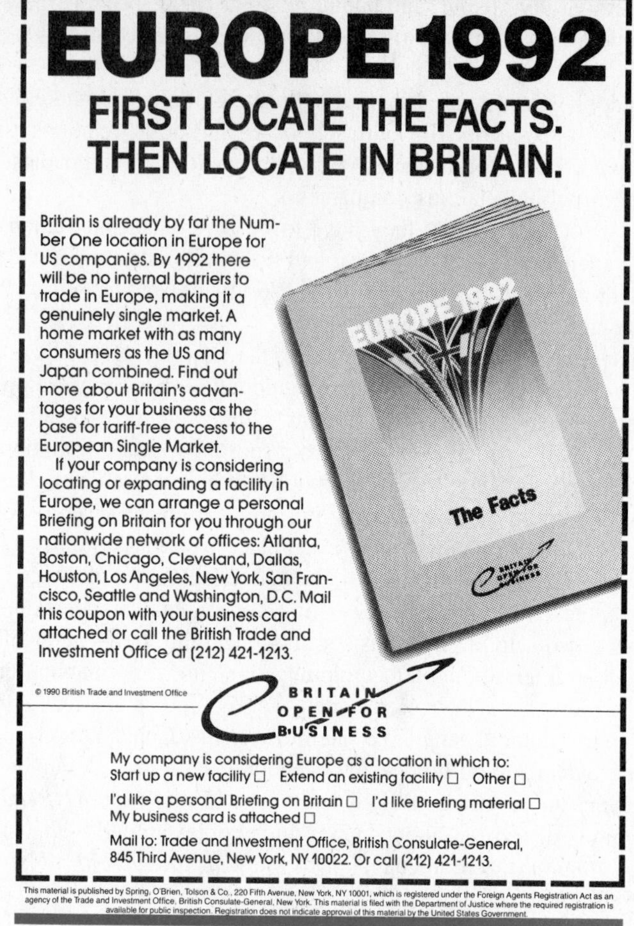

FIGURE 16.1
This advertisement was one of several published in U.S. newspapers and magazines as part of a campaign to induce American business firms seeking European Common Market trade to locate in Great Britain. (Courtesy of Spring, O'Brien, Tolson & Co. Inc., New York, registered under the Foreign Agents Registration Act as an agent of the British Trade Development Office of the British Consulate General, New York.)

year on training tapes and traveling teams of trainers and seminars, to foster a uniform approach to client projects.

Much of the new business jousting has taken place on West European terrain, where the advent of a commercially unified European Community (EC) in 1992 has attracted enormous attention. Active measures are being taken to attract businesses (see Figure 16.1). Belli predicted that by then EC countries would spend more than $3 billion a year on public relations, triple that of 1989. Much of the public relations expenditures were expected to accompany the expansion of commercial television resulting from widespread deregulation, the desire of viewers for more varied programming, satellite technology, and new EC business patterns. By 1992, it is predicted, West European television will have exploded to about 100 channels and total programming of 500,000 hours annually. Satellite TV, through cable systems, reaches 30 million people; one of its most striking changes involves the direct transmission of programming to homes by high-powered satellites, bypassing conventional networks, local stations, and cable systems. On the print side, the business press is growing about 20 percent every year, and there are about 15,000 trade publications in Western Europe.

Although the EC promotes the phrase "a single Europe" after 1992, corporations and public relations firms will still face the complex task of communicating effectively to 320 million people in 12 countries speaking nine languages. Adding to the complexity of the problem are often mutually incompatible national bureaucracies, legal systems, and cultural traits. Said Eddie Crockett, a senior partner in a Brussels public relations firm:

> It is frequently claimed that English is the language of business. There is some truth in this, much to the relief of UK and North American nationals, whose foreign language track record is, at best, abysmal. But English is not the language of commerce: marketing, public relations, advertising, product specifications, legal and accounting documents, annual reports, and the like—all have to be communicated in the language of the country in which a company is operating.

In the wake of the liberalization movements in the Soviet Union and Eastern Europe, corporations are moving to establish financial, manufacturing, and distribution bases in countries where free enterprise has not been practiced for decades. Coca-Cola planned a $140 million investment in East Germany. And U.S. telecommunications companies, with visions of tapping new markets for consumers and developing low-cost businesses, proposed deals to lay fiber-optic lines across the Soviet Union, establish cellular telephone service in Budapest, give Hungary its first workable telephone system, and take cable television to Poland. These are only examples of the innumerable instances of aid provided.

Because USSR laws prohibit taking rubles out of the country, corporations have encountered difficulties in establishing operations in the Soviet Union. Initial enterprises were based on barter arrangements. PepsiCo, Inc., for example, concluded a $1 billion trade agreement with the Soviet Union to "trade" Pepsi for vodka and Russian freighters. Soviet monetary restrictions, however, are expected to be relaxed in a few years. In 1987 the Soviet Parliament approved the establishment of joint ventures with foreign corporations. A year later the USSR signaled its desire for mutually beneficial nonstrategic trade with the United States by placing an eight-page supplement labeled "USSR: Facets of Perestroika" in the *Wall Street Journal*. In 1989 McDonald's achieved worldwide publicity when it opened its first Golden Arches fast-food restaurant in Moscow.

Pravda, the official Soviet Communist Party newspaper with a circulation of 8 million, in 1990 began accepting corporate advertising from American companies, charging $50,000 for a full-page advertisement.

LANGUAGE, CULTURAL, AND OTHER PROBLEMS

Fundamentally, companies operating in foreign countries are confronted with essentially the same public relations challenges as those in the United States, as Figure 16.2 shows. These include (1) the formation and maintenance of favorable climates for their operations, involving relationships with local and national government officials, consumer groups, the financial community, and employees; (2) the monitoring and assessment of potentially adverse situations and the establishment of ways to counteract them; and (3) the containment of crises before serious damage is done.

These problems, however, may be aggravated by conditions such as the following:

- Differences in languages and the multiplicity of languages in some countries
- Longer chains of command, stretching back to the home country
- Evident and subtle differences in customs
- The varying levels of development of the media and public relations
- Antipathy expressed toward ''multinationals,'' a pejorative word in many countries

FIGURE 16.2
This advertisement for a position in England shows the similarity between qualifications and objectives for public relations work in the United States and in other countries.

PUBLIC AFFAIRS CONTROLLER

To develop high profile Public Relations for leading music industry organisation

c.£38,000, mortgage assistance + car **Central London**

Held in high regard in the British music industry, this organisation plays a major role in supporting creative talent. To increase public awareness of this and its many other roles, we have been asked to fill a new position, which will report directly to the Chief Executive. Its essence is the development of innovative, co-ordinated strategies for all aspects of internal and external PR – and the direction of their implementation. Administrative and organisational support is already in place, producing highly professional corporate information and arranging sponsorship, exhibitions, and award ceremonies. We are looking for a cerebral, even inspirational, input, to add immediate spark and long-term fire. Ideal candidates, probably mid thirties/early forties, will almost inevitably be graduates (they'll certainly have graduate intellect) and will have outstanding inter-personal skills and communication flair. They will have already established high personal credibility with the media, including broadcasting, and will have first hand experience of a wide range of PR activities; their track record will demonstrate all this quite clearly. We would like to see some experience in broadcasting or publishing, while a real, if amateur, interest in music would be a distinct advantage.
It's a growth organisation and this is a growth job: above all, it's an exciting one (a cliché we promised ourselves we'd never use, but this time it's really justified!). Please send full career details, quoting reference WE 0143, to Judy Brasier, Ward Executive Limited, Academy House, 26-28 Sackville Street, London W1X 2QL. Tel: 071-439 4581.

WARD EXECUTIVE
LIMITED
Executive Search & Selection

- A dislike grounded in such factors as national pride, past relationships, envy, and apprehension, especially in regard to the United States, concerning foreign cultural, economic, political, and military influence

The following are some examples of the types of language problems encountered:

- Chevrolet executives could not figure out why the Chevy Nova was not selling well in Latin America. Then they learned that although *Nova* means "new" in Spanish, *No va* means "It doesn't go."
- A Deere & Company marketing manager, addressing a group of German dealers, chose the German word for *mouth* to describe the feeder opening of a forage harvester, inadvertently declaring that "John Deere is the biggest braggart."
- Informed that in the Soviet Union cosmetics and politics do not mix, a U.S. firm decided not to call its Moscow-bound lipstick "Perestroika Pink."
- An interpreter assigned during President Jimmy Carter's visit to Poland was fired for saying in Polish that the president "has a lust for Polish women" rather than "admires Polish women."
- American practitioners in some foreign countries also have discovered that much local conversation and writing is in Pidgin English, of which Figure 16.3 is an example.

Cultural differences provide additional pitfalls, as shown by the following examples:

- In China, tables at a banquet are never numbered. The Chinese think such tables appear to rank guests, so it is better to direct a guest to the "primrose" or "hollyhock" table.
- German and Swiss executives think a person is uncouth if he or she uses first names, particularly at public events.
- The English start and end their work later in the day, so breakfast meetings are unpopular.
- The proper etiquette for drinking in Korea is to fill your neighbor's glass as well as your own.
- News releases in Malaysia should be distributed in four languages to avoid alienating any segment of the press.
- Americans, perhaps because of their strong freedom-of-expression tradition, tend to be perceived throughout the world as extremely vocal and opinionated—traits not particularly admired or emulated in many cultures.
- In the Middle East, the color white signifies mourning, so no executive should be pictured in white. In that same region care also must be taken in portraying or photographing women.

AIDS • SIDA

SIK IA AIDS I KILIM MAN.
I NO GAT MERESIN.
SIK IA I PAS LONG TAEM WE
MAN I SLIP WETEM WOMAN.
LUKAOT!

BLOKEM SIK IA AIDS

1. Stap kwaet wetem woman o man blong yu nomo.
2. Sipos yu no save gud laef blong wan fren, man i mas putum kondom (o plastik) fastaem.

Helt Edukesen, Vanuatu.

Vanuatu AIDS warning in pidgin. "Look out! Prevent AIDS. Stay with your partner. Use a condom." Adapted from a Vanuatu government poster.

FIGURE 16.3
The campaign against AIDS has many international ramifications. The Vanuatu government distributed this poster in Pidgin English urging precautions against the disease. Read it carefully and you probably can decipher its message. If not, a translation appears in small print beneath the poster.

- If an American executive lacks time to have a negotiating proposal typed and submits a handwritten version, Arabs may consider the gesture so bizarre that they will analyze the proposal intensely, seeking significant messages, or conclude that the American considers the contract unimportant.
- When Americans make a business proposal, Japanese executives generally react with silence, giving themselves time to reflect—a sign of interest. Americans unfamiliar with this custom may be offended.
- When Japanese executives suck in air through their teeth and exclaim, "*Sa*! That will be *very* difficult," they really mean just plain "no." The Japanese consider an absolute "no" offensive and try to respond euphemistically.
- When an Asian business executive changes the date of a projected meeting, the

American executive should not be offended; the Asian may simply have consulted with a religious adviser who urged a more auspicious date for the visit.

- In some countries, such as Japan and those in Latin America, it is almost impossible to get a news story published or a television interview aired unless it has been prepared by a local unionized journalist.
- Americans, generally punctual, must learn not to be offended when people in many other countries arrive a half-hour or more late for an appointment. Time traditionally has a different meaning in those nations.
- Americans tend to separate their business and social lives. In many countries, however, business is an indirect outcome of a lengthy personal relationship; one does business with a friend, or only after a long social evening.

All of these illustrations indicate that Americans not only must learn the customs of the country to which they are assigned but should rely on native professionals to guide their paths. And, although they should study the language both before and after their arrival, they must realize that only by residing in the country for many years will they be free—if ever—of language problems.

Courses of study to prepare Americans to conduct business in other countries have been developed at a number of universities. Since 1970 the business school at New York University has nearly tripled its international business faculty. The University of South Carolina and the University of Denver, among others, have greatly expanded their international business programs, as has also the Georgetown Center for Strategic and International Studies. The American Graduate School of International Management in Glendale, Arizona, is devoted entirely to preparing students for world business careers. The nonprofit Business Council for International Understanding produces films that help Americans learn about practices in other countries. The Language and Intercultural Research Center at Brigham Young University publishes a variety of booklets which, though intended primarily for missionaries of the Church of Latter Day Saints, are useful for international business purposes.

Corporations, too, have done their homework. Their public relations experts overseas have helped them establish good rapport with the people in countries where they do business.

REPRESENTING FOREIGN CORPORATIONS IN THE UNITED STATES

Industries in other countries frequently employ American public relations firms to advance their needs in this country. Carl Levin, vice president and senior consultant, Burson-Marsteller, Washington, D.C., tells why:

- To hold off protectionist moves threatening their company or industry.
- To defeat legislation affecting the sale of a client's product.
- To support expansion of the client's markets in the United States.

- To provide ongoing information on political, sociological, and commercial developments in the United States that could bear on the client's business interests, not only here but worldwide. In the well-organized foreign company, this information is factored into day-to-day policy decisions as well as periodic strategic plans.

More than 25 counseling firms are registered by the U.S. Department of Justice as doing work for Japanese companies, more than for any other nation. When the sales of imported automobiles soared and those of U.S. manufacturers declined during the 1980s, the Japan Automobile Manufacturers Association mounted a public relations campaign to counteract rising public sentiment in America for curbs on the sale of imported cars. The campaign included a series of full-page advertisements in leading U.S. newspapers containing interviews with American economists and consumer-group leaders who defended auto imports and free-trade policies. Said a Japanese automaker: "We wanted to start communicating with the American public."

As Japanese companies began to build their cars in the United States with American labor, additional public relations efforts were required. With Chrysler Corporation sales suffering, Lee A. Iacocca, Chrysler president, personally headed a two-month advertising and public relations media blitz in 1990. The "Advantage Chrysler" campaign was based on a surprising research finding that new car buyers preferred Chrysler cars over those of the highly rated Honda Motor Company. The campaign provoked considerable debate since the notion that Chrysler vehicles were superior to those of Honda ran counter to vast industry research and public perception that had given Honda vehicles the highest rating for quality—far ahead of Chrysler—for several years. Honda's reply was voiced by a Detroit spokesman: "The sales speak for themselves."

In 1987 Toshiba Corporation conducted a quiet campaign of damage control among U.S. lawmakers after the political uproar over disclosures that its subsidiary had sold sensitive technology to the Soviet Union. Part of the Japanese manufacturer's strategy was a series of one-page ads in American newspapers apologizing for the lax management of the subsidiary.

In 1989 Japan's Sony Corporation purchased Columbia Pictures Entertainment Company for $3.4 billion after earlier acquiring CBS Records. Japanese government officials and business executives were taken aback by the negative publicity that followed. Some of them contended that the American reaction amounted to racism toward the Japanese.

Meanwhile, Japanese business interests increased their real estate investments in the United States to a total exceeding $10 billion. Japan's wealthy Mitsubishi Estate Company reportedly was so sensitive to American reaction that it obtained only a 51 percent interest instead of a planned 80 percent interest in its 1990 acquisition of New York's Rockefeller Center. Even so, American reaction was intense because, as one correspondent put it, Rockefeller Center is "a symbol for New Yorkers and for most Americans" that contains "the most beautiful illuminated Christmas tree in the West." In the deal Mitsubishi also acquired 51 percent of the Time & Life Building, half of the McGraw-Hill Building, and vacant land behind the Exxon Building.

Less pronounced was U.S. public reaction to the purchase later in 1990 of MCA Inc., one of the nation's largest entertainment companies, by Matsushita Electric Industrial Company of Japan for $6.13 billion and stock in a television station. It was by far the largest U.S. acquisition by the Japanese. Although most financial experts approved the purchase as in the United States' interest, a number of persons said they were disturbed by the thought of Japanese owning two American movie companies.

Among the public relations tactics employed by the Japanese to allay American fears of their business moves was to place special advertising supplements in U.S. magazines and newspapers emphasizing the contribution that Japanese companies were making to the U.S. economy. For example, statements were made that Japanese-owned companies employ more than 300,000 Americans and that about 70 percent of parts in a Japanese car built in the United States are American-made. In seeking to counter the widespread perception that Japanese interests were "buying America," the point was made that direct Japanese investment in the United States represented less than 20 percent of total foreign investment in the country.

REPRESENTING U.S. CORPORATIONS IN OTHER COUNTRIES

On a global basis, public relations as an occupation has achieved highest development in the industrialized nations of the world—United States, Canada, Western Europe, and parts of Asia. It emerges more readily in nations that have multiple-party systems, considerable private ownership of business and industry, large-scale urbanization, and relatively high per capita income levels—which also relate to literacy and educational opportunities.

By the same token, public relations as a specialized activity is less developed in Third World nations in which the vast majority of the citizens are still rural villagers—a situation often accompanied by little industrialization, low levels of personal income, government ownership of major industries, and political activity limited to one official party or a military government.

U.S. and other Western public relations firms began exporting their expertise to the People's Republic of China during the mid-1980s. Hill & Knowlton, active in Asia for almost 30 years, began its Beijing operation with three U.S. expatriates and a locally hired employee dispatching news releases and organizing receptions and conferences from headquarters in a hotel. (A case study later in this chapter tells how the firm helped an international soft-drinks manufacturer achieve its goals in China.) Although a number of corporations ceased their operations in China after the government used tanks and rifles against student democracy demonstrators in Tiananmen Square on June 4, 1989, others remained, with their public relations efforts largely directed at local news media.

In the Republic of China on Taiwan public relations experienced rapid growth in recent years, paralleling the economic growth of the country and its financial services industry.

Australia and New Zealand have public relations industries that are among the most active and developed in the Western world, according to David Potts, a senior public relations counselor in Sydney, Australia. Global public relations firms, as well as many small and medium-sized companies, operate in the two countries. "Some overseas corporations, however, make the mistake of assuming that public relations styles and campaigns which have worked overseas, especially in the U.S.A., will work in [these countries]," said Potts. "They don't always."

Potts has additional observations about public relations in other Pacific Rim countries:

- Hong Kong, because of its international financial, trading, and tourist links and the fact that Western management techniques are widely used, exhibits a widespread understanding of public relations. There are more advertising and public relations practitioners in Hong Kong than in any other Asian country. Their expertise, however, will stand its greatest test when Britain relinquishes the country to China late in the decade.
- Singapore and Malaysia enjoy well-developed public relations practices, both local and global. Singapore operations are heavily oriented to visual public relations, and many firms have strong graphics capabilities. The press is freer in Malaysia, and the intricacies of federal, state, and local politics offer wide scope for public relations activity.
- In Indonesia public relations consultancies and advertising agencies must be domestically owned.
- Thailand has a great deal of foreign investment and international tourism. The public relations industry, however, is handicapped by a lack of skilled practitioners and an overwhelming emphasis on defining public relations as publicity.
- Unlike most major Asian countries, no global public relations firm operates in the Philippines; instead outside companies work through local firms on a referral basis. P. A. Chanco III, of the Orientations firm in Manila, advises public relations representatives of foreign corporations to "know the Filipino culture and how it works before anything else." He adds: "The best motives can be misunderstood with disastrous results because the Filipino is highly sensitive and personalistic."
- In Japan public relations practice is centered on reaching the media through one or more of the 400-plus reporters' "clubs," with about 12,000 members representing 160 news-gathering organizations. Japan has no public relations tradition. Public relations is identified almost entirely with product publicity, according to Kosuke Ohashi, president of Dentsu New York, a branch of Japan's Dentsu, one of the world's largest advertising agencies.

Dentsu has joined Burson-Marsteller to form two joint ventures that provide public relations services to Western clients in the country and to Japanese clients in the United States. The partnerships replaced Burson-Marsteller/Tokyo, opened in 1973. James H. Dowling, president and chief executive of Burson-Marsteller, said the arrangement "makes Burson-Marsteller Japanese in Japan" and helps Western corporations solve regulatory problems, market Western goods and services, and recruit employees.

On the continent of Africa, South Africa is the only nation that has a sufficient industrial base to support an extensive number of public relations professionals. Although media relations and product publicity were their main concerns in the past, South African practitioners are increasingly getting involved in employee communications, issues management, community relations, and investor relations.

The new orientation of South African practitioners, of course, is related to factors in the environment of that nation. More than one million South African workers, predominantly black, have joined trade unions since the right to organize was granted in 1979. Now, for the first time, South African industry must deal with large organized groups that want more pay and better employment opportunities. At the same time, the nation is running out of skilled workers to fuel its robust economy. This means increased competition among companies for the available pool of skilled workers.

Productivity is another aspect. South Africa, like many other nations, must raise productivity to compete with foreign markets. One way to do this is to motivate workers through effective communications. Consequently, there is considerable interest in newsletters for the rank-and-file, increased training programs, and even pressure to alter government apartheid policies that restrict the recruitment of black workers. (South Africa also will be discussed later in this chapter.)

INTERNATIONAL GOVERNMENT PUBLIC RELATIONS

INFLUENCING OTHER COUNTRIES

The governments of virtually every country have one or more departments involved in communicating with other nations. Much effort and millions of dollars are spent on the tourism industry—attracting visitors whose expenditures aid their hosts' economies. Even larger sums are devoted to lobbying efforts to obtain favorable legislation for a country's products; for example, Costa Rica urged the U.S. Congress to let its sugar into the nation at favorable rates, and the Department of State threatened to enact trade sanctions against countries such as Korea and Taiwan that persisted in "pirating" U.S. products such as computers and books without payment.

Many countries send short-wave broadcasts throughout the world to achieve several objectives, including fostering their national interests and prestige, keeping in touch with nationals abroad, disseminating news, and influencing the internal affairs of other nations.

For decades people throughout the People's Republic of China have listened to Western radio broadcasts, particularly those of the U.S.-based Voice of America (VOA) and the British Broadcasting Corporation (BBC). During and after the prodemocracy uprisings in China in 1989, the VOA's 24-hour service in English and particularly its nearly 13 hours of Mandarin and Cantonese broadcasts each day helped get the facts out to the Chinese population even as the state- and Communist Party-controlled media tried to hide them. The BBC supplemented its regular English-language broadcasts with two and one-half hours of programming in Chinese each day.

For more than 40 years the broadcasts of the VOA, BBC, other European stations, and America's Radio Liberty, which transmitted programs in 14 languages from Munich, Germany, have conveyed Western-style news and values to the Soviet Union and other Eastern bloc nations. Despite the jamming that persisted into the late 1980s, millions of Soviet citizens listened. The effect of these broadcasts and of TV programming from West Germany in helping to provide the climate for acceptance of Mikhail Gorbachev's perestroika and glasnost campaigns in the midst of economic deprivations may never be known, but many consider it substantial.

For four decades Radio Free Europe in Munich transmitted programs in native languages to Eastern-bloc nations. In Romania, where demonstrations in December, 1989, ended with the capture and execution of President Nicolae Ceauşescu and his co-dictator wife Elena, student leaders told reporters they would not have taken to the streets had they not been listening for months to British and American short-wave reports about changes taking place elsewhere in Eastern Europe. Said a national student magazine editor: "There was something like a wind of liberty coming from the radio stations from other countries."

The U.S. Information Agency (USIA) operates the Voice of America, and Radio Liberty and Radio Free Europe also are financed by Congress. With the communist threat to world peace virtually eliminated, Congress and an interagency group working under the National Security Council in 1990 debated the future of the stations. The USIA budget was cut severely. The agency's director, Bruce S. Gelb, was offered the option of eliminating VOA programs for one day a week in all of the 43 languages in which it broadcasts. He chose to keep the VOA on the air seven days a week and to make up the more than $1 million shortage by trimming other USIA projects such as cultural exchange programs with other nations.

In 1990 the United States also reaffirmed its 1985 decision to withdraw from membership in the United Nations Educational, Scientific, and Cultural Organization (UNESCO) on grounds of mismanagement, politicization, and "endemic hostility" toward a free press, free markets, and individual human rights. A State Department announcement stated that the United States would continue to support educational, scientific, cultural, and communications activities through other global agencies.

Since the mid-1970s, Department of State officials have been aided materially by American news media organizations, operating mainly through the World Press Freedom Committee, to respond to complaints of Third World countries. These nations have sought, among other goals, independence and equity in access to global communication resources in order that their own views, values, and developmental efforts might be reported more fully. U.S. media leaders have counseled government representatives during debates on a proposed New World Order of Communication, conducted at UNESCO assemblies and other conferences.

Soviet Union In the USSR, after decades during which the "vulgarity" of Western capitalism and advertising was condemned, Soviet television in 1988 carried commercials by Visa, Pepsi, and Sony during a five-part series examining life in the United States. In 1989 the Soviet government newspaper *Izvestia* began running advertisements weekly in its foreign and Moscow editions. The Soviet Union even offered advertising space on the side of a space shuttle.

Public relations practice began gradually under government monitoring as USSR firms entered into partnership arrangements with foreign companies. The government itself, under President Mikhail Gorbachev's remarkable public relations leadership, had begun a broad-based public relations program in the mid-1980s designed to improve its world image. "The Soviets are waking up to the fact that they can adopt Western-style public relations and dress up their world," said Stuart Loory of Cable News Network. One of the opening shots in the Soviet public relations offensive was cosponsorship with CNN owner Ted Turner of a major sports event in Moscow, aired in the United States and elsewhere, and repeated in the United States in 1990. Soviet spokespersons appeared on U.S. network television programs, including ABC-TV's "Nightline" and the "MacNeil–Lehrer News Hour" on PBS. Numerous other U.S.–Soviet exchanges followed.

The epitome of glasnost occurred when the USSR opened the doors of its infamous Lubyanka prison to journalists in 1990. KGB General Alexander Karbayinov, the first chief of the KGB's newly created public relations department, welcomed the visitors to the security agency's facility. Other elements in the public relations drive included newspaper interviews with KGB officials, magazine articles about outstanding Soviet spies, and even a television phone-in. "The point of the public relations department is to show that society is no longer subordinate to the KGB or to the state," Karbayinov said, adding that Soviet citizens now have the right to shout "Down with the Communist Party" at the top of their lungs without arrest.

The public relations turnaround was in marked contrast to the secrecy that followed the disaster at the USSR's Chernobyl nuclear power plant in 1986 that forced evacuation of 100,000 people and spread radiation throughout much of Western Europe. Initial reports in the Western press were labeled "malicious mountains of lies."

South Africa The Republic of South Africa, in response to rising worldwide criticism of its apartheid policies, for many years has engaged in an extensive information and lobbying campaign in the United States and Western Europe. Its aim is to forestall severe trade sanctions while the government seeks a solution to its multiracial problem. In the United States, TransAfrica, a Washington-based lobbying organization, devised strategies to increase pressure on the South African government to hasten the end of apartheid. As the movement gained momentum, Congress passed a law in 1986 that banned new U.S. investments in South Africa, prohibited imports of ore and farm products, and revoked the landing privileges of South African Airways. And by 1990 more than 150 colleges and universities, 26 states, 17 counties, and 80 cities had divested their stock in companies doing business with South Africa.

President F. W. deKlerk, elected in 1989, became the chief architect of improving South Africa's image abroad by canceling many of the petty apartheid laws and releasing Nelson Mandela, president of the African National Congress (ANC), from a 27-year imprisonment. As preliminary negotiations began in 1990 to end ANC-South Africa hostilities, the 71-year-old Mandela undertook an extended tour of the United States and Great Britain. Among other objectives, he sought (1) assurances that economic sanctions would not be loosened until further gains were achieved, (2) contributions to help the ANC change from a militant underground force to an above-ground political organization, and (3) strong support for a new constitution that would for the first time enfranchise the 26 million blacks who represent 68 percent of South Africa's population.

The eight-city U.S. tour, highlighted by standing ovations during a joint session of Congress, was proclaimed a triumph. For many Americans the tour was marred only by Mandela's refusal to disavow ANC violence as a measure of defense and by his praise for Yassir Arafat and the Palestine Liberation Organization (PLO), Fidel Castro and Cuba's communist government, and Libya and its leader, Muammar Gaddafi. In reply to criticisms, Mandela pointed out that Arafat, Castro, and Gaddafi had "supported our struggle to the hilt."

PUBLIC RELATIONS IN BEHALF OF FOREIGN GOVERNMENTS

For fees ranging upward of $1 million or more per year, more than 150 American public relations firms work in this country for other nations. In recent years, for example, Hill & Knowlton has represented Indonesia and Morocco; Burson-Marsteller, Argentina, Costa Rica, Hungary, and the USSR (the latter mainly in trade fairs); and Ruder, Finn & Rotman, El Salvador, Israel, and Japan. Especially active in representing foreign countries is Doremus & Company, whose clients have included Egypt, Iran, Jordan, the Philippines, Saudi Arabia, and Tunisia.

The Countries' Goals What do these countries seek to accomplish? Burson-Marsteller's Carl Levin says that, among other things, the countries pursue several goals:

FIGURE 16.4
Indicative of the greatly improved relations between the United States and the Soviet Union, this exhibit of the Moroccan paintings of Henri Matisse was a joint USA/USSR project, organized by four leading museums in the two countries.

MATISSE IN MOROCCO
The Paintings and Drawings, 1912–1913
a USA/USSR Joint Project

National Gallery of Art, Washington
The Museum of Modern Art, New York
State Pushkin Museum of Fine Arts, Moscow
The State Hermitage Museum, Leningrad

FOR IMMEDIATE RELEASE

CONTACT: Katie Ziglar
Deb Spears
(202) 842-6353
Updated information

MATISSE'S ART INSPIRED BY MOROCCO

TO BEGIN USA/USSR TOUR AT NATIONAL GALLERY

SHOW INCLUDES NEWLY DISCOVERED WORKS

Washington, D.C., January 30, 1990 -- An exhibition of paintings and newly discovered drawings executed by Henri Matisse in Morocco in 1912 and 1913 will be held in the East Building of the National Gallery of Art March 18 through June 3, 1990. Matisse in Morocco, The Paintings and Drawings, 1912-1913, A USA/USSR Joint Project, organized by the National Gallery of Art, The Museum of Modern Art, New York, the State Pushkin Museum of Fine Arts, Moscow, and The State Hermitage Museum, Leningrad, will be the first exhibition worked out in all phases jointly by western and Soviet curators.

The most comprehensive show ever devoted to this pivotal phase of the artist's career, Matisse in Morocco is made possible by a generous grant from the Richard King Mellon Foundation.

The exhibition is made possible by a generous grant from the Richard King Mellon Foundation

- more -

- To advance political objectives
- To be counseled on the United States' probable reaction to the client government's projected action
- To advance the country's commercial interests—for example, sales in the United States, increased U.S. private investment, and tourism
- To assist in communications in English
- To counsel and help win understanding and support on a specific issue undermining the client's standing in the United States and the world community
- To help modify laws and regulations inhibiting the client's activities in the United States

Under the Foreign Agents Registration Act of 1938, all legal, political, fund-raising, public relations, and lobbying consultants hired by foreign governments to work in the United States must register with the Department of Justice. They are required to file reports with the attorney general listing all activities on behalf of a foreign principal, compensation received, and expenses incurred.

Action Programs Normally hired by an embassy after open bidding for the account, the firm first gathers detailed information about the client country, including past media coverage. Attitudes toward the country are ascertained both informally and through surveys conducted by a specialist such as George Gallup, Lou Harris, or Daniel Yankelovich.

PLENTY OF FOREIGN BUSINESS FOR U.S. PUBLIC RELATIONS FIRMS

American public relations firms handle a variety of international accounts. The following is a sampling of clients reported in *Jack O'Dwyer's Newsletter* in 1990:

Client	Public Relations Firm	Contract
Northern Ireland Industrial Development Board	Shandwick	$5.7 million
Korea Industrial Development Board	Burson-Marsteller	$4.5 million
Kenya	Black, Manafort, Stone & Kelly	$750,000
Chile Quality Export Committee	Hill & Knowlton	$400,000
Caribbean Tourism Organization	Marcella Martinez Associates	$129,833
Friends of Democracy in Pakistan Ltd.	Robinson, Lake, Lerer & Montgomery	$100,000

The action program decided on likely will include the establishment of a national information bureau to provide facts and published statements of favorable opinion about the country. Appointments are made with key media people and other influential citizens, including educators, business leaders, and government officials. These people often are invited to visit the client country on expense-paid trips, although some news media people decline on ethical grounds. (Ethical questions are discussed in more detail shortly.)

Gradually, through expert and persistent methods of persuasion and the expenditure of what may run into millions of dollars, critical public attitudes may be changed or reinforced. Success is difficult to judge. So high are the stakes that although the nations may change agencies from time to time, the image-polishing and fact-dissemination operation generally is made permanent.

Problems and Rewards The toughest problems confronting the firm often are as follows:

- Deciding to represent a country, such as Argentina, whose human rights violations may reflect adversely on the agency itself.
- Persuading the heads of such a nation to alter some of its practices so that the favorable public image sought may reflect reality.
- Convincing officials of a client country, which may totally control the flow of news internally, that the American press is independent from government control and that they should never expect coverage that is 100 percent favorable.
- Deciding to represent an autocratic head of state, such as Mobutu Sese Seko of Zaire, whose lavish living and large Swiss bank accounts stand in stark contrast to an average family income among the lowest in the world.

Amnesty International, the Nobel Prize–winning human rights monitor, picketed Burson-Marsteller's offices because of the Argentine account. The Council on Hemispheric Affairs criticized Ruder, Finn & Rotman for working for the government of El Salvador. Norman Wolfson, chairman of Norman, Lawrence, Patterson & Farrell, fled Nicaragua with would-be assassins close on his heels after serving during most of 1978 as the public relations counselor for the late dictator General Anastasio Somoza. A Doremus & Company executive working for the economic development of the Philippines, whose government, headed by Ferdinand Marcos, had placed the country under military law, also was threatened with death.

Why then do these firms work for unpopular governments? Wolfson put it this way: "I felt that I was performing a better service for my country by trying to help Americans understand Somoza than I did even by serving my country in the Navy during the Second World War." Said Burson-Marsteller's Carl Levin: "I do not think it is overreaching to state that in helping friendly foreign clients we also advance our national interests. And we help in ways that our government cannot." Black, Manafort, Stone & Kelly felt the same way, but dropped its $950,000 contract with an agency close to former Philippines President Ferdinand Marcos when President Reagan called on Marcos to resign. And, of course, retainers are large: Wolfson earned $20,000 to $30,000 per month, including expenses; Sydney S. Baron & Company was paid $650,000 annually, plus expenses, to promote investment opportunities in South Africa; and Burson-Marsteller received more than $800,000 a year to improve Argentina's reputation.

Publicity for Antigovernment Groups Although public relations counsel is usually retained by foreign governments, groups opposed to a foreign government also use public relations. The *Wall Street Journal,* in an editorial titled "Guerrilla P.R.," thought it interesting that the guerrillas battling the government in El Salvador had their own press kit. The editorial said, in part: "A few days ago, U.S. editors received a slick-looking press packet bearing the imprint of 'Fenton Communications' on behalf of something called the 'El Salvador Education Project.' It was a job any Madison Avenue house would have been proud of. What it said was that the Salvadoran guerrillas aren't participating in the elections because they are afraid of the 'death squads.'"

The Ethical Questions Gift-giving, entertainment, hospitality, and junkets are long-established practices of foreign governments, or the public relations and lobbying firms that represent them. Those who attend these parties—whether members of Congress and their staffs, regulatory agency personnel, members of the President's cabinet, business leaders, or even members of the press—do so advisedly, for there is a thin line between hospitality and bribery or illegal "influence peddling." For example, several members of a congressional committee responsible for foreign aid have been guests of President Mobutu Sese Seko at his palace in Zaire.

It is generally conceded that the wheels of government are lubricated by countless receptions and cocktail parties in capitals around the world, and there is generally no ethical problem for those attending. Adlai E. Stevenson, when he was chief American delegate to the United Nations, said that "protocol, Geritol, and alcohol" were endemic to a diplomat's life.

In the mid-1970s, however, the ambassador for the then–Shah of Iran stretched the rules considerably by staging lavish parties that included gifts of Persian carpets, diamond earrings, and cases of caviar and champagne for the guests. Reporters also were recipients of such gifts, and magazine writer Nicholas Burnett cited a number of instances of favorable publicity that followed.

"Gift-giving" by American corporations also reached an all-time high in the 1970s, and Congress passed the 1977 Foreign Corrupt Practices Act that forbids corporations from giving major gifts or bribes to foreign business contacts or government officials. (Acceptance of such payments is a widely condoned practice in some countries.) In 1982, for example, Boeing pleaded guilty to federal charges of failing to disclose more than $7 million in payments by top-level executives to overseas agents. Today, corporations are extremely careful about giving expensive gifts to potential foreign clients, and often set the corporate policy of only token gifts valued at no more than $25 to $100. (A full discussion of other ethical concerns involved in American firms' representing foreign interests is provided in Chapter 6.)

Intervention Tactics Placing full-page advertisements in major papers such as the Washington *Post* and New York *Times* is almost invariably the first action taken by agents of foreign governments in seeking to influence American public opinion during a crisis (see Figure 16.5). Surveys have shown that a high percentage of the nation's lawmakers and administrators read the *Post* before or soon after arriving in their offices each weekday morning. The *Times*, in particular, is read by opinion leaders not only in the East but throughout the country, and the advertisements gain important visibility, influencing editorial writers and others. Members of Congress often use these political statements in addresses to their colleagues and obtain permission to insert their remarks in the *Congressional Record*. The advertisements generally are followed by personal visits and telephone calls by foreign government agency people and their key supporters. Arrangements are made to place representatives on broadcast network programs. Press conferences are arranged, and newsletters are hastily dispatched to media, government, and other leaders.

For example, after the Israeli invasion of Lebanon in 1982, the Gray & Company public relations firm—hired by the Arab Women's Council and using contributions received from various Arab embassies—placed full-page advertisements in the New York *Times* calling attention to allegations of Israeli violations of human rights in Lebanon. The Arab League and representatives of other Middle East countries mounted similar campaigns. On the other side, the Hannaford Company—retained by the Lebanese Informational and Research Center, which represented conservative Lebanese militia who generally shared Israel's goals—countered with its own campaign, joined by the United Jewish Appeal and other groups.

Other examples:

- An advertisement by the American Council for Palestine Affairs charged that U.S. taxpayers, through the government's reported $10-million-per-day grant to Israel, were subsidizing the killing of Palestinians (see Figure 16.6).

- An advertisement ''coordinated by the ad hoc committee of Jewish labor leaders, rabbis and activists'' made ''A Jewish Call in Support of Middle East Peace.'' The ad listed the names of 250 persons supporting the official American readiness to open ''substantive contacts'' with the Palestine Liberation Organization to resolve the Israel–PLO conflict.

- An appeal to legal and human rights organizations ''and peace-loving people'' to contact Saudi Arabian representatives to condemn the reported past and prospective beheading of political prisoners in that country

- Coincidental with a visit of Mikhail Gorbachev to the United States, two large advertisements appeared. One, signed by the Joint Committee for the Preservation of Jewish Heritage in the Soviet Union, expressed hope that remaining human rights issues (the emigration of Jews) would be resolved. The other, noting that ''Soviet Armenian men, women and children are being burned out of their homes, threatened, beaten and murdered,'' urged Soviet government protection of Armenians from further Azerbaijan assaults.

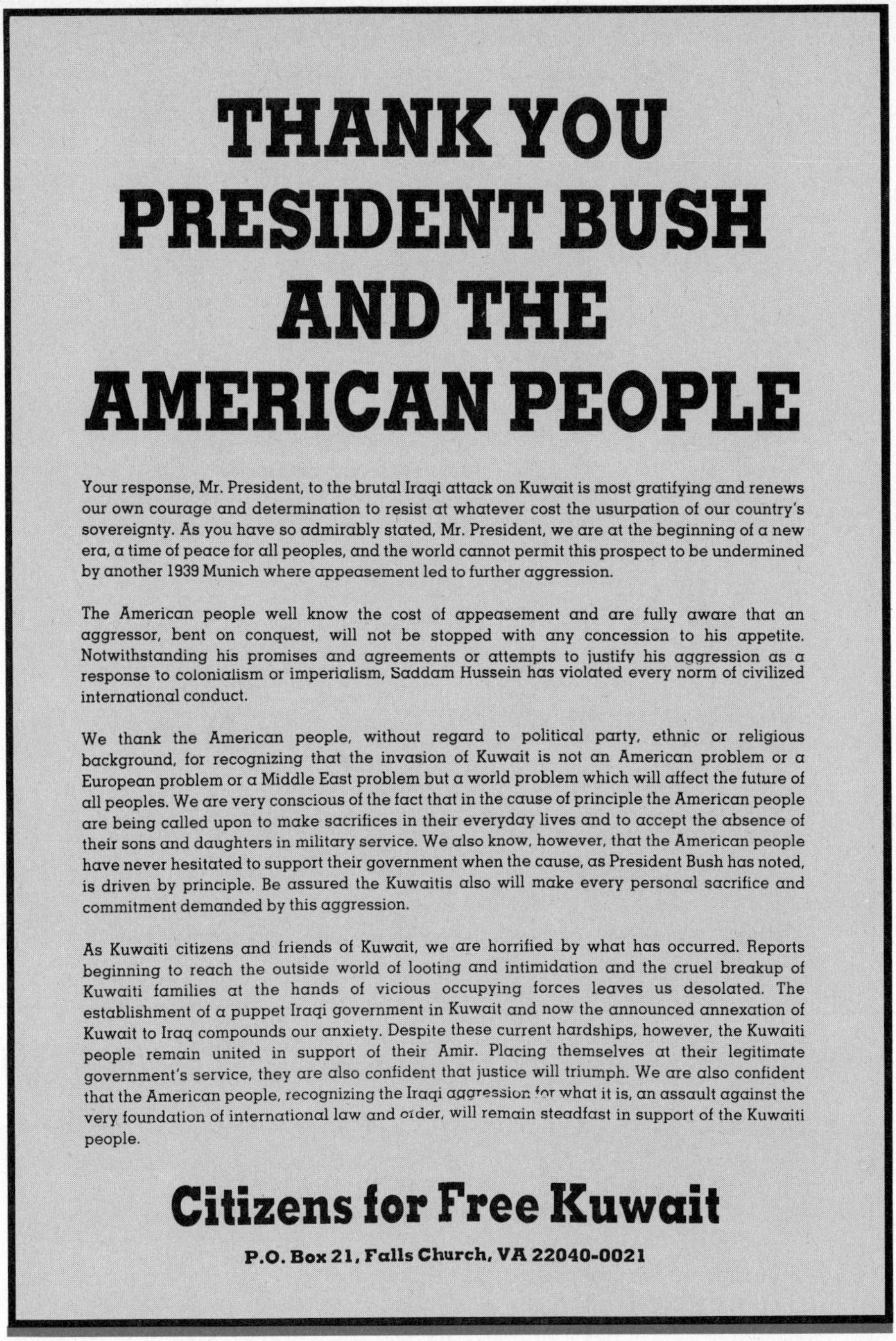

THANK YOU PRESIDENT BUSH AND THE AMERICAN PEOPLE

Your response, Mr. President, to the brutal Iraqi attack on Kuwait is most gratifying and renews our own courage and determination to resist at whatever cost the usurpation of our country's sovereignty. As you have so admirably stated, Mr. President, we are at the beginning of a new era, a time of peace for all peoples, and the world cannot permit this prospect to be undermined by another 1939 Munich where appeasement led to further aggression.

The American people well know the cost of appeasement and are fully aware that an aggressor, bent on conquest, will not be stopped with any concession to his appetite. Notwithstanding his promises and agreements or attempts to justify his aggression as a response to colonialism or imperialism, Saddam Hussein has violated every norm of civilized international conduct.

We thank the American people, without regard to political party, ethnic or religious background, for recognizing that the invasion of Kuwait is not an American problem or a European problem or a Middle East problem but a world problem which will affect the future of all peoples. We are very conscious of the fact that in the cause of principle the American people are being called upon to make sacrifices in their everyday lives and to accept the absence of their sons and daughters in military service. We also know, however, that the American people have never hesitated to support their government when the cause, as President Bush has noted, is driven by principle. Be assured the Kuwaitis also will make every personal sacrifice and commitment demanded by this aggression.

As Kuwaiti citizens and friends of Kuwait, we are horrified by what has occurred. Reports beginning to reach the outside world of looting and intimidation and the cruel breakup of Kuwaiti families at the hands of vicious occupying forces leaves us desolated. The establishment of a puppet Iraqi government in Kuwait and now the announced annexation of Kuwait to Iraq compounds our anxiety. Despite these current hardships, however, the Kuwaiti people remain united in support of their Amir. Placing themselves at their legitimate government's service, they are also confident that justice will triumph. We are also confident that the American people, recognizing the Iraqi aggression for what it is, an assault against the very foundation of international law and order, will remain steadfast in support of the Kuwaiti people.

Citizens for Free Kuwait

P.O. Box 21, Falls Church, VA 22040-0021

FIGURE 16.5

This advertisement in the *Wall Street Journal* was part of a multifaceted public relations campaign by Hill & Knowlton for its client, Citizens for Free Kuwait. This group, formed after Iraq's invasion of Kuwait, paid the firm $1 million a month to rally public support for massive American intervention. Techniques used by Hill & Knowlton included press conferences, mailings to Congress, video news releases, press kits, and even distribution of "Free Kuwait" T-shirts and bumper stickers at college campuses across the country.

U.S. TAXPAYERS SUBSIDIZE KILLING OF PALESTINIANS

Israelis killed 15 Palestinians and injured more than 700 on May 20, 1990. The next day, 4 more Palestinians were killed, including a woman beaten to death by Israeli soldiers, and 150 wounded. On the same day, 1.5 million Palestinians were placed under curfew in the Occupied Territories.

Since the Intifada began on December 9, 1987:

- 900 Palestinians have been killed by the Israeli army
- An estimated 87,500 Palestinians have sustained injuries
- At least 50,000 have been arrested and 15,000 remain in prison
- 1,417 homes have been demolished or sealed
- Universities and most schools have been closed for almost 3 years; home instruction is punishable as a crime

In addition, Israel has:

- Expropriated 56% of the land in the West Bank
- Seized 88% of Palestinian water resources
- Established over 120 illegal settlements

AID TO ISRAEL ($10 million per day)
compared with some other U.S. programs

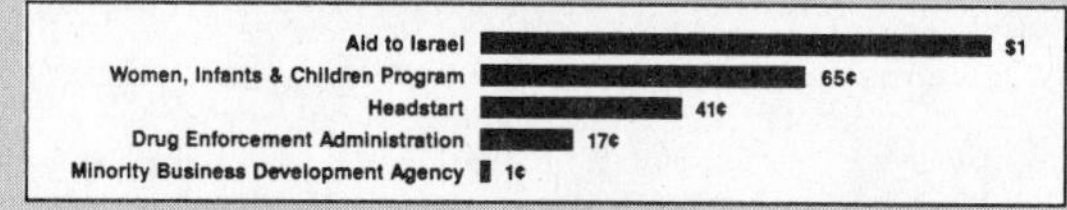

With our money Israel is systematically violating the human rights of the Palestinians. These outrages continue despite the fact that the Foreign Assistance Act of 1961 requires aid recipients to comply with international human rights standards in order to receive U.S. funds.

These violations will go on as long as the occupation lasts, and the occupation will go on as long as Americans are willing to pay for it. So long as Palestinians cannot vote, cannot travel freely, cannot carry their own passports, cannot build houses or go to school, the Intifada will not end.

The Bush Administration initially blocked an attempt by the United Nations Security Council to send a mission to investigate the treatment of Palestinians in the Israeli-occupied West Bank and Gaza. Instead of being timid with Israel, the U.S. government must recognize that international pressures and sanctions are effective. They have worked with South Africa. They can work with Israel.

The President and Congress should require Israel, as a recipient of American foreign aid, to uphold the human rights of the Palestinian population. We should support the call for U.N. protection of the civilian population of the Occupied Territories. The Palestinian people are entitled to self-determination and independence. The only way the peace process can go forward is through face to face negotiations between the P.L.O. and Israel.

Express your opinion. Call:
The White House (202) 456-1414
The State Department (202) 647-6575
The Congress (202) 224-3121

American Council For Palestine Affairs
570 Riverside Drive, Suite 9415
New York, NY 10031

FIGURE 16.6
An example of the Palestinian campaign against U.S. aid to Israel, this advocacy advertisement urges Americans to telephone the White House, the State Department, and Congress to support the Palestinian cause.

INTERNATIONAL GROUP PUBLIC RELATIONS

Hundreds of noncorporate groups depend upon international support for their undertakings. Such organizations as the International Red Cross, World Council of Churches, International Council of B'nai B'rith, and International Chamber of Commerce, along with numerous foundations, educational enterprises, labor unions, and government-support agencies, maintain vigorous public relations programs. For effective operation, their image must be kept as spotless as possible; like corporations, they must constantly monitor their environments, maintain proper relationships with the governments and publics of the countries in which they operate, and be prepared to handle crises.

The International Red Cross often is plagued with reports that relief goods and services are diverted into private hands or that aid has not been forthcoming as quickly as it might have been in major disasters around the world. Rumors that Red Cross representatives sold rather than gave cigarettes to troops in past wars still provide people who heard those reports years ago with an excuse for not giving.

UNICEF, a United Nations agency that provides food, medical supplies, and other aid for millions of children on three continents, constantly must respond to charges, leveled mainly by those who dislike the United Nations, that too many of the dollars raised through card and gift sales and Halloween door-to-door solicitations are used improperly, in part to pay heavy administrative expenses.

When the World Council of Churches gave $85,000 to the Patriotic Front, a Marxist guerilla organization fighting the white-dominated regime in Rhodesia, the organization was severely criticized in a *Reader's Digest* article and the CBS-TV program ''60 Minutes.'' In a detailed rebuttal, the council replied that the money was used for education, health, and agricultural programs in Botswana, Mozambique, and Zambia, and that allegations that the Front was responsible for the murder of missionaries had never been substantiated.

FOREIGN PUBLIC RELATIONS ORGANIZATIONS

In virtually every country where public relations has become an economic and social force, practitioners have organized to exchange information, maintain and improve standards of professional performance, and aid in the development of international public relations. Codes of conduct are commonplace, and many organizations seek to enhance the standing of their members through certification and accreditation programs. Journals or newsletters are published, awards recognize outstanding performance, and scholarships and other assistance are provided to educational centers.

Public relations associations have been formed in about 70 countries. In Great Britain more than 2500 practitioners belong to the British Institute of Public Relations, founded in London in 1948. Other European groups include the Association Française des Relations Publiques (France), Deutsche Public Relations Gesellschaft (West Germany), Federazione Italiana Relazioni Publiche (Italy), and Sociedada Portugesa de Relacoes Publicas (Portugal). The Public Relations Society of Japan includes well over 1000 members. Other examples are the Public Relations Institute of South Africa, Zimbabwe Institute of Public Relations, Public Relations Society of India, and the Public Relations Association of Trinidad and Tobago.

In addition to these national public relations groups, many nations also have organizations comparable to the International Association of Business Communicators (IABC) in the United States before it enlarged the scope of its operations. They include the Society of Business Communicators in Australia, Danish Association of Industrial Editors, Finnish Association of Organizational Communicators, and Asociacion Mexicana de Comunicaciones Internas (Mexico).

There also are regional groups of public relations practitioners. Some examples are the Federation of African Public Relations Associations, Federation of Asian Public Relations Organizations, Federation Inter-American of Public Relations Associations, and the Pan Pacific Public Relations Federation.

On a global basis, there is the International Public Relations Association (IPRA), founded in 1955, an individual membership society for professionals with overseas interests. IPRA has almost 1000 members in more than 60 countries and is seeking further expansion, primarily in Latin America, the Middle East, and Asia. Every third year IPRA sponsors a World Congress of Public Relations, which often attracts 600 or more practitioners. IPRA has its own code of ethics. IABC (discussed in Chapter 5) is primarily a North American organization, but it has chapters in Great Britain, Belgium, Hong Kong, the Philippines, and southern Africa.

In addition to the various associations that have been noted, numerous networks of public relations agencies provide clients with services almost anywhere in the world. One of the largest is IPR, which links agencies in almost 50 countries.

OPPORTUNITIES IN INTERNATIONAL WORK

The 1990s, according to many experts, will be the golden age of global marketing and public relations. The 1992 opening of the European Market, coupled with recent economic and social reforms in East European countries and the Soviet Union, will hasten the reality of a global economy.

All of these developments led Jerry Dalton, immediate past president of the Public Relations Society of America, to say, ''I think more and more American firms are going to become part of those overseas markets, and I expect a lot of Americans in public relations will be living overseas.'' Indeed, Dalton believes that the fastest-growing career field for practitioners is international public relations. He adds: ''Students who can communicate well and are fluent in a foreign language may be able to write their own ticket.''

But the coming of the ''global village,'' as Marshall McLuhan once described it, still means that there will be a multiplicity of languages, customs, and values that public relations professionals will have to understand. Corporations and public relations firms are seeking employees who have obtained substantial knowledge in international aspects of the social sciences, humanities, business, law, cross-cultural communications, and public relations.

Many transnational corporations, putting an increased emphasis on international customer relations, are hiring ''corporate protocol'' officers to be responsible for doing everything from booking hotels, planning banquets, and hiring limousines to scheduling plant tours, arranging security, and selecting gifts for foreign officials and major customers. They even brief company executives on current events, advise on the correct protocol for greeting royalty, and ''hand out sheet music for sing-alongs at Korean banquets,'' according to a New York *Times* article.

Its author, Paul Finney, says, ''Corporations tend to fill their protocol jobs with people who have backgrounds in public relations, marketing, [and] meeting planning and who have a knowledge of the industry.'' Although knowledge of foreign languages is a plus, it is not a prerequisite. One protocol officer is quoted as saying, ''At AT&T,

we're dealing with over 100 countries. You can rent language skills—interpreters, translators—if you need them.''

Gavin Anderson, chairman of Gavin Anderson & Company, which has several offices abroad, is an expert in international public relations. He writes:

> Practitioners of either global or international public relations are cultural interpreters. They must understand the business and general culture of both their clients (or employers) and the country or countries in which they hope to do business. Whether as an outside- or in-house consultant, the first task is to tell a U.S. company going abroad (or a foreign party coming to the United States) how to get things done. How does the market work? What are the business habits? What is the infrastructure? The consultant also needs to understand how things work in the host country, to recognize what will need translation and adaptation. . . .
>
> The field needs practitioners with an interest in and knowledge of foreign cultures on top of top-notch public relations skills. They need a good sense of working environments, and while they may not have answers for every country, they should know what questions to ask and where to get the information needed. They need to know where the potential dangers are, so as to not replenish the business bloopers book.

The decision to seek an international career should be made during the early academic years, so a student can take multiple courses in international relations, global marketing techniques, the basics of strategic public relations planning, foreign languages, social and economic geography, and crosscultural communication. Graduate study is an asset. Many students serve internships with international corporations as a desirable starting point.

Taking the U.S. Foreign Service Officers' examination is the first requirement for international government careers. Foreign service work with the innumerable federal agencies often requires a substantial period of government, mass media, or public relations service in this country before foreign assignments are made.

INTERNATIONAL CRISIS COMMUNICATIONS

Union Carbide faced an international public relations nightmare in December of 1984, when a tragic gas leak at its plant in Bhopal, India, resulted in the almost immediate deaths of more than 2,500 of an estimated half-million people in the affected area, caused another 50,000 or more to be treated, and brought lingering illness for lung damage and other complications from chemical poisoning to tens of thousand others. By 1990 the death toll exceeded 3,600.

This was the worst industrial disaster in history. *Time* magazine reported, ''There is no way to put a price tag on the damage done to Union Carbide's image in 38 countries, from Nigeria to New Zealand, where it has factories, and the 130 nations in which it sells products.''

But Union Carbide was able to generate a level of public respect in the days immediately following the disaster by implementing a crisis communication plan that portrayed genuine company concern for the victims.

The corporation chairman, Warren M. Anderson, flew to India within hours of the accident. Serving as the company's chief spokesperson on the disaster, he made himself available to hundreds of reporters clamoring for information. Reporters were impressed with his open manner and found him believable when he said the disaster was Union Carbide's ''highest priority.''

To back up his statements, Anderson pledged $1 million in immediate relief funds for victims and their families. In addition, he offered a team of technical experts to the Indian government probing the disaster and volunteered to close the company's methyl isocyanate plants around the world. Operations at a similar plant in West Virginia were immediately suspended until the cause of the gas leak was determined.

Contributing to Union Carbide's credibility in the crisis was the company's reputation for safety concerns. The *Wall Street Journal,* for example, reported, "A study by the not-for-profit Council on Economic Priorities, which monitors corporate activities, rated Union Carbide first among the nation's eight largest chemical concerns in compliance with Occupational Safety and Health Administration standards between 1972 and 1979." Other third-party testimonials in the press also referred to Union Carbide's voluntary efforts to make its plants safer and less polluting than legislation required.

All this activity—quick action, genuine concern, openness with the press, Anderson as a central spokesperson, and the company's record of corporate responsibility—illustrated the basic concepts of effective crisis communications on an international level.

Union Carbide's legal and public relations problems in India, however, were just beginning. The Indian government filed suit for victims' compensation in the United States, but a federal judge in 1986 refused to accept the case, saying that India was the proper site for the trial. In 1989 the Indian Supreme Court ordered Union Carbide to pay $470 million to the government for relief for the victims.

The settlement was negotiated by Union Carbide and the government of Prime Minister Rajiv Gandhi. Contentions that the sum was inadequate helped Gandhi's opponent, V. P. Singh, defeat the prime minister in his November, 1989, re-election bid.

The new government began distributing $210 million of the award in the form of individual payments of $12 per month for three years. The remaining $260 million was to be distributed only after India's Supreme Court ruled on motions by the government and victims' advocates to overturn the settlement in the hope of winning a larger one.

AUSTRALIA INVITES THE WORLD TO EXPO

Australia may be "down under" for most of the world, but thousands of visitors, including more than 5000 media representatives from 20 nations, found their way to Brisbane for World Expo 88, thanks to a full-blown public relations and marketing campaign.

Planning Several years in advance, the organizing committee established a communications division to create national and international awareness and anticipation of the exposition. Its departments—community relations, information services, media relations, media operations, entertainment publicity, and promotions—worked up a comprehensive program.

Execution *Media Alert,* a press kit and media guide, was prepared, and the Australian media were invited to a series of briefings before Expo opened.

A full-staffed media center was created. It included a briefing auditorium, photo darkroom, broadcast facilities, telex machines, phone banks, and computers.

Publications. Specialized magazines, brochures, and newsletters included:

- *Expo Down Under*—sent monthly to the media, travel industry, and national and international corporations

- *Travel Industry Update*—distributed to national and international travel people. Targeted were travel agents, recipients also of a six-page brochure printed in six languages and a brochure called a ''travel shell,'' on two blank pages of which the agents could work up their own tour packages.
- A newsletter for Australian school children, encouraging group travel
- *Neighborhood Update*—a community newsletter advising area residents about logistics and how Expo organizers were working to assure that local neighborhoods would suffer a minimum of disruption

In addition, feature stories and photos were distributed to in-flight magazines and Australian civic club publications.

Video. A 10-minute promotional video briefed media representatives and accompanied talks about Expo to service clubs throughout the country. For the foreign market: four-minute videos in Japanese, French, and German.

Direct marketing. Australians were invited to nominate friends and relatives abroad to compete for free trips to Expo. The approximately 125,000 names and addresses submitted produced a mailing list for Expo promotional materials.

Results The 5000 media representatives from 20 countries included a contingent of 293 reporters and photographers from Japan, accompanying Japan's Prime Minister Noboru Takeshita. Other large media delegations accompanied King Juan Carlos of Spain and Prime Minister Margeret Thatcher of England. Interpreters were provided.

The Expo staff compiled approximately 22,000 newspaper and magazine clippings from around the world and received reports of about 2,000 television and 3,000 radio stories.

World Expo 88 showcased Australia and served as the catalyst for a record year of international visitors.

CASE STUDY: CHINA—A PUBLIC RELATIONS SUCCESS STORY

An international soft-drinks manufacturer turned to Hill & Knowlton Asia Ltd. to handle and publicize events marking the opening of its second bottling plant in China and a six-day tour of that country by the company's international board of directors. The activities took place before the prodemocracy uprisings in 1989 disrupted much outside business involvement in the country.

Hill & Knowlton staff members in Hong Kong and Beijing researched and prepared an extensive briefing booklet for the directors, senior executives, and their spouses. The booklet included daily agendas, biographies of key guests, current events, history, cultural pointers, and economic briefs on the five cities to be visited. The more than 30 production items included glossy bilingual brochures, banquet invitations, bus banners, and gift items such as calligraphy books, lapel pins, and bottle-opener pens.

A satellite feed was arranged from Guangzhou, site of the plant opening, for broadcast to key media in Asia, Europe, South America, and the United States. Invitations to local media were dispatched, and 19 journalists from Hong Kong's leading

A COMMUNITY RELATIONS LESSON IN PAPUA NEW GUINEA

Poor community relations by an international company in a host nation can mean a major financial loss and even the closing of a plant, as BCL Industries of Australia sadly learned.

BCL had operated an open-pit copper mine on the island of Bougainville, in the North Solomon group off the coast of Papua New Guinea, since the 1970s. It had to close the mine in 1989, however, after local residents mounted a virtual rebellion against the company and its partner, the country's government.

The dispute flared over the belief of local landowners that they were not receiving a fair share of royalties from the mine and that the government was not doing enough to improve living conditions. BCL fueled the fire by violating several tenets of effective community relations:

- The company bypassed the community by hiring two-thirds of its employees from other parts of the island.
- It refused to meet with newly formed activist groups representing the disgruntled local residents. Reported the *Far Eastern Economic Review:* "Early hostility among the island people was ignored. And when the need to communicate was realized, efforts were bedeviled by placing liaison officers in the local community, leading to accusations of 'spying.'"
- The company failed actively to encourage its expatriate employees, mostly Australian, to blend in with the local community. The expatriates lived in their own company compounds, and their attitude, according to the publication, was "unashamedly 'colonial,' with a great deal of emphasis on a closed social circle devoted to sport, food, drink, and good times." "Ironically," the article continued, "the expatriates are very inclined to sneer that [Papua New Guinea] people cannot hold their beer and often land in jail on pay day, while simultaneously boasting of their own monumental drinking sprees and gross behavior."

The rebellion cost the lives of 20 people and forced BCL to close the mine. The closure wiped out the company's annual revenue of about $10 million as well as 45 percent of Papua New Guinea's exports, representing 17 percent of the country's total revenues.

The outcome was an expensive lesson to the company in how *not* to conduct community relations.

English and Chinese media, including an Associated Press photojournalist with portable transmission equipment, were flown to Guangzhou for the major press conference and other activities.

Hill & Knowlton drafted, edited, and translated more than 17 speeches and releases, issued simultaneously during the six-day period throughout Hong Kong, China, and the United States. A comprehensive bilingual press kit, including lead releases, backgrounders, speeches, and photos, was prepared for each of the five cities visited.

Advance teams of bilingual executives ensured that all media, banqueting, and logistical arrangements were set before arrival of the board, which included directors who also represented five of the world's top corporations.

More than 100 stories were published by newspapers and magazines in Hong Kong and Beijing alone, including dailies with circulations exceeding 2.5 million. CCTV, the leading television station in China, broadcast a two-minute clip reaching an estimated 200 million viewers. Radio Beijing, on both its Chinese and English channels, aired a two-minute report heard by an estimated 80 percent of its 800 million listeners.

Hill & Knowlton's expertise and experience in government affairs resulted in confirmed attendance at the client-hosted banquets by top government officials, a feat reportedly unheard of in China. Even Premier Zhao Ziyang participated, delivering a major policy statement during a meeting with the board members. He reaffirmed the commitment of the People's Republic of China to its "open door" policy to foreign investment and continued commitment to expanding the soft-drink industry.

With the help of the New York office of Hill & Knowlton, the satellite feed was transmitted to major stations on four other continents. From Hong Kong, news clips were sent to major broadcast stations throughout Asia.

Major U.S. newspapers covered the events, and *Fortune* magazine ran a four-page exclusive story in its national and international editions about the bus tour.

In terms of both business advancement and public exposure, the client rated the project a resounding success and established an ongoing public relations program through Hill & Knowlton's Hong Kong and Beijing offices.

CASE STUDY: A 90-COUNTRY CAMPAIGN—THE DALKON SHIELD STORY

By court order the A. H. Robins Company had *only six weeks* in which to notify users of its Dalkon Shield contraceptive device *in 90 countries,* by public relations means alone, that claims of infection-related deaths and other health problems allegedly associated with the device had to be filed by a certain date.

After four years of worldwide distribution, the company had withdrawn the device in 1974. Numerous lawsuits followed. A decade later there was concern that some women were still using it, so Robins conducted a national campaign to urge women with the device to have it removed.

The financial strain of continuing litigation, however, forced Robins to file for reorganization under Chapter 11 of the U.S. Bankruptcy Code. In November 1985, the federal judge in the case set April 3, 1986, as the date after which no further claims could be filed. Declaring that advertising would be too expensive, the judge ordered that a public relations program be designed and executed in all countries where the 4.5 million devices had been distributed. The notification program, he said, had to be completed by January 31, 1986.

Robins conducted an informational campaign in the United States during January 1986. The company then asked Burson-Marsteller to design and execute a public relations program in the 90 other countries—the largest such targeted problem in history.

Strategy/Research Working with the Robins staff, Burson-Marsteller decided to reach as many people as possible through a simultaneous, multiple-tiered notification program directed at the media, medical associations, and health officials. Each of the audiences would receive special packets of explanatory materials written in local official languages. Press conferences were planned in 16 cities regarded as international media centers, from which the message could be spread.

Planning The 90 countries were divided among 29 Burson-Marsteller offices and affiliates. The Washington, D.C., office coordinated and monitored the planning, which included preparation of a news release, background document, letter to U.S. ambassadors, letter to medical organizations, and print and broadcast public service announcements (PSAs). The Berlitz Translation Services translated materials into 29 languages, and the New Zealand affiliate later translated them into four languages used in the southern Pacific islands. Nine Robins officials were trained during a two-day session to serve as spokespersons.

Execution Each Burson-Marsteller field office compiled targeted media, medical, and other lists, made dialectal adjustments to the translated materials, distributed the information, arranged press conferences, and prepared to document contacts.

Obstacles that had to be overcome included (1) accomplishing everything within six weeks, including religious holidays; (2) censorship and intervention by some countries; (3) documentation in countries where no such services existed; and (4) international politics (for example, the Bahrain office could not work in Israel, and the Robins spokesperson in South Africa could not attend a press conference in Nigeria).

Evaluation The program generated worldwide coverage: 352 reporters attended the 16 press conferences; more than 4800 news media outlets received the information directly; 570 medical organizations, 447 Planned Parenthood organizations, and more than 7000 other groups received the materials; more than 2000 news clippings were obtained; and 300 instances of broadcast coverage were documented.

In all, more than 25,000 potential claims were filed from foreign countries, far more than the court had anticipated. The judge proclaimed the effort an overwhelming success. And Burson-Marsteller completed the assignment $200,000 below its allocated $1 million budget.

By March 1990, nearly 100,000 women had been notified of their options for collecting from a $2.4 billion trust fund set aside as compensation. The almost-two-decade dispute neared an end.

CASE STUDY: THE NESTLÉ INFANT FORMULA CONTROVERSY

Successive public relations campaigns have become a way of life for Nestlé, S.A. Until the late 1970s the Swiss conglomerate ''had virtually no public relations programs and felt no need for anything resembling issues management,'' a company official said.

Since then activists have conducted a seven-year boycott of the company's products sparked by its infant-formula-marketing practices in Third World countries. The boycott ended in 1984 but was renewed in 1989. In that same year attorneys general in three states began investigating whether the marketing and advertising of Good Start H.A., a new infant formula made by Nestlé's Carnation unit, were deceptive.

Nestlé learned its damage control lessons the hard way. Fighting accusations in the early 1970s that "thousands of babies in Third World countries have died or suffered malnutrition" because of its marketing and publicity practices, Nestlé at first treated the matter as a nutrition issue. That defense was dismissed as self-serving and simply not to be believed. Then Nestlé made the mistake of suing a Swiss activist group for libel. The prolonged trial was a public relations disaster that led directly to the first boycott.

Church and charitable groups, concerned scientists, consumer advocates, labor organizations, leftist activists, and other groups were drawn into the boycott, initiated by the Minnesota-based Infant Formula Action Coalition (INFACT).

The scientific case against Nestlé and other infant formula companies (although Nestlé was the sole target of the boycott) was based on five major assumptions, according to Carol Adelman, writing in the *Policy Review* publication of the Heritage Foundation:

> (1) There had been a dramatic decline in breastfeeding in developing countries: (2) bottlefed infants came largely from the poorest families in developing countries; (3) bottlefed babies in both developing and developed countries had higher disease and death rates than those breastfed; (4) mother's milk was the "perfect" food; and finally (5) corporate promotional practices contributed significantly to a mother's decision to bottlefeed.

None of these assumptions had been proved, but emotions ran high as INFACT supporters angrily charged that Nestlé's publicity and advertising tactics were causing infant malnutrition and disease from nonsterile bottle-feeding. Activists joined in the wave of Third World protests against transnational corporations and the institution of advertising itself.

Stunned by the highly organized protests, Nestlé in 1980 hired Rafael D. Pagan, Jr., to formulate a public relations campaign to resolve the dispute. Pagan embarked upon what he termed a *social action management* program designed, as he put it, "to listen with political antennae to the concerns of others . . . to bridge the gap between opposing perceptions involving the corporation and the public." The following steps were taken:

1. The issues were defined and a diagnosis made of the nature of the criticizing groups—"ideologues . . . trendy clergy and lay persons . . . and [those] who were sincerely and morally concerned regarding the problems of poverty and hunger," according to Pagan.

2. A strategy was developed to deal with perceptions, not with facts alone, in the highly emotional environment. "Bold new approaches and flexibility were required to seize the initiative," Pagan told the Public Relations Society of America at a national conference. "High levels of risk in terms of market share losses and a high corporate visibility had to be accepted by management."

3. A decision was made to ''stick to the issue'' at all costs and ''not be distracted by the obviously preposterous claims of some critics''—essential to avoid counterproductive confrontation.

4. The social base of the controversy was expanded. ''A good number of highly credible church leaders, scientists and opinion makers, who were not in agreement with the critics' questionable tactics and arguments, had remained silent for too long. They now had to be encouraged to speak out.''

Two key decisions helped shift the initiative to Nestlé:

1. The company organized the Nestlé Coordination Center for Nutrition, Inc., with Pagan as president. The aim was to focus Nestlé's activities ''on the positive task of performing its nutrition work so as to benefit the mothers and babies of the world—especially the Third World. . . . ''

2. In addition to steps previously taken to change its marketing policy, Nestlé in 1981 accepted the aims of the World Health Organization's recommended Code of Marketing Breastmilk Substitutes. Detailed instructions enforcing the code were sent to all field managers.

In order to gain complete credibility, the company created an independent audit commission, with former U.S. Secretary of State Edmund Muskie as chairman. The commission met with successive groups of critics and dispatched members to countries throughout the world to monitor Nestlé's implementation of the code and to suggest changes in practices on the basis of new interpretations of the code provisions.

In 1982 the American Federation of Teachers recommended withdrawal from the boycott. Several months later the National Council of the United Methodist Church recommended that in light of Nestlé's changed attitudes and actions, the church not join the boycott and that Methodist units already involved discontinue their activity. Several other groups reached the same conclusion. All except hard-line activists, it seemed, were being won over.

''We discovered that because business is viewed as aloof, smug, and happiest when left alone to make money,'' Pagan said, ''people are willing to believe the most ridiculous charges against us.

''But once we became aware of the world around us and opened up to human political give-and-take, we were listened to. More important, we were ourselves changed by the process, and we feel better off for it.''

The first boycott ended when the International Nestlé Boycott Commission cited Nestlé's progress in adopting standards of the World Health Organization Code of Marketing Breastmilk Substitutes and called on member organizations to cease activities.

But the issue of marketing infant formula in the Third World did not go away. Five years later, opponents began a second boycott, claiming that Nestlé had not done enough and that problems still existed. The company retained Ogilvy and Mather Public Relations, which recommended a major campaign to improve Nestlé's image. This was rejected. Instead, Nestlé pursued a less aggressive information campaign to explain how it was conforming to standards set by the World Health Organization.

By early 1991, however, protracted criticism by various public interest groups and pressure from Nestlé's independent infant-formula audit commission caused the company to announce a new policy. It committed Nestlé to stop providing free or low-cost formula in developing nations "except for the limited number of infants who need it."

Nestlé had been providing formula to Third World hospitals on a request basis. Over the next several years, according to the *Wall Street Journal*, "the company intends to halt virtually all such supplies and to help government officials define the infants who are truly at risk if the free formula is discontinued."

Nestlé had learned an important public relations lesson: company performance speaks louder than words.

CASE PROBLEM

As part of the liberalization of Eastern Europe, Czechoslovakia is now a republic with a freely elected government. To improve the country's economy, the Czech Tourist Agency wants to promote Prague as the premier tourist destination in Eastern Europe for foreign tourists.

Czechoslovakia has many features to recommend it. Much of the country was spared extensive bombing during World War II, and it has ancient castles, buildings, and medieval churches that are among the finest in Europe. Prague, the capital, is a particularly beautiful city with Old World charm. Food and lodging are relatively inexpensive, in comparison to costs in other European capitals.

Your public relations firm is retained by the Czech Tourist Agency to attract American tourists. What are your recommendations regarding (1) specific audiences to be reached, (2) key themes that should be emphasized, and (3) the publicity and promotional techniques that would be used?

QUESTIONS FOR REVIEW AND DISCUSSION

1. What is meant by international public relations? What are some of the reasons for its growth in recent decades?

2. Organizationally, in what several ways do public relations firms operate internationally?

3. What are some of the difficulties that a corporation is likely to encounter when it conducts business in another country? Enumerate some of the pitfalls that may await its public relations, advertising, and marketing personnel in such enterprises. How may these be partially or fully overcome?

4. What public information activities on an international scale does the U.S. government conduct?

5. Name three reasons why the United States and many other countries engage in short-wave broadcasting.

6. List some examples of how the Soviet government has used public relations and advertising under its new policy of openness.

7. List several objectives that foreign governments may have in conducting public relations programs in the United States. How do they seek to achieve their goals? What legal steps are required?

8. What problems did Burson-Marsteller encounter in informing Dalkon Shield users and former users in 90 countries about the deadline for filing claims?

9. Enumerate the steps taken by Hill & Knowlton to publicize the opening of a soft-drink bottling plant in China.

10. How did Australia attract thousands of visitors and obtain international publicity for its World Expo 88?

SUGGESTED READINGS

Anderson, Gavin. "A Global Look at Public Relations." *Experts in Action,* edited by Bill Cantor. New York: Longman, 1989, pp. 412–422.

Baldwin, William H. "As the World Turns." *Public Relations Journal,* March 1987, pp. 12–13. Public relations at the United Nations.

Carr, Steve. "How to Deal With the Japanese Media." *Public Relations Journal,* January 1989, pp. 27–28.

"Crackdown in China Stalls Growth of Budding Public Relations Business." *Public Relations Journal,* September 1989, pp. 7–8.

Crockett, Eddie. "A Single Europe: So Far and Yet So Near." *Communication World,* May–June 1990, pp. 123–128. Profile of the European Community.

Cutlip, Scott. "Pioneering Public Relations for Foreign Governments." *Public Relations Review,* Spring 1987, pp. 13–34.

Farinelli, Jean L. "Needed: A New U.S. Perspective on Global Public Relations." *Public Relations Journal,* November 1990, pp. 18–19, 42.

Fry, Susan L. "How to Succeed in the New Europe." *Public Relations Journal,* January 1991, pp. 17–21.

Gargan, Edward A. "Chinese Propaganda Turns Black into White: Seeing Is Not Believing." *Far Eastern Economic Review,* July 13, 1989, pp. 57–58. Propaganda efforts of the Chinese government after the Tiananmen Square massacre.

Halmos, Tony. "Campaign Aims to End Hong Kong Brain Drain." *Communication World,* September 1990, pp. 14–15.

Lindheim, James B. "1992: Meeting the Communication Challenge." *Communication World,* July–August 1990, pp. 35–39. Public relations in the European Community.

Lipman, Joanne. "Pravda Opens Party's Pages to U.S. Firms." *Wall Street Journal,* May 17, 1990, p. B1.

Liss, Richard. "How Do You Develop Pan-European Communication?" *Communication World,* August 1990, pp. 18–20.

Malik, Michael. "Island Insurrection." *Far Eastern Economic Review,* August 3, 1989, pp. 20–22. Community relations problems for a mining company on the island of Bougainville in the South Pacific.

McIntyre, David J. "When YOUR National Language Is Just Another Language." *Communication World,* May 1991, pp. 18–21. The value of foreign language training.

Pound, Edward T. "Zaire's Mobutu Mounts All-Out PR Campaign to Keep His U.S. Aid." *Wall Street Journal,* March 7, 1990, p. 1, A20.

Reed, John M. "International Media Relations: Avoid Self-Blinding." *Public Relations Quarterly,* Summer 1989, pp. 12–15.

Zaretsky, Gregory. "What's New in Machine Translation?" *Communication World,* August 1990, pp. 31–34. Use of translation services to reach foreign audiences.

CHAPTER

17

Membership Organizations

Corporations often pursue their goals not only individually but in groups called *trade associations*. Similarly, workers band together in labor unions; doctors, lawyers, and so on form professional societies; and business firms within cities join forces in chambers of commerce. Although their membership may be diverse, these organizations have in common the fact that they spend a high percentage of their budgets on public relations and communications.

Indeed, communications—to create unity of action—is the principal purpose for which most of these groups are established. They circulate and share information among their members, speak for them in public forums, educate the public about their members' work, and seek to influence government policies and legislation.

These associations legally are nonprofit organizations. They differ from most nonprofit bodies, however, because they seek to enhance the financial well-being of their members, whether they be individuals or companies.

Activist environmental groups constitute a different type of membership organization. Their goal of saving the environment from the ravages of exploitation often puts them in conflict with corporations and trade associations.

This chapter will examine how the various types of membership organizations function and the ways in which they use public relations methods.

TRADE ASSOCIATIONS

At last count, there were about 6000 trade and professional associations in the United States. Because federal laws and regulations often can affect the fortunes of an entire

industry, about one-third of these groups are based in the Washington, D.C., area. There, association staffs can monitor congressional activity, lobby for or against legislation, communicate late-breaking developments to the membership, and see government officials on a regular basis.

The membership of a trade association usually consists of manufacturers, wholesalers, retailers, or distributors in the same field. The following is a sampling of trade groups:

- Chocolate Manufacturers Association
- Edison Electric Institute (utilities)
- National Association of Manufacturers
- American Newspaper Publishers Association
- American Hotel & Motel Association
- Direct Marketing Association
- American Quarter Horse Association
- National Shoe Retailers Association
- Printing Industries of America

Although individual members may be direct rivals in the marketplace, they work together to promote the entire industry, generate public support and share information of general interest to the entire membership.

A TYPICAL PROGRAM

To understand how a trade association uses public relations, let us examine the program of a group representing the plastics industry, the Council for Solid Waste Solutions.

Like similar bodies, the council is financed by assessments and dues from companies in the plastics industry. It has a board of directors and a paid staff, and uses the services of a public relations firm. The council's primary objective is to create a political climate conducive to the marketing of plastic products.

The plastics industry has been under attack by consumer and environmental groups because plastic containers and products contribute to solid waste and are not biodegradable. In order to head off possible legislation, the council was formed to find effective, long-term solutions to the solid waste management headache. The plastics industry sought to position itself as committed to producing recyclable products.

The council's objective was to become an information/educational resource available to waste management policy-makers and influential people. Its 36-page booklet *The Solid Waste Problem: No Single Cause, No Single Solution* traces the history of American waste management practices. Factsheets were developed on topics relating to plastics, and an advertorial (combined advertising and editorial) insert, *The Urgent Need to Recycle,* appeared in such magazines as *Time*. Direct mailings to elected officials introduced the council and its programs. A conference of policy-makers discussed the problems of solid waste management.

Survey data later showed that more than a third of the opinion leaders perceived the plastics industry to be committed to producing recyclable products, up from about 20 percent before the program.

A VARIETY OF APPROACHES

Trade associations communicate to the public in a number of ways. One is the preparation of news stories and features for newspapers. Thus, the Air Conditioning and Refrigeration Institute prepares consumer tips on how to use an air conditioner economically in the home, while the Distilled Spirits Council of the U.S. distributes a recipe for cheese fondue that calls for two ounces of Scotch or bourbon. The catfish industry promotes itself with the Catfish Institute and such activities as crowning a Miss Catfish at its annual World Catfish Festival in Mississippi. Recently it held a luncheon at the United Nations in New York to introduce metropolitan tastebuds to the fish.

Trade groups of food growers are particularly adept at getting information in the food sections of newspapers and magazines. They send to editors a steady stream of recipes, features, and photographs of products arranged in mouth-watering servings. Typical is the following, published in a newspaper food section:

> Men and women in their sixties and seventies need about one-third less calories than they did in their twenties. However, the need for nutrients apparently does not decline but may actually increase. The National Broiler Council notes that chicken is an ideal protein source for the elderly because it contains fewer calories and has a lower fat content than most red meat. . . .

An extensive multimedia campaign was launched one year by the California Pistachio Commission. The purpose was to sell more nuts. Public relations activities included (1) production of a 7½-minute film for students in junior and senior high schools on how pistachio nuts are grown; (2) distribution of recipe books and articles about using pistachio nuts in salads, pasta, and microwave fudge; (3) dissemination of information to restaurant chains on use of the nut in menus; and (4) appearance of commission representatives on radio and television talk shows. The slogan for the campaign was "You can't say no to a Pistachio." Another slogan under consideration was "Pistachio: Not Just Another California Nut," but the commission thought it might be misinterpreted.

Another kind of public information campaign was launched by the National Institute of Infant Services, a rather grandiose name for a trade association of diaper-supply companies. After its business had been devastated by the highly advertised use of disposable plastic and paper diapers, the institute began a public relations campaign to bring young parents back to using professionally laundered cotton diapers.

The institute's approach was to employ a child-care writer to prepare recorded radio spots and newspaper columns in which the virtues of the reusable diaper are emphasized. The writer talked about such problems as comforting a teething child and hiring babysitters, while working in her suggestions about diapers. Newspapers and radio stations used these advice items without charge. The writer also prepared a booklet,

"The ABCs of Diaper Rash," distributed by members of the trade association. As a result of this campaign, the companies stopped the trend toward exclusive use of disposable diapers and increased their own business.

Makers of cloth diapers have also gained ground competitively by depicting disposable plastic diapers as an environmental hazard that clutters trash landfills. Disposable diaper companies retorted that their rivals exaggerated, because used throw-away diapers constitute only about one percent of trash in landfills. What's more, they told the press, washing diapers uses scarce water. Numerous states are considering bans or taxes on disposable diapers, urged on by cloth diaper manufacturers.

Other trade groups may spend the bulk of their money on advertising campaigns. To combat the perception that the chemical industry is an air polluter, the Chemical Manufacturers Association prepared a full-page magazine advertisement dominated by the photograph of a young man holding his small daughter in a swing. The headline stated, "I'm a chemical industry engineer in charge of my plant's air quality. We breathe that air. You can be sure I keep it clean."

Even the American Association of Advertising Agencies used an advertising campaign to debunk myths about its business after surveys found that 70 percent of the public said that they distrust advertising. One ad, attacking the claim that advertising uses subtle sexual messages to plant ideas in the consumers' subconscious, showed a glass of ice cubes with the headline: "People have been trying to find breasts in these ice cubes since 1957." Figure 17.1 shows an organization's poster aimed at college audiences.

WORKING TO REPEAL A LAW

So far, this discussion has focused on the way trade groups publicize services and products. A vivid example of how trade associations can rally public opinion and influence legislation occurred when the American Bankers Association and the U.S. League of Savings Institutions led a campaign to repeal the federal law requiring financial institutions to withhold 10 pecent of interest and dividend payments made to their investors.

The money withheld would go into the federal treasury as advance payments on the investors' annual income tax. The law was designed to catch cheaters who failed to report dividend and interest income on their returns. An estimated 400 million interest-bearing accounts exist in the United States, most of which would be affected by the withholding law.

The banks and other financial institutions disliked the law because it required additional paperwork for them, and they would lose use of money that ordinarily would stay on account until tax time. Consequently, banks and savings and loans, traditionally strong competitors, banded together through their national trade groups, to seek repeal of the law.

The American Bankers Association provided members with protest postcards and form letters demanding repeal, for their customers to send to Congress. Form letters-to-the-editor also were distributed. In addition, the association supplied a series of advertisements that member banks could place over their own signatures in local newspapers. The headline on one of these advertisements read:

CONGRESS WANTS A PIECE OF YOUR SAVINGS; WHAT THEY NEED IS A PIECE OF YOUR MIND

FIGURE 17.1
A college fraternity, Pi Kappa Phi, created this poster featuring the classic *Rape of the Sabine Women* as a contribution to the campaign against a campus social problem. (Courtesy Pi Kappa Phi.)

The impact of the campaign on Congress was potent. More than 11 million protest letters and postcards deluged Capitol Hill. The same Congress that had passed the law succumbed to the pressure and repealed it a year later. Leaders of the campaign believed that their efforts drew such a huge response because the law hit a raw public nerve—that citizens hated to give the government 10 percent of their investment income months before the annual April 15 tax deadline. This was an instance in which individual self-interest coincided with an industry's self-interest. (Letter-writing campaigns are also discussed in Chapter 15.)

Soon after this success, the U.S. League of Savings Institutions was confronted with a critical public relations problem when the savings and loan industry scandals broke in the early 1990s. The fact that waste, fraud, and unwise investments by some institutions will cost taxpayers billions of dollars put the industry into an extremely defensive position.

A LOCAL CAMPAIGN

The city of Blooming Prairie, Minnesota—population 2500—was the site of a week-long demonstration of energy-saving, conducted by the Natural Gas Council of Minnesota in conjunction with the local Lions Club, supported by numerous other civic organizations.

By making a single community the focus of its conservation program, the Natural Gas Council dramatized the fact that a concerted campaign can reduce individual energy bills. The council is a nonprofit group composed of representatives from various investor-owned utility companies. Its sole purpose is energy conservation education. This effort was intended to show that the utility companies care for the public welfare and don't coax customers into using unnecessary gas.

By working with them on this money-saving community project, the Natural Gas Council sought to establish good long-range relationships with civic leaders as well as regional and state government officials.

Called "Less-Energy Days," the Blooming Prairie project was publicized by multiple stories in the local newspaper and by news releases to regional newspapers and television and radio stations, all prepared by the council. Articles described the various events and listed tips for saving energy.

Other methods used included the following:

- Formation of a local energy committee, through which a special publication on money-saving methods was issued and participation encouraged.
- Publication of endorsements from state and federal energy authorities, making local residents feel "special."
- Provision of free home energy audit services to residents and distribution of a home energy audit questionnaire.
- Construction of a large thermometer in the center of the city that indicated daily energy usage. This injected a competitive spirit into the week.
- Distribution of packets on energy-saving to the local schools for students to read.

Aided by local enthusiasm, the campaign achieved an 11.5 percent reduction in natural gas consumption and a 7.1 percent reduction in use of electricity. Blooming Prairie received the President's Award for Energy Efficiency, a national distinction that created pride in the community.

On another level, membership groups often cooperate with a manufacturer to educate and inform the public. The American Veterinary Medical Association (AVMA) cooperated with Merck & Co., makers of a pill to prevent heartworm disease in dogs. The company offered each chapter of AVMA a $5000 grant to generate heartworm awareness among pet owners, and gave veterinarians kits of publicity materials for distribution to local media.

As a result of a nationally coordinated campaign, conducted primarily at the local level, an additional three million dogs were tested and placed on preventive medication. The program increased the business of veterinarians and helped to cause a 27 percent increase in prescriptions for Merck & Co.'s product. This campaign, conducted by Ketchum Public Relations, generated 22 million print and broadcast impressions.—that is, the total circulation and listening audience of the print and broadcast media that used the firm's material.

LABOR UNIONS

Since the mid-1970s, labor unions in the United States have suffered serious losses in membership and consequently in political clout. A perception of unions as money-hungry, inflexible, lacking in concern for public interest, and at times arrogant created a severe image problem. Media coverage often showed union members in negative, adversarial positions that sometimes inconvenienced the public.

Today total union membership amounts to less than 17 percent of all American workers; the figure among private sector workers is only 12 percent, slightly less than half what it was in 1973.

Nevertheless, labor unions still are very much a part of the American scene, and they are using public relations tools in an attempt to regain strength and influence.

Shifts in American industry contributed to the unions' decline. So did several particularly unpopular strikes. Traditional heavy industry strongholds of unionism have suffered severe reductions in employment, while nonunionized fields have enlarged their work forces. In addition, the unions' problems were increased by the strong antiunion attitude of the Reagan administration and by cutbacks in union workforces by some corporations during the flurry of acquisitions and mergers in the 1980s. Thus the unions must try to increase their appeal among white-collar workers and those in light industry.

Recognizing this challenge, the AFL-CIO in 1988 began a two-year, $13 million advertising and public relations campaign built around television commercials starring Jack Lemmon. The theme was ''UNION, YES!'' Union leaders, whose relations with the media often have been chilly, have sought to improve them. Several unions began formal training programs on media practices. Two large unions in particular—the Communications Workers of America and the United Steelworkers of America—showed a creative flair with videos, television spots, and other techniques used by corporations.

Like corporations, union managements need to employ public relations extensively with their internal audiences. They must keep their memberships informed about what they receive in return for their dues, including social and recreational programs and the representation to company management the union leadership supplies. As a whole, the unions' internal public relations have been more effective than their external relations.

It is too early to tell if increased communication activity will help solve the challenges facing labor unions today. Public relations and advertising campaigns can focus the spotlight on the positive functions that unions are undertaking, but real success will depend on how the public perceives the various messages and how the unions are able to reconceptualize themselves in the coming years.

PROFESSIONAL ASSOCIATIONS

Members of a profession or skilled craft organize for mutual benefit. In many ways, their goals resemble those of labor unions in that they seek improved earning power, better working conditions, and public acceptance of their role in society. Unlike their labor union counterparts, however, members of professional organizations place emphasis on setting standards for professional performance, establishing codes of ethics, determining requirements for admission to the field, and encouraging members to upgrade skills through continuing education.

In some cases, professional organizations have quasilegal power to license and censure members. This is true of organizations such as the American Medical Association and the American Bar Association. In most cases, however, professional groups use the techniques of peer pressure and persuasion to police the particular profession or skilled craft.

In general, professional associations are national in scope with district, state, or local chapters. Many scientific and scholarly associations, however, are international, with chapters in many nations. A good example is the International Communication Association (ICA), a group of academics and communication experts. Another is the International Communications Executives Association. There is even an international association of executives who specialize in managing trade groups and professional societies.

Organizations such as the Public Relations Society of America and the International Association of Business Communicators are classified as professional associations. Here is a sampling of other organizations:

- Society of Automotive Engineers
- American Library Association
- American Nuclear Society
- American Public Health Association
- National Association of Life Underwriters
- American Surgical Association

Public relations specialists for these organizations use the same techniques as their colleagues in other branches of practice. They address both internal and external audi-

FIGURE 17.2
This sampling of logos indicates the wide range of national trade, professional, and membership organizations that cultivate public support for their products and causes. (Logos courtesy of the organizations shown. The Seal of Cotton is a registered trademark/service mark of Cotton Incorporated.)

ences through a variety of communication tools, including newsletters, brochures, videotapes, slide presentations, radio and television spots, news releases, and direct mail packets.

Like their counterparts in trade groups and labor unions, professional associations are responsible for monitoring legislation that may affect the status or earning power of members. Many professional associations maintain a Washington office or one in the state capital and employ lobbyists to advocate positions. One of the most politically active groups is the American Medical Association.

Public service is the hallmark of many professional associations, and a number of programs make pertinent information available to the public. The Philadelphia Bar Association, for example, offers Dial-Law, which answers common legal questions over the telephone with taped messages on more than 70 topics. It informs callers about the association's Lawyer Referral and Information Service. More than 30,000 calls a

MEDICAL JOURNAL APOLOGIZES

Maintaining good relations with the news media is a basic policy for professional associations. Forgetting that principle, the *Journal of the American Medical Association* tried to punish the Miami *Herald* for allegedly violating a release date. After months of wrangling and bad publicity, the medical journal had to issue a public apology.

The *Herald* carried a story by its science editor about an AIDS study two days before the AMA *Journal* published a report on the same study. Advance copies of the medical journal containing a detailed release date had been mailed to newspapers, including the *Herald*. The medical association angrily issued a news release charging the newspaper with bad faith. The *Herald* writer said that he had obtained a copy of the AIDS study through his own sources weeks before the *Journal* article appeared and that he had been out of the state when the advance copy arrived.

To punish the newspaper, the AMA dropped the *Herald* from its mailing list and canceled the newspaper's subscriptions to the *Journal* and other specialty medical magazines.

The newspaper, vehemently denying the accusation, retaliated by obtaining advance copies of the *Journal* from another source each week and publishing stories from it several days before the release date.

After four months, the AMA yielded to the newspaper's demand and apologized in a news release for its charges. The public relations lesson is clear: *Be cautious about publicly condemning a media outlet, and be absolutely certain of your facts before doing so.*

year are received. To publicize the service, the bar association prepared radio and television announcements featuring Joseph A. Wapner, a white-haired retired judge widely known to viewers for his judicial role on ''The People's Court.'' The number of annual calls doubled when the Wapner announcments were aired. Several other local bar associations have produced simple brochures on how to write a will, establish a trust fund, or file a grievance in small claims court. A number of local medical societies also offer advice and referral by phone.

Both the Public Relations Society of America and the International Association of Business Communicators maintain a reference library available to the public or to answer queries by telephone. Another method of public service is a speakers' bureau directory, listing members willing to talk at meetings of civic and business groups. Such a directory was published, for instance, by the Society of Die Casting Engineers. The Scientists' Institute for Public Information has a toll-free referral service; journalists who dial it are given names of scientists from among the 20,000 experts on call who will answer the journalists' particular questions. Figure 17.3 shows one way the American Dental Association promotes good dental practices.

Public relations activity on behalf of individual professionals is a relatively new development. Traditionally, lawyers and medical doctors did not advertise or seek to publicize themselves in any way. The taboo arose in part from the rules and regulations of the professional societies. Until recently, many medical societies prohibited their members from hiring public relations firms. The Supreme Court, in several cases, however, said that such regulations infringed on free speech. And the Federal Trade

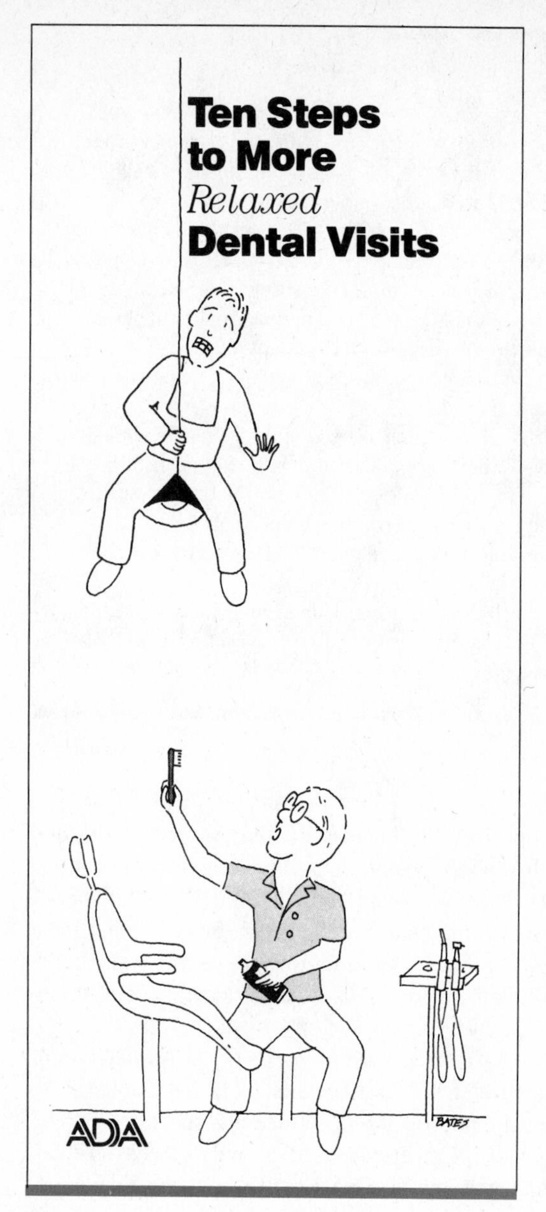

FIGURE 17.3
Clever graphics draw attention to an American Dental Association publication that urges readers to practice good dental care. (Compliments of the American Dental Association.)

Commission ruled in 1980 that the American Medical Association couldn't tell its members not to advertise.

Many attorneys and physicians still feel uncomfortable about advertising their services, but competition for clients and patients is breaking down the traditional taboos. A survey by *Attorneys Marketing Report,* for example, shows the majority of lawyers using Yellow Pages advertising. In descending order of frequency, they also use (1) entertainment of clients, (2) brochures, (3) seminars, and (4) newsletters.

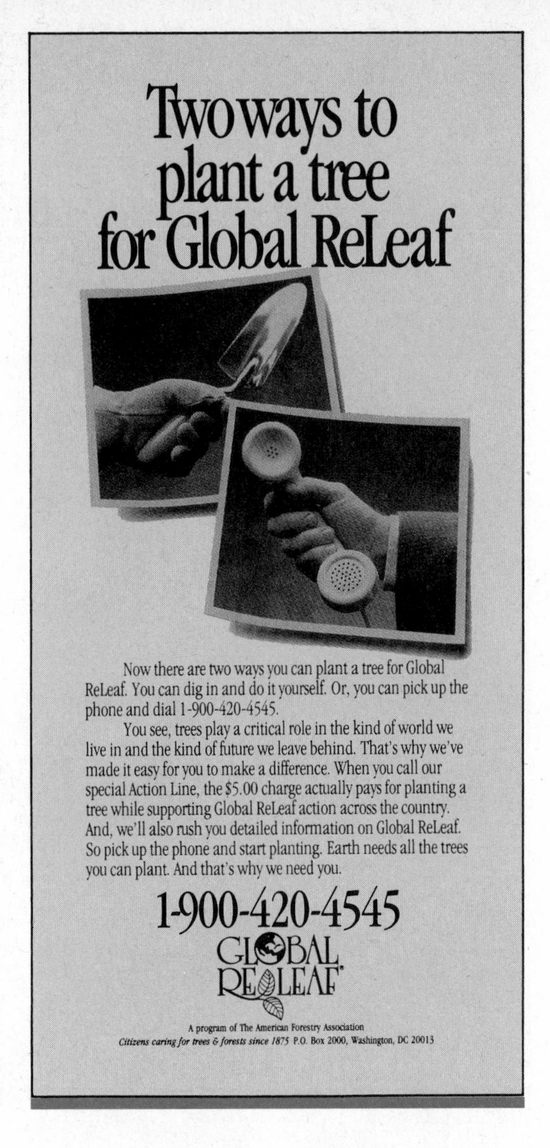

FIGURE 17.4
Tree-planting is a popular activity of the environmental movement because it is a simple, easily accomplished step individuals can take. Global ReLeaf is a program of the American Forestry Association.

ment. President Bush's decision in 1990 to ban virtually all additional off-shore oil drilling until the next century was made after intense lobbying at the White House by environmental groups against the oil industry's plans to drill new wells at sea. Passage of ordinances forbidding smoking in public buildings represents similar effort at the local level.

- *Litigation*. Through litigation, organizations file suits seeking court rulings favorable to their projects, or attempting to block unfavorable projects. The Sierra Club did so in a years-long action that resulted in a decision by the U.S. Fish and Wildlife Service declaring the northern spotted owl a threatened species. While the

AND ON THE EIGHTH DAY, WE BULLDOZED IT.

The oldest rainforests date back to the dinosaurs, 100 million years. Today they offer the last refuge for half of all plant and animal species on earth.

But how much time do rainforests have left? Millions of acres have been bulldozed and burned. Unless we act now, the last traces of original, irreplaceable paradise will vanish in a single human lifespan.

A miracle of creation will be wiped out, thousands of species doomed to extinction. And nobody will gain.

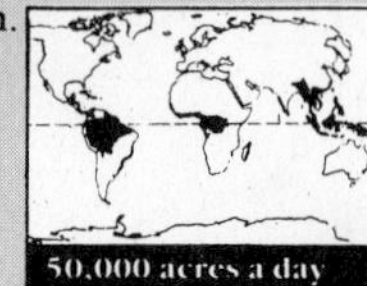

Rainforest soils are too shallow for agriculture, their complex ecology too fragile for humans to exploit without turning our planet's richest natural regions into eroded wastelands. Short of sustainable uses, leaving the rainforests alone would be the most promising development.

What can you do to save the rainforests?

You can support activist organizations in a dozen nations compaigning to conserve the splendid variety of living things which depend on these endangered environments.

Elusive jaguars, rarest orchids, colorful birds of paradise. And the latest arrivals on the scene: the children of humankind.

Save the rainforests and safeguard the survival of half of the species on earth, including our own. Here's my donation of ☐ $25 ☐ $50 ☐ $75 ☐ $100 ☐ ________

NAME ________________
ADDRESS ________________
CITY ________ STATE ____ ZIP ______

RAINFOREST ACTION NETWORK TNR-4

300 BROADWAY, SAN FRANCISCO, CA 94133

Public Media Center

FIGURE 17.5
The Rainforest Action Network is an example of a single-cause group. Here a provocative headline and a striking illustration attract donors to this appeal for preservation of the world's rain forests. (Courtesy of the Rainforest Action Network)

Sierra Club rejoiced at the ruling, the lumber industry asserted that it would cost thousands of lumber industry employees their jobs.

- *Mass demonstrations.* Designed to demonstrate public support for a cause and in some cases to harass the operators of projects to which the groups object, mass demonstrations require intricate public relations organizational work. Organizers must obtain permits, inform the media, arrange transportation and housing, plan programs, and provide crowd control. Earth First! organizers have gained much news attention from their confrontational tactics used to counter clear-cutting of California forests.
- *Boycotts.* ''Hit them in the pocketbook'' is the principle underlying use of the boycott to achieve a goal. Group members in particular, and the public in general, are urged not to purchase or use the products or services of companies accused of environmental offenses. Some boycotts achieve easily identifiable results. Others stay in effect for years with little evident success because too few people participate. One environmental success story occurred when the Rainforest Action Network boycotted Burger King for buying Central American beef raised in cleared rain forests. The fast-food chain agreed to stop such purchases.

FUND-RAISING

Direct mail fund-raising and publicity campaigns are a basic tool of environmental groups. Raising money to conduct their programs is an unending and costly problem for them. Early in the 1990s Greenpeace was sending out 4.5 million pieces of mail a month for this purpose. With so many groups in the field, competition for donations is intense. Some professional fund-raisers believe that as a whole the groups depend too much on direct mail and should place more emphasis on face-to-face solicitation from wealthy individuals, foundations, and environmentally concerned corporations.

SOCIAL ISSUE ORGANIZATIONS

Similar to the environmental groups in structure, but with social and behavior-modification goals, are several widely known organizations. They use public relations methods such as those just described.

Mothers Against Drunk Driving (MADD) is one such group. The National Rifle Association, extremely powerful politically, is another. The antiabortion Right to Life movement and the prochoice National Organization for Women (NOW), bitter enemies, frequently clash in rival public demonstrations. The Animal Rights movement resorts at times to extreme confronational tactics such as raiding animal research laboratories and seeking to shame the wearers of fur.

Other groups, such as the American Family Association, pressure advertisers to drop sponsorship of television shows that they consider contrary to family values. As a result of massive letter campaigns by this group, Coca-Cola and Procter & Gamble decided to cancel commercials on ''Married, With Children.'' Members of the AFA also pressured Pepsi to cancel its Madonna ads after seeing the star's video clip for her song ''Like a Prayer.'' Cancellation of the contract with Madonna cost Pepsi $5 million, according to the *Wall Street Journal,* but probably preserved sales among members of fundamentalist groups.

CASE STUDY: A NEW IMAGE FOR PRUNES

The Problem Prunes have always been the ugly duckling of fruits. Wiseacres call them Texas raisins, and they are perceived widely as laxatives. Sales had been declining steadily since the 1950s.

The Attack The California Prune Board, a group of packers and growers, hired Ketchum Public Relations for a broad-based effort to reposition prunes as a sleek ''good-tasting, high-fiber fruit.'' Recent scientific studies had shown a link between fiber consumption and cancer prevention, and prunes are one of nature's most complete sources of fiber.

The Public Relations Program The strategy of Ketchum Public Relations was to combine prune sampling with third-party endorsement from the medical community and exposure in consumer magazines and newspapers. Ketchum research showed that consumers often try new foods in restaurants before using them in their own kitchens, so the firm teamed up with Doubletree Inns to test-market high-fiber ''breakfast samplers'' nationwide.

Six consulting physicians reviewed all public relations materials for accuracy. Two doctors who had written a book on nutrition were commissioned to produce a four-page brochure, ''The Physician's Guide to Fiber,'' which was mailed to 7000 physicians. They also became the spokespersons for a 15-city media tour.

Other program tactics included (1) a ''harvest tour'' for national editors to see prunes being picked for the market, (2) free samples of prunes on Air California flights between San Francisco and Los Angeles, (3) prune recipes and photos sent to food editors of daily newspapers, (4) news releases about the high fiber content of prunes, and (5) promotion of Prune Breakfast Month through press kits and news releases.

The Result ''High fiber'' prune publicity generated 395 million impressions. Included in this number were a recipe and photo carried by the Associated Press that generated 10.5 million impressions, and the press kit on Prune Breakfast Month sent to 400 editors, resulting in 8 million impressions. Four news releases on the nutritional aspects of prunes produced 34.5 million print impressions. The media tour by the two physicians resulted in 24 television, 27 radio, and 15 print interviews for a total ''potential'' audience of 85 million consumers. In other areas, the mailing of the brochure to physicians generated 2450 requests to receive prune information kits for their patients.

The most important statistic of all, however, is that prune sales rose 12 percent in the first year and continued to increase.

CASE PROBLEM

The Turkey Producers of America (TPA) constantly is seeking new ways to sell more of its product to the American consumer on a year-round basis. TPA has noted the decline of red meat consumption among Americans and the increase of fish and chicken in the diet.

Research shows that turkey has much in its favor. A 3.5-ounce serving of cooked turkey breast, for example, has only 175 calories and less total fat than any other commercial meat. In addition, turkey is economical, and the various parts can be prepared in numerous ways.

Your public relations firm is retained to emphasize turkey as a "healthy" source of protein. What do you suggest for a national public relations program? Mention key publics, message themes, strategies, and communications tactics.

QUESTIONS FOR REVIEW AND DISCUSSION

1. Trade associations, like other membership organizations, often have headquarters in Washington, D.C., or a state capital. Why?

2. Describe how the Council for Solid Waste Solutions seeks to influence public opinion about the role of plastic.

3. In what ways do organizations of food growers try to influence homemakers through newspapers and on the broadcast media?

4. How did the diaper industry increase the public demand for commercially laundered cotton diapers?

5. What did the American Bankers Association do to generate public support for the repeal of a federal law?

6. What challenges do labor unions face today?

7. What are the differences and similarities among trade groups, labor unions, and professional associations?

8. What decisions stimulated the trend for members of the professions to use public relations counsel?

9. Chambers of commerce often are described as the public relations arm of city government. Why?

10. What are four principal methods environmental organizations use to achieve their goals?

Cosco, Joe. "Unions: Polishing a Tarnished Image." *Public Relations Journal,* February 1989, pp. 17–21.

Gray, Patricia. "More Lawyers Reluctantly Adopt Strange New Practice—Marketing." *Wall Street Journal,* January 30, 1987, Section 2, p. 1.

Grunig, James. "Sierra Club Study Shows Who Become Activists." *Public Relations Review,* Fall 1989, pp. 3–24.

Neuman, Connie. "The 'Lady' Moves Engineers, Long in the Wings, to Stage Center." *Public Relations Quarterly,* Summer 1987, pp. 17–20. The engineering profession adopts public relations.

Shribman, David, and Wermiel, Stephen. "Activists on Abortion Take Their Crusades to the 50 Statehouses." *Wall Street Journal,* April 26, 1989, p. 1.

Sterne, Diana. "Many Environmental Groups Slow to React to Growth, Critics Say." *Non Profit Times,* April 1990, pp. 1, 16. Charts showing membership and budgets of major environmental groups.

CHAPTER

18

Social and Cultural Agencies

Much of society's effort to enrich contemporary life and to improve each individual's well-being is carried on by nonprofit organizations that depend heavily upon volunteer help and financing. Skillful public relations is crucial to the success of these organizations.

This chapter examines the role of public relations in this field, whose motivating forces are service, charity, and education. The diverse categories of organizations grouped under this broad heading are analyzed. The public relations goals of nonprofit agencies are listed and the methods by which practitioners achieve them are studied.

Without donations to finance their work, nonprofit social, cultural, health-care, educational, and religious agencies would collapse. Raising money is a constant challenge in which public relations representatives are directly or indirectly involved. This chapter explains fund-raising principles and methods. It closes with an examination of hospital public relations as an example of how practitioners employed by social agencies carry out their tasks.

THE CHALLENGES OF PUBLIC RELATIONS FOR PHILANTHROPIC ORGANIZATIONS

Social service, cultural, medical, educational, and religious organizations exist to improve the human condition. Communication is essential to the success of these organizations. Since these groups are not profit-oriented, the practice of public relations in their behalf differs somewhat from that in the business world.

As discussed in Chapter 14, public relations in business life includes a defensive element, to protect the company or client from attack, as well as an assertive element, to improve the company's reputation with both external and internal audiences. Significant political, economic, and social forces are at work against the corporate community as a whole and portions of it in particular. Suspicion exists among many individuals and groups that companies, especially large corporations, make excessive profits and gouge the public. The "green movement," for example, pressures manufacturers to control toxic waste, eliminate air pollution, and purify water used in industry.

Most social agencies are not seriously troubled by such negative image problems. Usually the agencies are regarded as the "good guys" of society. This is not universally true, though. The causes some of them espouse generate emotional opposition from persons who hold conflicting views. Also, tax-exempt organizations that maintain a high profile with mass-market fund-raising operations such as telethons and direct mail sweepstakes offering huge prizes stir doubts among many members of the public concerning their credibility. Suspicious citizens ask, "Is most of the money raised really going to the cause? Or is it being eaten up by administrative costs or diverted for someone's private benefit? Are minorities getting their fair share of funds raised?" Occasional news stories reporting misuse of nonprofit funds give some substance to these concerns. Fortunately, such suspicions do not rub off on most of the many thousands of well-motivated, carefully operated nonprofit social agencies. Their public relations representatives, however, should prevent trouble by emphasizing the open nature of their financing and operations. A good approach is, "If you have any questions, ask us. We will show you precisely how we work."

The word *nonprofit* should not be construed to mean that these agencies are free from money worries. Quite the opposite is true. For many of these groups, obtaining operating funds is a necessity that dominates much of their effort. Without generous contributions from companies and individuals whose money is earned in the marketplace, nonprofit organizations could not exist. As an indication of the scope of philanthropy in the United States, and of the money needed to keep voluntary service agencies operating, American contributions to charity rose to $114.7 billion in 1989, according to the American Association of Fund-Raising Counsel (see Figure 18.1).

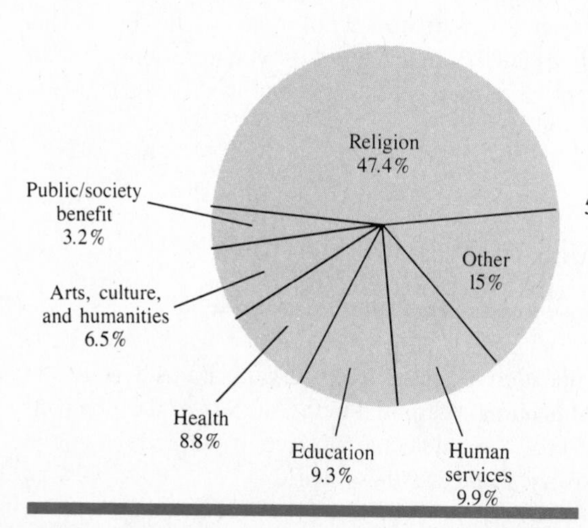

FIGURE 18.1
This pie chart shows how the $114.7 billion given to charity in 1989 was allocated. Individual gifts accounted for 84.1 percent of the total amount given; foundations, 5.8 percent; bequests, 5.7 percent; and corporations, 4.4 percent. (Giving USA, 1990, published by the AAFRC Trust for Philanthropy.)

Additional funds are donated to specialized nonprofit organizations that do not fall under the "charity" mantle, and still more are contributed by federal, state, and local governments. Competition among nonprofit agencies for their share of donations is intense.

In general terms, nonprofit organizations are of two types—*service,* typified nationally by the Visiting Nurse Association and the Boys Clubs of America, and *cause,* whose advocacy role is exemplified by the National Safety Council and the National Association for the Advancement of Colored People (NAACP). Frequently organizations have dual roles, both service and advocacy.

Demands on volunteer service agencies to enlarge their programs of aid to the needy are growing, in part because of efforts in recent years to reduce federal welfare services and shift increased responsibility for humanitarian work to service organizations.

THE SEVEN CATEGORIES OF SOCIAL AGENCIES

For purposes of identification, nonprofit organizations and their functions may be grouped into seven categories:

1. *Social service agencies.* Serving the social needs of individuals and families in many forms are social service agencies. Among prominent national organizations of this type are Goodwill Industries, the American Red Cross, Boy Scouts and Girl Scouts of America, and the YMCA. Local and regional chapters of these organizations carry out national programs at the community level.

2. *Health agencies.* Many health agencies combat a specific illness through education, research, and treatment, while others deliver generalized health services in communities. Typical national organizations include the American Heart Association, the American Cancer Society, the National Multiple Sclerosis Society, and the March of Dimes.

3. *Hospitals.* Public relations work for hospitals is a large and expanding field. The role of a hospital has taken on new dimensions. In addition to caring for ill and injured patients, hospitals conduct preventive health programs and provide other health-related social services that go well beyond the traditional institutional concept. Hospitals may be tax-supported institutions, nonprofit organizations, or profit-making corporations.

4. *Religious organizations.* The mission of organized religion, as perceived by many faiths today, includes much more than holding weekly worship services. Churches distribute charity, conduct personal guidance programs, provide leadership on moral and ethical issues in their communities, and operate social centers where diverse groups gather. Some denominations operate retirement homes and nursing facilities for the elderly. At times, religious organizations assume political roles to further their goals. The nondenominational Salvation Army provides the needy with shelter, food, and clothing. It has a vigorous public relations program to generate support and raise funds.

Churches in particular feel the pressure for increased private agency participation in welfare work. President Reagan cut back federal humanitarian services in the early 1980s; state budgets also were strained to meet welfare needs. Some churches operate food lines, and as the number of homeless Americans multiplied in the late 1980s and early 1990s, churches have taken a prominent role in providing shelters for them.

A recent study by the Brookings Institution, *Fiscal Capacity of the Voluntary Sector,* stated in this regard: ''Because religion occupies a stable, central role in American life, religious institutions will be looked to as a backup finance and delivery mechanism by other subsectors . . . particularly . . . in the human service field.''

Commenting on these developments in a speech to the Baptist Public Relations Association, Don Bates, a prominent New York public relations counselor, pointed out: ''Certainly the shift from government to private initiative provides more opportunities to serve people in need and to prove a case in the process for what your organization does and how it benefits the community.''

5. *Welfare agencies.* Most continuing welfare payments to persons in need are made

FIGURE 18.2
Social and cultural agencies such as those whose logos are shown here depend on extensive fund-raising programs to finance their work. (Easter Seal logo courtesy of National Easter Seal Society; other logos courtesy of organizations named)

by government agencies, using tax-generated funds. Public information officers of these agencies have an important function, to make certain that those entitled to the services know about them and to improve public understanding of how the services function.

6. *Cultural organizations*. Development of interest and participation in the cultural aspects of life falls heavily into the hands of nonprofit organizations. So, in many instances, does operation of libraries, musical organizations such as symphony orchestras, and museums of art, history, and natural science. Such institutions frequently receive at least part of their income from government sources; many are operated by city, state, and federal governments. Even government-operated cultural institutions depend upon private-support organizations such as Friends of the Museum to raise supplementary funds and help operate their facilities.

Regardless of their ownership and management, government or private, cultural institutions require vigorous public relations activity. Creation and publicizing of programs, formation of support groups, development of a volunteer staff, and fund-raising involve the public relations staff either directly or on a consulting basis.

7. *Foundations*. The hundreds of tax-free foundations in the United States constitute about 6 percent of total charitable giving. Money to establish a foundation is provided by a wealthy individual or family, a group of contributors, an organization, or a corporation. The foundation's capital is invested, and earnings from the investments are distributed as grants to qualified applicants in the field for which the foundation was established. Often foundations offer matching grants, in which recipient organizations are given money equal to the amount they raise from other sources. A variation is the challenge grant, in which the foundation offers a gift of a specified amount if the recipient organization can raise an identical sum.

The public knows about such mammoth national organizations as the Ford Foundation, the Rockefeller Foundation, and the National Science Foundation. It is probably not aware, however, of many smaller foundations, some of them extremely important in their specialized fields, that distribute funds for research, education, public performances, displays, and similar purposes.

Giving away money constructively is more difficult than most people realize. Again, public relations representation has a significant role. The requirements of a foundation must be made known to potential applicants for grants. Inquiries must be handled and announcements of grants made. In the case of the very large national foundations, at least, general information explaining the organization's work and its social value needs to be circulated. This is necessary, among other reasons, to allay uneasiness among some persons who suspect that the tax-exempt status of foundations is a device to avoid paying a fair share of the tax burden. In small foundations, public relations work is handled by the executive secretary, but most larger foundations have a public relations staff of one or more persons.

From this summary, the student can see what diverse, personally satisfying opportunities are available to public relations practitioners in the social agency fields.

PUBLIC RELATIONS GOALS

Every voluntary agency should establish a set of public relations goals. In doing so, its management should heed the advice of its public relations staff members, for they are trained to sense public moods and are responsible for achieving the goals. Emphasis on goals will vary, depending on the purpose of each organization. In general, however, nonprofit organizations should design their public relations to achieve these objectives:

1. Develop public awareness of the organization's purpose and activities
2. Induce individuals to use the services the organization provides
3. Create educational materials—especially important for health-oriented agencies
4. Recruit and train volunteer workers
5. Obtain funds to operate the organization

The sections that follow discuss ways in which each of these goals can be pursued.

PUBLIC AWARENESS

The news media provide well-organized channels for stimulating public interest in nonprofit organizations and are receptive to newsworthy material from them. Newspapers usually publish advance stories about meetings, training-sessions, and similar routine activities. Beyond that, much depends upon the ingenuity of the public relations practitioner in proposing feature articles and photographs. Television and radio stations will broadcast important news items about organizations and are receptive to feature stories and guest appearances by organization representatives who have something interesting to tell. *Stories about activities are best told in terms of individuals, rather than in high-flown abstractions*. Practitioners should look for unusual or appealing personal stories—a retired teacher helping Asian refugee children to learn English, a group of Girl Scouts assisting crippled elderly women with their shopping, a volunteer sorting donated books for a Friends of the Library booksale who discovers a rare volume. A physician who speaks to the American Heart Association and explains warning signs for a certain heart ailment in an unusually compelling manner perhaps would be willing to give the same lecture on a local magazine-type television show.

Creation of events that make news and attract crowds is another way to increase public awareness. Such activities might include an open house in a new hospital wing, a concert by members of the local symphony orchestra for an audience of blind children, or a Run-for-Your-Life race to publicize jogging as a protection against heart trouble. A museum of history may sponsor a history fair for high school students with cash prizes for the best papers and projects.

Novelty stunts sometimes draw attention to a cause greater than their intrinsic value seems to justify. For example, a bed race around the parking lot of a shopping center by teams of students at the local university who are conducting a campus fund drive for the March of Dimes could be fun. It would draw almost certain local television coverage and raise money, too. Each team would have a banner over the bed it pushed, and a streamer across the finish line would proclaim the cause. The possibilities of event publicity are countless.

Publication and distribution of brochures explaining an organization's objectives, operation of a speakers' bureau, showings of films provided by general headquarters of national nonprofit organizations, and periodic news bulletins distributed to opinion leaders are quiet but effective ways of telling an organization's story. Fund-raising, which will be discussed later, always stimulates public awareness.

USE OF SERVICES

Closely tied to creation of public awareness is the problem of inducing individuals and families to use an organization's services. Free medical examinations, free clothing and food to the urgently needy, family counseling, nursing service for shut-ins, cultural programs at museums and libraries, offers of scholarships—all these and many other services provided by nonprofit organizations cannot achieve their full value unless potential users know about them.

The news media are valuable in this work. So is word of mouth. Boys and girls become interested in joining the Scouting organizations when they hear about the good times their friends are having in them. Awareness of Planned Parenthood's counseling services and Meals on Wheels food delivery to shut-ins is spread in neighborhood conversations.

Because of shyness or embarrassment, persons who would benefit from available services sometimes hesitate to use them. Written and spoken material designed to attract these persons should emphasize the ease of participation and, in matters of health, family, and financial aid, the privacy of the consultations. A health organization attracts clients with material describing the symptoms of a disease and urging those who suspect such symptoms in themselves to see a physician or to inquire at the organization's office. The American Cancer Society's widely publicized warning list of cancer danger signals is an example of this approach.

CREATION OF EDUCATIONAL MATERIALS

Public relations representatives of nonprofit organizations spend a substantial portion of their time preparing written and audiovisual materials. These are basic to almost any organization's program.

The quickest way to inform a person about an organization is to hand out a brochure. Brochures provide a first impression. They should be visually appealing and contain basic information, simply written. The writer should answer a reader's obvious questions: What does the organization do? What are its facilities? What services does it offer me? How do I go about participating in its activities and services? The brochure should contain a concise history of the organization and attractive illustrations. When appropriate, it may include a membership application form or a coupon to accompany a donation.

Organizations may design logos, or symbols, that help them keep their activities in the public eye. Another basic piece of printed material is a news bulletin, usually monthly or quarterly, mailed to members, the news media, and perhaps to a carefully composed list of other interested parties. This bulletin may range from a single duplicated sheet to an elaborately printed magazine. Tax-exempt organizations that meet Postal Service standards as religious, educational, scientific, philanthropic, agricultural, labor, veterans', or fraternal groups may be able to obtain special bulk third-class nonprofit rates that let them mail their bulletins at approximately one-third the first-class rate.

A source of public relations support for national philanthropic organizations is the Advertising Council. This is a not-for-profit association of advertising professionals who volunteer their creative and technical skills for organizations such as the American Red Cross, the National Alliance of Business, and the National Committee for the Prevention of Child Abuse. The council creates public service advertising campaigns in the public interest. Figure 18.3 shows an American Red Cross educational poster.

The council handles more than 30 public service campaigns a year for nonsectarian, nonpartisan organizations, chosen from 300 to 500 annual requests. Newspapers and radio and television stations publish or broadcast free of charge the advertisements the council sends them. The sponsoring agency reimburses the council for the cost of campaign materials.

One of the best ways to tell an organization's story succinctly and impressively is with an audiovisual package. This may be a slide show or a video, usually lasting about 20 minutes, to be shown to community audiences and/or on a continuing basis in the organization's building. As described earlier, an organization can create its own slide show and perhaps make its own videotape program, or specialists may be hired to do the work. Local chapters of national organizations usually are able to obtain audiovisual materials from their national headquarters.

VOLUNTEER WORKERS

A corps of volunteer workers is essential to the success of almost every philanthropic enterprise. Far more work needs to be done than a necessarily small professional staff can accomplish. Recruiting and training volunteers, and maintaining their enthusiasm so they will be dependable long-term workers, is an important public relations function. Organizations usually have a chairperson of volunteers, who either answers to the public relations (often called community relations) director or depends upon the director for assistance.

The statistics are impressive. One in five American adults volunteers time for charitable causes, according to a 1989 Bureau of Labor Statistics survey. The median weekly time volunteers contribute is slightly more than four hours. Yet the demand for more volunteers is intense. President Bush tried to stimulate recruiting by his talk about "a thousand points of light." A major problem is that since so many women now hold jobs and have less free time, they can do less volunteering than earlier generations did.

The concept of voluntary, private charity activity, so strongly developed in the United States, is spreading to other parts of the world. It has taken root recently in Eastern Europe and in those Asian countries that are prospering with new wealth. Volunteerism long has been a factor in Western Europe.

More than 400 U.S. voluntary agencies also do work overseas. The fundamental changes in the global political and social picture, led by the collapse of communism in

FIGURE 18.3
This striking poster featuring singer Patti LaBelle was issued by the American Red Cross and the U.S. Public Health Service as part of the campaign to educate Americans about the causes of AIDS, the deadly acquired immune deficiency syndrome.

Eastern Europe, have created new opportunities and challenges for them. Experts foresee the development of worldwide voluntary organizations that may substantially replace government-operated foreign programs. Rotary International, for example, has raised millions of dollars in a drive to eliminate polio from the world by the year 2000.

What motivates men and women to volunteer? The sense of making a personal contribution to society is a primary factor. Volunteer work can fill a void in the life of an individual who no longer has business or family responsibilities. It also provides

FIGURE 18.4
A promotional campaign built around a popular cartoon figure is an excellent way for a social agency to attract volunteer workers, because the familiar character gives the agency an aura of significance. Legal permission from the cartoonist before such use is essential. (DENNIS THE MENACE® used by permission of Hank Ketcham and © by North America Syndicate)

social contacts. Why does a former business leader living in a retirement community join a squad of ex-corporate executives who patrol its streets and public places each Monday, picking up wastepaper? The answer is twofold: pride in making a contribution to local well-being and satisfaction in having a structured activity that partially replaces a former business routine. For the same reasons, the retired executive spends another day each week as a hospital volunteer, working in the supply room. Those motives are basic to much volunteerism.

Social prestige plays a role, too. Appearing as a model in a fashion show that raises funds for scholarships carries a social cachet. So does selling tickets for a debutante ball, the profits from which go to the American Cancer Society. Serving as a docent, or guide, at a historical museum also attracts individuals who enjoy being seen in a prestigious setting. Yet persons who do well at these valuable jobs might be unwilling to stuff envelopes for a charity solicitation or spend hours in a back room sorting and mending used clothing for resale in a community thrift shop—jobs that are equally important. Such tasks can be assigned to those volunteers who enjoy working inconspicuously and dread meeting the public.

Religious commitment is another powerful motivating force. Churches provide the base for many social service organizations that depend on workers who donate their time.

Retirees Make Excellent Volunteers Retired men and women, who are increasing in number, form an excellent source of volunteers. The Retired Senior Volunteers Program (RSVP) operates 750 projects nationwide, staffing them from its membership of 365,000. The largest organization of seniors, American Association of Retired Persons (AARP), directs its members into volunteer work through its AARP Volunteer Talent Bank. With 30 million members, AARP also operates an insurance program for older citizens, publishes the magazine *Modern Maturity,* and provides discounts on drugs and travel.

How to Recruit Volunteers Recruiters of volunteers should make clear to potential workers what the proposed jobs entail and, if possible, offer a selection of tasks suitable to differing tastes. A volunteer who has been fast-talked into undertaking an assignment he or she dislikes will probably quit after a short time.

The public relations practitioner can help in recruiting by supplying pamphlets, slide shows, speakers, and other information resources to explain the organization's purpose, to show the essential role its volunteers play, and to stress the sense of achievement and social satisfaction that volunteers find in their work. Testimony from successful, satisfied volunteers is an excellent recruiting tool. Instruction materials and speakers should be provided to train new volunteers. Those who meet the public may receive small badges with their names and the word *Volunteer* printed on them.

Like all persons, volunteers enjoy recognition, and they should receive it. Certificates of commendation and luncheons at which their work is praised are just two ways of expressing appreciation. Hospital auxiliaries in particular keep charts showing how many hours of service each volunteer has contributed. Service pins or similar tokens are awarded for certain high totals of hours worked. Whatever form of recognition it chooses, every organization using volunteers should make certain that it says "Thank you!"

Active, satisfied volunteers do more than provide a workforce for an organization. They also form a channel of communication into the community.

Because fund-raising is one of the key goals of all voluntary agencies, it warrants more developed discussion here.

At board meetings of voluntary agencies, large and small, from coast to coast, the most frequently asked question is, ''Where will we get the money?'' Discussion of ways to maintain present programs and to add new ones revolves around that inevitable query. Obtaining operating funds is a never-ending problem for organizations, except for a few blessed with endowments sufficient for their needs.

Although some voluntary organizations receive funds from government sources, many depend entirely upon money they raise in contributions. Because agencies receiving government funds frequently find the subsidies inadequate, they must join in the scramble for donations.

Fund-raising has been elevated to a highly developed art involving sales psychology, financial skill, ingenuity, and persistence. It may be as simple as the sale of raffle tickets to neighbors, or as complex as intricate forms of accounting that provide donors with cherished tax shelters. Although the largest, most publicized donations are made by corporations and foundations, the total of individual contributions far exceeds combined corporate and foundation giving, amounting to about 84 percent of the more than $100-million annual U.S. philanthropic donations. Depending on their needs, voluntary organizations may try to catch minnows—hundreds of small contributions—or angle for the huge marlin—large gifts from big-money sources.

Public relations representatives participate directly in fund-raising by organizing and conducting solicitation programs, or they may serve as consultants to specialized development departments of their organizations. If their needs are substantial, organizations often employ professional firms to conduct their campaigns on a fee basis. In that case, the organization's public relations representatives usually have a liaison function.

Fund-raising on a major scale requires high-level planning and organization. Various departments and divisions, each with a particular area of responsibility, may be set up. An organizational chart for a typical fund-raising campaign is shown in Figure 18.5.

THE RISKS OF FUND-RAISING

Fund-raising involves risks as well as benefits. Adherence to high ethical standards of solicitation and close control of money-raising costs, so that expenses constitute only a reasonable percentage of the funds collected, are essential if an organization is to maintain public credibility. Numerous groups have suffered severe damage to their reputations from disclosures that only a small portion of the money they raised was applied to the cause they advocated. The rest was consumed in solicitation expenses and administrative overhead.

These fund-raising and administrative costs fluctuate widely among organizations, depending on circumstances, and it is difficult to establish absolute percentage standards for acceptable costs. New organizations, for example, have special start-up expenses. In general, an organization is in trouble if its fund-raising costs are more than 25 percent of what it takes in, or if fund-raising and "administrative overhead" exceed 40 to 50 percent.

Some examples among respected national organizations include the following: the American Cancer Society applies 78.2 cents of every dollar it raises to its anticancer work; solicitation costs are 12.1 cents and administrative overhead 9.7 cents. The American Heart Association applies 75 cents to its work, with 14 cents for solicitation and 11 cents for administration. The Girl Scouts of America applies 71 cents to its work; 1.9 cents go to solicitation and 27.1 cents to administration. The United Way of America averages about 13 percent for fund-raising and overhead costs.

In contrast to these performances, the United Cancer Council, Inc., raised $5.1 million in 1985, of which a mere $15,000 went into cancer research and treatment. The organization spent 97 percent of its income to solicit more funds. In Washington, a speech by President Reagan added glamour to a 1986 dinner at which $219,525 was pledged to help Nicaraguan refugees. An accounting revealed that the tax-exempt Nicaraguan Refugee Fund in the end sent only $3,000 worth of food and clothing to the

FIGURE 18.5
This chart shows the basic structure of a fund drive. Specialized groups should be added in each division as necessary to meet local geographical and organizational needs.

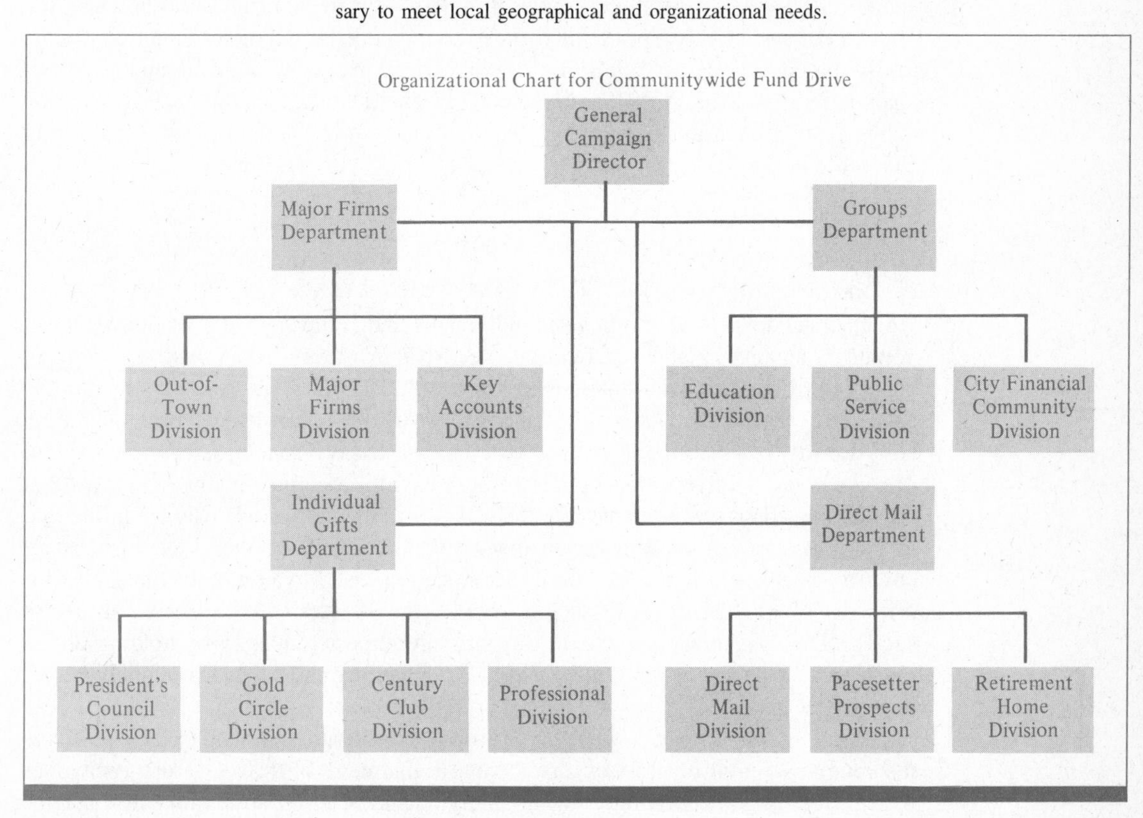

refugees. The rest of the announced donations went for expenses or failed to materialize because individuals failed to pay their pledges.

The National Charities Information Bureau, which reported the cancer organization's performance, sets a standard that 70 percent of funds raised by a charity should go into programs.

Even the most prestigious charity organizations encounter trouble when news reaches the public of incidents that give an impression of misspent money. After the news media revealed that the Los Angeles–area United Way of America had lent more than $300,000 in charitable funds to its executives, more than 2000 contributors canceled their pledges. United Way hastily hired a veteran public relations specialist to guide it through the official investigations that followed, and a public relations firm volunteered to help rebuild the United Way image during the next annual fund-raising campaign.

To protect its reputation, a social agency should publish an annual report that specifies expenses as well as income. It should encourage its solicitors to know the financial facts so they can answer questions. Reputable agencies do this (see Figure 18.6).

Charitable groups should be extremely cautious about lending their names to promoters and telemarketing firms that sell merchandise or conduct events on their behalf, using their names. Often the marketing firm takes 80 to 90 percent of the funds raised, and the charitable organization receives only 10 to 20 percent. The charity's credibility often is damaged by deceptive, high-pressure methods the promoter employs. In one California city, a telemarketing firm used a collection agency in an attempt to collect pledges for a staged softball tournament to benefit abused children. The resulting public anger and unfavorable media coverage dealt a crippling blow to the sponsoring charitable agency.

MOTIVATIONS FOR GIVING

An understanding of what motivates individuals and companies to give money is important to anyone involved in fund-raising. An *intrinsic desire to share* a portion of one's resources, however small, with the needy and others served by philanthropic agencies is a primary factor—the inherent generosity possessed in some degree by almost everyone. Another urge, also very human if less laudable, is *ego satisfaction*. Those who are motivated by it range from donors to large institutions who insist that the buildings they give be named for them, down to the individuals who are influenced to help a cause by the knowledge that their names will be published in a list of contributors. *Peer pressure* is a third factor; saying "no" to a request from a friend is difficult. The cliché about "keeping up with the Joneses" applies here, openly or subtly. Some organizations exploit this pressure almost ruthlessly by holding dinner meetings at which those present are urged to announce their pledges publicly before their fellow guests.

While many companies are truly desirous of contributing a share of their profits to the community well-being, they also are aware that news of their generosity improves their images as good corporate citizens. Individuals and corporations alike may receive

FIGURE 18.6
The March of Dimes builds public confidence in its integrity and efficiency by inviting possible donors to request audited financial statements showing how it spends the contributions it receives. (Courtesy of March of Dimes Birth Defects Foundation)

income tax deductions from their donations, a fact that is less of a motivating factor in many instances than the cynical believe.

Fund-raisers know that while many contributors desire nothing more than the personal satisfaction of giving, others like to receive something tangible—a plastic poppy from a veterans' organization, for example. This fact influences the sale of items for philanthropic purposes. When a neighbor high school girl rings the doorbell, selling candy to raise a fund for a stricken classmate, multiple forces are at work—instinctive generosity, peer pressure (not to be known in the neighborhood as a tightwad), and the desire to receive something for the money given. Even when householders are on a strict diet, they almost always will accept the candy in return for their contribution rather than merely give the money.

THE COMPETITIVE FACTOR

The soliciting organization also should analyze the competition it faces from other fund-raising efforts. The competitive factor is important. The public becomes resentful and uncooperative if approached too frequently for contributions. Deserving causes may fail in their campaigns if other organizations have been vigorously in the field ahead of them. That is why the United Way of America exists, to consolidate solicitations of numerous important local service agencies into a single unified annual campaign.

The voluntary United Way management in a community, with professional guidance, announces a campaign goal. Pledges are collected from corporation managements, from their employees through voluntary payroll deduction, from other individuals, and from any additional available sources during a specified campaign period. The money is distributed among participating agencies according to a percentage formula determined by the United Way budget committee.

LOOK-ALIKE ORGANIZATIONS

A vexing problem for major, nationally known organizations is the growing number of look-alike groups. Using names almost like the well-known ones, they solicit funds by direct mail, siphoning off donations the givers thought they were sending to the long-established groups.

The Cancer Fund of America, with a name that imitates the renowned American Cancer Society, even used a return mail address on Peachtree Street in Atlanta, the street on which the American Cancer Society headquarters is located. The big organizations try to combat such diversionary tactics through public education and legal actions.

TYPES OF FUND-RAISING

There are several principal types of fund-raising used by philanthropic organizations:

- Corporate and foundation donations
- Structured capital campaigns
- Direct mail
- Sponsorship of events
- Telephone solicitations
- Use of telephone numbers with "800" & "900" area codes for contributors
- Entrepreneurship

Corporate and Foundation Donations Organizations seeking donations from major corporations normally should do so through the local corporate offices or sales outlets. Some corporations give local offices a free hand to make donations up to a certain amount. Even when the decisions are made at corporate headquarters, local recommendation is important. Requests to foundations generally should be made to the main

TRENDS IN NONPROFIT ORGANIZATIONS

	1980	1989
Charities registered with the Internal Revenue Service	319,826	447,525
Nonprofit sector's share of gross national product	5.5%	6.4%
Total charitable giving	$48.7 billion	$104.3 billion
Total hours contributed by volunteers	11.5 billion	19.5 billion
Pieces of third-class mail sent by nonprofit organizations	8 billion	11.9 billion

Source: Data from *Chronicle of Philanthropy,* January 9, 1990

office, which will send application forms if the organization's request falls within the scope of the foundation's purpose.

Corporations make donations estimated at more than $5 billion a year to all causes, of which roughly 40 percent goes to education. Much of this is distributed in large sums for major projects, but an increasing amount is going to smaller local programs. A directory, *Guide to Corporate Giving,* published by the American Council for the Arts in New York, describes the contribution programs of 711 leading corporations, which provide $1 billion of the more than $5 billion total. As an example, in a typical recent year the largest contributor was PPG Corporation, with $120 million over five years to the Scripps Research Clinic. Corporations often fix the amount they will contribute each year as a certain percentage of pretax profits. This ranges from less than 1 percent to more than 2.5 percent. The timing of applications is important, because many corporations set aside money for donations in their annual budgets. Corporate years often begin on July 1, so requests should be made well in advance of that date.

Increasingly, corporations make donations on a matching basis with gifts by their employees. The matching most commonly is done on a dollar-for-dollar basis; if an employee gives $1 to a philanthropic cause, the employer does the same. Some corporations match at a 2-to-1 rate or higher. This system tends to spread corporate gifts on a wider basis in a community to smaller, less prominent, voluntary agencies in which individual employees take an interest. By the early 1990s, nearly 900 companies had matching-gift programs, although some were limited to higher education.

Corporations make contributions to charities in less direct ways, too, some of them quite self-serving. (The practice of cause-related marketing was explained in Chapter 14.) Recently 13 million consumers received a mailing from the Arthritis Foundation containing cents-off coupons for pain-relief consumer products from two pharmaceutical companies. One company offered to donate 25 cents to the Arthritis Foundation for each coupon it received, up to $50,000, and the other offered 50 cents each, up to $100,000.

The Arthritis Foundation's local chapters strongly supported the program, and the foundation permitted use of its logo in grocery ads.

Structured Capital Campaigns The effort to raise major amounts of money for a new wing of a hospital, for an engineering building on a campus, or even for the reconstruction and renovation of San Francisco's famed cable car system is often called a capital campaign.

Because of the significant amounts involved, campaign organization and fund-raising techniques become much more sophisticated than soliciting funds through bulk direct mail or selling candy and cookies from door to door. In a capital campaign, emphasis is placed on substantial gifts from corporations and individuals. One key concept of a capital campaign, in fact, is that 90 percent of the total amount raised will come from only 10 percent of the contributors. In a $10 million campaign to add a wing to an art museum, for example, it is not unusual that the lead gift will be $1 or $2 million.

Capital campaigns require considerable expertise and, for this reason, many organizations retain professional fund-raising counsel. There are a number of firms in the country that offer these services, but the most reputable are those belonging to the American Association of Fund-Raising Counsel.

Traditionally, professional fund-raisers were paid by organizations for their work either in salary or by a negotiated fee. In a controversial decision, however, the National Society of Fund-Raising Executives changed its code of ethics in 1989 to permit its members to accept commissions based on the amount of money their drives raise. It did so because its attorney said the old arrangement violated federal antitrust law as a restraint of trade.

The preparation for a capital campaign, whether managed by a professional counseling firm or by the institution's own development staff, is almost as important as the campaign itself.

The first step is a survey among community leaders and influential people to determine support for the proposed campaign. Do community leaders, particularly those who will be asked to make major donations, think the cause is just and needed by the community? Is this the right time for a capital campaign? Do the proposed plans make sense? In many cases, this kind of feedback causes revision in plans and cost of the project. A finding that community leaders are not sold on the idea signals the need for an intensive cultivation program to brief potential backers thoroughly on the project and to get their support. Cultivation programs also (1) encourage community leaders to participate in the project at an early stage and (2) identify major donor prospects.

The next step is to compile a list of companies and wealthy individuals who will personally be approached for a major contribution. It is common practice for campaign organizers to establish a specific amount of money they will request from each leading potential donor. It is also an axiom of capital fund-raising that prospective donors are asked to contribute by someone who is their peer. Thus the president of one major company will solicit the president of another leading firm. It is also a principle of effective fund-raising that those who ask for gifts have already made their own pledge.

The fund campaign usually is organized on quasi-military lines, with division leaders and team captains. An advance gifts division concentrates on anticipated large donors, so that when the campaign is formally kicked off the leadership can announce that a substantial amount already has been pledged toward the goal. This provides impetus and inspiration to the bulk of the volunteer solicitors, and it creates a bandwagon effect for community support.

Donors often are recognized by the size of their gifts—and terms such as *patron, contributor,* or *founder* are used. In addition, major donors may be given the opportunity to have rooms or public places in the building named after them. Hospitals, for example, prepare ''memorial'' brochures that show floor plans and the cost of endowing certain facilities.

Direct Mail Direct mail is an expensive form of solicitation because of the costs of developing or renting mailing lists, preparation of the printed matter, and postage. An organization can conduct an effective local, limited direct mail campaign on its own if it develops an up-to-date mailing list of ''good'' names known to be potential donors and can provide enough volunteers to stuff and address the solicitation envelopes. Regional and national organizations, and some large local ones, either employ direct mail specialists or rent carefully chosen mailing lists from list brokers.

The old days when direct mailing pieces came addressed to ''Occupant'' are largely gone, thanks to the wonders of computerized mailing lists. Now the letters arrive individually addressed. Inside, the appeal letter may bear a personalized salutation and include personal allusions within the text, such as: ''So you see, Ms. Smith, that this opportunity. . . .''

WRITING DIRECT MAIL LETTERS

A large percentage of fund-raising for charitable institutions is conducted through the direct mail letter. The purpose of the letter, of course, is to produce a response—that is, a donation. Writers of fund-raising letters have learned the best approaches:

1. Make use of an attention-getting headline.
2. Follow with an inspirational lead-in on why and how a donation will benefit clients of the charitable agency.
3. Give a clear definition of the charitable agency's purpose and objectives.
4. Humanize the cause by giving an example of a child or family that benefited.
5. Include testimonials and endorsements from credible individuals.
6. Ask for specific action, and provide an easy method for the recipient to respond. Self-addressed stamped envelopes and pledge cards often are included.
7. Close with a postscript that gives the strongest reason for reader response.

The abundance and diversity of mailing lists for rent is astounding. One company offers more than 8000 different mailing lists. A common rental price is $30 per thousand names. Other lists cost more, depending on their special value. The best lists contain donors to similar causes. Direct Media List Management Group, for example, offers a list of almost 1.5 million ''aware'' women who have contributed to at least one of 27 causes. Or a person can order the Doris Day Animal League list of 400,725 donors. These people are described as ''compassionate animal lovers who have responded to a direct mail appeal requesting donation and petition signatures to protect animals from unnecessary laboratory experimentation.''

In direct mail campaigns, economic success depends on getting the mailing pieces into the hands of potential donors while not wasting postage in mailing to those who probably are not. Marketing research firms feed demographic, geographic, and psychographic information into computers; the computers then produce mailing lists focused on the desired audience. Such targeting greatly increases the predictable percentage of successful contacts from the mailing. A response of one percent on a mailing usually is regarded as satisfactory; two percent is excellent.

One marketing research firm, for example, identified 34 human factors such as age, gender, education, and levels of economic well-being. It fed these factors into computers along with a list of 36,000 ZIP code markets and produced 40 neighborhood types. An organization interested in reaching one of these types—the supereducated top income level, for example—could use suitable mailing lists broken down to postal area routes.

Attractive, informative mailing pieces that stimulate recipients to donate are keys to successful solicitation. The classic direct mail format consists of a mailing envelope, letter, brochure, and response device for making a contribution, often with a postage-paid return envelope.

Another essential factor in direct mail solicitation is getting recipients to open the mailing piece. This need has resulted in development of many attention-getting graphic and psychological devices. One attention-getting device that generates curiosity is to omit the name of the organization on the envelope. An address is given, but the receiver must open the envelope to determine who sent the letter. Once a well-chosen recipient has been induced to open the envelope and begin reading the message, much of the selling work has been done. After that, the appeal of the message and the degree of ease with which the recipient can respond will determine the result.

Direct Mail List Rates and Data, updated bimonthly by Standard Rate & Data Service, Inc., is a basic reference book for direct mail lists.

Sponsorship of Events The range of events a philanthropic organization can sponsor to raise funds is limited only by the imagination of its members.

Participation contests are a popular method. Walkathons and jogathons appeal to the current American emphasis on using the legs for exercise. Nationally, the March of Dimes holds an annual 32-kilometer WalkAmerica in 1100 cities on the same day. Local organizations do the same in their own communities. Bikeathons are popular, too. The money-raising device is the same in all such events: each entrant signs up sponsors who promise to pay a specified amount to the fund for each mile or kilometer the entrant walks, jogs, runs, or cycles. If an entrant obtains several sponsors, at rates from a few cents up to $1 a mile, the contributions mount up.

Staging of parties, charity balls, concerts, and similar events in which tickets are sold is another widely used approach. Often, however, big parties create more publicity than profit, with 25 to 50 percent of the money raised going to expenses. Other methods include sponsorship of a motion picture opening, a theater night, or a sporting event. Barbecues flourish as money-raisers in western cities. Used-book sales can be excellent profit-makers. Raffles, either on their own or in connection with a staged event, are profitable. So are home tours. This is only a sampling of methods popular with smaller organizations, which normally do the work themselves without professional assistance.

Sale of a product, in which the organization keeps a portion of the selling price, ranges from the church baked-goods stand, which yields almost 100 percent profit because members contribute homemade products, to the massive national Girl Scout cookie sale, which grosses about $375 million annually. Light bulbs, candy, grapefruit, Christmas fruitcake, and magazine subscriptions are other commodities sold in this manner.

A key to success in all charity-fund sales is abundant publicity in the local news media. Posters, movable-letter signs, and announcements at organization meetings also help. Use of paid advertising rarely is worthwhile because its cost eats seriously into the profit margin.

Direct solicitation of funds over television by *telethons* is used primarily in large cities. A television station sets aside a block of air time for the telethon, sponsored by a philanthropic organization. During the telethon, the host and a parade of well-known guests take turns making on-the-air appeals for contributions. Donors telephone an announced number, where a battery of volunteers record the pledges. Mixed in with the appeals are bits of entertainment by the guests and prearranged on-camera presentations of large checks by corporations and other givers. Best known of the national telethons is the one conducted annually by comedian Jerry Lewis for muscular dystrophy. Telethons have become increasingly expensive to stage and usually are suitable only for organizations that can command entertainment talent. Collection of the telephoned pledges also may be a problem.

Telephone Solicitations Solicitation of donations by telephone is a relatively inexpensive way to seek funds but of uncertain effectiveness. Many groups hold down their cost of solicitation by using a WATS (Wide Area Telephone Service) line that provides unlimited calls for a flat fee, without individual toll charges. Some people resent receiving telephone solicitations. If the recipient of the call is unfamiliar with the cause, it must be explained clearly and concisely—not always easy for a volunteer solicitor to do. The problem of converting verbal promises by telephone into confirmed written pledges also arises. The normal method is for the sponsoring organization to send a filled-in pledge form to the donor for signature as soon as possible after the call, reminding him or her of the promise to contribute and enclosing a reply envelope.

Use of "800" or "900" Telephone Numbers Toll-free telephone numbers with area codes of 800, permitting callers to phone an organization long distance without cost to themselves, have been in use for years. Recently a 900 code has been added by the telephone companies that requires users to pay a fee for each call placed. The phone company takes a service charge from this fee, and the remainder goes to the party being called.

Charitable organizations increasingly are using "900" numbers in fund-raising. Although the callers must pay for their calls, they have the convenience of making a pledge without having to read solicitation material and write a response. Public television station WNET in New York used a 900 number in its annual pledge drive and received $235,000 in contributions through it.

Entrepreneurship Operation of gift shops, bookstores, coffee shops, and similar businesses is another source of revenue for nonprofit organizations. Museums, hospitals, and institutions of learning often use this method. Some large nonprofit organizations carry this approach much further by participating in real estate syndicates, publishing magazines that carry paid advertising, and entering the cable television business. Volunteer help often staffs the service businesses, enabling them to be profitable. However, many voluntary organizations lack the experience required to enter more complicated ventures than the gift shop level and may lose money if they do so. Another problem is opposition from commercial firms if the nonprofit organization's project impinges substantially on their fields of livelihood.

Any nonprofit organization contemplating operation of a business should check the tax laws, which require that the enterprise be "substantially related" to the purpose of the nonprofit group.

CASE STUDY: A LESSON IN FUND-RAISING

The Old Globe Theater in San Diego's Balboa Park is an integral part of the city's cultural life. It attracts about 300,000 playgoers a year to its 325 evening performances and has a splendid professional reputation.

The theater's board of directors knew that it needed rehearsal space, refurbishing, and a concession area. They also wanted to pay off debt incurred from rebuilding part of the theater damaged by fire in 1984 and to acquire a $2 million endowment and reserve fund.

The board decided to conduct a $10 million capital fund campaign. An article in *The Chronicle of Philanthropy* tells how they did so successfully despite severe obstacles.

First, the directors conducted a feasibility study. This showed that San Diego's community leaders did not regard the theater's financial needs as compelling; it also showed that the theater's volunteer leadership lacked members who could make large personal contributions and solicit major campaign gifts.

After a delay caused in part by the death of the theater's campaign consultant, Robert B. Sharp took the job and the campaign was revitalized. New volunteer leaders were recruited. Several events then occurred:

- A four-color brochure was published to be given to donor prospects.
- A few donors made large gifts as a nucleus of the drive.
- At cocktail parties, board members and major donors heard a presentation about the campaign. They were asked to pick names of people they knew from a list of 20,000 season ticket holders. This provided a list for solicitation.
- A precise goal was set for each prospect—two to five percent of the donor's estimated "adjusted gross worth." The campaign hired a researcher to examine various credit and public records to determine what these goals should be.

With this list, the campaign reached full speed. The co-chair made a challenge gift of $500,000 that required the theater to raise $1.5 million within seven months.

Prospective donors were invited to dinner and a play, taken backstage, and given a slide presentation before seeing the play. The campaign used slides rather than a videotape because they enabled the speaker to pause during the presentation for questions.

Solicitors went after the largest gifts first, then moved step by step to the smaller prospects. They had a gift model showing the various sizes of gifts sought, from a high of $1 million down to $1000, and the number of prospects for each size (three for $1 million, 1500 for $1000). Actual donors in each category proved to be about one-third of the category's prospects.

So far, everything had been done on a personal basis without major publicity. A total of $8.5 million was raised from individuals, corporations, and foundations.

Then the campaign went public with a media blitz to solicit gifts under $10,000 from the general public. The final phase involved sending direct mail pieces to theater constituents who had not contributed.

Large donors were recognized by having their family coats of arms incorporated in the design of the new facilities and they received framed versions of the coats of arms. An importing company donated research to find coats of arms for families lacking them.

A crucial part of this successful campaign was the identification of potential large donors and the analysis of how much each might donate, so that solicitors could make their calls with specific money targets in mind.

HOSPITAL PUBLIC RELATIONS

GROWTH OF MARKETING

The practice of public relations for hospitals is a vigorous, expanding field, because the public is deeply concerned about health care and hospitals have adopted aggressive competitive marketing.

Hospital managements in both nonprofit and commercial institutions seek to offset rising costs of operation and the pressures of competition by marketing their product, health care. Like hotels, hospitals need high room-occupancy rates, but storefront emergency medical facilities, health maintenance organizations, and other alternative medical services have cut into their business. Innovative public relations programs are essential for hospitals' well-being.

Hospital public relations practitioners must not only deal with specific projects and problems, but they must also try to overcome widespread public concern about the extremely high cost of American medical care. In general, the American people endorse the quality of medical care they receive but are deeply disturbed about its cost.

A large number of U.S. hospitals now are owned by corporations, rather than by various types of community nonprofit organizations or local governments. The idea of a corporation making a profit from treating the seriously ill jars some people, who see the corporate money-making drive as a reason for their high hospital bills.

When, to cite a fairly typical example, a family receives a $22,000 bill for a patient's two-week hospital stay, with the doctor bills extra, and then must wait uneasily more than six months to get all their insurance payments, they instinctively say, "There must be something wrong here!"

Practitioners face a challenge in explaining why medical advances cost so much and emphasizing the high quality of care their hospitals provide.

The public relations staff of a hospital has two specific roles: (1) to strengthen and maintain the public's perception of the institution as a place where medical skill, compassion, and efficiency are paramount, and (2) to help market the hospital's proliferating array of services. Going further, the public relations staff should try to identify additional publics for the hospital to serve and to develop new programs to reach them.

Health care in all its manifestations is a $400-billion-a-year industry, consuming more than 10 percent of the U.S. gross national product. Truly, it is big business.

Expansion of the health-care field has created additional public relations jobs and has improved salaries. Approximately two-thirds of the public relations personnel in hospital and other health care work are women, according to a survey published by *PR Reporter*.

In some hospitals the public relations staff also handles the advertising program; in others the public relations director answers to the marketing director. The name *community services department* sometimes is used to cover all these functions.

Because hospitals sell a product (improved health), parallels exist between their public relations objectives and those of other corporations. Both focus on diverse audiences, external and internal; involve themselves in public affairs and legislation because they operate under a mass of government regulations; and stress consumer relations. In the case of hospitals, this involves keeping patients and their families satisfied, as well as seeking new clients. Hospitals produce publications for external and internal audiences. They have an additional function that other corporate public relations practitioners don't need to handle—the development and nurturing of volunteer organizations whose help keeps hospitals functioning smoothly.

NEW ROLES FOR HOSPITALS

Today's hospitals reach far beyond their traditional role of treating the ill and comforting the dying. As community health centers they provide a range of social services, preventive medicine, counseling, and in some cities senior citizen housing. Each of these roles requires the support of public relations skills.

In addition to increasingly complex medical treatments, hospitals provide many supplemental services. These include alcoholism rehabilitation, babysitter training, childbirth and parenting education, home care, hospices for the terminally ill, pastoral care, sexual dysfunction treatment, a smokers' hotline giving advice on how to quit, speech pathology, a physician referral service, rental of infant car seats for safety, and Tel-Ed. (Tel-Ed informs telephone callers on scores of health topics such as ''Understanding Headaches'' and ''Are Old-Age Freckles Dangerous?'')

Hospital public relations programs have four basic *audiences:* patients, medical and administrative staffs, news media, and the community as a whole. The four audiences overlap, but each needs a special focus. Careful scrutiny can identify significant subaudiences within these four—for example, the elderly; women who have babies or soon will give birth; victims of heart disease, cancer, and stroke who need support groups after hospitalization; potential donors of money to the hospital; and community opinion leaders whose goodwill helps to build the institution's reputation. Each group can be cultivated by public relations techniques discussed in this textbook.

PUBLIC RELATIONS EFFORTS BY HOSPITALS

The reputations of some hospitals are damaged by public perception that they are cold institutions that don't care enough about individual patients. Word-of-mouth complaints by patients about poor food and brusque nurses are damaging, too. Again, public relations staffs are challenged. Emphasis on the human touch in hospital care is vital.

Public relations departments of typical U.S. hospitals have taken some specific steps to explain the work of their institutions and to defuse criticism (other hospitals use the same or similar methods):

- A "Direct Line" telephone extension within the Sutter Community Hospitals, Sacramento, California, allows patients and community members to register complaints and suggestions to the administration 24 hours a day.
- A market research survey for the North Mississippi Medical Center at Tupelo disclosed that 25 percent of the respondents believed the hospital to be less concerned with its patients' well-being than other area hospitals were. In response, the administration began a public relations program called "Close enough to care." An advisory committee of employees was formed. Staff members were asked to sign a "caring pledge" and were given a daily checklist and lapel care pin. An audiovisual presentation, shown to all employees and 3000 community members, depicted how healing is enhanced when caring and compassion are evident. Ratings on the "caring" question were high in later patient surveys. Simultaneously, monthly employee turnover decreased, indicating improved staff morale.
- Patients at Mercy Hospital, Cedar Rapids, Iowa, pay a small fee to play bingo twice a week over a closed-circuit television system. Cash prizes are awarded. These games brighten the patients' days.
- Eager to obtain as much television coverage as possible, the public relations staff of St. Joseph Medical Center, Burbank, California, organized a team of health-care representatives ready to provide local television stations with immediate comments on health-oriented news stories. The staff also proposes medical story ideas to the stations. Assignment editors find the group such a quick, authentic, and willing source that hospital representatives have appeared on local television an average of 225 times a year—a splendid way to build public awareness, especially considering that southern California has 278 other hospitals.
- Another way is conducting a community health fair with free screenings to detect symptoms of certain diseases and comprehensive blood tests for a nominal fee, perhaps five dollars. Chevron U.S. has underwritten numerous health fairs.

WRITING A "CASE FOR SUPPORT"

Charitable organizations requesting major funds from wealthy individuals, foundations, and corporations usually prepare a ''case for support.'' The following is an outline of what should be contained in such a document.

Background of the Organization

- Founding date
- Purpose and objectives
- What distinguishes the organization from similar organizations
- Evolution (development) of objectives, services

Current Status of Organization's Services

- Number of paid, volunteer staff
- Facilities
- Number of clients served annually
- Current budget
- Breakdown of how budget is allocated
- Geographical areas served

Need for Organization's Services

- Factual and statistical evidence
- Availability of similar services
- Evidence showing seriousness of the problem
- Uniqueness of the program

Sources of Current Funding

- Public donations
- Foundations and corporations
- Government funding

Administration of the Organization

- Background of executive director
- Qualifications of key staff
- Board of directors (names and titles)

Tax Status of Organization

Community Support

- Letters from satisfied clients
- Letters from community leaders
- Favorable media coverage of programs

Current Needs of the Organization

- Specific programs
- Specific staffing
- Financial costs
- Amount of financial support needed
- Sources of possible funding

Benefits to Community with New or Expanded Program

Request for Specific Amount of Funds

- Need for donor's participation
- Benefits to the donor

STEPS IN RUNNING A CAPITAL CAMPAIGN

Robert B. Sharp, California professional consultant, recommends these steps in running a capital campaign:

Conduct a Feasibility Study Commission an objective review of the cause behind the proposed campaign. The study should . . . provide a monetary goal for the campaign, as well as a ''gift model''—a chart breaking down the goal into individual gift amounts and indicating how many of each are needed.

The study may also suggest breaking the campaign into phases for ''sequential solicitation,'' starting with the largest donations and working down to smaller and smaller gifts.

The review should also lead to the development of a clear ''case statement,'' setting out the goals for the campaign.

Get the Board's Approval for and Support of the Feasibility Study The board should review the feasibility study, give final approval to the case statement and the goal, and take steps to carry out the recommendations. (This often results in delay.) . . .

Enlist Volunteer Leadership Recruit volunteer leaders who are capable of making significant gifts to the campaign. Choose a campaign chairman and a committee made up of such volunteers. These volunteers will carry the campaign through a private phase, during which a major portion of the goal is achieved before seeking support from the general public.

Begin Soliciting Gifts Using the feasibility study's gift model and suggested campaign phases, begin the solicitation of prospects, moving from attempts to get larger gifts to efforts to obtain lesser ones. In some cases, larger-gift solicitation will continue throughout the campaign, with smaller-gift phases being added.

Stop for a Mid-Point Evaluation This evaluation, taking place well into the campaign, should make needed adjustments in the drive's time line, financial goal, or strategy. It is here that the campaign is usually announced to the public through the media. Announcement of the campaign should be made only when the goal is assured. Solicitation of the general public, however, will not come until later. Many groups do not go through a formal evaluation or erroneously think that adjustments mean they have failed. . . .

Determine Closing Strategies This phase usually means more adjustments as volunteers and staff members determine what changes need to be made to meet or exceed the original goal. They should also determine when and how they will begin to solicit the general public.

Honor Volunteer Leadership Draw up plans for how the volunteers who led the campaign will be acknowledged with special events and permanent recognition. . . .

Perform ''Administrative Wrap-up'' Because many large gifts may be divided into pledge payments that will continue to come in for some time after the campaign closes, the staff should set up procedures to process them and encourage timely payment. And staff members, volunteers, and board members should review what the campaign has achieved and then consider the campaign's implications for future fund-raising efforts.

Source: Condensed from *Chronicle of Philanthropy,* February 2, 1990

FARM AID CONCERTS RAISE MILLIONS

Farm Aid, founded by country singer Willie Nelson, has raised $10.3 million as of 1990 on behalf of needy farmers and farm advocacy groups with concerts every April since 1986.

Two major factors contribute to the concerts' success. First, ticket sales largely cover the annual $1.6 million production cost. Second, the event is the focal point of a national campaign. During the live concert cable telecast, "800" and "900" telephone numbers (for example, 800–FARM AID) to which donations may be phoned are flashed on the screen. The numbers also are broadcast by major television networks that cover the concert.

Concert organizers say that more than 200,000 individuals have made donations, most around $25.

Source: Chronicle of Philanthropy, April 3, 1990

NONPROFITS IN THE 1990s

Challenges and issues facing charitable organizations in the 1990s will require leaders and public relations experts to be more creative in problem-solving. Nonprofit leaders surveyed made the following predictions:

- Competition to raise money will be fierce as more nonprofits form and use sophisticated fund-raising techniques.
- Environmental issues will get the most increased donor support. Efforts to alleviate poverty and improve education will continue to get attention.
- Traditional charities, such as those that raise money for major diseases, may face increased resistance from donors.
- Donors will take a harder look at charity appeals and ask more questions before making a donation.
- There will be increased efforts to recruit outstanding administrators, and salaries for personnel will go up.
- More people will be interested in volunteering, but they will expect more responsibility and autonomy from the organizations they help.
- Rising costs and new federal regulations will make raising money through the mail more difficult.
- Fund-raising by telephone will become more sophisticated.
- Charities will do more extensive research on the backgrounds of prospective donors and emphasize planned-giving techniques to take advantage of tax benefits.
- There will be more battles about on-the-job solicitation, and other groups will challenge United Way's traditional dominance in community fund-raising.

(*Continued*)

- The federal government will increase its scrutiny of charities involved in commercial ventures.
- Foundations will give cluster grants to address a variety of social needs, instead of making grants that deal with a single issue.
- American charities will increasingly become involved in international philanthropic efforts.

Source: The Chronicle of Philanthropy, January 9, 1990

CASE PROBLEM

The facts: For 20 years a western city of 150,000 population has operated a volunteer Meals on Wheels program, taking food to shut-ins. However, financial contributions to help support the project have dwindled, as has the force of volunteers to deliver the meals, endangering continuation of this humanitarian service. Your public relations firm has been hired by a local church to revitalize the program.

Following the four-step process explained in Part Two of this book, develop a program to achieve this objective. Define the audiences you should address. Explain specifically what you would seek to learn during your research, describe the plan of action you would use, tell how you would communicate your message, and draw up a plan of evaluation.

QUESTIONS FOR REVIEW AND DISCUSSION

1. Give examples of a service-oriented nonprofit organization and a cause-oriented nonprofit organization.

2. How did President Reagan's campaign to cut back on federal welfare programs affect the role of churches?

3. What is a challenge grant?

4. Why do large foundations need public relations representatives? List some of the tasks these practitioners handle.

5. Social agencies depend heavily on volunteer help. What motivates individuals to volunteer?

6. Why is it important for a nonprofit organization that solicits money from the public to put out a detailed annual financial report?

7. Name three factors that motivate individuals and companies to make contributions.

8. In what ways do capital campaigns differ from routine fund-raising for an organization's operating expenses?

9. List several types of fund-raising events often staged by smaller organizations using volunteer help.

10. What are the basic audiences of a hospital public relations program?

SUGGESTED READINGS

"Challenges for the 1990s." *Chronicle of Philanthropy,* January 9, 1990, pp. 1, 12. Trends in philanthropy and nonprofit organizations.

Chapel, Gage W. "Ethiopian Relief: A Case Study in Failed Public Relations." *Public Relations Review,* Summer 1988, pp. 22–31.

Crossen, Cynthia. "Organized Charities Pass Off Mailing Costs as Public Education." *Wall Street Journal,* October 29, 1990, pp. 1, A4.

Fuchsberg, Gilbert. "Charities Are Stepping Up Recruiting as Good Help Grows Harder to Find." *Wall Street Journal,* March 6, 1990, p. B1.

Goss, Kristin A. "Donations in 1989: Over $114 Billion." *Chronicle of Philanthropy,* June 12, 1990, p. 1, 12.

Goss, Kristin A. "Public's Perception Worries Fund Raisers." *Chronicle of Philanthropy,* June 26, 1990, pp. 19–22. Includes charts showing salaries in the field.

Greene, Elizabeth. "Farm Aid, with $10.3 Million Raised, Shows Someone Cares." *Chronicle of Philanthropy,* April 3, 1990, pp. 5, 11.

Greene, Stephen. "Worldwide Upheavals Offer Opportunities for American Voluntary Agencies." *Chronicle of Philanthropy,* May 29, 1990, pp. 1, 14.

Hall, Holly. "900-Area-Code Telephone Services Gain Popularity." *Chronicle of Philanthropy,* March 20, 1990, pp. 4, 8.

Lewton, Kathleen L. "Health Care: Critical Conditions." *Public Relations Journal,* December 1989, pp. 18–22.

Lublin, Joann S. "More Charities Reach Out for Corporate Sponsorship." *Wall Street Journal,* October 1, 1990, p. B1.

McMillen, Liz. "Americans Gave More to Charity Again in 1989: Total Topped $100 Billion for 2nd Straight Year." *Chronicle of Higher Education,* June 13, 1990, pp. 1, A23.

Millar, Bruce. "Hispanics Seek More Help from United Ways and Other Groups." *Chronicle of Philanthropy,* April 3, 1990, pp. 4, 10.

Montague, William. "Proliferating 'Look-Alikes' Cause Headaches for Many Charities." *Chronicle of Philanthropy,* January 9, 1990, pp. 25–26. Charities with similar names.

Overkamp, Sunshine. "Not-for-Profits: A New Ball Game." *Public Relations Journal,* January 1990, pp. 22–23. Trends in the 1990s.

Rouner, Donna, and Camden, Carl. "Not-for-Profits Appear to Lack PR Sophistication." *Public Relations Review,* Winter 1988, pp. 31–34.

"State Laws Governing Charitable Solicitations." *Chronicle of Philanthropy,* June 12, 1990, p. 33.

CHAPTER

19

Education

To inform a wide variety of publics, to interpret programs, and to cultivate support—that is the mission of public relations specialists on college campuses and in public school systems. This chapter discusses both types of operations.

The college public relations office provides news and publications services, coordinates special events including tours and exhibits, and performs a multitude of other tasks such as writing speeches and reports and responding to requests for information. These are the main functions of public school communication specialists as well, although generally on a much smaller scale. In addition, a university development staff works with alumni and other groups, and raises money; both are extremely important tasks, because every institution needs increased financial support.

Members of a college public relations office interact with a number of publics: students, faculty and staff, parents, alumni, the community, boards of control, foundations and other research and support agencies, government bodies, business executives, secondary schools, and other colleges, to name the principal ones. The public schools have their own set of publics—teachers, students, parents, staff, and the community. The chapter describes some school systems that have been especially successful in creating good relations with these groups.

COLLEGES AND UNIVERSITIES

DEVELOPMENT AND PUBLIC RELATIONS OFFICES

The president (or chancellor) is the chief public relations officer of a college or university; he or she sets policy and is responsible for all operations, under the guidance of the institution's governing board.

In large universities the vice president for development and university relations (that person may have some other title) supervises the office of development, which includes a division for alumni relations, and also the office of public relations; these functions are combined in smaller institutions. Development and alumni personnel seek to enhance the prestige and financial support of the institution. Among other activities, they conduct meetings and seminars, publish newsletters and magazines, and arrange tours. Their primary responsibilities are to build alumni loyalty and raise funds from private sources.

The public relations director, generally aided by one or more chief assistants, supervises the information news service, publications, and special events. Depending upon the size of the institution, perhaps a dozen or more employees will carry out these functions, including writing, photography, graphic design, and broadcasting.

Figure 19.1 shows the organization of a public relations staff at a typical middle-sized university.

In addition, scores of specialists at a large university perform diverse information activities in agricultural, medical, engineering, extension, continuing education, and other such units, including sports.

PUBLIC INFORMATION BUREAU

The most visible aspect of a university public relations program is its public information bureau. Among other activities, an active bureau produces hundreds of news releases, photographs, and special columns and articles for the print media. It prepares programs of news and features about faculty activities and personalities for broadcast stations. It provides assistance and information for reporters, editors, and broadcasters affiliated with the state, regional, and national media (see Figure 19.2). The staff responds to hundreds of telephone calls from members of the news media and the public seeking information.

SERVING THE PUBLICS

In order to carry out their complex functions, top development and public relations specialists must be a part of the management team of the college or university. At some institutions this is not so, and the public relations program suffers. Ideally, these leaders should attend all top-level meetings involving the president and other administrators, learning the whys and wherefores of decisions made and lending counsel. Only then can they satisfactorily develop action programs and respond to questions from the publics those programs concern. They are indeed the arms and voice of the administration.

Faculty and Staff As noted in previous chapters, every sound public relations program begins with the internal constituency. Able college presidents involve their faculty in decision-making to the fullest extent possible, given the complexities of running a major institution. It is a maxim that the employees of a company or institution serve as its major public relations representatives because they come into contact with so many people. Good morale, a necessity, is achieved in large measure through communication.

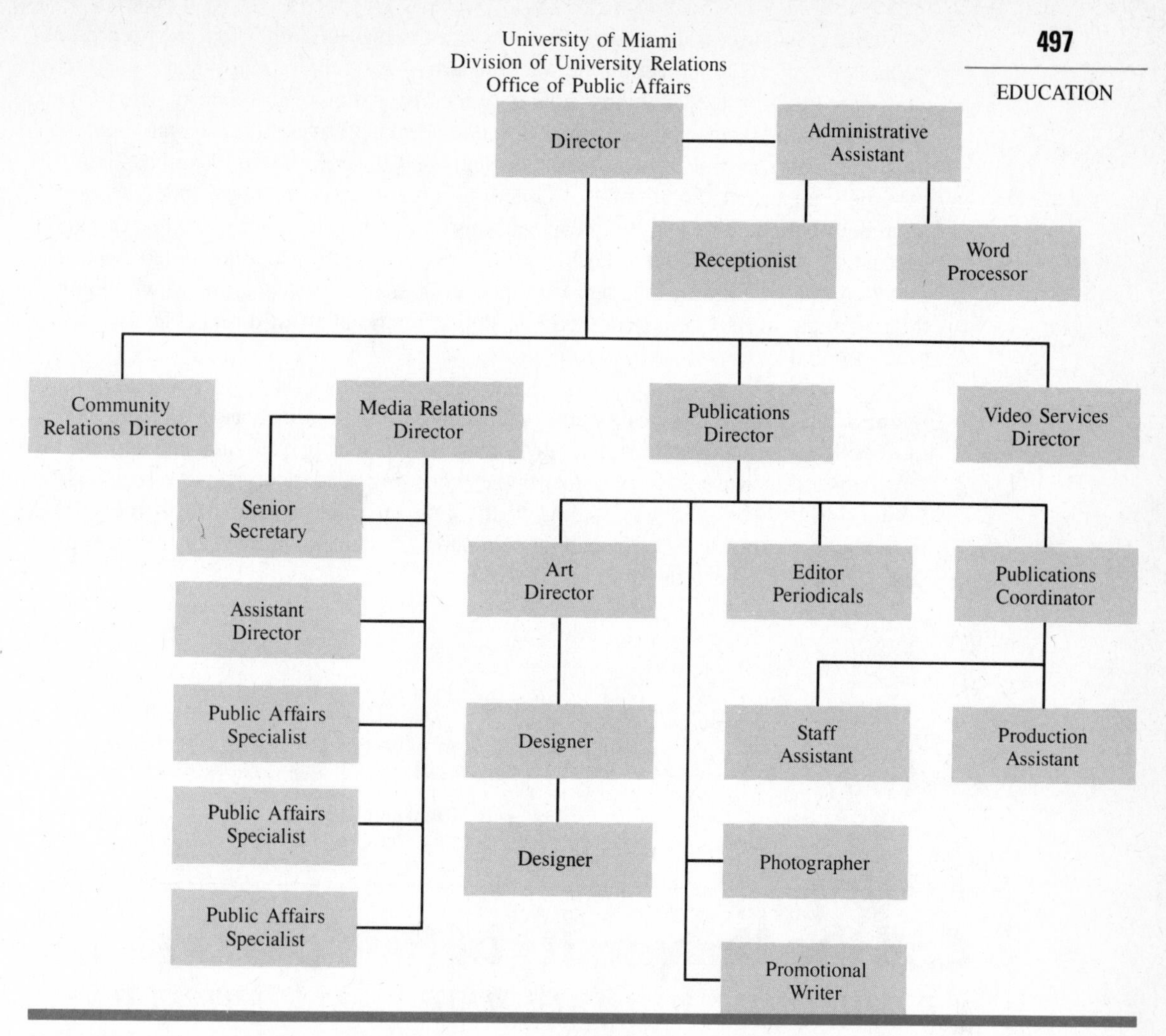

FIGURE 19.1
Organizational chart for the University of Miami's public affairs office, showing the division of responsibility for the various areas of the operation. (Courtesy of University of Miami)

Colleges communicate with their faculty and staff members through in-house newsletters and newspapers; journals describing research, service, and other accomplishments (which also are sent to outside constituencies); periodic meetings at which policies are explained and questions answered; and in numerous other ways.

Faculty and staff members who fully understand the college's philosophy, operations, and needs generally will respond with heightened performance. For example, when the University of Georgia sought to obtain $2.5 million in contributions from its faculty members as part of an $80 million bicentennial enrichment campaign, they responded with a generous outpouring of nearly $6 million—a signal to outside contributors that helped ensure the success of the program.

Students Because of their large numbers and the many families that they represent, students make up the largest public relations arm—for good or bad—that a university has. The quality of the teaching which they receive is the greatest determinant of their allegiance to the institution. However, a sound administrative attitude toward students, involving them as much as possible in decisions that affect their campus lives, is extremely important. So are other forms of communication, achieved through support of student publications and broadcast stations and numerous other ways. When, upon graduation, they are inducted en masse into the university's alumni society, chances are good that, if they are pleased with their collegiate experience, many will support the university in its future undertakings. Public relations effort directed at students is thus essential.

Alumni and Other Donors Fund-raising activities have increased dramatically at most colleges and universities in recent years. As a result, private financial support for these institutions rose 8.8 percent over the preceding academic year to a record $8.9 billion during 1988–1989, according to the Council for Financial Aid to Education. Individuals contributed nearly half of this sum, 25 percent more than the preceding year. Alumni giving totaled about $2.3 billion.

FIGURE 19.2
Some universities try to increase public awareness of themselves by having faculty members quoted in the media as experts when news develops in their special fields. In this advertisement published in the *Directory of Experts, Authorities & Spokespersons,* the University of Buffalo invites the media to use its services. (Courtesy of the University of Buffalo)

Call the University at Buffalo first...
for authorities with proven media experience in

☐ Asthma/Allergies
☐ U.S.-Canada Trade
☐ Current Legal Issues
☐ Educational Issues
☐ Pediatric Medicine/Surgery
☐ The Great Lakes
☐ Cancer and Nutrition
☐ Dental Research
☐ Human Body Implants
☐ Earthquake Engineering Research
☐ Environmental Problems
☐ Problems of Aging
☐ Human Sexuality
☐ Trauma Care
☐ Geographic Information Systems

and hundreds more!

Call: The University at Buffalo
News Bureau
136 Crofts Hall
Amherst, New York 14260
716-636-2626
FAX: 716-636-3765

UNIVERSITY AT BUFFALO
State University of New York

MEDIA RESOURCE GUIDES AVAILABLE ON REQUEST

With the stakes so high, the demand for experienced fund-raisers has created a shortage among those qualified, and salaries in some instances have skyrocketed well beyond $100,000 or more annually, accompanied by elaborate fringe-benefit packages.

Colleges and universities use the money mainly to attract and pay new faculty, to buy equipment and provide support for faculty research, and to attract and offer financial aid for students. A common complaint is that few grants are provided to repair or replace aged structures, re-equip obsolete science laboratories, and provide additional classroom and library space. These pressures are accompanied by a number of complications: societal demands that costs be trimmed and management streamlined; rising costs for salaries and benefits for faculty and staff (particularly in health fields); growing public concern over tuition increases; the cost of serving increasingly diverse student bodies including remedial programs and provisions for disabled students; and new developments in scholarship such as the increasing faculty collaboration in combined, expensive research projects across disciplines.

The placement of universities' endowment funds, investments totaling more than $1.7 billion, often poses a public relations problem. During the last decade or so, groups opposed to South Africa's apartheid system have persuaded many universities and other entities to sever financial ties with the nation. In 1990, for example, organizations such as the Tobacco Investment Project persuaded Harvard University and the City University of New York to sell their highly profitable stock holdings in the tobacco companies.

The movement's spread brought a similar dilemma to other universities: how and if they could withdraw their holdings in tobacco companies without sacrificing the firms' large annual grants. Particularly at risk was the United Negro College Fund, which has been receiving a total of nearly $500,000 annually from the Philip Morris Companies and RJR Nabisco.

In addition to annual operating expense drives, universities increasingly conduct long-range capital fund campaigns for very large sums, such as the $1.15 billion goal at Columbia University and the $1.1 billion goal at Stanford University.

Many institutions employ students to participate in fund-raising phonothons. At the University of Michigan students called 970,000 alumni and raised $8.3 million during a recent nine-month period.

At most institutions letters are mailed to specific graduating classes over the names of members who have agreed to be class agents for that purpose (one of the most unusual is shown in Figure 19.3).

Sought are not only year-by-year contributions but bequests and annuities as well. In return, the colleges publish honor rolls listing donors, invite contributors to join honorary clubs (the President's Club, for example), and name rooms and buildings for the largest givers. Educational events and tours to foreign countries often are arranged to build and sustain alumni interest. Class reunions are said to be the most powerful instruments in getting alumni to give.

Universities often use matching grants to make a donor's contribution go further—and thus make giving more attractive. For instance, a donor in Dallas, who wanted to remain anonymous, contributed $8 million toward the establishment of faculty enrichment chairs at the University of Texas at Austin. The sum was matched by foundations, and the entire $16 million, in turn, was matched by the university, making possible the

Billy Clyde Puckett

SEMI-TOUGH EX-HORNY TOAD

Dear Fellow and Female Alumnis and Alumnuses:

My name is Billy Clyde Puckett, who I used to semi-doughpop Longhorns and Mustangs for you on the football field, and our old school has asked me to talk to you a minute about your basic upfront whipout, which is what I call money.

Like you, I been getting all this mail through the years, which I throw away unopened, because I know somebody in a vest and tie with his hair parted in the middle wants me to help keep TCU afloat by making a contribution.

Sometimes I do and sometimes I don't — just like you — depending on whether my wallet looks like an elephant has slept on it.

But I've thought about it lately and I've decided that TCU can't survive and prosper and flourish, and maybe even go to the Cotton Bowl again someday, unless we break the death grip on our moneyclips. TCU is a private university, as some of us intellectuals are aware, which means that every time the Frogs need something, they can't go plowing their way through the polyester of the state legislature and getting what they want like some of those other universities can, which is what you might call the sissy way to do it.

Naw, we got to dig down and take care of our own selves. That's the only way TCU can outlast the state schools. Do you want to be outlasted by some farm schooler? I say TCU deserves to grow if for no other reason than to preserve the memories of Sam Baugh and Davey O'Brien — and all the coffee Maxine spilled on everybody at the old drugstore.

The best thing is, TCU ain't proud. The old school will accept $10 from you, $25, $100, on up. Nobody's saying you got to give as much as them high rollers do. What's important about a lot of us giving *something* is that it impresses them corporations and foundations who look and see how enthusiastic the alumnis are before they decide how much of their own cheese they're gonna turn loose of.

Do it like I do. I write a check and I put "gift" or "research" on it so I can deduct it, then I stick a pin in the upper righthand corner so the bank's computer will spit it out and send it back, and then I re-mail it and that gives your paycheck time to let the swelling go down. If enough of us contribute, maybe one of them corporations will buy us a quarterback who throws darts and a halfback who don't run sideways. Even some books and test tubes, what the hell!

All of this is part of what every college calls the Annual Fund Drive, which is a businesslike way to describe begging. But it's necessary when you consider that it costs about $45 million a year to run the joint. Actually, the figure is closer to $46 million if you count the student parking tickets that don't get paid and the library books that get stole.

Anyhow, haul off and give something, no matter how small, and make all those tests you cheated on and all that beer you drank stand for something!

Sincerely,

Billy Clyde

Billy Clyde Puckett

(as dictated to Dan Jenkins, '53)

FIGURE 19.3

This unusual alumni solicitation letter was written by Dan Jenkins, a 1953 journalism graduate of Texas Christian University and longtime *Sports Illustrated* writer and editor. (Billy Clyde Puckett is a character in Jenkins's novel *Semi-Tough*.)

establishment of 32 new chairs. Such support is essential in order for good universities to become great universities.

Influential alumni and other important friends of colleges and universities also are encouraged, through personal contact and correspondence, to provide political clout with legislative bodies and boards of regents, in support of the institutions' financial and other objectives. Such support also is important in the recruitment of students with outstanding academic or athletic achievement.

STANFORD GETS A BLACK EYE

A university's good relations with many of its key publics—government, alumni, corporations, and faculty—can be easily upset when the institution is charged with improprieties.

Stanford University's credibility and reputation were tainted after a congressional subcommittee found that it had used funds earmarked for overhead costs on government research contracts to pay for receptions and household items, including an antique commode, at its president's home.

According to media reports, Stanford president Donald Kennedy made matters worse when, in his congressional testimony, subcommittee members perceived him to be "uncooperative" and somewhat "arrogant" about the university's accounting methods. More bad publicity followed when it was reported that Stanford was attempting to charge the government for performing an audit of its own books.

Realizing all the negative publicity in what the *Chronicle of Higher Education* called a "political and public relations fiasco," Stanford then began the slow process of mending fences and doing "damage control" by hiring Hill & Knowlton for counsel and advice. Of particular concern to the university were its alumni, many of whom worried about the university's possible misuse of their contributions.

Government State and federal governments often hold the vital key to whether universities receive sufficient monies to maintain facilities, faculty, and programs. Most large institutions have someone who regularly monitors the state legislature on appropriations and issues ranging from laboratory experiments on animals to standardized tests and taxes. Their work includes (1) competing with other state institutions for money, (2) defending proposed increases in higher-education budgets and protecting against cuts, (3) establishing an institution's identity in the minds of legislators, and (4) responding to lawmakers' requests for favors. Said Robert Dickens, coordinator of government relations for the University of Nevada at Reno: "When I say I'm a lobbyist, some people look at me as if I need a shower. It's a new business with the universities, and some people think it's a dirty business. But nothing's dirtier than not having resources."

The declining federal support for higher education since the 1960s also has led to an increase in the number of government relations experts representing universities in Washington, D.C. Their work complements that of the American Council on Education, the National Association of Land-Grant Universities, and the Association of American Universities. They not only lobby members of Congress regarding legislation that might have an adverse or favorable effect on their clients but also seek information from federal agencies about new programs and uncommitted funds.

The Community As in the case of industry, a college or university must maintain a good relationship with the members of the community in which it is situated. The greatest supporters that an institution may have are the people within its immediate sphere of influence, many of whom mingle with its faculty, staff members, and students. Tax dollars are also an immense benefit, although the fact that university property is tax exempt may impose a strain unless the institution voluntarily agrees to some form of compensation for services such as fire and police protection.

The amicable ''town-gown'' relationship so avidly sought by city leaders and university officials alike generally is tested in other ways as well, including students' loud parties and careless driving. University and local officials cope with these problems as well as they can.

In order to bridge the town-gown gap often evident, faculty and staff members are encouraged to achieve community visibility through work with civic and other organizations. Business groups often take the lead. The Chamber of Commerce in Lawrence, Kansas, for example, for many years sponsored an annual barbecue, including various other activities, to give faculty and townspeople an opportunity to get to know each other better.

Prospective Students Suffering from declining revenues, increased costs of operation, and a dwindling pool of prospective students occasioned by lower birthrates, many colleges have turned to highly competitive recruiting methods. Some, in the ''hard-sell'' classification, use extensive advertising in print and broadcast media and on billboards. Other colleges and universities have replaced their catalogues and brochures with four-color, slick materials that use bright graphics and catchy headlines to lure students.

Various other recruiting devices are used. Vanderbilt University sent personalized videotapes to about 40 highly coveted high school seniors. The College of the Atlantic took prospective students on a 90-foot sailing yacht party. Stanford University was host to 750 high school students who stayed overnight in dormitory rooms, visited classes, attended a musical program, and participated in a campus scavenger hunt. Brown University each spring sponsors a party for up to 250 prospects on an Amtrak train traveling between Washington and Providence, Rhode Island. As competition for students has increased, so have the costs of recruiting them. Expenditures on admissions and recruitment have run about $700,000 or more for private universities and in excess of $600,000 for public universities. This high level of activity creates many opportunities for employment in public relations and development.

The purchase of mailing lists is a common tool of student recruitment. Each of approximately 900 colleges annually buys from 10,000 to 15,000 names and addresses of high school students who have taken College Board Examinations. The most sought-after prospects are National Merit Scholarship winners, and it is not uncommon for competing universities to shower a prospect with such lures as free tuition for four years, a private dorm room, guarantees of priority registration, and so on.

Other Publics Examples of other groups requiring special attention are shown in Figure 19.4.

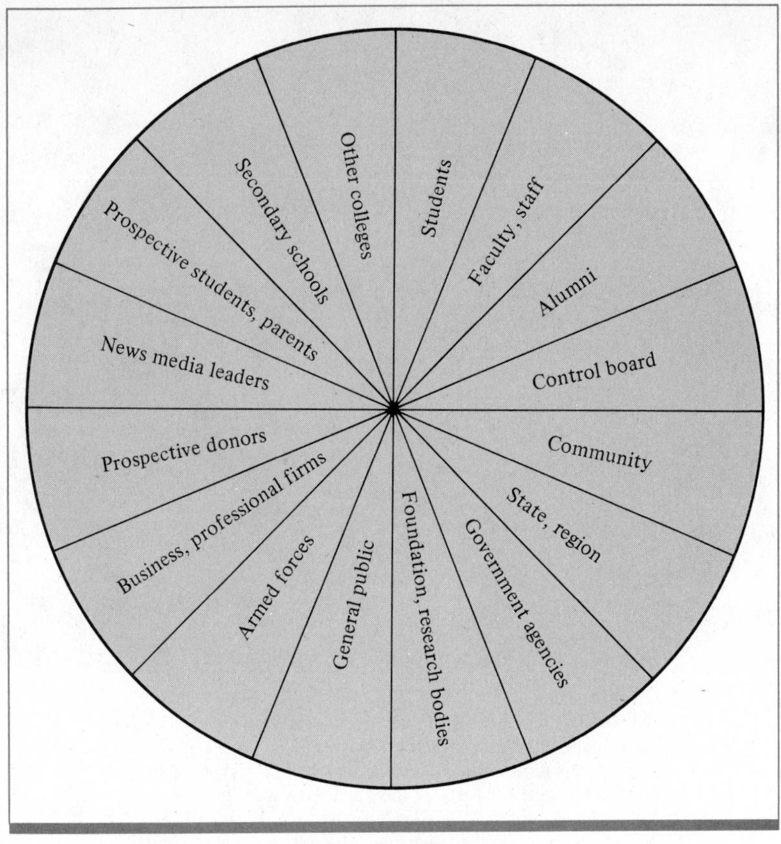

FIGURE 19.4
The wheel shows most of the publics with which college public relations offices endeavor to maintain two-way communication.

SUPPORT FOR ADVANCEMENT OFFICERS

Most public relations, alumni, and development leaders—known euphemistically as *advancement officers*—enjoy the many services of the Council for Advancement and Support of Education (CASE), with headquarters in Washington, D.C. The aims of CASE are described as building public understanding, stepping up the level of alumni involvement and support, strengthening communication with internal and external audiences, improving government relations, and increasing private financial support. Among CASE current objectives are (1) helping leaders at historically black institutions advance in their careers, (2) publicizing a code of ethics, (3) developing gift and expenditure reporting standards, (4) improving the communication of university research to the public, and (5) studying the impact of new technologies.

Representing more than 2400 institutional members, CASE serves nationally as a principal public affairs arm for education, monitoring federal rights legislation and regulations and working with the American Council on Education and other associations on education-related issues. The organization provides district conferences and

FIGURE 19.5
The Cornell University news service cleverly obtained extensive publicity for a laboratory apparatus developed by researchers to grow fleas, replacing dogs and cats kept for that purpose. It called the device the "artificial dog" and distributed this photograph by Claude Levet of a laboratory cat, Amie, in front of the apparatus. The release created such headlines as "Research team embarks on flea-ting project." (Courtesy of Cornell University and Claude Levet.)

institutes, evaluation and critique services, a certification program, awards, reference materials, and placement opportunities. Thousands each summer attend its four-day assembly, replete with workshops.

ELEMENTARY AND SECONDARY SCHOOLS

RESPONSE TO CONTEMPORARY ISSUES

In 1983 the National Commission on Excellence in Education, citing "a nation at risk," called for massive educational reform. The resulting nationwide debate represented the latest in a series of public examinations that education in America has undergone during the last several decades. Integration, busing, accountability, book censorship, sex education, discipline, drugs, and vandalism—all these issues have commanded continuing public attention.

The 18-member commission made recommendations in five major areas, based on the belief that everyone can learn, that everyone is born with an urge to learn that can be nurtured, that a solid high school education is within the reach of virtually all, and that lifelong learning will equip people with the skills required for new careers and for citizenship. Among the recommendations were the following:

1. ***Content.*** State and local high school graduation requirements should be strengthened, and all students seeking a diploma should be required to take four years of English, three years of mathematics, three years of science, three years of social studies, and one-half year of computer science. Two years of foreign language are strongly recommended for the college-bound.

2. ***Standards and expectations.*** Schools, colleges, and universities should adopt more rigorous and measurable standards, and higher expectations, for academic performance and student conduct, and four-year colleges and universities should raise their admission requirements.

3. ***Time.*** Significantly more time should be devoted to learning the New Basics. This would require more effective use of the existing school day, a longer school day, or a lengthened school year.

4. ***Teaching.*** Teacher candidates should be required to meet high educational standards, and demonstrate an aptitude for teaching and competence in an academic discipline. Salaries should be made more competitive and market-sensitive, with promotion, tenure, and retention tied to teacher evaluation. Teachers should be under 11-month contract. Career ladders should be developed. Substantial nonschool personnel resources should be used to help overcome the shortage of math and science teachers. Incentives should be developed to attract outstanding students to teaching. Master teachers should help design teacher preparation programs and supervise beginning teachers.

5. ***Leadership and fiscal support.*** Citizens should hold educators and elected officials responsible for providing the leadership necessary to achieve these reforms, and citizens should provide the fiscal support and stability required to bring about the reforms.

Although stung by the commission's indictments, school officials welcomed the nationwide interest aroused. They were hopeful that the spotlight thrown on educational needs would result in another post-Sputnik-type wave of support, which indeed followed.

News of the commission's recommendations reached the offices of thousands of school superintendents almost immediately over the Education U.S.A. Newsline and Information Network, an electronic news and advisory service of the National School Public Relations Association (NSPRA). When local media people called shortly thereafter, many of the more alert superintendents and their communication coordinators were prepared to offer reactions.

NSPRA followed its newsline alert with a special bulletin to members describing the recommendations more fully. The bulletin contained a statement by its president, William J. Banach, urging educators to "initiate the movement toward better educational programming by matching the commission's recommendations against what exists in local districts. Then they should take their findings to the people, explain the value of a well-educated society, and work with citizens, business people, governmental leaders, and others to generate support for the kinds of schools America needs and deserves.''

Also enclosed was a telephone survey questionnaire prepared by Banach for use by school public relations people to ascertain community attitudes toward the recommendations—a necessary first step in the coordination of local school response with anticipated state and federal legislation and recommendations.

These actions, and others taken throughout the nation, provided a striking example of the vastly increased appreciation of the role of public relations that has swept many school districts and state and federal school offices in recent years.

And it has come none too soon. Questions had steadily mounted over the teaching of basic reading, writing, and computation skills; the requirements for graduation; the toughness of courses; and more. California's Proposition 13 had been preceded and followed by taxpayer revolts elsewhere in the nation that brought tightened purse strings for school maintenance and the defeat of one capital improvement bond issue after another. Busing and integration—the major problems of the 1960s and 1970s—remained key issues. The campaign seeking tax credits for parents of children enrolled in private schools was troublesome. There were fewer students, more citizens without school-age children, more one-parent families. School-building closings and boundary shifts brought protests.

The issues facing school administrators, teachers, and public relations coordinators became even more complex as the nationwide movement to increase the accountability and efficiency of teachers grew, with quality-based education (QBE) programs sweeping through most state legislatures. Even more pressure resulted from the 1986 report of a 14-member task force appointed by the Carnegie Forum on Education and the Economy. The report called for a wholesale restructuring of the teaching corps designed to provide a profession of ''well-educated teachers prepared to assume new powers and responsibilities to redesign schools for the future.'' Its two major proposals were to (1) set up a national board to certify teachers who meet standards and (2) confine training to graduate school, eliminating the bachelor of education degree.

The pressure for school reform increased in 1989 when the Carnegie Foundation, in a report titled ''Turning Points: Preparing American Youth for the 21st Century,'' declared that schools, community groups, and businesses should work together to educate adolescents between the ages of 10 and 15 to become productive workers, healthy citizens, and responsible members of society.

''Young adolescents are far more at risk for self-destructive behaviors—educational failure, drug and alcohol abuse, school-age pregnancy, contraction of sexually transmitted disease, violence—than their age group ever was before,'' the report stated.

Schools were urged to create challenging, interdisciplinary curricula that stress health and citizenship, as well as basic education in science, math, history, and English. The report, among other things, recommended that schools be restructured to allow students and staff to meet in small groups, and that every student have an adult adviser.

Meanwhile, increasing amounts of financial aid were being funneled to K–12 (kindergarten through twelfth grade) schools, with corporate contributions rising from \$33.9 million in 1987 to \$51.9 million in 1988, according to the Council for Aid to Education. Hundreds of corporations, however, were demanding a greater voice in deciding what reforms were needed and how they would be implemented.

In 1990 the monthly *Partnerships in Education Journal* reported the formation of about 140,000 ties between business firms and schools. Many were year-by-year "Adopt-a-School" arrangements, but some extended for ten years or longer. This longer commitment signals strong business concerns, among others, that future employees would be ill prepared for demanding industry and service jobs. *Public Relations Journal* reported that programs financed included combating illiteracy, bolstering the recruitment of minority students, providing leadership and technical training for teachers, reducing the dropout rate, using computers as learning tools, and creating innovative plans for urban schools.

The larger, more progressive public school systems and independent, private schools, as well as thousands of smaller ones, had long maintained public relations programs in an effort to increase public awareness of their critical needs. Budgetary squeezes, however, had constricted many of those programs. But the necessity for sound community relations—at the heart of both management and public relations—was more evident in the 1990s than ever before. If funds were not available or the system too small to warrant a full-fledged public relations program, then a sole information specialist was employed, full- or part-time. School public relations had come into its own.

REACHING THE PUBLICS

The primary publics of a school system are teachers, children, parents, staff, and the community. As in all public relations, research, planning, action, and evaluation comprise the essential steps with which to reach these publics. On the desks of information directors, communication coordinators, and school-community relations specialists (or whatever the title may be, and it varies widely) are booklets prepared by national and state offices detailing hundreds of ways in which they may carry out their mission. Perhaps the best way to describe school public relations in its major aspects is to examine some of the outstanding programs accorded the Gold Medallion award of the National School Public Relations Association.

Analysis of Public Opinion Formal opinion surveys for schools often cost from $7,500 to $15,000, but the Utica (Michigan) Community Schools system conducts Project HEAR (Householder Educational Attitude Reactions) at a cost of only about $250 per year. The system uses volunteers to telephone a random sample of approximately 300 persons and ask questions for about 15 minutes.

Many of the questions are borrowed from the annual Gallup poll of the Public's Attitudes Toward the Public Schools and from a countrywide survey conducted by the Macomb (Michigan) Intermediate School District; other questions reflect local school district issues. A computer generates the phone numbers from names on a voter registration list, and the questions are pretested for proper phrasing. The persistent but courteous callers have achieved a remarkable 100 percent response rate, thus ensuring the reliability of the random-selection method, even though it is restricted to registered voters and does not include the community at large. The responses are used to readjust school programs each year.

Face-to-Face Communication Supplementing the newsletters and brochures distributed by all systems, the Fairfax County (Virginia) Public Schools, a large district in suburban Washington, emphasizes face-to-face communication. The superintendent meets monthly with advisory councils representing all categories of employees, bimonthly with a planning council representing citizen organizations, and regularly with a countywide student advisory council.

Members of the office of community relations (1) help the PTA county council conduct semiannual school-community nights, (2) maintain regular contact with other local groups, (3) operate a speakers' bureau equipped with a slide-tape presentation, (4) conduct administration building tours for school staffs, and (5) arrange student award ceremonies at school board meetings with accompanying publicity.

Confronted with the potential defection of parents of preschool children to private schools, the system conducted "kindergarten roundup" programs and tours in all elementary schools. The invitations to parents were accompanied by a brochure describing five preschool classes as well as free vision and hearing tests. Slide-tape shows were screened at the open houses and questions answered. The result: a record kindergarten enrollment the following fall.

The Fairfax County system won a Gold Medallion for its total public relations program because of, among other achievements, its good relationship with the news media, including service to 100 media outlets—suburban weeklies as well as metropolitan dailies and dozens of radio and television stations.

The system's winning techniques included (1) close personal daily contact with news people; (2) special orientations for new press representatives; (3) distribution of systemwide news stories, feature story tips, and memoranda concerning future events; (4) public service announcements for radio and television; (5) weekly taped radio programs about the school system; (6) press packets for board meetings; (7) distribution of photographs; and (8) interviews with board and key staff people.

Public Forums For only $35 each, the New Jersey School Board Association prepared a kit containing a 33-minute filmstrip, introductory comments, instructions on how to guide a discussion period, and an in-depth questionnaire with which to obtain valuable feedback at public and in-school meetings, as well as a take-home brochure. It was designed so that any volunteer could conduct such a forum. The filmstrip stars students, teachers, and others and relates how public education seeks to respond to social change.

Marketing of Public School Education A pioneer in public opinion surveying in education, William J. Banach, administrative director at the Macomb Intermediate School District in Mount Clemens, Michigan, developed a two-year plan designed to discover what the public wants in its schools. The plan also sought ways to respond to those desires and to educate citizens about actions the school could and could not take. Banach based the campaign on what he termed "the 90-7-3 concept of school communication":

> Ninety percent of the school's image is who we are and what we do 24 hours a day. How school people think, act, and appear and what they say are key factors in marketing. This is why staff training is an integral part of a marketing program—to help people understand their communication roles and how important they are.

Seven percent of the marketing effort is listening—tuning in to find out what people like, don't like, want, don't want. Anything we do to know more about our "customers" is worth doing.

Three percent of marketing is outbound communication—publications, posters, news releases, and other visible and tangible items.

In successive phases, the marketing plan was targeted at (1) elementary parents, with a focus on reading, writing, and arithmetic; (2) secondary students and their parents, emphasizing "the basics and beyond" and beginning with specific objectives based on survey results and meetings with student leaders; and (3) citizens without children in school.

Arrangements were made for teachers to apply "No. 1 apple" stickers to outstanding student papers, and all classroom papers were sent home each Friday. Posters welcoming visitors were placed at each school. The slogan "Your public schools . . . There's no better place to learn" was displayed on billboards, calendars, bookmarks, bumper stickers, T-shirt transfers, and thank-you cards.

A survey made a year after the campaign began revealed enhanced public confidence in the schools. The Macomb Plan, as it is called, has attracted national attention.

Campaigns to Finance the Schools When the academic year began in Springfield, Oregon, there was money for only three or four months of classes. Unemployment was high, and the district had already lost two finance campaigns in a row. Nevertheless, school leaders decided to seek a $12.6 million operating levy at an election in September and a new tax base guaranteeing up to $16.9 million in annual funding at the November general election.

Because state law prohibited use of public funds to advocate any election issue, the system's communications officer could only issue appeals through already authorized publications, make talks, and enlist volunteer help. Private sources provided a budget of about $1000 for each election. Past campaigns were analyzed and a new strategy was devised, built around two main points:

- Instead of emphasizing the money needed and aiming messages at male heads of households, all advertising was directed at women and stressed children rather than budgets. One advertisement showed a child's smiling face and the words, "Vote Yes! For Kids. District 19 Tax Base Nov. 4."
- Volunteers gained insight into voter preferences through a barrage of telephone calls. Persons indicating a negative response were ignored, while those favorable or undecided were sent pamphlets and contacted personally in an effort to sway or reinforce their decisions.

Elements of the campaigns also included paid media spots, a speakers' bureau with slide presentation, broadcast public affairs programs, internal communication among the district's employees, a focus on the black community, yard signs, endorsements by the board of realtors and other civic leaders, news media conferences, announcements on marquees, and T-shirts.

Both measures passed in surprisingly large voter turnouts. In evaluating the campaigns, system leaders concluded that the person-to-person element was the most effective of all. And the combined cost of both campaigns was only $900.

Crisis Communication For emergencies such as earthquakes, sudden loss of utilities, severe storms, hazardous material spills, explosions, fires, tornadoes, nuclear warnings, plane crashes, bomb threats—for all such crises a communication plan should be in readiness. For the Great Falls (Montana) Public Schools, situated in a city near an Air Force base and missile sites, Audrey Olson, the school district's information consultant, embarked on a project of integrating all emergency procedures into one comprehensive crisis procedure manual.

Communication procedures were provided in checklist form. In an attached envelope were important documents addressing unique situations facing individual schools. Copies of the manual were placed near every telephone in the district, and checklist instructions were made available in every classroom without a phone. A special alert radio was installed in the schools and the administration building.

Procedures were included for pupil dismissal, transportation, and media relations. The manual also contains policy statements by top officials and a letter with which explanations may be provided for parents.

CASE STUDY: RECRUITING MINORITY STUDENTS IN WISCONSIN

Nearly 160,000 students are enrolled in the 13 universities and 13 freshman–sophomore centers that comprise the University of Wisconsin System. Historically, however, minority enrollment has represented only 4 to 5 percent of that total; competition among the institutions for the same, relatively few minority students who desire to pursue higher education had not worked.

A new approach was then sought, sparked by UW System President Kenneth A. Shaw's goal, announced in 1987, for the number of new minority freshman and transfer students to be increased by 50 percent by 1993 and by 100 percent by 1998.

Research by the Wisconsin Department of Public Instruction indicated that students needed to be reached prior to high school. So University Relations Vice President Ronald C. Bornstein, Shaw, and Assistant to the President for Minority Affairs James Sulton, Jr., jointly agreed that the best way to meet enrollment goals was to design a campaign to reach minority *middle school* students in Wisconsin and let them know college was a real possibility.

Objectives Three objectives were set: (1) to reach minority young people in Wisconsin areas with the highest minority population, (2) to expose them to role models of young people like themselves who currently were attending college, and (3) to develop mechanisms for these young people to receive information and counseling on college admissions and financial aid.

The Approach Using a celebrity spokesperson was considered, but rejected. The key to a successful campaign, it was decided, would be showing people with whom

FIGURE 19.6
The University of Wisconsin's brochure promoting its ''Do College'' campaign for minority enrollment features a young man and woman in cap and gown on the cover. (Courtesy of University of Wisconsin System; photo by James Gill)

minority young people could most easily identify. The leaders then pondered how to reach the target audience. They decided that the primary focus would be on TV spots with top production values and a look, sound, and feel likely to appeal to the target audience. They would be run near programs that research indicated minority young people were most likely to watch.

The Campaign The campaign, with a ''Do College'' theme, was a multimedia effort produced over a 12-month period. The centerpiece was a series of seven 30-second TV spots. Each featured a minority student at a UW institution. The students were selected from auditions of more than 50 students recommended by minority/disadvantaged coordinators at each campus.

The students were asked to talk about the difficulties in being a minority student on a largely white campus and the satisfaction of achieving a college education. To lend authenticity, the spots were scripted from the students' own comments during their initial screen test. Having the students tell their stories in their own words was regarded as crucial to having the spots ring true. Each spot ended with the tag line, ''Do College.''

To reduce costs, all the spots were filmed in two UW–Madison dorm rooms. The students provided personal items as props and set dressing. Funders were given audio credits at the end of each spot. To keep credits short, only one funder was mentioned in any given spot.

Prior to airing, the video spots were field-tested among focus groups of minority young people in Milwaukee and Racine. Their response was overwhelmingly positive.

Radio spots also were produced using the same audio. In all, more than 1500 paid radio and TV ads ran during an 11-week period, September 11 to November 25, 1989. The spots were broadcast on commercial stations in the Milwaukee, Racine-Kenosha, and Janesville-Beloit areas.

In print, one image was used consistently—a photograph of two students in graduation caps and gowns—with the words "Do College." The same image was used in a four-color ad in a special tabloid section of the Milwaukee *Journal,* which went to 310,000 readers, with an extra 1,000 reprints distributed.

A brochure using the "Do College" image—along with photos of the seven young people shown in the TV spots—was produced. It gave concrete suggestions on how to pursue a college education and included the address and toll-free number for the Minority Information Center, a statewide resource for minority students. More than 12,000 brochures were distributed, mainly through school counselors in targeted areas.

More than 1300 "Do College" posters with the same image were distributed. They promoted a new toll-free number and included postcards to mail for information on financial aid, precollege programs, or college admissions.

Counselors at middle schools in the target areas received the posters and brochures for use in their efforts. In addition, the posters and brochures were distributed widely by the Minority Information Center and by a seven-member group of volunteers throughout the state. "Do College" also was featured on the cover of a faculty and academic staff quarterly magazine.

Resources Paid advertising, rather than public service announcements, was required because of the decision to place the TV spots around programs with the highest viewership among minority young people. Wisconsin Bell, Miller Brewing Company, and the Wisconsin Power & Light Foundation donated a total of $60,000, mainly to purchase airtime. Production costs of the spots were paid by John Roach, an Emmy-winning producer, and the Madison production firm of RW Video.

Miller Brewing Company's advertising agency, Frenkenberry, Laughlin and Constable, Inc., of Milwaukee, provided detailed media research and direction in placing ads to reach the desired demographic groups. Two UW System staff members coordinated production of the TV and radio spots and print materials. An in-house designer produced the print materials.

Results A followup survey of 3500 students in Milwaukee and Racine revealed what was termed "a phenomenal awareness" of the campaign. Eighty-two percent of the Milwaukee students and 77 percent of those in Racine had seen or heard the ads. The students were asked if the TV spots prompted them to send in a postcard, call the toll-free number, or talk to a school counselor. Thirty-two percent of the Milwaukee students and 8 percent of those in Racine said they had taken one or more of these actions.

The Minority Information Center received more than 300 postcards and almost 100 phone calls requesting information.

Recognition In 1990 the University Relations Division of the University of Wisconsin System won two gold medals, including the Grand Gold award, in the annual competition sponsored by the Council for the Advancement and Support of Education.

CASE PROBLEM

The office of Paul W. Hartman, former vice chancellor for university relations and development at Texas Christian University, mailed the fund-raising letter to alumni from ''Billy Clyde Puckett, semi-tough ex–horny toad,'' displayed in this chapter.

As shown at the bottom of the letter, Puckett is Dan Jenkins, a 1953 TCU journalism graduate. Jenkins is author of the novel *Semi-Tough* and other famous best-sellers and longtime associate editor of *Sports Illustrated*—so famous that in 1987 he was inducted into the Texas Walk of the Stars in Austin's Sixth Street entertainment district along with a football coach, state official, country singer, and other widely known sportswriters.

Many alumni laughed at the offbeat solicitation letter and forwarded contributions. Some others, however, sent Hartman what he termed ''hate'' mail, protesting the letter's nature.

Was the use of the letter justified? In your opinion, what are the special problems of raising university development funds from alumni and friends year after year?

QUESTIONS FOR REVIEW AND DISCUSSION

1. Who is the chief public relations officer on a college or university campus? Why?

2. A college news bureau is involved in a vast array of day-to-day public relations operations. Name five or six of these functions.

3. With what primary public does a sound university public relations program begin? Why? List eight other constituencies that must be addressed in such a program.

4. In what ways may powerful alumni and other friends provide support for an institution of higher learning? What is the role of the development office in gaining this support? What is CASE and what support does it provide for public relations and alumni officers?

5. The National Commission on Excellence in Education called for massive educational reform. What were its main concerns and how did school officials respond?

6. If you were to conduct a formal opinion survey, could you improve on the procedures followed by the Utica (Michigan) Community Schools system? Explain your answer.

7. Tell how the Fairfax County (Virginia) Public Schools system maintains effective community relations.

8. Do you agree with the marketing concept used by public relations people in the Macomb Intermediate School District in Mount Clemens, Michigan? Describe the key points of this plan in explaining your answer.

9. What public relations problems may be evident when a community turns down a bond issue to improve school financing? What public relations actions do you consider important in building and maintaining strong support of schools?

10. What key public relations planning decisions helped ensure the success of the minority recruitment campaign of the University of Wisconsin System?

SUGGESTED READINGS

''Anti-Smoking Groups Push Universities and Other Investors to Sell Holdings in Tobacco Companies and Refuse Gifts.'' *Chronicle of Higher Education,* June 20, 1990, pp. A1, 31–32.

''Columbia U. Opens Campaign to Raise $1.5 Billion: Cornell Is Said to Prepare for a $1.25 Billion Drive.'' *Chronicle of Higher Education,* October 3, 1990, pp. A33–34.

McMillen, Liz. ''Gifts to Colleges Rise 8.8% in Year, Reach Record $8.9 Billion.'' *Chronicle of Higher Education,* May 30, 1990, pp. 1, A26–27. Includes breakdown of major giving categories.

Putka, Gary. ''Meet the PR Man Who Took Candor Right to the Limit.'' *Wall Street Journal,* February 1, 1990, pp. 1, A9. Profile of Bob Beyers, former director of Stanford University News Service.

Sheldon, Keith A. ''Por Qué No Puede Leer Juanito?'' *Communication World,* May 1991, pp. 22–25. Language diversity of students in American schools.

Wilson, Robin. ''College Recruiting Gimmicks Get More Lavish as Competition for New Freshmen Heats Up.'' *Chronicle of Higher Education,* March 7, 1990, pp. 1, A34.

CHAPTER

20

Entertainment, Sports, and Travel

Use of promotional techniques to publicize individuals, entertainments, and sporting events is another facet of public relations work. Although occupying only a small segment of the public relations spectrum, personality buildup and entertainment "drum-beating" attract public attention because of their highly visible and sometimes flashy nature. Men and women engaged in what is known colloquially as "hype" need ample technical skills and an energetic approach because the work is highly competitive and subject to unpredictable changes in public mood.

Personal and entertainment publicity dates back to the early days of traveling theatrical troupes and circuses. Practitioners became known as press agents. Today's version of the craft is more complex and sophisticated, especially in its heavy use of television. This chapter examines how publicity methods are used to create awareness of personalities and to generate interest in entertainment and athletics. After discussing the concepts of the "personality" and "celebrity," it explores the question of ethics in this highly charged field. The steps in an entertainment publicity campaign are listed. The second part of the chapter takes a close look at sports publicity, examining the Super Bowl as the most extravagant example of this area of public relations.

The travel industry, another competitor for the consumer's recreational dollars, also depends upon public relations skills for its prosperity. The chapter closes with a discussion of travel promotion.

THE USE AND ABUSE OF PUBLICITY

Suddenly the name *Dick Tracy,* a movie about a largely forgotten comic strip detective hero, bombarded the American public from many directions. Within a two-week period at the height of the 1990 summer movie season, it appeared in newspaper stories, on magazine covers, in radio and television broadcasts. A *Dick Tracy* paperback book blossomed on the sales racks. So did a Tracy coloring book. Warren Beatty and Madonna, the film's stars, gave repeated interviews. A life-size cardboard cutout of Dick Tracy stood in every McDonald's, promoting the fast-food chain's tie-in Crimestoppers game. Shops sold Dick Tracy T-shirts, mugs, and hats.

A coincidence? Obviously not. The publicity campaign was the most extensive, intricately planned hype of an entertainment in many years, intended to create such an opening smash that the film would be a runaway box office success. After spending $46.5 million to make the picture, the Walt Disney Studios spent $54.7 million more to market and distribute it—with only mild success, incidentally.

Dick Tracy demonstrates in intensive form the work of public relations specialists whose job is to create attention for ''personalities'' and shows that, for a short time at least, may become household words.

The publicity buildup of individuals and events is an integral part of the American fabric, and those who engage in it must be creative and extremely hardworking. This area is outside the mainstream of public relations, however, and professional public relations practitioners often are embarrassed by the tactics of press agents and publicity experts. Although only a relatively small number of men and women are engaged in the promotion of entertainers, politicians, and ''beautiful people,'' the exaggerations and ''little white lies''—not so little, at times—that some of them use are wrongly viewed by uninformed people as representative of the public relations industry as a whole.

Nevertheless, all students of public relations should learn how the publicity trade functions. At some point in their careers, they may find a knowledge of its techniques useful—for example, if they are engaged to guide the career of a political aspirant or advise an ambitious professional person or business executive. When applied discreetly and honestly, the techniques of publicity can be useful in many situations. They fall into disrepute when employed to create false images and to substitute deceit for truth.

THE CULT OF PERSONALITY

In contemporary society, the cult of personality has attained enormous stature. Newspapers run daily columns of short items about people by whom their readers supposedly are fascinated. The magazine *People* achieved very large circulation quickly after its appearance. The same personalities turn up on television and radio talk shows all over the United States. Weekly gossip tabloids such as *National Enquirer* and *Star* peddle sensational revelations about the private lives of individuals.

Celebrity worship isn't new. A hundred years ago, press agents touring the small cities of the country ahead of traveling theatrical parties showered local editors with publicity stories—and often with gossipy, unprintable asides—about the stars of their shows. Their purpose was to stir public interest in the performers and create an audience for the forthcoming shows. The flamboyant P. T. Barnum was the first highly acclaimed press agent in the United States. His success in stirring public excitement about his performers, ranging from a giant elephant to the Swedish singer Jenny Lind, was immense because he knew how to tap the public's desire for entertainment (see Chapter 3).

The objective is the same today, but the methods for achieving it have expanded greatly, especially through television. And the electronic medium has become vital in politics as well as in entertainment. Increasingly, Americans are learning about their candidates through exposure on nightly newscasts and paid TV and radio advertisements. Much campaign coverage consists of ten-second "sound bites" in which a candidate makes an attention-getting statement without supporting facts or arguments.

THE MYSTIQUE OF "CELEBRITY"

WHAT MAKES A STAR?

What constitutes a celebrity? In some instances fame is based on solid achievement that has won recognition on its own merits, perhaps with an assist from professional publicists. In his time, Henry Ford was a celebrity, as were Charles Lindbergh and Admiral Richard Byrd, the polar explorer. Today, people such as Barbra Streisand, Lee Iacocca, Bill Cosby, and Dan Rather are considered celebrities because of their talents and staying power in the public eye.

Donald Trump, a New York real estate high-roller with an insatiable desire for publicity, emerged in the early 1990s as the ultimate example of the calculated personal buildup. He put his name on objects he purchased or built—the Trump Taj Mahal casino in Atlantic City, the Trump air shuttle, and the Trump Tower in New York, to name three.

Trump's announcement that he planned to divorce his wife, Ivana, leaving her with a mere $25 million of his reputed $1.7 billion wealth, received major nationwide coverage. The New York tabloids ran wild with the story, including intimate details of his reported romance with a young actress, Marla Maples.

As a master of self-aggrandizement, Trump had a personal press agent in addition to the Trump Organization's aggressive public relations department. He held frequent press conferences and telephoned reporters with stories about himself. Both his wife and his girlfriend had publicists. He published a book about "the art of the deal."

But fame is a slippery thing. Just when "The Donald," as he was nicknamed, was at the height of national attention, stories revealed that he was in financial trouble—overextended with a massive debt and inadequate flow of cash.

Reports about his scramble for new financing replaced those about his business triumphs. Worst of all, people began to tell jokes, not about his reported sexual prowess but about his money troubles. His second book, *Trump: Surviving at the Top,* was panned by critics.

One public relations specialist put it succinctly: "The mystique is off."

Publicity buildups of this nature led Barbara Goldsmith to write in the *New York Times Magazine:*

> The line between fame and notoriety has been erased. Today we are faced with a vast confusing jumble of celebrities: the talented and the untalented, heroes and villains, people of accomplishment and those who have accomplished nothing at all, the criteria of their celebrity being that

their images encapsulate some form of the American dream, that they give enough of an appearance of leadership, heroism, wealth, success, danger, glamour and excitement to feed our fantasies. We no longer demand reality, only that which is real-seeming.

Goldsmith adds, "The public appetite for celebrity and pseudo-event has grown to Pantagruelian proportions, and for the first time in history, the machinery of communications is able to keep up with these demands, even to outrun them, creating new needs we never knew existed. To one extent or another, all the branches of the media have become complicitous to this pursuit. . . . "

What she means is that the publicist and the press agent have a ready market for the materials, staged events, and hype that they constantly peddle to mass media outlets. A place on "The Tonight Show," which was hosted by Johnny Carson for many years, is the most sought-after publicity appearance on television because of the large audience—estimated at 20 million Americans nightly. Its host entertains a stream of guests who take advantage of the exposure to hype their latest book, song, or movie.

If a client is lucky, the publicity on "The Tonight Show," in *People* magazine, or in the Hollywood gossip columns becomes self-multiplying. A press mention confers celebrity status, and this in turn generates even more publicity and invitations to the right events. Through the efforts of a publicist, an aspiring actress may be invited to celebrity parties escorted by a celebrity male. A great deal of media exposure was generated, for example, by having Michael Jackson escort Brooke Shields to a Hollywood gathering. It is not certain which one of them got more publicity mileage from the photographs taken of the two together.

Eventually, the publicist's news releases begin to refer to the person as a celebrity. Presto, the client is a celebrity. Nobody officially proclaims the celebrity status, any more than some mysteriously remote Solomon on a high pinnacle sends down official word that a sports "star" has become a "superstar."

Indicative of the commercialization of personality is the success of Celebrity Service International, which keeps a 400,000-card data bank on well-known persons and publishes daily bulletins in five cities on their comings and goings. It also publishes an annual entertainment-industry contact book that gives the names of managers, lawyers, and publicists who represent celebrities. The daily bulletin, priced at $1250 annually,

Donald Trump stands among the glittering lights of his Trump Taj Mahal Casino in Atlantic City. (UPI/Bettmann)

ZSA ZSA PERFORMS IN COURT

Intense publicity does not always translate into public approval. A faded film actress whose Hungarian accent was perhaps her greatest talent, Zsa Zsa Gabor generated enormous public attention for herself by her arrogant conduct while being tried and convicted for slapping a police officer in Beverly Hills.

Sneers at her behavior were common. Yet from her point of view and that of her publicist, her courtroom performance brought her back into the public eye and created new career opportunities.

Dreyer's Ice Cream, for one, tried to capitalize on Zsa Zsa's publicity by hiring her as spokeswoman in its TV commercials. So many people complained, however, that the company dismissed her. "People didn't think using Zsa Zsa was consistent with our image," a company representative explained.

Zsa Zsa Gabor achieved extensive publicity, much of it unfavorable, for her behavior while on trial for slapping a police officer. The film actress exemplified the old adage of publicity seekers: "I don't care what you say about me. Just spell my name correctly." (UPI/Bettmann)

tips off the media as to what prominent people might be available for a television talk show or a feature interview. The contact book helps business, industry, and charities locate celebrities who might serve as a spokesperson or a charity chairperson, or add glamor to a hotel opening.

MAKING THE MOST OF CELEBRITY APPEARANCES

Celebrities attract crowds to special events, fund-raisers, conventions, and even grand openings of stores. Darcy L. Bouzeos in *Public Relations Quarterly* gives the following tips to assure the success of celebrity appearances and speaking engagements:

- Use the services of a consultant who regularly works with celebrities and knows which one might be appropriate for the event.
- Clearly define the event objectives; this helps the celebrity selection process.
- Make a careful study of the audience demographics. A football star may be good for a Lion's Club banquet but totally inappropriate for a convention of the American Association of University Women (AAUW).
- For a diverse audience, an entertainer, comedian, motivational speaker, or a well-known journalist may be the best selection.
- Avoid the temptation to seek the most popular celebrity of the day. He or she may not be suited to the needs and objectives of the event.
- Ask the celebrity's agent about prior engagements and how the person relates to various kinds of audiences.
- Have alternatives in mind if the first choice is not available.
- Be realistic about budgets. A top-name speaker such as Mike Ditka or Barbara Walters may cost $15,000 to $25,000 for a one-hour appearance.
- Be realistic about what to expect from a speaker or guest celebrity. Don't expect him or her to sign autographs for three hours, be present for the entire event, or talk for more than 30 minutes.
- Be aware of schedules. Television news anchors are rarely available for dinners. Newspaper writers have afternoon deadlines, and sports reporters attend games in the afternoon or evening. Baseball and football players rarely have free time during the season.
- Review contracts carefully. Information about the celebrity's transportation and hotel needs, the amount of the honorarium, and the length of the appearance should be spelled out.
- Have a back-up plan if the celebrity is delayed or cancels at the last minute.

A PRESS AGENT'S REVELATIONS

An entertaining source book on the activities of a Hollywood press agent is *Walking the Tightrope* by Henry Rogers (of Rogers & Cowan Public Relations). In the book, the author recounts how he attracted media attention to an aspiring actress named Rita Hayworth. The news angle was her fabulous wardrobe—even though he spent a week before the *Look* magazine interview borrowing clothes all over town for Hayworth's closet.

In more recent years, Rogers had Cheryl Tiegs, the famous model, as a client. The publicity campaign was to reposition her as a beauty and physical fitness expert, since she had reached the age of 30 and could no longer generate high modeling fees in a culture that emphasizes youth. Part of the firm's work involved (1) getting her on television talk shows to speak about beauty care and physical fitness, (2) convincing *Time* magazine that she would make an excellent cover story—which appeared, and (3) sending her on a multicity tour to publicize her book.

PSYCHOLOGICAL EXPLANATIONS

Psychologists offer varied explanations of why the public becomes impressed—often *fascinated* is the more accurate word—by highly publicized individuals. In pretelevision days, the publicity departments of the motion picture studios promoted their male and female stars as glamor figures who lived in a special world of privilege and wealth. Dreaming of achieving such glory for themselves, young people with and without talent came to Hollywood to crash the magical gates, almost always in vain. Thousands more back home spun fantasies about being Rita Hayworth or Cary Grant. They cherished machine-autographed pictures of their favorites and read with relish inflated stories about the stars in fan magazines, visualizing themselves in the glamor figures' places.

In the earlier days of personality buildup, *wish-fulfillment* was a compelling force. It still is. Their exposure on television in the intimacy of the family living room, however, makes personalities seem much closer to admiring viewers today than the remote gods and goddesses were in the glory days of the major motion picture studios. Such is the power of television, in fact, that reporters and news anchors who talk on camera about the activities of celebrities attain celebrity status themselves.

Many ordinary people leading routine lives yearn for heroes. Professional and big-time college sports provide personalities for *hero worship*. Publicists emphasize the performances of certain players, and television game announcers often build up the stars' roles out of proportion to their achievements; this emphasis creates hero figures for youthful sports enthusiasts to emulate. Similar exaggerated treatment is applied to entertainers and politicians. Syndicated gossip columnist Liz Smith once tried to explain the American cult of personality by saying, "Maybe it's because we all want someone to look up to or spit on, and we don't have royalty."

In addition to admiration for individual performers, members of the public develop a *vicarious sense of belonging* that creates support for athletic teams. Sports publicists exploit this feeling in numerous ways. A winning baseball team becomes "our" team in conversations among patrons of a bar. To signify their loyalty, children and adults alike wear baseball caps bearing the insignia of their favorite major league teams. Enthusiasts decorate their automobiles with bumper stickers and license-plate holders bearing the name of their favorite team. It isn't surprising that alumni of a university gnaw their fingernails while watching their school basketball team in a tight game, but the same intensity of support is found among fans who have no direct tie to the school. For many years, the vehement rooting from afar for Notre Dame's football team by its so-called sidewalk alumni has been notorious. A championship professional sports team stirs widespread community support.

Still another factor is the *desire for entertainment* most people feel. Reading fan magazines, or watching their favorite stars being interviewed, or lining up in front of a box office hours before it opens to be sure of getting a ticket—these are ways to bring variety and a little excitement into the daily routine of life.

A public relations practitioner assigned to build up the public image of an individual, either to increase the client's ego satisfaction or to stimulate sale of tickets to an event involving the individual, should analyze the ways in which these psychological factors can be applied. Since the client's cooperation is vital in promotional work, a wise publicist explains this background and tells the client why various actions are planned.

THE PRACTITIONER'S RESPONSIBILITY

DAMAGE CONTROL

A practitioner handling an individual client is responsible for protecting the client from bad publicity as well as generating positive news. When the client appears in a bad light because of misbehavior or an irresponsible public statement, the publicist must try to minimize the harm done to the client's public image. To use a naval term, the objective is damage control.

Often politicians who say something controversial in public, then wish later that they hadn't, try to squirm out of the predicament by claiming they were misquoted. This is a foolish defense unless the politician can prove conclusively that he or she was indeed quoted incorrectly. Reporters resent accusations of inaccuracy and may hold a grudge against the accuser. If the accused reporter has the politician's statement on tape, the politician appears even worse. A better defense is for the politician to explain what he or she intended and to express regret for the slip of the tongue.

ETHICAL PROBLEMS FOR PUBLICISTS

Personal misconduct by a client, or the appearance of misconduct, strains a practitioner's ingenuity and at times his or her ethical principles. Some practitioners will lie outright to protect a client, a dishonest practice that looks even worse if the media show the statement to be a lie. On occasion, a practitioner acting in good faith may be victimized because the client has lied. As a cynical old-time Hollywood publicist put it while describing how he helped cover up for a famous film hero (married) who found his actress girlfriend dead in her bedroom under strange circumstances, "We told him that before we could lie for him, he had to tell us the truth." Generally, experienced publicists advise their clients in trouble to remain out of sight and talk to as few persons as possible during the critical period.

Issuing a prepared statement to explain the client's conduct, while leaving reporters and their editors dissatisfied, is regarded as safer than having the client call a news conference, unless the client is a victim of circumstances and is best served by talking fully and openly. The decision about holding a news conference also is influenced by how articulate and self-controlled the client is. Under questioning, a person on the defensive may say something that compounds the problem. Guiding a personality through a period of trouble is an unpleasant, difficult aspect of a practitioner's job and may test his or her standards of good professional behavior. (Defensive news conferences are discussed more fully in Chapter 23.)

A campaign to generate public awareness of an individual should be planned just as meticulously as any other public relations project. This is the fundamental process, step by step, for the practitioner to follow.

INTERVIEW THE CLIENT

The client should answer a detailed personal questionnaire. The practitioner should be a dogged, probing interviewer, digging for interesting and possibly newsworthy facts about the person's life, activities, and beliefs. In talking about themselves, individuals frequently fail to realize that certain elements of their experiences have publicity value under the right circumstances.

Perhaps, for example, the client is a little-known actress who has won a role as a Midwestern farmer's young wife in a motion picture. During her get-acquainted talks with the publicist, she happens to mention in passing that while growing up in a small town she belonged to the 4-H Club. The feature angle can be the realism she brings to the movie role: when she was a member of the youth organization, she actually did the farm jobs she will perform in the film.

Not only must practitioners draw out such details from their clients, they must also have the ingenuity to develop these facts as story angles. When the actress is placed as a guest on a television talk show, the publicist should prompt her in advance to recall incidents from her 4-H experience. Two or three humorous anecdotes about mishaps with pigs and chickens, tossed into the TV interview, give it verve. The audience will remember her. The television show host should be tipped off to lead the interview in this direction.

PREPARE A BIOGRAPHY OF THE CLIENT

The basic biography should be limited to four typed pages, perhaps less. News and feature angles should be placed high in the ''bio,'' as it is termed, so an editor or producer can find them quickly. The biography, a portrait and other photographs of the client, and, if possible, additional personal background items should be assembled in a press kit for extensive distribution. Usually the kit is a cardboard folder with inside pockets to hold the contents.

PLAN A MARKETING STRATEGY

The practitioner should determine precisely what is to be sold. Is the purpose only to increase public awareness of the individual, or also to publicize the client's product, such as a new television series, motion picture, or book? Next, the practitioner should decide which types of audience are the most important to reach. For instance, an interview with a romantic operatic tenor on a rock-and-roll radio station would be inadvisable. But an appearance by the singer on a public television station's talk show would be right on target. A politician trying to project herself as a representative of minority groups should be scheduled to speak before audiences in minority neighborhoods and placed on radio stations whose demographic reports show that they attract minority listeners.

CONDUCT THE CAMPAIGN

The best course normally is to project the client on multiple media simultaneously. Radio and television appearances create public awareness and often make newspaper feature stories easier to obtain. The process works in reverse as well. Using telephone calls and "pitch" letters to editors and program directors, the publicist should propose print and on-air interviews with the client. Every such approach should include a news or feature angle for the interviewer to develop. Since magazine articles require longer to reach print, the publicist should begin efforts to obtain them as early as feasible, once the exposure process has begun to gain momentum.

News Releases News releases are an important avenue of publicity, but the practitioner should avoid too much puffery. *Bulldog Reporter,* a West Coast public relations newsletter, once gave a "fireplug" award to a press agent who wrote a release about a Frank Sinatra concert in the Dominican Republic. The release said, in part:

> The Sinatra concert represented the first time a legendary star has ever performed for a subscription pay television service. The historical event, in a balmy night that could only rival, not surpass, the audience's decibel level for enthusiasm, should overshadow any in-person star appearance ever offered on subscription television. The Sinatra and Santana/Heart doubleheaders may well be recorded as pay TV milestones.

Photographs Photographs of the client should be submitted to the print media as often as justifiable. Basic in the press kit is the standard head-and-shoulders portrait, often called a "mug shot." Photographs of the client doing something interesting or appearing in a newsworthy group may be published merely with a caption, without accompanying story. If the client seeks national attention, such pictures should be submitted to the news services so that, if deemed newsworthy, they will be distributed to hundreds of newspapers. (Newspaper and magazine requirements for photographs are discussed in Chapter 24.)

The practitioner and the photographer should be inventive, putting the client into unusual situations. The justification for a successful submission may be thin if the picture is colorful and/or timely. For example, the Associated Press distributed a photograph of actor Larry Hagman, villain of the television show "Dallas," and his Swedish-born wife, Maj, posing with three young women and a young man in Scandinavian national costumes. Two of the Scandinavians held small Swedish and Norwegian flags. Everyone was smiling. The pose resembled those found in hundreds of amateur snapshot albums. Although of little significance from either news or photographic points of view, the picture was published in newspapers a few days before Christmas because it was seasonal. The caption stated: "Actor Larry Hagman and his Swedish-born wife Maj pose with representatives of the Scandinavian community in Los Angeles Wednesday after the group presented Hagman and his wife with traditional holiday ornaments from their native countries." Obviously this was a contrived situation, but a pleasant one; it contributed to the desired image of Hagman as a nice fellow offscreen.

Sharply increased awareness among editors of women's concern about sexual exploitation has largely eliminated from newspaper pages "cheesecake" pictures—photographs of nubile young women in which the news angle often is as skimpy as their attire. At one time such pictures were published frequently as editors tried to spice up their pages. Occasionally such a picture shows up in print today, blatantly contrived and perhaps in bad taste, such as the one of a smiling man pointing to the replica of a check painted on the bare stomach of a belly dancer. The caption read: "Julian Caruso, an entertainment manager, arrived in court in Stafford, England, yesterday to pay a parking fine. He didn't want to pay the fine, the equivalent of $17, because, he said, Stafford lacks adequate parking. To emphasize his displeasure, he presented the court a check written on the stomach of a belly dancer, Sandrina. Court officials took a look at her—real name, Sandra Audley—and decided they couldn't handle the check in that form."

Stunts like this are a throwback to old-time gimmick press agentry, yet sometimes they succeed. The picture was distributed by the Associated Press and published large size in at least one metropolitan newspaper.

Cheesecake photographs still are printed in the trade press, even though they are seldom seen in daily newspapers. Certain British and Australian newspapers, however, continue to publish large photos of skimpily clad young women, often topless. Some practitioners persist in having bikini-clad models appear at trade shows and shopping center openings, but in doing so they risk having the events picketed.

Public Appearances Another way to intensify awareness of individual clients is to arrange for them to appear frequently in public places. The appearances may be as modest as cutting the ribbon at a new supermarket or attending opening ceremonies at a county fair.

Commercial organizations at times hire celebrities of various calibers to dress up dinner meetings, conventions, and even store openings. A major savings and loan association employs a group of early-day television performers to appear at openings of branch offices. Each day for a week, for two hours, an entertainer stands in a guest booth, signing autographs and chatting with visitors, who receive a paperback book of pictures recalling television's pioneer period. Refreshments are served. A company photographer takes pictures of the celebrity talking to guests. Later, visitors who appear in the pictures receive them as a souvenir. These appearances benefit the commercial sponsor by attracting crowds and help the entertainers stay in the public eye.

Awards A much-used device, but still successful, is to have a client receive an award. The practitioner should be alert for news of awards to be given and nominate the client for appropriate ones. Follow-up communications with persuasive material from the practitioner may convince the sponsor to make the award to the client. In some instances, the idea of an award is proposed to an organization by a practitioner, whose client then conveniently is declared the first recipient. The entertainment business generates immense amounts of publicity for individuals and shows with its Oscar and Emmy awards. Winning an Academy Award greatly strengthens a performer's career and means much additional box office revenue for a film. There is a myriad of lesser awards.

Question-and-Answer Columns Another source of exposure in print is the question-and-answer column in newspapers and magazines. The format is for well-known persons to answer questions that readers have submitted to the columnist. Some of the questions published do in fact come from readers; the columnist often asks public relations representatives of the personalities involved to supply answers. However, less legitimately, practitioners sometimes submit questions about their clients along with the answers, and the columnist publishes both—an easy way for the writer to fill a column.

Nicknames and Labels Creating catchy nicknames for clients, especially sports and entertainment figures, helps the practitioner get their names into print. Celebrity-worshipers like to call their heroes and heroines by nicknames, as though the practice denoted a personal relationship. Thus we see and hear such familiarities for professional basketball players as "Air Jordan" and "Magic," and "Old Blue Eyes" and "The Boss" for entertainers. Cliché-prone reporters and columnists help to perpetuate these appellations.

A questionable variation of the nickname consists of adding a descriptive word to the name of a person being publicized, to create a desirable image or career association. Sometimes this is done to provide a respectable veneer for a person of dubious background. In the Palm Springs resort area, to cite an instance, a socially active figure named Ray Ryan hired a practitioner whose task was to build up the image of Ryan as a well-to-do oilman. In every news release about Ryan and every telegram inviting social, business, and media individuals to Ryan's elaborate parties, the practitioner referred to his client as "oilman Ray Ryan." Publications in the area consistently printed "oilman Ray Ryan," giving the publicist the effect he desired. Actually, Ryan also was involved in big-time professional gambling—an involvement apparently responsible for the fact that when he turned the ignition key of his automobile one day, a bomb planted in the car killed him.

RECORD THE RESULTS

Those who employ practitioners want tangible results in return for their fees. The practitioner also needs to compile and analyze the results of a personality campaign in order to determine the effectiveness of the various methods used. Tearsheets, photographs, copies of news releases, and, when possible, videotape clips of the client's public appearances should be given to the client. Clipping services help the practitioner assemble this material. At the end of the campaign, or at intervals in a long-term program, summaries of what has been accomplished should be submitted. Estimates of the audiences reached, based on circulation figures of publications, audience estimates of radio and television stations, and similar statistical criteria often impress clients, although their value as indicators of a campaign's true effectiveness is doubtful (see Chapter 10).

PUBLICITY TO STIMULATE TICKET SALES

The primary goal of any campaign for an entertainment is to sell tickets. An advance publicity buildup informs listeners, readers, and viewers that an event will occur and stimulates their desire to attend it. Rarely, except for community events publicized in smaller cities, do newspaper stories and broadcasts about an entertainment include detailed information on ticket prices and availability. Those facts usually are deemed too commercial by editors and should be announced in paid advertising. Even pop singer Michael Jackson's managers found the press uncooperative when they requested newspapers to publish ticket application coupons free of charge for his ''Victory'' tour. However, some newspapers may include prices, times, and so on in tabular listings of scheduled entertainments. Performance dates usually are included in publicity stories.

Stories about a forthcoming theatrical event, motion picture, rock concert, or similar commercial performance should concentrate on the personalities, style, and

In a carefully staged setting, President Bush welcomes singing and dancing star Michael Jackson to the White House. Jackson's appearance was intended to help both men by increasing the President's appeal to youth and enhancing Jackson's stature as an international pop figure. (Reuters/UPI)

history of the show. Every time the show is mentioned, public awareness grows. Thus, astute practitioners search for fresh news angles to produce as many stories as possible. Even two-paragraph items are valuable if they mention the names of the show and its stars. Newspaper entertainment pages frequently use such short pieces.

AN EXAMPLE: PUBLICIZING A PLAY

Let us look at the way a new play can be publicized. The methods are the same, whether the work will be performed on Broadway by professionals or in the local municipal auditorium by a little-theater group.

Stories include an announcement that the play will be presented, followed by releases reporting the casting of lead characters, start of rehearsals, and opening date. Feature stories, or "readers," discuss the play's theme and background, with quotations from the playwright and director inserted to emphasize an important point. In print, radio, and television interviews the play's star can tell why he or she finds the role significant or amusing.

Photographs of show scenes, taken in costume during rehearsal, should be distributed to the media, to give potential customers a preview glimpse. As a reminder, a brief "opening tonight" story may be distributed. If a newspaper lists theatrical events in tabular form, the practitioner might submit an entry about the show, to make the editor's work easier and increase the likelihood that the listing will appear correctly.

THE "DRIP-DRIP-DRIP" TECHNIQUE OF PUBLICITY

Motion picture studios, television production firms, and networks apply the principle of "drip-drip-drip" publicity when a show is being shot. In other words, there is a steady output of information about the production. A public relations specialist, called a unit man or woman, assigned to a film during production, turns out a flow of stories for the general and trade press and plays host to media visitors to the set. The television networks mail out daily news bulletins about their shows to media television editors. They assemble the editors annually to preview new programs and interview their stars. The heaviest barrage of publicity is released shortly before the show openings.

One danger of excessive promotion of an event, however, is that audience expectation may become too high, so that the performance proves to be a disappointment. A skilled practitioner will be judicious in his or her use of publicity and stay away from "hype" that can lead to a sense of anticlimax.

A LOOK AT THE MOTION PICTURE INDUSTRY

By market research and interpretation of demographics and psychographics, motion picture public relations departments define target audiences they seek to reach. Most motion picture publicity is aimed at 18- to 24-year olds, where the largest audience lies. Seventy-five percent of the film audience is under age 39, although increased attendance by older moviegoers has become evident recently.

Professional entertainment publicity work is concentrated in New York and Los Angeles, the former as the nation's theatrical center and the latter as the motion picture center. (American television production is divided primarily between the two cities, with the larger portion in Los Angeles.)

A typical Los Angeles-area public relations firm specializing in personalities and entertainment has two staffs: one staff of "planters," who deliver to media offices publicity stories about individual clients and the projects in which they are engaged, and another staff of "bookers," whose job is to place clients on talk shows and in other public appearances. Some publicity stories are for general release; others are prepared especially for a single media outlet such as a syndicated Hollywood columnist or a major newspaper. The latter type is marked "exclusive," permitting the publication or station that uses it to claim credit for "breaking" the story.

A cardinal sin of "exclusive" publicity is to give a story to two media outlets simultaneously, in the hope that one or the other will use it. This practice is called "double-planting."

Another device is to provide supplies of tickets for a new movie or show to radio stations, whose disc jockeys award them to listeners as prizes in on-the-air contests. In the process, these announcers mention the name of the show dozens of times. Glamorous premieres and trips for media guests to distant points so that they can watch the filming or attend an opening are used occasionally, too.

For such services to individual or corporate entertainment clients, major Hollywood publicists charge at least $3000 a month, with a three-month minimum. The major studios and networks have their own public relations staffs.

SPORTS PUBLICITY

Professional and big-time college sports, especially football and basketball, are entertainment that must be sold like other shows. They compete for the consumer's time and dollars just as motion pictures, fairs, rock concerts, and plays do. Sports have a highly exploited star system in which colorful individual athletes are publicized as energetically as contract film stars of the major motion picture studios once were. As a result, a special field of sports public relations has developed, using the same principles as other entertainment publicity, but with angles all its own. A study sponsored by a brewery in the early 1980s found that nearly 70 percent of Americans watch, discuss, or read about sports daily.

COLLEGE AND UNIVERSITY SPORTS

In universities, the sports publicity director usually is an athletically inclined practitioner whose task is to build crowds for games, maintain alumni enthusiasm for the old school's teams, and assist in enticing high school athletic stars to enroll in the school. Among the standard tools of the sports publicity director are press kits, news releases, publicity photographs, interviews with coaches and sometimes with players, and press box tickets for games. At the start of each football practice season, a press day is held during which photographers take on-field pictures of the players in uniform and reporters talk with coaches and players.

Emphasis on individual stardom in college football and basketball is heavy because stars sell tickets, and college football is big-dollar business. Star-studded winning teams fill the seats, earn money and public attention from postseason games, and encourage alumni to make contributions. Thus the campaigns by sports practitioners to get college players named to all-American teams are intense, often employing attention-getting techniques that have little direct bearing on the games themselves. Coaches, too, are promoted as celebrity figures.

PROFESSIONAL SPORTS

Public relations departments of professional teams try to create images for their clubs that will catch the fans' attention; for example, the Los Angeles Dodgers feature Dodger Blue, the predominant color of their uniforms. Like other big league baseball teams, during the winter they send groups of their more articulate players on tours of cities in their audience area. The players speak to school assemblies, hold baseball clinics, attend service club luncheons, visit hospitals, shake hands, and sign autographs. Often they stress antidrug themes. Such personal contact builds fan loyalty. In Chicago each winter, baseball enthusiasts hold a Die-Hard Cubs Fan Convention, in which the team's management participates.

THE MARKETING OF SPORTS TEAMS

Marketing communications and corporate sponsorships play a vital role in the financial success of professional sports teams. Two examples are the Baltimore Orioles baseball team and the Brisbane, Australia, Broncos rugby team.

The Orioles, for whose games 85 percent of season tickets are purchased by corporations, also have 30 corporate sponsors that fund various "freebies" of products, special events, and purchase of billboards in the outfield. Such sponsorships cost $30,000 to $70,000. Marty Conway, the club's corporate marketing director, says, "They like to see their stuff distributed, and see the billboards in the outfield. Customers are impressed, and employees feel they are getting a benefit, since many of the tickets are distributed to them."

Corporations also are the mainstay of professional sports in Australia. The Brisbane Broncos receive about 75 percent of their revenues from corporate sponsorships. Powers Beer tops the list with a $1 million investment that, among other things, gives the brewery the exclusive right to sell its beer at home games. The Broncos also have corporate boxes at $25,000 each, a monthly luncheon for corporate executives during which they can talk to the players, and a magazine that features corporate supporters.

Shane Edwards, manager of marketing for the Broncos, says corporate sponsorships are a business proposition. Corporations are looking for increased exposure, linkage with the community, and product sales. "Let's face it, sports is a business and competes for the entertainment dollar," he says.

SUPERSPORTS: THE SUPER BOWL

The ultimate in sports hype is the National Football League's championship playoff game, the Super Bowl. A football game, frequently no more exciting and often less so than many regular season games, has been turned into a weeklong spectacular. To suggest stature and great importance, each year's game is known by a Roman numeral—not just Super Bowl 22 but Super Bowl XXII.

Print and electronic reporters fall over each other during the week before the game, hunting story angles. Raucous parties mark the week as free-spending ticketholders swarm into the host city. The telecast of the game itself is seen by more than 100 million viewers, according to the ratings. The network whose turn it is to broadcast the game uses more than 20 cameras, a dozen or so videotape machines for replays, and about 100 microphones to inundate viewers with pictures and commentary. ABC, which televised the 1991 Super Bowl, charged $1.6 million for a one-minute commercial.

Anyone responsible for staging a sports event, in fact, can benefit from studying the public relations effort at a Super Bowl, then reducing it in scope to fit the particular need.

At Super Bowl games, the National Football League usually issues more than 2200 media credentials. To offer adequate press service, the NFL public relations department supplements its staff by bringing in the publicity directors of several league teams. During the week preceding the game, the league runs buses for the media from hotels to the practice fields, and operates a central media headquarters in a hotel.

To assist sportswriters, publicity departments compile sets of facts about teams. At the stadium on game day, the league provides a main press box, an auxiliary press section, and extra workrooms below the stands. After the Sunday afternoon game, the department opens a large dining room at the headquarters hotel, to which news people are invited as NFL guests.

By paying close attention to detail, providing ample staff personnel, and arranging adequate working space, the NFL keeps the media throng satisfied in a situation that, poorly handled, could become chaos. Discussion of commercial sponsorship of sports appears in Chapter 14.

TRAVEL PROMOTION

With money in their pockets, people want to go places and see new things. Stimulating and harnessing that desire is the goal of the travel industry, and wise, innovative use of public relations techniques is a principal step in reaching that goal. Anyone doubting the size of the travel market need only face the mob in a major airport at Christmas or read the abundance of alluring cruise ads in magazines.

The federal government has estimated that $269 billion is spent annually on travel and tourism in the United States. Competition for these dollars among states, cities, transportation companies, hotels, theme parks, restaurants, and rental car firms is fierce.

FIGURE 20.1
Today's luxurious cruises have evolved from the days before overseas air travel, when ocean liners served as port-to-port transportation. The text of this 1932 advertisement includes the same glowing "selling" words seen in today's travel promotion, such as "luxury," "superb," and "prestige."

Like entertainment and sports, travel draws upon the public's recreational dollars. Often its promoters intertwine their projects with those of entertainment and sports entrepreneurs.

THREE PHASES OF TRAVEL PROMOTION

The practice of travel public relations can be divided into three steps:

1. Stimulating the public's desire to visit a place
2. Arranging for travelers to reach the place
3. Making certain that visitors are comfortable and well entertained when they get there

Stimulation is accomplished by travel articles in magazines and newspapers, alluring brochures distributed by travel agents and by direct mail, and travel films and videos. When a city or country convinces a motion picture producer to shoot a movie in its territory, the film automatically interests viewers in visiting the area. Encouraging companies and associations to hold conventions in a given place stimulates travel by groups. Figure 20.2 is an example of a magazine ad about Santa Fe, New Mexico.

Some publications have their own travel writers; others purchase free-lance articles and pictures. Well-done articles by public relations practitioners about travel desti-

HOW MANY "FREEBIES" TO ACCEPT?

Creation of newspaper and magazine stories about travel destinations, so essential in tourism promotion, poses a problem for writers and public relations people. Who should pay the writer's expenses in researching them?

Some large newspapers forbid their travel writers to accept free or discounted hotel rooms, meals, and travel tickets. They believe that such subsidies may cause writers to slant their articles too favorably, perhaps subconsciously.

Many smaller publications and most free-lance writers cannot afford such an expensive rule, however, and by following it would be unable to prepare travel articles. They contend that pride in their professional objectivity keeps them from being influenced by their hosts' "freebies." Some point to critical articles they have written on subsidized trips.

For the public relations director of a resort, cruise, or other travel attraction, the situation presents two problems: (1) How much hospitality can be given to the press before the "freebies" become a form of bribery? and (2) How does the director screen requests from self-described travel writers who request free housing or travel?

The Society of American Travel Writers (SATW) sets this guideline:

> Free or reduced-rate transportation and other travel expenses must be offered and accepted only with the mutual understanding that reportorial research is involved and any resultant story will be reported with the same standards of journalistic accuracy as that of comparable coverage and criticism in theater, business and finance, music, sports, and other news sections that provide the public with objective and helpful information.

FIGURE 20.2
Intriguing the potential visitor with an unusual feature of a vacation destination is an important aspect of travel public relations. With its rich Native American and Spanish traditions, Santa Fe, New Mexico, uses this approach to add allure to its travel advertisement. (Courtesy of Creative Images Limited and Santa Fe Convention & Visitors Bureau.)

nations often are published, too, if written in an informational manner without resort to blatant salesmanship and purple prose.

Arrangements for travel are made through travel agencies or by direct booking at airlines, airports, and rail and bus stations. Complicated tours and cruises are arranged most frequently by travel agencies, which charge customers retail prices for accommodations and receive a 10 percent commission from the travel supplier. Wholesalers create package tours that are sold by travel agencies.

To promote sales, travel agencies distribute literature, sponsor travel fairs, and encourage group travel by showing destination films at invitational meetings. Cities and states operate convention and travel departments to encourage tourism. Often these invite travel writers and convention planners on familiarization trips (called ''fam trips''), on which they are entertained by hotels and restaurants and shown local attractions. Figure 20.3 ''sells'' warmth to cold newspaper readers.

Good treatment of travelers is a critical phase of travel promotion. If a couple spend a large sum on a trip, then encounter poor accommodations, rude hotel clerks, misplaced luggage, and inferior sightseeing arrangements, they come home angry. And they will tell their friends vehemently how bad the trip was.

FIGURE 20.3
The Australian Tourist Commission received publicity in U.S. newspapers with this photo of Santa Claus at Bronte Beach in Sydney. Its message about the warm December weather in Australia is clear. The photo was released to 100 daily and weekly newspapers with circulations from 25,000 to 50,000 in various states except California, Texas, Arizona, and Florida—states with warm weather.

Even the best arrangements go awry at times. Planes are late, tour members miss the bus, and bad weather riles tempers. This is where the personal touch means so much. An attentive, cheerful tour director or hotel manager can soothe guests, and a "make-good" gesture such as a free drink or meal does wonders. *Careful training of travel personnel is essential.* Many travelers, especially in foreign countries, feel uneasy in strange surroundings and depend more on others than they would at home.

APPEALS TO TARGET AUDIENCES

As in other forms of public relations, travel promotion identifies target audiences and supplements its general appeals with special messages aimed at them. A few examples: In addition to its basic message urging visitors to see Britain's historic places and pageantry, British promotion focuses on such attractions as London theater tours, golf in Scotland, genealogical research on family roots, and tours of the cathedrals for persons with architectural or religious interests.

Similarly, Italy urges persons of Italian descent to visit the villages of their ancestors and promotes religious group visits to the Vatican. Ireland stresses family visits to ancestral homes, its picturesque pubs, and the greenness of its countryside. For Australia, the kangaroo is a national symbol; in addition, promotion draws water enthusiasts to the Great Barrier Reef and depicts the beauties of Sydney harbor. Other countries develop similar appeals. American travel promotion abroad urging people of other countries to visit the United States emphasizes New York, San Francisco, the Grand Canyon, and Washington, D.C., in particular.

The biggest special audience of all is older citizens. Retired persons have time to travel, and many have ample money to do so. Hotels, motels, and airlines frequently offer discounts to attract them.

A large percentage of cruise passengers, especially on longer voyages, are retirees. Alert travel promoters design trips with them in mind, including such niceties as pairing compatible widows to share cabins and arranging trips ashore that require little walking. Shipboard entertainment and recreational activities with appeal to older persons—nostalgic music for dancing rather than rock and roll, for example—are important, too. Public relations practitioners charged with creating interest in cruises can find numerous angles of this kind to emphasize.

Travel to Eastern Europe A vast new field for international travel opened in the early 1990s in eastern Europe. After living under severe restrictions for 40 years, a half-dozen former Soviet satellites opened their borders and heavy travel began in both directions. Czechoslovakia was the first of them to allow U.S. tourists to enter without a visa. Western travel in the Soviet Union, made easier during the late 1980s, increased greatly in the 1990s.

Public relations specialists needed to warn visitors to the former satellites, however, that the accommodations they would find in these countries often were far from luxurious, especially outside the main cities. Urging tolerance and a readiness to understand different cultures while traveling is part of the public relations message.

TIMES OF CRISIS

Public relations in travel has moments that require crisis management, just as corporation work does. When a popular destination area suffers a natural disaster, as Mexico City did with its 1985 earthquake, fear strikes timid tourists, many of whom cancel their reservations. Travel by Americans to Europe suffered a precipitous decline after terrorist attacks occurred on that continent and the U.S. government retaliated by bombing Libya. American travel overseas declined again in 1991 because people feared possible Iraqi terrorist bombings during the Persian Gulf War.

Mexico met its tourism crisis by using a large American public relations firm. These specialists arranged interviews on U.S., Canadian, and British television networks in which Mexican officials emphasized that only a few square miles of the country had been seriously damaged and that facilities for visitors still were excellent. Travel editors and travel agents were flown on tours of Mexico to see for themselves, and they brought back favorable reports.

Similarly, San Francisco suffered a sharp drop in tourism after its severe earthquake in 1989 but began to recover after a few months of spreading the word that tourist accommodations were abundant.

After suffering 27,000 more cancellations than bookings in the week following the U.S. bombing raid on Libya, British Airways responded with a spectacular promotion to regain the American tourist trade. Its newspaper advertisements offered the possibility of a free flight to Britain (the airline had plenty of empty seats). From 900,000 persons who sent in their names, the airline drew 5,791 winners. They received other discounts and free services in addition to the free flights, and 30 winners were entertained for tea at 10 Downing Street, where Prime Minister Margaret Thatcher personally served watercress sandwiches. Widespread favorable publicity in U.S. newspapers and broadcasts encouraged the perception that Britain was safe and hospitable, and the tourist trade began to recover.

CASE PROBLEM

Kitaro is a Japanese composer and musician in the field now widely known as "New Age" electronic music. One of his most popular compositions is the *Silk Road Suite,* which has been performed by such groups as the London Symphony Orchestra.

His electronic music blends the musical traditions of East and West, and his music is filled with the sounds of wind chimes, ocean surf, and wind rustling through the forest. His haunting melodies of distant places are popular among young professionals burned out on "hard rock."

Kitaro is planning a concert tour of ten major American cities, and you have been hired as his publicist. Your purpose is to make sure that his American tour receives extensive coverage in the mass media. This, ideally, will lead to increased popularity and sales.

What key publics will you try to reach? What communications strategies will you utilize? What media will be most appropriate for your purposes?

QUESTIONS FOR REVIEW AND DISCUSSION

1. Why do public relations students need to understand how the personal publicity trade functions, even if they do not plan to handle theatrical or sports clients?

2. What is the most sought-after publicity appearance on American television?

3. Name two psychological factors underlying the American obsession with celebrities.

4. When politicians say something they wish they hadn't and it is published, they often claim that they were misquoted. Why is this poor policy?

5. What is the first step in preparing a campaign to increase the public's awareness of an individual client?

6. What is a "bio"? What should it contain?

7. "Cheesecake" photographs once were commonplace in American newspapers, but few are published now. Why is this so?

8. A professional blunder committed by some entertainment practitioners is called "double planting." What does this mean?

9. Why do practitioners put emphasis on certain players on sports teams?

10. What are the three basic phases of travel promotion?

SUGGESTED READINGS

Antrobus, Edmund. "Back in the USSR and Eastern Europe." *Public Relations Journal,* May 1990, pp. 20–26. Travel and tourism.

Arab, Nancy H. "Integrated Marketing Repositions Toronto Hotel: Occupancy Soars." *Public Relations Journal,* March 1991, pp. 22–23.

Beyer, Lisa. "Destination Asia." *Time,* October 23, 1989, pp. 52–56. Tourism promotion by various Pacific Rim nations.

Bouzeos, Darcy L. "How to Make the Most of Celebrity Appearances." *Public Relations Quarterly,* Summer 1989, pp. 25–26.

Cox, Meg. "Literary World Is Debating How Much of a Huckster a Book Writer Should Be." *Wall Street Journal,* August 2, 1990, p. B1. Book promotion.

Culver, Marcia. "Sleazy Gossip: Then and Now." *Wall Street Journal,* March 7, 1990, p. A18. Historical perspective of Donald Trump divorce controversy.

Cutlip, Scott. "A Public Relations Footnote to the Pete Rose Affair." *Public Relations Review,* Winter 1989, pp. 46–48.

Donlon, Sally O. "PR Turns Media Spotlight on Historic City." *Communication World,* November 1988, pp. 33–35. How New Orleans won a major convention.

Fuchsberg, Gilbert. "Will U.S. Promoters Give Mandela Time to Fight Apartheid?" *Wall Street Journal,* March 13, 1990, pp. 1, A9. U.S. tour of Nelson Mandela and how it was promoted.

Fuhman, Candice Jacobson. *Publicity Stunt: Great Staged Events That Made the News.* San Francisco: Chronicle Books, 1989.

Horovitz, Bruce, and Biederman, Patricia. "Personal PR: Newest Necessity." Los Angeles *Times,* September 23, 1990, pp. A1, 33. Individuals now hiring public relations practitioners for personal publicity.

Landro, Laura. "Hollywood in Action: Making a Star." *Wall Street Journal,* February 16, 1990, pp. B1, 3. Actor Steven Seagal.

Lapin, Jackie. "How to Win with Sports." *Public Relations Journal,* February 1987, pp. 31–32. Corporate marketing.

Lynn, Donna M. "If the Shoe Fits." *Public Relations Journal,* February 1987, p. 16. Sports marketing.

Perilla, Bob. "How to Work with Celebrities." *Public Relations Journal,* April 1988, pp. 33–34.

Sklarewitz, Norman. "Cruise Company Handles Crisis by the Book." *Public Relations Journal,* May 1991, pp. 34–36.

Skolnik, Rayna. "U.S. Travel and Tourism Today." *Public Relations Journal,* March 1991, pp. 16–21.

PART FIVE
Tactics

CHAPTER

21

Public Relations and New Technologies

Enormous changes are occurring in the mechanics of communication. The technology available to public relations practitioners has expanded spectacularly. Therefore, this chapter begins by explaining these recently developed electronic methods.

The chapter focuses primarily on three major developments: (1) the computer, (2) satellite transmission, and (3) videotape. It explains how they operate and tells how they are used in public relations work. It also discusses facsimile transmission.

Within a public relations office, uses of the computer include preparation of news releases, dispatch of electronic mail, and maintenance of mailing lists and lists of contacts. The computer also is valuable in desktop publishing and in gathering information from outside sources, especially from databases.

Public relations organizations use satellite transmission for distribution of news releases and to conduct teleconferences. Videotape has innumerable applications; some examples are given in the chapter. Other new technologies described include teletext, videotex, and fiber optics.

THE COMMUNICATIONS EXPLOSION

Fortunately for public relations people, the communications explosion of recent years gives them an array of new tools with which to communicate their messages more rapidly, attractively, and precisely. The electronic revolution has added zest to their work. It challenges the ingenuity of practitioners to find new ways of applying technology to their jobs.

An earlier generation worked primarily with the telephone, typewriter, pencil, and mimeograph machine. The telephone remains vital. Imagine trying to work for a day without it! But the new technology has produced equipment that, if not entirely replacing the old standbys, works faster and more flexibly than they do. The word processor supplants the typewriter at desks, and the high-speed duplicating machine produces sleek printlike copies, sometimes in color, that are far superior to the output of the traditional mimeograph machine.

THE COMPUTER

By definition, a computer is a machine that accepts and processes information and supplies the results in a desired form. The digital computer processes the information with figures, using binary or decimal notation to solve mathematical problems at high speed. Development of the microcomputer and sophisticated software programs has added flexibility and convenience for users.

Since a computer can store, codify, analyze, and search out information at speeds far beyond human capability, its applications are enormous. When we add its ability to transmit information over long distances at fantastically high speeds, its potential becomes even greater. Still more astounding is the anticipated development of the ''thinking'' computer. This machine, designed to diagnose and solve problems, in addition to calculating and processing data as present computers do, is in the experimental stages in Japanese and American laboratories.

It is easy to become bewildered by all the fascinating applications of the computer, which has entered almost every phase of daily life (see Figure 21.1). The text will concentrate on the way public relations practitioners can make effective use of this new equipment.

WORD PROCESSING

The computer, often called ''the word processor'' by writers, is now standard equipment in the public relations business. Two of its principal values are: (1) the capacity to store created material in its memory system for instant recall and (2) the ability to make corrections, insert fresh material, and move material from one portion of a document to another. Ingenious software programs used in the computer greatly enhance the range of services it provides writers. Among these programs are Microsoft Word, Word Perfect, MultiMate, and Apple Write.

Material written on a computer can be transferred electronically to another person's computer for review, correction, and approval. By using a printer attachment, the writer can obtain a ''hard copy'' version printed on paper. Computer word processing can be used in public relations practice for business letters, news release processing, spelling and grammar correction, and electronic mail.

FIGURE 21.1
Product publicity photographs are important in the computer industry to help the consumer make the most suitable choice from the abundance of makes and models on the market. The caption accompanying this picture of the Macintosh™ SE emphasizes that it is a general-purpose business computer whose functions can expand with communications, video, or performing acceleration cards inserted in the system's open slot as the user's needs grow.

Business Letters The word processor can produce professional-quality business letters from material typed into the computer. If a counseling firm wishes to send an identical letter, except for a few personalized touches, to ten prospective clients, some taps on a keyboard will produce a different salutation on each plus individualized copy changes aimed specifically at each recipient. On the typewriter, this special attention would require the time-consuming typing of ten letters. With word processing, the result can be obtained with a small amount of keyboard punching. This instance is merely a sample of how writing business letters can be speeded up with a computer.

Processing of News Releases Word processing is valuable in preparation of news releases. Like letters, releases can be reworded by computer for different types of publications, such as trade magazines, daily newspapers, and the business press.

The draft of a news release can be placed in computer storage while the client makes revisions on a printout copy. These changes can then be made without the time-consuming process of retyping the entire release. Also, the draft of a news release can be entered in storage by its writer and later called up on another screen by the supervisor who must review and approve it.

Correction of Spelling and Grammar Special software programs—sets of instructions telling the computer what to do—can improve the public relations writer's work by correcting spelling and grammatical mistakes. Some programs contain a dictionary of more than 100,000 words and a thesaurus of more than 10,000 words. Not only will they detect errors, but they may suggest more appropriate words. Ordinarily, however, they will not catch a wrong word choice, such as "effect" when the writer should have used "affect." Writers should give anything on paper a thorough proofreading before submitting it.

Electronic Mail A piece of writing delivered from the originator's computer into the recipient's computer, instead of being sent by mail or messenger service, is called *electronic mail,* or simply "E-mail." When a writer creates copy for a brochure, the edited text can be recorded on a disk for delivery to the printing company. Or, if the printing company has suitable computer connections, the brochure copy can be transmitted electronically from the writer's computer into the printing company's computer. No paper is used. That computer in turn can feed the copy into a phototypesetting system, from which it will emerge as type on paper ready to be reproduced, with headlines included.

DESKTOP PUBLISHING

Recent advances in computer techniques make possible the creation of professional-looking newsletters and graphically illustrated material on a personal computer right in the office. This is known as desktop publishing.

Desktop publishing allows the public relations writer and editor to design and lay out reports, newsletters, brochures, and presentations by manipulating copy and graph-

FIGURE 21.2
Producing news releases on a computer speeds up production in a public relations office. This graph published in *Public Relations Journal* shows the steps and elapsed times from origination to finished release.

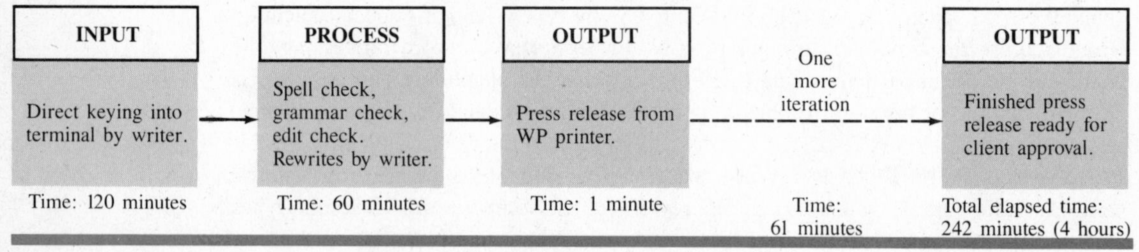

ics right on a computer screen instead of on a drawing board. It produces camera-ready pages for offset printing.

The primary advantages of desktop publishing are savings in cost and time. Less than $10,000 will buy all the components necessary for producing high-quality newsletters and graphics: a personal computer, a word-processing program, a graphics program, page-making software, and a laser printer. Producing camera-ready materials in-house reduces the fuss and expense of involving a commercial printer. Apple Computer, a leader in the field, maintains that its desktop publishing systems pay for themselves in six months, from production and cost savings alone. Apple estimates that a 16-page newsletter can be produced by the desktop method in eight hours, compared with 16 hours by the traditional commercial printing method.

MAILING LISTS

Up-to-date mailing lists are vital in public relations work. Lists of names are typed into a computer and stored in its memory. Changes of address or other alterations can be made by calling up a name and using a few keystrokes. When a mailing is to be made, the desired names on the master list can be activated and printed on adhesive labels or on the individual envelopes.

The capability to select groups of names from the master list assists the practitioner in reaching target audiences. Edward Reed, vice president of Claire Harrison Associates, wrote in *Public Relations Journal* that, typically, his firm maintains a mailing list of about 3500 names in its computer system. He explained, ''We have divided our list into 175 homogeneous groups, and we can pick specific groups for a specific mailing. Requesting this from the computer takes no time at all, and we can print on labels, envelopes, or even generate personalized letters.''

Public relations departments and firms may compile their own computer lists of media contacts or purchase standard diskettes from press-directory companies. The Gebbie Press media directory is available on PC compatible diskettes. One set contains the addresses of about 1,625 daily and 7,600 weekly newspapers in the United States; the other gives the addresses of 1,100 television stations and 10,000 AM and FM radio stations nationwide.

LISTS OF CONTACTS

In a related application, public relations offices use the storage and call-up facilities of computers to maintain ready-reference lists of individuals with their telephone numbers and addresses, job titles, and other personal data, which can be listed by category.

By keeping names and addresses on a computerized list, the public relations practitioner can easily add new names and make corrections—and the computer keeps everything in alphabetical order. This eliminates the traditional address card file.

With certain software programs, a person can summon a desired telephone number onto the screen and, with a single command, have the computer automatically dial the number.

ON-LINE CONFERENCES

When two or more persons tie their computers together by telephone line, they can hold discussions by exchanging a series of typed messages. In order to do so, their computers must be equipped with a *modem* (short for *modulator/demodulator*), an attachment that converts the computer's electronic signals into signals that can move along the telephone line.

On-line conferences are increasingly valuable in public relations work. Practitioners "converse" with clients and suppliers, or they participate in forums on professional matters with groups of their peers. The text of what has been said can be retained for the record in computer storage or typed out by a hard-copy printer.

As the number of personal computers in use expands, the frequency of on-line conferences will too. Because of their mobility—some are merely lap-size—properly equipped personal computers can be used in out-of-office situations, such as while traveling. The Phoenix (Arizona) *Gazette* created still another use by accepting into its computer system letters to the editor transmitted by personal computer.

DATABASES

With fact-finding and research essential in sophisticated practice today, the computer is becoming as important as a dictionary in a public relations office. Through it, personnel can extract information from an estimated 1500 databases that have in storage an enormous amount of current and historical information.

Public relations departments and firms use computer databases in several ways:

- Researching facts and figures to support a proposed project that requires top management approval
- Keeping up-to-date with news about clients and their competitors and markets
- Tracking the media campaigns of a company and the press announcements of its competitors
- Finding a special quotation or impressive statistic for a speech or report
- Tracking the press and business reaction to a company's latest actions
- Finding an expert for advice on a new promotional campaign
- Promoting more effectively and efficiently the products and services of a company
- Keeping top management apprised of current business trends and issues
- Learning the demographics and attitudes of target audiences

Databases range from the so-called commercial "supermarkets" that offer a broad assortment of information categories to specialized technical services. Local bulletin board databases operate in large cities, and interlocking regional networks have been created.

Here are some of the best known databases:

- *Dow Jones News/Retrieval*. A source of business information, it provides the full text of the *Wall Street Journal,* access to 185 other business and financial publications, profiles of 5000 companies, and Dun & Bradstreet reports on company credit ratings.
- *NEXIS*. This includes 8 million full-text articles from more than 125 magazines, newspapers, newsletters, and news services. It contains the full text of the New York *Times,* abstracts from leading international and foreign publications, and an advertising and marketing intelligence database.
- *CompuServe*. Considered the nation's largest vendor of computer services, it has a subscriber base of more than 200,000 and offers a number of specialized electronic bulletin boards, including those for advertising, marketing, and public relations.
- *The Source*. Similar to CompuServe, The Source's services include news, games, numerous categories of information, and electronic mail.
- *Dialog Information Retrieval Service*. This has more than 180 databases, many deriving from the space program, from which the user may choose. Newspaper and magazine indexes are included in its 80 million entries.
- *VU/TEXT*. Operated by Knight-Ridder Newspapers, Inc., VU/TEXT includes the contents and electronic libraries of numerous newspapers. A researcher can call up the entire text of the Washington *Post* on either VU/TEXT or NEXIS.

Several reference books provide lists of available database services. Two important sources for a listing of services are *The Computer Phone Book,* by Mike Cane, published by the New American Library, New York, and *The Directory of Online Databases,* put out by Cuadra Associates, Santa Monica, California.

Some public libraries offer computer search service for relatively small fees, to assist individuals who do not have computers or prefer to have a trained librarian conduct the search. Typically, a person can hunt through a magazine index to find listings of articles on desired topics, information on specified medical problems, and government reports—types of information a public relations practitioner often needs in formulating programs.

How Public Relations Firms Use Database Research Public relations firms use on-line database research in a number of ways. Regis McKenna, Inc., headquartered in Palo Alto, California, and specializing in high technology clients, provides a good example. One client, a software manufacturer, wanted to learn about the customer service and support policies of other software firms. Using NEXIS and Dialog, a researcher rapidly compiled a list of pertinent information that had appeared in business and trade magazines. The information helped the client develop its own customer support plans and position its services against the competition.

On another occasion, a microprocessor manufacturer, monitoring its entry into a relatively new market, wanted to learn if anything had been written about the use of its

GEMS FROM DATABASE RESEARCH

Databases contain masses of information available to assist public relations practitioners on difficult assignments who need answers to obscure questions. Specialists trained in database research usually can find the answers, often in a surprisingly short time.

Writing in *Communication World,* Hank Bachrach gave this sampling of questions database researchers have been requested to answer:

- What is the state-by-state tally of sheep slaughtered in the past year?
- How much underwear is produced in Malaysia?
- What is the heartbeat of an elephant? of a mouse?
- How many bottle caps are produced in the United States?
- What are the thermodynamic properties of potassium?
- How is a wife in a harem defined for tax purposes?

Drawing by Curt Hopkins in *Communication World*. (Reprinted courtesy of *Communication World*.)

product in industrial robots. And a manufacturer of microcomputer software used on-line database research to determine the product publicity activities of its competition. Clients also use database research to check dissemination of their own messages. What publications, for example, have mentioned the company? In what context?

Regis McKenna also uses on-line databases to research new clients. Retrieval of information about a company's products, sales, competition, management, and reputation enables account executives to be highly knowledgeable about the client in first meetings and also to recommend appropriate public relations programs.

A third use of on-line research at Regis McKenna is staff education. An account executive, just assigned a new account, can rapidly gain information about the client and its products by using a database. For example, an account executive wanted information about CAD/CAM systems (computer-aided design and computer-aided manufacturing) in preparation for a meeting with a client. Regis McKenna also maintains a library that subscribes to 250 newsletters and magazines in the electronic and business field so that the staff can easily find complete articles from a bibliography provided by on-line databases.

Government Databases A number of government databases are available, either directly from the federal government or through commercial databases that package the information for resale to subscribers. Data from the U.S. Census Bureau, particularly valuable for demographic and economic information, can be purchased on computer tapes and diskettes.

A California charity, for example, employed census facts to determine areas of the state with households earning more than $20,000 and thus more likely to make contributions. And the public relations department of a large corporation used census data to determine the size of the Spanish-speaking audience in major cities where the company had plant sites.

The Environmental Protection Agency operates an issues information file, open to the public. The file contains material on the background, current status, impact, and implications of 72 key environmental issues. A public relations person assigned to write a speech for a client on an environmental topic, for example, can quickly tap up-to-date information.

GRAPHICS

Use of computers to design for publications eye-catching colored graphics—drawings, graphs and charts, and text—has emerged as a new technology in public relations practice. Recent developments in computer software make such graphics possible, although they remain expensive.

Attractive graphics give visual impact to annual reports and employee publications, as well as to video programs and slide presentations. The techniques of computer graphics are still evolving and somewhat complicated, but the imaginative visual effects that experts can obtain are astonishing.

Slide presentations in particular can be enhanced dramatically with computer-generated graphics. Representations of people, designs, and charts add visual zest that stimulates audiences. Increasingly public relations departments and firms employ such graphics to dress up transparencies used in presentations to gain management approval for their ideas. Still another application of computer graphics is in news releases, especially those reporting on corporate sales and earnings. (Preparation of slide shows is discussed in Chapter 24.)

FACSIMILE TRANSMISSION

An invaluable new tool in public relations practice is facsimile transmission, commonly called *fax*. Such frequently heard remarks as ''I'll fax it to you'' have added a new verb to the language.

Facsimile transmission moves an exact copy of printed matter and graphics by telephone circuit from a machine in one office to one in another office, across town or to the other side of the world. A news release, a draft of a client's newsletter, instructions from headquarters to a branch office: these are merely three among scores of ways in which practitioners use fax. Office workers even fax their lunch orders to nearby restaurants.

Fax transmission is a tremendous timesaver. Delivery is almost immediate, compared to two days or more by mail. Some machines can deliver copies of an item to multiple addresses.

Indicative of the heavy use of fax machines, the Washington, D.C., office of the Daniel J. Edelman public relations firm sent out nearly 2500 faxes in a recent month and received somewhat fewer than that. During the 1990 Soviet-American summit meeting, the Soviet embassy in Washington on some days sent newspapers 30 to 40 pages of faxed material about President Mikhail Gorbachev's visit. This led to one newspaper headline: ''Soviets burying the West—with reams of fax paper.''

A word of caution: Discretion should be used in sending news releases to editors by facsimile. Send only those you consider to be truly important and urgent, Editors complain, often quite sharply, about the amount of ''junk fax'' they receive. They say that the inpouring of materials useless to them, including advertisements and irrelevant announcements, ties up their machines and may delay delivery of important news material. Some states have enacted laws restricting distribution of unsolicited fax items.

SATELLITE TRANSMISSION

Text messages and pictures can be flashed around the world in seconds by using satellite transmission, a fact of enormous significance to public relations communicators.

Satellite transmission on a reliable 24-hour basis became possible when a satellite was shot aloft to the altitude of 22,300 miles above the equator. There a satellite has an orbital period of 24 hours. It thus remains stationary above a fixed point on the earth's surface, available for relaying back to receiving dishes on the earth the transmissions beamed up to it from originating points on the ground. So valuable is satellite transmission that a constantly growing number of satellites are being parked above the equator in what scientists call the *geostationary belt*.

When information is dispatched by computer through a ground ''uplink'' station to a transponder pad on a satellite, then bounced back to a receiving dish on the ground and into a receiving computer, enormous amounts of material can be transmitted over great distances at breathtaking speeds. One computer can ''talk'' to another via satellite about 160 times faster than can be done over landlines, and at much lower cost. For instance, transmission of a long novel by this method requires only a few seconds.

The *Wall Street Journal,* New York *Times,* and *USA Today* use satellites to transmit entire page layouts to regional printing plants. The Associated Press, United Press International, and other news services transmit their stories and pictures by satellite. The television and radio networks deliver programs in the same manner.

In public relations practice, satellite transmission has become a tool of impressive dimensions in several ways.

NEWS RELEASE DELIVERY

More than a dozen American companies deliver news releases electronically to large newspapers and other major news media offices. In the receiving newsrooms these releases are fed into computers, to be examined by editors on video display terminals for possible publication or broadcast.

The difference between news release delivery firms and the traditional news services such as the Associated Press is this: newspapers, radio, and television stations pay large fees to receive the reports of the news services, which maintain staffs of editors and reporters to gather, analyze, select, and write the news in a neutral style. On the other hand, the news release delivery companies are paid by creators of news releases to distribute those releases to the media, which pay nothing to receive them. These delivery services are prepaid transmission belts, not selectors of material. They do enforce editing standards and occasionally reject releases as unsuitable.

One of the largest news release companies is Business Wire. Using electronic circuits and satellite communications, the company can simultaneously reach more than 1600 media points in the United States and Canada and more than 500 in Europe, Latin America, the Far East, and Australia. In addition, Business Wire provides rapid dissemination of financial news releases to more than 600 securities and investment community firms worldwide. The company sends an average of 175 news releases daily for a roster of more than 9000 clients.

Electronically delivered news releases have an advantage over the conventional variety. Releases transmitted by satellite tend to receive closer, faster attention from media editors than those arriving by mail.

The largest of the news release delivery companies, PR Newswire, was the first to distribute its releases by satellite. Using time on the SATNET satellite system of the Associated Press, PR Newswire's computers distribute releases and official statements from more than 7500 organizations directly into the newsroom computers of the media. Each day it transmits approximately 150 such releases. The releases by PR Newswire go into several commercial databases. Satellite delivery of public relations news material undoubtedly will increase as other distributors adopt the method.

VIDEO AND AUDIO NEWS RELEASE DISTRIBUTION

Transmission by satellite also makes possible fast distribution of video news releases (VNRs). The picture-and-voice releases are sent primarily to cable television networks, local cable systems, and local television stations. Nearly 30 companies produce

FIGURE 21.3
Indicative of the attention a video news release can achieve, this VNR from the California Raisin Advisory Board reached 20 million TV viewers nationwide. The singing figure is "Michael Raisin," a claymation raisin in Michael Jackson's image. The VNR was distributed by Medialink.

and distribute hundreds of video news releases for clients. Only relatively few of the most newsworthy, technically superior VNRs succeed in obtaining airtime. (See Chapter 24 for a discussion of video news releases.) These are two examples of successful VNRs:

- J.C. Penney distributed a video news release showing Prince Charles and Princess Diana touring a store in Springfield, Virginia, during a visit to the United States.
- *Sports Illustrated* amassed extensive television publicity about its annual swimsuit issue by transmitting a video news release that featured interviews with two of the models and a *Sports Illustrated* editor, as well as footage of all the photographs in the article, and even some outtakes.

Voice-and-sound news releases for use on radio are also distributed by satellite. Business Wire and Audio Features, Inc., to name two suppliers, send releases over the satellite/audio circuits of the Associated Press and United Press International.

GLOBAL TRANSMISSION OF MESSAGES

Still another use of satellite communication is found in *global electronic mail*. For example, Apple Computer of California regularly communicates with its foreign offices through a Tym-Net system that allows a public relations manager to type a message into an Apple Computer in California and, through a modem, electronically transmit that message via satellite anywhere in the world within seconds.

Some American corporations send facsimile pages of annual reports by satellite to printing firms in Japan and Korea. These corporations find that the cost of overseas transmission, printing, and air shipment back to the United States is lower than if the printing were done by American companies.

TELECONFERENCING

The most spectacular use of satellite transmission for public relations purposes is *teleconferencing,* also called *videoconferencing*. Through it, groups of conferees separated by thousands of miles can interact instantaneously with strong visual impact.

Use of this technique is growing rapidly. *TeleSpan* newsletter estimated in 1988 that more than 15,000 videoconferences had taken place, and by 1989 there were 60 videoconferencing networks. Around the United States 19,500 sites were equipped to handle such events. A traditional conference consists of a group of men and women assembled at a central location for discussion, exchange of information, and inspiration. Participants frequently come from distant points. Their travel costs and hotel bills are often high, they may be plagued by the nuisances of flight reservations and connections, and they may be away from their offices for days.

Satellite-relayed television has changed this concept radically. Now the conferees can remain at their home offices, or gather in groups in nearby cities, and hold their conferences by television. Travel time and cost are reduced or eliminated. In one five-year period, the Boeing Company used teleconferencing for 5699 meetings and eliminated the need for more than 1.5 million miles of travel.

Long-distance discussions among widely separated groups began in the 1930s when the telephone company created conference calls that enabled three or more parties to talk among themselves. The American Telephone & Telegraph Company had videoconferencing in mind when it introduced the ill-fated Picturephone in 1964, but the high cost kept the idea from taking hold.

Now, however, satellites and fiber optics have dropped transmission costs to several hundred dollars per hour, and a company can easily arrange a teleconference by employing a firm that specializes in this form of communication. A company such as Visnews charges less than $2000 for a 30-minute New York-to-Los Angeles videoconference and about $2500 for a New York-to-London connection.

The most widely used form of teleconferencing blends one-way video and two-way audio. This one-way video technology, a form of direct broadcast satellite (DBS), broadcasts a live presentation to many locations simultaneously. DBS is the least expensive method because cameras, transmitters, and other expensive equipment are needed only at one end. The video signal can be received by small, relatively inexpensive antennas at locations around the world via satellite. Figure 21.4 shows, in schematic form, how the satellite transmission works.

Guests at receiving locations view the presentation on large screens. Regular telephone circuits back to the point of origin enable the guests to ask follow-up questions. Teleconferencing also has great potential for employee relations. Ford Motor Company, for example, has installed a $10 million system connecting more than 200 Ford locations in North America over which executives in Detroit can speak. Many other large companies have their own internal corporate satellite systems.

Here are examples of teleconferencing in operation:

- The Whirlpool Corporation in the United States and an N. V. Philips division in the Netherlands needed to explain their new $2 billion joint venture agreement. So

FIGURE 21.4
The diagram explains how satellite teleconferencing operates. (Courtesy of VideoStar Connections, Inc.)

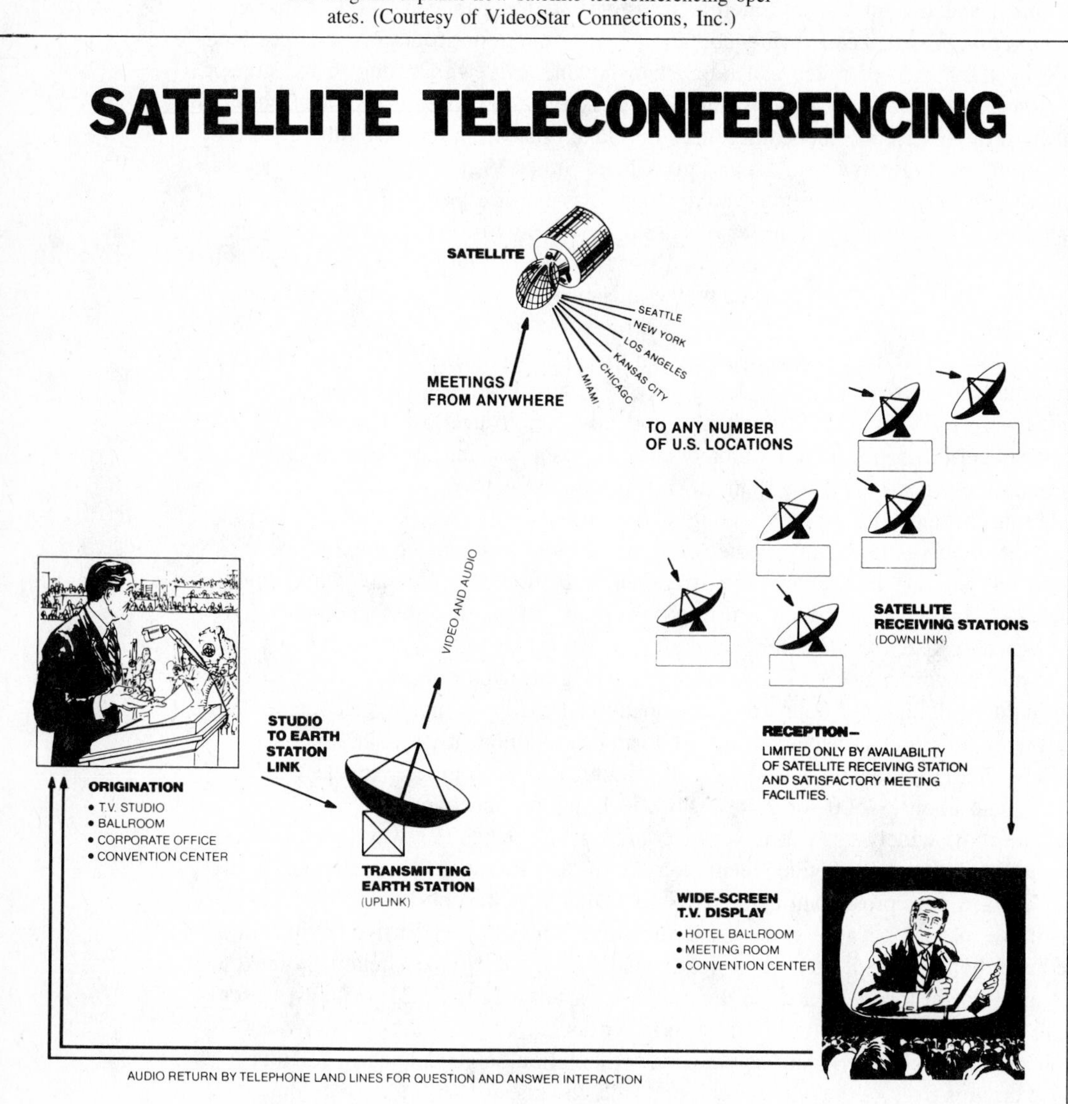

they held an international teleconference for their respective stockholders and employees, the media, and financial analysts.

- Hill & Knowlton, on behalf of several government agencies, arranged a two-hour conference between Cairo, Egypt, and five U.S. cities that permitted several hundred U.S. investors to talk directly with high-ranking Egyptian officials about private investment in that nation.
- When the Rev. Theodore M. Hesburgh retired as the president of the University of Notre Dame, his farewell speech, made on campus, was distributed by satellite to 123 sites in the United States, Canada, and Mexico where alumni, parents, and students gathered to see and hear it. During the program, the university introduced its multimillion-dollar development plan to the audience of prospective contributors.
- To introduce a newly developed hepatitis B vaccine, Merck Sharp & Dohme used a teleconference beamed to more than 400 locations where doctors, health-care workers, and reporters had gathered. After watching the presentation, the invited guests telephoned questions to a panel of experts.

Technical refinements of teleconferencing are still being developed. Voice-activated cameras can focus on participants in a conference for closeups as each speaks. Hard (printed) copies of documents under discussion can be transmitted from one conference point to another. A more economical system is the "slow scan" conference. This provides for transmission of still pictures or slides over a telephone circuit between conference points, with voice transmission over a separate line.

To decide whether a teleconference will be cost-effective, a potential user should obtain quotations on all expenses involved, and should then compare these figures to the price of travel, lodging, and entertainment if all employees or invited guests were brought to a central conference location. To these travel costs should be added the intangible one of work time lost by employees away from their offices. International teleconferencing is especially attractive for multinational corporations because of the high cost of overseas travel. (For additional information, see Chapter 16.)

Those who use teleconferencing emphasize that it is most effective for reaching large audiences for such purposes as introduction of a product, sales meetings, and announcement of new corporate policies. Like other electronic methods of communication, though, it lacks the personal warmth that comes from a handshake and a face-to-face conversation.

Satellite Media Tours Instead of having a personality—an actor or author, for example—crisscross the country on an expensive, time-consuming promotional tour, public relations sponsors increasingly use the so-called satellite tour.

The personality is stationed in a television studio, and TV reporters interview him or her by satellite from their home studios. Two-way television is used, permitting a visual dialogue. Each station's reporter is put through to the personality at a specified time; thus a series of interviews, 5 to 10 minutes each, can be done in sequence.

Actor Christopher Reeve set an endurance record by doing 45 consecutive interviews at one sitting. Tiresome mentally and physically, no doubt, but much faster and cheaper than visiting all those cities!

HEWLETT-PACKARD: A LEADER IN SOPHISTICATED VIDEO COMMUNICATION

Hewlett-Packard, with headquarters in Palo Alto, California, spends more than $1 million annually on video communications and produces some of the nation's most sophisticated industrial television.

The company began teleconferencing in 1981 by using a satellite transmitter to reach more than 80 plant and sales sites around the nation, which enabled an executive to address many audiences at the same time.

More recently, Hewlett-Packard took teleconferencing one step further with ''point-to-point'' capability. With this technology, up to seven people in three locations can be connected by satellite to see one another on a television screen.

Another application of video by HP involves use of a video disk, which combines the visuals of a video with the ''brains'' of a computer to allow random access to information. The method is called *interactive video* because the information portrayed is determined by the viewer's response to certain questions. It resembles a videogame, in which the response often determines the outcome.

To communicate with employees, Hewlett-Packard produces a slick video magazine. Released six times a year at a cost of $25,000 per show, ''H-P Video Magazine'' is formatted after television's ''Evening Magazine.'' ''After surveying our employees, we found that our print magazine, *Measure,* was appealing primarily to the professional and managerial ranks,'' says Brad Whitworth, manager of internal communications. ''We wanted to reach the baby boomers, the production, and the clerical workers and felt that television would be a more effective medium.''

VIDEOTAPE

The third major tool not available to earlier generations of public relations people, but invaluable in contemporary practice, is videotape. It has replaced motion picture film under most circumstances because it is less expensive and more convenient. Furthermore, these desirable attributes make videotape useful in situations where motion picture film could not be considered.

Videotape is plastic tape coated with iron oxide on which visual and audio signals are recorded in magnetic patterns. The tape is small, easily edited, and ready for immediate playback after a scene has been shot. Television news programs use videotape, often in combination with satellite transmission. A military incident recorded on videotape in the Persian Gulf and transmitted to the United States by satellite can be shown to American viewers nationwide within a few minutes. The home viewer can record the scene from the family television set with a videocassette for later replay.

The uses of videotape in public relations work are limited only by the imagination of the practitioner. A few examples: for its distributors, Coors Brewery in Golden, Colorado, produces a monthly half-hour videotaped show in magazine format that presents news sales plans and shows departments of the company at work. Also, the brewery supplies television stations with unedited half-hour videotapes of brewery operations, from which the news departments can use footage as desired to illustrate stories. In still a third use, the company shows videotapes to employees in training programs. Similarly, Atari, the electronic game manufacturer, issued a video news release to announce a new game.

Just coming into trial use for promotional and sales purposes is the disposable videocassette. Made cheaply of cardboard instead of plastic, the lightweight cassette wears out after about 10 viewings, but by that time its message has either succeeded or failed. Its creators promote it as an effective direct mail tool.

Numerous other uses of videotape are mentioned in this book, especially in Chapters 23 and 24.

OTHER TOOLS

Electronic methods of communication are expanding rapidly as new techniques become available. Any attempt to name them all is futile, since new developments make the list out-of-date almost instantly, Even so, it is useful to examine a few of the recent additions that are of particular interest to public relations people.

TELETEXT

Teletext is one form of the recently developed concept of *information on demand*. By pushing a few keys, viewers can summon onto the screen indexes of material stored in a computer. From these indexes, the viewers call up what they wish to see. In addition to news, a major component in teletext, the viewer may wish to look for entertainment guides, community service listings, or capsule reviews of restaurants, all of which are targets for public relations practitioners publicizing their clients' services. Teletext is a one-way information service, sender to viewer.

VIDEOTEX

This more complex form of on-demand service is a two-way, or interactive, system. On videotex, viewers call up on a screen what they wish to watch; then by using telephone circuits they can respond to what they have seen.

Videotex usage is still developing as the systems come into commercial service. Among the applications are conducting two-way banking operations, ordering goods displayed on the screen, and having viewers answer poll questions put to them.

In the area of corporate information, videotex has significant potential. Reporting the ideas of Perry Jaffe, director of the Pratt Center for Computer Graphics and Design, Bill Hunter tells in *Communication World* how videotex can be applied in this sphere:

> If an employee wants to see the latest company newsletter, he or she might simply hit a button on a computer terminal and get the information, supplemented by computer graphics or video strips of the company president delivering a speech to shareholders.
>
> At the end of a segment, the employee might be invited to press a button to see portions repeated or to hear additional comments about some specific issue. Or employees might be asked to communicate back about whether they understand the points the president was trying to make. Press Y for "yes" and N for "no."

FIGURE 21.5
A whimsical touch in public relations photography, as in this picture of a rider using a cellular phone while clearing a jump, catches the eye of editors. The caption under the photo in the *GTE Shareholder News* said, "You can use a GTE Mobilnet cellular phone on any mode of transportation." The rider is Tom Howland; the horse, Shadow. (Courtesy of GTE Mobilnet Incorporated.)

FLOPPY DISKS

The latest form of the informational brochure is the floppy disk, which a person "reads" on a personal computer. Buick, for example, mailed 20,000 floppy disks to users of Apple personal computers to tell them about its new models.

Breakthroughs in software design made it possible for recipients of the Buick floppy disk to "interact" with the information presented. By pushing a few buttons, computer users could load the trunk with luggage and ask questions about mileage, standard equipment, and how the Buick compared with other auto makes.

A "press disk," the floppy disk version of a press kit, has been sent out by at least one company, but reporters made little use of the novelty. They found it less convenient and more time-consuming than traditional printed material. Lack of technical standardization also restricts their use. A more efficient use of the disk technique is distribution by corporations of their annual reports on diskettes.

ELECTRONIC BLACKBOARDS

Blackboards with chalk now belong to the past as companies begin to use "whiteboards" that serve the same function as facsimile machines. A person can write on a whiteboard with a liquid marker during a presentation, and the image is electronically scanned to allow a printer rapidly to produce multiple copies of the image for future reference by members of the audience.

Xerox is taking this concept one step further by experimenting with something called a "liveboard." Each desk in a meeting room has a computer terminal on which a person can draw or type something that is automatically produced on the large "liveboard" for everyone to see.

CELLULAR PHONES

While driving, a public relations practitioner can conduct business by using a cellular telephone. A cellular system has interlocking low-power transmitters; as a motorist moves from one zone to another, calls from the car are switched by computer into the next zone, permitting continuous nonfading conversations. Interview calls to radio stations by clients from a practitioner's moving car are one attention-getting use of the system (see Figure 21.5). A cellular phone system with a range enabling communication from one part of the world to another has been announced.

FIBER OPTICS

Transmission of messages is being revolutionized by the use of *fiber optics*. Instead of sending signals by wire, this system uses highly transparent strands of glass thinner than human hair. Replacing electronic signals, pulses of light flash along these glass strands at the rate of 90 million per second. So fine are these strands that 240,000 telephone calls can be transmitted at one time through a single fiber optics cable (see Figure 21.6). The probable extension of fiber optics lines into homes in coming years should open the way for new public relations applications.

FIGURE 21.6
A fiber-optic cable the size of a finger (right) can carry 100 times more telephone calls than the standard 3½-inch copper cable. (Courtesy of Pacific Bell.)

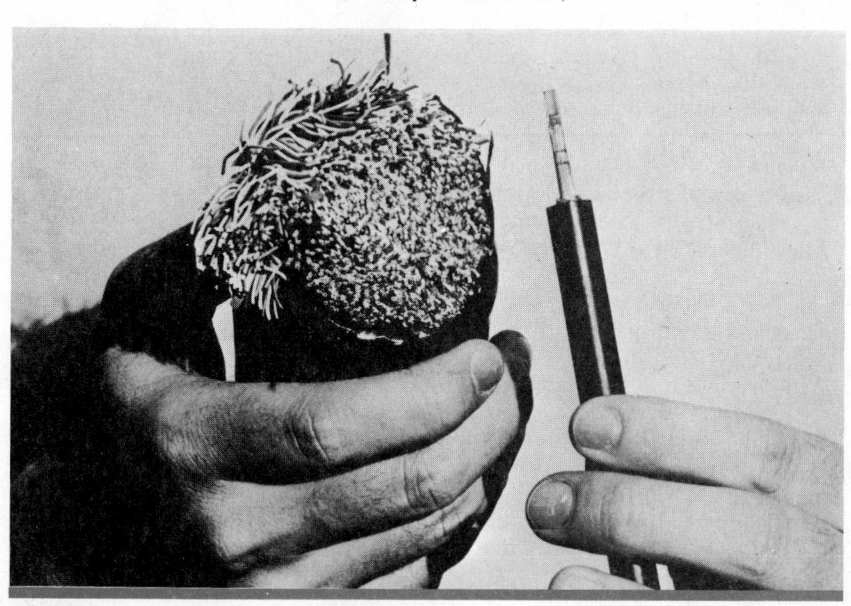

CASE PROBLEM

Ace Chemical Company publishes and distributes a report to its 10,000 employees on an annual basis. The report reviews the company's progress in the past year, honors employees who made a significant contribution to productivity, and discusses topics of employee interest such as opportunities for advancement, increased benefits, and what the company is doing to make the workplace even safer.

Readership of this annual report has declined in recent years. There is no specific reason, but one comment frequently heard is, ''It's a dull report to read.'' One suggestion is to put the annual report on a videotape; another is to upgrade the current printed report with computer graphics; yet another suggestion is to put the entire report on a floppy disk and mail it to employees who could put the report on a personal home computer.

What are the pros and cons of each of these suggestions? What would you ultimately recommend?

QUESTIONS FOR REVIEW AND DISCUSSION

1. What are the principal values of the word processor?

2. Define such terms as *electronic mail, direct broadcast system (DBS), interactive video, desktop publishing, modem, database, teleconference, slow scan, teletext,* and *videotex.*

3. In what ways are computer databases used in public relations?

4. Satellites are placed in geostationary orbit. What does that mean?

5. What is the difference between a news release delivery system such as Business Wire and a news service such as the Associated Press?

6. Teleconferencing is growing in popularity. Explain how it operates and give some examples.

7. What are the advantages of videotape over motion picture film?

8. Why has facsimile become such a popular method of communication?

9. As a public relations practitioner, how might you use on-line computer conference calls?

10. Why is transmitting signals by fiber optics superior to sending them over an ordinary telephone line?

Calloway, Linda Jo. "Survival of the Fastest: Information Technology and Corporate Crisis." *Public Relations Review,* Spring 1991, pp. 85–92.

"Computerized Press Kits: Wave of the Future?" *Public Relations Journal,* October 1989, pp. 13–14.

Dirks, Douglas. "Setting Up an International Conference . . . Online." *Communication World,* March 1991, pp. 28–29.

Finley, Michael. "The New Meaning of Meetings." *Communication World,* March 1991, pp. 25–27. Using computer software for more productive meetings.

"Four Ways to Make Desktop Work." *Communication World,* November 1988, pp. 19–26. Practical applications of desktop publishing.

Glazer, George. "Beam It Over and Out—Via Satellite." *Communication World,* March 1988, pp. 14–15.

Green, David, and Wall, Don. "Group Meetings: In-Person vs. Satellite TV." *Communication World,* March 1988, pp. 22–25.

Green, Richard, and Shapiro, Denise. "A Video News Release Primer." *Public Relations Quarterly,* Winter 1987–1988, pp. 10–13.

Grundberg, Andy. "Ask It No Questions: The Camera Can Lie." New York *Times,* August 12, 1990, Section 2, pp. 1, 29. Computer imaging can change photographs.

Lehrman, Celia K. "Videoconferencing Comes Down to Earth." *Public Relations Journal,* April 1989, pp. 23–27.

Lipman, Joanne. "Direct Mailers Study Disposable Videos." *Wall Street Journal,* May 30, 1990, p. B6.

Maxwell, Linnea. "Taking Desktop Publishing One Step Further." *Communication World,* November 1988, pp. 30–32. Newsletters on computer disks.

Pintak, Larry. "VNRs Go Abroad, Sometimes." *Communication World,* January 1991, pp. 15–17. International distribution of video news releases.

Restivo, Peter J. "Suffering from Video Technophobia." *Communication World,* March 1990, pp. 27–30.

"A Revolution in Search of Revolutionaries." *Communication World,* March 1991, pp. 15–24. The uses of computer databases in public relations.

Shell, Adam. "VNR Update: An Easy Guide to VNR Suppliers." *Public Relations Journal,* December 1990, pp. 28–32.

Sims, Paul. "Satellite Technology Boosts TV News Coverage of Company-Sponsored Community Events." *Public Relations Quarterly,* Winter 1990–1991, pp. 23–24.

Solomon, Julie. "Business Communication in the Fax Age." *Wall Street Journal,* October 1988, p. B1.

Teague, Walter F. "Video Extravaganza: Pulling Out All the Stops." *Communication World,* February 1988, pp. 16–19. A large audience production for a conference.

CHAPTER

22

Written Tactics

Of all the tools a public relations practitioner uses, the news release is the most common. It is the primary written method of conveying news to the media for publication or broadcast. As such, the news release requires careful preparation and judicious distribution so that its information will be delivered to the right places in an accurate, timely, easily usable, and attractive manner.

This chapter begins with a discussion of the techniques of the news release. Then it examines other types of written communications used in public relations. It explains the purpose of each kind, the methods employed in developing it, and its relative value in campaigns to reach specified audiences. The materials described include factsheets, press kits, newsletters, company magazines and newspapers, publications such as brochures and handbooks, information distributed within organizations (staff bulletins and employee home mailing pieces, for example), annual reports, and corporate advertising. Many, indeed, are the ways to use the written word!

THE NEWS RELEASE

Basically, a *news release* is a simple document whose purpose is the dissemination of information in ready-to-publish form. Editors of print and broadcast media to whom news releases are sent judge them on the basis of news interest for their audience and timeliness, and in some instances on their adaptability to the medium's form. No payment is made to the publication or station if the material appears in print or on the air. If an organization or individual purchases space in a publication to present its material, this is a paid advertisement and the purchaser controls the content.

Releases should be prepared so that the media can relay their news content to audiences easily, with confidence in their accuracy. Editors want the main facts stated succinctly in the opening paragraph of a release, for quick recognition. A news release is a purveyor of information, not an exercise in writing style, except in those cases of longer releases that are clearly intended to be feature stories. The writer of a basic news release should leave the clever writing to staff members of the media.

A news release faces intense competition when it arrives on an editor's desk, against scores or even hundreds of other releases. As they scan the releases, editors make almost instant decisions, assigning each release to one of three categories:

1. *Obvious news.* Copy that is certain to be used.

2. *Maybe.* Stories possibly worth developing if a reporter has the time. A sharp news angle in a release may put it in the "obvious-news" category instead of the risky "maybe" pile. Potentially good stories placed in the "maybe" pile face the danger of being thrown away after a second reading if the key information is poorly developed.

3. *Discard.* Releases of insufficient interest to the receiving editor's audience and those of marginal value that would require too much effort to develop. These go into the recycling box or the wastebasket.

News releases that are prepared according to the criteria described in the following sections have the best chance of being accepted for publication, assuming that their content is newsworthy.

PHYSICAL APPEARANCE

There is a standard format for news releases:

- Use plain white 8½-by-11-inch paper.
- Identify the sender in the upper-left-hand corner of the page, listing name, address, and telephone number. Especially if the sender is a large organization, also give the name of an individual within the organization as a point of contact. It is important that the listed phone be answered by an informed person, usually a public relations specialist, not by a recording.
- Below the identification state *For Immediate Release* if the material is intended for immediate publication, as most news releases are. If a time restriction is necessary, as with an advance copy of a speech to be delivered at a specified hour, indicate the desired publication time; for example, *For Release at 6 p.m. EST Feb. 12.* This is called an *embargo.* Media recipients of embargoed material have no legal obligation to obey its restrictions, but they normally do so out of courtesy and mutual convenience unless they believe that the embargo is an obvious effort to manipulate the news. Embargoes should be used only when genuinely necessary.

The standard form for the heading looks like this:

Wilson Furniture Co.
3325D Healy Drive
Winston Salem, NC 27103
(704) 555-8561
Contact: Evelyn Richards

For immediate release

- Leave two inches of space for editing convenience before starting the text.
- Start the text with a clearly stated summary lead containing timely, relevant, important information.
- Leave wide margins. Double-space the copy to give editors room in which to edit the material.
- Never split a paragraph from one page to the next. Put (*more*) at the bottom of each unfinished page.
- Place an identifying slugline and page number at the top of each page after the first.

Some public relations practitioners place a summary headline above the text, for quick identification and possible use by the editor. Others use no headline, in the belief that headline-writing is entirely the editor's business.

CONTENT

There are a few essential rules for content:

- Begin the news release with a tightly written summary lead and state the fundamentals—who, what, when, where, and why—early in the copy. The first sentence should state the most important point in the story. *Do not bury the lead.*
- Be concise. Edit the copy to remove excess words and ''puff'' terminology. A competent editor would cut them out, anyway. Few news releases need to be more than two pages long; most can be written in a single page. A reporter may obtain additional details by telephoning the number listed at the beginning.
- Caution: Avoid clichés and fancy phrases. When editors receive a news release using such terms as ''blonde dynamo'' and ''West Coast lingerie doyenne'' about a fashion designer, they almost automatically throw it away.
- Never use excessively technical language in a release for a general audience.
- Be absolutely certain that every fact and title in the release is correct and that every name is spelled properly. Check the copy closely for grammatical errors. Errors can be embarrassing and costly. In a news release announcing a Mexican cruise, distributed nationally, Cunard Lines mistakenly listed the 800 telephone number

of a San Francisco optical company instead of its own. The optical company received more than two thousand calls in the first week; its phone lines were tied up and it had to assign personnel to redirect the calls. Cunard compensated for its blunder by giving the optical proprietor and his wife a free cruise to Europe.

For protection against errors and misunderstandings, a public relations counselor is wise to have the client initial a file copy of each news release before its distribution. In company public relations departments, similar initialing by a superior is desirable and in some cases mandatory.

Those who issue news releases welcome follow-up inquiries from reporters and are happy to provide additional information about the news situation. They desire the fullest exposure possible for their stories. Figure 22.1 shows a typically well-presented news release.

When a story is controversial, and the organization or individual issuing the news release is in a defensive position, this openness sometimes diminishes or even vanishes. The attitude of some upper-management executives toward the media in controversial situations is, "Tell them only what we want the public to know. Let them find out the rest for themselves, if they can." This attitude on the part of management may persist even to the point of having the public relations department omit relatively simple information from routine releases, raising questions every good reporter should want answered.

Citing "company policy," Quadrex Corporation refused to answer press inquiries about how many people were being laid off. An editorial in the local newspaper called the company to task. It said, in part: "A public company should be relatively open. There is no reason or excuse—except short-term stonewalling to harbor the company's stock from truth—to withhold such information as the number of persons in a layoff. . . . In the long run, Quadrex would generate a better public image by disclosing rather than withholding information."

This management attitude of playing it close to the vest is a source of mistrust among the media toward companies that follow the practice. A survey by a unit of the J. Walter Thompson advertising agency showed that 55 percent of the business editors who responded criticized corporate press releases for burying important information.

$3 MILLION PRINTING ERROR

Kraft USA's failure to catch a printing error cost the company more than $3 million and much controversy. The episode illustrates the need for meticulous checking of public relations, marketing, and other printed matter a company issues.

The Kraft sales promotion contest was designed to award a Dodge Caravan to the top winner, and bicycles and skateboards to lesser winners. But the printing error made nearly every coupon in specially marked Kraft packages a winner.

Nearly 10,000 persons turned in winning coupons for the van and more than 5,000 for bicycles. Kraft declared the contest void and offered alternative prizes of $250 cash to the apparent van winners and $50 to the bicycle winners.

Many accepted, but several hundred filed a class action suit against Kraft instead, creating heavy legal expense for the company and possibly the cost of more vans.

Santa Clara Valley Water District

5750 ALMADEN EXPRESSWAY
SAN JOSE, CALIFORNIA 95118
TELEPHONE (408) 265-2600
FACSIMILE (408) 266-0271

AN AFFIRMATIVE ACTION EMPLOYER

News Release

Contact: Teddy Morse, Public Information Representative
Office: 408/265-2600, ext. 279 (After Hours - 408/269-6172)
Home: 408/268-4847

Date: July 17, 1990

SANTA CLARA COUNTY WATER CONSUMERS CONTINUE TO SAVE WATER

The Santa Clara Valley Water District released its water conservation figures for the month of June today, and the news is good. Consumers used 30 percent less water in June 1990 than in June 1987.

The need to cutback on water use is the result of the fourth year of below average rainfall in Santa Clara County and reductions in imported water available to the district. The rainfall season ended June 30. Santa Clara County rainfall figures ranged between 65 and 71 percent of average, and water district reservoirs are at near record low levels.

"Everyone is pitching in to encourage conservation," said Ronald R. Esau, water district general manager. "Most water companies are imposing financial incentives and the cities and county are restricting how water can be used."

For its part the Santa Clara Valley Water District contracted with PRx, a San Jose-based public relations/advertising firm, to create and implement a water conservation advertising campaign. The Smothers Brothers, comedians who started their career in the Bay Area, were hired to publicize the campaign. Bus boards, radio and television spots, and newspaper ads are being used to remind consumers of the need to conserve.

-more-

FIGURE 22.1
This news release issued by the Santa Clara Valley Water District is typical of competent news releases. It states clearly the name and telephone numbers of the person to be called for further information.

Frequently, as news-oriented persons, public relations practitioners wish they could be more informative in their releases than management policy permits. As the influence of upper-level public relations executives on corporate policy-making increases, which it is doing gradually, many firms are adopting a more forthright approach. A company has no reason to wash its dirty linen in public in a voluntary outburst of confession. Yet greater frankness in news releases and willingness to volunteer answers to reasonable questions that good reporters will ask anyway help to build a company's credibility in the eyes of media and public.

DELIVERY OF NEWS RELEASES

News releases should be conveyed to the media in a timely and effective manner. As pointed out in Chapter 12, releases should be addressed to recipients by name whenever possible. Releases may be sent in a broadside manner to large numbers of recipients, in an approach called *macrodistribution,* or to carefully selected target media sources, in the *microdistribution* technique. The high cost of postage and of specialized delivery services causes most public relations practitioners to select recipients of their news releases with care, not sending to those unlikely to use the material. Therefore, practitioners should familiarize themselves with the appropriate media sources for their firm or their clients.

Locally, releases should be sent first-class if mailed, or delivered by messenger if they contain urgent material. Use of bulk mail to save postage is unwise. Delivery is subject to delay, and recipients of bulk mail tend to dismiss it as of little importance.

Delivery of releases regionally or nationally is more complicated because of timing problems and the need to reach the proper outlets and individuals in areas where the sender lacks knowledge of local situations. Accurate, current mailing lists substantially influence the amount of exposure a news release obtains. For this reason, many organizations employ distribution firms to handle their mailings.

Recent developments in computer techniques give the creator of a release numerous options for its delivery, depending upon the importance of the release and budget allocations. Distribution by mail still is the cheapest, most common, and least attention-getting method. Overnight delivery by Federal Express, Express Mail, or United Parcel Service by messenger is more expensive but gives the news release an aura of importance. Releases also are delivered by facsimile. Faxed messages are a popular way of delivering invitations to meetings and events.

Electronic Delivery As pointed out in Chapter 21, distribution of news releases electronically is one result of the satellite and computer revolution. Companies whose services are based on computer programming offer various types of news release delivery, usually aimed at carefully targeted lists of recipients. The public relations practitioner writes a news release and turns over the copy to one of these distribution companies. Depending upon the type of distribution the practitioner chooses, the commercial firm either prints and mails it to a selected mailing list or distributes it by high-speed private wire to outlets chosen by the author. The release arrives in newsrooms on special public relations printers in the same ready-to-publish form as if it had been mailed. Recognizing the growing dependence on computers in newsrooms, distribution companies also will dispatch news releases from their computers directly into the computers of newsrooms, just as news services send copy to most newspapers.

In the growing number of instances in which the public relations practitioner has suitable word processing equipment, the release can be composed on the writer's video screen, transmitted into the distribution firm's computer, checked there, and dispatched into the computers of designated recipients. Not a word has appeared on paper from the originator to the ultimate recipient. Such electronic distribution is much more expensive than the traditional mailings. However, distribution firms offering the service claim better usage of a release sent electronically. Recipients include commercial databases, whose clients such as stockbrokers and banks may call up the information.

Editorial Promotion Services Still another way of distributing news about products, services, and events nationally is through an editorial promotion service. A company or firm sends a featurized news release about its project or product to the promotion service. If the service's editors deem the content to be newsworthy and written in competent news story style, they include the release in one of their periodic mailings to newspaper editors. Photographs and appropriate drawings may be included to illustrate the release. Brand names are permitted, although they usually are placed inconspicuously well down in the stories. Smaller newspapers in particular use editorial promotion service copy as textual matter in special advertising sections on such themes as gardening, home repair, Mother's Day, auto repair, and fashions. To win acceptance by an editorial promotion service, copy must be free of hard-sell "puffery," concentrating instead on an informational approach.

An example of the material distributed is this story excerpt from a Stamps-Conhaim service mailing for Clairol:

> Anyone who is trying to finance an education today cannot be too happy with the budget cut news coming from Washington. With cutbacks in student aid, one thing is for sure—federal money for a college education is a lot harder to come by and the competition is nothing short of fierce.
>
> Certainly budget cuts will hurt the traditionally aged college students, but the effect will be that much more devastating on the older students who have been flocking back to the classroom in record numbers these past few years to train for new careers. Finding established funding has always been difficult for this group, who today comprise over 40 percent of all college enrollment.
>
> One good source of aid for female students over 30 is the Clairol Loving Care Scholarship Program. Established in 1974 as part of Clairol's policy to support the efforts of women, the scholarship program awards scholarships of up to $1000 to qualified women over 30 for studies leading to a career goal on the undergraduate and master's levels, in the professional schools and for vocational training. . . .

At the end of the story, readers are told where to write for information about scholarship applications. While publicizing the Clairol name and hair-coloring product, which is sold heavily to women over 30, the story has legitimate news interest. A good likelihood exists that it will be published in numerous newspapers. By arriving on editors' desks under the auspices of the editorial promotion service, rather than as a mailed news release, its chances of receiving attention are enhanced. Clairol's scholarship program is a good example of how a manufacturer can publicize a product in a socially significant manner.

LOCALIZING A NEWS RELEASE

National corporations realize that when the releases they send out are localized, media use will be substantially higher. The local angle should be placed in the lead if possible. Inclusion of local names or statistics attracts editors; they know it interests readers. For example, a corporation with offices and plants in 20 cities sends out a release reporting that it currently has 30,000 employees systemwide, who last year received total wages and health benefits of stated amounts. The release may be published rather inconspicuously in the newspapers of some company cities but will receive little or no broadcast attention because it is too general. Even company employees will have difficulty relating to it. However, if the releases sent to the media in each company city tell how many employees the company has in that locality, and how much these workers receive in payroll and health benefits each year, likelihood of widespread use will be high.

Lack of local application in the news releases they receive was a major cause of complaint by business editors surveyed by *Editor & Publisher*. The magazine reported: "The editors noted the vast majority of the hundreds or more press releases they receive each day are completely unrelated to their needs. They are consistent in reporting that 95 percent of the material they receive has no relevance to local companies, industries, or interests and consequently is trashed."

Despite their desirability, localized releases traditionally have been expensive to prepare and send out. Computerization has changed this somewhat. Now a corporation can prepare a standard national news release giving general information for use by all recipients. It also can prepare paragraphs containing the local information for each company city. These paragraphs are inserted by computer appropriately into the releases intended for each specific city. The media outlets in that city receive only the releases especially tailored for them.

GETTING EXTRA MILEAGE FROM NEWS RELEASES

Shrewd practitioners find ways to get extra value from published news releases. Clipping services they employ send them stories in newspapers and magazines based on their releases. Some distribution firms also offer clipping services. By sending photocopies of these clippings appropriately to sales representatives and company officials in each territory, practitioners keep the field force informed about what is being published concerning the company and its products. The same system is useful for trade and professional associations. When an individual is mentioned favorably in a news story based on a release, the practitioner can please the individual by sending a copy of the story to him or her with a note of congratulation.

A discussion of television news releases appears in Chapter 24.

THE FACTSHEET

Although factsheets are distributed by public relations personnel to the same media as news releases are, and somewhat resemble releases physically, they are in outline form instead of in news story format.

A *factsheet* is essentially a quick reference tool for reporters: it summarizes the key points about an event, a product, or a company to help reporters get a quick grasp or overview. A file of factsheets proves useful as reference material.

Press kits (discussed in the next section) often contain factsheets, and the sheets may also accompany a single news release or a letter suggesting a story idea to a reporter or editor.

Figure 22.2 shows a factsheet giving basic facts about Napa Valley Wine Train Incorporated.

FIGURE 22.2
Public relations offices distribute two kinds of factsheets. The corporate profile contains basic information about a company, as shown by this opening page of a release from the Napa Valley Wine Train; the event factsheet provides facts and figures about a forthcoming activity.

FROM: Bob Glantz (415) 984-6297
David Emanuel (415) 984-6326
Ketchum Public Relations
55 Union Street
San Francisco, CA 94111-1217

RELEASE AT WILL
January 25, 1990

CONTACT: Jack McCormack (707) 253-2160
Napa Valley Wine Train

FACT SHEET

Organization: Napa Valley Wine Train Incorporated, a California corporation.

Incorporated: 1984

Purpose: Napa Valley visitor attraction operating as a common carrier railroad. Gourmet luncheon and dinner trains begin service September 16, 1989. Future offerings will include excursion trains with stops at pre-selected points to allow passengers to visit wineries.

Management: Vincent DeDomenico, chairman, former owner of Golden Grain Macaroni Company, major shareholder in the Napa Valley Wine Train.

John C. (Jack) McCormack, president, veteran businessman and entrepreneur with 25 years experience with such companies as American Honda Motor Company, The Ventana Group and American Eagle products. Time magazine noted "Mr. McCormack is a high octane director."

Background: Napa Valley Wine Train, Inc. acquired 21 miles of track and 125 acres of right-of-way land for $2.25 million in April 1987 from Southern Pacific Railroad, which had owned the line for more than 100 years.

The line runs from Roctram (south of the city of Napa) to north of the Krug Winery, north of the city of St. Helena. Proposed stops on the line are at Yountville, Oakville, Rutherford, and St. Helena.

Special Designation: The Napa Valley Wine Train enjoys an "interchange" agreement with the Southern Pacific Railroad, an interstate carrier. Terms of the acquisition agreement call for the Napa Valley Wine Train to receive such privileges as tie-ins with interstate ticketing agencies. These privileges elevate the Napa Valley Wine Train beyond a "tourist train" operation.

- (more) -

Susan Antilla, New York bureau chief of *USA Today's* money section, said in *Jack O'Dwyer's Newsletter,* "PR people can really help a lot by providing background on companies . . . good factsheets are considered gold and are kept on file."

THE PRESS KIT

A *press kit* is often prepared when a company announces a new product or sponsors a major event; frequently elaborate, it gives media representatives a thorough background and provides information in various formats. Press kits may be sent to the media or distributed at a news conference (discussed in the next chapter).

The basic format consists of a large folder cover with pockets inside that contain news releases, factsheets, backgrounders (background articles), collateral company materials, black-and-white publicity photos, color slides, and even article reprints. The folder usually is visually attractive, incorporating graphic design, color, and the name of the company.

Typical of such press kits is one prepared by LMS International, a new company formed as a joint venture of Control Data and Philips corporations. The public relations objective was to announce the new organization and develop a stronger understanding among the electronic trade media of its products; consequently, the press kit contained the following materials:

- Backgrounders on (1) the company/management team, (2) product areas/markets, and (3) major new products
- Separate news releases on each new product
- A six-page, four-color brochure on glossy paper about the new company and its products
- Black-and-white product publicity photos of major products
- Color slides of major products

The budget for the press kit was $10,000. One thousand press kits were distributed to (1) senior editors and reporters of the computer press around the world, (2) business and financial editors covering computer technology, and (3) market researchers and analysts. As a result, articles and photographs about the company appeared in more than 200 publications worldwide. Secondary articles appeared in more than 400 publications; also, the company received more than 100 requests for special features, industry trend/position articles, and technical articles.

Levi Strauss & Co. also prepared a fairly elaborate kit to publicize the results of a national survey about the fashion and lifestyle tastes of today's college students. The survey, conducted on 25 campuses among 7700 undergraduates, was called the Levi's 501 Report.

This kit contained (1) four news releases, (2) a factsheet on Levi's 501 jeans, (3) a backgrounder on the statistical findings of the survey, and (4) a sampling of fashion publicity photos of college-age models wearing, of course, jeans. A special press kit cover and letterhead were also designed.

The cost to write, produce, and distribute the press kit was $20,000. The cost of the survey was $25,000. The package was distributed to fashion editors at the top 500 newspapers around the United States, the news services, college media news services, and radio syndicates. Within three months, 345 articles appeared.

THE NEWSLETTER

Designed as an informal publication to deliver information to a target audience at regular intervals, the newsletter is precisely what the two portions of its name indicate: *news* transmitted in the chatty, brisk style of a *letter*. Newsletters are used frequently by corporations to communicate with employees and stockholders, by nonprofit agencies and associations to reach members and friends, and by sales organizations to deliver information and personnel chit-chat to representatives in the field. Expert opinion and inside advice in specialized fields also are sold to subscribers in newsletter form by commercial publishing firms. The cover shown in Figure 22.3 is of a well-edited newsletter.

The typical newsletter is a four-page folder of 8½-by-11-inch pages, often set in computer type rather than regular printer's fonts. This style projects an air of informality and urgency. Ample use of white space increases readability.

The newsletter can be double-folded into a No. 10 business envelope, or it can be a self-mailer—that is, when folded, it has space on an outside surface for the address and stamp. A piece of tape sometimes is used to hold the self-mailer shut. While envelope mailing generally is considered to have greater impact, the self-mailer is more economical. The choice is a question of budget. Some newsletters have three holes punched along the fold so that they can be filed in ring binders.

Newsletters for internal audiences typically report to employees on trends in their field of work, forthcoming events, personnel changes and policy announcements within the organization, news from field offices, introduction of new products, unusual achievements by employees, results of surveys, and new publications. The goal is to make employees feel that they are informed about company affairs, right up to the minute.

A newsletter aimed at an outside audience, members of an organization, or both, may contain items about political trends that could affect the organization or field of interest, announcements of new programs and policies, brief human interest stories about personnel or recipients of organization services, promotions and retirements—whatever news the editor believes of interest to readers that can be told succinctly. On complicated stories, the newsletter should give the basic facts and indicate where readers can write or telephone for additional details. A newsletter is a brisk compilation of highlights and tidbits, not a place for contemplative essays or detailed professional discussion.

Punchiness in writing style is essential for a successful newsletter. Sentences are short and direct. The writing is authoritative and no-nonsense in tone, from a busy writer to a busy reader. Another secret of the successful newsletter is to cover several topics that will appeal to a wide variety of readers. The single-topic edition should be avoided as too limited in interest.

VISIONS

BISHOP RANCH
BUSINESS PARK

BR

BISHOP RANCH SET FOR BIG EXPANSION

Bishop Ranch Business Park is booming with business as it readies for the grand opening this fall of Bishop Ranch 7 and the full completion of Bishop Ranch 8.

Opening September 1, the third and final building at Bishop Ranch 8 will welcome 400 employees of Impell Engineers into 60% of the building's 190,000 square feet. The five-story building's impressive interior features a covered atrium surrounded by walkways overlooking a beautiful water sculpture and tranquil sitting area. Its bold, angular exterior faces a carefully landscaped courtyard with fountains, across which sit the structure's two siblings.

According to Gabe Ciccone, Sunset Development Company's vice president of construction, the three buildings at BR 8 are among the business park's finest structures. "The interior atriums are quite impressive, providing a feeling of openness," Ciccone said. The 27-acre Bishop Ranch 8 complex is located at 5000 Executive Parkway between the Toyota and Pacific Bell facilities.

Opening in November, Bishop Ranch 7, adjacent to the Heliport at 2527 Camino Ramon, offers 220,000 square feet of leasable space in its three stories. Single floor sizes of 75,500 square feet are available.

The building sits on 13.5 acres and features a beautifully landscaped half-acre courtyard accessible through front and rear lobbies. Showers and lockers for employees who jog during their lunch hour, a restaurant and an abundance of free parking are among the amenities offered. The $34 million project will be the sixth Bishop Ranch complex of 11 planned by Sunset Development Company.

Aerial view of Bishop Ranch 7 (below) highlights the building's half-acre courtyard. Bishop Ranch 8 (right) nears completion.

CHOPPER CHOPPER CHOPPER CHOPPER CHOPPER SERVICE LANDS AT BISHOP RANCH

It's a bird, it's a plane, no . . . it's a helicopter. And, because of this new amenity, tenants at Bishop Ranch now can fly in and out of the business park via charter chopper.

The Bishop Ranch Heliport, at 2565 Camino Ramon near the intersection of Executive Parkway, is home to a four-passenger Bell Jet Ranger helicopter operated by Aris Helicopters of San Jose.

According to Jon Miller, the company's primary pilot for Bishop Ranch, the helicopter is available for business and pleasure for employees at Bishop Ranch. "We can fly to any airport in the Bay Area, north to Sacramento and south to the San Joaquin Valley."

Flight time to Oakland's airport is eight minutes and 15 minutes to both San Jose and San Francisco airports, he said. Cost to charter the helicopter is $435 per hour. "It's a bigger toll than taking other forms of transportation, but it's certainly faster, less aggravating, more fun and much more convenient."

Bishop Ranch's helicopter charter service operates from 7 a.m. to 6:30 p.m. Monday to Friday and 9:30 a.m. to 5 p.m. on Saturdays.

For more information contact Jon Miller at Bishop Ranch 2, 2682 Bishop Drive #110, 275-8045.

FIGURE 22.3
The newsletter is more informal in appearance and content than a magazine and is usually produced more quickly. Like magazines, newsletters can be designed for various special audiences. This six-page newsletter from the Bishop Ranch Business Park is exceptionally strong visually.

For internal use among departments and branches of large corporations with extensive word processing facilities, the electronic newsletter has made its appearance. The editor composes the letter in the usual way. The copy then is coded into the computer system, dispatched, and delivered to everyone on the receiving list on hard copy from the recipients' printout machines.

THE ADVERTORIAL

Illustrated editorial inserts in newspapers and magazines, underwritten by a sponsoring company and known as *advertorials,* have become increasingly common. These usually attempt to emulate the look and tone of the publication, so as to appear an integral part of it. In one instance, a one-page pre-Olympics article in *Time* was underwritten by Visa International.

Some editors oppose having advertorials appear in their publications, contending that the corporate sponsorship blurs the traditional line separating editorial and advertising content.

COMPANY PERIODICALS

Hundreds of well-written, well-edited, and attractive periodicals published in the United States never are seen by the general public. They are produced by public relations departments of companies or their counseling firms and distributed free to carefully selected audiences. Whether designed to be read by employees, stockholders, customers, or combinations of these audiences, periodicals are among the most effective channels of continuing communication that a company can use. Like any publication issued at regular intervals, the company magazine or newspaper creates a sense of anticipation of its arrival. This helps to strengthen the ties between management and the groups its seeks to inform and influence.

Although it is commonly accepted that employees with long-term service in a company are the most avid readers of company newsletters and magazines, research has disputed this. Professor John Pavlik, formerly of Penn State University, studied employees of Honeywell, Inc., in Minneapolis and found that an employee's career aspirations are a much better predictor of readership. Quite simply, Pavlik says, "An employee with higher career aspirations tends to place greater importance on reading to keep track of changes in management and to find out what is going on in the company generally."

The research found that the purpose of reading the company publication varies with gender. Women seem to show strong interest in reading to keep track of their friends, while men primarily want to follow the company's business activities. Of course, this finding may be skewed in the respect that traditionally women have been assigned more to lower-level clerical functions, and many have had no real career path in the company.

Experts emphasize the importance of four elements in maintaining a good relationship between management and employees—employee recognition, communication, a sense of belonging, and emotional security. When all of these elements function well, productivity tends to rise. Workers who believe that their jobs are secure and their personal worth recognized will contribute more than disgruntled ones.

Along with other forms of internal communication—including company brochures, staff-management meetings, audiovisual presentations, and memoranda—company periodicals help substantially in the development of all four elements. The periodicals communicate information and decisions from management to employees. They increase the workers' feeling that they know what is going on in the company, and why. Management can use the periodicals to influence the attitudes of employees. However, this purpose must be accomplished with caution and finesse. If employees sense that management is talking down to them and using the periodical merely as a propaganda vehicle, the publication may become an object of derision rather than a tool for achieving the two-way communication management desires. Periodicals also can serve as channels for communication from employees to management through letters to the editor, question-and-answer features, and similar editorial devices.

Major corporations sometimes produce sleek, sophisticated-appearing magazines that are in the forefront of contemporary design. Four-color covers and splashy graphics help to attract readers in this age of visual emphasis. Examples of this lavish approach are AT&T's management-oriented *AT&T Magazine* and Transamerica Corporation's *Transamerica*.

From this elaborate and expensive format, company publications range down to four-page folders in black and white that resemble a small tabloid newspaper. The publication interval may be weekly, biweekly, monthly, or quarterly. Decisions on format and frequency depend on the size of the public relations budget and the audience management seeks to reach. Some companies have found that their blue-collar employees get more satisfaction from a periodical which is simple in design and presentation than from an elaborate, multicolored, sophisticated-looking magazine such as those distributed to stockholders and others the company seeks to impress.

Large corporations frequently publish several periodicals, each designed for a different audience. Usually the objective of a publication is stated in small type in its masthead. Typically, *Chevron World,* published quarterly by Standard Oil Company of California, states, ''The *Chevron World* is published and distributed by the company's Public Affairs organization for the information of shareholders, employees, and other interested parties.'' Knowledge of this stated purpose helps a person to scrutinize the content of a periodical and analyze why various elements were included. (*Chevron World* is described in detail later in the chapter.)

Nonprofit organizations publish periodicals for much the same purposes that corporations publish theirs. Instead of trying to please stockholders and customers, nonprofit organizations must seek the support of contributors. Their product is service. Therefore, periodicals aimed at contributors and possible donors emphasize the quality and social value of the service the organization delivers. Internal periodicals fill the same role in management–employee relations that company periodicals do. In the discussion of company periodicals that follows, therefore, those of nonprofit organizations are included for simplicity.

Company magazines fall into four major categories, grouped by the audience they serve. To illustrate how the various types function, the following sections analyze the contents of typical magazines in each category: those for employees and retirees, for stockholders and employees, for marketing staff and wholesaler customers, and customers and association members.

MAGAZINES FOR EMPLOYEES AND RETIREES

The employee magazine is a means by which management can inject a personal touch into company affairs. As a humanizing tool, it helps to offset the feelings of some employees, especially in large corporations, that they have little significance as individuals to management. Through its pages, the company can recognize the achievements and personal milestones of those who work for it. A well-edited employee periodical helps to instill an attitude among employees that they are part of the company. At the same time, the magazine offers management an opportunity to report its policies and explain why they were adopted. When the publication is in newspaper format, the appearance is different but the goals are the same (see Figure 22.4).

Employee publications, like most periodicals, usually have stated objectives. The Clorox Company publishes a quarterly magazine, *The Diamond,* for its 4800 employees. *The Diamond* has the following objectives:

- To assist management in securing employee understanding and support for the company's operations, activities, objectives, and plans
- To recognize employee accomplishments on and off the job to maintain high morale and develop a sense of participation in the company's affairs and its relationship with local communities
- To educate employees about subjects such as the U.S. economic system, safety, and the obligations of responsible citizenship to make employees more valuable members of the Clorox family and their communities.

The editor of *The Diamond* follows a story mix intended to recognize people in different divisions, departments, and various locations while covering issues important to the company such as safety, quality, productivity, cost reduction, and community involvement. One edition of *The Diamond,* for example, contained the following stories:

- *Clorox Community Service*. An article about a company community service project that received a national presidential citation.
- *Pasta Plant in Pennsylvania*. A feature about the operations of a company manufacturing facility. A sidebar article features a salad-dressing plant in West Virginia. Photos show employees at work.
- *Volunteers Helping Kids*. A short employee feature about a Clorox employee who volunteers her time at a shelter for troubled youngsters.

FIGURE 22.4
Magazines published for employees are a valuable channel of communication within a company. This cover is from one of the excellently designed and edited employee magazines being issued today. Because IBM, which publishes it, is a global corporation, the content of *Think* has a strong international flavor. (Courtesy of IBM Corporation)

- *A Day in the Life of . . .* A feature about the work of the Cincinnati regional sales manager.
- *Company Profits.* An economic education feature that explains how company profits are reinvested in areas of safety and new plant equipment.

- *A Healthy Heart.* A true-false Q&A article to educate employees about heart disease.
- *Service Anniversaries.* Names of employees who have worked 20, 15, 10, and 5 years for the company.
- *Doer's Profile.* An article highlighting how a manufacturing facility in Chicago slashed workers' compensation costs by more than 99 percent with a well-organized safety campaign.

The Clorox *Diamond* exemplifies effective employee communication with a limited staff and budget. In a primarily one-person operation, the editor plans content, interviews people, writes all copy, handles all approvals, takes most photographs, and supervises design, production, and printing. The editor also handles all phases of a monthly two- to four-page newsletter.

MAGAZINES FOR STOCKHOLDERS AND EMPLOYEES

Because a magazine of this type is aimed at two audiences, its approach must be broader. Although stockholders and employees share concern about the success of their company, their interests are not identical. News about the activities and milestones of individual employees does not interest stockholders. The magazine's focus needs to be more on technical and economic developments in the corporation's field and on the company's strategy to take advantage of them. A magazine distributed to stockholders as well as to employees usually is more visibly management-oriented than one for employees only. It must be kept in mind that many employees also are stockholders, often as participants in company-sponsored stock purchase programs.

An example of the company periodical distributed to both stockholders and employees is *Chevron World,* published quarterly by Standard Oil of California as a colorfully printed, 30-page, slick-paper magazine.

A typical issue of *Chevron World* contains a policy statement by the chairman of the board about oil exploration, articles about natural gas reserves and oil taxation, and a feature about Chevron's TV school in which the company instructs its executives on how to appear on television programs. Other material includes a brilliantly illustrated story about oil exploration in Arctic waters and one about bird life on the company's North Sea oil platforms.

The difference in approach between *Chevron World* and the magazines edited exclusively for employees is obvious. In this publication, employees are given a carefully crafted picture of their company's ambitious search for new energy sources. Their pride in the company's size and ingenuity is stimulated. They receive strong exposure to management's views on taxation and legislation. Corporate image-building is the dominant theme. Another company periodical, *Standard Oiler,* is distributed only to employees and retirees. A 34-page slick-paper bimonthly, it contains individual milestone information, queries from readers, and information about company operations that is of direct value to employees.

MAGAZINES FOR MARKETING STAFF MEMBERS AND WHOLESALERS OF COMPANY PRODUCTS

These periodicals are unabashedly promotional, edited to encourage sales through inspirational essays and how-to-do-it articles.

An excellent example of these direct sales-booster periodicals is *Team Talk,* published by Anheuser-Busch of St. Louis to promote its group of beers. Articles contain cheerleader sentences of a type the reader would be unlikely to find in the magazines previously analyzed. These quotations from wholesalers are included in articles about their activities:

> Everybody loves a winner and wants to be associated with a class organization . . . our retailers and the general public know we are proud of our products. Anheuser-Busch is a winner, and we want to be one, too.

Team Talk is a 24-page bimonthly magazine illustrated with large color photographs and striking drawings. The contents of an issue not only show the editorial approach but provide intriguing insight into the way a successful company sells its products in an intensely competitive market:

- *Cover*. The single word *IMAGE* in bright blue on a black background is reflected upside down, as in a mirror. A subtitle at the bottom of the cover states, ''A Reflection of Quality'' and refers to a story on page 2.
- *The Look of the Leader*. This mirror-image device on the cover is duplicated in smaller type as a headline. This article tells how beer wholesalers can enhance their image as the purveyors of quality products by placing company-specified signs on their warehouses and trucks and by having their drivers and other employees wear clean, well-tailored uniforms.
- *A-B Gets High Marks on College Campuses*. A pair of articles describe how Anheuser-Busch wholesalers promote the sale of their beers in universities, one on a large campus and the other at a smaller university. The articles carefully point out how the sellers obey state laws against selling beer to students under the minimum age in each state.

In general, the content of *Team Talk* urges marketing people to exploit established events by pushing exposure of their products and to create special events for the same purpose. Its goal is stimulation of its readers. In *Team Talk,* the corporate communications department functions as a clearinghouse through which sales ideas are disseminated.

MAGAZINES FOR CUSTOMERS AND ASSOCIATION MEMBERS

As a psychological link to their customers, to remind them of company products and services, some firms publish magazines addressed exclusively to this group. Magazines published by national organizations for their members are similar in purpose and character, although in some instances somewhat wider in editorial range. The cost of a membership magazine normally is included in the annual dues.

The customer magazine is not a catalogue, although it may contain pages offering services or products, often packaged in special offers. Primarily its objective is to present a favorable image of the company, rather than direct selling.

A colorful example of the customer magazine is *Silver Circle,* a 48-page quarterly published by Home Savings of America and distributed free to members of its Silver Circle. The Circle is a device designed to increase deposits in this very large savings and loan association. Home Savings depositors who have at least $10,000 in accounts become Silver Circle members. They receive the magazine and a membership card entitling them to discounts on numerous travel and entertainment items.

The editors of *Silver Circle* can make several important assumptions about their audience: (1) those who receive the magazine have at least a moderate amount of spare money; (2) members may be expected to have substantial interest in travel; (3) all probably have at least a fundamental understanding of financial matters. Relative affluence, money awareness, concern about health, interest in travel: those attributes of the *Silver Circle* audience are the framework on which the magazine is built.

Because of the national worry about failures in the savings and loan industry, a typical issue opens with a reassuring statement by the chairman of Home Savings about the company's financial strength and long-term growth. One article exposes get-rich-quick schemes, another tells how to set up a home fitness center, and a third describes a cruise to South America. Financial tips and medical news items are presented attractively. The magazine also includes a lengthy hotel and resort guide listing places that offer Silver Circle discounts, and discount coupons from amusement centers.

The interlocking tie-ins between the magazines and the hotels, restaurants, and amusement parks offering discounts in it illuminate the techniques of entertainment sales promotion. Those who give discounts know they are reaching an audience with money to spend. Home Savings in turn earns goodwill from magazine recipients by offering such bargains. When presented in the context of a sleek magazine, the discounts avoid the look of being gimmicks that may have a catch in them somewhere.

Another group of magazines in this category are aimed specifically at target audiences of importance to a corporation or association, such as *WEcology* by McDonald's, sent to 4.5 million students and teachers.

BROCHURES AND HANDBOOKS

Writing informational publications to fill innumerable needs is among the most common duties of public relations practitioners. Some printed pieces are issued at stated intervals, such as quarterly reports to stockholders and college catalogues. The majority, however, are designed to last for indefinite periods, subject to updating as required. Most of this material is distributed free, although price tags may be placed on more elaborate and expensive items such as museum catalogs.

Whatever their purpose, these publications share clearly defined writing requirements. Clarity is essential. Frequently the writer must explain technical material or simplify complex issues for a reader who knows little about the topic. This calls for explanations that are straightforward, shorn of jargon, and stated in terms of reference that a casual reader can comprehend quickly. Paired with clarity is conciseness. Informational writing should be tightly done; elaborate literary devices should be left to the fiction writer. The person who delivers information needs to pare excess verbiage from sentences and paragraphs.

Every brochure, handbook, or other form of printed information should be organized on a firm outline that moves the reader forward comfortably through unfamiliar territory. Frequent subheads and typographical breaks are desirable. The writer often operates under budget restrictions that dictate the size of the publication—perhaps a 4-page folder, perhaps a large-format brochure of 30 pages consisting primarily of illustrations with short blocks of type. Space limitations should be regarded as a challenge to the writer's skill at condensation.

The following are the types of publications in this category that a public relations writer is most frequently called upon to create.

INFORMATIONAL BROCHURES

These describe the purposes, policies, and functions of an organization. Tour-guide folders given out at museums are an example of this form.

GUIDELINES FOR BROCHURES AND HANDBOOKS

Plain English and basic design enhance the communication effectiveness of any document. These attributes not only increase goodwill with key publics but also reduce complaints and confusion among employees and consumers.

The following are research-based criteria for enhancing readability and comprehension:

- Use 8- to 10-point type. Readers often ignore text that is too small.
- Use plenty of white space. Wide margins, indents, and occasional short pages keep the document from looking crowded and too difficult to read.
- Use ragged right, rather than justified, margins. This gives the document a relaxed, contemporary look.
- Use short lines. Optimal line length for most text is 50 to 70 characters.
- Use boldface for emphasis. It is easier to read than a word in all capital letters.

Source: Based on material from the Document Design Center of the American Institute for Research, Washington, D.C., as presented in *PR Reporter*.

HANDBOOKS

More elaborate than basic brochures, these usually include policy statements, statistical information, and listings of significant facts about the issuing organization and its field of operation. Handbooks often are designed for distribution primarily to news media sources as handy references for a writer or broadcaster in a hurry. Trade associations and large corporations are among the most frequent users of the handbook as a public relations tool.

Typical examples of the handbook are the following:

- *''Sharing the Risk,'' published by the Insurance Information Institute.* Nearly 200 pages describe property and casualty insurance concepts, regulations, and policies, ranging from homeowners' losses to nuclear risks.
- *''Oil & Gas Pocket Reference,'' published by Phillips Petroleum Company.* This is a 60-page small-format booklet of statistics about the oil industry. Included are such lists as the top 10 U.S. oil-producing states; the top 15 oil-producing nations, with amounts; oil and gas imports by year; and significant reference dates.

CORPORATE BROCHURES FOR EXTERNAL USE

Frequently aimed at specific audiences rather than at the general public, these may be such items as the inserts utility companies include with their bills, financial documents such as quarterly reports to stockholders and proxy statements for potential stock purchasers, owners' manuals, and teaching materials that help students learn about the issuing industries.

CORPORATE BROCHURES FOR INTERNAL USE

To inform and train their employees, companies issue a broad range of brochures and handbooks. These may be distributed at in-plant meetings or to individuals at work, or mailed to the employees' homes. In simplest form, information sheets may be posted on company bulletin boards. Readership of these boards is high; anything posted there will be noticed and probably will become a topic of conversation on the job.

Examples of in-company brochures and manuals include the following:

- *Atlantic Richfield Company's 12-page booklet to assist older employees make the transition from work to retirement.* It answers questions that concern every employee approaching retirement, such as financial planning, use of leisure time, and health benefits.
- *A manual describing proper telephone techniques, given to employees of Washington Federal Savings and Loan Association in Seattle.* Employees discuss the manual in seminars during which they see a 25-minute film depicting ''telephone traps'' in which they might find themselves.

GLOSSARIES

Trade associations and corporations in technical fields often issue pamphlets defining terms, including jargon as well as standard words, commonly used in their work. Like handbooks, glossaries are distributed extensively to the news media, to help writers understand the special language and use it accurately. Glossaries sometimes are included in other corporate publications.

An oil industry glossary, for example, includes words and terms such as *desiccation, dispersant, huff-and-puff,* and *wrinkle chaser*—hardly the language that a nonspecialist writer runs across in daily life. (*Huff-and-puff* is descriptive of techniques to recover oil by steam injection. A *wrinkle chaser* is a geologist.) These examples were taken from a glossary published by Phillips Petroleum.

THE ANNUAL REPORT

''The principal purpose of the annual report is to tell the company's story to a multiplicity of audiences,'' says David F. Hawkins, a professor at the Harvard Business School. ''It's a public relations document with a regulatory requirement.''

Indeed, preparation of a corporation's annual report is a major function of a company's public relations department or counseling firm and is probably the company's most expensive written contact with its stockholders and the financial community. According to a study by the National Investor Relations Institute, investor relations executives devote about 13 percent of their time to preparing annual reports. The estimated 10,000 public companies in the United States spend an average of $3.52 a copy to produce a glossy publication of abundant color, with striking graphics and impressive photography, averaging 44 pages. (See Figure 22.5.)

Technically, the corporate annual report is an informational document required by the Securities and Exchange Commission of all publicly traded companies. But there is no legal requirement that annual reports be extravaganzas. Under Rule 14a–3 of the Securities Exchange Act, publicly traded companies are required to include only basic financial information and other material such as a list of directors and the auditor's opinion letter. Once these requirements are met, the rule states, ''the report may be in any form deemed suitable by management.''

Companies publish expensive and attractive annual reports for public relations purposes. These include (1) impressing current and potential stockholders that the company is well managed and successful, (2) encouraging potential investors to purchase stock, and (3) using the annual report as a vehicle for recruiting new employees. In other words, annual reports help showcase the company's accomplishments and management philosophy.

Some evidence exists, however, that costly expenditures on such reports don't really influence potential investors. A Hill & Knowlton survey of 501 investors concluded that only 3 percent found annual reports to be the best source of investment information. In that respect, annual reports ranked behind periodicals, stockbrokers, statistical services, friends, and relatives. Some companies recently have reduced the scope of their annual reports, even down to summary size.

A corporate annual report is divided into two general sections:

1. *Detailed financial information about the company's condition and performance during the past year*. A consolidated balance sheet and management's discussion of the financial condition are essential elements. A letter from the corporation's auditing firm

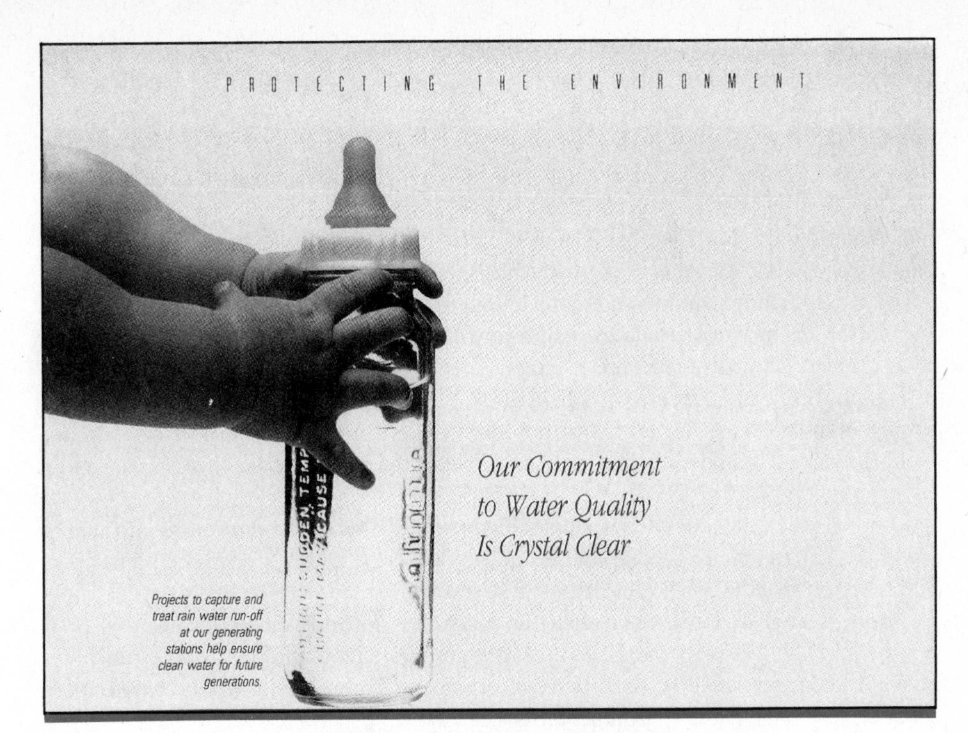

FIGURE 22.5
This illustration in New York State Electric & Gas Corporation's 1990 annual report achieves the double purpose of emphasizing the company's environmental concern and adding human interest to the yearly financial document. (Courtesy of New York State Electric & Gas Corporation)

attesting to the validity of the figures is included, along with separate breakdowns of certain financial aspects. The statistical material in this section is prepared by the financial department and approved by top management. The material is coldly objective and must be completely accurate, but some companies also use a profusion of numbers that often confuse everyone except specialists in accounting.

To cite one case, an annual report of Koppers Company had a mass of numbers, charts, and graphs—and even a ten-year financial comparison of 45 items. Yellow lines highlighted the most favorable statistics that the company wanted to emphasize.

Other relevant information about the corporation is published in this section for reference. This may include lists of key executives and their salaries, names of major stockholders, lists of plant sites, and major subsidiaries. Because specific financial data are required by the Securities and Exchange Commission in an annual report, a specialist in financial public relations should be assigned to compile the reports.

2. *Management's presentation of accomplishments during the past year, its goals and outstanding problems*. This material, appearing in the first portion of the report just after a one-page summary of financial highlights, is designed to give a good impression of management's work. While the prose is restrained, use of striking color

photographs and other graphics, often in full-page size, helps to suggest corporate vigor and achievement.

The centerpiece of this front section is a report to stockholders by the chairman of the board or the chief executive officer. This is the "message," and it is sometimes used to rail against government regulation, or to extol the company's contribution to making America a leader of the "free world."

When companies have had a bad year financially, or have been involved in an embarrassing episode, they frequently bury that fact in their annual reports, so that only a close reading—not too common among ordinary stockholders—will disclose it.

Others discuss their troubles with refreshing candor. In the LSI Logic company's 1989 report, Chairman Wilfred Corrigan told stockholders, "this past year was a disappointment, and I'm glad it's behind us." Similarly, Walter Elisha, chairman of Spring Industries, the big textile corporation, commented, "In sum for the '80s, we would, if asked, grade ourselves a 'B' . . . better than most but not yet measuring up to our own standards."

In general, trends in annual reports during the 1990s are toward more informality in writing, more focus on employees, and, when a company's operations justify it, emphasis on its role in the international market.

This section of the annual report also contains information about new projects, new acquisitions, new products, and areas of corporate philanthropy. Many companies also comment on social responsibility efforts to hire more minorities, promote more women, and deal with environmental issues.

On occasion, a company breaks out of the usual mold with a creative approach. BellSouth, for example, used an annual report to focus on the year 2000 by including essays from nationally known authors, commentators, and experts about our lives now and in the future. And First Hawaiian, Inc., a bank-holding group, used color photos of its executives in Hawaiian shirts instead of three-piece suits.

As supplements to printed annual reports, but never as replacements for the financial section, some companies issue videotaped annual reports for showing to employees, stockholders, and financial groups. Teleconferencing an annual meeting is an increasingly common practice. But evidence shows that although a video can provide basic information, comprehension is increased if an executive is present to explain and field questions. Emhart Corporation, which pioneered videotaped annual reports, is now going back to printed summaries because it found that information communicated on video is not conducive to reflective study and people don't "reread" video.

CORPORATE ADVERTISING

Traditionally, *advertising* is defined as purchased space or time used to sell goods or services, while public relations space in the media is obtained free. The line of demarcation becomes fuzzy when a company engages in *corporate advertising,* also called *institutional advertising*. Such advertising is processed and purchased in the regular manner. Its purpose, however, is not to sell the company's products or services directly but to enhance public conception of the company or to advocate a company policy (see Figure 22.6).

A corporate advertisement, as defined by Leading National Advertisers, a checking service, must deal with a company's policies, functions, facilities, objectives, ideas, and standards; build favorable opinions of the company's management, skill, technology, or social contributions; enhance the investment qualities or financial structure of the company; or promote it as a good place to work.

Recently some corporate advertising has been used to push products, sometimes rather subtly, to the extent that the distinction between product and corporate advertising becomes blurred.

FIGURE 22.6
This blunt apology by Lee Iacocca of Chrysler Corporation, published as a two-page advertisement in newspapers and magazines, was the automaker's head-on response to public criticism after disclosure of a deceptive company practice. Surveys by the company found media comment on the advertisement to be 90 percent favorable. Almost 70 percent of the public group surveyed said that Chrysler had dealt adequately with the problem. (Courtesy of Chrysler Corporation.)

"Testing cars is a good idea. Disconnecting odometers is a lousy idea. That's a mistake we won't make again at Chrysler. Period."

Lee Iacocca

LET ME SET THE RECORD STRAIGHT.

1. For years, spot checking and road testing new cars and trucks that come off the assembly line with the odometers disengaged was standard industry practice. In our case, the average test mileage was 40 miles.
2. Even though the practice wasn't illegal, some companies began connecting their odometers. We didn't. In retrospect, that was dumb. Since October 1986, however, the odometer of every car and truck we've built has been connected, including those in the test program.
3. A few cars–and I mean a few–were damaged in testing badly enough that they should not have been fixed and sold as new. That was a mistake in an otherwise valid quality assurance program. And now we have to make it right.

WHAT WE'RE DOING TO MAKE THINGS RIGHT.

1. In all instances where our records show a vehicle was damaged in the test program and repaired and sold, *we will offer to replace that vehicle* with a brand new 1987 Chrysler Corporation model of comparable value. No ifs ands or buts.
2. We are sending letters to everyone our records show bought a vehicle that was in the test program and offering a free inspection. If anything is wrong because of a product deficiency, we will make it right.
3. Along with the free inspection, we are extending their present 5-year or 50,000-mile protection plan on engine and powertrain to 7 years or 70,000 miles.
4. And to put their minds completely at ease, we are extending the 7-year or 70,000-mile protection to *all major systems:* brakes, suspension, air conditioning, electrical and steering.

The quality testing program is a good program. But there were mistakes and we were too slow in stopping them. Now they're stopped. Done. Finished. Over.

Personally, I'm proud of our products. Proud of the quality improvements we've made. So we're going to keep right on testing. Because without it we couldn't have given America 5-year 50,000-mile protection five years ahead of everyone else. Or maintained our warranty leadership with 7-year 70,000-mile protection. I'm proud, too, of our leadership in safety-related recalls.

But I'm not proud of this episode. Not at all.

As Harry Truman once said, "The buck stops here." It just stopped. Period.

We just want to be the best.

The largest percentage of corporate advertising is done on television, with consumer magazines a close second. Radio, outdoor advertisements, and newspaper supplements receive much smaller amounts, and daily newspapers receive the least.

Corporate advertising may be divided into three basic types: (1) *general corporate image-building,* (2) *investor and financial relations programs,* and (3) *advocacy.*

IMAGE-BUILDING

Image-building advertising is intended primarily to strengthen a company's identity in the eyes of the public and/or the financial community. Conglomerates whose divisions market unrelated products seek through such advertising to project a unified, readily recognized image. Others use it to correct an unfavorable public impression. Increasingly, corporations use institutional advertising to show their concern for the environment, and by doing so seek to demonstrate what good corporate citizens they are.

Chevron, for example, published a series of advertisements titled ''People Do'' in which the oil corporation emphasized that its construction crews avoid disturbing nature. One of these image advertisements, built around a drawing of a sage grouse, read:

THE PIPELINE AND THE DANCING BIRD

At sunrise in Western Wyoming, the strange and spiky male Sage Grouse does its mating dance.

It's the beginning of a process of life that could be endangered if anything enters his breeding grounds.

That's why people building a pipeline stopped construction. They worked further down the line and came back to finish the job after the chicks had hatched.

Sometimes doing what's required doesn't make work easier, but it can make it feel more worthwhile.

Do people really put aside human plans so nature can take its course?

People Do.

CHEVRON

A warning: Any corporation that strikes a pro-environmental posture, then is caught polluting or otherwise damaging the environment, immediately becomes the object of derision for hypocrisy.

In one instance, Mobil Chemical Company sought to attract environmentalists by advertising that its Hefty brand plastic trash bags are degradable and break down when exposed to the elements. Calling the advertising false, the attorney generals of seven states sued to halt its use and asked civil penalties of at least $500,000 against the company. With its image damaged by the publicity, the company agreed to drop the claim until agreed terminology could be worked out.

FINANCIAL RELATIONS PROGRAMS

The second form of corporate advertising is aimed straight at the financial community. The advertiser tries to depict its financial strength and prospects so favorably that securities analysts will advise their clients to purchase its stock. When a corporation has millions of shares outstanding, even a fractional improvement in their price is beneficial. Such advertising is used extensively during proxy fights for control of companies, or when a company is undertaking a major reorganization and needs to keep the financial community informed.

ADVOCACY

The third, sometimes controversial, form of corporate advertising is advocacy. In such advertisements, a corporation or association tries to influence public opinion on a political or social issue. Only a small portion of corporate advertising expenditure goes into advocacy advertising, but because these advertisements sometimes touch public sensibilities, they receive considerable attention.

Mobil has been among the most vocal corporations in its advocacy advertising, emphasizing its aggressive positions on matters of energy control and chiding the media for what Mobil's advertising has called ''irresponsible reporting.'' The tone of this advertising brought criticism against the giant oil corporation.

Chase Manhattan Bank also encountered criticism for some of its advocacy advertising, as it conceded frankly in a full-page newspaper advertisement. This advertisement was dominated by a drawing of several of the Founding Fathers, above the headline:

In accordance with the wishes of our founding fathers, we'll continue to speak out.

The text stated, in part:

In the past year, Chase has been running a series of advertisements which expressed our views on some of today's important economic issues. These included the need for greater productivity . . . the need to stimulate research and development . . . tax incentives to spur investment, generate capital and modernize our industrial plant . . . government overregulation . . . inflation. And the spurious rhetoric about ''excessive'' corporate profits.

Since then, these topics have become central issues in this critical election year. For that we're grateful, because the American public surely deserves a full and open debate as to how best these pressing national problems can be solved.

On the other hand, it's caused us to go through some soul-searching in recent weeks. We've frankly asked ourselves whether an institution such as ours should continue to speak out on important and sometimes sensitive issues in the middle of a national election.

So we went back to the First Amendment to our Constitution and took a long and thoughtful look. As a result, we've decided to go right on speaking out, even though we obviously risk causing controversy or alienating a constituency. . . .

EVALUATING CORPORATE ADVERTISING

How effective is corporate advertising? Because of its abstract nature, measurement of results is difficult. In this sense it resembles public relations programs more than it does traditional advertising, which can be evaluated in terms of units sold.

Ogilvy & Mather, a major advertising agency, studied corporate advertising. It announced these conclusions:

We have learned that good corporate advertising can:

- Build awareness of a company
- Make a favorable impression on investors and securities analysts
- Motivate employees and attract recruits
- Influence public opinion

- Strengthen relations with dealers
- Influence legislation

We have learned that corporate advertising cannot:

- Gloss over a poor record or a weak competitive position
- Boost the price of your stock next month
- Swiftly turn the tide of public opinion

There are no quick fixes. Advertising can spread the truth about your company but cannot *conceal* it.

Thomas F. Garbett, a recognized authority on the subject, offered this justification for corporate advertising, in an article published in the *Harvard Business Review:*

Although many companies assume that the safest course is to keep a low profile, this may in fact be a dangerous tack. If some inadvertent disclosure brings high visibility or even incidental exposure, an unknown company maintains little credibility as it moves to counter public criticism . . . When people first get acquainted with a company through an unfortunate disclosure, they often distort what little they know and make generalizations about missing information. The less filled out a company's image is, the more subject that image is to wild distortions.

CASE PROBLEM

A new 550-room hotel, the Fairmont, will be built in downtown San Jose, California's fourth-largest city, with a population of 800,000. The hotel, to cost an estimated $30 million, is part of a downtown redevelopment effort that includes a light rail system and a $110 million convention center now under construction.

The hotel, part of the Fairmont chain, will have four restaurants, a health club, lobby bar, and banquet facilities for up to 2000 people. The architect is Skinner and Associates, and the contractor is BK Industries. Estimated completion date and grand opening of the hotel will be in about 18 months. Hotel executives and city officials say that the hotel is the cornerstone of the downtown's revival.

Write a news release on behalf of the hotel chain to announce the decision to build a new facility in San Jose. Use appropriate quotations from hotel and city officials as you deem necessary.

QUESTIONS FOR REVIEW AND DISCUSSION

1. What is an *embargo* on a news release? Does it have any legal standing?
2. What are the physical requirements for an attractive news release?

3. A public relations counselor should have a client initial a file copy of each news release before distribution. Why?

4. Describe the difference between a news release and a factsheet.

5. To what audiences might a corporate public relations department send a newsletter?

6. As editor of a company magazine intended for employees and retirees, what would be your objectives?

7. Handbooks are issued frequently by corporations and trade associations. What types of material do they usually contain?

8. To what federal agency must corporate annual reports be submitted?

9. Corporate or institutional advertising differs in purpose from ordinary advertising. Explain this difference.

10. What risk does a corporation take when it uses aggressive advocacy advertising?

SUGGESTED READINGS

Bernstein, Gail. "Meet the Press." *Public Relations Journal,* March 1988, pp. 28–32. A reporter's view of news releases.

Brockway, Laurie Sue. "Employee Annual Reports: Thriving Amidst Corporate Change." *Public Relations Journal,* July 1989, pp. 21–24.

Horton, James L. "Using Computers to Increase Productivity." *Public Relations Journal,* July 1989, pp. 26–29. Using word processors to do news releases.

Howard, Elizabeth. "Preparing Annual Reports in the 1990s." *Public Relations Journal,* May 1991, pp. 26–27.

Kemper, Gary W. "Employee Publications: Are They a Poor Investment for Many Organizations?" *Communication World,* April 1991, pp. 17–23.

Lewis, Jan. "How to Write Corporate Ads." *Public Relations Journal,* September 1988, pp. 45–46.

Minter, Bobby. "Starting a Newsletter." *Public Relations Journal,* July 1989, pp. 30–32.

Morton, Linda. "Effectiveness of Camera-Ready Copy in News Releases." *Public Relations Review,* Summer 1988, pp. 45–49.

Otterbourg, Robert K. "Banishing Boredom." *Public Relations Journal,* July 1990, pp. 21–24. Effective writing in annual reports.

Parker, Robert. "How Do You Play the Annual Report Game?" *Communication World,* September 1990, pp. 24–29. Trends.

Ranly, Don. ''How Organization Editors Regard Their Jobs and Their Profession.'' *Journalism Quarterly,* Winter 1989, pp. 949–953.

Sethi, S. Prakash. *Handbook of Advocacy Advertising Concepts: Strategies and Applications.* Cambridge, MA: Ballinger Publishing, 1987.

Taylor, Anne Marie. ''Putting On a Happy Face.'' *Communication World,* September 1990, pp. 20–23. Annual reports.

Waltzer, Herbert. ''Corporate Advocacy and Political Influence.'' *Public Relations Review,* Spring 1988, pp. 40–45.

CHAPTER

Spoken Tactics

Long before prehistoric men and women scratched picture messages on rocks, they communicated with each other by voice. The words may have been little more expressive than the ''ughs'' cartoonists put into the mouths of cave dwellers, but they delivered information and expressed feelings.

The spoken word is humanity's most ancient form of communication, except perhaps for hand gestures and facial expressions. Under many circumstances it is still the most powerful form. Speech is a basic tool for the public relations practitioner; this chapter examines ways to use it.

The text provides down-to-earth advice on ways to carry out assignments that practitioners face every day: how to write and stage a speech, help a management representative hold a news conference, give a press party, assist a client in preparing for an interview, and run an effective meeting.

At the close, word-of-mouth publicity and ways to combat the often insidious effects of rumors are discussed.

FACE-TO-FACE DISCUSSION

A conversation face-to-face between two persons is widely regarded as the most effective form of interpersonal communication. This is certainly true in the world of work. The chemistry of personality that can develop during a business call is not easily defined but can be tremendously valuable.

Visualize these typical situations: a salesperson soliciting an order from a customer at lunch; a public relations representative at an editor's desk explaining the reasons for her hospital client's fund drive; a corporate vice president for public affairs calling on a city council member to urge the opening of a new street to reduce traffic congestion outside the company's manufacturing plant. In each case, the logic of the persuader's arguments is reinforced (or undermined) by the impact of the individual's personality. Sincerity impresses the listener. An aggressive, demanding approach arouses irritation. A smile, perhaps a casual quip, and a friendly but respectful manner help immeasurably in getting one's message across.

The personal call is among the most potent methods a public relations practitioner can use. It may fail, however, no matter how good the cause, if the caller arrives ill-prepared and handles the presentation clumsily. Here, from a veteran newspaper editor who has listened to hundreds of across-the-desk public relations presentations, is advice on how to present a case effectively:

1. *Telephone in advance for an appointment.* Then be on time. Don't walk in ''cold'' and expect a hearing.

2. *Identify yourself and your purpose immediately.* Present a business card if possible, so the recipient has your name and affiliation at hand during the discussion and for filing later.

3. *Be concise.* Editors, program directors, and other opinion-makers on whom you call are busy. Even those who appear relaxed and casual have other work waiting to be done. Make your presentation succinctly. Describe what your client plans to do, explain the purpose of the program, tell how it will help the public, and state specifically what support you hope to receive from the person you are addressing. Respond to your host's questions without meandering up side conversational paths, politely seek a commitment if that seems appropriate, then leave. Unless the listener judges your proposal to be excessively commercial or self-serving, you can expect a sympathetic hearing in most instances.

4. *Don't oversell.* Don't plead. Persons who receive presentations dislike being pressured and instinctively build defense mechanisms against excessively emotional ''pitches.'' Never say, ''You must help us!'' Persons whose aid you seek resent being told that they ''must'' do anything.

5. *Express appreciation for your host's time and for anything he or she can do to assist your cause.*

6. *Leave behind written material—a brochure, a news release, a factsheet—for your host to study later.* Be certain that the material includes a telephone number at which you can be reached for further information. Asking your host to read the material while you sit there is a poor tactic, unless it is very short; the result may be a hasty, reluctant scanning rather than the thoughtful reading you desire.

If the presentation can be made at lunch, over coffee or perhaps over a drink, outside the office setting, its impact may be stronger—assuming that the person being solicited will spare the necessary time.

7. *Follow up with a note of appreciation for the reception, expressing hope that the recipient can use the information you left.* It subtly reminds the person to read the material, if that hasn't happened, and to do something about it.

If you are working with an editor or program director in a small community, or with a person you know well, the approach can be more informal. However, conciseness, restraint, and the delivery of printed information are important in every situation.

Face-to-face discussion also is an essential tool for open communication within business organizations. Such conversations between management representatives and supervisors, supervisors and foremen, management and union officers, spread understanding of a company policy or a new product among the employees. Slightly less intimate, but almost as effective if well done, is the small-group discussion directed toward the same goal. Internal communication through staff study meetings, employee training sessions, and department meetings creates a more competent, motivated workforce and identifies areas of employee dissatisfaction. (A discussion on how to conduct an effective meeting appears later in this chapter.)

A blind spot in company management, in small firms as well as large ones, is the too-frequent assumption that employees down the line know the reasons for company policies. The cynical wisecrack "There's no reason for it, it's just company policy" shows a weakness of management that need not exist if verbal channels of internal communication are used frequently and intelligently. Explaining *why* something is done is just as important as explaining *how* it should be done.

Vital as they are in reaching opinion leaders, person-to-person conversations form only one segment of a campaign to inform the public and mold opinion through the spoken word. A public relations campaign usually must reach many persons at the same time. This can be done orally through speeches, news conferences, and appearances of representatives on radio and television. Although the impact of a speaker's personality on individual listeners may diminish when the message is delivered in a large meeting hall or filtered through a receiving set, the sheer abundance of simultaneous contacts speeds up distribution of the message. Repetition of a message in several forms creates greater awareness, and use of several methods helps to reinforce the message among selected audiences.

Each of these spoken methods will be discussed in detail. The text will first examine the speech: how to plan it, how to write it, and how to assist the speaker who delivers it.

ASSIGNMENT: SPEECHWRITING

Public relations practitioners frequently are called on to write speeches for their employers or clients. As speechwriters, their role is a hidden one. They labor silently to produce the words that may sparkle like champagne when poured forth by their employers from the lecterns of convention halls. In the White House, the wraps of anonymity usually are drawn around the writers who churn out speeches and statements for the president of the United States. A president who utters a memorable phrase gets the credit, but some unknown writer in a back office probably created it. There is nothing discreditable about this. Presidents have more urgent tasks than to think up catchy quotations. Although speechwriters rarely receive ego-building recognition, they find personal satisfaction in creating competent speeches for someone else. Speechwriting is a highly skilled craft.

Most of the largest corporations employ speechwriters, some of whom receive annual salaries from $70,000 to $120,000. Free-lance writers often command from $1,000 to $10,000 for a speech. The life of a speechwriter is not easy, however; the writer's copy must be approved by numerous executives, and it sometimes becomes badly mangled in editing battles.

Turning loose a speaker, especially an inexperienced one, before an audience without a text, or at least a careful outline, may be an invitation to boredom. The ''and . . . uhs'' and ''as I was sayings'' will proliferate like rabbits. The audience will squirm, inwardly at first and then conspicuously in their chairs, as the speaker stumbles along. The opportunity to deliver a message that informs, persuades, and entertains listeners has been thrown out the window. That is why speakers who lack the time or the skill to do their own preparation need able speechwriters.

Some speakers prefer to work from notes rather than read a text. In that event, the writer should prepare a full speech for the speaker to study, then reduce the main elements of it to note cards arranged in proper sequence. Talking from notes increases the air of spontaneity, if the speaker is experienced and comfortable before an audience. It also magnifies the risk, however, that the speaker will meander and lose control of the time.

A written speech should reflect the personality and voice patterns of the speaker, not those of the writer.

Speeches come in many sizes and serve many purposes. The writer may be called on to prepare a light 20-minute talk for the service club luncheon circuit, a provocative 10-minute statement to open a panel discussion, or a scholarly 45-minute lecture for delivery before a university audience. Possibly the assignment may be for ''just a few remarks'' to welcome foreign visitors on a plant tour. Or it could be for a hard-sell pitch to raise money for a local charity campaign.

THE BASIC POINTS OF SPEECHWRITING

Whatever the assignment, here are basic points for the speechwriter to keep in mind:

1. *A speech should say something of lasting value.* Even a talk intended to entertain, full of fluffy humor, should be built around a significant point. A speech needs both content and style; without the former, the latter is empty.

One veteran speechwriter for a large corporation and an influential trade organization applies what he calls the ''Door Test'' to the speeches he writes. After hearing a dinner speaker, the listeners go out the door of the banquet room and on entering the doors of their homes are greeted by their spouses and asked what the dinner speaker said. In reply, the listeners give the essence of the speech as they remember it. Was there a message clear and concise enough to remember? Did the speech pass the Door Test?

2. *A speech should concentrate on one, or at most two, main themes.*

3. *A speech needs facts.* The information must be accurate. The writer's skill as a researcher is put to the test, to dig up information that will illustrate and emphasize the

speaker's theme. Before a speaker makes a statement, the information in it should be verified beyond any doubt.

4. *The type of audience should influence the style and content of the speech.* When a company celebrates its fiftieth anniversary with a reception and dinner dance for its employees, they don't want to hear the president drone on for 30 minutes about the corporate financial structure. The setting calls for some joking, a few nostalgic stories, references to some individuals by name, words of appreciation for what the employees have contributed, and a few upbeat words about the future. On the other hand, the president may ask the writer for a speech about the company for delivery at a meeting of securities analysts. This is not the place for droll stories. The audience wants facts on which to base investment decisions, not entertainment.

5. *Clarity in speechwriting is essential.* If the listeners don't understand what the speaker is saying, everyone's time is wasted. This happens when the speech contains complicated sentences, technical information that the speaker fails to explain in terms the audience can comprehend, and excessive jargon or ''inside'' talk. The speechwriter's challenge is to simplify and classify the speaker's message without destroying its significance.

AN EXAMPLE OF SPEECHWRITING

To determine how the speechwriting process works, consider how a specific assignment could be handled. The assistant public relations director of a large regional restaurant chain is assigned to prepare a speech for the general manager to deliver at a chamber of commerce banquet in a middle-size city where the company has recently opened a luxury restaurant. What does the practitioner do?

First, she must know what the speaker desires to emphasize. The management has heard extensive word-of-mouth criticism about the high dinner prices the new restaurant charges. Some business has been lost because of this. The general manager sees the speech invitation as an opportunity to explain why the restaurant must charge these prices and to stress what good values the dinners really are. To do so, he must give the audience a frank behind-the-scenes look at the restaurant business—an opening for the speechwriter to spice up the necessary financial information with whimsical backstage anecdotes.

Twenty minutes of such material, brightly presented, will entertain and inform this business-oriented audience. It will demonstrate that the restaurant organization is efficiently run and does its best to provide residents with a distinctive place to dine at the lowest feasible cost. Indeed, here is an excellent public relations moment.

The speechwriter rarely talks with the general manager. So she must use her speech-planning appointment with him not only to learn what he wants to say but to study his style. Does he speak intensely or in a casual, wry manner? Is his speech staccato or a bit fulsome? The words she writes should be shaped to his natural style. Probably he can provide her with one or two of his favorite restaurant anecdotes. She can talk later with other officials of the company to obtain additional stories.

With this guidance in hand, how does the practitioner organize and write the speech?

A speech is built in blocks, joined by transitions. The following pattern for assembling the blocks provides an all-purpose outline on which most speeches can be built:

1. *Introduction (establishment of contact with audience)*
2. *Statement of main purpose of speech*
3. *Development of theme with examples, facts, and anecdotes*. Enumeration of points in 1, 2, 3 order is valuable here. It gives a sense of structure and controlled use of time.
4. *Statement of secondary theme, if there is one*
5. *Enunciation of principal point to which speaker has been building, the heart of the speech*
6. *A pause at this plateau, with an anecdote or two*. This is a soft place while audience absorbs principal point just made.
7. *Restatement of theme in summary form*
8. *Brief, brisk conclusion*

This plan of speech organization is *deductive;* that is, the central theme is stated almost at the beginning, and the points that follow support and illustrate the theme. A less common type of organization is *inductive*. In it the speaker presents points of information and arguments leading up to a statement of the principal theme near the end of the speech.

Introduction Following the preceding deductive outline, the speechwriter uses the first 2 minutes of the allotted 20 to build rapport between the general manager and the audience. The manager explains that when his company first considered coming to this city, he doubted that the area would support the luxury type of restaurant it operates. But the chamber of commerce convinced him that it would, and he is delighted that he had the good sense to listen (a light, slightly self-disparaging touch). He congratulates the chamber on the excellent statistical material it provided, thanks the membership for the organization's aid in solving the problems of setting up business, and mentions by name a few individuals who were especially helpful.

Then come the building blocks leading up to the conclusion.

Statement of Main Purpose The speaker says he wants to tell the audience about how a luxury restaurant operates, what its problems are, and why the customer sees things done a certain way. A summary of purpose in a single theme sentence at this point gives the speech a solid foundation. Almost as an aside he remarks, ''Perhaps this will help you understand why our dinners cost as much as they do.''

Development The manager states his company's total investment in opening this restaurant and reveals the number of people needed to run it . . . mentions kitchen jobs the diner never knows about . . . lists how many potatoes, steaks, heads of lettuce, and pounds of coffee are consumed in a week . . . relates a story about the night when the maitre d' had a full book of reservations and the salad chef walked out in a huff after a quarrel with his waitress girlfriend . . . describes how the chain's bill for pork and beef has soared.

Statement of Secondary Theme The speaker explains how the restaurant chooses its menus. He describes research into which entrees sell well or poorly, nutritional factors, and the difficulties in finding reasonable prices for the high-quality foodstuffs that will maintain the restaurant's standards of excellence.

Enunciation of Principal Point Operation of a top-flight restaurant in a time of high labor costs and rising food prices is a risky business, subject to the vagaries of weather, the economy, and the largely unpredictable turns of public fancy. By its steady growth, his organization has proved that a significant percentage of the public, "including here in this city," will patronize a restaurant that serves fine food with alert service in a distinctive setting. "Our challenge is to provide these things at the lowest prices we can offer while earning a legitimate profit from our investment."

Pause on Plateau The manager relates an anecdote about a diner who tried to steal some silverware, only to have it drop out of his pocket near the front door. The story illustrates problems of operating a restaurant.

Restatement of Theme The speaker's summary emphasizes his pride in the way local diners have patronized the new restaurant, proving his belief that the establishment provides the city with a type of high-quality dining that its citizens want and appreciate.

Brief Conclusion The audience hears a bit of news: the speaker announces that the restaurant has arranged to receive ample supplies of a popular but relatively rare fish. Next week the restaurant will add the fish, prepared in an unusual manner, to the menu at a special low introductory price. He invites everyone to come and try it.

One more step remains to make this a thoroughly successful public relations appearance. The speaker knows that the audience will be invited to ask questions; he has had the speechwriter give him a list of antagonistic queries he may receive. These include such challenges as, "Why do you hold people with dinner reservations in the bar so long before seating them—to make more money on liquor?" and "Is it true that you require waitresses to surrender a percentage of their tips to management?" His ability in answering the tough ones will improve or detract from the good impression his speech has made.

SPEECHWRITING TECHNIQUES

THE DIFFERENCE BETWEEN THE WRITTEN AND SPOKEN WORD

The first principle in writing words to be spoken is to make them flow in the way a person usually talks. Writing intended for the ear must be simpler in construction and more casual in form than writing meant for the eye. Instead of saying, "the Chicago man,'' make it ''the man from Chicago''; it sounds more natural. Contractions such as *don't* and *won't* increase the sense of informality.

Short, straightforward sentences are best. To provide variety, an occasional long sentence is acceptable if its structure is simple. So is a scattering of sentences beginning with brief dependent clauses. Often the ear fails to comprehend as fully and quickly as the eye does because the listener is easily distracted or may not hear clearly. The audio channel becomes clogged. Complex grammatical constructions should be avoided. A person can read a complicated sentence again and again until its meaning is clear. A listener who hears that same sentence spoken has no opportunity to hear it again because the speaker has moved ahead to new material. Thus a speaker, especially when handling difficult information, should repeat key points of the speech, couching them if possible in slightly different form.

Studies indicate that the average person listens four times as rapidly as the average person speaks. Thus the listener may be thinking about other matters while hearing the speaker. Even for a skillful speaker, holding the listener's undivided attention is extremely difficult; recapitulation of main points helps the listener retain at least the main thrust of the speech.

Here, for example, is a sentence from a published news story that would be unacceptable in a speech text because of its intricate structure:

> Wright, who has agreed to pay the fine, said she believes the commission's action, which comes three weeks before the Nov. 2 election, will have no effect on her reelection campaign against Democrat C. D. (Dick) Stine.

If the material were written as follows, listeners could comprehend it far more easily:

> Wright has agreed to pay the fine. The commission's action comes only three weeks before the November 2nd election. But Wright believes that it will not affect her campaign for reelection against Democrat Dick Stine.

An excellent way to grasp the concept of writing for speech is to close your eyes and listen to people around you talk. Do the same thing while hearing a radio newscast, which has been written especially for the ear. Visualize how the words you are hearing would appear on paper. Notice how often people use fragments of sentences. The words that would complete the sentences are implied, a kind of verbal shorthand. Such fragments in a speech increase the feeling of naturalness.

The incomplete sentence is used quite effectively in this excerpt from a speech by John C. Bedrosian, president of the American Federation of Hospitals. His topic, the high cost of medical care, was complex, and he dealt with the problem in depth. A brief text, however, kept the speech from bogging down. Brief sentences, sentence fragments, and short words are used to offset such necessary long ones as *catastrophic* and *ambulatory:*

> Hospital care is expensive. There is no denying that. It is essentially designed to provide care to the critically ill. Catastrophic illnesses. Major surgeries. Serious injuries. Any institution that is equipped and staffed to provide the highest level of care is by its very nature not economically appropriate for low-level care.

That's why we are witnessing the growth of alternative care and treatment sources. Satellite clinics, for example, surgi-centers, and other ambulatory care facilities. Skilled nursing homes for recuperation from illness or surgery. Home health care, a concept that has really only gotten started.

All of these are approaches that match the level of care to the need, and at a significant reduction in cost.

A speaker normally delivers a text at the rate of about 150 words a minute. A standard page of pica-sized typewriter copy contains about 250 words. So, when preparing a 20-minute speech, the writer must produce about 3000 words, approximately 12 typewritten pages. If the speaker is an especially fast talker, this wordage might be increased a bit. Pauses for emphasis and laughter, however, tend to make a speaker's delivery before an audience slower than during practice run-throughs.

SOME TIPS FROM PROFESSIONALS

Here are tips on writing from professional speechwriters:

- *Read aloud the words you have written, to be certain that they sound natural to the ear.*
- *Avoid clauses that complicate sentences.* Instead of writing, "John Williams, chairman of the State Highway Commission, said, etc.," eliminate the clause by writing, "Chairman John Williams of the State Highway Department said, etc."
- *Use smooth transitions to move from one section of the speech to the next, as in these examples:*

"And while discussing the fine art of communications, Japanese style, I would like to mention the role of the press." (K. M. Chrysler of *U.S. News & World Report*)

"Now I'd like to move to a second major challenge facing us—crime." (James B. Jacobson of Prudential Insurance Company of America in a speech on "Challenges and Choice—Inflation and Crime")

- *Use rhetorical questions.* They provide change of pace and are a good device to introduce new ideas. An example:

"Is it too difficult to develop a curriculum whereby students can be fully educated? I think not. It has been done before and quite well." (Benjamin H. Alexander, president of the University of the District of Columbia)

- *Draw verbal pictures.* Help the audience to visualize scenes, color, movement.
- *Be wary of jokes.* Some speakers tell them well, others fumble. Never let your speaker use that bromide, "That reminds me of a story." If used, jokes should be woven into the text, not telegraphed in advance. Those involving racial and religious topics are likely to offend some members of the audience. Don't use them. The light touch desired in a speech can be obtained by anecdotes or quips that provoke a smile or a chuckle.

PRO ATHLETES GIVE SPEAKING HINTS

Articulate professional athletes are popular public speakers. Audiences like to see them in person and hear behind-the-scenes stories of sports. Many are scheduled through the *Sports Illustrated* Speakers Bureau.

Three famous sports speakers handled by *Sports Illustrated* describe how they organize their talks and establish personal contact with audiences.

Billy Casper, golfer I have found that most people like to hear me talk about some behind-the-scenes aspects of golf. I try to relate the humorous side of the game and give my audience some insight into what we go through in a normal working day. I would suggest that unless a person is extremely experienced in speaking before large audiences, he avoid telling jokes. But, as any athlete knows, there are enough situations in sports that are funny by themselves and do not need forced attempts at humor. If I feel that my audience will appreciate and respond to a more serious subject, I cut down on the humor and talk on the role of sport in our society.

Harmon Killebrew, former major league baseball star I usually begin by some reference to people in the audience and try to keep my whole talk on as much a personal level as possible. Since my main function as a speaker is to entertain the listeners, I stay away from a complicated approach. I try to keep the subject of my talk to one point and build up that point in various ways. For example, if my main point is the difficulties faced by an athlete in professional sports, I would begin by telling an anecdote that points this out. I would then establish my own point of view and follow this up with some further stories which illustrate my premise. I try to maintain interest by relating humorous or generally little-known stories and then end my speech by restating the original premise.

Bart Starr, professional football coach I try to cement as strong relationships as possible with the people to whom I talk. After my talk I try to stay around as long as possible and talk with people from the audience. I've found that doing this establishes a personal rapport with the people, and often leads to further assignments. *I always send the chairman of the group a short note thanking him for his hospitality* [emphasis added].

- *Quote statistics sparingly*. Provide them in graphic terms when possible. Dixy Lee Ray, former chairperson of the Atomic Energy Commission, did it this way: the amount of energy now being consumed in the United States by one person in one day is equivalent to what would be produced by the human muscle of approximately 300 slaves working all 24 hours, consuming no energy themselves.

ESTABLISHING A BOND WITH THE AUDIENCE

Use of the second-person form of direct address is a clever tool for speakers trying to establish a personal bond with the audience. A physicist delivering a university lecture would avoid such a device; it might subtly lower the intellectual level of his speech. Politicians use it frequently.

Writing in *Speechwriter's Newsletter,* Stephen R. Maloney pointed out how skillfully President Ronald Reagan used the ''you and I together'' approach in a broadcast speech promoting a tax increase bill. A year earlier he had pushed through a major tax reduction bill. Reagan's task was to explain and justify his reversal of tax policy in a period of national recession. This was the opening paragraph of the Reagan speech:

There is an old saying we've all heard a thousand times about the weather and how everyone talks about it but no one does anything about it. Well, many of you must be feeling that way about the present state of our economy. Certainly there's a lot of talk about it, but I want you to know that we are doing something about it. And the reason I wanted to talk to you is because you can help us do something about it.

Maloney wrote:

What the President does in his introduction is to plant a powerful suggestion—one that he reinforces throughout the speech—in the mind of his listeners that the tax increase was somehow *their* idea.

Through a repeated use of the words ''we'' and ''ours'' the President stresses the bond of commonality—not *his* economic program but ''*our* economy.'' The repetition of the word ''you'' also serves to involve the audience, drawing them into the discussion, breaking down their resistance, and enlisting them in the cause.

Late in the speech Reagan returned to the direct-address style he used in the opening paragraph. He said, ''You helped us to start this economic recovery program last year, when you told your representatives you wanted it. You can help again. . . . ''

Analyzing this statement, Maloney pointed out, ''The implication is: This isn't *my* tax increase; it's part of *our* (yours and mine) economic program.''

Of such niceties of language are successful speeches of persuasion made.

VISUAL AIDS FOR A SPEECH

A speech often can be strengthened by use of visual devices. Graphs and charts, a common kind of visual aid, are only as good as their visibility to the audience. A chart too complicated for easy comprehension or too small to be read from the rear of the room is almost useless. Slides projected onto a screen are frequently used. They must be simple in content; holding a slide on the screen long enough for the audience to study involved information creates restlessness. (Audiovisual aids are discussed in Chapter 24.)

Use of objects is still another form of visual aid for a speaker. The model of a new company product displayed near the lectern is an example. A blown-up reproduction of a United Way fund drive emblem hung behind the head table is another. President Jimmy Carter tried a similar technique by wearing a cardigan on camera, instead of the usual presidential suitcoat, during a nationally telecast speech urging energy conservation. The device was so obvious, however, that criticism of the presidential image-building effort severely weakened its effect.

STAGING A SPEECH

Effective speeches don't just happen. They have to be rehearsed and prepared—or, in the language of the theater, ''staged.'' Organizations frequently rely upon a practitioner's understanding of potential audiences to ensure that a speaking engagement helps the organization get a positive message across. And to create a pool of talented speakers, some organizations establish training programs.

THE PRACTITIONER'S ROLE

Public relations practitioners who write speeches are frequently called upon by management to give their opinion about whether the company should accept an invitation to speak and, if so, how the firm should use such a forum to present its views and policies in the most favorable light.

When an invitation arrives, the first decision to be made is whether a speech should be delivered at all. This is where the practitioner's advice may be sought by company management. Thought should be given as to whether the occasion provides a suitable opportunity to further the speaker's cause, and whether the size and significance of the audience justify the time and effort involved. Although this may sound a little arrogant, it is only a matter of practicality.

On the other hand, a public relations representative whose employer desires to make speeches can create ample opportunities. Waiting for invitations is unnecessary. Offers to make a speaker available to organizations without charge may be made discreetly by letter, telephone, or word-of-mouth. The approach is to suggest that the speaker has an unusual message that should be of special interest to the group being solicited. If the speaker is a corporation executive, the hosts should be assured that they will not be subjected to a heavy sales pitch.

Management also is likely to seek out the practitioner's opinion when a speaker must appear before a hostile audience—a real test of public relations skill. While not always pleasant, the experience can pay dividends. A utility company president who proposes construction of a nuclear power plant in the neighborhood cannot expect a cordial welcome when addressing an antinuclear alliance. If the official can command respect by a pleasant, frank manner, however, some in the audience may realize that the company president is not the ogre they had imagined. Having achieved this, the speaker can lay out the pronuclear arguments before the opponents and at least make them aware of the utility's reasoning.

George Graff, former president of McDonnell Douglas, a manufacturer of aircraft, often found himself before hostile audiences who regarded him as a leader in the armaments race. He met this antagonism head-on by opening his speeches thus: ''I'd rather have an industry making toasters, but we're in the real world. I'd like to talk to you about that real world.'' Surprised by this approach, his listeners would give him their attention. People usually respect frankness in others and, while not always admitting it, may grudgingly admire a person for voluntarily facing up to enemies.

Members of the public are not the only audiences an organization's speaker may be called upon to address. Management representatives—including public relations staff members—frequently make speeches within the organization, as part of an employee relations program. Although the atmosphere normally is friendly, the speaker still must maintain good rapport with the audience. Practitioners themselves may address a group, or they may offer guidance to other speakers in presenting the message. During times of internal hostility such as labor disputes, public relations expertise may be essential.

SPEECH TRAINING PROGRAMS

Even a brilliantly written speech can fail if it is delivered poorly. Upper-echelon executives for whom speeches are a required part of the job should be offered training by professionals in the techniques of public speaking. Progressive organizations also search among their employees for men and women who can be trained to speak effectively.

Employees selected may be assigned to attend on-the-job training sessions in speechmaking. They are instructed in such basics as diction, stage presence, voice projection, reading audience reaction, and handling questions. Videocassette tapes and other teaching aids enhance the instruction.

When a company needs to explain its policy to employees and seek their cooperation, top-echelon officials aren't always the best ones to do it. A well-trained fellow worker in a department may succeed better in convincing his or her colleagues to authorize automatic payroll deduction for United Way contributions than a speaker sent out from the executive offices. When management trains speakers from various work levels, provides them with well-written speeches appropriate for their needs, and gives them a suitable setting, they can fill a valuable role in the internal communication chain. What's more, they can give management enlightening feedback from their colleagues.

HELPING THE SPEAKER POLISH AND PRESENT THE SPEECH

After writing a draft of a speech, the writer should go over it with the speaker, who may request changes. By listening to the speaker read the material aloud, the writer can detect clumsy portions and smooth them out. The more frequently a speaker reads the text aloud in practice, the better the on-stage performance will be. A videotape made of a practice session will show the speaker where improvement is needed.

The finished version of a speech should be typed on $8\frac{1}{2}$-by-11-inch pages in easily read type, without excessive crowding. Some speakers prefer that the typescript cover only the upper two-thirds of a page, to prevent them from dropping their heads too low as they read. If the bottoms of the typed pages are crimped a bit, the speaker can turn them without having two stick together.

Writing an introduction and sending it to the person who will present the speaker is a good tactic. This assures that the information about the speaker will be correct. Although the introducer may alter the material, the content probably will be approximately what the public relations representative desires.

At the scene of the speech, the public relations representative should take several actions:

- *The microphone and other apparatus should be tested.* The audiovisual equipment should be set up and checked and the slide projector focused. Charts or flipcards should be arranged in correct order on an easel.
- *Extra copies of the speech should be brought along.* Additional copies are for distribution to the news media and to listeners who request a copy.
- *The speech should be recorded on tape.* The tape can be used to settle any disputes over what the speaker said, to provide ''actuality'' excerpts for local radio stations, and to assemble material for a postmortem session between speaker and writer analyzing the performance. If the speaker is well known, especially if he or she is from out of town, the public relations representative may arrange for radio, television, and newspaper interviews as well as provide taped excerpts to the stations.

Two other steps can be taken to obtain additional exposure for an important speech: (1) copies can be mailed to a selected list of opinion leaders and (2) the speech can be rewritten as an article for a company publication or submitted to a suitable trade magazine (see Figure 23.1).

SPEAKERS' BUREAUS AND HOTLINES

Speakers' bureaus operated by trade associations, social agencies, and corporations constitute an important instrument for bringing speakers and audiences together (see Figure 23.2). They function something like a company's pool of internal speakers, but on a more elaborate scale. Speakers developed within an organization are made available by the bureaus upon request. The bureaus also seek to place speakers before influential audiences. Utility companies, which have a constant need to build friendly community relations, are especially heavy users of the speakers' bureau concept. Typically, a telephone company in Illinois has a bureau with 42 trained speakers who talk before all types of clubs and civic organizations. Before being sent out to represent the company, the speakers receive professional training and must pass auditions.

Talent-booking agencies that place professional speakers for a fee sometimes also call themselves speakers' bureaus. The roles of these two types of speakers' bureaus are quite dissimilar: one provides speakers without charge, to promote the cause of the corporation or organization that operates it, while the other does so on a direct profit-making basis. It is important to distinguish between the two.

Somewhat related to the organizational speakers' bureau is the telephone hotline service operated by some trade associations and companies to provide quick answers, especially to the news media (see Figure 23.3). This facility generally offers toll-free telephone service using the 800 prefix. The following advertisement by the Edison

BankAmerica Corporation

The Matter of Survival

Remarks by

Ronald E. Rhody

Senior Vice President
Bank of America

As delivered at the

Public Relations Society of America Management Seminar
Palm Springs, California

June 26, 1990

Fellow toilers in the vineyards of truth, good morning ... and thank you.

I'm not quite sure how I got myself in this position, and even less sure how I'm going to get myself out of it.

It must have been one of those cozy, the-world-is-a-wonderful-place, fog-bound San Francisco mornings when Tom Sanger called and invited me to speak here today. Clearly, I didn't hear him clearly. Who, in their right mind, would undertake to advise an audience like this on survival ... personal survival I've come to understand ... in situations of mergers, acquisitions, downsizings, or takeovers?

Never mind that said situation is our normal work world these days. Never mind that we're plying our trade in an environment in which uncertainty is the only certainty. And never mind that the role and importance of this craft you and I practice is probably the most widely misunderstood of all management tools.

Never mind all that. The fact is that the decade we're entering is going to be the most competitively punishing any of our institutions has faced. The pressures on costs across the full range of the institution's activities are going to be uncompromisingly severe. And the demands for results, particularly from cost centers like public relations and communications, are going to be unrelenting and unforgiving.

If you think that is the case already and that things can't get much more intense – grab hold of something, you're in for a ride.

So I guess the question of survival is appropriate – whether merged, acquired, downsized, taken over, or simply trying to do your day-to-day job as best you can in a world you never made.

Unfortunately, I don't have any answers.

I do have some suggestions that may help improve the odds a little, though, and that's where I want to focus my remarks ... on improving the odds.

From this point on I'm going to be borrowing liberally from the ideas and experiences of several of our colleagues who have played through the roughest parts of the game, played admirably, and who are survivors. But not just survivors. Survival, alone, isn't much of an objective. Being a key player – now that's an objective. And that's what they are.

The people I'm plagiarizing are: David Fausch of Gillette, Bob Irelan of Kaiser Aluminum, and Kurt Stocker of Continental Bank, by way of United Airlines. They are veterans of some of the most dramatic downsizings, acquisitions, and hostile

FIGURE 23.1

A spoken communication can reach an important additional audience when printed and sent to opinion leaders such as newspaper editors, government officials, academicians, and people who speak for industry. This is the first page of a speech reprint distributed by the BankAmerica Corporation.

Electric Institute Information Service in *Editor & Publisher,* the newspaper trade journal, illustrates how the hotline functions:

YOU DON'T NEED A PRESS CONFERENCE TO GET THE ENERGY STORY

Let's have a conference right now.

And it won't even cost you a dime.

One of our experts is ready to help you with your newsbreak, feature, or editorial.

Ask for facts, background, and the national perspective on electric energy.

Ask about energy sources, economics, and the environment.

Because energy is one of the crucial issues in American life today, there's someone on the hotline, 24 hours a day, 7 days a week.

Just think. By using the phone, you'll be saving energy while writing about it.

Call toll-free 800-424-8897.

SPECIAL TYPES OF SPEAKING OPPORTUNITIES

THE NEWS CONFERENCE

A speaker addressing an audience represents one-way communication. Listeners receive the message, either accepting or rejecting it, but do not engage in a dialogue during which they can challenge the speaker's statements. The speaker commands the situation. The only exception occurs when a speaker agrees to accept questions from the floor—a practice that some speakers relish but others avoid either because they realize that they do not perform well spontaneously or they desire to avoid embarrassing questions.

At a news conference, communication is two-way. The person speaking for a company or a cause submits to questioning by reporters, usually after a brief opening statement. A news conference makes possible quick, widespread dissemination of the sponsor's information and opinions through the news media. It avoids the time-consuming task of presenting the information to the news outlets individually and assures that the intensely competitive newspapers and electronic media hear the news simultaneously. From a public relations point of view, these are the principal advantages of the news conference. Against these important pluses must be weighed the fact that the person holding the conference is open to severe and potentially antagonistic questioning.

In public relations strategy, the news conference can be either an offensive or a defensive device, depending on the client's need.

Most news conferences—or press conferences, as they frequently are called—are *positive* in intent; they are affirmative actions to project the host's plans or point of view. A corporation may hold a news conference to unveil a new product whose manufacture will create many new jobs, or a civic leader may do so to reveal the goals and plans for a countywide charity fund drive she will head. Such news conferences should be carefully planned and scheduled well in advance under the most favorable circumstances.

Public relations specialists also must deal frequently with unanticipated, controversial situations. A business firm, an association, or a politician becomes embroiled in difficulty that is at best embarrassing, possibly incriminating. Press and public demand

FIGURE 23.2
Recognizing the immense ethnic diversity in its service area, Southern California Edison Company operates a speakers' bureau, the Multi-Lingual Speakers Task Force, consisting of company employees. Speakers are available in several Asian languages and in Spanish. More than 26 percent of Edison customers speak Spanish with limited English capability, and 16 percent speak an Asian language. The language in this illustration is Vietnamese. (Courtesy of Southern California Edison Company)

an explanation. A barebones printed statement is not enough to satisfy the clamor. This is the moment for a news conference that is *defensive* in nature, an effort to put out the fire with the least damage possible. The person who holds the conference will face uncomfortable minutes under sharp questioning. However, the alternative of ''stone-

RAILROAD
FACTS, FAST:

CALL (202) 835-9550/9555.

If you want more facts for your railroad story, call us. We'll be glad to update your information about America's freight railroads.

FREIGHT RAILROADS
ARE ON THE MOVE.

FIGURE 23.3
Trade associations place advertisements in media journals, such as this one in *Editor & Publisher,* to encourage use of their telephone hotlines. (Reprinted by permission of Association of American Railroads.)

walling'' silence is worse. It leaves public and press with a feeling of evasion and a suspicion that the truth is even worse than it actually is. A well-prepared spokesperson may be able to achieve a measure of understanding and sympathy by issuing a carefully composed printed statement when the news conference opens.

Former Mayor Marion Barry of Washington used both the news conference and written statement techniques when arrested in 1990 for drug offenses. First he met the press on the courthouse steps, coolly dismissing the charge of possessing crack cocaine as insignificant and politically motivated. Pressed by reporters to explain the circumstances of his arrest, he evaded their questions by asserting that he could not do so because the matter was before a court. Then he said he must get back to governing the city, implying business as usual.

Almost immediately thereafter, Barry went into isolation in an alcohol and drug treatment center in Florida. While he was there, a federal grand jury indicted him on additional drug charges. This time his response to the media was a statement issued by his attorney that the charges were "a continuation of the political lynching and excesses of the Justice Department." That is a classic defense tactic of trying to divert attention by attacking the attacker.

Barry was convicted on one misdemeanor charge of cocaine possession, but he was acquitted on another charge, and the jury failed to reach a verdict on the other 12 charges. He declared the trial outcome a personal victory and made himself frequently available to reporters, stressing a call for "a time of healing" and talking about his political future. He did not have much to say later, however, when he was sentenced to six months in jail.

No matter how trying the circumstances, the person holding the news conference should create an atmosphere of cooperation and project a sincere intent to be helpful. The worst thing he or she can do is to appear resentful of the questioning. The person never should succumb to a display of bad temper. A good posture is to admit that the situation is bad and that the organization is doing everything in its power to correct it. (Further discussion of crisis public relations appears in Chapter 14.)

Rarely, an organization or public person caught in an embarrassing situation foolishly attempts to quiet public concern by holding a news conference that really isn't a news conference. The host reads a brief, inadequate statement, then refuses to answer questions from reporters. This practice alienates the press, which feels cheated. Suspicions of the host's conduct are increased, not minimized. If, for a valid reason, only a brief statement can be issued at the time, this should be done by distribution of a news release rather than by summoning reporters to a nonproductive conference.

Two more types of news conferences are held occasionally. One is the spontaneous conference arising out of a news event: the winner of a Nobel Prize meets the press to explain the award-winning work . . . a runner who has just set a world's record breathlessly describes his feelings . . . a woman appointed to a high-court judgeship tells reporters about her legal philosophy . . . a candidate for mayor makes an election night claim of victory. The other type is the regularly scheduled conference held by a public official at stated times, even when there is nothing special to announce. Usually this is called a briefing—the daily State Department briefing, for example.

Planning and Conducting a News Conference First comes the question, "Should we hold a news conference or not?" Frequently the answer should be "No!" The essential element of a news conference is *news*. If reporters and camera crews summoned to a conference hear propaganda instead of facts, or information of minor interest to a limited group, they go away disgusted. Their valuable time has been wasted—and it *is* valuable. Editors complain that they never have enough staff hours available to cover everything they would like to cover; if they send reporters to a conference that has been called merely to satisfy the host's sense of self-importance, they resent the fact. The next time, they probably won't send reporters.

If the material involved fails to meet the criteria of significant news, a wise public relations representative will distribute it through a press release. The information has a chance of being published based on its degree of merit without irritating editors and reporters.

Notices usually are sent by mail, but some organizations use telegrams or electronic delivery methods for major conferences in the belief that the extra impact justifies the additional cost. Every news outlet that might be interested in the material should be invited. An ignored media outlet may become an enemy, like a person who isn't asked to a party. The invitation should describe the general nature of the material to be discussed so an editor will know what type of reporter to assign.

What hour is best? This depends upon the local media situation. If the city has only an afternoon newspaper, 9:30 or 10 A.M. is good, because this gives a reporter time to write a story before a midday deadline. If the city's newspaper publishes in the morning, 2 P.M. is a suitable hour.

Another prime goal of news conference sponsors is the early evening newscasts on local television stations, or even network TV newscasts if the information is important enough. A conference at 2 P.M. is about the latest that a television crew can cover and still get the material processed at a comfortable pace for inclusion in a dinner-hour show. This time period can be shortened in an emergency, but the chances of getting on a show diminish as the processing time dwindles.

A warning: a public relations representative in a city with only an afternoon newspaper who schedules a news conference after that paper's deadline, yet in time for the news to appear on the early evening television newscasts, makes a grave blunder. Newspaper editors resent such favoritism to television and have long memories. Knowledge of, and sensitivity to, local news media deadlines are necessary elements of a public relations representative's work.

Deadlines for radio news reporters are less confining than those for newspapers and television, because radio newscasts are aired many times a day. The conference hours suggested for newspapers and television are suitable for radio as well, though.

Here are two pieces of advice from longtime public relations specialists to persons who hold news conferences:

1. *The speaker should never attempt to talk off-the-record at a news conference.* If the information is so secret that it should not be published, then the speaker shouldn't tell it to reporters. Many editors forbid their reporters to honor off-the-record statements, because too often the person making them is merely attempting to prevent publication of material that is legitimate news but might be embarrassing. Any statement made before a group will not stay secret long, anyway. If one reporter present ignores the request and publishes the material, those who honored it are placed at an unfair competitive disadvantage.

2. *The speaker should never lie!* If he or she is pushed into a corner and believes that answering a specific question would be unwise, it is far better to say, "No comment" in some form than to answer falsely. A person caught in a lie to the media suffers a critical loss of credibility.

Preparing the Scene At a news conference, public relations representatives resemble producers of a movie or television show. They are responsible for briefing the spokesperson, making arrangements, and assuring that the conference runs smoothly. They stay in the background, however.

Bulldog Reporter, a West Coast public relations newsletter, suggests the following checklist for a practitioner asked to organize a news conference. The time factors given are normal for such events as new product introductions, but conferences concerning spot news developments for the daily press and electronic media often are called on notice of a few days or even a few hours.

- Select a convenient location, one that is fairly easy for news representatives to reach with minimal travel time. In some cities, this is the local press club; in others, it is a major hotel. On occasion, the organization's headquarters is appropriate.
- Set the date and time. Times between midmorning and midafternoon are good. Friday afternoons are deadly, as are days before holidays. Be sure to check media deadlines.
- When possible, issue an invitation to a news conference about six to eight weeks ahead of time, but one month is acceptable. The invitation should include the purpose of the conference, names of spokespersons, and why the event has significant news value. Of course, the date, time, and location must be provided.
- Distribute a media release about the upcoming news conference when appropriate. This depends on the importance of the event.
- Write a statement for the spokesperson to give at the conference and make sure that he or she understands and rehearses it. In addition, rehearse the entire conference, including introductions and presentation of the prepared statement.
- Try to anticipate questions so the spokesperson can readily answer difficult queries. Problem/solution rehearsals prepare the spokesperson for off-the-wall questions or ones that are designed to put the speaker on the defensive.
- Prepare printed materials for distribution at the conference. These should include a brief factsheet with names and titles of participants, a basic news release, and basic support materials. This is sometimes called a press kit.
- Prepare visual materials as necessary. These may include slides, transparencies, posters, or even a short videotape. Television crews particularly need something visual.
- Make advance arrangements for the room. Be sure that there are enough chairs and leave a center aisle for photographers. If a lectern is used, make certain that it is large enough to accommodate multiple microphones from radio and television crews.
- Arrive 30 to 60 minutes early to double-check arrangements. Test the microphones, arrange name tags for invited guests, and distribute literature.

Some organizations provide coffee and possibly sweet rolls for their media guests as a courtesy. Others find this gesture unnecessary because most of the newspeople are in a hurry, more concerned with getting the story than with enjoying social amenities. Liquor should not be served at a regular news conference. Such socializing should be reserved for the press party, discussed in the next section.

At some news conferences, still photographers are given two or three minutes to take their pictures before questioning begins. Some photographers complain that, thus restricted, they cannot obtain candid shots. If free shooting is permitted, as usually is the best practice, the physical arrangements should give the photographers operating space without allowing them to obstruct the view of reporters.

Relationships between print and television reporters sometimes become strained at news conferences. A practitioner should take particular care to arrange the room in such a way that the electronic equipment does not impede the print reporters. Some find it good policy for the speaker to remain after the news conference ends and make brief on-camera statements for individual TV stations, if their reporters request this attention. Such statements should not go beyond anything the speaker has said to the entire body of reporters.

A final problem in managing a news conference is knowing when to end it. The public relations representative serving as backstage timekeeper and watchdog should avoid cutting off the questioning prematurely. To do so creates antagonism from the reporters. Letting a conference run down like a tired clock is almost as bad. At every conference there comes a moment when the reporters run out of questions and the danger of dull repetition arises. A speaker may, or may not, recognize this. If not, the practitioner may step forward and say something like, ''I'm sorry, but I know some of you have deadlines to make. So we have time for just two more questions.''

Presidential press conferences do not have this problem. Long-standing custom limits these conferences to 30 minutes. At that point, the senior news service reporter present calls out, ''Thank you, Mr. President!'' and the conference ends. Everyone concerned with public relations should study a presidential press conference on television. The kinds of questions asked, the manner in which the president answers them, the nature of any opening announcements, and the physical facilities—all of these provide clues for organizing news conferences of a more mundane nature.

THE PRESS PARTY AND THE PRESS TOUR

In the straightaway news conference, the purpose is to transmit information and opinion from the conference speaker to the news media in a businesslike, time-efficient manner. Neither side wishes to turn the meeting into a social event. It is part of the day's work. Often, however, a corporation, an association, or a political figure wishes to deliver a message or build rapport with the media on a more personal basis; then a social setting is desirable. Thus is born the press party or the press trip.

The Press Party This gathering may be a luncheon, a dinner, or a reception. Whatever form the party takes, standard practice is for the host to arise at the end of the socializing period and make the ''pitch.'' This may be a hard-news announcement, a brief policy statement followed by a question-and-answer period, or merely a soft-sell thank-you to the guests for coming and giving the host an opportunity to know them better. Guests usually are given press packets of information, either when they arrive or as they leave. Parties giving the press a preview of an art exhibit, a new headquarters building, and so forth are widely used.

The press party is a softening-up process, and both sides know it.

The advantages of a press party to its host can be substantial under the proper circumstances. During chitchat over food or drink, officials of the host organization become acquainted with media people who write, edit, or broadcast material about them. Although the benefit from the host's point of view is difficult to measure immediately, opening the channels of communication with the media at multiple informal levels may prove highly advantageous in the future.

Also, if the host has an important policy position to present, the assumption—not necessarily correct—is that editors and reporters will be more receptive after a social hour. The host who expects that food and drink will buy favorable press coverage may receive an unpleasant surprise. Conscientious reporters and editors will not be swayed by a free drink and a plate of prime rib followed by baked Alaska. In their view, they have already given something to the host by setting aside a part of their day for the party. They accept invitations to press parties because they wish to develop potential news contacts within the host's organization and to learn more about its officials.

Until a few years ago, though, *free-loading* by news people at parties was widespread and accepted as normal practice. Often press guests were given expensive gifts. In large cities, the expectations of certain reporters, especially those covering business and entertainment, became absurdly high. One co-author of this book recalls attending a new-model announcement dinner for the press given some years ago by the Chevrolet division of General Motors. During dinner, the public relations director announced that there would be gifts for the guests when they went home. Each guest was asked to fill out a color preference card—blue, green, or tan.

One guest at the author's table asked another, quite seriously, ''Do you think they are going to give us cars?'' The other responded, with equal gravity, that perhaps they might. The actual gift proved to be an expensive blanket of the preferred color, packed in an individualized cedar chest. This type of payoff for attending the presentation became known as ''loot.'' None of the media guests refused to accept the gift. (Present practice concerning gifts will be described shortly.)

Here are two actual examples of press parties:

1. Officials of Blue Cross in a Midwestern state regularly hold a series of dinners in major cities for invited members of the local media. The guest lists include men and women who cover the health field, have a role in editing stories about it, or comment on it editorially. During a cocktail party before dinner, Blue Cross officials mingle with the guests. The public relations consultant accompanying them helps with introductions. During dinner, the host group spreads itself around to sit with guests.

After dinner, the chief executive speaks briefly, explaining what Blue Cross regards as the significant trends and problems in health care. Then he opens the meeting to questions. Inevitably, queries center on why medical costs are so high and what Blue Cross is doing to control them. Some questions are friendly, some barbed. The public relations consultant distributes packets of news releases, factsheets, and charts. No gifts are offered to the guests.

2. A land developer invited local media guests and civic leaders to a luncheon at which he disclosed plans for a major shopping center at the edge of the city. Printed invitations announced a reception at noon and lunch at 12:30. Acceptances by phone were requested by a certain date. Arriving guests received paste-on tags imprinted with

their names, large folders containing news releases, photographs of the developer and of an artist's rendering of the project's exterior and interior, and a factsheet giving the developer's biography and a list of projects he had built. The artist's renderings stood on easels around the room; a scale model of the project was displayed on a table. Drinks were served, followed by a large luncheon. After the meal, the developer spoke about the project and answered questions.

The normal adjournment hour for luncheon sessions is 1:30 P.M. This one ran a few minutes past that hour because of the number of questions. No press luncheon ever should run past 2 P.M.

"JUNKET JOURNALISM" AT DISNEY WORLD

Disney World in Florida threw a press party to celebrate its fifteenth anniversary, and more than 10,000 people came.

The fact that Disney World paid the entire expense of some guests—and offered to do so for all of them—created a debate on media ethics that almost overshadowed the celebration. The party, incidentally, was a classic example of a created news event.

Disney World was well aware of the trend in the media against allowing reporters to accept free trips because the gift might influence the tone of their stories. Its invitations, sent nationwide, offered guests three alternatives:

1. Disney World and its travel-promotion partners would pay a guest's entire travel, lodging, and food costs.

2. The hosts would pay $150 a day of a guest's expense, and the guest's company would pay the balance.

3. A guest's employer would pay his or her entire expense.

Some guests used each method, but Disney World refused to say how many.

The New York *Times* in an editorial claimed that media guests who accepted the free-trip offer had "debased" journalism and given the impression that the entire press was "on the take." The St. Petersburg *Times* called the party "junket journalism." Rebutting this position, some guests from smaller newspapers and broadcasting stations said that their companies could not afford such expensive travel, so this was the only way they could visit the entertainment center and write about it.

Disney World did not require its expense-paid guests to do anything in return. The park did receive a very large amount of publicity, generally favorable except for the media-ethics dispute. News coverage was stimulated by the presence of former U.S. Chief Justice Warren Burger, who opened the bicentennial celebration of the U.S. Constitution during the party, and Nicholas S. Daniloff, an American correspondent just released after a controversial arrest in Moscow.

The total cost to Disney World and its cosponsors was estimated at around $7.5 million, according to *Editor & Publisher*.

The Press Tour There are three kinds of press tours. The most common is a trip, often disparagingly called a "junket," during which editors and reporters are invited to inspect a company's manufacturing facilities in several cities, ride an inaugural flight of a new air route, watch previews of the television network programs for the fall season in Hollywood or New York, or view military exercises in Europe. The host, whether IBM or the United States Air Force, picks up the tab for transporting, feeding, and housing the reporters.

A variation of the press tour is the familiarization trip. ''Fam trips,'' as they are called, are offered to travel writers and editors by the tourism industry (see Chapter 20). Convention and visitor bureaus, as well as major resorts, pay all expenses in the hope that the writers will report favorably on their experiences. Travel articles in magazines and newspapers usually result from a reporter's ''fam trip.''

In the third kind of press tour, widely used in high technology industries, the organization's executives travel to key cities to talk with selected editors; for example, top Apple Computer executives toured the East Coast to talk with key magazine editors and demonstrate the capabilities of the new Macintosh computer. Depending on editors' preferences, the executives may visit a publication and give a background briefing to key editors, or a hotel conference room may be set up so that the traveling executives may talk with editors from several publications at the same time.

The Ethics of Who Pays for What In recent years, severe self-searching by media members, as well as by professional public relations personnel who feel it is unethical to offer lavish travel and gifts, has led to increased self-regulation by both groups as to when a press tour or ''junket'' is appropriate and how much should be spent.

The policies of major dailies forbid employees to accept any gifts, housing, or transportation; the newspapers pay all costs associated with a press tour on which a staff member is sent. In contrast, some smaller dailies, weeklies, and trade magazines willingly accept any and all offers for an expense-paid trip. The managers of these publications maintain that they don't have the resources of large dailies to reimburse an organization for expenses and such trips are legitimate if the reporter is covering a newsworthy activity.

Some newspapers with policies forbidding acceptance of travel and gifts don't extend the restrictions to all departments. Reporters in the ''hard news'' area, for example, cannot accept gifts or travel, but such policy may not be enforced for reporters who write ''soft news'' for sports, travel, and lifestyle sections. Few newspapers, for example, pay for the press box seats provided for reporters covering a professional football game, nor does the travel editor usually pay the full rate for rooms at beach resorts that are the focus of travel articles.

Given the mixed and often confusing policies of various media, the public relations professional must use common sense and discretion. He or she, first of all, should not violate the PRSA code of ethics that specifically forbids lavish gifts and free trips that have nothing to do with covering a legitimate news event. Second, the public relations person should be sensitive to the policies of news outlets and should design events to stay within them. A wise alternative is to offer a reporter the option of reimbursing the company for travel and hotel expenses associated with a press tour. Hewlett-Packard, when it invites an editor to have a hosted lunch with an executive during a press tour, even asks the editor to select the restaurant, so the company cannot be accused of trying to ''buy'' favorable coverage by taking the editor to the most expensive restaurant in town.

In terms of gift-giving, the sensible approach is a token of remembrance such as a pen, note pad, or a company paperweight. (Ethics are discussed extensively in Chapter 6.)

Organizing a Press Party or Press Tour The key to a successful event is detailed organization. Every step of the process should be checked out meticulously.

In planning the press event, the practitioner has to consider a variety of details. Menus for a luncheon or dinner should be chosen carefully. Do any of the guests have dietary restrictions? Has the exact hour of serving been arranged with the restaurant or caterer, to allow sufficient time for the program? The usual check on microphone and physical facilities is essential.

Even such a seemingly trivial item as a name tag requires the practitioner's careful attention. Paste-on tags written in advance are lined up on a check-in table at the entrance to the room. A host or hostess hands the tags to the arriving guests. A guest who can be welcomed by name, without having to state it, feels subtly flattered. Almost inevitably, though, some name tags will be unclaimed because individuals who accepted fail to show up. In a perfect world, absentees would telephone to cancel their acceptances, but public relations life doesn't work that way. Occasionally, an invited person who failed to answer the invitation will arrive unexpectedly; blank name tags should be kept available for such a situation. (Arrangements with the restaurant should include agreement on the percentage of meals ordered that can be canceled at the last moment without charge. Press kits should be sent to the absentees.)

Fouled-up transportation is perhaps the worst grief for a person conducting a press tour. Buses that fail to arrive at the departure point on time and incorrect booking on airliners irritate the guests and give tour managers gray hairs. Some guests may be prima donnas with inflated egos who will be dissatisfied with almost any hotel room assigned to them. None of the tour guests should be allowed to feel that others are receiving favored treatment. Booking and maintaining a firm tour schedule is essential. When stops are made, the host should specify their length, then begin to round up the strays a few minutes before departure time. Otherwise, the trip may bog down in confusion.

As much as possible, the tour host should ''walk through'' the entire route to confirm arrangements and look for possibly embarrassing hidden troubles. When North American Aviation introduced a new jet fighter to the national press at the Palmdale, California, airport in the Mojave desert, it asked the pilot to impress the guests by diving and creating a sonic boom. He did so—and pieces of glass went flying through the reception area from windows broken by the impact of the boom. The pilot climbed to do it again, but the public relations hosts stopped him in time by yelling into the radio, ''Call it off!''

THE INTERVIEW

Another widely used spoken method of publicizing an individual or a cause is the interview, which may appear in print form in newspapers and magazines or be transmitted electronically via television and radio. In both versions, the ability of the person being interviewed to communicate easily is essential to success. Although required to stay in the background during a client's interview, with fingers crossed that all goes well, a public relations specialist can do much to prepare the interviewee for the experience.

Andrew D. Gilman, president of CommCore in New York City, emphasizes the need for preparation. Said he: "I would no more think of putting a client on a witness stand or through a deposition without thorough and adequate presentation than I would ask a client to be interviewed by a skillful and well-prepared journalist without a similar thorough and adequate preparation."

Techniques for arranging interview appearances by clients are discussed in Chapter 12. This section will examine the steps the public relations representative can take to increase the odds for an effective performance.

In all interviews, the person being questioned should say something that will inform or entertain the audience. Otherwise, the public exposure is wasted. The practitioner should prepare the interviewee to meet this need. An adroit interviewer attempts to develop a theme in the conversation—to draw out comments that make a discernible point or illuminate the character of the person being interviewed. The latter can help the interviewer—and his or her own cause as well—by being ready to volunteer specific information, personal data, or opinions about the cause under discussion as soon as the conversational opportunity arises.

In setting up an interview, the public relations person should obtain from the interviewer an understanding as to its purpose. Armed with this information, the practitioner can assemble facts and data for the client to use in the discussion. The practitioner also can aid the client by providing tips about the interviewer's style and approach.

A significant difference exists between interviews in print and those on radio and television. In a print interview, the information and character impressions the public receives about the interviewee have been filtered through the mind of the writer. The man or woman interviewed is interpreted by the reporter, not projected directly to the audience. On radio and television, however, listeners hear the interviewee's voice without intervention by a third party. During a television interview, where personality has the strongest impact of all, the speaker is both seen and heard by the audience. Because of the intimacy of television, a person with a weak message who projects charm or authority on the air may influence an audience more than one with a strong message who does not project well. When a charismatic speaker is armed with a strong message, the impact can be enormous.

The following sections describe these two types of interview in detail.

When an organization or individual is advocating a particular cause or policy, opportunities to give newspaper interviews are welcomed, indeed sought after. Situations arise, however, when the better part of public relations wisdom is to reject a request for an interview, either print or electronic. Such rejection need not imply that an organization has a sinister secret or fails to understand the need for public contact.

For example, a corporation may be planning a fundamental operational change involving an increase in production at some plants and the closing of another, outdated facility. Details are incomplete and company employees have not been told. A reporter, either suspecting a change or by sheer chance, requests an interview with the company's chief executive officer.

Normally, the interview request would be welcomed, to give the executive public exposure and an opportunity to enunciate company philosophy. At this moment, however, public relations advisers fear that the reporter's questions might uncover the changes prematurely, or at least force the executive into evasive answers that might hurt the firm's credibility. So the interview request is declined, or delayed until a later date, as politely as possible. The next week, when all is in place, the chief executive announces the changes at a news conference. *Avoiding trouble is a hidden but vital part of a public relations adviser's role*. At a later time, the public relations representative might make a special effort to do the would-be interviewer a favor on a story, to remove any lingering feeling of having been slighted.

An alternative approach would be for the chief executive officer to grant the interview, with the understanding that only topics specified in advance would be discussed. Very rarely is such an approach acceptable, however, because reporters usually resent any restrictions and try to uncover the reasons for them.

The Print Interview An interview with a newspaper reporter may last about an hour, perhaps at lunch or over coffee in an informal setting. The result of this person-to-person talk may be a published story of perhaps 400 to 600 words. The interviewer chooses bits from the conversation, weaves them together in direct and indirect quotation form, works in background material, and perhaps injects personal observations about the interviewee. The latter has no control over what is published, beyond the self-control he or she exercises in answering the interviewer's questions. Neither the person being interviewed nor a public relations representative should ask to approve an interview story before it is published. Such requests are rebuffed automatically by newspapers as a form of censorship.

A talk with an entertainment personality is among the most common forms of newspaper interview. Many personality interview stories carrying Hollywood or New York datelines are proposed by practitioners endeavoring to build up a performer's image or to publicize a new motion picture or television series.

Excellent promotional results can be achieved in far less popular fields of endeavor than entertainment when the person interviewed has something unusual to offer. The following excerpt from an interview with a grower of kiwis demonstrates the point. Many readers, uncertain what kiwis are, would never guess that a man could become a millionaire by growing them. Notice how well prepared the grower was with quotable comments and pertinent facts about his unusual business. Publication of this San Francisco *Chronicle* interview was timed to the kiwi harvesting season; interest it created could be translated readily into purchases at the food store.

KIWI PIONEERS HAVE LAST LAUGH

When the three Tanimoto brothers planted their first acre of kiwi fruit 17 years ago, "we put it in back of our peach groves so people wouldn't laugh at us," recalled George Tanimoto.

"Everybody laughed anyway, and we laughed too," Tanimoto said last week. "Now they say he's laughing all the way to the bank and it's true."

Year after year, the Tanimoto brothers waited for a crop. Finally, in 1970—after 5 years of fruitless ridicule—the first fuzzy brown egg-shaped pods of kiwi appeared on their vines.

Tanimoto sold his maiden kiwi crop to Frieda Kaplan, a Los Angeles fruit dealer who happened to be allergic to kiwi. At first, he shipped the fruit south in three wooden boxes that looked suspiciously like coffins, then individually wrapped them in packages called "flats," because kiwis are very sensitive and will shrivel and shrink when exposed to gas fumes or other ripening fruit.

Today, the 56-year-old Tanimoto is a millionaire because he didn't quit on what he affectionately calls the "Ugly Fruit.". . .

This interview is not a direct hard-sell job, nor can it be described as outright "puffery." The purpose from the newspaper's point of view was to tell readers something interesting. From a public relations point of view, the story distributes knowledge of the product involved, with the possibility that this knowledge will stimulate purchases of the product.

Magazine interviews usually explore the subject in greater depth than those in newspapers, because the writer may have more space available. Most magazine interviews have the same format as those in newspapers. Others, such as those published in *Penthouse* and *U.S. News & World Report,* appear in question-and-answer form. These require prolonged questioning of the interviewee, sometimes at several tape-recorded sessions, by one or more writers and editors. During in-depth interviews, the person interviewed must be alert against letting down his or her guard and saying something that has unfortunate repercussions.

Such an instance occurred when Jimmy Carter was running for president against President Gerald Ford. Carter was a deeply religious man, a fact his public relations advisers emphasized by publicizing his work as a Sunday School teacher and lay preacher in a Southern Baptist church. When they sensed that these pursuits made Carter appear too sanctimonious to voters less religiously inclined, his advisers sought to have him offset this image by being interviewed in *Playboy*.

In the published interview Carter, although happily married, admitted that he had "looked upon a lot of women with lust" and "committed adultery in my heart many times." Angry reactions from his conservative followers were swift. He had besmirched their perceived image of him. Although this frank admission of a common enough male trait made Carter seem more "human" to some voters, overall the interview statements damaged his campaign. He was, of course, elected anyway.

A third, even more elaborate, form of magazine interview story is the long profile, such as those published in *The New Yorker*. Reporters doing profiles usually travel with the interviewee, observing the subject at close range over extended periods. Before trying to interest a magazine in doing such a profile on a client or employer, the public relations adviser should be satisfied that the intended subject of the profile is willing to accept the interviewer on an intimate basis for long periods and will wear well under close scrutiny. Outbursts of anger, a dictatorial manner toward assistants, excessive drinking, and similar private habits produce a bad effect when revealed in print. The profile when published might have a negative result instead of a positive one.

Radio and Television Interviews With more than 10,000 AM and FM radio stations operating in the United States, the possibilities for public relations people to have their clients interviewed on the air are immense. The current popularity of talk shows, both on local stations and syndicated satellite networks, provides many opportunities for on-air appearances in which the guest expresses opinions and answers call-in questions from listeners. Chapter 12 discussed the public relations opportunities radio and television provide. This discussion will be concerned with the preparation and techniques of on-the-air appearances.

A successful radio or television broadcast interview appearance has three principal requirements:

1. *Preparation.* Guests should know what they want to say.

2. *Concise speech.* Guests should answer questions and make statements precisely and briefly. They shouldn't hold forth in excessive detail or drag in extraneous material. Responses should be kept to 30 seconds or less, because seconds count on the air. The interviewer must conduct the program under severe time restrictions.

3. *Relaxation.* ''Mike fright'' is a common ailment for which no automatic cure exists. It will diminish, however, if the guest concentrates on talking to the interviewer in a casual person-to-person manner, forgetting the audience as much as possible. Guests should speak up firmly; the control room can cut down their volume if necessary. (Personal appearances on television are discussed in more detail in Chapter 24.)

A public relations adviser can help an interview guest on all of these points. Answers to anticipated questions may be worked out and polished during a mock interview in which the practitioner plays the role of broadcaster. If a tape recording or videotape can be made of a practice session, the guest-to-be will have an opportunity to correct weaknesses in manner and content that may be revealed.

All too often, the hosts on talk shows know little about their guests for the day's broadcast. The public relations adviser can overcome this difficulty by sending the host in advance a factsheet summarizing the important information and listing questions the broadcaster might wish to ask. On network shows like David Letterman's, nationally syndicated talk shows like Oprah Winfrey's, and local programs on metropolitan stations, support staffs do the preliminary work with guests. Interviewers on hundreds of smaller local television and radio stations, however, lack such staffs. They may go on the air almost ''cold'' unless provided with volunteered information.

Training business executives in speaking techniques, described earlier in the section on speechmaking, also helps to prepare them for broadcast appearances.

CONDUCTING A MEETING

Meetings are a major public relations tool in contemporary American life. They can be an extremely effective form of communication, or they can be incredible bores. Speakers who drone on too long and discussions that degenerate into petty quibbling act as soporifics on the audience. The hardness of chairs seems to increase by geometrical progression as the presiding officer introduces speaker after speaker. Collective attempts at mental telepathy by audience members urging the chairperson, ''Please, please, let us go home,'' never seem to work. Far from accomplishing a worthwhile purpose, such meetings alienate their audiences. Everyone's time is wasted.

Meetings held for public relations purposes take many forms and vary greatly in size. Sessions may be informational and friendly, they may be heated and controversial, or they may be largely formalized gatherings such as banquets and dedications. Within a company or an organization, they are held to explain and discuss policy, to plan programs, and to train employees. Half a dozen persons may participate, or more than a hundred. Whatever the size and form of a meeting, good planning and an alert presiding officer can assure that the meeting accomplishes its purpose without leaving participants glassy-eyed with fatigue.

A computer information magazine, *MIS,* estimated after a survey that 12 million meetings are held in North America every business day. The survey also reported that executives spend an average of 16 hours a week in meetings for a total of 21 weeks a year. Many of these meetings, called for informational purposes, could be avoided by distribution of the material in printed form.

Guidelines for Meetings Preparation and firmness discreetly applied can control the dynamics of a meeting. The program should move briskly toward a goal. Few people have ever been heard to complain that a meeting was too short. Participants should have a feeling of movement without the appearance of hurry. By following these 12 guidelines, the organizers and presiding officer can create an effective session:

1. If the meeting is open to the public, an audience should be built through distribution of news releases and through other forms of publicity such as posters and announcements at clubs.

2. An agenda should be made and followed.

3. The meeting should start promptly at the announced hour.

4. Speakers should be allotted specified amounts of time and urged to cooperate.

5. Physical arrangements of the hall should be checked in advance—acoustics, seating of the audience so that it is centered in front of the speakers, adequate lighting and fresh air, advance placement of visual aids, and the like.

6. If possible, the reading of minutes and reports should be avoided. Distribution of these documents in printed form is one way to solve this time-consuming problem.

7. Printed material should be distributed to an audience at the start or the close of a meeting, not while the session is in progress. The latter is distracting.

8. Discussion should be controlled even-handedly so that the audience has adequate opportunity to express itself but isn't allowed to wander from the theme. In a controversial situation, a time limit should be set on each speaker from the floor—5 minutes, perhaps—and enforced. When the discussion lags, it should be cut off. One or two verbose individuals should not be permitted to dominate a discussion.

9. In a panel discussion, the presiding officer should give all panel members equal opportunity to be heard. The moderator should try to distribute questions from the floor equitably among the panelists.

10. In long meetings such as a seminar or a training session, periodic recesses should be called; the meeting should resume promptly after the allotted time. A recess should be at least 10 minutes, 15 or 20 if the crowd is large. Comfortable chairs should be provided.

11. The meeting should be brought to a constructive conclusion. If there are several speakers, the best one should be scheduled last, if possible. At the end of a discussion, the presiding officer should summarize for the audience what was said. If a motion for action will be needed, arrangements may be made in advance for someone to offer it.

12. A closing time should be set and strictly adhered to, especially if it has been announced in advance.

AUDIO NEWS RELEASES

Another form of spoken public relations is the audio news release, sent to radio stations in ready-to-broadcast form. The following release distributed by the North American Precis Syndicate for Visa is typical.

At the top of the page, the release specifies how much air time the announcement will consume, information essential to a radio station.

108 words, 43 seconds

IF YOU HAD A MILLION. . .

What would you do if you suddenly found yourself with a credit card worth a million dollars? According to a recent survey, most people would buy a new car. The survey was taken by Visa U.S.A., which is offering a free million dollar card as the grand prize in its ''Our Treat'' sweepstakes. Every time you use a Visa card for the rest of the year, you've entered the contest. The instant millionaire will be randomly selected in January. You can also enter the sweepstakes by mailing in an entry. To learn the rules write Visa ''Our Treat'' Sweepstakes Rules, Post Office Box 8-5-4-0, Prospect Heights, Illinois 6-0-0-7-0.

WORD-OF-MOUTH

Often called ''interpersonal communication'' by academics, ''word-of-mouth'' is an ephemeral form of spoken communication difficult to isolate or measure but which has a major impact on the formation of public opinion. (See Chapters 9 and 11.)

Research shows that people seldom accept new ideas or products unless friends and relatives also endorse them. Studies also show that informal conversations among peers and friends influence our thinking and behavior more than television commercials or newspaper editorials do.

What people tell one another about a political candidate, a product, a play, or a movie often circumvents the multimillion-dollar expenditures of advertising and marketing experts. Critics may pan a movie, but if enough people report to friends that it is great and shouldn't be missed, it will be a box office success. Such was the case of the foreign film *The Gods Must Be Crazy,* which was a winner at the box office despite a lack of advertising and reviews and which later had a successful sequel. It is also noteworthy that this entertainment film, produced in South Africa, won international popularity despite sanctions against many South African products because of the government's apartheid policies.

Word-of-mouth is instrumental in making or breaking many products. The American automobile industry provides an example. The message traveled by word-of-mouth that imported cars were more reliable and better crafted than American cars. Despite massive advertising campaigns to change public perception, American automakers lost millions of buyers.

One study shows that a person dissatisfied with a product tells a minimum of 10 to 15 people about the experience; in turn, these people tell others in an ever-widening ripple effect that condemns the product. On the other hand, if word-of-mouth designates a product as "trendy," sales soar. The Mexican beer Corona, for example, gained national popularity with virtually no advertising or promotion.

THE INSIDIOUS PROBLEM OF RUMORS

Every professional communicator should understand how rumors start and, more important, how to combat them.

Simply stated, rumors are pieces of "information" that cannot be confirmed or verified by personal experience or a highly credible secondary source. They thrive when a combination of uncertainty and anxiety exists and authentic, official information is lacking or incomplete.

When a company's future is in doubt because of a takeover or merger, employees invariably start a number of rumors about layoffs. The same thing occurs when information is released that the company had a bad fiscal year. The rumors will persist until official information confirms them ("Yes, there will be layoffs") or denies them ("No layoffs are planned"). The key is whether employees trust management to tell the truth. If trust is low, even company announcements may not curtail or kill the rumor.

A rumor has kept circulating in Europe, especially in France, that ten popular brands of food products, including Coca-Cola and Cadbury-Schweppes, are carcinogenic. The rumor began in 1976 in an anonymous leaflet that cited research at a certain hospital. Although the hospital issued repeated denials, the rumor continued to circulate by word-of-mouth and was printed in local publications and newsletters.

Researchers found a significant impact from the pamphlet among homemakers in one neighborhood where the leaflet was circulated. About 70 percent of them had further disseminated the rumor, and 19 percent admitted avoiding certain products after reading the leaflet. Sociologists attributed the persistence of the rumor to widespread distrust of modern food technology, including the use of additives.

James Esposito and Ralph Rosnow, writing in *Management Review,* give four strategies for defusing rumors in a company:

1. *Keep employees informed.* Employees are especially sensitive about situations that may affect them directly, such as management–union relations, job advancement, opportunities for relocation, and potential layoffs. Be fully honest, because half-truths encourage additional rumors and destroy the credibility of official spokespersons.

2. *Pay attention to rumors.* If the source of employee anxiety can be determined, the underlying cause of the rumors is obvious. Then, by giving feedback to employees—

letting them know how the situation is being dealt with—their fears should be allayed and the prospect of future rumors reduced.

3. *Act promptly*. Rumors become more difficult to control as they harden with time. Get the facts out rapidly but don't repeat a false rumor, because repetition may foster belief. If the rumor is true, it must be confirmed.

4. *Educate personnel*. Actually, conducting a workshop on rumors and their destructive potential can help to stop rumors before they get started. This is especially true when a situation arousing anxiety arises, such as a new boss.

External rumors are more difficult to control, and they can have a devastating effect on a company or its products. A bank in New York City's Chinatown experienced a large outflow of deposits because of a rumor that the bank was in financial trouble. When Johnny Carson did a joke about a supposed toilet-paper shortage, people rushed to the supermarket to stock up. Long lines at the bank and empty shelves at the supermarket tended to reinforce the rumors.

PROCTER & GAMBLE FIGHTS A RUMOR

Despite elaborate efforts to disprove the lie, Procter & Gamble continues to be plagued by a malicious, damaging rumor that it promotes devil worship.

The falsehood is based in part on the soap and food company's circular trademark, which shows a man-in-the-moon face in profile, looking at a field of stars representing the original American colonies. Rumormongers claim that this represents Satan.

Anonymous pamphlets distributed in schools and churches are the chief source of the rumor. They claim that a P & G executive appeared on a nationally televised talk show and pledged the company's profits to the Church of Satan.

The rumor became so intense in 1982 that the company received 15,000 calls in one month about it.

Procter & Gamble struck back with statements from the talk show producers that no P & G executive had ever appeared on their programs, and letters of support from ministers. As a last report, it filed suits against a dozen persons it identified as rumormongers and won judgments against all of them, ordering them to cease.

Throughout the 1980s the rumor kept breaking out—on the East Coast, in the South, the Pacific Northwest, and Indiana. In the early 1990s it surfaced again, in the Southeast and Chicago.

The company immediately mailed "truth packets" to hundreds of churches, schools, newspapers, and radio stations in those areas. These included testimonials for it from the Revs. Jerry Falwell and Billy Graham.

Yet the rumor rolls on. During 1990, the company received about 350 calls a day about it. Altogether, P & G had handled much more than 100,000 phone calls concerning the rumor.

In 1991 the company won its first damage award—$75,000—from a couple found guilty of spreading the rumor. It also slightly revised the trademark.

TIPS ON COMBATING RUMORS

Here are general guidelines for combating rumors:

1. Analyze the nature and impact of the rumor before taking corrective action. Many rumors are relatively harmless and dissipate within a short time.

2. Attempt to track the cause of the rumor and the geographical locations where it is prominent. This will help determine whether the rumor should be dealt with on a local, state, or national level.

3. Compile complete, authentic information that will either refute or confirm the rumor.

4. When denying a rumor, avoid repeating it more than necessary.

5. Use outside experts and credible public agencies to refute the rumor. The public views the U.S. Food and Drug Administration as more trustworthy than the president of a company defending the firm's product. If the rumor is only among certain highly identifiable groups, enlist the support of the groups' leaders.

Rumors that cannot be tracked to any particular cause are more difficult to deal with. McDonald's had to cope with a rumor that its ground beef contained earthworms as a protein supplement, and General Mills had to contend with the rumor that its Pop Rocks candy was explosive.

Little evidence exists to support the suspicion by many people that rumors are started by commercial competitors. Instead, social psychologist Frederick Koening says, "Rumors validate the world view of those who believe them. If you believe in Satan—and many people do—you're likely to welcome a rumor that he's alive and well in Akron, Ohio."

People spread rumors by word-of-mouth for a number of reasons: (1) they are advocates of conspiracy theories and distrust all institutions of society; (2) they feel victimized by a complex, uncaring society and have high anxiety; (3) they seek recognition from peers by claiming to have "inside" information; and (4) they find the rumor somewhat plausible.

The environmental context is also a major factor. The run on the New York bank began shortly after the bank was closed for Election Day and newspaper articles had appeared about the failures of banks in Hong Kong. Many depositors, ethnic Chinese, put these facts together and reached the wrong conclusion.

Another example of environmental context is the continuing recall of products from the American marketplace. People increasingly express anxiety about the general safety of food products they are consuming, and from there it is only a short step to rumors about a particular product.

MEASURING THE EFFECTS OF WORD-OF-MOUTH COMMUNICATION

Although efforts to measure the specific effects of word-of-mouth communication have been relatively few, and of minor value, the Coca-Cola Company did obtain enlightening information from a study it sponsored concerning public reaction to its handling of consumer complaints.

Questionnaires were sent to hundreds of persons who had filed complaints with Coca-Cola's consumer affairs department. Responses showed that individuals who felt that their complaints had not been resolved satisfactorily told a median of nine to ten persons about their negative experience. Those who were completely satisfied told a median of four to five persons about their good results—a word-of-mouth distribution of bad news over good by a ratio of approximately two to one. Nearly 30 percent of those who felt that their complaints had not been resolved satisfactorily said they no longer bought Coca-Cola products. On the other hand, nearly 10 percent of the satisfied complainers reported that they now bought more Coca-Cola products as a result of the good treatment. Two lessons for companies trying to preserve a favorable image with customers emerge from this survey:

1. The best service possible should be given so that complaints are held to a minimum.

2. Complaints should be handled promptly and thoroughly, so that customers feel the company really cares about them. Not only may unhappy customers become noncustomers, but their word-of-mouth criticism may drive away other potential purchasers—how many, no one ever knows. As an example, an eight-year-old girl sued the makers of Crackerjack because she didn't find a prize in a box she purchased. She had written to the company about the mistake, but it failed to answer the letter. The lawsuit she brought gave the company bad nationwide publicity.

CASE PROBLEM

The national headquarters of Continental Oil Company is in Los Angeles. For the past month, a false rumor has been circulating that the company will move its headquarters to Houston. In fact, plans are on the drawing board for a new, larger headquarters building in Los Angeles.

The rumor probably started because the company had a managers' conference in Houston several months ago. This was rumored to be a high-level meeting to take a look at Houston real estate and decide on a site for the new headquarters. The rumor is beginning to affect employee morale in Los Angeles.

The president of Continental Oil, upon the advice of public relations counsel, decides to put the rumor to rest in a speech at the annual employee recognition banquet next week. You are assigned to write the ten-minute speech for the president.

Would you include in the speech a direct reference to the rumor? Would you take the opportunity to ridicule the rumor? Write a draft of the speech for the president.

QUESTIONS FOR REVIEW AND DISCUSSION

1. List three tasks a public relations representative should perform when preparing for and making a face-to-face presentation to an editor.

2. How many themes should a speech have?

3. What are some key building blocks a writer uses in constructing a speech?

4. Which type of sentence structure should a speechwriter use? Explain your answer.

5. Why do companies sometimes use fellow workers rather than high executives to address audiences of employees?

6. How should a company executive prepare to hold a news conference?

7. Should a spokesperson speak off the record at a news conference? Why or why not?

8. What might a corporate host hope to accomplish by holding a press luncheon instead of a morning news conference?

9. How can a public relations representative help a client prepare for a television interview?

10. A company may be harassed by malicious rumors about its policies. If it decided to strike back, how might it do so?

SUGGESTED READINGS

Ailes, Roger. *You Are the Message: Secrets of the Master Communicators.* New York, Dow Jones-Irwin, 1987.

Burns, Robert E. "Combating Speech Anxiety." *Public Relations Journal,* March 1991, pp. 28, 30.

Cone, Russ. "Reporter Interviews Media Trainers." *Communication World,* January 1987, pp. 32–35.

DeVito, Joseph A. *Messages: Building Interpersonal Communication Skills.* New York: HarperCollins, 1990.

Gildea, Robert L. "Speaker, Writer—Let the Twain Meet." *Public Relations Quarterly,* Summer 1988, pp. 21–22.

Klepper, Michael. "What Are You Talking About?" *Communication World,* October 1990, pp. 20–22. Organizing a speech.

Newman, Joyce. "Speaker Training: Twenty-Five Experts on Substance and Style." *Public Relations Quarterly,* Summer 1988, pp. 15–20.

Sheldon, Keith A. ''Build Bridges with a Multilingual Speaker's Bureau.'' *Communication World,* August 1990, pp. 21–23.

Sklarewitz, Norman. ''Press Junkets: Sound Marketing Method or Boondoggle?'' *Communication World,* February 1988, pp. 32–35.

Solomon, Jolie. ''Executives Who Dread Public Speaking Learn to Keep Their Cool in the Spotlight.'' *Wall Street Journal,* May 4, 1990, p. B1.

Spalding, Jeannette. ''Speech Writers in the Thick of It.'' *Communication World,* October 1990, pp. 23–27.

''Survey: CEO Speechwriters' Median Salary Is $75,000.'' *Public Relations Journal,* February 1990, p. 12.

Swasy, Alecia. ''P&G Once Again Has Devil of a Time with Firm's Logo.'' *Wall Street Journal,* March 26, 1990, p. B3. Rumor control.

Tarver, Jerry, and Geigel, Sara. ''It Is with Great Pleasure That I Introduce . . .'' *Communication World,* June 1988, pp. 30–32. How to introduce a speaker.

Winter, Grant. ''Improving Broadcast News Conferences.'' *Public Relations Journal,* July 1990, pp. 25–26.

''Writing Speeches with Impact.'' *Public Relations Journal,* September 1990, pp. 31–33. Using statistics and visuals.

CHAPTER

Visual Tactics

The third major form of public relations communication is *visual,* in which the message is delivered to the recipient through the eye by fixed or moving images. Frequently, the form is *audiovisual,* when sound accompanies the visual message.

This chapter examines the visual and audiovisual methods. Television is the most pervasive, because virtually every home in the United States and Canada has at least one television set. With the swift growth of cable television and transmission by satellite, the possibilities of television as a public relations tool are proliferating.

Motion pictures are another method with many applications; so are videotapes. Generally grouped under the term *audiovisual aids*—still images for projection—are slides and filmstrips, usually with live or recorded narration. Still photography delivers public relations messages in the print media. Outdoor displays and corporate design are other forms of visual but silent communication.

TELEVISION

The human eye is a magnificent channel for communication, carrying messages to the brain at astounding speeds, often so subtly that the recipient is not consciously aware of absorbing them. These images are stored in the brain, combining with the intake of audible and tactile impressions to help form opinions, trigger decisions, and generate actions. Since these are the goals of public relations, the role of visual communication in public relations practice obviously is vital.

Television is the dominant form of visual communication in contemporary life.

Early in the 1990s, the Nielson survey reported that the average American family had its TV set turned on slightly more than seven hours a day.

Chapter 12 examined how the television industry is organized and listed ways in which public relations practitioners can use television to advance their causes. This chapter will look more closely at techniques employed for this purpose and will discuss the growing use of television for internal corporate communication.

NEWS RELEASES

Practitioners can provide news releases to television stations in several ways, ranging from a simple sheet of paper to an expensively produced videotaped story ready to go on the air. The type of news material, the time factor, and the originator's budget will determine which method is best for each story.

The Printed News Release Identical to that sent to newspapers, the so-called handout frequently is sufficient (see Chapter 22). If the news director or assignment editor at a station judges the material to be newsworthy, a staff member is assigned to handle the story, rewriting it briefly in television style or, if the material justifies, going to the scene with a camera crew to obtain visual support for the facts. When a television reporter and crew come on assignment in response to a news release, the public relations practitioner who sent out the release should do everything possible to assist them, such as providing an authoritative spokesperson who will appear on camera to state the facts and answer questions, and helping to arrange other shots the reporter and photographer may request.

A fundamental difference between a news story on television and one in a newspaper is *motion*. Stories that can be illustrated easily and effectively often will receive more air time than ones that cannot. The rule for a practitioner trying to place a news story on television is: *think pictures!* The representative never should tell a reporter and photographer what pictures to shoot or what questions to ask but may discreetly suggest possible picture and story angles.

The other primary factor in television news coverage is *brevity*. A story that runs 400 words in a newspaper may be reported in only two or three sentences in a newscast. If a television crew spends an hour shooting a story with a practitioner's help, and the story then receives 30 seconds or less of air time, the inexperienced public relations representative may feel let down. All that work, with such a brief result! As any veteran will advise, however, there is no reason for disappointment. The impact of even a very brief item on a popular newscast can be heavy.

The Prepared Script This second, more elaborate, form of television news release is accompanied by one to four slides to illustrate the text. In this method, the public relations representative does most of the television news department's work on the story. Smaller stations with limited news staffs may be especially willing to air such ready-to-use material if it is newsworthy, perhaps even if only marginally so. In preparing scripted news releases, the writer should avoid terminology that sounds like advertising or ''puff'' publicity. Graphics created by computers can be used effectively in news releases (see Figure 24.1).

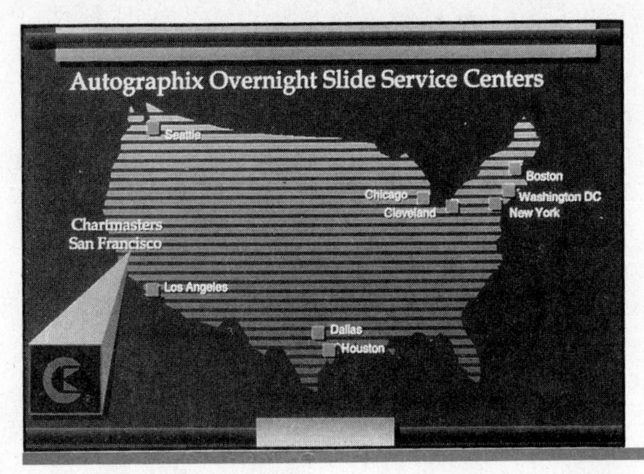

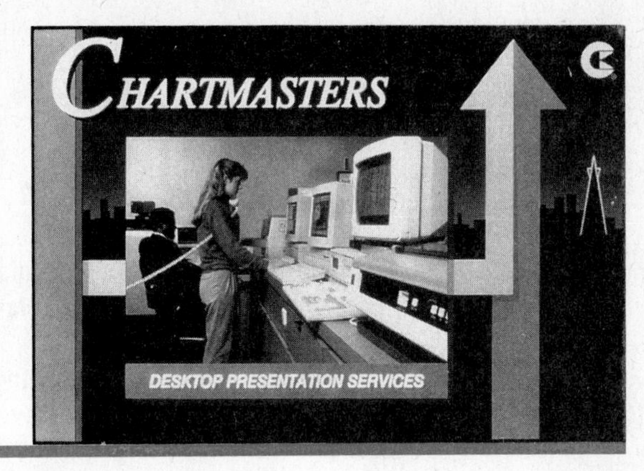

FIGURE 24.1
Colorful computer graphics deliver information effectively and add visual impact to news releases for television. (Graphics courtesy of Chartmasters.)

For a fee, specialist commercial firms will prepare a news release script with slides from a practitioner's material, send the script to television stations, and report on the use they made of it.

Videotaped excerpts from local speeches made by the practitioner's client, delivered to a television station along with a written news release explaining the circumstances in which the speech was made, may be used in the station's newscasts if the content is significant or provocative. Prospects for use of the material are improved if it is delivered quickly after the event for same-day use.

The Videotaped News Release The most elaborate and expensive form of news delivery to television stations is the videotaped news release (VNR). This ready-to-use report prepared by a public relations organization presents news about a product, a service, or an idea, usually in featurized style. In its most highly developed form, the videotaped news release may cost $10,000 to $30,000 to produce and distribute. Location shots by film crews and other production work resemble that done for television commercials.

Several factors should be considered before an organization commits that much money to a news release. Is the story sufficiently newsworthy, so that many of the stations receiving the release probably will put it on the air? Can the story be told well visually? Does the producer have sufficient time to prepare the release? As much as six weeks may be needed to create an outline, shoot the videotape, edit the release, and distribute it. Visual footage for use in videotaped releases often may be obtained from government and commercial archives to supplement freshly shot footage.

Michael Klepper, chairman of a marketing company, writing in the *Wall Street Journal,* listed several factors to be considered in deciding whether to produce a videotaped news release:

- The corporation/organization should be involved in a legitimate medical, health, or scientific breakthrough.

- Visual material can be provided that the television stations cannot obtain on their own.
- The VNR contains an interview segment that television stations cannot get on their own.

He described how a company obtained mass exposure for a new talking doll by producing a release about the history of artificial voice synthesis, using the doll as an example of the technology. Television news directors liked the release because it was slanted to new technology.

Similarly, Visa U.S.A. gained a wide audience with a video news release describing the conceptual research involved in designing a super Visa card with a built-in computer chip and keyboard.

In producing videotaped news releases, the sponsoring organizations must present the material as *news*. Advertising sales-pitch techniques should be scrupulously avoided; so should glorifying adjectives. The benefit to the producing organization is indirect, by making known to the public the existence of the service, the idea, or the product. Sales efforts must be handled separately. If stations receiving the release view it as an obvious attempt to obtain free advertising, they will throw it away.

Ethical Problems in Use of VNRs. Although often cleverly produced to look like neutral news stories at first glance, most video news releases are designed to present the sponsoring company's story in a favorable light, subtly or more obviously.

This fact makes many television news directors, especially those at the networks and large stations, reluctant to use VNRs. They are particularly wary of any VNR in which a narrator's voice reading a script prepared by the sponsor is attached to the visual portion in such a way that the script cannot be edited.

Ethical responsibility for the airing of video news releases lies equally with those who produce the VNRs and the television stations that run them.

Public relations people should label the source of the material and make certain that the facts are neither inaccurate nor misleading. Leading public relations firms emphasize that they clearly identify sponsors of their releases sent to TV stations.

The stations in turn should tell their viewers the source of a video news release. Too many stations that use VNRs, especially those with small staffs, fail to meet this responsibility. They run the tapes unedited and attempt to give viewers the impression that their own staff reporters have created the stories. Cable systems often are frequent users of VNRs.

Television stations with high editing standards normally use staff announcers, reading staff-prepared scripts, when they broadcast part or all of a VNR's visual portion. Knowing this, astute makers of VNRs send a printed script or a list of story points, which the station can rewrite to its own taste, along with unedited visual footage (known as *B-roll footage*) from which the station can choose what it desires. The easier VNR sponsors make it for stations to exercise editorial control, the greater the likelihood that a VNR will get on the air.

An expanded form of VNR, called an *infomercial* or *advertorial,* is a lengthy presentation made to look like an editorial examination of a topic when in reality it is a sales pitch for a product or service. Such programs often turn up on the screen in the after-midnight hours.

NEWS ON CABLE TELEVISION

Newscasts on cable television provide fresh opportunities for public relations exposure. Innovative practitioners can find ways to place their news stories before cable-viewing audiences in addition to viewers of the over-the-air television stations and networks.

Numerous newspapers have obtained local cable channels on which they produce newscasts, using their own staff-gathered material as resources. Videotaped news releases, as described above, have a possibility of receiving air time on these newscasts. Using satellite distribution, nationwide superstations such as WTBS-TV in Atlanta and WGN-TV in Chicago, and networks such as Cable News Network, reach large numbers of cable viewers from coast to coast. These outlets are worthwhile targets for the public relations practitioner.

PERSONAL APPEARANCES ON TELEVISION

Anyone invited to appear on television in a talk show or for an interview should prepare for the occasion. The beaming red light of a television camera aimed at a guest, indicating that he or she is on the air, can have a terrifying effect on an inexperienced performer. The throat goes dry. The words won't come out. The guest projects discomfort and uncertainty to thousands of viewers, precisely the opposite of the effect desired. A valuable opportunity is wasted.

Public relations practitioners can help their clients avoid this unpleasantness by coaching them in what to say and how to behave. Playing the role of interviewer in practice sessions, the coach can rehearse the guest by asking anticipated questions. If the subject matter is controversial, the practitioner should fire antagonistic questions to test the guest's mettle. As much as possible, the guest's prepared responses should be honed down to 30 seconds or less. (Preparation for appearances on television is discussed in Chapter 23).

In general, guests on television should dress conservatively. On most shows a business suit is appropriate for men; for women, a suit or dress of simple pattern without conspicuous ornamentation. White clothing, including shirts, should be avoided, as should metallic decorations—all might reflect studio lights. On shows featuring entertainers and sports figures, dress is more informal, to the point of conspicuous casualness. By watching a show in advance or asking production personnel, the public relations person can advise a client how to dress suitably for the appearance.

Professional coaches who prepare guests for television appearances make these suggestions for their personal conduct:

- *Use of gestures*. The guest should create movement for the camera, even though seated, by changing facial expressions and by moving the hands, arms, head, and shoulders to emphasize points. Potential guests can observe these tricks by watching professional actors on talk shows.

- *Use of eye contact*. The guest should look at the interviewer, as in a private conversation. If the camera is focused directly at the guest, he or she should talk to it. The trick is to think of the camera eye not as an electronic device but as another person whom the speaker is trying to inform or convince.

Madonna, with her audacious costumes and energetic singing style, is an exception to the rule that guests on television should dress conservatively. (Reuters/Bettmann)

- *Proper placement of the body*. Persons being interviewed should not cross their legs; the position is awkward. It is better to sit with one foot in front of the other. Leaning forward in the chair makes a person appear more aggressive. Keeping the hands apart allows the guest to use them for gesturing. Guests also should be coached to mention key points about the event or product several times.

TELEVISION FOR RESTRICTED AUDIENCES

Television can be used to tell a story to the general public through news releases and personal on-the-air appearances. This is the external face of the medium, aimed at viewers who choose their programs by flicking the dial from channel to channel. Less well known, but growing enormously, is use of television to reach controlled private audiences in selected locations without having the program content seen by the general public.

The uses of *closed-ciruit television,* tremendously enlarged by development of satellite transmission, are multiplying. Corporations employ it to deliver information and training material to their employees, to conduct sales meetings, to present financial information to securities analysts and shareholders, to show the proceedings of their annual meetings, and to hold long-distance news conferences. Surgeons, engineers, and other professional groups employ television to discuss technical developments and to solve problems.

BUSINESS USES OF VIDEOTAPE

As described in Chapter 21, videotape has become a communication method of great importance. Its flexibility and low cost enable commercial firms and nonprofit organizations to deliver their messages visually to internal and external audiences in ways that never were feasible before the tape technique was created.

A few examples:

- Levi Strauss, clothing manufacturer, had its executives masquerade as Batman, Superman, David Letterman, and Jeopardy! game contestants in company videos to give financial and performance results.
- Vantage Travel in Massachusetts offered as a gift to customers a ten-minute video of a tour to Australia and New Zealand, which it described as "an electronic travel brochure."
- The Atlanta delegation used videos and computer graphics in the presentation that won the city the right to hold the 1996 Summer Olympic Games.
- Louisiana State University raised money for its athletic program with a video, sold commercially, in which a quartet consisting of the governor of Louisiana, a former governor, and two LSU coaches sang four LSU songs about football and basketball.

Following are descriptions of several videotape techniques used by corporations for sales and informational purposes.

WEST COAST UTILITY EXPANDS USE OF VIDEO

Pacific Gas & Electric Company, PG&E, with headquartters in San Francisco, is increasingly making video its major tool of communications. In 1976 the company's video capabilities included just two cameras and one employee. Today the company uses 31 employees and about $2 million of equipment fo this purpose.

PG&E now produces more than 100 video programs annually; many of them are geared to informing its employees at 350 locations throughout northern California. Every Pacific Gas & Electric Company facility of nine or more employees has at least one VCR and one tape recorder. In addition, the company's video center tapes more than 4000 hours of locally broadcast television news and information programs to monitor the tone and substance of news coverage about the company.

The company anticipates using fiber optics and satellite soon to transmit signals live throughout most of its system.

VIDEOTAPED FINANCIAL REPORTS

Corporations increasingly are putting their financial information onto videotape for showing to shareholders and securities analysts. Videotaping of annual meetings is one aspect of this trend. Specially prepared reports with graphs and other visual aids also are taped.

Distribution of videotaped material needs as much attention as preparation of the content. Videocassettes may be mailed to brokers and other financial specialists for their individual viewing. Perhaps more effective is a personal showing of the videotaped material by a company executive to groups of invited guests, who can ask questions after viewing the tape. Another method is to invite interested investors and brokers to request a loan copy of the videotape.

INTERNAL CORPORATE TV NEWS PROGRAMS

Large corporations with thousands of employees scattered in many locations keep hunting for ways to give their employees a sense of company pride and common purpose. Among the print media, company newspapers and magazines have that goal. The audiovisual equivalent is the corporate television news program.

Such programs need a strong professional touch in production: hence, they are expensive to create. They should have a well-defined formula for content. Management-oriented material should be presented discreetly in news style. The techniques of brevity, visual story-telling, human interest, and touches of humor that mark a successful commercial television newscast need to be applied to a corporate news program—not an easy task. Television consultant firms may be employed to produce the program or to provide technical assistance.

Showing of these programs to employees on a voluntary basis is done at lunch hours or other convenient times. Videotape cassettes of the shows can be distributed to sales and other employees working in the field. Playing the programs on cable television in cities where corporate plants are located is another possibility.

VIDEOTAPED TRAINING AND MARKETING PROGRAMS

An estimated $3 billion is being spent annually on employee video programs in the 1990s, according to the American Society for Training and Development. The flexibility and economy of videotape makes it an ideal vehicle for training employees and updating their work skills.

VIDEOTAPED SALES MESSAGES

A recent development as the electronic revolution changes publicity methods is distribution of sales messages on tape to selected potential customers. *Videocassettes* are mailed upon request to prospective buyers who can play these illustrated sales messages on home recorders. A stamped, self-addressed envelope for return of the cassettes to the firm may be included. Because of the costs involved, this method is used primarily for higher-priced items, by companies selling direct to the consumer rather than through retail outlets.

Looking into the future, some electronics enthusiasts predict that a prospective purchaser, after seeing an item advertised, will be able to dial a toll-free number on a home telecomputer, watch the sales demonstration on the home television screen, and order the item by pushing the proper button on the computer terminal. Payment for the item will be drawn by computer from the customer's bank account. Whether or not future sales methods follow this precise line, the use of electronic demonstration and selling inevitably will grow. Meanwhile, home-shopping channels on cable TV offer a similar service.

HOME VIDEO

More than 50 percent of American families now have videocassette recorders (VCRs) with which they record television shows or view rented or purchased movies. A Newspaper Advertising Bureau study showed that VCR owners rented an average of 108 movies a year while the average American visited a movie theater only five times annually.

Taking advantage of this viewing potential, a growing number of organizations and companies now use videotape to reach key audiences.

In politics, candidates and groups use videotapes as today's ''high-tech leaflet.'' A Massachusetts congressional candidate distributed a 15-minute videotape of himself for campaign workers to show in voters' homes. In Orinda, a community across the bay from San Francisco, pro-incorporation forces produced a videotape on the advantages of being a city, for showing at neighborhood meetings and in homes. The incorporation measure passed, and the city's first mayor credited the videotape as a major factor in the victory.

Increasingly, employees can check out videotapes of company-produced materials from the corporate video news magazine to view such material as an explanation of the new health benefits. This gives the company an opportunity to communicate with the employee's family. Stockholders are routinely offered videotape cassettes reporting on company affairs.

On another level, a corporation may subsidize production of a videotape to be sold to the public at a nominal charge. The Red Lobster seafood chain, for example, underwrote a videotape featuring quick recipes taken from *Bon Appetit* magazine's column ''Too Busy to Cook.'' The informative video sold for $19.95; Red Lobster created goodwill and was able to show its restaurant settings. Instructive tapes on health and similar topics, frequently underwritten by corporations, are loaned rent-free at some video stores.

MOTION PICTURES

Hollywood commercial feature films viewed by millions of customers in theaters constitute only a fraction of the films produced in the United States and Canada every year. Hundreds of motion pictures, often equal in quality to theatrical films, are made annually by sponsors for showing to selected audiences. Only a handful of these ever will appear on commercial theater screens, and then only as supporting films on programs of mass market entertainment.

Sponsored films have a major role in public relations work, as noted in Chapter 12. Designed to inform, instruct, and persuade, often subtly, they play to a huge cumulative audience. Unlike commercial films, most of them are shown to viewers without charge. The makers of these films, and in some instances the organizations showing them, bear the cost in order to further their purposes directly or indirectly.

Public relations practitioners can make use of mass market entertainment motion pictures and, more important, of sponsored nontheatrical films.

HOLLYWOOD ENTERTAINMENT FILMS

Moviegoers are frequently exposed to publicity projects in the films they watch, although they rarely are aware of it. Public relations specialists who arrange mentions of their clients' products or causes in movies obtain high visibility because Hollywood motion pictures often are seen by millions of viewers (see Chapter 20).

Such mentions dropped into the middle of the story line are not accidental. They are arranged by negotiations between public relations specialists and the film's producer, in which the filmmaker receives payment in money or services. The show business weekly *Variety* calls the practice "product *pluggola*."

Some recent examples:

- *In Teenage Mutant Ninja Turtles* when the heroes eat pizza, it is clearly indentified as Domino's Pizza, and they receive a Domino's discount for late delivery. The pizza company paid a high price for the exposure.
- In *Baby Boom,* the disposable diapers used are clearly identified as Huggies.
- The Disney Company sent letters to manufacturers offering placements in its film *Mr. Destiny* for prices ranging from $20,000 to $60,000—the lower price if the product were just shown, the higher price if an actor actually used it.

Benefits of such appearances often are difficult to evalute in terms of sales, but product exposure even at high prices is regarded as a bargain for participants if the film proves to be a hit. When E.T., the lonesome waif from space, ate Reese's Pieces in *E.T., The Extra-Terrestrial* the makers of that candy, Hershey Food Company, reported a 65 percent increase in sales of the brand.

SPONSORED FILMS AND VIDEOS

The range of films and videos made to be shown free of charge, or to be rented or purchased for showing to external audiences, is immense. A well-produced film or video, with minimal commercial emphasis, is an excellent way for companies and organizations to reach members of school, church, social, cultural, professional, and business groups.

Sponsored films and videos, despite their expense, serve several public relations purposes. They can (1) inform audiences about a topic of educational interest, (2) create understanding of a company or organization's activities, and (3) generate goodwill and name recognition among important audiences. Charms Candy, for example, reached an important audience, schoolchildren, by producing a film on school-bus safety that school administrators often show in school assemblies.

Cable television is another important outlet for sponsored films. Consumer education films and videos in which the company's commercial message is reduced to perhaps just the opening and closing credit lines find widespread acceptance by cable operators who need to fill broadcast time at minimal expense.

Production of sponsored films and videos, also called *industrial films,* is a substantial industry involving an estimated 600 firms around the world. Their filming techniques and equipment in many instances are highly advanced and on a par with any Hollywood or television network studio. Indeed, potential viewers are so accustomed to professional television that even a company's training film cannot be amateurish.

Motion pictures are produced in four sizes, from 70 millimeter down to 8 millimeter. The Hollywood-type entertainment picture usually is made on 35-millimeter film for large-screen projection in theaters. Some sponsored films are 35 millimeter, but the majority are produced on 16-millimeter width, the format of the standard movie projector used in classrooms. Increasingly companies are also making films available in video format, and it is often difficult to determine whether a production was originally produced on motion picture film or videotape.

A limiting factor on use of videotape is the projection method. Unless a large group meeting place is equipped with a large television screen or multiple television monitors, viewing is difficult. School-assembly or service-club rooms rarely have large television monitors. And even if the group is small enough for a standard television monitor, there is the problem of standardization in tape size and equipment. Some players take ½-inch tape, others take ¾-inch; the Beta and VHS cassettes are incompatible, with VHS the more popular form. Although the availability of playback equipment is improving, the standard movie projector is still the workhorse in classrooms and small membership organizations. Recently TV monitors have been installed in many classrooms by Whittle Communications and cable TV systems so students can watch their programs.

The length of sponsored films and videos varies greatly. A survey by Modern Talking Picture Service, however, shows a strong audience preference for films 21 to 30 minutes in length. But there are exceptions. "Where's the Cap'n?" is a four-minute music video sponsored by the Quaker Oats Company to develop awareness among children 6 to 12 years old about a cereal promotion. The video was used on nationally and locally produced video music programs, reaching an estimated audience of 7.9 million viewers.

At the other end of the spectrum, Pepsi-Cola sponsored a 40-minute film titled *Amber Lights* that received widespread acclaim as a high-school assembly program. It combined popular film clips and music in an MTV format to address the No. 1 killer of teenagers in the United States—drunk drivers. The company estimates that 3 million teenagers saw the film during one school year.

A Corporate-Image Film Bechtel Corporation's *Jungle Gold* depicts the company's gold-mining operations in New Guinea. The film discusses a school and a hospital built there by Bechtel and reflects the company's interest in showing that private-sector initiatives can be catalysts in developing countries.

A Government Social-Problem Film The Utah Department of Health produced a frank film about a serious social problem. *If You Want to Dance . . .* concerns an unwed teenage couple faced with the consequences of an unplanned pregnancy. Candid but constructive, the 14-minute film opens with a locker-room scene in which three high school boys talk about sex, then shifts to a hospital room where two pregnant unwed teenage girls discuss their problems. Much praised, the film has been widely shown to high school classes, church groups, and community organizations. A discussion guide is distributed with the film, which is available for loan or purchase on both 16-millimeter film and ¾-inch videocassette.

STILL IMAGES FOR PROJECTION

Slides, filmstrips, and transparencies—all of them methods for projecting still images onto a screen—often are referred to as *audiovisual aids*. Properly, the word *audiovisual* encompasses all forms of sound-and-picture projection, including motion pictures, but in practice it frequently is applied only to these simpler forms. Inclusion of such visual aids in programs stimulates audiences.

Audiovisual aids are much cheaper than motion pictures and videotapes and have simple projection requirements. All that is needed are a relatively inexpensive slide projector, an electrical outlet, and a small screen. A presentation of still images accompanied by live or recorded narration often is the most efficient method for bringing a message to a small audience. Public relations practitioners find scores of uses for such presentations.

SLIDE SHOWS

Slide presentations range upward from Uncle Chester showing the dinner guests slides he made during his trip to Europe—usually too many and occasionally upside-down—to the projection of intricate triple-screen, three-dimensional productions issued by some corporations.

For his performance before the captive audience in the living room, Uncle Chester selects the slides he likes best and delivers a rambling ad-lib narration about them as they flash on the screen. This is the exact opposite of the way a professional slide show should be constructed.

A slide show should be built on a well-defined theme, to tell a story and deliver a message. The script should be written and approved first, then the visual elements should be developed to illustrate and emphasize points in the script. Standard technique is for a visually oriented person to study the script, marking places in it that lend themselves to illustration by photograph or drawing. An artist then creates rough storyboards, indicating the illustration perceived for each point. More detailed and refined storyboards may be developed in subsequent story conferences. Photographer and artist go to work, producing 35-millimeter slides that meet the requirements of the storyboards. Slides and motion picture film can be coordinated.

Depending on its purpose, a slide show might consist of photographs, as in a program made by a state tourist board to publicize the scenic attractions of the state.

VISUAL AIDS IMPROVE MEETING RESULTS

Speakers who use visual aids such as slides, filmstrips, and overhead transparencies not only keep their audiences more interested but also accomplish greater results. A study sponsored by the Wharton School of Business at the University of Pennsylvania showed the following percentages:

	With Visuals	**Without Visuals**
Speaker's goal achieved	67%	33%
Group consensus reached	79%	58%
Information retained	50%	10%
Average meeting length	19 minutes	28 minutes

Or, if intended to explain retirement benefits to an internal audience of employees, it might be made entirely with drawings and explanatory text slides. A combination of photographs, drawings, and text also can be effective. Leasing of stock shots of scenery, people, and events from commercial firms such as *Time* specializing in this work is a convenient way to fill out the picture requirements of a show. Some large picture firms have from 2 to 5 million still photos and slides on file to fill requests.

Whatever form the slide show takes, inclusion of humorous bits creates audience interest. These might be cartoons or candid photographs in which individuals are caught in laughable situations.

Text-only slides often help to give a presentation cohesion and to emphasize key points. The content of each text slide should be brief, making a single clear statement in a maximum of 25 words, preferably fewer. A slide containing ten words or fewer can be powerfully effective. Color slides containing text and/or drawings need strong contrast, usually a dark background of blue, black, or brown with letters and pictures in white or yellow.

A narrator may deliver the script of a slide show live, or it may be accompanied by a taped voice synchronized with the progression of slides. Slides can be shown on an automatic projector controlled by a button the speaker presses to change them.

If a company or organization has competent writing, photographic, or graphic talent on its staff, it may be able to produce an attractive slide show using its own resources. Outside graphic talent may be hired, or the sponsor may employ a firm specializing in audiovisual work to handle the entire production. Specialist organizations are able to produce elaborate slide shows with dramatic graphic effects. Animation and masking that reveals only part of a picture at a time add visual zest, and use of multiple screens and projectors provides dramatic impact.

FILMSTRIPS

A filmstrip consists of a series of 35-millimeter or 16-millimeter slides reproduced in sequence on a short piece of film. The strip can be advanced slowly, one frame at a time, in an inexpensive projector, with each frame held on the screen as long as desired. Filmstrips are economical, small, and easily transported. They are especially useful as instructional tools for single concepts. If a recorded narration accompanies the filmstrip, the frames must be advanced at a coordinated speed.

OVERHEAD TRANSPARENCIES

A simple, economical form of audiovisual aid is a sheet of transparent acetate or similar material on which illustrations and/or lettering have been placed. When this sheet is laid on a flat glass surface in the projector, the images are reproduced on a screen behind the speaker by light transmitted by mirrors and lenses. Overhead transparencies are especially good in classrooms and small discussion groups because of their flexibility. They can be made by running a master on regular paper through a photocopier onto the acetate plastic. Large type should be used on overheads and only a few words of copy.

Masking a transparency permits a speaker to show several steps in a process with only one transparency. If the same series of steps were shown by slides, a separate slide would be necessary for each step.

When a speaker wishes to show the operation of a piece of machinery, for example, masking can be done in the following way: The transparency contains a diagram of the entire machine. A piece of onionskin or white opalescent plastic is laid over each portion of the diagram and taped lightly into place. As the blanked-out transparency appears on the screen, the speaker removes each sectional overlay progressively and explains the revealed portion of the diagram, until the entire diagram is visible. The speaker can draw or write on a transparency while it is being displayed on the screen.

STILL PHOTOGRAPHY

A story in the print media, especially newspapers and magazines, may, and frequently should, be told in pictures as well as words. Still photography is an essential tool for every practitioner who works with publications.

NEWSPAPER REQUIREMENTS

Newspaper editors like to receive black-and-white photographs of persons mentioned in news releases. The presence of a photograph with a release sometimes increases the likelihood that the story will be published. Or, as frequently happens, a photograph of a newsworthy individual or group will be published without an accompanying story, the necessary information having been condensed into the photo caption (see Figure 24.2).

The type of photograph most easily placed in a newspaper by a practitioner is the head-and-shoulders portrait of a client. These portraits, known in the trade as *mug shots,* frequently are published in one-column or half-column size to illustrate textual material. Group shots are published less often than individual pictures because they require multiple-column space. Practitioners submitting group photographs should keep the number of persons in a picture small and have them tightly grouped—a maximum of three or four persons unless the picture is a highly unusual one.

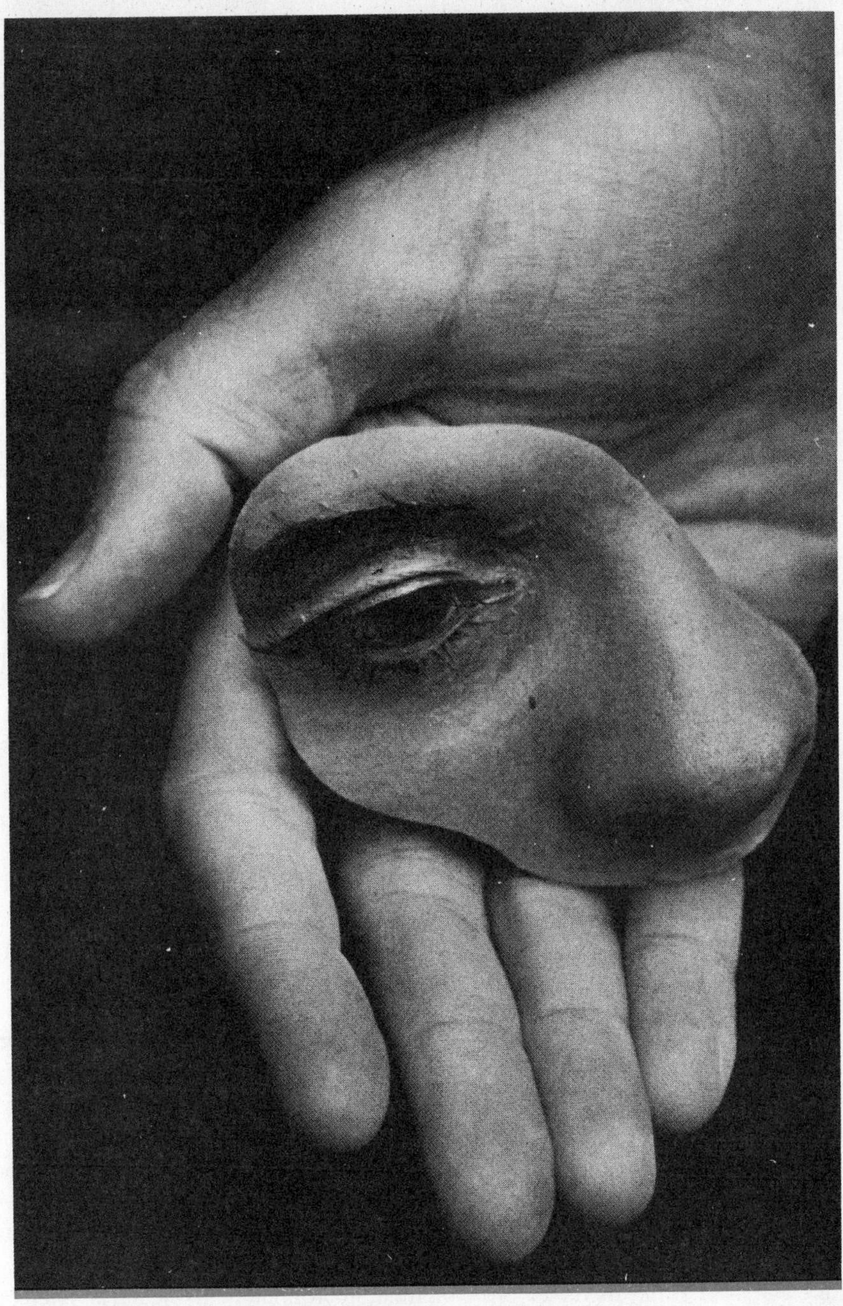

FIGURE 24.2
An imaginative photograph accompanying a news release may be decisive in convincing an editor to use the story, or it may be published alone with a caption. This photo typifies the high quality of feature pictures distributed by BW Photos, a service of BusinessWire. It shows that synthetic prosthetic replacements for facial bones and skin, eyes, ears, noses, and cheeks for people with facial trauma are a reality. (Courtesy of BusinessWire)

Photographs on the main news pages of a newspaper usually are taken by staff photographers or are provided by the news picture services. They stress spot-news action. The chances for a public relations practitioner to have a submitted photograph published in these up-front pages are relatively small, except for one-column portraits. When spot news is involved, the practitioner is better advised to telephone the photo editor of a newspaper and call attention to a picture possibility that a staff photographer can cover. Staff photographers know their editors' requirements, space limitations, and deadlines. They can respond very quickly to fast-breaking news situations.

Other sections of a newspaper provide abundant opportunities for publication of photographs submitted by practitioners.

The business pages regularly include photographs of meetings, new products, and individuals appointed to new positions. Sports editors welcome photographs of athletes and coaches in various poses. Entertainment editors need pictures of performers, individually and in groups, and publish still photos taken from scenes in locally playing motion pictures and television shows. Travel editors desire photographs of interesting scenes and modes of transportation.

An especially broad target for the practitioner is the section of a newspaper called "Family Living," "Life Styles," "Today's Scene," or something similar. For many years these sections were referred to as "women's," "society," or, in newspaper jargon, "sock." They concentrated on engagements and weddings, parties and club meetings, food, beauty, and fashion. Now their appeal is greatly enlarged, aimed at men as well as women.

While retaining the traditional elements, these sections have added material about family life and problems, personal finances, careers, and contemporary lifestyles. This broadened appeal has multiplied the photographic possibilities for the public relations practitioner, both to submit photographs and to query editors with ideas for illustrated feature stories by staff members about activities of their clients.

"Family Living" sections often publish pictures of groups planning charity events, civic affairs, and social organization parties. These pictures generate interest in the event, help to sell tickets, and incidentally serve as an ego payoff to workers who appear in them. Unfortunately, far too many such pictures belong to the waxworks school of photography—stilted, self-conscious poses in which the participants appear ramrod-stiff and painfully artificial. A photographer's ingenuity is challenged to invent an interesting piece of business for the participants to do, and to coax them to relax.

When shooting a publicity shot, a clever photographer will include, if possible, a prop that helps to carry the message. A picture promoting a Red Cross blood drive, for example, would be strengthened by inclusion of a Red Cross poster or similar symbol.

Publicity shots may be submitted by the practitioner, or arrangements may be made with an editor for a staff photographer to handle the assignment. If a staff photographer is assigned, the practitioner must make certain that all participants in the picture assemble at the appointed place on time, appropriately dressed. The photographer is busy and, in a sense, the editor is doing the organization a favor.

Creativity also should be applied to news pictures submitted for publication. Groundbreakings, installations of officers, delivery of donation checks—routine events that frequently fall within the domain of the public relations worker—are notorious sources of cliché photos. For that reason, some newspapers refuse to publish photographs of these events. A practitioner taking a picture of such an event, or a

FIGURE 24.3
Staged publicity photos sometimes receive good media space when they include basic, attractive elements. This picture of two smiling Australians and a koala succeeded for that reason. It was taken by a staff photographer of the Brisbane, Australia, *Courier-Mail*.

commercial photographer hired to do so, should use every ounce of innovative skill to find a new camera angle or piece of action.

Photographs submitted to newspapers normally are 8 by 10 inches in black and white, with caption material attached either to the back or bottom of the picture. *The practitioner should be absolutely certain that the names in the caption are spelled correctly and match up in left-to-right sequence with the photograph itself.* An added precaution is to count the number of persons in the picture and the number of names in the caption, to be sure that they correspond. Smaller prints usually are acceptable for head-and-shoulders portraits.

Use of Color Many newspapers publish pictures in color daily, and the practice is growing. Although spot pictures, such as those showing fires and wrecks, usually are taken by staff photographers, excellent public relations opportunities exist to place color pictures in feature sections. Living sections often run color photos of prepared foods; travel sections show enticing color shots of destinations.

The practitioner should submit color slides, not color prints. To increase the chances that a picture will be used, it is a wise precaution to determine in advance from the picture editor or chief photographer what special technical requirements for color work the newspaper may have.

Keep File Pictures Current Since newspapers maintain large files of published and unpublished photographs, it is not unusual for a mug shot of a newsworthy personality to be published more than once—a bonus for the practitioner who submitted it. Individuals change in appearance as they age, and occasionally an editor will reach into the files in a hurry and publish an obviously outdated picture of a news figure. The public relations person handling a prominent individual can avoid this embarrassment by submitting an up-to-date photograph from time to time, with a request that it replace the old one.

The importance of including a selection of photographs in a press kit introducing such projects as a new shopping center, a sales program, a political campaign, or a fund drive is obvious. The kit should contain pictures of the key persons involved and of physical aspects of the projects.

On a national or regional basis, the alert practitioner may obtain space by appealing to newspaper editors' interest in hometown angles. At trade conventions or sales conferences, the public relations staff can run a ''production line'' in which individual delegates are photographed in company with a celebrity. A mattress manufacturer, for example, hired Vanna White, the sexy, glamorously gowned costar of the TV game show ''Wheel of Fortune,'' to sit on a new model mattress at a trade show. Company salesmen were invited to come up one by one and pose on the mattress beside her. The opportunity delighted them. One elderly participant exclaimed, ''What an experience! Me on a bed with Vanna. I must tell my grandchildren.''

At least rudimentary knowledge of photographic techniques is an important asset for all men and women working in public relations. The best way to obtain this is to take a college course in news photography. If this cannot be done, courses in photography are available in many adult education programs. Membership in a camera club is another way.

MAGAZINE REQUIREMENTS

Magazine requirements resemble those of newspapers, although emphasis is primarily on feature photographs. Some magazines use only color photographs, some only black and white, some both. The practitioner should study each magazine before submitting pictures to it. Color slides rather than prints should be sent.

Trade and professional magazines frequently use submitted photographs of individuals, new products, and industrial installations. When sending in a proposal for a feature story about a client, the practitioner should offer to provide photographs to accompany the text, regardless of whether the story is written by the practitioner, by a free-lance writer, or by a magazine staff member. Many magazines do not have photographic staffs, or budgets and facilities for acquiring pictures, and so depend upon submitted pictures. Attractive photographs accompanying a manuscript enhance the possibility that it will be accepted for publication.

Public relations departments and counseling firms should include in their annual budgets a substantial amount for photographic service. In addition to submitting pictures to the media, representatives often find it effective to send souvenir prints of these pictures to persons appearing in them and to important persons such as dealers and customers. Such small gestures have a flattering effect.

COMIC BOOKS AND CARTOONS

Another eye-catching way to deliver visual messages in print is to use comic books and cartoons. The artwork must be of professional quality, however, or the effect is diminished. Drawings are especially good for illustrating steps in a process, as in an owner's instruction manual. If an artist can create a whimsical cartoon character that symbolizes the service or objective, entire campaigns can be built around it.

A variation is the coloring book, which E. F. Hutton sent to its employees with mixed results. The purpose was to boost employee morale battered by Hutton's guilty plea to a check-overdraft scheme. But one employee told *Time* magazine that he thought the coloring-book idea was disgusting and that management should communicate in an adult fashion.

A note of warning: published cartoons and comic strips are covered by copyright and may be reproduced only by permission, which the copyright holders often are reluctant to give.

FIGURE 24.4
A touch of humor brightens certain types of publicity releases and increases their chances of publication. The California Strawberry Advisory Board uses this method effectively, showing a strawberry cartoon character in whimsical poses.

OUTDOOR DISPLAYS

Although billboards, building signs, and other forms of outdoor announcements are erected primarily for advertising and identification, they have potential uses as public relations tools. Billboards may remind motorists and pedestrians of a citywide charity fund drive in progress. A changing electric sign outside a bank showing time and temperature performs a public service and creates good will for the bank; so does a signboard on which announcements of forthcoming civic events are placed. An ingenious practitioner working for a nonprofit organization may be able to find numerous outlets of this type to deliver a message, at little or no cost.

A public relations specialist should know the fundamentals of billboard design and economics, in case a situation arises in which outdoor displays will fit into a publicity program. The standard billboard of the type seen along streets and on buildings is 12 by 25 feet. The colorful paper posters pasted onto it are slightly smaller, leaving a white frame around them. The standard poster is called a 24-sheet, because at one time 24 sheets of paper were needed to cover the space on a full-sized billboard. Modern printing processes do it with 10 sheets. Small posters called 3-sheets are designed to attract pedestrian readers at sidewalk level. Recent development of computer-controlled painting on vinyl billboards permits use of larger boards.

Outdoor advertising companies rent display space on their billboards on the basis of what they call a *100-showing*—that is, the number of boards in a market area calculated to expose the advertiser's message to approximately 100 percent of the people at some time during the 30 days it is posted. The number of boards that constitute a 100-showing fluctuates from market to market, based on traffic studies.

When messages are painted onto the billboards instead of being pasted on, their effective life is longer and the space rental price higher.

Successful billboard copy must be short and illustrations simple, because the duration of viewing time as motorists pass is brief. Eye-catching impact is the goal. That requires powerful design and strong colors. Two lively examples: ''Heaven Can Wait. . . Wellness Works'' and ''We Don't Do That in Clarke County,'' an antilittering billboard in Georgia. One message was five words long, the other seven, quickly absorbed. Perhaps the greatest advantage of billboards is their reinforcement value in support of a program using other methods as well. Design and preparation of billboard posters are handled by advertising agencies, while physical placement is done by the billboard companies.

CORPORATE DESIGN

The need to present a unified visual image to the world is becoming increasingly evident to corporations and nonprofit organizations. Especially among corporations that have grown rapidly by acquiring many subsidiaries, the uncoordinated proliferation of letterheads, signs, publication symbols, news release sheets, packages, and other visual public representations of the organization gives a jumbled, unfocused appearance.

Creation of a simple, powerful logotype for use on all printed matter and signs projects an image of the company as a tightly knit contemporary operation. An impressive logo suggests quality and strength.

In the acquisition-minded climate of corporate life today, companies often add so many subsidiaries that the original names of the parent firms become inadequate to describe their overall function. So these corporations adopt generalized names, usually of one or two words. United States Steel Corporation changed its name to USX Corporation, and American Machinery & Foundry Company became AMF Incorporated.

Because it no longer makes cans but has moved into such varied fields as life insurance, direct mail, recorded music and stock brokerage, the American Can Company decided to change its name. It paid Lippincott & Margulies consultants $200,000

FIGURE 24.5
Evolution of the City Bank of New York's symbol over 180 years is demonstrated in this series of pictures. The designs reflect the artistic taste of the periods in which they were used. In today's version the name has been shortened to Citibank; the type is simple, strong, and suggestive of movement. (© 1985 Citibank, N.A., Member FDIC)

to help it choose a new one. The choice was Primerica, a synthetic word intended to reflect the company's "prime" growth prospects and ability to finance them.

Corporate redesign usually involves coordinated effort by the public relations and marketing departments. First, management must define the objectives to be sought in the new design. Should the graphic style be ultramodern, formal and conservative, or perhaps old-fashioned to suggest historical continuity? A counseling firm and graphics specialist usually are brought into the discussion. A detailed audit of existing printed materials and signs is necessary, to establish the areas where the new design will be used. In a corporation with numerous divisions, the logotype may be color-coded—a different color for each division, with identification of the division in type below.

As companies enter the international market, they often find that their traditional identifying logotypes are unsuitable in foreign countries because of language complications and cultural differences. So they seek logos that are easily identified around the world. The Fuji Bank of Japan, for example, replaced its symbol using Japanese letters with a simple design consisting of a drawing of Mount Fujiyama and the words Fuji Bank.

Corporate designers also must wrestle with the need to create symbols and designs that are effective on computer screens and other electronic outlets, as well as on traditional paper.

Creation of a symbolic person to represent a corporate product is another effective graphic method (see Figure 24.6). Practitioners working with smaller companies and nonprofit organizations can achieve visual unity and focus public attention, just as the huge corporations do.

Goodwill Industries, for example, formerly had as its symbol a cartoon character, a smiling young man, feather in his hat and a lunch box in his hand, pictured rolling along in a wheelchair. The national help-the-handicapped organization found that the symbol, while clever, did not print well and lacked sales appeal on signs outside its retail outlets. The design consultant Goodwill employed replaced the symbol with a rectangular logo in which a large lowercase *g* in the upper-left corner looks like half of a smiling face.

In another piece of clever public relations and marketing, Goodwill put a "Morgie" label on the used jeans it sells, thereby spoofing the current fad for designer jeans that bear high-fashion labels. Sales of the used jeans rose, and Goodwill received excellent national press coverage.

Creation of a graphics standards manual helps a large organization to enforce its unified designs throughout all its operations. Such a manual gives the specification of exact colors, the proper use of stationery, the size of lettering on signs, and similar information.

CASE PROBLEM

The local chapter of the American Lung Association needs to update its ten-minute slide presentation about the activities and services of the organization. Do some research on the American Lung Association and what it does. Then write the script on the right side of the paper. On the left, briefly describe the slides that would be keyed to the basic points of the script.

Johnson, Marti. "Thanks for the Memory." *Communication World,* July–August 1988, pp. 44–45. How to write video scripts.

Kern-Foxworth, Marilyn. "Plantation Kitchen to American Icon: Aunt Jemima." *Public Relations Review,* Fall 1990, pp. 55–67. Historical evolution of a Quaker Oats trademark.

Landro, Laura. "Audubon Society Hopes Music Videos and Movies Get Its 'Green' Message Out." *Wall Street Journal,* April 10, 1990, p. B1.

McDowell, Edwin. "America Is Taking Comic Books Seriously." New York *Times,* July 31, 1988, p. E7.

McGreevy, Ralph W. "Maximizing Trade Show Exposure." *Public Relations Journal,* August 1989, pp. 29–30.

Olins, Wally. "How a Corporation Reveals Itself." New York *Times,* October 14, 1990. Corporate identity programs.

Poe, Randall. "Company Shows Face the Music." New York *Times* Business World supplement, June 10, 1990, pp. 25, 30, 50. Using musicals to convey information to employees, stockholders.

Shell, Adam. "Reaching Out to the TV Generation." *Public Relations Journal,* November 1990, pp. 28–30, 32. Corporate video programs.

Stecki, Ed, and Corrado, Frank. "How to Make a Video, Part I." *Public Relations Journal,* February 1988, pp. 33–34.

Stecki, Ed, and Corrado, Frank. "How to Make a Video, Part II." *Public Relations Journal,* March 1988, pp. 35–36.

Tolley, James L. "Corporate Identity Programs." *Experts in Action,* edited by Bill Cantor. New York: Longman, 1989, pp. 80–90.

Walter, Kate. "Moving Your Photos on the Wires." *Public Relations Journal,* March 1989, pp. 33–35.

Afterword: The Future of Public Relations

BY ROBERT L. DILENSCHNEIDER
Former President and Chief Executive Officer
Hill & Knowlton, Inc.

The rapid and fundamental change that so strongly influenced business and society in the 1980s has, if anything, speeded up in the 1990s. The recession and Persian Gulf war have had profound effects on both the nature and the content of public relations. Those of us in the business are under pressure to absorb and react to technological evolution, even while we join the rest of society in experiencing uncertainties that are almost unprecedented. We must adapt speedily to the ever-shifting relationships that the institutions we represent have with the society to which we speak on their behalf. Any attempt to visualize an unknowable future—with possibly even more radical changes in store—must be tentative.

As the last decade ended, I had expected growth of 20 percent to 30 percent per year for the counseling branch of the public relations business in the years ahead. The Persian Gulf war and the recession have changed the psychology of business and the public. Perhaps that expected growth will slow down. But I am optimistic that some growth will continue for as long as I can glimpse into the future—a few years at best.

Those public relations professionals working directly for other employers, as distinguished from counseling firms, may or may not be facing as promising a future. It will depend upon the gross trends in society, including its affluence, its degree of specialization, the development of organizational philosophy, and alterations in the direction of higher education. My guess is that public relations in the business, government, and nonprofit areas will grow at a slower pace because clients are finding economies and other advantages in the use of counseling firms of all kinds, including public relations firms.

The future is not without risks for public relations people and, in fact, for the very existence of public relations as a specialty. We have always occupied a narrow spectrum between legal counsel and management consultants. We are lately squeezed also by investment bankers, particularly in financial public relations. As public relations itself expands beyond its traditional communication functions and becomes more advisory in nature, it invites the attention, and sometimes the greedy impulses, of others who vie for the ears, attention, and respect of management.

Unfortunately, we in public relations counseling have lost status in the executive suites of some major companies. This is evidenced in the published weekly list of lost business that so frequently reminds us about a certain inability in the field to sustain lasting relationships. That may help companies like mine that are well established and enjoy enduring reputations, but it does not say anything positive about our field as a whole.

Another problem is that turnover exceeds 15 percent annually, and in some firms it is an appalling 50 percent. Our industry has a reputation of chewing up young people, particularly those who want to pursue public relations as a career. The low salary structure, especially at the entry level, makes it tough for public relations firms and departments to compete with law firms, consulting firms, and investment bankers for the best young talent.

And we have another built-in problem that must be solved if we are to be confident of the future for public relations and for ourselves. That is the failure, in too many cases, of public relations executives to think strategically in the first place and to provide management with some tangible measurement of results in the second place. Both are symptoms of the shallowness of which we are so often accused.

Finally, the old bugaboo of low stature for public relations people, departments, and counselors still dogs us. Public relations has come a long way in the past generation, but the depressing truth is that too many people heading communications report to top management indirectly. Every step away from the executive suite is a step closer to the technician's status. I would not be happy with that as our field's destiny, and I am sure few reading this volume would be either.

So there is nothing assured about our progress into the twenty-first century: it will be there only if we create new opportunities and overcome old problems. I am optimistic that the business—or profession, if you prefer—will find the leadership to accomplish this, but that will not happen without a general recognition in the field of the need for constant progress and improvement in our perceptions and techniques.

Assuming that we can anticipate the flowering of public relations in the years ahead, we can attribute it, I believe, to several characteristics of society that show signs of accelerating rather than slowing down:

- The growing complexity of society, including international relations. Who could imagine, only a couple of decades ago, that we would be concerned about the structure of government in Fiji, the religious alignment in Iran, and statecraft in South Africa? Or that America would be allied with the USSR and many other nations in a confrontation in the Middle East?

- The fractionalization of society. The audiences for management are growing smaller, even as their importance is burgeoning. Politics is no longer a two-party game; it is dominated by ticket-splitters and independents. No clear line divides environmentalists and polluters; individuals are grouped by issues. Noise abatement environmentalists duel with clean air advocates. Middle management fights for unemployment benefits while rank and filers become the technocrats of computer-aided manufacturing. Society has evolved into hundreds, and perhaps thousands, of these different power groups that affect institutions.

- Sophistication in communications. The technological capabilities and the constantly upgraded stylistic demands are unending and require understanding and handling by specialists, i.e., public relations people. No U.S. institution is free today to ignore criticism from quarters abroad that once rarely figured in American thinking.

- Institutional oversight. Of all the reasons the public relations industry will grow, none is more potent than the nearly universal demand that institutions justify themselves to the people they touch. That demand reaches to governments, to business, to the health and other professions, to nonprofit institutions, and to every segment of society everywhere in the world. (As I write this, West and East Germany have just unified into a single country, becoming probably the most economically powerful nation in the West, after the United States.)

Most leading countries of the free world have recently, or soon will, turn over their governments. The potential new realignment of power and redirection of policies and bureaucracies are unimaginable. And more diligent citizen watchfulness will obviously be felt nearly everywhere at the local level and in states and communities, as well as in school districts and other subdivisions of government close at hand for taxpayers.

In the corporate world there is a trend toward the taking over of large U.S. companies by committees of outside directors. Chief executive officers will, I believe, truly be answerable to the pleasure of the directors, who will be strictly charged to represent shareholder interests and to respect employee interests—something that rarely concerns them now. This fragmentation of power within companies will place increasing pressure on communications to establish and maintain a working consensus.

The media, instrumental in bringing about much change, are themselves becoming an important target of scrutiny and criticism. The public is uneasy about incursions into private lives and into national security, bringing into conflict the constitutional right of free speech with personal concepts of decency and honor. It would appear that the press is increasingly regarded not as an institution but as a product line of the communication industry. Its stature may decline, as public demand for better protection of the individual and of national security may multiply.

Our insight into the future is hampered by our experience of the past. All of us who have been in public relations for more than a few years are keenly conscious of the distance we have traveled. Public relations has been transformed by all those aspects of living that have invaded the awareness of vast numbers of people, both at home and abroad.

We think of all the movements that have virtually forced public relations upon our institutions: equal rights, feminism, environmentalism; the drives for workplace safety, human treatment of prisoners, improved public education, preservation of natural resources; government legislation mandating EPA, OSHA, ERISA, FERC, and all the rest. We are mindful particularly of federal regulation of the markets and other aspects of business operation, including mergers and acquisitions. We think seriously about the severe effect the attention of Congress, or of the media, or of an adversary group often has on the reputation of an individual, a company, or an institution. And we recognize immediately that all of this strongly spurred the growth of public relations both in its spread throughout society and in its importance.

But it would have been most difficult to foresee those developments before they occurred, just as it is most difficult today for us to foresee how and in what way similar growth can be expected in the future. We know only that what deeply concerns society will become a professional concern of public relations people. We are, for example, only beginning to sense what kind of tidal wave AIDS will wreak on the nation and indeed on the world.

AIDS was identified only in 1981, but expected to infect and therefore maim or kill more than 365,000 Americans alone by 1992, and with the faster rate at which HIV infections are being found, that may be a conservative estimate. Rand Corporation estimates that the resulting annual healthcare cost, spread across the entire population, will amount to $500 per capita. Forget, for a moment, the human suffering. This new disease will probably eradicate whatever personal income gains those agonizing years of tax reform debate may have yielded. We will all be touched, financially and socially, as this new element goes to work more devastatingly throughout the world. Even now, as this process begins, it is widely recognized that the most urgent need arising from AIDS is for public education as to its nature—a public relations function.

We hope that AIDS may be the last plague upon the people of the world, but as intelligent craftsmen we know that many unforeseen things are going to affect the way we think and function as our planet spins new years through our lives. That is going to create problems (read that as business) for public relations men and women, no matter what elements of society they may represent, and whether they work inside their institutions or as advisers to them.

Traditionally, Hill & Knowlton has represented business organizations and their trade associations, although its clientele is broadening out to embrace governments and nonprofit institutions. So my own orientation is heavily to commerce and industry. And I believe that the growth and welfare of business public relations will depend more and more as time passes on the practitioners' ability to learn how to measure the results of public relations undertakings.

Advertising has been using measurement successfully for six decades, and it is my conviction that it will be required from public relations if we are to do large-scale corporate positioning. I see an increasing flow of investment in the United States coming from the rest of the world, along with foreign managers who do not understand our culture but who do understand positioning. It may well be performance based on measured results that will buy public relations firms and individuals access to the international marketplace. Measuring results from our kind of work is not easy, nor have any universal standards evolved that we can all adopt. I believe those firms, like mine, that are diligently trying to develop such standards can count on prosperity in the future.

Public relations is fast becoming a worldwide activity. When John Hill first began setting up overseas arrangements a generation ago, it was barely known even in such sophisticated nations as Britain, France, and Germany. Not so today. Public relations thrives around the world, and it is outside the United States that its greatest surge has yet to come. But here at home, if we recognize the traps and manage to avoid them, if we have the good sense to identify ourselves more closely with the strategy of the institutions we represent and therefore gain the respect and support of our managements, and if we continue to stay a step ahead of progress by improving our technology and our techniques and by sharpening our thinking, public relations does have a very bright future. Indeed, if we can attract the right young people and motivate them with goals and adequate compensation, I believe no other profession has more to offer.

We can make a difference in the world!

Filmstrip Sequence of film frames that, when advanced one by one in a projector, presents a topic on a screen; used as a training tool.

Flack Derogatory term applied primarily to a person who publicizes entertainment events and personalities. (See *Press agentry*.)

Focus group Panel of persons, representative of the audience a public relations practitioner desires to reach, who are asked to give their opinions of proposed programs.

Free-loading The practice of some reporters and editors to accept gifts, entertainment, and travel from organizations seeking to influence them.

Gatekeeper Editor, reporter, news director, or other person who decides what material is printed, broadcast, or otherwise offered to the public.

Gross impressions Total circulation and listening audience of the print and broadcast media that use a news release.

Hierarchy of needs Abraham Maslow's definition of an individual's five levels of needs, a basis for planning appeals to self-interest.

Hotline In public relations, a toll-free telephone number set up by a trade association or corporation to provide quick answers, especially to the news media.

Hype The promotion of movie and television stars, books, magazines, and so forth, through shrewd use of the media; used as both noun and verb. (See *Press agentry*.)

Hypodermic needle theory The belief that people receive information directly without any intervening variable, as in a vacuum.

Image-building Protection and enhancement of the reputation of an organization or individual.

Impression Exposure of an individual to a news release through the print or broadcast media. (See *Gross impressions*.)

Information on demand Computerized information on requested topics called up on a television or computer screen by the user.

Information retrieval Act of obtaining desired pieces of information from material stored in a computer.

Institutional advertising Advertising intended to strengthen a company's image, rather than to stimulate immediate sales of its products or services. (See *Corporate advertising*.)

Internal publication One designed for distribution primarily to employees. (See *External publication*.)

Internship Temporary employment by a student to obtain professional work experience.

Interpersonal communication Exchange between two or more persons in close proximity using conversation and gestures.

Issues management Program of identifying and addressing issues of public concern in which a company is, or should be, involved.

Libel Mainly defamation by written or printed words; but also, as interpreted by the courts, by broadcast. (See *Slander*.)

Line function Pursuit of management objectives through supervision, delegation of authority, and work assignments. (See *Staff function*.)

Literary agent Person who represents an author in dealings with publishers.

Lobbyist Person who presents an organization's point of view to members of Congress or other government bodies.

Marketing communications Product publicity, promotion, and advertising.

Marketing public relations Use of public relations techniques to support overall advertising and marketing objectives of a company or client.

Message entropy Tendency for a message to dissipate, or lose information, as it is disseminated.

Muckrakers Writers who seek to expose corrupt and immoral conduct by companies, institutions, and governments; specifically, a group of early 1900s writers and publications in America.

Mug shot Slang term for a head-and-shoulders photograph of an individual for newspaper publication.

News conference Meeting at which the spokesperson for an organization delivers information to reporters and answers their questions; often called a *press conference*.

News release Timely information about an activity of a public relations practitioner's client or organization, distributed in ready-to-use form.

Off-the-record Practice of giving reporters confidential information with the demand that it not be published.

100-showing Number of billboards needed to expose a message to approximately 100 percent of the population in a designated area within 30 days.

Opinion leader Articulate person knowledgeable about specific issues whose opinions influence others.

Pattern speech Basic speech written so that several speakers can deliver it to different audiences with only minor variations.

People meter A device for measuring how much a person watches television, used in determining the size of TV audiences.

Pilot test Tryout of a public relations message and key copy points on a small audience before general distribution.

Planter Publicist who delivers news releases to media offices and urges their use.

Positioning The practice of creating corporate identity programs that establish a place in the market for a company and its products. Also, the effort to get ahead by doing something first.

Press agentry Term applied primarily to the publicizing of entertainers and shows; often used in a derogatory sense. (See *Hype*.)

Press conference (See *News conference*.)

Press kit Folder containing news releases, photographs, and background information, distributed to media representatives.

Preventive public relations Efforts to maintain goodwill for an organization or individual through reinforcing messages.

Probability sample Survey in which every member of the targeted audience has a chance of being selected for questioning.

Product recall Act of calling back from consumers a company's product found to be defective, for repair or replacement.

Public affairs Term used primarily to describe work in the areas of government and community relations.

Public information Term used primarily by government agencies, social service organizations, and universities to describe their public relations activities.

Publisher Chief official of a newspaper who directs financial, mechanical, and administrative operations, and sometimes news and editorial operations as well.

Purposive sampling Selection of opinion leaders to be interviewed; usually used when approval of the group is necessary for success of a public relations campaign.

Quota sampling Selection of a group to be polled that matches the characteristics of the entire audience.

Royalty fee Amount of money received by an author for each copy of a book sold, usually 10 or 15 percent of the retail price; also money received by program distributors for materials used in broadcasting.

Satellite transmission Method of transmitting text, pictures, and sound by beaming an electronic signal to a transponder on a satellite orbiting 22,300 miles above the earth, from which it bounces back to receiving dishes on the ground.

Semantic noise Inept language usage that impedes the receiver's ability to comprehend a message; for example, use of trade jargon to a general audience.

Semantics Study of words and their use and interpretation.

Slander Oral defamation of character. (See *Libel*.)

Social contract Popular term for a corporation's set of responsibilities to the public.

Source credibility Use of representatives who have expertise, sincerity, and charisma to win acceptance from an audience.

Split message Exposure of two or three different appeals to separate audiences, to determine which is most effective.

Sponsored film Motion picture paid for by an organization to deliver information or a message, usually shown without charge.

Staff function Pursuit of management objectives through suggestions, recommendations, and advice. In corporate organization, public relations is a staff function. (See *Line function*.)

Talk show Television or radio program on which a host or hostess chats with guests or telephone callers.

Teleconference Presentation or discussion by television, involving groups assembled at scattered receiving points, usually with telephone or television channels that permit distant viewers to ask questions or express reactions.

Teletext System of delivering news and other information to a television screen, in which the viewer can select certain portions of the material to watch.

Telethon Fund-raising program on television lasting several hours, in which appeals for donations are mixed with entertainment.

Trade journal Magazine designed and edited for a special-interest commercial or professional group.

Trademark Name, symbol, or other device identifying a product, officially registered and legally restricted to the use of the owner or manufacturer.

Transfer Technique of associating a person, product, or organization with individuals or situations of high or low credibility, depending on the intention of the message.

Transparency Sheet of transparent acetate or similar material on which text or graphic material is placed, for showing on an overhead projector.

Videocassette Small container of videotape that can be inserted in a playback machine for projection.

Videoconference (See *Teleconference*.)

Video news release (VNR) Pictorial news release distributed on videotape, with or without accompanying spoken commentary.

Videotape A recording of moving images and sound on magnetic tape.

Videotex Two-way communication system in which a viewer receives information on a screen and sends messages by keyboard.

BIBLIOGRAPHY

This selected list of recent books is based, in part, on an annual bibliography compiled by the Information Center of the Public Relations Society of America, 33 Irving Place, New York, NY, 10003.

GENERAL BOOKS

Ailes, Roger, and Kraushar, John. *You Are the Message: Secrets of the Master Communicators*. New York: Simon & Schuster, 1988.

Aronoff, Craig, and Baskin, Otis. *Public Relations: The Profession and the Practice*. 2nd edition. Dubuque, IA: Brown, 1988.

Awad, Joseph. *The Power of Public Relations*. Westport, CT: Greenwood, 1985.

Beals, Joseph. *Expose Yourself: Using the Power of Public Relations to Promote Your Business and Yourself*. San Francisco: Chronicle Press, 1990.

Botan, Carl H., and Hazelton, Vincent. *Public Relations Theory*. Hillsdale, NJ: Lawrence Erlbaum, 1989.

Brody, E. W. *The Business of Public Relations*. Westport, CT: Greenwood, 1987.

Brody, E. W. *Public Relations Programming and Production*. New York: Praeger, 1988.

Cantor, Bill. *Experts in Action: Inside Public Relations*. 2nd edition. White Plains, NY: Longman, 1989.

Crable, Richard, and Vibbert, Steven. *Public Relations As Communication Management*. Fort Lee, NJ: Burgess, 1986.

Cutlip, Scott M., Center, Allen H., and Broom, Glen M. *Effective Public Relations*. 6th edition. Englewood Cliffs, NJ: Prentice-Hall, 1985.

Dilenschneider, Robert, and Forrestal, Dan. *Public Relations Handbook*. 3rd edition. Chicago: Dartnell, 1987.

Grunig, James E., and Hunt, Todd. *Managing Public Relations*. New York: Holt, Rinehart and Winston, 1984.

Haberman, David, and Dolphin, Harry. *Public Relations: The Necessary Art*. Ames: Iowa State University Press, 1988.

Haller, Robert T. *Creative Power! Grow Faster with New Proactive Tactics in Advertising and Public Relations*. Hamlin, PA: Leister and Sons, 1988.

Harris, Thomas L. *The Marketer's Guide to Public Relations*. New York: Wiley, 1991.

Hausman, Carl, and Benoit, Philip. *Positive Public Relations*. Blue Ridge Summit, PA: Tab Books, 1990.

Haynes, Colin. *A Guide to Successful Public Relations*. Glenview, IL: Scott, Foresman, 1989.

Hiebert, Ray E. *Precision Public Relations*. White Plains, NY: Longman, 1988.

Hill, Dennis. *Power PR: The No-Nonsense, No-Holds Barred Guide to Profitable Public Relations*. Hollywood, FL: Fell, 1990.

Jefkins, Frank. *Planned Press and Public Relations*. Philadelphia: Trans-Atlantic, 1986.

Lesly, Philip. *Lesly's Handbook of Public Relations and Communications*. New York: AMACOM, 1991.

Mercer, Laurie, and Singer, Jennifer. *Opportunity Knocks: Using PR*. Radnor, PA: Chilton, 1989.

Nager, Norman, and Allen, T. Harrell. *Public Relations: Management by Objective*. White Plains, NY: Longman, 1984.

Newsom, Doug, Scott, Allen, and Vanslyke, Judy. *This Is PR: Realities of Public Relations*. 4th edition. Belmont, CA: Wadsworth, 1989.

Reilly, Robert T. *Public Relations in Action*. 2nd edition. Englewood Cliffs, NJ: Prentice-Hall, 1987.

Seitel, Fraser P. *The Practice of Public Relations*. 4th edition. Columbus, OH: Merrill, 1989.

Simmons, Robert E. *Communication Campaign Management*. White Plains, NY: Longman, 1990.

Stevens, Art. *The Persuasion Explosion*. Washington, DC: Acropolis, 1985.

Wilcox, Dennis L., Ault, Phillip H., and Agee, Warren K. *Public Relations: Strategies and Tactics*. 3rd edition. New York: HarperCollins, 1992.

Winner, Paul. *Effective PR Management: A Guide to Corporate Success*. East Brunswick, NJ: Kogan Page, 1990.

SPECIAL INTEREST

BIOGRAPHY/MEMOIRS

Barmash, I. *Always Live Better Than Your Clients: The Fabulous Life and Times of Benjamin Sonnenberg*. New York: Dodd, Mead, 1983.

Dilenschneider, Robert. *Power and Influence: Mastering the Art of Persuasion.* Englewood Cliffs, NJ: Prentice-Hall, 1990.

Hiebert, Ray. *Courtier to the Crowd: Ivy Lee*. Ames: Iowa State University Press, 1966.

Rogers, Henry C. *Walking the Tightrope*. New York: Morrow, 1980. Life and clients of a Hollywood publicist.

Saxon, A. H. *P. T. Barnum: The Legend and the Man*. New York: Columbia University Press, 1990.

Wood, Robert, and Gunther, Max. *Confessions of a PR Man*. New York: New American Library, 1989.

BUSINESS/MANAGEMENT

Albrecht, Karl. *At America's Service*. Homewood, IL: Dow Jones–Irwin, 1988.

Atkins, Chris, and Sauerhaft, Stan. *The Visible Company: Creating Corporate Goodwill for Market Advantage*. New York: Wiley, 1989.

Brody, E. W. *Communicating for Survival: Coping with Diminishing Human Resources*. New York: Praeger, 1987.

Buchholz, Rogene. *Business Environment and Public Policy: Implications for Management*. Englewood Cliffs, NJ: Prentice-Hall, 1989.

Carter, David E. *American Corporate Identity*. New York: Art Direction, 1987.

Ciabattari, Jane. *Winning Moves: How to Survive (and Manage) a Corporate Shakeup*. New York: Penguin, 1989.

Drucker, Peter. *Management: Tasks, Responsibilities, Practices*. New York: Harper & Row, 1985.

Drucker, Peter. *Managing for Results*. New York: Harper & Row, 1986.

Garbett, Thomas F. *How to Build a Corporation's Identity and Project Its Image*. Lexington, MA: Lexington Books, 1990.

Gray, James G. *Managing the Corporate Image: The Key to Public Trust*. Westport, CT: Greenwood, 1986.

Hanan, Mack, and Karp, Peter. *Customer Satisfaction*. New York: AMACOM, 1989.

Hart, Norman. *Effective Corporate Relations: Public Relations in Business and Industry*. New York: McGraw-Hill, 1988.

Lesly, Philip. *Overcoming Opposition: A Survival Manual for Executives*. Englewood Cliffs, NJ: Prentice-Hall, 1986.

Napoles, Veronica. *Corporate Identity Design*. New York: Von Nostrand Reinhold, 1987.

Olasky, Marvin N. *Corporate Public Relations and American Public Enterprise*. Hillsdale, NJ: Lawrence Erlbaum, 1987.

Onkvist, Sak, and Shaw, John. *Product Life Cycles and Product Management*. Westport, CT: Greenwood, 1989.

Peters, Thomas, and Waterman, Robert. *In Search of Excellence*. New York: Warner Books, 1988.

Poppe, Fred. *50 Rules to Keep a Client Happy*. New York: Harper & Row, 1988.

Rukeyser, Louis, and Cooney, John. *Louis Rukeyser's Business Almanac*. New York: Simon & Schuster, 1988.

Selame, Elinor, and Selame, Joseph. *The Company Image: Building Your Identity and Influence in the Marketplace*. New York: Wiley, 1988.

Thomsett, Michael C. *The Little Book of Product Management*. New York: AMACOM, 1990.

Tomasko, Robert M. *Downsizing*. New York: AMACOM, 1990.

Vella, Carolyne, and McGonagle, John. *Improved Business Planning Using Competitive Intelligence*. Westport, CT: Greenwood, 1988.

Walton, Wesley, and Brissman, Charles. *Corporate Communications Handbook*. New York: Clark Boardman, 1989.

Wood, Donna J. *Business and Society*. Glenview, IL: Scott Foresman/Little, Brown, 1990.

CAREERS

Field, Sally. *Career Opportunities in Advertising and Public Relations*. New York: Facts on File, 1990.

Rotman, Morris. *Opportunities in Public Relations Careers*. Lincolnwood, IL: National Textbook, 1988.

CASE STUDIES

Capper, Alan, and Cunard, Peter. *The Public Relations Case Book: Major Campaigns in Action*. Woodstock, NY: Beekman, 1990.

Center, Allen, and Jackson, Patrick. *PR Practices: Managerial Case Studies and Problems*. 4th edition. Englewood Cliffs, NJ: Prentice-Hall, 1990.

Hendrix, Jerry A. *Public Relations Cases*. Belmont, CA: Wadsworth, 1988.

Simon, Raymond. *Public Relations Management: Casebook*. 3rd edition. Worthington, OH: Publishing Horizons, 1986.

Agee, Warren K., Ault, Phillip H., and Emery, Edwin. *Introduction to Mass Communications*. 10th edition. New York: HarperCollins, 1991.

Bateman, David, and Sigband, Norman. *Communicating in Business*. 3rd edition. Glenview, IL: Scott, Foresman, 1989.

Bittner, John. *Mass Communication*. 5th edition. Englewood Cliffs, NJ: Prentice-Hall, 1989.

Brody, E. W. *Communication Tomorrow: New Audiences, New Technologies, New Media*. New York: Praeger, 1990.

Clark, Ruth Anne. *Persuasive Messages*. New York: Harper & Row, 1984.

Creedan, Pamela J. *Women in Mass Communications: Challenging Gender Values*. Newbury Park, CA: Sage, 1989.

D'Aprix, Roger. *Communicating for Productivity*. New York: Harper & Row, 1982.

DeFleur, Melvin, and Ball-Rokeach, Sandra. *Theories of Mass Communication*. 5th edition. White Plains, NY: Longman, 1989.

DeVito, Joseph A. *Messages: Building Interpersonal Communication Skills*. New York: HarperCollins, 1990.

Goldhaber, Gerald. *Organizational Communication*. 5th edition. Dubuque, IA: Brown, 1990.

Hamilton, Seymour. *A Communications Audit Handbook: Helping Organizations Communicate*. White Plains, NY: Longman, 1987.

Hiebert, Ray, Ungulait, Donald, and Bohn, Thomas. *Mass Media VI*. White Plains, NY: Longman, 1991.

***International Encyclopedia of Communications*.** New York: Oxford University Press, 1989.

Jowett, Garth, and O'Donnell, Victoria. *Propaganda and Persuasion*. Newbury Park, CA: Sage, 1987.

Kreps, Gary L. *Organizational Communication*. 2nd edition. White Plains, NY: Longman, 1990.

Larson, Charles U. *Persuasion: Reception and Responsibility*. 5th edition. Belmont: CA: Wadsworth, 1989.

Merriam, John, and Makower, Joel. *Trend Watching*. New York: AMACOM, 1988.

Murphy, Kevin. *Effective Listening*. New York: Bantam, 1989.

Pasqua, Thomas, Buckalew, James, Rayfield, Robert, and Tankard, James. *Mass Media in the Information Age*. Englewood Cliffs, NJ: Prentice-Hall, 1990.

Petty, Richard, and Capioppo, John. *Communication and Persuasion*. New York: Springer-Verlag, 1986.

Reardon, Kathleen K. *Persuasion in Practice*. Newbury Park, CA: Sage, 1991.

Rice, Ronald, and Atkin, Charles K. *Public Information Campaigns*. 2nd edition. Newbury Park, CA: Sage, 1989.

Ross, Raymond. *Understanding Persuasion*. 3rd edition. Englewood Cliffs, NJ: Prentice-Hall, 1990.

Salmon, Charles T. *Information Campaigns*. Newbury Park, CA: Sage, 1989.

Samovar, Larry, and Porter, Richard. *Intercultural Communication: A Reader*. 6th edition. Belmont, CA: Wadsworth, 1991.

Severin, Werner, and Tankard, James. *Communication Theories: Origins, Methods, Uses*. 2nd edition. White Plains, NY: Longman, 1988.

Shockley-Zalabak, Pamela. *Fundamentals of Organizational Communication*. 2nd edition. White Plains, NY: Longman, 1991.

Winett, Richard. *Information and Behavior: Systems of Influence*. Hillsdale, NJ: Lawrence Erlbaum, 1986.

COMMUNITY RELATIONS

Kruckeberg, Dean, and Starck, Kenneth. *Public Relations and Community: A Reconstructed Theory*. Westport, CT: Greenwood, 1988.

Mayhall, P. *Police–Community Relations and the Administration of Justice*. New York: Wiley, 1985.

Yarrington, R. *Community Relations Handbook*. White Plains, NY: Longman, 1983.

COMPUTERS/DESKTOP PUBLISHING

Desktop Publishing/Teletypesetting. New York: Wiley Westerfield, 1987.

Felici, James, and Nace, Ted. *Desktop Publishing Skills*. Reading, MA: Addison-Wesley, 1987.

Freedman, Alan. *The Computer Glossary*. 5th edition. New York: AMACOM, 1990.

CONSULTING/COUNSELING

Brody, E. W. *Professional Practice Development*. New York: Praeger, 1989.

Cohen, William A. *How to Make It Big as a Consultant*. 2nd edition. New York: AMACOM, 1990.

Connor, Richard. *Getting New Clients*. New York: Wiley, 1988.

Davidson, Robert L. *Contracting Your Services*. New York: Wiley, 1990.

Holtz, Herman. *The Consultant's Guide to Proposal Writing*. 2nd edition. New York: Wiley, 1990.

Marcus, Bruce. *Competing for Clients*. Chicago: Probus, 1985.

Nager, Norman, and Truitt, Richard. *Strategic Public Relations Counseling*. White Plains, NY: Longman, 1987.

Putnam, Anthony O. *Marketing Your Services*. New York: Wiley, 1990.

Shenson, Howard L. *The Contract and Fee Setting Guide for Professionals and Consultants*. New York: Wiley, 1990.

Shenson, Howard L. *Shenson on Consulting: Success Strategies*. New York: Wiley, 1990.

Weiner, Richard. *Professional's Guide to Public Relations Services*. 6th edition. New York: AMACOM, 1988.

CRISIS/EMERGENCY COMMUNICATIONS

Bernstein, Alan. *Emergency Public Relations Manual*. 3rd edition. Highland Park, NJ: PASE, 1988.

Charles, Michael, and Kim, John. *Crisis Management: A Casebook for Survival*. Gettysburg, PA: C. C. Thomas, 1988.

Fink, Steven. *Crisis Management: Planning for the Inevitable*. New York: AMACOM, 1986.

Irvine, Robert B. *When You Are the Headline: Managing a News Story*. Homewood, IL: Dow Jones–Irwin, 1987.

Janis, Irving L. *Crucial Decisions: Leadership in Policy Making and Crisis Management*. New York: Free Press, 1988.

Meyers, Gerald. *When It Hits the Fan: Managing the Nine Crises of Business*. Boston: Houghton Mifflin, 1986.

Pinsdorf, Marion. *Communicating When Your Company Is Under Siege*. Lexington, MA: Lexington Books, 1986.

DEMOGRAPHICS

Ambry, Margaret K. *1990–91 Almanac of Consumer Markets: The Official Guide to the Demographics of American Consumers*. Ithaca, NY: American Demographics Press, 1989.

Crispell, Diane. *The Insider's Guide to Demographic Know-How*. Ithaca, NY: American Demographics Press, 1990.

DIRECT MARKETING

See also ''Marketing'' section.

Benson, Richard. *Secrets of Successful Direct Mail*. Lincolnwood, IL: National Textbook, 1989.

Encyclopedia of Telemarketing. Englewood Cliffs, NJ: Prentice-Hall, 1989.

Gottleib, Richard. *The Directory of Mail Order Catalogs*. 4th edition. Lakeville, CT: Grey House Publishing, 1990.

Gram, Rene. *Rene Gram's Direct Mail Workshop*. Englewood Cliffs, NJ: Prentice-Hall, 1989.

Gross, Martin. *The Direct Marketer's Idea Book*. New York: AMACOM, 1989.

Linchitz, Joel. *The Complete Guide to Telemarketing Management*. New York: AMACOM, 1990.

Ljungren, Roy G. *Business to Business Direct Marketing Handbook*. New York: AMACOM, 1988.

Shepard, Dave. *The New Direct Marketing . . . How to Implement a Profit Driven Database*. Homewood, IL: Dow Jones–Irwin, 1990.

EDUCATION

Bonus, Thaddeus. *Improving Internal Communications*. Washington, DC: Council for Advancement and Support of Education (CASE), 1984.

Bortner, Doyle. *Public Relations for Public Schools*. Rochester, NY: Schenkman, 1983.

Kotler, Philip, and Fox, Karen. *Strategic Marketing for Educational Institutions*. Englewood Cliffs, NJ: Prentice-Hall, 1985.

Rowland, A. W. *Handbook of Institutional Advancement*. 2nd edition. San Francisco: Jossey-Bass, 1986.

Rudman, Jack. *Public Relations Director*. Syosset, NY: National Learning, 1989.

Topor, Robert. *Institutional Image: How to Define, Improve, Market It*. Washington, DC: CASE, 1986.

West, Philip. *Educational Public Relations*. Newbury Park, CA: Sage, 1985.

EMPLOYEE RELATIONS

See also ''Writing in Public Relations'' section.

Bland, Michael, and Jackson, Peter. *Effective Employee Relations*. London: Kogan Page Ltd., 1990.

Brown, Kathleen, and Turner, Joan. *AIDS: Policies and Programs for the Workplace*. New York: Van Nostrand Reinhold, 1989.

Reuss, Carol, and Silvas, Donn. *Inside Organizational Communications*. 2nd edition. White Plains, NY: Longman, 1984.

Smith, Alvie L. *Innovative Employee Communication*. Englewood Cliffs, NJ: Prentice-Hall, 1991.

ENVIRONMENT

Blakey, H. Allen. *Environmental Communications and Public Relations Handbook*. Rockville, MD: Government Institute, 1990.

Fazio, James, and Gilbert, Douglas. *Public Relations and Communications for Natural Resource Managers*. Dubuque, IA: Kendall-Hunt, 1986.

ETHICS

See also "Legal" section.

Christians, Clifford, Rotzoll, Kim, and Fackler, Mark. *Media Ethics*. 3rd edition. White Plains, NY: Longman, 1991.

Day, Louis A. *Ethics in Mass Communications: Case and Controversies*. Belmont: CA: Wadsworth, 1991.

Fink, Conrad. *Media Ethics*. New York: McGraw-Hill, 1988.

Karp, R. *Corporate Morality and Executive Ethics*. Lexington, MA: Ginn, 1985.

Walton, Clarence. *The Moral Manager*. New York: Harper Business, 1990.

Ward, Gary. *Developing and Enforcing a Code of Business Ethics*. Babylon, NY: Pilot, 1989.

FINANCIAL/INVESTOR RELATIONS

Berry, Leonard. *Bankers Who Sell: Improving Selling Effectiveness in Banking*. Homewood, IL: Dow Jones–Irwin, 1985.

Dumitrescu, Claudia. *Public Relations for Financial Marketers*. Chicago: Financial Institute Marketing Association, 1990.

Furlong, Carla. *Marketing Money*. Chicago: Probus, 1989.

Graves, Joseph. *Investor Relations Today*. Glen Ellyn, IL: Investor Relations, 1985.

Nichols, Donald. *The Handbook of Investor Relations*. Homewood, IL: Dow Jones–Irwin, 1989.

Taggert, Philip, and Alexander, Roy. *Taking Your Company Public*. New York: AMACOM, 1991.

Winter, Elmer L. *A Complete Guide to Preparing a Corporate Annual Report*. New York: Van Nostrand Reinhold, 1985.

FUND-RAISING/DEVELOPMENT

Broce, Thomas. *Fund Raising*. Norman: University of Oklahoma Press, 1986.

Kelly, Kathleen S. *Fund Raising and Public Relations: A Critical Analysis*. Hillsdale, NJ: Lawrence Erlbaum, 1991.

Nichols, Judith E. *Changing Demographics: Fund Raising in the 1990s*. Chicago: Bonus Books, 1990.

Payton, Robert. *Philanthropy: Four Views*. New Brunswick, NJ: Transaction Books, 1988.

Seymour, Harold J. *Designs for Fund Raising*. Washington, DC: The Taft Group, 1988.

Smith, William J. *The Art of Raising Money*. New York: AMACOM, 1985.

Stolper, Carolyn, and Hopkins, Karen. *Fundraising: A Handbook for Arts and Cultural Organizations*. Phoenix, AZ: Oryx, 1989.

GRAPHICS/DESIGN

Baird, Russell. *The Graphics of Communication*. 5th edition. New York: Holt, Rinehart, & Winston, 1987.

Beach, Mark. *Getting It Printed: How to Work with Printers and Graphic Arts Services*. Portland, OR: Coast to Coast Books, 1987.

Bohle, Robert. *Publication Design for Editors*. Englewood Cliffs, NJ: Prentice-Hall, 1990.

Conover, Theodore. *Graphic Communications Today*. St. Paul, MN: West, 1990.

Crow, Wendell. *Communication Graphics*. Englewood Cliffs, NJ: Prentice-Hall, 1986.

Shapiro, Ellen. *Clients and Designers*. New York: Watson-Guptill, 1990.

White, Jan. *Mastering Graphics: Design and Production Made Easy*. Ann Arbor, MI: Bowker, 1983.

INTERNATIONAL

Cateora, Philip. *International Marketing*. Homewood, IL: Business One–Irwin, 1990.

Chang, Won Ho. *Mass Media in China: The History & the Future*. Ames: Iowa State University Press, 1989.

Hornik, Robert C. *Development Communication: Information, Agriculture, and Nutrition in the Third World*. White Plains, NY: Longman, 1988.

Lamont, Douglas. *Winning Worldwide: Strategies for Dominating Global Markets*. Homewood, IL: Dow Jones–Irwin, 1990.

Quelch, John. *The Marketing Challenge of 1992*. Reading, MA: Addison-Wesley, 1990.

Reed's Worldwide Directory of Public Relations Organizations. Washington, DC: Pigafetta Press, 1990.

Ryans, John, and Rau, Pradeep. *Marketing Strategies for a New Europe*. Chicago: American Marketing Association, 1990.

Samovar, Larry, and Porter, Richard. *Communication Between Cultures*. Belmont: CA: Wadsworth, 1991.

Weber, Robert. *The Marketer's Guide to Selling Products Abroad*. Westport, CT: Greenwood, 1989.

Wiklund, Erik. *International Marketing Strategies: How to Build International Market Share*. New York: McGraw-Hill, 1987.

Williams, Robert. *The World's Largest Market: A Business Guide to Europe 1992*. New York: AMACOM, 1990.

ISSUES MANAGEMENT

Chase, Howard. *Issues Management: Origins of the Future*. Stamford, CT: Issues Action Publications, 1984.

Ewing, Raymond P. *Managing the New Bottom Line: Issues Management for Senior Executives*. Homewood, IL: Dow Jones–Irwin, 1987.

Heath, Robert. *Strategic Issues Management: How Organizations Influence and Respond to Public Interests and Politics*. San Francisco: Jossey-Bass, 1988.

Heath, Robert, and Nelson, Richard. *Issues Management*. Newbury Park, CA: Sage, 1985.

LEGAL

Banta, William. *AIDS in the Workplace: Legal and Practical Answers*. Lexington, MA: Lexington Press, 1990.

Lawrence, John, and Timberg, Bernard. *Fair Use and Free Inquiry: Copyright Law and the News Media*. 2nd edition. Norwood, NJ: Ablex Publishing, 1989.

Lively, Donald E. *Modern Communications Law*. Westport, CT: Greenwood, 1991.

Middleton, Kent, and Chamberlin, Bill. *Law of Public Communication*. 2nd edition. White Plains, NY: Longman, 1991.

Rome, Edwin, and Roberts, William. *Corporate and Commercial Free Speech*. Westport, CT: Quorum Books, 1985.

Walsh, Frank. *Public Relations and the Law*. New York: Institute for Public Relations Research and Education, 1988.

Watkins, John J. *Mass Media and the Law*. Englewood Cliffs, NJ: Prentice-Hall, 1990.

Werner, Ray. *Legal and Economic Regulation in Marketing*. Westport, CT: Greenwood, 1989.

Wilson, Lee. *Make It Legal*. New York: Allworth Press, 1990.

MARKETING

See also ''Direct Marketing'' section.

Bingham, Frank, and Raffield, Barney. *Business to Business Marketing Management*. Homewood, IL: Business One–Irwin, 1990.

Bonoma, Thomas, and Kosnik, Thomas. *Marketing Management: Text and Cases*. Homewood, IL: Business One–Irwin, 1990.

Boyd, Harper, and Walker, Orville. *Marketing Management: A Strategic Approach*. Homewood, IL: Dow Jones–Irwin, 1990.

Cravens, David, and Lamb, Charles. *The Marketing Plan: How to Prepare It, What Should Be In It*. Homewood, IL: Business One–Irwin, 1990.

Davidson, Jeffrey P. *The Marketing Sourcebook for Small Business*. New York: Wiley, 1989.

Debelak, Don. *Total Marketing*. Homewood, IL: Dow Jones–Irwin, 1989.

Duro, Robert. *Winning the Marketing War*. New York: Wiley, 1989.

Francese, Peter, and Piierto, Rebecca. *Capturing Consumers*. Ithaca, NY: American Demographics Press, 1990.

Fuld, Leonard. *Monitoring the Competition: Finding Out What's Really Going On Over There*. New York: Wiley, 1988.

Goldman, Jordan. *Public Relations in the Marketing Mix*. Lincolnwood, IL: National Textbook, 1985.

Hamper, Robert, and Baugh, Sue. *Strategic Market Planning*. Skokie, IL: NTC Business Books, 1990.

Hiebing, Roman, and Cooper, Scott. *How to Write a Successful Marketing Plan*. Skokie, IL: NTC Business Books, 1990.

Kotler, Philip, and Armstrong, Gary. *Marketing: An Introduction.* Englewood Cliffs, NJ: Prentice-Hall, 1987.

Lazarus, George, and Wexler, Bruce. *Marketing Immunity: Breaking through Customer Resistence.* Homewood, IL: Dow Jones–Irwin, 1987.

McCarthy, Jerome, and Perreault, William. *Basic Marketing.* 10th edition. Homewood, IL: Business One–Irwin, 1990.

McKenna, Regis. *The Regis Touch.* Reading, MA: Addison-Wesley, 1986.

Powers, Tom. *Marketing Hospitality.* New York: Wiley, 1990.

Quelch, John A. *How to Market to Consumers.* New York: Wiley, 1989.

Ries, Jack, and Trout, Al. *Bottom-Up Marketing.* New York: McGraw-Hill, 1989.

Ross, Marilyn, and Ross, Thomas. *Big Marketing Ideas for Small Service Businesses.* Homewood, IL: Business One–Irwin, 1990.

Shaw, Robert, and Stone, Merlin. *Database Marketing.* New York: Wiley, 1990.

Shimp, Terence, and DeLozier, M. Wayne. *Promotion Management and Marketing Communications.* Hinsdale, IL: Dryden, 1986.

Stanley, Thomas J. *Marketing to the Affluent.* Homewood, IL: Dow Jones–Irwin, 1988.

Vladimir, Andrew. *The Complete Travel Marketing Handbook.* Lincolnwood, IL: National Textbook, 1987.

Wilson, Jerry. *Word of Mouth Marketing.* New York: Wiley, 1990.

MEDIA/PRESS RELATIONS

See also ''Publicity/Promotion'' section.

Biagi, Shirley. *Media Impact.* Belmont: CA: Wadsworth, 1990.

Blohowiak, Donald W. *No Comment! An Executive's Essential Guide to the News Media.* New York: Praeger, 1987.

Blyskal, Jeff, and Blyskal, Marie. *PR: How the Public Relations Industry Writes the News.* New York: Morrow, 1985.

Corrado, Frank. *Media for Managers.* Englewood Cliffs, NJ: Prentice-Hall, 1984.

Evans, Fred J. *Managing the Media: Proactive Strategy for Better Business and Press Relations.* Westport, CT: Greenwood, 1987.

Garner, Gerald. *Chief, The Reporters Are Here.* Gettysburg, PA: Thomas, 1987. Police public relations.

Hannaford, Peter. *Talking Back to the Media.* New York: Facts on File, 1986.

Howard, Carole, and Matthews, Wilma. *On Deadline: Managing Media Relations.* Prospect Heights, IL: Waveland, 1988.

Irvine, Robert. *When You Are the Headline: Managing a Major News Story*. Homewood, IL: Dow Jones–Irwin, 1987.

Schmertz, Herb. *Good-bye to the Low Profile: The Art of Creative Confrontation*. Boston: Little, Brown, 1986.

Weiner, Richard. *Webster's New World Dictionary of Media and Communications*. Englewood Cliffs, NJ: Prentice-Hall, 1990.

NONPROFIT/CHARITABLE GROUPS

Connors, Tracy. *Non-Profit Organization Handbook*. 2nd edition. New York: McGraw-Hill, 1988.

Kotler, Philip, and Anderson, Alan. *Strategic Marketing For Nonprofit Organizations*. Englewood Cliffs, NJ: Prentice-Hall, 1987.

Kotler, Philip, and Clarke, Roberta. *Marketing for Health Care Organizations*. Englewood Cliffs, NJ: Prentice-Hall, 1987.

Lewton, Kathleen L. *Public Relations in Health Care: A Guide for Professionals*. Chicago: American Hospital Association, 1991.

Malinowsky, Robert, and Perry, Gerald. *The AIDS Information Sourcebook 1989–90*. Phoenix, AZ: Oryx Press, 1989.

Marlowe, David. *Building a Foundation for Effective Health Care Market Research*. Chicago: American Marketing Association, 1988.

Ruffner, R. *Handbook of Publicity and PR for the Nonprofit Organization*. Englewood Cliffs, NJ: Prentice-Hall, 1985.

Topor, Robert. *Your Personal Guide to Marketing a Nonprofit Organization*. Washington, DC: Council for Advancement and Support of Education (CASE), 1988.

PUBLIC AFFAIRS/GOVERNMENT

Armstrong, Richard. *The Next Hurrah: The Changing Face of the American Political Process*. New York: Morrow, 1988.

Gollner, Andrew. *Social Change and Corporate Strategy: The Expanding Role of Public Affairs*. Stamford, CT: IAP, 1984.

Kern, Montague. *30-Second Politics: Political Advertising in the Eighties*. Westport, CT: Greenwood, 1989.

Mack, Charles S. *Lobbying and Government Relations: A Guide for Executives*. Westport, CT: Quorum Books, 1989.

Marcus, Alfred. *Business Strategy and Public Policy*. Westport, CT: Greenwood, 1987.

Remmes, Harold. *Lobbying for Your Cause*. Babylon, NY: Pilot Books, 1986.

Post, James, and Mahon, John. *Corporate Public Affairs*. New York: Ballinger, 1989.

Wittenberg, Ernest, and Wittenberg, Elisabeth. *How to Win in Washington*. Washington, DC: Basil Blackwell, 1990.

PUBLICITY/PROMOTION

See also "Writing in Public Relations" section.

Barhydt, James D. *The Complete Book of Product Publicity*. New York: AMACOM, 1987.

Brough, Bruce. *Publicity and Public Relations Guide for Business*. Grants Pass, OR: Oasis Press, 1986.

Doty, Dorothy I. *Publicity and Public Relations*. Haupauge, NY: Barron, 1990.

Feirman, Jeffrey, and Blashek, Robert. *Sweepstakes, Prizes, Promotion Games, and Contests*. Homewood, IL: Dow Jones–Irwin, 1986.

Freisleben, Christine G. *The Publicity Process*. 3rd edition. Ames: Iowa State University Press, 1989.

Fuhrman, Candace J. *Publicity Stunts*. San Francisco: Chronicle Books, 1989. Historical overview.

Hart, Norman. *Practical Advertising and Publicity*. New York: McGraw-Hill, 1989.

Ramacitti, David F. *Do-It-Yourself Publicity*. New York: AMACOM, 1990.

RESEARCH METHODOLOGY/STUDIES

Bradburn, Norman, and Sudman, Seymour. *Polls and Surveys*. San Francisco: Jossey-Bass, 1988.

Breen, George, and Blakenship, A. B. *Do-It-Yourself Marketing Research*. 3rd edition. New York: McGraw-Hill, 1989.

Brody, E. W., and Stone, Gerald. *Public Relations Research*. Westport, CT: Greenwood, 1989.

Broom, Glen, and Dozier, David. *Using Research in Public Relations*. Englewood Cliffs, NJ: Prentice-Hall, 1990.

Dillon, William R. *Marketing Research in a Marketing Environment*. Homewood, IL: Business One–Irwin, 1990.

Emmert, Philip, and Barker, Larry. *Measurement of Communication Behavior*. White Plains, NY: Longman, 1989.

Gorton, Keith, and Doole, Isobel. *Low Cost Marketing Research: A Guide for Small Business*. New York: Wiley, 1989.

Grunig, James, and Grunig, Larissa. *Public Relations Research Annual*. Volume 2. Hillsdale, NJ: Lawrence Erlbaum, 1990.

Grunig, James, and Grunig, Larissa. *Public Relations Research Annual*. Volume 3. Hillsdale, NJ: Lawrence Erlbaum, 1991.

Lowery, Shearon, and DeFleur, Melvin. *Milestones in Mass Communications Research*. 2nd edition. White Plains, NY: Longman, 1988.

Pavlik, John V. *Public Relations: What Research Tells Us*. Newbury Park, CA: Sage, 1987.

Soares, Eric. *Cost Effective Marketing Research*. Westport, CT: Greenwood, 1988.

Stempel, Guido, and Westley, Bruce. *Research Methods in Mass Communication*. 2nd edition. Englewood Cliffs, NJ: Prentice-Hall, 1989.

Templeton, Jane. *Focus Groups: A Guide for Marketing and Advertising Professionals*. Chicago: Probus, 1990.

Van Minden, J. R. *The Dictionary of Marketing Research*. Chicago: St. James Press, 1990.

SPECIAL EVENTS

***Chase's Annual Events*.** Chicago: Contemporary Books, 1991.

Harris, April. *Special Events: Planning for Success*. Washington, DC: Council for Advancement and Support of Education (CASE), 1988.

SPEECHES/PRESENTATIONS

Allen, Steve. *How to Make a Speech*. New York: McGraw-Hill, 1986.

Burleson, Clyde. *Effective Meetings: The Complete Guide*. New York: Wiley, 1989.

DeVito, Joseph A. *The Elements of Public Speaking*. 4th edition. New York: HarperCollins, 1990.

Fletcher, Leon. *How to Design and Deliver a Speech*. 4th edition. New York: HarperCollins, 1990.

Glenn, Ethel, and Forman, Sandra. *Public Speaking: Today and Tomorrow*. Englewood Cliffs, NJ: Prentice-Hall, 1990.

Howell, William, and Bormann, Ernest. *The Process of Presentational Speaking*. New York: Harper & Row, 1988.

Kaplan, Burton. *The Corporate Manager's Guide to Speechwriting*. New York: Free Press, 1988.

Kelly, Lynne, Lederman, Linda, and Phillips, Gerald. *Communicating in the Workplace: A Guide to Business and Professional Speaking*. New York: Harper & Row, 1989.

McKenzie, John K. *It's Show Time*. Homewood, IL: Dow Jones–Irwin, 1989.

McMahon, Tom. *Big Meeting, Big Results*. Skokie, IL: NTC Business Books, 1990.

Rafe, Stephen C. *How to Be Prepared to Think on Your Feet*. New York: Harper Business, 1990.

Richardson, Linda. *Winning Group Sales Presentations*. Homewood, IL: Dow Jones–Irwin, 1989.

Smith, Terry C. *Making Successful Presentations*. 2nd edition. New York: Wiley, 1990.

Verderber, Rudolph F. *Essentials of Persuasive Speaking: Theory and Concepts*. Belmont: CA: Wadsworth, 1991.

VIDEO/BROADCASTING

See also ''Writing in Public Relations'' section.

Block, Mervin. *Writing Broadcast News Shorter, Sharper, Stronger*. Chicago: Bonus Books, 1987.

Degan, Clara. *Understanding and Using Video*. White Plains, NY: Knowledge Industry, 1985.

Hausman, Carl. *Institutional Video: Planning, Budgeting, Production, and Evaluation*. Belmont, CA: Wadsworth, 1991.

Hilliard, Robert L. *Writing for Television and Radio*. 5th edition. Belmont: CA: Wadsworth, 1991.

MacDonald, R. H. *Broadcast News Manual of Style*. White Plains, NY: Longman, 1987.

WRITING IN PUBLIC RELATIONS

Beach, Mark. *Editing Your Newsletter*. 3rd edition. Portland, OR: Coast to Coast Books, 1988.

Beach, Mark. *Getting It Printed: How to Work with Printers/Graphic Art Services*. Portland, OR: Coast to Coast Books, 1986.

Berg, Karen, and Gilman, Andrew. *Get to the Point*. New York: Bantam, 1989.

Bivins, Tom. *Handbook for Public Relations Writing*. Lincolnwood, IL: National Textbook, 1987.

Brill, Laura. *Business Writing: Quick and Easy*. Detroit: Gale, 1989.

Brody, E. W., and Lattimore, Dan L. *Public Relations Writing*. New York: Praeger, 1990.

Cohen, Paula. *A Public Relations Primer: Thinking and Writing in Context.* Englewood Cliffs, NJ: Prentice-Hall, 1987.

Hutchison, Earl R. *Writing for Mass Communication.* White Plains, NY: Longman, 1986.

Majors, Randall E. *Business Communication: Writing, Interviewing, and Speaking at Work.* New York: HarperCollins, 1990.

Newsom, Doug, and Carrell, Bob. *Public Relations Writing: Form and Style.* 3rd edition. Belmont: CA: Wadsworth, 1991.

Newsom, Doug, and Wollert, James. *Media Writing: Preparing Information for the Mass Media.* 2nd edition. Belmont: CA: Wadsworth, 1988.

Rayfield, Robert, Acharya, Lalit, Pincus, David, and Silvis, Donn. *Public Relations Writing: Strategies and Skills.* Dubuque, IA: Brown, 1991.

Roman, Kenneth, and Raphaelson, Joel. *Writing That Works.* New York: Harper & Row, 1985.

Stovall, James G. *Writing for the Mass Media.* Englewood Cliffs, NJ: Prentice-Hall, 1990.

Tucker, Kerry, and Derelian, Doris. *Public Relations Writing: A Planned Approach for Creating Results.* Englewood Cliffs, NJ: Prentice-Hall, 1989.

Walsh, Frank. *Public Relations Writer in the Computer Age.* Englewood Cliffs, NJ: Prentice-Hall, 1986.

Wilcox, Dennis L., and Nolte, Lawrence W. *Public Relations Writing and Media Techniques.* New York: HarperCollins, 1990.

Williams, Patricia A. *Creating and Producing the Perfect Newsletter.* Glenview, IL: Scott, Foresman, 1990.

DIRECTORIES

Directories are valuable tools for public relations personnel who need to communicate with a variety of specialized audiences. Media directories, for example, can provide the names, addresses, telephone numbers, and even fax numbers of key editors in thousands of publications. Other directories can provide the demographics of a specific publication, or even the address of a national trade organization. The following is a selected list of the leading national and international directories.

MEDIA DIRECTORIES

All TV Publicity Outlets: Nationwide. Resource Media, Box 307, Kent, CT 06766.

Bacon's Publicity Checker: Magazines/Newspapers. Bacon Publishing Company, 332 S. Michigan, Chicago, IL 60604.

Bacon's Radio/TV Directory. Same address as above.

Black Media in America. Hall Company, 70 Lincoln, Boston, MA 02111.

Broadcasting/Cablecasting Yearbook. Broadcasting Publications, 1705 DeSales NW, Washington, DC 20036.

Burrelle's Special Directories: Black Media, Hispanic Media, and Women's Media. Burrelle Company, 75 E. Northfield, Livingston, NJ 07039.

Cable & Station Coverage Atlas. Warren Publications, 2115 Ward Court NW, Washington, DC 20037.

Cable Contacts. BPI Media Services, Box 2015, Lakewood, NJ 08701.

Directory of the College Student Press in America. Oxbridge Communications, 150 Fifth Ave., New York, NY 10011.

Directory of Newsletters. See above address.

Directory of US Trade Journals. Low Associates, Box 149, Pittstown, NJ 08867.

Editor & Publisher Directory of Syndicated Services. Editor & Publisher, 11 W. 19th St., New York, NY 10011.

Editor & Publisher International Year Book. See above address. Listing of weekly and daily newspapers.

Gale's Directory of Publications and Broadcast Media. Gale Research Company, Box 441914, Detroit, MI 48244–9980.

Gebbie Press All-in-One Directory. Gebbie Press, Box, 1000, New Paltz, NY 12561.

Hispanic Media USA. Media Institute, 3017 M St. NW, Washington, DC 20007.

Hudson's Newsletter Directory. Hudson Company, 44 W. Market St, Rhinebeck, NY 12572.

Just the Fax: A Media Directory. Public Access, 2000 L St. NW, Washington, DC 20036.

National Directory of Magazines. Oxbridge Communications, 150 Fifth Ave., New York, NY 10011.

National Directory of Community Newspapers. American Newspaper Representatives, 84 S. 6th St., Minneapolis, MN 55402.

National Radio Publicity Outlets. Resource Media, Box 307, Kent, CT 06766.

Oxbridge Directory of Newsletters. Oxbridge Communications, 150 Fifth Ave., New York, NY 10011.

Print Media Editorial Calendars. SRDS, 3004 Glenview Rd., Wilmette, IL 60091.

Radio Contacts. BPI Media Services, Box 2015, Lakewood, NJ 08701.

Standard Periodical Directory. Oxbridge, 150 Fifth Ave., New York, NY 10011.

Syndicated Columnists Contacts. BPI Media Services, Box 2015, Lakewood, NJ 08701.

Talk Show Selects. Broadcast Interview, 2233 Wisconsin St. NW, Washington, DC 20007.

TV Contacts. BPI Media Services, Box 2015, Lakewood, NJ 08701.

TV News Contacts. See above address.

Working Press of the Nation. National Research Inc., 130 S. Willard St., Burlington, VT, 05401. Five volumes, covering newspapers, magazines, radio, and television.

INTERNATIONAL DIRECTORIES

Bacon's International Publicity Checker. Bacon Publishing, 332 S. Michigan, Chicago, IL 60604.

Benn's Media Directory. Benn Business Information Service, Box 20, Sovereign Way, Tonbridge, Kent, England TN9, 1RW. Volume 1 is the United Kingdom, and Volume 2 is international media.

Editor & Publisher International Year Book. Editor & Publisher, 11 W. 19th St., New York, NY 10011.

Hollis Press and Public Relations Annual. Contact House, Lower Hampton Rd., Sunbury-on-Thames, Middlesex, England TW16, 5BR.

International Literary Market Place. R. R. Bowker Company, 245 W. 17th St., New York, NY 10011.

International Media Guides: Newspapers Worldwide, Consumer Magazines Worldwide, Business Publications Asia/Pacific, Europe, The Americas, Middle East/Africa. International Media Enterprises, 22 Elizabeth St., South Norwalk, CT 06856.

Ulrich's International Directory. R. R. Bowker Company, 245 W. 17th St., New York, NY 10011.

World Radio/TV Handbook. Billboard, 1515 Broadway, New York, NY 10036.

OTHER DIRECTORIES

Awards, Honors, Prizes. Gale Research Company, Box 441914, Detroit, MI 48244–9980.

Business Organizations, Agencies, and Publications Directory. See above address.

Celebrity Register. See above address.

Charitable Organizations of the United States. See above address.

Chase's Annual Events. Contemporary Books, 180 N. Michigan Ave., Chicago, IL 60601.

Directories in Print. Gale Research Company, Box 441914, Detroit, MI 48244–9980.

Encyclopedia of Associations. See above address.

Encyclopedia of Governmental Advisory Organizations. See above address.

The Foundation Directory. The Foundation Center, 79 Fifth Ave., New York, NY 10003.

Holidays and Anniversaries of the World. Gale Research Company, Box 441914, Detroit, MI 48244–9980.

Literary Marketplace. R. R. Bowker Company, 245 W. 17th St., New York, NY 10011.

National Directory of Corporate Public Affairs. Columbia Books, 1350 New York Ave. NW, Washington, DC 20005.

National Trade/Professional Associations. See above address.

O'Dwyer's Directory of Corporate Communications. O'Dwyer Company, 271 Madison Ave., New York, NY 10016.

O'Dwyer's Directory of Public Relations Firms. See above address.

Professional's Guide to Public Relations Services. AMACOM, 135 W. 50th St., New York, NY 10020.

Reed's Worldwide Directory of Public Relations Organizations. Pigafetta Press, Box 39244, Washington, DC 20016.

Standard Rate and Data Services: Business Publications Rates and Data, Community Publication Rates and Data, Newspaper Rates and Data, and Spot Radio Rates and Data. SRDS, 3004 Glenview Rd., Wilmette, IL 60091.

Trade Shows and Professional Exhibits Directory. Gale Research Company, Box 441914, Detroit, MI 48244–9980.

Washington Lobbyists Directory. Columbia Books, 1350 New York Ave. NW, Washington, DC 20005.

PERIODICALS

Broadcasting. 1735 DeSales St. NW, Washington, DC 20036. Weekly.

CASE Currents. 11 Dupont Circle, Washington, DC 20036. Monthly publication of the Council for the Advancement and Support of Education.

Communication World. IABC, One Hallidie Plaza, Suite 600, San Francisco, CA 94102. Monthly publication of the International Association of Business Communicators.

Community Relations Report. Box 924, Bartlesville, OK 74005. Monthly.

Environmental Marketing Report. 315 East 65th St., New York, NY 10021. Bimonthly.

Investor Relations Update. NIRI, 1730 M St. NW, Suite 806, Washington, DC 20036. Monthly publication of the National Investor Relations Institute.

Jack O'Dwyer's PR Newsletter. 271 Madison Ave., New York, NY 10016. Weekly.

O'Dwyer's PR Services Report. See above address. Monthly.

PR Reporter. Box 600, Dudley House, Exeter, NH 03833. Weekly.

Public Relations Journal. PRSA, 33 Irving Place, New York, NY 10003. Monthly publication of the Public Relations Society of America.

Public Relations News. 127 E. 80th St., New York, NY 10021. Weekly.

Public Relations Quarterly. Box 311, Rhinebeck, NY 12572. Quarterly.

Public Relations Review. JAI Press, 55 Old Post Road, Greenwich, CT 06836–1678. Quarterly.

Ragan Report. 407 S. Dearborn, Chicago, IL 60605. Weekly.

Special Events Report. 213 W. Institute Pl., Chicago, IL 60610. Twice a month.

Video Monitor. 10606 Mantz Rd., Silver Spring, MD 20903. Monthly.

Index